Index to
American Reference Books Annual
1975-1979

Index to American Reference Books Annual 1975-1979:

A Cumulative Index to Subjects, Authors, and Titles

Christine L. Wynar

1979

Libraries Unlimited, Inc.
Littleton, Colo.

Copyright ©1979 Libraries Unlimited, Inc.
All Rights Reserved
Printed in the United States of America

No part of this publication may be reproduced, stored in a retrieval system, or transmitted, in any form or by any means, electronic, mechanical, photocopying, recording, or otherwise, without the prior written permission of the publisher.

LIBRARIES UNLIMITED, INC.
P.O. Box 263
Littleton, Colorado 80160

ISBN 0-87287-199-1

ISSN 0192-6969

This book is bound with Scott Graphitek®–C Type II nonwoven material. Graphitek–C meets and exceeds National Association of State Textbook Administrators' Type II nonwoven material specifications Class A through E.

TABLE OF CONTENTS

Preface vii

Authors and Titles 1

Subjects 199

PREFACE

American Reference Books Annual (ARBA) is well established as the most comprehensive source for reviews of all types of reference books published or distributed in the United States. The ten annual volumes of ARBA, beginning with 1970, contain 17,178 reviews of reference books. These titles include books on any topic and in a variety of reference formats—encyclopedias, dictionaries, bibliographies, indexes, handbooks, etc.

Access to books reviewed in each annual volume of ARBA is provided through its index of authors, titles, and subjects, and through five-year indexes. The first five-year cumulative index, *Index to American Reference Books Annual 1970-1974*, was prepared as a wholly new work by Joseph Sprug and was published in 1974. The 1970-1974 index provided separate indexes of both authors and titles. The subject index was a thorough and detailed analysis of the 8,796 titles reviewed during 1970-1974.

This second five-year cumulation, *Index to American Reference Books Annual 1975-1979*, provides full author, title, and subject access to every review published in ARBA during that five-year period. The cumulative indexing brings together for quick reference a wealth of information about recent reference publications. Readers familiar with ARBA recognize that consultation of an ARBA review will yield complete bibliographic information, an evaluation of the book, and citation to other early published reviews. Thus, the uses of this cumulative index extend far beyond that of a locator device for ARBA reviews of reference books.

A nearly complete list of reference books published in the United States (1975-1979) is presented through the authors and titles index. Students, librarians, bibliographers, and scholars will find the array of titles listed by subjects an invaluable tool for locating current reference aids on specific topics, for developing bibliographies, and for collection development. Publishers and writers will also find special uses for the subject analysis of recent reference publications.

This second five-year index, covering 8,382 books reviewed during 1975-1979, is restructured, expanded, and hopefully easier to consult and access desired information. The entry form is simplified. ARBA review citations are given at the end of the entry and show ARBA year and entry number (n). Slashes are used to separate the elements of the entry: author/title/review citation:

Fisk, M/Encyclopedia of associations/77n85

To keep the index to a reasonable size, it was necessary to use short titles and to abbreviate words in titles. This shortening of titles allowed an expansion of the authors and titles index (see below) and should not detract from the main purpose of the index.

AUTHORS AND TITLES

Treatment of authors and titles is expanded and improved. The authors and titles index contains both author-title and title-author access. In the 1970-1974 index, separate author-only and title-only indexes were provided. Another change in the present index is the inclusion of both personal and corporate authors.

Author entries include all single and joint authors, editors, and compilers. Author entries give: surname, initials/shortened title/ARBA citation:

Lowery, G H/Louisiana birds/75n1505

Authors with the same surnames and initials are listed as separate entries, not misleadingly combined as one. Book titles are shortened to the first three words. Titles provide identification but not full bibliographic information.

Title entries provide the fullest form of the title used in the index, but in somewhat shortened form. Subtitles are usually deleted, as are editions, unless required to distinguish two or more listings. Only the first author is cited in a title entry. Title entries give: title/author/ARBA citation:

Costume design in the movies/Leese/78n952

SUBJECTS

Following the pattern of the 1970-1974 index, the subject index lists precise headings that reflect the contents of a reference book as a whole. In addition, when an ARBA review (or a title itself) indicates additional topics, supplementary headings are provided for them. Two or more headings are assigned to each title.

Subheadings are used infrequently in the 1975-1979 index, with the aim of simplifying the search for an appropriate heading. Long lists of entries are subdivided by form (bibliography, dictionaries and encyclopedias, etc.), topic, country or geographic area, as appropriate.

Main subject headings are printed in all caps at the left margin of the column; subheadings are printed in all caps and are indented. (However, the heading UNITED STATES has additional subdivisions printed in italics.) *See* and *See also* references are printed, as needed, directly following a subject heading.

Subject headings were chosen from the 1970-1974 ARBA index and from several standard sources, especially *Library of Congress Subject Headings*, 8th edition. Terminology found in the ARBA reviews as well as current usage noted in journals was considered in the choice of subject headings. Works such as Marshall's *On Equal Terms* suggested some adaptations to standard subject heading terminology. An effort was made to avoid inverted headings and to adopt, wherever possible, natural word order. So, for example, AMERICAN ART and AMERICAN AUTHORS are used. Cross references under ART and under AUTHORS direct the reader to the chosen heading. Qualifiers are used with subject headings as needed, e.g., BULBS (botany).

The information given in the subject entries is presented in shortened form and includes: author/title/ARBA citation:

>CHILDREN'S LIBRARIES
>*See also* School libraries
>Baker/School & public library media
>programs for children & YAs/78n178

ACKNOWLEDGMENTS

Although a number of people contributed to this index, special recognition is due Janet Littlefield, author-title editing; Louise Stwalley, filing and assistance in indexing; Roberta Depp, assistance in subject indexing; Susan Kohlman, author-title indexing. Judy Caraghar was responsible for design and typesetting. Proofreading was done by Koert C. Loomis, Jr. Some errors inevitably are overlooked in a project of this kind extending over a five-year period. The editor welcomes any comments or suggestions for improvement of the index from its users.

CLW
May 1979

AUTHORS AND TITLES

A-V connection/78n245
A-Z of astronomy/Moore/78n1234
AA gd to camping & caravanning on the continent/Kelly/79n711
AAAS sci bk list suppl/Wolff/79n1294
AAAS sci film catalog/Seltz-Petrash/77n1280
Aaron, S/Wine buyers/79n1516
Aaronson, P B/College gd/79n459
Abajian, J de T/Blacks and/76n342/Blacks in/78n385
Abbey, K/Bibliography of language/78n587
Abbott, C S/Marianne Moore/78n1147
Abbott, I A/Marine algae/77n1365
Abbott, R T/American malacologists/75n1498/American seashells/75n1522/Caribbean seashells/77n1396
Abbreviations & acronyms in medicine & nursing/Garb/77n1475
Abbreviations dict/De Sola/75n114; 79n105
Abbreviations in Greek inscriptions/Oikonomides/76n285
Abbreviations in medicine/Schertel/79n1466
Abbreviations in the African press/75n1297
ABC of indoor plants/Baines/75n1698
ABC pol sci/Garrison/78n436
ABC's of the consumer product safety act/75n929
ABC's wide world of sports ency/Benagh/75n720
Abdullah, O/Black playwrights/79n1009
Abdulrazak, F/Arabic historical/78n366
Abel, B/Guide to state/78n353
Abell, M D/Collective bargaining/78n161
Abernethy, G L/Pakistan/76n264
Abernethy, P L/English novel/77n1227
Abidi, S A/Fifty years/76n359
Abingdon Bible hndbk/Blair/76n1095
Abler, T S/Canadian Indian/75n863
Abo, T/Marshallese-English/78n1062
Aboriginal tribes of Australia/Tindale/75n870
Abortion bibliography/Floyd/76n1516
Abraham, G & K/Organic gardening/76n1581
Abrahams, R D/Afro-American/79n453
Abramowitz, M/Elie Wiesel/76n1253
Abse, J/Art galleries/77n868

Abstract of land grant surveys of Augusta & Rockingham Counties, VA/Kaylor/77n467
Abstracts & indexes in sci & tech/Owen/75n1432
Abstracts from the *Pennsylvania Gazette*/Scott/78n410
Abstracts of alternatives to lab animals/Andrla/76n1369
Abstracts of papers/Amer Chem Soc/76n1388
Abstracts of pop culture/79n1084
Abstracts of the collected works of C.G. Jung/Rothgeb/79n1431
Abstracts of the std ed of the complete psychological works of Sigmund Freud/Rothgeb/75n1596
Academic libraries by the yr 2000/Poole/78n168
Academic library/Farber/75n180
Academic who's who, 1975-76: univ teachers in the British Isles in the arts, educ & social sciences/77n641
Acadian church records/De Ville/76n430
ACC/Directory of craft/75n1029
Access: for disabled Americans/Bruck/79n840
Access index to little magazines/Burke/78n19
Access: sup index periodicals/Burke/76n28
Access to periodical resources/Assoc of Research Libraries/75n230
Access to the world/Weiss/79n623
Accountants' index/Kubat/78n719/78n720; 79n827
Accounting desk bk/76n841
Accounting desk bk/Casey/79n824
Accounting hndbk for nonaccountants/Nickerson/76n844
Accredited institutions of postsecondary educ & programs/76n632
Aceto, V J/Film lit/76n1063; 77n1014
Achabal, C/Craftworker's market/79n938
Ackerman, J S/Bible-related/77n1049
Acklen, J T/Tennessee records/75n405
Ackroyd, P R/Cambridge hist/76n1097
Ackroyd, T J/Health &/79n795
Acquisitions/Grieder/79n254
Acquisitions from the Third World/Clarke/76n173
Acquisitions of maps & charts published by the US gov/Low/77n245

2—Authors and Titles

Acri, M J/Death/78n1426
Acronyms, initialisms, & abbreviations dict/ Crowley/78n108
Actor gd to the talkies/Aros/78n953
Actors/Arnott/76n52
Actors' TV credits/Parish/79n1179
Acupuncture/Liao/77n1464
Adamovich, S G/Reader in/76n175
Adams, C F/Encyclopedia of food/79n1529/ Nutritive value/77n1548
Adams, C J/Reader's gd/78n969
Adams, L/Norman Mailer/76n1245
Adams, L/Shoot-em-ups/79n1031
Adams, R E/Venezuelan hist/78n374
Adams, R F/Language of/79n1114
Adams, S/Information for/75n134
Aday, L A/Development of/77n1453
Adelberg, E A/Review of medical/79n1475
Adell, J/Guide to non-/77n1142
Adelmann, M/Musical Europe/75n1144
Adjustment to widowhood/Strugnell/75n852
Adkins, R/Beginning writer's/79n1169/ Writer's market/76n1175
Adler, M J/Great treasury/78n85
Adloff, R/Historical dict/76n250
Administration of gov docs collections/ Harleston/75n214
Administration of justice in the courts/Klein/ 77n537
Administration of the college lib/Lyle/76n139
Administrative aspects of educ for librarianship/Cassata/76n220
Admission requirements of US & Canadian dental schools/77n1479
Admissions, financial aid, & placemt procedures at colleges that use college brd services/ 77n607
Adoption bibliog & multi-ethnic sourcebk/Van Why/78n657
Adults & the Pratt Library/Martin/77n188
Advances in info systems sci/Tou/78n1520
Advances in librarianship/Voight/75n153; 78n140
Advena, J C/Drug abuse/75n1652; 76n1547
Adventure trip gd/75n592
Adventuring with bks/Cianciolo/78n189
Advertiser's gd to scholarly periodicals/Black/ 79n16
Advertising law hndbk/Wooley/75n913
Adwick, K/Dictionary of golf/76n747
Aelfric/White/75n1380
Aestheticism & decadence/Dowling/78n1089
Aesthetics for dancers/Kaprelian/78n924

Aetiology of psychoactive substance use/ Fazey/79n1454
Afflerbach, L/Emerging fld/78n214
Aflalo, F G/Encyclopedia of sport/77n670
Afre, S A/Ashanti region/76n252
Africa/75n327; 76n244
Africa: bibliog of geography/Bederman/75 n568
Africa contemporary record/Legum/75n326; 76n243
Africa south of the Sahara/76n268; 77n307
Africa yr bk & who's who/78n275
African & Black American studies/Birkos/77 n431
African-Asian reading gd for children & young adults/Hotchkiss/77n1152
African authors/Herdeck/76n1215
African bk world & press/Zell/79n45
African bks in print/Zell/76n13
African ency/75n314
African music & oral data/Stone/77n962
African social psychology/Armer/76n1485
African trade unionism/Martens/78n769
Africano, L/Businessman's gd/79n815
Afro-American ency/Rywell/76n377
Afro-American folk culture/Szwed/79n453
Afro-American hist/Smith/75n360
Afro-American singers/Turner/79n977
Afro-Americana, 1553-1906/75n816
Afro-Americans & Africa/Helmreich/78n386
Age of Jewett/Harris/76n209
Aggarwal, N K/Bibliography of studies/79 n1411
Aging/McIlvaine/79n1456
Aging bibliog/Schwartz/79n739
Agner, D/Books of WAD/78n52
Agricultural atlas of Nebraska/Lawson/78 n1448
Agricultural credit/78n1449
Agricultural enterprises management in an urban-industrial society/Christian/79n1512
Agricultural outlook/77n1508
Agricultural sci in the Netherlands/76n1556
Agricultural statistics/77n1509
Agricultural terms/79n1510
Agriculture/Satyaprakash/79n1513
Agrindex/77n1512
Aguilera, F/Archive of/75n1429
Aguolu, C C/Nigeria/75n285/Nigerian civil/ 75n390
Aharoni, Y/Macmillan Bible/78n988
AIAW directory/Assoc for Intercollegiate Athletics for Women/79n648

AIBS directory of biosci departmts & faculties in the US & Canada/77n1293
Aids to media selectn for students & teachers/Moses/77n657
Ainslie, T/Ainslie's complete/76n740/Ainslie's ency/79n720
Ainslie's complete Hoyle/Ainslie/76n740
Ainslie's ency of thoroughbred handicapping/Ainslie/79n720
Ainsworth Rand Spofford/Cole/76n208
Air conditioning, heating & refrigeration dict/Zurick/79n1549
Air conditioning testing & balancing/Gladstone/75n1806
Air facts & feats/Taylor/76n1683; 79n1590
Air pollution control: gdbk for managemt/Rossano/75n1541
Air pollution control: gdbk to US regs/Hertzendorf/75n1539
Air quality abstracts/75n1554
Airman's info manual/75n1818; 79n1581
Airplanes/Angelucci/75n1819
Aitchison, J/Unesco thesaurus/79n344
Aiyepeku, W O/Geographical lit/75n567
Akeroyd, J V/Alternatives/77n104/Where are/78n1117
Akers, S G/Akers' simple/78n217
Akers' simple lib cataloging/Akers/78n217
ALA yrbk/77n188; 78n139; 79n170
Alabama birds/Imhof/78n1319
Alain Robbe-Grillet/Fraizer/75n1415
Alaska, a bibliog/Tourville/75n387
Alaska fishing gd/75n758; 76n726
Alaska hunting gd/75n774; 76n753
Alaska-Yukon wild flowers gd/White/75n1473
Alaskan mushroom hunter's gd/Guild/78n1300
Albert, S/Mokilese-English/78n1063
Albrecht, G/Internationale bibliographie/79n1276
Albright, J A/Southeastern bibliographic/79n169
Alcantara, R R/Filipinos in/78n388
Alcohol educ materials/Milgram/77n1465
Alcoholism digest annual/75n1586
Alconcel, N S/Filipinos in/78n388
Alden, D W/French XX/79n1266
Aldous, J/International bibliog/76n781
Alexander, A/Operanatomy/76n1021
Alexander, G L/Guide to atlases/78n510
Alexander, P/Eerdman's family/79n1065
Alexander, S/State-by-/76n512
Alexander, S F/Psychotropic drugs/75n1656
Alexis Bespaloff's gd to inexpensive wines/Bespaloff/77n1519

Alexis Lichine's new ency of wines & spirits/Lichine/76n1562
Alfonsi, F & S/Annotated bibliog Moravia/77n1270
Alfred North Whitehead/Woodbridge/78n1005
Alfred William Pollard/Roper/77n283
Algae abstracts/75n1555
Ali, S/Handbook of birds/77n1373
Ali, S M/Agriculture/79n1513/Indian sci/78n1221
Alibrandi, T/Meditation hndbk/77n1446
Alkire, L G/Periodical title/78n13
All about motorcycles/Alth/76n1617
All about repairing major household appliances/Squeglia/76n1644
All-Asia gd/Lynch/79n619
All-in-one TV alignmt hndbk/Shane/75n1789
All-romanized English-Japanese dict/75n1273
All together now/Castleman/77n978
Allaby, M/Dictionary of environment/79n1393
Allan, D/Illustrated guide common/77n1431
Allan, S/Atlas of Oregon/78n521
Allen, C G/Manual of European/77n1189/Rulers &/79n512
Allen, G P/National directory/76n70
Allen, G W/New Walt/77n1217
Allen, H B/Linguistic atlas/76n1115; 77n1058/Linguistics &/78n1024
Allen, J/Good earth/76n1567
Allen, J C/Collective bargaining/75n639
Allen, J L/Aviation &/76n64/Stamp collector's/75n1087
Allen, J S/Literature on/77n860
Allen, M L/Media report/77n1107
Allen, R D/Mental health/79n1435
Allende yrs/Williams/78n11
Allergy in the world/Roth/79n1476
Allied escort ships of WWII/Elliot/79n1601
Allied occupation of Japan/Ward/75n544
Allison, A F/Titles of/77n333; 78n9
Allworth, E/Soviet Asia/77n345
Alman, M/Periodicals from/78n277
Almanac of American politics/Barone/75n480; 76n474
Almanac of dates/Millgate/78n88
Almanac of liberty/Schemmer/76n336
Almanac of Virginia politics/Crater/78n456
Almanac of world military power/Dupuy/76n1677
Almanack for the yr of Our Lord 1974/Whitaker/75n88
Almanzar, A F/Coins &/75n1071

4—Authors and Titles

Almasy, E/Comparative survey/78n270
Almstedt, R F/Bibliography of Diegueno/75n802
Alonso, R C/Annotated bibliog interorganizational/78n640
Alperin, M S & S/US medical/79n1471
Alpern, R/Pratt gd/75n857
Alphabetical listing of 1972 presidential campaign receipts/US Gen Accounting Off/75n498
Alphanumeric filing rules for business docs/Hoffman/79n819
al-Qazzaz, A/Women in/78n279
Alred, G J/Business writer's/78n816
ALSED directory of specialists & research institutions/75n662
Alt, M S/Encyclopedia of Ohio/79n90
Altbach, P G/Comparative higher/77n573/Higher educ/76n573
Alternate sources of energy/Harrah/76n1454
Alternative America: directory of alternative lifestyle groups/Gardner/78n92
Alternative careers in info-library services/Minor/79n324
Alternative educ/Fantini/77n572; 78n537
Alternative press index/76n78
Alternative shopping: gd to handcrafted wares/Eddy/75n1033
Alternatives: gd to newspapers/Akeroyd/77n104
Alternatives in print/75n97; 76n79; 79n110
Alternatives to college/Hecht/76n622
Alternatives to trad'l library services/Bundy/79n286
Alth, M/All about/76n1617
Altick, R D/Selective bibliog for/76n1180
Altman, E/Data gathering/78n172
Altoma, S J/Modern Arabic/77n1252
Aluri, R/US gov/77n1295
Am I not a man & a brother/Burns/78n335
AMA drug evaluations/79n1495
Amago, B/Centeno collection/79n1285
Aman, M M/Arab states/75n221/Librarianship and/78n251
Amateur astronomer's hndbk/Muirden/75n1445
Amateur navigator's hndbk/Townsend/75n752
Amber, J T/Handloader's digest/76n754
Amble, J/Executive's digest/79n825
Ambrose-Grillet, J/Glossary of/79n1094
Ambrosi, H/Where the/77n1518
Amelia Gayle Gorgas/Johnston/79n186
America: history and life/Boehm/76n328; 76n329/5-yr index/Boehm/79n415

America in maps/Klemp/77n542
America in time/Jensen/78n349
America votes/Scammon/78n449
American almanac/Linton/78n348
American & British genealogy & heraldry/Filby/77n449
American & British writers in Mexico/Gunn/75n1308
American antique glass/Oliver/78n856
American architects from the Civil War to the first world war/Wodehouse/77n879
American architects from the first world war to the present/Wodehouse/78n805
American architectural bks/Hitchcock/78n802
American architecture & art/Sokol/77n876
American art directory/75n1007; 79n883
American Assoc of Community & Junior Colleges/Microform hndbk/76n226
American Assoc of Museums/Statistical survey/78n71
American Assoc of Univ Women/Journal index/79n673
American bench/Reincke/79n570
American bibliog of Slavic & East European studies...
    1968-69/Naylor/75n303
    1970-72/Scanlan/76n271
    1973/Kraus/76n272
    1974/Kraus/78n307
American biking atlas & touring gd/Browder/75n736
American biographical notes/75n122
American biographies/Preston/75n373
American black women in the arts & social sciences/Williams/79n454
American bk prices current/75n61; 77n68
American bk publishing record/75n4
American bk review/79n1216
American bk trade directory/76n47; 79n46
American car spotter's gd/Burness/75n1825; 76n1664; 79n1551
American Chem Society directory of grad research/Com on Profes Training/78n1251
American chemists & chemical engineers/Miles/78n1257
American clock/Distin/78n867
American composers/Hughes/75n1117
American constitutional developmt/Mason/78n445
American Correctional Assoc/Directory of juvenile/77n709
American dance band discography 1917-42/Rust/76n994

American diaries in manuscript/Matthews/ 75n361
American diplomatic hist since 1890/Fowler/ 76n311
American dissertations on foreign educ/Parker/77n578; 77n579; 78n544
American doctoral dissertations on the Arab world 1883-1974/Selim/78n282
American drama criticism, suppl II/Eddleman/77n987
American drug index/Billups/78n1434
American ethnic groups/Kinton/76n390
American Fed of Labor & Congress of Industrial Organizations pamphlets/ Woodbridge/78n774
American fiction, 1900-50/Woodress/76n1220
American fiction to 1900/Kirby/77n1194
American film directors/Hockman/75n1210
American Film Institute catalog of motion pictures/Krafsun/77n1006
American Film Institute gd to college courses in film & TV/Bohnenkamp/79n1029/ Grogg/77n1004
American folklore/Flanagan/78n1012
American folklore films & videotapes/ 77n1052
American Genealogical Research Institute Staff/How to trace/76n420
American genealogical resources in German archives/Smith/78n412
American genealogist, being a catalogue of family histories/77n453
American Geological Institute/Dictionary of geological/77n1425
American gov 73/74 ency/75n479
American gd to British soc sci resources/ Levine/77n301
American hndbk of psychiatry/Arieti/76 n1497
American Heritage school dict/79n1107
American Hospital Assoc/Health manpower/ 75n1613
American Hospital Assoc gd to the health care field/78n1402
American humanities index/78n20
American Indian/75n803
American Indian almanac/Terrell/76n811
American Indian & Eskimo authors/Hirschfelder/75n805
American Indian & the US/Washburn/75 n369
American Indian ref bk/78n380
American Indian: study gd/Dunn/76n412
American Jewish landmarks/Postal/78n528

American Jewish yr bk/Fine/75n321; 76n378
American left/Kehde/77n505
American Library Assoc/1974 Directory of gov/ 75n157/Guidelines for audiovisual/76n144/ Recommendations for/76n145
American lib developmt 1600-1899/Stone/78 n263
American lib directory/MacKeigan/75n158; 77n174; 79n165
American lib hist/Harris/79n328
American lib laws, 2d suppl/Ladenson/79n174
American lib philosophy/McCrimmon/76n116
American literary manuscripts/Robbins/78 n1118
American literary scholarships/Robbins/75 n1337/Woodress/78n1114
American lit/Leary/78n1111
American malacologists/Abbott/75n1498
American manuscripts 1763-1851/Cripe/78 n61
American marriage records before 1699/ Clemens/76n427
American medical ethnobotany/Moerman/78 n1280
American medicinal plants/Millspaugh/76 n1377
American men & women of science...13th edition. 7v./77n1297
   agricultural, animal & vet sciences/75n1660
   biology/78n1212
   chemistry/78n1213
   consultants/78n1214
   discipline index; social & behavioral sciences/75n346
   economics/75n900
   medical & health sciences/78n1215
   medical sciences/76n1542
   astronomy, mathematics, statistics, & computer sci/78n1216
   social & behavioral sciences/79n347
   urban community sciences/75n858
American metric construction hndbk/Lytle/ 77n1567
American Museum of Natural Hist gd to shells/Emerson/77n1394
American music before 1865 in print & on records/77n964
American music hndbk/Pavlakis/75n1150
American nautical art & antiques/Kranz/76 n962
American Navy/Smith/75n1851; 75n1852; 78n1853
American organ music on records/Rowell/ 77n966

American ornithological bibliog/Coues/75n1503
American overseas lib tech assistance/Brewster/77n277
American painting/Keaveney/75n1028
American pewter/Kerfoot/77n900
American Philosophical Soc yr bk/76n1105
American picturebks/Bader/78n1119
American political dict/Plano/77n507
American political sci research gd/Johnson/79n521
American printmakers/75n1024
American Psychiatric Assoc/Psychiatric glossary/76n1494
American publisher's directory/79n47
American radical press 1880-1960/Conlin/75n1293
American ref bks annual/Wynar/75n1; 76n1
American revolution/Shy/75n359
American revolution in drawings & prints/Cresswell/77n373
American sailing coasters of the North Atlantic/Morris/75n1830
American Schools Assoc/Directory of college/75n672
American sculpture/Ekdahl/78n821
American seashells/Abbott/75n1522
American Soc for Info Sci/Proceedings/75n272
American Soc for Testing & Materials/Unified numbering/76n1612
American Soc of Composers, Authors & Publishers/Copyright law/78n53; 79n54
American-Southern African relations/El-Khawas/77n526
American sporting collector's hndbk/Liu/77n935; 78n832
American stage to WWI/Wilmeth/79n1012
American state governors, 1776-1976/Kallenbach/78n458
American statistics index/76n818
American students & teachers abroad/McIntyre/76n616
American studies: topics & sources/Walker/77n334
American symbols/Schnapper/75n444
American travelers' treasury/Lord/78n527
American trucks of the early thirties/Vanderveen/76n1667
American universities & colleges/Songe/79n640
American woman's gazetteer/Sherr/77n724
American women & the labor movemt/Soltow/77n841
American women . . . biographical dict/Howes/75n849
American women . . . biographies/Willard/75n853
American women writers/White/79n1211
American writers/Unger/75n1350
American youth hostels bike-hike bk/77n681
American's tourist manual for the People's Republic of China/Felber/77n565
American's tourist manual for the USSR/Felber/76n557; 77n566
America's backpacking bk/Bridge/75n754
America's birthday/Peoples Bicentennial Commission/75n1243
America's 50 safest cities/Franke/75n833
America's soaring bk/76n730
America's tennis bk/Casewit/76n761
America's thousand bishops/Liederbach/75n1226
Ames, D/Indexes to New/76n930
Ammer, C & D S/Dictionary of business/78n706
Amnesty in America/Sherman/75n478
Amos, S W/Radio, TV/79n1567
Amstutz, M R/Economics and/79n796
Anais Nin/Franklin/75n1416
Analysis & atlas of travel in the US/Hudman/78n735
Analysis of info systems/Meadow/75n281
Analytic dict of Chinese & Sino-Japanese/Karlgren/76n1151
Analytic index of présence Africaine (1947-1972)/Ojo-Ade/78n276
Analytical access/Hyman/79n262
Analytical gd & indexes to . . .
    Alexander's Magazine 1905-1909/75n29
    Colored American Magazine 1900-1909/75n30
    Voice of the Negro 1904-1907/75n31
Analytical gd to the bibliographies on . . .
    Islam, Muhammad, & the Qur'an/Geddes/75n290
    Arab fertile crescent/Geddes/76n253
    Arabian peninsula/Geddes/75n291
Analytical index to the publications of the Institution of Civil Engineers/Holstrom/78n1516
Analytical methods: IV, cooking liquors/Pollock/77n1325
Analytical survey of Anglo-American trad'l erotica/Hoffmann/75n1321
Anatomy, descriptive & surgical/Gray/76n1530
Anatomy of antiques/Kelley/76n961
Anatomy of wonder/Barron/77n1173
Anchor atlas of world hist/Kinder/76n297; 79n401

Ancient hist/Harvard Univ Library/76n295
Ancient man/Corliss/79n394
Anderman, N/US Supreme/77n540
Anders, M E/Libraries &/77n148
Andersen, A W/Norwegian-Americans/76n415
Andersen, H H/Bibliography & index/79n1329
Andersen, R/Development of/77n1453
Anderson, A G/New Zealand/79n597
Anderson, A J/Problems in/75n229
Anderson, B/SportSource/77n663
Anderson, C B/Bookselling in/76n40/Manual on/75n47
Anderson, D/Book of slang/76n1127
Anderson, D/Universal bibliographic/76n195
Anderson, D A/Privacy &/77n531
Anderson, D K/Charles T./79n981
Anderson, D L/Symbolism/77n1124
Anderson, E N/Revised, annotated/79n773
Anderson, E R/Contemporary American/77n970
Anderson, F J/Private press/79n28/ Submarines, diving/76n1687
Anderson, G B/Freedom's voice/79n958
Anderson, I G/Directory of European/76n66; 77n77
Anderson, J E/Grant's atlas/79n1443
Anderson, L/Libraries for/79n238
Anderson, M/Coins of/75n1070
Anderson, M/Conscription/77n1625
Anderson, N C/Putnam's contemporary/75n1268
Anderson, P B/Annotated bibliog twentieth-/78n1154
Anderson, P J/Research gd/75n1292
Anderson, R J B/Anglo-Scandinavian/78n500
Anderson, S B/Encyclopedia of educ'l/76n591
Anderton, R L/Doctoral research/76n581
Andreoli-deVillers, J-P/Futurism &/77n861
Andrew, H E/Arco ency/79n939
Andrews, C J/Fell's internat'l/75n1060;77n902
Andrews, E L/Subject index/79n1195
Andrews, G E/Theory of/78n1224
Andrews, J/Shells &/78n1334
Andrews, J A C/Almanac of/76n1677
Andrews, L/Dictionary of Hawaiian/75n1280
Andrews, P M/Microanatomy of/79n1336
Andrews, R C/Dictionary of reading/75n651
Andrews, T/Bibliography of drug/78n1435/ Bibliography of socioeconomic/76n1511
Andriot, D & L/Guide to US/78n1355
Andriot, J L/Township atlas/78n462
Andrla, O J/Abstracts of/76n1369

Angel, J L/Directory of American/77n779/ Directory of inter-/76n893
Angeletti, S/Seas &/79n927
Angelucci, E/Airplanes/75n1819
Angier, B/Color field/78n1311/Field gd edible/75n1465
Angione, H/AP stylebk/79n127
Angione, P V/Continuing lib/78n255
Anglo-American & German abbreviations in sci & tech/Wennrich/78n1202; 79n1301
Anglo-Irish lit/Finneran/78n1193
Anglo-Saxon England/Clemoes/77n403
Anglo-Scandinavian law dict of legal terms used in prof & commercial practice/Anderson/78n500
Angry buyer's complaint directory/White/75n939
Angus, I/Fell's gd/75n1061
Animal facts & feats/Wood/79n1368
Animal kingdom/Pollack/79n901
Animals & their colors/Fogden/75n1495
Anker, J/Bird bks/75n1025
Ann Landers ency/79n1427
Annals of Buffalo Valley, PA/Linn/76n436
Annals of Newberry (SC)/Chapman/75n410
Anniversaries & holidays/Gregory/76n1108
Annotated bibliographies of mineral deposits in Africa, Asia, & Australasia/Ridge/77n1439
Annotated bibliog for child & family developmt programs/79n743
Annotated bibliog of . . .
    Aspen Institute publications/Kuhn/78n543
    automation in libraries & info systems/MacCafferty/77n168
    Canadian air pollution lit/Sparrow/77n1420
    Chicano folklore from the southwestern US/Heisley/78n1013
    Chinese painting catalogues & related texts/Lovell/75n989
    cryptography/Shulman/77n1105
    French language & lit/Bassan/77n1260
    Greek & Roman art, architecture, & archaeology/Coulson/77n862
    homosexuality/Bullough/78n650
    interorganizational studies/Bell/78n640
    John Dryden/Zamonski/76n1274
    John Updike criticism/Olivas/76n1250
    Moravia criticism in Italy & the English-speaking world/Alfonsi/77n1270
    Oceanic music & dance/McLean/79n960

8—Authors and Titles

Annotated bibliog of . . . (cont'd)
  papers from the Addiction Research Center/79n1496
  Shakespearean burlesques, parodies, & travesties/Jacobs/77n1240
  texts on writing skills/Burns/77n1067; 78n588
  twentieth-cent critical studies of women & lit/Backsheider/78n1154
  the British army 1660-1914/Bruce/77n1641
  the literature on resource sharing computer networks/US Dept of Commerce/77n1586
  the published writings of W E B DuBois/Aptheker/75n356
Annotated bibliography on . . .
  movemt educ/Rizzitiello/78n547
  precipitation measuremt instruments/World Meteorological Organization/75n1571
  the ecology & reclamation of drastically disturbed areas/Czapowskyj/78n1339
  the economic hist of India/79n797
Annotated calendar of the letters of Charles Darwin in the lib of the American Philosophical Soc/Carroll/77n1345
Annotated checklist of Osleriana/Nation/78n1389
Annotated gd to basic ref bks on the black American experience/Westmoreland/76n399
Annotated gd to the works of Dorothy L. Sayers/Harmon/78n1181
Annotated Mahabharata bibliog/Lal/75n1421
Annual bibliog of British & Irish hist/Elton/77n404; 79n431
Annual bk of ASTM stds/76n1604
Annual index to pop music record reviews/Armitage/75n1169; 77n976; 77n977
Annual of industrial property law/Warden/76n519
Annual of new art & artists/Sandberg/75n1006
Annual of psychoanalysis/75n1587
Annual register: world events/Hodson/75n84
Annual register of grant support/Sclar/75n667; 79n80
Annual report to the President & Congress/National Com on Libraries & Info Sci/79n151
Annual review of . . .
  anthropology/Siegel/76n808
  astronomy & astrophysics/Burbidge/75n1444; 76n1335

Annual review of . . . (cont'd)
  biochemistry/Snell/76n1339
  biophysics & bioengineering/Mullins/76n1348
  earth & planetary sciences/Donath/76n1468
  ecology & systematics/Johnston/76n1357
  energy/Hollander/77n1415
  English bks on Asia/Ferguson/78n294
  entomology/Smith/76n1409
  fluid mechanics/Van Dyke/77n1602; 77n1603
  genetics/Roman/77n1342
  info sci & tech/Williams/78n141; 79n171
  lignin chemistry/Pearl/77n1334
  materials sci/Huggins/77n1564; 77n1565
  medicine/Creger/76n1527
  microbiology/Starr/76n1358
  neuroscience/Cowan/79n1474
  nuclear sci/Segrè/76n1349
  pharmacology/Elliott/76n1548
  physical chemistry/Eyring/76n1340
  physiology/Comroe/76n1359
  phytopathology/Baker/76n1375
  plant physiology/Briggs/76n1376
  psychology/Rosenzweig/76n1496
  sociology/Inkeles/76n775
  UN affairs/Vambery/78n432
Annual summary of info on natural disasters/76n1469
Anson, W S W/Mottoes &/77n482
Antarctic bibliography/Thuronyi/78n1203/indexes to vols 1-7/Thuronyi/79n1307
Antebellum black newspapers/Jacobs/77n432
Anthony, J D/Historical &/77n315
Anthony, L J/Journal of/78n158
Anthropological & cross-cultural themes in mental health/Favazza/78n1373
Anthropology & educ/Burnett/75n865
Anthropology in the New Guinea highlands/Hays/77n739
Anti-Filipino movemts in Calif/DeWitt/77n442
Antinoro-Polizzi, J/Ghetto &/75n859
Antione, G H/Guide to graduate/79n661
Antique American country furniture/Voss/79n924
Antique collecting in the midwest/Simonsgaard/78n841
Antique restorer's hndbk/Grotz/78n836
Antique shops & dealers USA/Doherty/78n835
Antiques & collectibles, 16th cent to 1976/Franklin/79n913
Antiques: browser's hndbk/Mullenix/78n839

Antiques, illus & priced/Hudson/79n915
Apaches/Melody/79n781
Apanasewicz, N/Education in/76n574
APhA drug names/77n1500
Apparatus for F. Scott Fitzgerald's *The Great Gatsby*/Bruccoli/75n1355
Appel, M/Baseball's best/79n706
Appleby, J A/Training programs/79n852
Appleton, W S/Boston births/79n474
Applications of minicomputers to lib & related problems/Lancaster/76n232
Applications of operations research models to libraries/Chen/77n236
Applied & decorative arts/Ehresmann/78n827
Applied sci & tech index/Toom/76n1325
Approval plans & academic libraries/McCullough/78n165
Apte, V S/Student's English/75n1281
Aptheker, H/Annotated bibliog published/75n356/Documentary hist/75n810
Aquatic & wetland plants of southwestern US/Correll/76n1382
Aquatic plants of Australia/Ashton/75n1468
Arab Islamic bibliog/Grimwood-Jones/78n278
Arab-Israeli conflict/DeVore/77n417; 79n439
Arab states author headings/Aman/75n221
Arabic historical writing/Abdulrazak/78n366
Arano, L C/Medieval health/77n69
Arasteh, A R & J D/Creativity in/78n1361
Arata, E S/Black American playwrights/77n986/Black American writers/76n1226
Arbuthnot, M H/Children &/79n218
Archaeological atlas of the world/Whitehouse/77n351
Archaeologists' yr bk/75n400
Archaeology/Day/79n395
Archaic & classical Greek coins/Kraay/77n912
Archaicon: collection of unusual archaic English/Barlough/75n1256
Archer, D H R/Jane's infantry/78n1570/Jane's pocket/79n1607
Architectural & building trades dict/Putnam/75n1021
Architectural preservation in the US/Tubesing/79n894
Architectural strategy for change/Holt/77n214
Architecture bk/White/77n878
Architecture of Frank Lloyd Wright/Storrer/79n893
Architecture schools in North America/Hegener/78n798
Archive-library relations/Clark/77n153

Archive of Hispanic lit on tape/US LC. Hispanic Foundation/75n1429
Archives of the pioneers of Tazewell County, VA/Schreiner-Yantis/75n362
Archuleta, A J & M J/Hyperactive child/75n1645/Sudden infant/76n1512
Arco ency of crafts/Andrew/79n939
Arctic bibliog/Martna/77n1343
Ardis, B/AV source/79n1467
Area handbook for the . . .
    Persian Gulf states/Nyrop/79n357
    Philippines/Vreeland/78n300
Arem, J E/Color ency/79n1420
Arenstein, M/Do you/77n643
Argentina: chronology & fact bk/Fitzgibbon/75n339
Argumentation & debate/Kruger/76n1177
Arid lands research institutions/Paylore/79n1405
Arieti, S/American hndbk/76n1497
Arighi, M S & S/Wildwater touring/75n745
Arijon, D/Grammar of/78n947
Aristotle's rhetoric/Erickson/76n1106
Arizona blue book/75n503
Arizona gathering II/Powell/75n385
Arkin, F/Kitchen wisdom/78n1467
Arkin, H/Handbook of/75n904
Arlott, J/Oxford companion/76n701
Armed forces of the world/Sellers/78n1561
Armenians in America/Wertsman/79n447
Armer, M/African social/76n1485
Armitage, A D/Annual index/75n1169; 77n976; 77n977/Canadian essay/77n1135/Popular music/77n983
Armour, R/Happy bookers/77n149
Armoured fighting vehicles of the world/Foss/78n1562
Arms control & disarmament/Burns/79n550
Arms control, disarmament, & economic planning/Roswell/75n1837
Arms trade with the Third World/Stockholm Internat'l Peace Research Institute/76n870
Arms traffic/Gillingham/78n1555
Army badges & insignia of WWII/Rosignoli/77n1644; 77n1645
Army uniforms of WWII/Mollo/75n1849
Arnason, D E/John Updike/75n1371
Arndt, K J R/German language/77n444
Arno, S F/Northwest trees/79n1358
Arnold, D B/Education-psychology/76n584
Arnold, D V/Management of/79n249
Arnold, P/Check list/75n1646/Illustrated bk/76n741

10 — Authors and Titles

Arnold Bennett: annotated bibliog 1887-1932/Miller/78n1166
Arnott, J F/Actors/76n52
Arora, S L/Proverbial comparisons/79n1147
Aros, A A/Actor gd/78n953/Title gd/78n954
Arpan, J S/Directory of foreign/76n894
Arpin, G Q/John Berryman/77n1200
Arrowsmith, N/Field gd little/78n1008
Art & crafts market/Lapin/78n874
Art & Indian individualists/Monthan/76n936
Art at auction/Wilson/75n1002
Art at educ'l institutions in the US/Fundaburk/75n1009
Art directors' workbk of type faces/Biegeleisen/77n880
Art educ/Bunch/79n627
Art galleries of Britain & Ireland/Abse/77n868
Art in the US Capitol/US Congress/77n867
Art index/Patten/76n929
Art/Kunst 1: internat'l bibliog of art bks/75n987
Art Libraries Soc of North America/Matter of/78n826
Art library manual/Pacey/78n260
Art nouveau/Kempton/78n785
Art of pre-Columbian Mexico/Kendall/75n988
Art of Walt Disney/Finch/75n1190
Art of the . . .
 librarian/Jeffreys/75n141
 Pacific Northwest from the 1930's to the present/US Smithsonian Inst/75n1013
 printed book 1455-1955/Blumenthal/75n63
Art pottery of the US/Evans/75n1080
Artel, L/Positive images/78n955
Artibise, A F J/Western Canada/79n375
Articles on women writers/Schwartz/78n1092
Artillery of the world/Foss/77n1642
Artis, B/Bluegrass/76n1022
Artists' & illustrators' ency/Quick/78n788
Artist's & photographer's market/Lapin/77n856
Artist's market/Polking/76n927/Wones/79n886
Artists of early Michigan/Gibson/76n935
Artists of the American West/Dawdy/75n1012
Arts managmt hndbk/Reiss/75n1005
Asamani, JO/Index Africanus/76n245
ASCAP symphonic catalog/78n921
Ash, B/Visual ency/79n1202/Who's who science/77n1172
Ash, D/Dictionary of British/77n896

Ash, I/Formulary of/78n1253
Ash, I & M/Formulary of/79n1320
Ash, J/Health/77n1454
Ash, L/Subject collections/76n131
Ash, M/Formulary of/78n1253
Ash, R L/Motion picture/75n1207
Ashabraner, J/Collectors ency/78n866
Ashanti region of Ghana: annotated bibliog/Afre/76n252
Asheim, L/Library's public/77n213
Asher B. Durand/Lawall/79n907
Ashley, R/Dictionary of nutrition/77n1469
Ashton, H I/Aquatic plants/75n1468
Ashton, J/Harriet Beecher/78n1149
Ashworth, L S/Dell ency/75n1678
Asia & Pacific planning bibliog/Chang/75n298
Asian Americans: annotated bibliog/78n384
Asian Americans: study gd/Dunn/76n395
Asian animal zodiac/Sun/75n1607
Asian/Pacific literatures in English/McDowell/79n364
Asiedu, E S/Public admin/78n469
Asimov, I/Asimov's biographical/77n1298
Asimov's biographical ency of sci & tech/Asimov/77n1298
Askew, T A/Small college/75n640
Askland, C L/Lyons' ency/77n1609
ASLA report on interlibrary cooperation/77n173; 79n162
Aslib Transport & Planning Group & Library Assoc/New directions/77n1617
Aspects of Jewish life/Goodman/76n381
Aspen hndbk on the media/Rivers/77n1102
Assaf, K & S A/Handbook of mathematical/75n1440
Assessing the learning disabled/Mauser/79n672
Assessing the need for short courses in lib-info work/Slater/78n253
Associated Press stylebk & libel manual/Angione/79n127
Association for Asian Studies/Dictionary of Ming/77n398/South Asian/77n243; 77n244
Association for Childhood Educ Internat'l/Yearbook/76n688
Association for Computing Machinery/Graduate assistantship/75n673
Association for Intercollegiate Athletics for Women/AIAW directory/79n648
Association of American Library Schools/Davis/75n262

Association of American Publishers/Industry statistics/77n46
Association of Research Libraries/Access to/ 75n230/Methods of/75n231/System for/ 75n232
Association of Track & Field Statisticians annual/Potts/77n700
Astin, H S/Women/75n843; 76n786
Astley, S/Sourcebk of/77n1590
Astronauts & cosmonauts biographical & statistical data/US Congress/77n1571
Astronomy/Roth/77n1310
Ataturk & Turkey/US LC/75n526
Atherton, A L/International organizations/ 78n428
Atherton, P/Librarians and/79n299/ONTAP/ 79n264
Atid bibliog/79n457
Atiyeh, G N/Contemporary Middle/77n308
Atkins, B T/Collins-Robert/79n1134
Atkins, J M/Audio-visual/77n714
Atkins, T V/Cross-ref/75n222
Atkinson, F/Dictionary of literary/78n1096/ Dictionary of pseudonyms/76n1183/ Librarianship/75n135
Atkinson, J/Eugene O'Neill/75n1362
Atlanta: 1813-1976/Lankevich/79n426
Atlantic alliance/Gordon/79n552
Atlantic bridge to Germany/Hall/75n417
Atlantic liners/Emmons/75n1828
Atlas of . . .
   Africa/Chi-Bonnardel/75n576
   ancient archaeology/Hawkes/75n402
   American hist/Jackson/79n410
   Atlanta/Murray/75n880
   binary alloys/Staudhammer/75n1454
   classical archaeology/Finley/78n317
   discovery/Roberts/75n351
   early American hist/Cappon/77n375
   early man/Hawkes/78n327
   fantasy/Post/75n1328
   gallium-67 scintigraphy/Johnston/75n1643
   head & neck surgery/Loré/75n1644
   insects/Tweedie/75n1518
   Irish hist/Edwards/75n396
   issues in the Middle East/US Central Intelligence Agency/75n330
   Japan/75n573
   Kentucky/Karan/78n520
   landforms/US Military Academy/75n581
   maritime hist/Lloyd/76n1688; 78n328
   Maryland/Thompson/79n593
   medical anatomy/Langman/79n1477
   Mercury/Cross/78n1235

Atlas of . . . (cont'd)
   metro-Atlanta/Murray/77n545
   Michigan/Sommers/78n522
   Mississippi/Cross/75n574
   optical transforms/Harburn/77n1338
   Oregon/Loy/78n521
   pediatric echocardiography/Gutgesell/79 n1446
   physical & chemical properties of Puget Sound & its approaches/Collias/75 n1576
   protein spectra in the ultraviolet & visible regions/Kirschenbaum/75n1451
   representative stellar spectra/Yamashita/ 79n1315
   stereochemistry/Klyne/76n1345
   US trees/Little/78n1305
   weapons & war/Williams/78n1554
   Wisconsin/Robinson/75n580
   world population hist/McEvedy/79n786
Atlas of the . . .
   American Revolution/Nebenzahl/75n364
   Arab-Israeli conflict/Gilbert/76n358
   central nervous system in man/Miller/79 n1448
   flora of the Great Plains/Great Plains Flora Assoc/78n1283
   Pacific Northwest/Highsmith/75n578
   planets/de Callatay/76n1336
   sea/Barton/75n1575
   second world war/Young/75n1843
Attic black-figure vase-painters/Beazley/79 n903
Attinelli, E J/Bibliography of American/77 n903
Atwood, E/Who's who Alaskan/79n540
Aubrey, R H/Selected free/77n647
Auchard, J/American lit/78n1111
Auchterlonie, P/Union catalogue/78n29
Audi service, repair hndbk/Jorgensen/75n1735
Audio-visual equipmt directory/Herickes/79 n677
Audio-visual gd to American holidays/Emmens/ 79n1086
Audiovisual materials in support of info sci curricula/Klempner/79n305
Audio-visual resources for population educ & family planning/Atkins/77n714
Audiovisual resources for teaching instructional tech/Dodge/79n680
Audubon, J J/Quadrupeds of/76n1410
Audubon Soc fd gd to North American birds: eastern region/Bull/78n1315/western region/Udvardy/78n1323

Auerbach gd to retail point-of-sale systems/ 75n921
Aufdenkamp, J A/Special libraries/76n165
Auger, C P/Engineering eponyms/76n1651/ Use of/76n1306
Auger electron spectroscopy/Hawkins/79n1316
Austin, J O/Genealogical dict/79n475
Austin, W K/Comprehensive bibliog/77n1503
Australia/White/75n619
Australia: 1606-1976/Castles/79n429
Australian bibliog/Borchardt/77n22
Australian bks in print/Nicholson/75n6; 79n9
Australian bush birds in colour/Morcombe/ 76n1426
Australian dict of biography/76n108
Australian libraries/Balnaves/76n212
Australian literature/Lock/79n1259
Author biographies master index/La Beau/79 n135
Author index of mathematical reviews/76 n1331
Author index to Esquire/Baron/77n1190
Author index to selected British "little magazines"/Bloomfield/77n1133
Author-number index to the LC classification schedules/Olson/79n277
Authors & printers dict/Collins/75n51
Author's gd to journals in psychology, psychiatry & soc work/Markle/78n1369
Author's gd to journals in sociology & related fields/Sussman/79n737
Authors in the news/Nykoruk/77n1108
Auto electronics simplified/Hallmark/76n1613
Auto enthusiast directory/Black/77n926; 77n927
Autographs: collector's gd/Patterson/75n1100
Automated lib circulation systems/Dranov/79 n288
Automatic data processing hndbk/78n713
Automation in libraries/Kimber/76n231
Automobiles of the world/Lewis/79n1553
AV source directory: health sci/Ardis/79n1467
Avallone, E A/Marks' std/79n1577
Avant-garde choral music/May/78n895
Avant gardener/Powell/76n1601
Aviation & space dict/Gentle/75n1721
Aviation & space museums of America/Allen/ 76n64
Avis gd to skiing in Europe/76n760
Avi-Yonah, M/Encyclopedia of archaeological/ 77n347; 79n393/Illustrated ency classical/ 77n364/Macmillan Bible/78n988
AVMP 1977 AV market place/78n553

Avocational activities for the handicapped/ Overs/76n604
Awards, honors, & prizes/Wasserman/76n71; 76n72
Axford, L B/English language/77n1539/ Weaving, spinning/76n947
Ayer directory of publications/75n21
Ayer glossary of advertising & related terms/ 79n828
AYH hostel gd & hndbk/76n542; 77n557
Ayling, R/Sean O'Casey/79n1279
Azad, H S/Industrial wastewater/77n1605
Azevedo, R E/Labor economics/79n853

Babb, L L/Washington Post/77n558
Baby & child care/Spock/77n1499
Bacharach, J L/Near East/78n280
Bacheller, M A/CBS News/77n97
Bachman, J/Quadrupeds of/76n1410
Back, K/Oral hist/78n323
Back, P/Complete bk herbs/75n1484
Backe, T/Concise Swedish-/75n552
Backer, T E/New career/78n773
Backpacking with small children/Stout/76 n722
Backscheider, P/Annotated bibliog twentieth-/ 78n1154
Backyard treasure hunting/Lowery/75n1051
Bader, B/American picturebks/78n1119
Badges & insignia of the British armed services/May/76n1678
Baeckler, V/GO, PEP/77n211/PR for/79n284
Baedeker's handbk(s) for travellers/76n539
Baer, E A/Titles in/75n2
Baer, W E/Labor arbitration/75n973
Baerwald, J E/Transportation &/77n1618
Baetzenr, W H/Naturalists' directory/76n1368
Bagnasco, E/Submarines of/79n1598
Baguley, D/Bibliographie de/79n1267
Bahat, D/Historical atlas/76n356
Bahr, A H/Book theft/79n250/Microforms/ 79n332
Baig, A/Current accounting/77n796
Bailey, A/World atlas/77n1543
Bailey, E Z/Hortus third/78n1485
Bailey, F L/Complete manual/76n513
Bailey, L H/Hortus third/78n1485
Bailey, L P/Broadside authors/75n1334
Bailey, M J/Special librarian/78n192
Bailey, R/Good Housekeeping/75n1697
Bailey, R B/Guide to Chinese/75n1413
Bailie, J M/British crossword/79n1122
Bailly, O/What to/77n1530

Authors and Titles—13

Bain, R C/Convention decisions/75n487
Baines, J/ABC of/75n1698
Bair, F/Biography news/75n117
Bair, F E/Weather almanac/75n1568; 78n1353
Baird, D/English novel/76n1256
Baird, L Y/Bibliography of Chaucer/78n1169
Baird, S F/Water birds/75n1499
Bakalla, M H/Bibliography of Arabic/77n1059
Baker, A/Storytelling/79n205
Baker, C/Modern American/75n1288
Baker, C O/Earned degrees/76n633
Baker, D P/School and/78n178
Baker, J A/Index to criticisms/75n1332
Baker, K F/Annual review/76n1375
Baker, R A/US Senate/78n455
Baker, R F/Handbook of highway/76n1662
Baker, R K/Introduction to library/79n1268
Baker, R L/Indiana place/76n453
Baker, S L/Collector's bk/77n928
Baker, W/George Eliot-/78n1160
Baker, W A/Maine shipbuilding/75n376
Baker's pocket atlas of the Bible/Pfeiffer/75n1233
Baker's pocket dict of religious terms/Kauffman/76n1084
Bakewell, K G B/Management principles/79n869
Bakó, E/Guide to Hungarian/75n304
Balachandran, M/Guide to trade/78n727
Balandier, A/Comparative survey/78n270
Balandier, G/Dictionary of black/75n315
Baldo, F R/US Senate/78n455
Baldwin, C M & DE/Yoruba of/77n735
Baldwin, J K/Collector's gd/75n1078
Baldwin, J L/Weather atlas/76n1479
Baldwin, N/Observer's bk/76n1663
Balfour, M/Good earth/76n1567
Ball, J M/Bibliography for geographic/77n547
Ballard, R F/Directory of Manhattan/79n889
Ballet gd/Terry/76n1040; 78n935
Ballparks/Shannon/76n706
Bally, A W/Stratigraphic atlas/78n513
Balnaves, J/Australian libraries/76n212
Balzer, H M/Official baseball/79n707
Bamber, C/Durations/79n99
BAMEG reviews/79n222
Band music gd/77n951
Banerji, S C/Companion to/78n1192
Banes, D/Chemist's gd/75n1449
Banes, S/Sweet home/75n602
Banfield, A W F/Mammals of/76n1443
Bangert, W V/Bibliographical essay/77n1021
Banks, A/Military atlas/76n296/World atlas/75n1842

Banks, A S/Political hndbk/76n468; 79n510
Banks, F R/Penguin gd/79n611
Banks, R F/Maine during/76n343
Banned bks/Haight/79n310
Banov, A/Book of successful/76n1636
Bantam great outdoors gd to the US & Canada/Landi/79n712
Barabas, S/Zondervan pictorial/76n1104
Barbara Kraus dict of protein/Kraus/76n1576
Barber, C J/Minister's library/75n1213; 77n235/Minister's library: periodic suppl/79n1047
Barber, E A/Ceramic, furniture/78n830
Barber, M/Index to letters/77n1041
Barber, P/Trees around/76n1400
Barbour, F M/Concordance to sayings/75n1356
Barbour, L B/Families of/78n396
Barbour, R L/Who's who public/77n1109
Barbour, R/Mammals of/75n1519
Barclay, J M/Emily Brontë/75n1382
Barclay, W/New Testament/75n1228
Bard, A J/Encyclopedia of electrochemistry/75n1450; 76n1343; 79n1318
Bard, R/Atlas of Pacific/75n578
Barefoot, P/Community services/79n1458
Barefoot librarian/Wijasuriya/76n218
Bareham, T/Bibliography of George/79n1238
Bargain hunting in L.A./Partridge/75n953
Bargain hunting in San Francisco/Socolich/75n954
Barker, L M/Pears cyclopaedia/76n62; 79n78
Barker, W P/Who's who church/79n1076
Barleycorn, M/Moon-shiners/76n1560
Barlough, J E/Archaicon/75n1256
Barlow, A R/English-Kikuyu/77n1093
Barlow, H/Dictionary of opera/78n911
Barnes, C A/Atlas of physical/75n1576
Barnes, D L/Rape/78n673
Barnes, L/Handbook of wealth/78n729
Barnes, M/Best detective/76n1202/Youth library/77n212
Barnes, R W/Marriages &/79n477/Maryland marriages/76n423; 79n476
Barnett, B J/New Mexico/76n22
Barney, R D/Pacific islands/75n1303
Barnhart, C L/Scott, Foresman/77n1078/Thorndike Barnhart/76n1122/World Book/77n1075
Barnhart, R K/World bk dict/77n1075
Baron, B/Bibliography of bks/79n223
Baron, H/Author index/77n1190/Concordance to poems/76n1231

Barone, M/Almanac of American/75n480; 76n480
Barr, A H/Painting &/79n877
Barr, E S/Index to biographical/75n1437
Barr, G/Who's who Bible/76n1094
Barr, K/Essays on/76n207
Barraclough, G/Times atlas/79n583
Barrett, H/Viola/79n989
Barron, N/Anatomy of/77n1173
Barron's guide to . . .
  graduate business schools/Miller/79n659
  graduate schools: soc sciences & psychology/76n634
  law schools/Epstein/79n657
  medical, dental, & allied health sci careers/Wischnitzer/75n1635; 78n1409
  two-year colleges/75n674
Barron's handbook of . . .
  American college financial aid/Proia/76n635
  college transfer info/Proia/76n636
  junior & community college financial aid/Proia/76n637
Barron's how to prepare for the . . .
  admission test for graduate study in business/Jaffe/76n597
  MCAT medical college admission test/Seibel/77n608
Barron's profiles of American colleges . . .
  descriptions of the colleges/76n638; 79n649
  Midwest/76n639
  Northeast/76n640
  South/76n641
  West/76n642
Barros, J/International law/75n1535
Barrow, G B/Genealogist's gd/79n466
Barry, T E/Marketing &/77n807
Bartels, N K/Bradford bk/77n918
Bartholomew/Scribner atlas of Europe/Browne/75n575
Bartlett, J R/Word index/79n1277
Bartlett, L/William Everson/78n1138
Barton, J J/Brief ethnic/77n421
Barton, R/Atlas of sea/75n1575
Barzman, S/Madmen &/75n488
Barzun, J/Modern American/75n1288/ Modern researcher/78n322
Baseball ency/75n729; 77n673
Baseball's best/Appel/79n706
Basic bibliog on marketing research/Ferber/76n864
Basic bk of antiques/Michael/75n1057
Basic docs of American public admin/Mosher/78n438
Basic electrocardiography hndbk/Lyon/78n1413

Basic food & brand-name calorie counter/Kraus/75n1691
Basic food & brand-name carbohydrate counter/Kraus/75n1692
Basic gd to research sources/O'Brien/77n13
Basic hndbk on mental illness/Milt/75n1594
Basic info about higher educ institutions in the middle states region/75n675
Basic mathematics/Lerro/77n1303
Basic ref sources/Taylor/75n246
Basic statistics for librarians/Simpson/76n122
Basic tools of research/Vitale/78n1094
Basil, D C/Purchasing info/78n732
Basile, P S/Energy demand/77n1398
Baskin, B H/Notes from/78n179/Special child/77n216
Basler, B K/Health sciences/78n197
Basler, R P/Guide to study/77n338/Muse and/75n260
Basler, T G/Health sciences/78n197
Bason, F T/Bibliography of writings/75n1394
Basova, I M/Publications on/76n229
Bassan, F/Annotated bibliog French/77n1260
Basseches, B/Bibliography of Brazilian/79n1
Bassett, F E/Farwell's rules/78n1573
Bassett, M/Profiles &/77n509
Batch, D L/Fishes of/75n1512
Bates, J D/Fishing/75n759
Bate, J G/Faber medical/76n1524
Bates, S L/Concordance to poems/79n1243
Bateson, F W/Guide to English/78n1088
Batson, W T/Guide to genera/79n1341
Battista, O A/Quotoons/79n94
Battle maps & charts of the American revolution/Carrington/76n321
Battleships/Dulin/77n1649
Batts, J S/British manuscript/77n405
Batty, D/Knowledge &/77n150
Batty, L/Retrospective index/76n1061
Batz, L/Running Press/78n750
Bauer, C F/Handbook for/78n180
Bauer, E A/Hunting with/75n775
Bauer, N S/William Wordsworth/79n1257
Baugh, A C/Chaucer/78n1170
Baum, S J/Practical gd/75n981
Bauman, M K/Blindness, visual/79n1449
Baumeister, T/Mark's std/79n1577
Bäuml, B J & F H/Dictionary of gestures/76n1167
Baumol, W J/Economics of/75n176
Bavier, R N/New yacht/75n750
Bawden, L-Z/Oxford companion/77n997
Bay, K E/How to tie/76n727
Bayerl, E/Interdisciplinary studies/78n560

Bayliss, G M/Bibliographic gd/78n329
Baynton, R A/Who's who British/75n1720
Beach, E L/Naval terms/79n1603
Beach, M/Bibliographic gd American/76n575
Beale, H P/Bibliography of plant/77n1513
Beale, W H/Old and/77n1219
Beall, K F/Kaufrufe und/78n806
Bean, L J/California Indians/78n676
Bean, W J/Trees and/75n1490
Beard, H J & J B/Turfgrass bibliog/79n1347
Beard, J/Cooks' catalogue/76n1568
Beard, T F/How to find/79n467
Bearse, R/Canoe camper's/76n714
Beasley, J C/English fiction/79n1227
Beatles again?/Castlemen/79n997
Beaty, H W/Standard hndbk/79n1546
Beaumont, A G/Handbook for/75n653
Beazley, J D/Attic black-/79n903
Bechtel, H/Cactus identifier/78n1486
Beachtle, T C/Dissertations in/79n1078
Beck, C/Political sci/76n464
Beck, J H/Rail talk/79n1115
Beck, L/Bibliography of African/76n1164
Beck, T-D/Foundation center/76n571
Becker, C H/Plant manager's/75n1809
Becker, H K/Law enforcement/78n497
Becker, J/Handbook of data/76n230
Beckerman, J/Inside the/77n938
Beckett, G & K/Illustrated ency indoor/78n1487
Beckman, R/International directory/75n1550
Beckson, K/Literary terms/76n1184
Beckwith, J/Contemporary Canadian/77n971
Bederman, S H/Africa/75n568
Bedford, E G/Concordance to poems/76n1282
Bedford, F/Twentieth-century/75n1120
Beebe, T/Who's who new/79n1077
Beede, B R/Independence docs/79n518
Beeler, R J/Evaluating library/77n265
Beer, A/Astronomy/77n1310
Beer, R L/Michigan legal/75n545
Beer can collecting/Cady/77n929
Beer can collector's bible/Martells/77n936
Beers, V G/Children's illus/78n989
Beethoven abstracts/MacArdle/75n1158
Beetles of America/Headstrom/78n1329
Beeton, D R/Dictionary of English/77n1083
Beetz, K H/John Ruskin/77n1239/Wilkie Collins/79n1236
Beginners' dict of Chinese-Japanese characters/Rose-Innes/78n1052
Beginner's gd to the skies/Cleminshaw/79n1314
Beginning writer's answer bk/Polking/79n1169

Behn, W/Kurds in/78n284
Behrends, S/Travel research/78n742
Beinecke rare bk & manuscript library/76n57
Belch, J/Contemporary games/75n697
Belgium's 500 largest companies/76n895
Bell, E C/Annotated bibliog interorganizational/78n640
Bell, I F/English novel/76n1256
Bell, J E/Hawaiian language/79n389
Bell, J K/Bell &/77n1086
Bell, J P/Our Quaker/77n454
Bell, L C/Cumberland parish/75n406/Sunlight on/75n407
Bell, M V/Reference bks/79n178
Bell, S P/Biographical index/76n1606/Dissertations on/76n366
Bell & Cohn's hndbk of grammar/Bell/77n1086
Bellamy, J M/Dictionary of labour/79n574
Bellassai, M C/Access to/75n230
Belt, F H/Yearbook of consumer/75n1791
Belzer, J/Encyclopedia of computer/76n1626; 78n1523
Bemis, V/Energy gd/78n1337
Ben Abba, D/Signet Hebrew/79n1140
Ben Johnson/Brock/75n1387
Ben Jonson's London/Chalfant/79n1244
Ben K. Green/Wilson/78n1139
Benagh, J/ABC's wide/75n720
Bender, A E/Dictionary of nutrition/78n1468
Bender, T K/Concordance to Conrad's/79n1237/Concordance to Conrad's Lord/77n1231
Bendick, J & R/Consumer's catalog/76n882
Benedict Arnold/Gocek/75n358
Benefit-cost analysis of alternative library delivery systems/Hu/77n248
Benito Pérez Galdós/Woodbridge/77n1277
Benjamin, C G/Candid critique/79n29
Benjamin, S G W/Our American/78n794
Bennett, A/College gd/78n564
Bennett, A/New color-/79n1108
Bennett, A G/Five centuries/78n861
Bennett, G F/Environmental lit/75n1556
Bennett, H/Chemical formulary/78n1254/Concise chemical/76n1342
Bennett, H/Complete short/75n1202
Bennett, J C/Environmental lit/75n1556
Bennett, J R/Catalogue of vocal/79n969
Bennett, P J/Fifty-year index/75n371
Bennett, S/Victorian periodicals/79n1226
Bennett, T/NFL's official/78n624

Bennie, F/Learning centers/79n206
Benoliel, D/Northwest foraging/76n1381
Benson, R C/Handbook of obstetrics/75n1626
Bentinck-Smith, W/Building a/77n276
Bentley, E P/Index to 1800/79n478
Bentley, G E/Bibliography of George/76n1271
Benton, A A/Church cyclopaedia/76n1080
Beraha, J A/Writer's market/79n1168
Berberi, D/Cortina/Grosset/77n1092
Berelson, B/Library's public/77n213
Bergaust, E/National outdoorsmen's/76n715
Berger, A J/Fundamentals of/78n1324
Berger, A/Learning disabilities/79n692/Rates of/77n574
Berger, A H/Dictionary of psychology/78n1366
Berger, J/Filipinos in/78n388
Berger, J L/Educators gd audio/78n591/Educators gd tapes/76n675
Bergeron, D M/Shakespeare/76n1284
Bergman, W H/Handbook of manpower/75n974
Bergstrom, L V/Women and/76n797
Berisiner, Y/Collector's gd/79n933
Berkowitz, F P/Popular titles/76n983
Berkowitz, T/Who's who where/76n787
Berlin, I N/Bibliography of child/77n1457
Berlitz, C/Dictionary of foreign/76n1118
Berman, L/Evolution of/79n524
Berman, R/Reader's gd/75n1396
Bernard Shaw companion/Hardwick/75n1401
Bernardo, G A/Philippine retrospective/76n14
Bernier, B A/Popular names/77n115
Bernier, C L/Indexing concepts/79n330
Bernstein, I M/Handbook of stainless/78n1544
Bernstein, J E/Books to/79n744
Bernstein, S/Dog digest/77n1526
Bernstein, T M/Bernstein's reverse/76n88
Bernstein's reverse dict/Bernstein/76n88
Berra, T M/William Beebe/78n1271
Berridge, R I/Community educ/75n654
Berry, D M/Bibliographic gd educational/76n576
Berry, T E/Plots and/78n1196; 79n1282
Berryman, P/Guide to global/77n712
Bertrand, P/Books with/77n1143
Besançon, R M/Encyclopedia of physics/75n1456
Besford, P/Encyclopaedia of swimming/78n631
Bespaloff, A/Alexis Bespaloff's/77n1519
Bessinger, J B/Concordance to Anglo-/79n1231
Bessis, M/Corpuscles/75n1642

Best bks for children/Gillespie/79n230
Best buys in print/79n32
Best detective fiction/Barnes/76n1202
Best, encore/Passel/78n89
Best musicals/Jackson/79n1036
Best of the best/Scherf/77n1144
Best ref bks/Wynar/77n16
Best restaurants of L.A. and Southern Calif/Dills/77n1541
Best restaurants of San Francisco & Northern Calif/Killeen/77n1542
Best yrs catalogue/Biegel/79n839
Besten der besten/Scherf/77n1144
Besterman, T/World bibliog African/76n2/World bibliog Oriental/76n3
Betancourt, J/Women in/76n1054
Bettelheim, J/Worldwide directory/75n169
Betts, D A/Chess/75n767
Beuscher's law & the farmer/Hannah/76n1557
Beyond the lions/NY Public Library/75n189
Bezer, C A/Russian &/75n334
Biagi, A/English-Italian/75n1272
Bianchini, F/Health plants/79n1351
Bible in order/Rhymer/77n1047
Bible interpretation/Megivern/79n1043
Bible-related curriculum materials/Warshaw/77n1049
Biblical refs in *The Faerie Queene*/Shaheen/77n1245
Bibliografia Chicana/Trejo/76n404
Bibliografie/Stichting Druckwerk in de Marge/79n41
Bibliographia Canadiana/Thibault/75n394
Bibliographia cartographica/Zogner/78n511
Bibliographia oziana/Hanff/77n1187
Bibliographic citations for nonprint materials/Fleischer/76n87
Bibliographic control/Davinson/76n197
Bibliographic guide to . . .
  American colleges & universities from colonial times to the present/Beach/76n575
  art and architecture/77n1
  black studies/77n2
  business & economics/77n3
  conference publications/77n4
  dance/77n5
  educational research/Berry/76n576
  gov publications—foreign/77n7
  gov publications—US/77n6
  law/77n8
  lit of contemporary American poetry/Gershator/77n1195

Bibliographic guide to . . . (cont'd)
  music/77n9
  population geography/Zelinsky/77n758
  psychology/77n10
  Spanish diplomatic hist/Cortada/79n551
  technology/77n11
  theatre arts/77n12
  the two world wars/Bayliss/78n329
Bibliographic index: cum bibliog of bibliographies/Case/76n29
Bibliographical essay on the hist of the Soc of Jesus/Bangert/77n1021
Bibliographical essays in medieval Jewish studies/77n1022
Bibliographical guide to . . .
  history of Indian-white relations in the US/Prucha/78n345
  self-disclosure lit/Moss/79n1425
  study of the lit of the USA/Gohdes/77n1186
Bibliographical hist of electricity & magnetism/Mottelay/76n1631
Bibliographical index of the Ukrainian press outside Ukraine/Fedynskyj/76n1163
Bibliographical notes for understanding . . .
  military coup in Chile/Riesch/76n497
  transnational corporations & the Third World/Strharsky/76n828
Bibliographical studies & notes on rare books . . . of the Jewish Theological Seminary of America/Marx/79n67
Bibliographie de la critique sur Émile Zola/Baguley/79n1267
Bibliographie des français dans l'Inde/Bibliog of the French in India/Scholberg/77n399
Bibliographie du genre romanesque français/Martin/78n1186
Bibliographie zur sozial-wissenschaftlichen erforschung Tanzanias/Bibliog for soc sci research on Tanzania/Hundsdörfer/76n256
Bibliography & index of experimental range & stopping power data/Andersen/79n1329
Bibliography & indexes of US Congressional committee prints 1911-69/Field/79n117
Bibliography & reel index: gd to the US decennial census publications/77n755
Bibliography: bks for children/Markun/75n1347
Bibliography: clay/75n1039
Bibliography: corporate responsibility for soc problems/75n790
Bibliography: enamel/75n1048
Bibliography for . . .
  Adlerian psychology/Mosak/76n1488
  beginners/Gore/75n244

Bibliography for . . . (cont'd)
  finite elements/Whiteman/76n1603; 77n1562
  geographic educ/Ball/77n547
Bibliography: glass/75n1049
Bibliography in the history of . . .
  American women/Lerner/77n720
  European women/Kelly/77n401
Bibliography of . . .
  African broadcasting/Head/76n1164
  African freshwater fish/Matthes/75n1515
  Africana/Panofsky/76n247
  aggressive behavior/Crabtree/79n1424
  American ethnology/Cashman/77n422
  American lit/Blanck/77n1335
  American numismatic auction catalogues/Attinelli/77n903
  appraisal lit/MacBride/76n858
  Arabic linguistics/Bakalla/77n1059
  Arthur Machen/Goldstone/75n1391
  Asian studies/76n257
  audiotapes & tape-slide programs applicable to undergrad medical educ/Zubkoff/75n1621
  bibliographies on India/Kalia/76n5
  bioethics/Walters/76n1520; 78n1385; 78n1386
  books for children/Baron/79n223
  Brazilian bibliographies/Basseches/79n1
  British history 1714-1789/Pargellis/78n370/1789-1851/Brown/78n368/1851-1914/Hanham/77n410
  business ethics/Jones/78n701
  California Indians/Heizer/78n679
  Cameroon/DeLancey/76n249
  cello ensemble music/Kenneson/76n1016
  Chaucer/Baird/78n1169
  child psychiatry & child mental health/Berlin/77n1457
  child study/Wilson/76n1489
  Chinese newspapers & periodicals in European libraries/77n318
  collective bargaining in hospitals & related facilities/Rothman/77n840
  Colorado State Univ imprints in the Colorado State Univ libraries/Kolesar/78n12
  computer applications in music/Kostka/75n1129
  contemporary linguistic research/Gazdar/79n1089
  contemporary North American Indians/Hodge/77n742

Bibliography of . . . (cont'd)
  continental drift & plate tectonics/Kasbeer/ 75n1565
  corporate soc responsibility: programs & policies/78n696
  creative African writing/Jahn/77n1251
  cultivated trees & shrubs/Rehder/79n1364
  Delaware/Univ of Delaware, Morris Lib/ 78n311
  Dickensian criticism/Churchill/76n1272
  Diegueno Indians/Almstedt/75n802
  discographies, classical/Gray/79n970
  dissertations in classical studies/Thompson/ 78n551
  drug abuse, including alcohol & tobacco/ Andrews/78n1435
  energy conservation in architecture/Lee/ 78n803
  English hist to 1485/Gross/77n408
  English-language sources on Estonia/Parming/ 75n305; 76n273
  English translations from medieval sources/ Ferguson/75n350
  Eric Gill/Gill/75n72
  Festschriften in religion published since 1960/O'Brien/76n1074
  finance & investment/Brealey/75n955
  food & agric'l marketing/79n1511
  French revolutionary pamphlets on microfiche/Thompson/76n365
  geography/Harris/77n548
  George Berkeley Bishop of Cloyne/Keynes/ 77n1027
  George Crabbe/Bareham/79n1238
  George Cumberland/Bentley/76n1271
  German lang legal monograph series/ Schwerin/79n567
  Horace Walpole/Hazen/75n1406
  Indo-English lit/Karkala/77n1267
  industrial relations in the railroad industry/ Morris/76n905
  insurance hist/Nelli/79n851
  international law/Delupis/77n535
  Ismāʻīlī lit/Poonawala/79n1052
  John Middleton Murry/Lilley/76n1279
  language arts materials for native North Americans/Abbey/78n587
  Latin American bibliographies published in periodicals/Gropp/77n339
  Latin American theater criticism 1940-74/ Lyday/79n1010
  law-related curriculum materials/Davison/ 78n494
  liquid column chromatography/Deyl/ 78n1239

Bibliography of . . . (cont'd)
  literature from Guyana/McDowell/76 n1302
  Matthew Arnold, 1932-70/Tollers/76 n1266
  microwave optical tech/Harvey/78n1266
  modern British novelists/Stanton/79n1230
  modern Icelandic lit in translation/Mitchell/77n1266
  modern Irish & Anglo-Irish lit/Kersnowski/ 77n1269
  New Mexico state politics/Wolf/76n493
  new religious movemts in primal societies/ Turner/78n977
  noise for 1973/Floyd/76n1452
  Norman Mailer/Sokoloff/75n1361
  nursing lit/Thompson/75n1619
  paper & thin-layer chromatography/ Macek/77n1324
  philosophical bibliographies/Guerry/78 n1000
  Pidgin & Creole langs/Reinecke/77n1060
  plant viruses & index to research/Beale/ 77n1513
  printed battle plans of the American Revolution/Nebenzahl/76n313
  programming langs/Stock/75n1777
  prostitution/Bullough/78n643
  psychohistory/deMause/76n1487
  publications issued by Unesco or under its auspices/75n111
  quantitative ecology/Schultz/77n1409
  recreational mathematics/Schaaf/79n1310
  research studies in educ/US Off of Educ/ 75n650
  Russian composers/Moldon/78n896
  science fiction/Sween/75n1329
  selected statistical sources of the American nations/Inter-American Statistical Institute/75n873
  seventeenth cent bibliographies/Weeks/ 79n5
  Shelley studies/Dunbar/77n1244
  skiing studies/Goeldner/78n629
  songsters printed in America before 1821/ Lowens/77n1821
  sources & applications/Murrell/76n910
  sources for the study of ancient Greek music/Mathieson/75n1131
  southern Appalachia/Ross/78n312
  studies & translations of modern Chinese lit, 1918-42/Gibbs/76n1293
  studies on Hindi lang & linguistics/Aggarwal/79n1141

Bibliography of ... (cont'd)
  Targum lit/Grossfeld/79n1049
  vocational educ/Cordasco/78n538
  water colour painting & painters/
    Lucas/78n819
  water pollution control benefits & costs/
    Unger/76n1455
  William Cullen Bryant & his critics 1808-
    1972/Phair/76n314
  women's periodicals/75n844
  writings by & abt Harold Frederic/
    O'Donnell/76n1238
  writings by & abt John Ford & Cyril
    Tourneur/Tucker/78n932
Bibliography of the ...
  Criollo cattle of the Americas/Müller-
    Hayes/79n1524
  Golden Cockerel Press 1921-41/77n52
  history of medicine/79n1450
  literature on British & Irish labour law/
    Hepple/76n904
  literature on North American climates of
    the past 13,000 yrs/Grayson/76n1478
  Naval Arctic Research Lab/Gunn/75n1524
  New York bight/US Natl Oceanic &
    Atmospheric Admin/75n1563
  published works of J V Cunningham/
    Gullans/75n1353
  socioeconomic aspects of medicine/
    Andrews/76n1511
  Soviet soc sciences/Heiliger/79n385
  urban modifcation of the atmospheric &
    hydrologic environment/US Environ-
    mental Data Service/75n1529
  writings & criticisms of Edwin Arlington
    Robinson/Lippincott/75n1366
  writings of E. E. Evans-Pritchard/Evans-
    Pritchard/76n803
  Walter H. Pater/Wright/76n1281
  W. Somerset Maugham/Bason/75n1394
  Wyndham Lewis/Morrow/79n1246
Bibliography on ...
  accountability/75n641
  atomic energy levels & spectra/Hagan/
    78n1267
  atomic transition probabilities/Fuhr/79
    n1330
  deafness/Fellendorf/79n1455
  divorce/Israel/76n782
  geographic thought, philosophy, & metho-
    dology/Wheeler/77n550
  land settlement/79n787
  major aspects of the humanisation of work
    & the quality of working life/79n854

Bibliography on ... (cont'd)
  oral history/Waserman/77n383
  taxation of foreign operations & for-
    eigners/Owens/78n783
  the common law in French/Blaustein/
    75n546
  the genetics of drosophila/Herskowitz/
    75n1460
  urbanization in India/Bose/78n641
  women/Davis/75n846
  women & drug related issues/76n788
Bibliography-1: fine arts/78n784
Bibliography: tiger or fat cat?/Dunkin/76
  n198
Bibliography without footnotes/Hoffman/
  78n104
Bibliography: Wood/75n1044
Bibliotherapy in rehabilitation, educat'l, &
  mental health settings/Zaccaria/79n309
Bibliotherapy sourcebk/Rubin/79n307
Bicentennial almanac/Linton/79n331
Bicentennial bk/Lawlor/76n551
Bicentennial city: Philadelphia/Marion/75
  n611
Bicentennial gd to the American Revolution/
  Stember/75n599
Bicentennial Philadelphia/Gales/75n606
Bickel, W/Hering's dict/76n1573
Bickner, M L/Women at/75n845
Bicultural heritage/Schon/79n462
Bidmead, M/Use of computers/77n287
Bidwell, R/Bidwell's gd/75n516; 75n517
Bidwell's gd to gov ministers: Arab world/
  Bidwell/75n516
Bidwell's gd to gov ministers: British Empire/
  Bidwell/75n517
Biegel, L/Best yrs/79n839
Biegeleisen, J I/Art directors'/77n880
Biery, T L/Venomous arthropod/78n1327
Biesenthal, L/Canadian bk/77n196
Big bk of halls of fame in the US & Canada/
  Soderberg/78n603
Big name hunting/Hamilton/75n1096
Bigelow, H E/Mushroom pocket/75n1486
Bilboul, R R/Retrospective index/78n1222;
  79n1306
Bilingual bicultural educ for the Spanish
  speaking in the US/Trueba/78n548
Bill, E G W/Calendar of/77n1033/Catalogue of
  manuscripts/77n1023
Billups, N F/American drug/78n1434
Bilsborrow, R E/Population in/78n684
Bindoff, S T/Research in/77n406
Binford, L C/Birds of/75n1500

Binstock, R H/Handbook of aging/78n648
Biographia Nigeriana/Orimoloye/78n117
Biographical-bibliographical directory of
 women librarians/Cummings/78n154
Biographical cyclopaedia of American women/
 Cameron/76n104
Biographical dictionaries & related works,
 suppl/Slocum/79n134
Biographical dictionaries master index/La
 Beau/76n91; 77n120
Biographical dict of . . .
 actors, actresses, musicians, dancers,
  managers & other stage personnel in
  London, 1660-1800/Highfill/75n1188;
  76n1045; 79n1022
 American educators/Ohles/79n695
 American labor leaders/Fink/75n975
 American music/Claghorn/75n1155
 film/Thomson/77n1017
 Japanese literature/Hisamatsu/77n1271
 railway engineers/Marshall/79n1585
 scientists/Williams/76n1330
 Scottish grads to A.D. 1410/Watt/79n441
 Southern authors/Knight/79n1219
Biographical dictionary of the . . .
 Confederacy/Wakelyn/78n364
 federal judiciary/Chase/77n541
 phonetic sciences/Bronstein/79n1157
Biographical directory of the . . .
 Divina Commedia of Danta Alighieri/
  Locock/76n1297
 fellows & members of the American
  Psychiatric Assn/75n1603; 78n1368
 governors of the US 1789-1978/79n543
 South Carolina House of Representatives/
  Edgar/75n484
 US Executive Branch 1774-1977/Sobel/
  78n451; 79n541
Biographical history of Lancaster County
 (PA)/Harris/75n420
Biographical index of American artists/Smith/77
 n870
Biographical index of British engineers in the
 19th century/Bell/76n1606
Biographical register of the Confederate Congress/Warner/76n341
Biographical register of the Univ of Oxford
 A.D. 1501 to 1540/Emden/75n691
Biographical subj index to the LC classification schedules/Olson/79n278
Biography/79n136
Biography news/Bair/75n117
Biological & agricul'l index/Brooks/76n1370
Biological indicators of environmental quality/
 Thomas/75n1528

Biological sciences/77n1344
Biology of perceptual systems/Carterette/75
 n1588
Biomedical, scientific & tech bk reviewing/
 Chen/78n1381
Birchfield, M E/Consolidated catalog/78n429
Bird, J/Effective library/77n215
Bird, M M/Industrial marketing/78n737
Bird, P/Vintage car/78n865
Bird, W/Library telecommunications/78n134
Bird bks & bird art/Anker/75n1025
Bird life/Rowley/76n1431
Bird life of Texas/Oberholser/76n1427
Birds in New Zealand/Robertson/76n1430
Birds of . . .
 California/Small/75n1520; 76n1432
 New Jersey/Leck/76n1424
 Seychelles & the outlying islands/Penny/
  76n1428
 western North America/Carlson/75n1500
Birds of the . . .
 Bahamas/Brudenell-Bruce/76n1415
 New York area/Bull/77n1374
 Southwest Pacific/Mayr/79n1374
 West/Clarke/77n1375
 world/Clements/75n1502; 79n1370/
  Short/77n1387
 world on stamps/Stanley/75n1091
Birdwatcher's gd to wildlife sanctuaries/
 Kitching/77n1382
Birkos, A S/African and/77n431/East
 European/76n821/Historiography,
 method/76n284/Soviet cinema/77n1007
Birnbaum, M/Comparative gd American/77
 n611; 79n650/Comparative gd two/78
 n567/Counselors' comparative/77n612
Birth, marriage, divorce, death/78n654
Bishop, A C/Larousse gd/78n1359
Bishop, M/Sachs engine/75n1740
Bishop, R/American clock/78n867
Bishop, R/How to know/75n1073
Biskup, P/Australian libraries/76n212
Bissainthe, M/Dictionnaire de/75n295
Biteaux, A/New consciousness/76n1508
Bittman, S/Recipes for/75n1801
Bitton, D/Guide to Mormon/78n971
B-J paperback bk gd/Blow/77n195
Black, D V/Directory of academic/77n209
Black, H A/Modern accountant's/78n721
Black, J A/Your Irish/75n435
Black, J D/Blathwayt atlas/76n367
Black, L/Auto enthusiast/77n926
Black, R A/Advertiser's gd/79n16
Black African traditional religions & philosophy/Ofori/77n1029

Black American fiction/Fairbanks/79n1215
Black American lit/Whitlow/75n1336
Black American playwrights/Arata/77n986
Black American ref bk/Smythe/77n435
Black American writers, 1773-1949/Matthews/76n398
Black American writers past & present/Rush/76n1226
Black Americans/Dunn/76n397
Black Americans in autobiography/Brignano/75n811
Black children & their families/Dunmore/77n715
Black defenders of America/Greene/75n813
Black experience/Blazek/79n448
Black experience in children's bks/Rollock/76n163
Black family in the US/Davis/79n449
Black genealogy/Blockson/78n397
Black higher educ in the US/Chambers/79n628
Black lit resources/Clack/77n1188
Black names in America/Puckett/77n488
Black parents' hndbk/McLaughlin/77n1495
Black playwrights/Hatch/79n1009
Black rhetoric/Glenn/77n1122
Black-white racial attitudes/Obudho/77n427
Black woman in American society/Davis/76n396
Black world in lit for children/Mills/76n160; 77n1159
Blackall, W E/How to know/76n1387
Blackburn, G/Illustrated ency ships/79n1582/Illustrated ency woodworking/75n1045
Blackburn, L & M/Index to poetry/79n1189
Blackburn, M/Index to poetry/79n1189
Blackey, R/Modern revolutions/77n359
Blackmore, R M/Cumulative index/77n111
Blacks & their contribution to the American West/Abajian/76n342
Blacks in American movies/Powers/76n1051
Blacks in Minnesota/Taylor/77n437
Blacks in selected newspapers, censuses & other sources/Abajian/78n385
Blacks in the US armed forces/MacGregor/79n452
Blacks in white & black/Sampson/78n950
Black's medical dict/Thomson/76n1522; 77n1470
Blackstock, P W/Intelligence, espionage/79n501
Blackstone, T/Social policy/77n703
Blackwell, E/Celebrity register/75n118
Blackwell, T E/College law/75n564
Blair, E P/Abingdon Bible/76n1095

Blair, P/Development in/78n296
Blake, E R/Manual of neotropical/78n1316
Blake, G N/Chisholm's hndbk/76n832
Blake, J/Great perpetual/77n648
Blake, M C/Boston postmarks/75n1088
Blake, P/Art of/75n1190
Blakemore, F/Who's who modern/76n931
Blanck, J/Bibliography of American/75n1335
Bland, R C/How to know/79n1379
Blandford, P W/Country craft/75n1030
Blanford, C J/Economic hist/75n926
Blaser, B R/College chemistry/78n1252
Blathwayt atlas/Black/76n367
Blaustein, A P/Bibliography on common/75n546/Constitutions of/78n427/Independence documents/79n518
Blavatsky, H P/Theosophical glossary/75n1234
Blaze, W/Guide to alternative/76n643
Blazek, R/Black experience/79n448/Influencing students/77n217
Blejwas, S A/East Central/75n335
Bles, A de/How to distinguish/76n925
Blevins, R B/Processors of/75n968/Wholesale dealers/75n928
Bleznick, D W/Sourcebook for/75n1426
Blindness, visual impairment, deaf-blindness/Bauman/79n1449
Blinking eye/Covo/75n1354
Blishen, E/Junior pears/79n73/Thorny paradise/77n1145
Bliss, E M/Encyclopedia of missions/76n1081
Bliss bibliographic classification . . .
education/Mills/78n225
introduction & auxiliary schedules/Mills/78n224
religion, the occult, morals & ethics/Mills/78n226
social welfare/Mills/78n227
Block, A/Children's lit/77n1150
Block, M H/Text-atlas/77n1455
Blockson, C L/Black genealogy/78n397
Blomquist, L L/Improving access/75n234
Bloomberg, M/Introduction to classification/77n250/Introduction to public/78n231/Introduction to technical/75n247; 77n269/World war/76n289
Bloomfield, B C/Author index/77n1133
Bloomfield, J/Concise dict/79n1522
Bloomfield, J/Social sciences/77n304
Bloomfield, L/Menomini lexicon/76n1148
Bloomfield, V/Commonwealth elections/78n476

Blouin, L P/May Sarton/79n1223
Blow, B/B-J paperbk/77n195
BLS hndbk of methods for surveys & studies/ US Bureau of Labor Statistics/78n691
Bludworth, E/300 most/75n1653
Blue & white stoneware, pottery & crockery/ Harbin/79n948
Blue bk: leaders of the English-speaking world/76n95
Bluegrass/Artis/76n1022
Blumenson, J J-G/Identifying American/78n799
Blumenthal, J/Art of/75n63/Printed bk/78n32
Boalch, D H/Makers of/76n1012
Board of Music Trade of the USA/Complete catalogue/75n1121
Boase, T S R/Book illustrators/77n66
Boating facts & feats/Johnson/77n684
Boatner, M M/Encyclopedia of American/75n365/Landmarks of/76n326
Bobbs, H/Bows and/76n763
Bobinski, G S/Dictionary of American/79n185
Bocchetta, V E/Follett vest-/79n1142
Bock, H/Complete ency/76n750
Bodnar, J E/Ethnic hist/76n386
Boehm, E H/America/76n328; 76n329; 79n415
Boesch, M/Careers in/76n598
Bogart, G L/Jr. high/76n159/Short story/77n1134
Boger, L A/House and/75n1053
Boggs, W S/Postage stamps/75n1089
Bogomolny, R L/Handbook on/76n1549
Bogus, R J/Doubleday dict/76n1120
Bohne, H/Canadian bks/75n8/Subject gd/75n9
Bohnenkamp, D R/American Film/79n1029
Boisture, J B/Sources of/76n277
Bolin, D L/Ohio Valley/77n455
Boll, J J/Introduction to cataloging/75n223
Bolté, C G/Libraries and/79n146
Bolton, C K/Founders/77n456/Real founders/75n408
Bolton, K/Classics illus'd/75n1317
Bolz, R E/Handbook of tables/75n1713
Bombers in service/Munson/77n1639
Bond, D F/Eighteenth century/76n1257
Bond, H L/Encyclopedia of antiques/77n897
Bond, J E/Plea bargaining/76n514
Bond, O F/University of/78n1070
Bond, P S/Modern military/77n1627
Bond, R G/CRC handbk/75n1536

Bonds, R/Encyclopedia of land/78n1557
Boner, M/Reference gd/77n532
Bongartz, R/New England/79n386
Bonk, W J/Building library/75n219
Bonn, G S/Changing times/79n147
Bonnefoy, C/Dictionnaire de littérature/79n1269
Book browser's gd: Britain/Lewis/76n54
Book catalog/Minneapolis. Public Library/75n1531
Book collecting/Peters/78n50
Book collector's fact bk/Haller/77n63
Book collector's hndbk of values/Bradley/77n62
Book illustrators in 18th cent England/ Hammelmann/77n66
Book of . . .
  American trade marks/Carter/78n733
  ballet/Guillot/77n994
  firsts/Patrick/75n94
  flags/Campbell/76n449
  gadgets/Grossinger/75n92
  kings/McNaughton/76n446
  owls/Walker/75n1508
  slang/Anderson/76n1127
  successful painting/Banov/76n1636
  the road/76n543
  the states/77n519; 79n532
  women's achievements/Macksey/77n722; 78n671
Book publishers directory/Geiser/78n43
Book publishing/Dessauer/75n45
Book review digest/Samudio/76n30/Author-title index/Dunmore-Leiber/77n37
Book review index/Tarbert/75n32; 76n31; 76n32; 76n33; 78n21/Thomas/75n33
Book review index to social sci periodicals/ Rzepecki/79n346
Book selection/Lunati/76n186/Spiller/75n220
Book theft & library security systems/Bahr/79n250
Book trade in Canada/79n48
Book trade of the world/Taubert/77n51
Bookfinder: children's lit about problems of youth/Dreyer/78n1100
Bookhunter's gd to the . . .
  Northeast/Reynolds, 78n47
  West, Southwest/Reynolds/79n56
Bookman's glossary/Peters/76n46
Bookman's gd to Americana/Heard/78n49
Bookman's price index/McGrath/78n48; 79n59
Books about books/Webber/75n70; 76n56

Books about Hawaii/Day/78n313
Books afloat & ashore/Skallerup/75n271
Books and history/Downs/75n136
Books by mail/Kim/78n143
Books for . . .
   college libraries/76n141
   cooks/Patten/77n1549
   public libraries/76n147
   secondary school libraries/77n231
   the teen age/79n224
   you/Donelson/77n232
Books: from writer to reader/Greenfeld/77n49
Books in . . .
   English on the Soviet Union/Jones/76n278
   other languages/Wertheimer/78n206
   print/76n7; 79n6
   series in the US/78n1
   series suppl/79n2
   Spanish for children & young adults/Schon/79n1292
Books of WAD: books designed by W. A. Dwiggins/Agner/78n52
Books on . . .
   American Indians & Eskimos/Lass-Woodfin/79n464
   Buddhism/Yoo/77n1036
   demand author gd/79n33
   demand subj gd/79n34
   demand title gd/79n35
Books to help children cope with separation & loss/Bernstein/79n744
Books with options/Bertrand/77n1143
Bookselling in America & the world/Anderson/76n40
Bookstein, A/Prospects for/78n215
Booms, B H/Benefit-cost/77n248
Boone, S A/West African/75n638
Booth, L/Collection, use/78n888
Booth, M/Catalogue of Louis/76n1255
Booth, R E/Personnel utilization/76n183
Booz, Allen & Hamilton, Inc./Organization &/75n177
Borchardt, D H/Australian bibliog/77n22
Borden, G A/Directory of college/75n677
Borklund, E/Contemporary literary/79n1207
Borko, H/Indexing concepts/79n330
Borkowski, M V/Library technical/77n151
Born, W/Concise atlas/75n1670
Born in the spring/Roberts/78n1297
Bose, A/Bibliography of urbanization/78n641
Bossart, J K/Health organizations/79n1472

Boston, G/Directory of criminal/78n506/Terrorism/78n642
Boston births, baptisms, marriages, & deaths, 1630-99, and Boston births, 1700-1800/Appleton/79n474
Boston Children's Medical Center/Child health/76n1543
Boston: chronological & documentary hist/Lankevich/75n507
Boston marriages from 1700 to 1809/McGlenen/78n406
Boston postmarks to 1890/Blake/75n1088
Boswell, J C/Milton's library/76n1278
Botanical classifications/Swift/76n1371
Bott, J F/Handbook of chemical/78n1255
Botterweck, G J/Theological dict/76n1096; 79n1064
Bottorff, R M/Popular periodical/75n34
Boulding, E/Handbook of internat'l/78n669
Boulton, J T/Research in/77n406
Bowden, H W/Dictionary of American/78n999
Bowden, J A/Contemporary authors/79n138
Bowe, F/French lit/79n1270
Bowers, P M/US navy/78n1577
Bowker annual of library & book trade info/Glick/79n172/Miele/77n190
Bowker serials bibliog suppl/75n22; 77n33
Bowker's medical bks in print/75n1612; 76n1513; 77n1458
Bowles, S E/Index to critical/76n1062
Bows & arrows: archery bibliog/Bobbs/76n763
Boyce, B N/Real estate/76n851
Boyd, J R/Facts and/79n1500
Boyd, M A/Mail-order/76n948
Boydston, J A/Checklist of/75n642
Boyer, C/Ship passenger lists, national/79n479/Ship passenger lists, New/79n480
Boyer, M/Nelson's new/79n1118
Boyer, M V/Texas collection/79n1006
Boykin, R E/Union list/77n1441
Boyle, D/Children's media/79n225/Expanding media/78n246/North American/77n186
Boys' & girls' bk of clubs & organizations/Kujoth/76n696
Brabec, B/Guide to craft/76n949
Brace, E R/Illustrated dict/79n715/Nelson's new/79n1459
Brace, P/Glossary of environment/78n1342; 79n1394
Bradford bk of collector's plates/Bartels/77n918

24 — Authors and Titles

Bradley, C J/Reader in/75n201
Bradley, P/Index to Waverley/76n1283
Bradley, V A/Book collector's/77n62
Brady, E A/Eric Gill/75n71
Brady, G S/Materials hndbk/78n1539
Bramley, G/Library services/79n285/World trends/76n219
Branch library serv/Perkins/79n259
Brand-name hndbk of protein, calories, & carbohydrates/Wade/78n1479
Brandon, D H/Data processing/76n1623
Brandon, J/Wierd America/79n1085
Brandt, P/Oregon biography/77n390
Branford, J/Dictionary of South/79n1116
Branscomb, H/Teaching with/75n178
Branson, B A/Fishes of/75n1512
Brant, C A/Transistor ignition/77n1572
Brantner, J P/Practical gd/76n1499
Brantz, M H/Health sciences/79n1451
Brasch, I W & W M/Comprehensive annotated/75n1245
Brass bk/Schiffer/79n937
Brater, E F/Handbook of hydraulics/77n1604
Bray, W/Penguin dict/77n348
Bray, W D/Controversy over/78n486
Brazer, C W/Essays for/78n859
Brazil: chronology & fact bk/Fitzgibbon/75n340
Brazil 1980: Protestant hndbk/Read/75n1224
Brazilian-American business review directory/78n708
Brazilian serial documents/Lombardi/75n109
Brealey, R A/Bibliography of finance/75n955
Breed, P F/Annotated bibliog French/77n1260
Breedlove, J M/Guide to holdings/75n864/Holdings of Stanford/75n1247
Breen, W/Penny whimsy/77n915/Walter Breen's/79n918
Bregman, J I/Handbook of water/77n1422
Breit, M/Thomas Merton/75n1215
Breivik, P S/Open admissions/78n162
Bremer, H F/Richard Nixon/76n332
Brench, A C/Putnam's contemporary/75n1268
Brennan, J A/Guide to Harper/76n350/Guide to Henry/76n351/Guide to Edward/76n349
Brennan, P C/Descriptive inventory/79n407
Brenni, V J/Essays on/76n196
Bressett, K E/Guide bk/77n904
Brewer, A M/Book publishers/78n43/Dictionaries, encyclopedias/76n1114
Brewer, T M/Water birds/75n1499
Brewster, B J/American overseas/77n277
Brewster, J W/Index to book/76n303; 77n368; 79n405
Brewton, J E/Index to poetry/79n1189
Breyer, S/Guide to Soviet/79n1599
Brichford, M J/Manuscripts gd/77n28
Bricker, G W/Bricker's internat'l/76n644; 77n609
Bricker's internat'l directory of univ-sponsored executive developmt programs/Bricker/76n644; 77n609
Brickey, C/Almanac of Virginia/78n456
Bricklin, M/Practical ency/78n1433
Brickman, W W/Jewish community/78n389
Briden, J C/Mesozoic and/78n1357
Bridge, R/America's backpacking/75n754/Freewheeling: bicycle/75n735/Tourguide to/76n716
Bridgeman, H/Encyclopedia of Victoriana/76n958
Brief ethnic bibliog/Barton/77n421
Briggs, G/National heraldry/75n439; 76n448
Briggs, J/Collector's Beethoven/79n982
Briggs, K/Encyclopedia of fairies/78n1009
Briggs, W R/Annual review plant/76n1376
Briggum, S M/Concordance to Conrad's/79n1237
Brigham, C S/History &/77n1110
Brightbill, G D/Communications &/79n1159
Brignano, R C/Black Americans/75n811
Brimer, J B/Home gardener's/77n1553
Brisman, S/History &/79n458
Bristol and America/Hargreaves-Mawdsley/79n485
Britannica ency of American art/75n996
Britannica jr ency/78n64
Britchky, S/Restaurants of/75n685; 79n599/Seymour Britchky's/77n1540
British & American tanks of WWII/Chamberlain/76n1684
British architects/Wodehouse/79n895
British bk sale catalogues 1676-1800/Munby/79n60
British bks in print/75n7; 76n15; 79n10
British children's authors/Jones/77n1225
British comic catalogue/Gifford/77n1169
British crossword puzzle dict/Bailie/79n1122
British directory of little magazines & small presses/England/75n24
British economic / soc hist/Chaloner/77n407
British hist/Harvard Univ. Library/76n369
British insurance business/Cockerell/79n849
British invasion of Maryland, 1812-15/Marine/78n405
British library hist: bibliog/Keeling/76n225

British library resources/Downs/75n148
British manuscript diaries of the 19th cent/ Batts/77n405
British music hall/Busby/78n942
British music yrbk/Jacobs/76n998
British novel: Conrad to the present/Wiley/75n1379
British novel: Scott through Hardy/Watt/75n1378
British official publications/Pemberton/75n110
British place-names in their historical setting/ McClure/75n451
British pottery/Godden/77n919
British qualifications/Priestley/76n664
British scientific documentation services/ British Council/78n1217
Britt, S/Illustrated ency jazz/79n996
Britton, J/US military/77n1629
Broad system of ordering/Coates/79n300
Broadcast antenna systems hndbk/75n1780
Broadcast communications dict/Diamant/75n1201; 79n1161
Broadribb, V/Modern parents'/75n1647
Broadside authors & artists/Bailey/75n1334
Broadway in the West End: London/Stanley/79n1021
Broadway's greatest musicals/Laufe/79n1004
Broce, T E/Directory of Oklahoma/75n78
Brock, D H/Ben Jonson/75n1387
Brockman, J/Home computer/79n1564
Broderick, D M/Library work/78n181
Broderick, R C/Catholic ency/77n1037
Brodsky, J/Trustee$ of/77n595
Brody, E/Music gd Austria/77n945/Music gd Belgium/78n889/Music gd Italy/79n956
Brohough, W/Photographer's market/79n954/ Songwriter's market/79n978
Bromley, J/Clockmakers' library/79n934
Bromwich, R/Medieval Celtic/76n1258
Bronstein, A J/Biographical dict/79n1157
Brontë companion/Pinion/76n1269
Brook, C/Music gd Austria/77n945/Music gd Belgium/78n889/Music gd Italy/79n956
Brook, M/Reference gd/75n377
Brooke, J/General index/75n476
Brooks, B/Biological and/76n1370
Brooks, H/Illustrated ency/77n1577
Brooks, J S/Public library/75n183
Broos, B P J/Index to formal/79n904
Brophy, P/COBOL programming/77n288
Broster, E J/Glossary of applied/76n908
Broughton, V/Bliss bibliographic/78n224; 78n225; 78n226; 78n227

Browder, S/American biking/75n736/New age/75n446
Brower, D J/Management and/76n801
Brown, A G/Introduction to subject/77n251; 77n252
Brown, A P/Carlo D'Ordonez/79n983
Brown, B E/Canadian business/77n765
Brown, C/New internat'l/77n1043; 78n995
Brown, C F/Ethiopian perspectives/79n352/ Howard Univ/78n979
Brown, C S/Glossary of Faulkner's/77n1202/ Reader's companion/75n1307
Brown, D R/Puerto Rico/77n336
Brown, G DeW/FORTRAN to/76n1624
Brown, G W/Dictionary of Canadian/76n109
Brown, J/Let's go/79n617
Brown, J F/Dictionary of speech/76n1523; 77n1471
Brown, J M/Helicopter directory/77n1619
Brown, J W/Educational media/75n656; 76n599; 79n669/Nonprint media/78n247
Brown, K R/Library, documentation/77n36
Brown, L/New York/79n1176
Brown, L/Weeds in/78n1309
Brown, L G/Core media/76n156
Brown, L M/Bibliography of British/78n368
Brown, M G/Freethought in/79n1079
Brown, M R/Guide to grading/76n965
Brown, M W/Neuropsychiatry and/77n1459
Brown, P L/Energy info/76n1464
Brown, R E/Joetta community/76n146
Brown, R F/Putnam's contemporary/75n1278
Brown, S J/Getting into/75n1636; 77n610
Brown, V/Illustrated gd/77n1431
Brown, V/Reptiles and/76n1447
Browne, D/Housebuilding bk/75n1763
Browne, G S/Bartholomew/Scribner/75n575
Browne, R A/Rose-lover's/75n1699
Brownell, J A/Directory of selected/77n1062
Browning music/East/75n1137
Brownings' correspondence/Kelley/79n1233
Brownrigg, E B/Colonial Latin/79n443
Brownstone, D M/Film review/76n1064
Bruccoli, M J/Apparatus for/75n1355/First printings/78n1110/Ring Lardner/77n1209
Bruce, A P C/Annotated bibliog British/77n1641
Bruck, L/Access/79n840
Brudenell-Bruce, P G C/Birds of/76n1415
Brueckner, J H/Brueckner's French/76n1139
Brueckner's French contextuary/Brueckner/76n1139
Brumbaugh, G M/Maryland records/76n424

Brunk, G G/World countermarks/77n905
Bruns, R/Am I/78n335/Congress investigates/76n307
Bruntjen, C & J/Checklist of American/76n8; 78n6
Brunton, D W/Index to contemporary/76n21
Brunvand, J H/Folklore/78n1010
Brunyate, R/Concise ency modern/75n997
Brusaw, C T/Business writer's/79n816
Bruun, B/Dell ency/75n1501/Larousse gd/79n1369
Bruyn, H B/Handbook of pediatrics/77n1486
Bruzelius, A/Concise Swedish-/75n552
Bryan, H/University libraries/77n201
Bryer, J R/Hamlin Garland/75n1359/Louis Auchincloss/78n1130/Sixteen modern/75n1338
Bryfogle, R C/City in/77n726/City in suppl 1/77n727
Bryfonski, D/New England/76n544/Twentieth-century/79n1183
BUC book: used boat directory/76n708
Buchanan, B/Glossary of indexing/77n170
Buchanan, J E/Miami/79n421/Phoenix/79n422
Buchanan, W W/Cumulative subject/75n102
Buchanan-Brown, J/Cassell's ency/75n1315
Buchwald, V F/Handbook of iron/77n1432
Buck, J O/Pedigrees of/75n425
Buckeye, N M/International subscription/79n49
Buckingham, J/Atlas of stereochemistry/76n1345
Buckley, J C/Retirement hndbk/75n930; 79n841
Buckley, J H/Victorian poets/78n1155
Buckley, J W/Executive's digest/79n825
Buckley, M/Color theory/76n914
Buckley, M H/Executive's digest/79n825
Buckman, T R/Issues in/75n218
BUC's 1976 new boat directory/77n682
Budd, R/Sailing boats/75n746
Buder, L/New York/77n602
Budge, E A W/Egyptian hieroglyphic/79n1133
Budge, R S/Analysis and/78n735
Budgetary control in academic libraries/Martin/79n199
Budgeting for school media centers/Loertscher/77n226
Buenker, J D/Immigration and/78n375
Building a children's lit collection/Quimby/76n1195
Building a great library/Bentinck-Smith/77n276

Building construction hndbk/Merritt/76n1620
Building ethnic collections/Buttlar/78n376
Building library collections/Carter/75n219
Building technology publications/US Natl Bureau of Stds/78n1519
Bull, J/Audubon Society/78n1315/Birds of/77n1374
Bull, S/Index to biographies/75n1152
Bullinger, E W/Critical lexicon/78n990
Bullock, A/Harper dict/78n83
Bullock, C/Ethnic serials/78n379
Bullough, V L/Annotated bibliog homosexuality/78n650/Bibliography of prostitution/78n643
Bunch, C/Art educ/79n627
Buncher, J F/CIA and/77n510
Bundy, M L/Alternatives to/79n286/Guide to soc literature/78n646/Investigative methods/75n243/National children's/78n659/National prison/76n778; 77n710; 78n505/Prison group/76n777
Bunker, M P/Long Island/77n457
Bunting, J/Climbing/75n755
Bunting & Lyon's gd to private schools/77n598
Burack, A S/Writer's hndbk/76n1168
Burack, E/Atlas of central/79n1448
Burbank, R/Day by/79n403
Burbidge, G R/Annual review astronomy/75n1444; 76n1335
Burchell, R W/Environmental impact/77n1416
Burchfield, R W/Supplement to/77n1073
Burckel, N C/Immigration and/78n375
Bureau of Radiological Health publications index/79n1478
Burger, M A/Annotated gd works/78n1181
Burgess, R/Library lit/76n113
Burgess, R A/Construction industry/75n1757
Buried genealogical data/Scott/78n411
Buried past/Ichioka/75n819
Burk, J L/Environmental concerns/78n1338
Burke, C G/Collector's Haydn/79n984
Burke, J/Genealogical and/78n393
Burke, J B/Burke's Irish/78n417/General armory/77n483
Burke, J G/Access/76n28/Access index/78n19/Children's library/75n192/Dictionary of contemporary/77n90/Guide to ecology/77n1403
Burke, J H/80 years/78n37
Burke, J M/Civil rights/75n796
Burke's... American families with British ancestry/76n425/Family index/78n418/Irish family records/Burke/78n417/Presidential families of the US/76n426

Burkett, E M/Writing in/78n101
Burkhalter, P K/Nursing care/76n1528
Burks, B D/Mayflies/76n1439
Burlingame, D F/College learning/79n192/
  Library and/79n251
Burma, J H/Spanish-speaking/75n817
Burn, B/Practical gd/77n1528/Whole horse/
  79n1525
Burnam, T/Dictionary of misinformation/77
  n89/American car/75n1825; 76n1664;
  79n1551
Burnett, J H/Anthropology and/75n865
Burnham, R/Burnham's celestial/79n1312
Burnham's celestial handbook/Burnham/79
  n1312
Burnim, K A/Biographical dict/75n1188; 76
  n1045; 79n1022
Burns, R D/Arms control/79n550/Vietnam
  conflict/75n463
Burns, S/Annotated bibliog texts/77n1067;
  78n588
Buros, O K/English tests/76n562/Foreign
  language/76n563/Intelligence tests/76
  n564/Mathematics tests/76n565/Person-
  ality tests/76n566/Reading tests/76n567/
  Science tests/76n568/Social studies/76
  n569/Tests in/75n1601/Vocational tests/
  76n570
Burrell, T W/Communication studies/75n156
Burrill, B/Who's who boxing/75n753
Burrington, G A/How to find/76n238
Burroughs, P/Nantucket/75n603
Burt, R/Congressional hearings/75n489
Burt, W H/Field gd mammals/77n1392
Burton, J A/Owls of/75n1507
Burton, M/Purnell's first/78n1314
Burton, P E/Dictionary of microcomputing/
  78n1521
Burton, R/Living sea/77n1371
Busby, R/British music/78n942
Busby, T/Musical manual/78n898
Busch, J C/Directory of unpublished/79
  n1430
Bush, C L/Dictionary of reading/75n651
Busha, C H/Intellectual freedom/78n266
Busher, W H/Furlough from/75n840
Business & financial planning tables desk bk/
  77n791
Business atlas of western Europe/76n838
Business bks & serials in print/78n697
Business control atlas of the US & Canada/75
  n899
Business history collection/76n822
Business info services/Campbell/76n852; 77
  n767

Business media gd international:
  Africa & Middle East/Levite/75n905
  Asia & Russia/Levite/75n906
  Europe/Parrin/75n907; 75n908
  Latin America/Meyer/75n909
  newspaper-newsmagazines/Parrin/75n910
  North America & Oceania/75n911
Business of publishing/77n47
Business people in the news/Nykoruk/77n795
Business periodicals index/Third/76n839
Business services & info/79n817
Business writer's hndbk/Brusaw/79n816
Businessman's entertainmt gd/75n593
Businessman's guide to . . .
  dealing with the fed gov/75n888
  the Middle East/Africano/79n815
  Washington/Ruder/76n836
Buske, M R/Significant American colonial/
  77n128/Significant American presidents/
  77n136
Bustanoby, J H/Dictionary of sexology/75
  n1580
Butchart, I/Non-book/79n148
Butcher, J N/Handbook of cross-/77n1447
Buteau, J D/Nonprint materials/77n1103
Butler, B/Dictionary of tarot/77n1450
Butler, B/Library automation/76n233
Butler, L A/Films for/79n373/Learning
  resource/75n216
Butler, P/Encyclopedia of antique/75n1054
Butterflies afield in the Pacific Northwest/
  Neill/78n1331
Butterick, G F/Where are/78n1117
Butterick fabric hndbk/Kleeberg/76n875
Butterick home decorating hndbk/Kleeberg/
  77n941
Butterick kitchen equipmt hndbk/Knees/78
  n1474
Butterick sewing machine hndbk/Courtney/
  78n877
Butterworths medical dict/Critchley/79n1460
Buttlar, L/Building ethnic/78n376/Encyclo-
  pedic directory/76n394/Guide to ethnic/
  79n446
Buttons/Houart/79n936
Buttress, F A/World gd/76n89
Buttrey, T V/Guide bk/78n843
Buvinic, M/Women and/78n662
Buy books where–sell books where/Robin-
  son/79n61
Buyer's gd to environmentl media/75n1545
Buyer's gd to environmentl media: energy/
  75n1546
Buying antiques in Europe/Kennedy/78n837

By hand: gd to schools & careers in crafts/ Coyne/75n1031
Byers, D M/Readings for/76n1072
Byrne, J H/Mrs. Bryne's/75n1257
Byron, D/Firearms price/78n849
Byron & the Bible/Looper/79n1234

C. G. Jung & analytical psychology/Vincie/ 78n1365
C. S. Lewis/Christopher/75n1390
Cabeceiras, J/Multimedia library/79n244
Cabello-Argandona, R/Chicana/77n440
Cable TV: gd to fed regulations/Rivkin/76n1179
Cactus identifier, including succulent plants/ Bechtel/78n1486
Cadillac modern ency/Shapiro/75n73
Cady, L/Beer can/77n929
CAIN online user's gd/Gilreath/77n255
Calasibetta, C/Fairchild's dict/76n978
Calculator hndbk/Feldzamen/75n1769
Calculator user's gd & dict/Sippl/77n1582
Calendar of festivals/78n1019
Calendar of the papers of Charles Thomas Longley, 1862-68/Sayers/77n1033
Calhoun, J/Louisiana almanac/76n490
California/Heizer/79n785
California catalogue/Rapoport/78n529
California environmental directory/78n1346
California experience/Hoskin/79n388
California hndbk/Trzyna/76n492
California Indian hist/Heizer/76n804
California Indians/Bean/78n676
California legal research hndbk/Henke/76n516
California local hist/Rocq/77n394
California mushrooms/Thiers/76n1399
California: patterns on the land/Durrenberger/ 77n543
Calkins, C C/Reader's Digest/79n1542
Call for action: survival kit for New Yorkers/ Sohmer/76n884
Callaghan, B/Van Nostrand/75n1203
Callaham, L I/Russian-English/76n1341
Callender, J H/Time-saver/75n1015
Callow, J T/Guide to American/78n1115/From its/78n1116
Calvert, S/Children's media/79n225
Camber, R/Collectors and/79n878
Camblos, R/Shopping round/75n941
Cambodian-English dict/Headley/79n1129
Cambridge ancient hist/Edwards/76n357; 79n396

Cambridge bibliog of English lit/Watson/75n1375
Cambridge ency of astronomy/Mitton/79n1313
Cambridge hist of the Bible/Ackroyd/76n1097
Cambridge Info and Research Services/Sources of/79n798
Cameron, A/Plan for/75n1248
Cameron, M W/Biographical cyclopaedia/76n104
Cameron, W W/Handbook of swimming/75n1758
Camp, A J/Everyone has/79n498
Camp, R A/Mexican political/78n485
Camp, W L/Guide to periodicals/76n585
Campaigns of the American Revolution/ Marshall/77n377
Campbell, B/Dictionary of birds/76n1416
Campbell, D/American manuscripts/78n61
Campbell, D J/Small tech/75n202
Campbell, G/Book of flags/76n449
Campbell, H H/James Thomson/77n1247
Campbell, I/Minerals/76n1480
Campbell, J E/Pottery and/79n946
Campbell, M J/Business info/76n852/Manual of business/76n166
Campbell, S/Let it/76n1582
Camper's favorite campgrounds/Steinberg/ 75n598
Camper's hndbk/Power/75n635
Campground gd/Chase/76n717
Camphouse, M/Guide-book/76n545
Campo, A/William Everson/78n1138
Campo, C A/Maine union/78n27
Canada and the French/Riseborough/76n504
Canada year bk/78n303
Canadian almanac & directory/Walters/78n304
Canadian annual review of politics and public affairs/Saywell/75n338; 76n500
Canadian bk review annual/Tudor/77n196
Canadian bks for children/McDonough/77n1256
Canadian bks for young people/McDonough/ 79n1192
Canadian bks in print/Bohne/75n8/Pluscauskas/77n23; 77n24; 79n11
Canadian business & economics/Brown/77n765
Canadian essay & lit index/Armitage/77n1135
Canadian essays & collections index/77n1253
Canadian fiction/Fee/77n1255

Canadian Indian bibliog/Abler/75n863
Canadian juvenile fict & the library market/ Wilkinson/77n1259
Canadian libraries in their changing environment/Garry/79n313
Canadian library directory/75n159
Canadian library systems & networks/75n254
Canadian music/Jarman/77n957
Canadian postage stamps & stationery/ Howes/75n1090
Canadian ref sources: suppl/Ryder/76n6
Canadian selection/Jarvi/79n181
Canadian serials directory/Pluscauskas/78n14
Canadian tokens & medals/Hoch/75n1067
Canadian writer's market/Goodman/79n1167
Canadiana/79n12
Candid critique of bk publishing/Benjamin/ 79n29
Caney, S/Steven Caney's/76n764
Canham, K/Film actors/78n960
Canney, M/University of/76n823
Canning, B/State constitutional/78n457
Cannons' bibliog of lib economy/Jordan/77n167
Canoe camper's hndbk/Bearse/76n714
Cantwell, Z M/Instructional tech/75n698
Capital contacts in consumerism/78n745
Caplan, F/Parents' yellow/77n745
Caplan, H H/Classified directory/78n790
Cappon, L J/Atlas of early/77n375
Capps, D/Psychology of/77n1024
Caras, R/Venomous animals/76n1411
Carbone, L/Dictionary of sewing/79n943
Cardwell, P/Index of model/78n876
Care & conservation of collections/Rath/78n321
Care & maintenance of paper machine clothing/Ewing/78n1258
Career educ pamphlets/Shaffer/77n654
Career gd to prof associations/77n834
Careers in the outdoors/Boesch/76n598
Carey, H B/Gateways to/77n1166
Carey, R J P/Library guiding/75n233
Cargas, H J/Holocaust/79n436
Caribbean investmt hndbk/Jonnard/75n916
Caribbean seashells/Warmke/77n1396
Carl H. Milam & the Amer Library Assoc/ Sullivan/77n284
Carl H. Milam & the UN Library/Dale/77n278
Carlander, K D/Handbook of freshwater/78n1325
Carleton Varney decorates from A to Z/ Varney/79n942

Carlo D'Ordonez, 1734-86/Brown/79n983
Carlson, G E/Architectural and/75n1021
Carlson, H S/Nevada place/76n454
Carlson, K L/Birds of/75n1500
Carlson, R A/Educational TV/75n1192
Carlson, R K/Enrichment ideas/77n642
Carman, W Y/Badges and/76n1678/Dictionary of military/78n1556
Carmichael, C W/Literature and/78n1099
Carmichel, J/Modern rifle/76n755
Carmony, M/Indiana place/76n453
Carnahan, D/Guide to alternative/79n111
Carnell, H/Oxford literary/78n1159
Carnovale, N/Twentieth-century/76n1013
Caroline drama/Fordyce/79n1008
Carpenter, A/Index to US/75n103
Carpenter, R L/Statistical methods/79n336
Carr, J J/CET license/77n1589
Carrick, P/Encyclopaedia of motor-/78n635
Carrington, D K/Map collections/79n236
Carrington, E M/Women in/76n337
Carrington, G C/Plots and/77n1205
Carrington, H B/Battle maps/76n321
Carrington, I de P/Plots and/77n1205
Carroll, F L/Library at/79n326
Carroll, P T/Annotated calendar/77n1345
Carroll, V/Nukuoro lexicon/75n1282
Carrubba, R W/Directory of college/75n677
Carson, B/Principal's hndbk/79n213
Cartano, T/Dictionnaire de littérature/79n1269
Cartel annotated bibliog of bilingual bicultural materials/78n589
Carter, C/Guide to ref/75n273
Carter, D E/Book of American/78n733
Carter, E/Records in/76n1000
Carter, E F/Dictionary of inventions/77n1288
Carter, G A/Local hist/75n265
Carter, G M/From protest/75n520; 78n471
Carter, M D/Building library/75n219
Carter, W C/Concordance to oeuvres/79n1271
Carterette, E C/Biology of/75n1588
Cartier, M K/Mental health/79n1435
Cartledge, T M/National anthems/77n950
Cary, E/NYCLU gd/79n763/Rights of/75n560
Cary, N M/Guide to US/77n1646
Casada, J A/Dr. David/77n309
Casale, J T/Diet food/76n1569
Case, A M/Bibliographic index/76n29
Case, B/Illustrated ency jazz/79n996
Case, R N/Curriculum alternatives/75n193
Casewit, C W/America's tennis/76n761

Casey, W J/Accounting desk/79n824/Lawyer's desk/76n515/Life insurance/76n901/Real estate/76n853
Cashman, M/Bibliography of American/77n422
Caskey, J D/Samuel Taylor/79n1235
Cass, J/Comparative gd American/77n611; 79n650/Comparative gd two/78n567/Counselors' comparative/77n612
Cassara, E/History of USA/78n341
Cassata, M B/Administrative aspects/76n220/Reader in/78n232
Cassell's ency of world lit/Buchanan-Brown/75n1315
Casserley, H C/Observer's bk/76n1669
Cassis, A F/Twentieth-century/78n1162
Cassorla, A/Skateboarder's bible/78n636
Castagno, M/Historical dict/76n254
Castillo, C/University of Chicago/78n1070
Castillo, E D/California Indian/76n804
Castle hotels of Europe/Long/79n618
Castleman, H/All together/77n978/Beatles again?/79n997
Castles, A C/Australia/79n429
Caswell, J/Coutumes of/79n563
Cat catalog/Fireman/77n1527
Catalog of . . .
  American antiques/Ketchum/79n917
  federal domestic assistance/77n109
  federal educ assistance programs/78n554
  federal loan guarantee programs/US. House of Representatives/79n874
  federal programs related to community educ/US Off of Educ/78n571
  federal youth programs/78n658
  Filipiniana at Valladolid/Tubangui/76n279
  food/Feinman/78n1471
  free things/Feinman/77n91
  magic/Kaye/79n723
  published concert music by American composers/Eagon/75n1124
  resource material on community educ/79n678
  US gov produced AV materials/76n668
  Verdi's operas/Chusid/75n1165
Catalog of the . . .
  Communications Library, Univ of Illinois/76n1166
  Conservation Library, Denver Public Library/76n1457
  diptera of the Oriental region/Delfinado/78n1328
  Jean Piaget archives, Univ of Geneva/76n1492

Catalog of the . . . (cont'd)
  Library of the American Hospital Assn/77n1460
  library of the French Biblican & Archaeological School/76n19
  Social & Behavioral Sciences Monograph Section of the Lib of the Inst for Sex Research, Indiana Univ/76n1493
  theatre & drama collections/NY Public Library/77n989
  unusual/Hart/75n100
Cataloging phonorecordings/Daily/76n188
Cataloging with copy/Dowell/77n253
Catalogo dei libri in commercio/77n25; 78n7
Catalogs of the Sophia Smith Collection, Women's Hist Archive, Smith College, Northampton, MA/76n789
Catalogue de la bibliothèque de L'Ecole Biblique et Archéologique Française, Jerusalem, Israel/76n19
Catalogue de reproductions de peintures 1860 à 1973/76n916
Catalogue of . . .
  American catalogues/De La Iglesia/75n944
  American portraits/NY Hist'l Society/76n918
  Arabic manuscripts, Princeton Univ Library/Mach/78n60
  books and manuscripts, Italian 16th cent/Harvard College Library/76n58
  British family histories/Thomson/78n422
  Italian drawings in the art museum, Princeton Univ/Gibbons/78n808
  manuscripts in Lambeth Palace Library/Bill/77n1023
  medieval Armenian manuscripts in the US/Sanjian/78n62
  members: League of Canadian Poets/77n1254
  persons named in German heroic lit (700-1600)/Gillespie/75n1420
  reproductions of paintings 1860-1973/76n916
  steam locomotive types/Long/75n1833
  vocal recordings from the 1898-1925 German catalogues of the Gramophone Co/Bennett/79n969
Catalogue of the . . .
  Anglo-Saxon ornamental metalwork, Ashmolean Museum/Oxford Univ/75n994
  earlier Italian paintings in the Ashmolean Museum/Lloyd/78n818

Catalogue of the . . . (cont'd)
   history of sci collections of the Univ of Oklahoma Libraries/Roller/77n1281
   Imperial College of Tropical Agriculture; Univ of West Indies, Trinidad/76n1555
   Louis Zukofsky manuscript collection/Booth/76n1255
   medieval & renaissance manuscripts of the Univ of Notre Dame/Corbett/79n66
   printed music & music manuscripts before 1801 in the Music Library of the Univ of Birmingham Barber Inst of Fine Arts/Fenlon/77n953
   South/Phillips/75n98
   Travistock Joint Library; London/76n1521
   tract collection of Saint David's Univ College/77n369
   translator's library of the Dept of Trade & Industry/Hamilton/77n766
   world's most popular coins/Reinfeld/78n844
Cataloguing practice/Ranganathan/76n193
Catching up/Veley/79n101
Catholic almanac/Foy/76n1086
Catholic ency/Broderick/77n1037
Cathon, L E/Storeis to/75n198
CATV and its implications for libraries/Thomassen/75n242
Causes & effects of anti-Semitism/Grosser/79n437
Cavaliers and pioneers/Nugent/79n491
Cavalry journal/armor cum indices/Young/75n1841
Cave, R/Rare book/77n191
Cavendish, R/Encyclopedia of unexplained/75n1604
Cawker, R/Canadian fiction/77n1255
Cawkwell, T/World ency/76n1053
Cayne, B S/Encyclopedia Americana/77n72
CBS news almanac/Westerman/76n76; 77n97
Cebuano literature/Mojares/78n1195
Celebrating with books/Polette/78n191
Celebrations: treasury of holiday ideas/Cordello/78n1020
Celebrity register/Blackwell/75n118
Cello/Cowling/76n1014
Census of pensioners for revolutionary or military services/US Dept of State/75n432
Centennial anniversary vol of the American Neurological Assn/Denny-Brown/76n1510
Centeno collection: lit of Spain & Hispanic America/Amago/79n1285
Central America by recreation vehicle/Hardaway/76n558

Century of service: librarianship in the US & Canada/Jackson/77n157
Ceramic, furniture, & silver collectors' glossary/Barber/78n830
Černý, J/Coptic etymological/78n1053
Certification model for prof school media personnel/77n218
Cervantes' place-names/Torbert/79n1293
Cesar Chavez & UFW/Fodell/75n976
CET license hndbk/Carr/77n1589
Ceux qui font l'edition/79n50
Ceynar, M E/Creativity in/76n1161
CFL official yearbook/Walker/75n764
Chadwick, J/Professional organizations/77n88
Chaff, S L/Women in/78n1387
Chairs/Pollack/79n923
Chairs: choosing, buying & collecting/Darty/75n1074
Chalfant, F C/Ben Jonson's/79n1244
Chalif, E L/Field gd Mexican/75n1509
Chalkley, L/Chronicles of/75n409
Challinor, J/Dictionary of geology/76n1471
Chaloner, W H/British economic/77n407
Chamberlain, A/Psychotropic drugs/75n1656
Chamberlain, P/British and/76n1684
Chamberlain, R L/Current index/79n792; 79n793
Chamberlin, W/Chronology and/77n493
Chambers, D/Cock-A-Hoop/77n53
Chambers, F/Black higher/79n628
Chambers, J F/Hey Miss!/79n226
Chambers dict of sci & tech/77n1289
Chan, L M/LC subject/79n268
Chandidas, R/India votes/75n518
Chandler, G/How to find/75n3
Chandler, S P/Living black/75n1349
Chandor, A/Dictionary of computers/79n1560
Chang, D/Asia and/75n298
Chang, F M/Team piano/77n952
Chang, H C/Selected, annotated/77n337/ Taiwan demography/75n871
Changing role of the special librarian in industry, business, & gov/Ladendorf/75n206
Changing times: changing libraries/Bonn/79n147
Chant, C/Encyclopedia of air/77n1637
Chapel, C E/Gun collector's/78n850
Chapin, S/Guide to recommended/75n604/New revised/76n546
Chaplin, A H/Organization of/75n225
Chaplin, J P/Dictionary of occult/78n1375
Chapman, B A/Marriages of/77n458

Chapman, C B/Physiology of/76n1514
Chapman, C F/Piloting, seamanship/76n709
Chapman, C O/Index of names/79n1251
Chapman, D H/Index to black/76n1211
Chapman, E A/Reader in/76n180
Chapman, J A/Annals of/75n410
Chapman, L/Directory of community/75n512/
 1974 suppl to/75n513
Chapman, R L/Roget's internat'l/78n1041
Chappell, J/Potter's complete/79n947
Charles, H/Encyclopedia of sport/77n670
Charles Ammi Cutter/Miksa/78n153
Charles F. Lummis/Sarber/79n1221
Charles T. Griffes/Anderson/79n981
Charles W. Chesnutt/Ellison/78n1136
Charles W. S. Williams/Glenn/77n1249
Charlton, J E/1975 std/75n1062
Charmet, R/Concise ency/75n997
Charnley, A & E/European chemical/76n896/
 European retail/77n809
Charvat, W/Prentice-Hall/79n130
Chase, H/Biographical dict/77n541
Chase, L & M/Campground gd/76n717
Chaston, G D/Genealogical records/75n423
Chatton, M J/Current medical/75n1609
Chatton, M J/Handbook of medical/75n1627
Chaucer/Baugh/78n1170
Chaucer dict/Dillon/75n1383
Check list for emergencies/Arnold/75n1646
Checklist & key to the amphibians & reptiles
 of Belize, Central America/Henderson/77
 n1397
Checklist of . . .
 American imprints for 1831/Bruntjen/76
  n8
 American imprints for 1832/Bruntjen/78
  n6
 editions of Moby-Dick/Tanselle/78n1146
 names for 3,000 vascular plants of economic importance/Terrell/79n1340
 painters, c1200-1976/79n905
 printed materials relating to French-
  Canadian lit/Tougas/75n1411
 science-fiction anthologies/Cole/76n1204
 the American Bar Assn materials in Crom-
  well Library of the American Bar Foun-
  dation/Pederson/78n498
 the Hogarth Press/Woolmer/77n1222
 the world's birds/Gruson/77n1379
 Virginia state publications/79n114
 writings about John Dewey/Boydston/75
  n642
Cheek, E/List of/75n959
Cheeks, J E/Practical gd/75n984

Cheese buyer's hndbk/O'Keefe/79n1532
Chekki, D A/Social system/76n260
Chemical & process tech ency/Considine/75
 n1755
Chemical formulary/Bennett/78n1254
Chemical kinetics of the gas phase combus-
 tion of fuels/Westley/78n1241
Chemical tables/Nemeth/77n1333
Chemical technology/Codd/77n1575
Chemist's gd to regulatory drug analysis/
 Banes/75n1449
Chemotaxonomy of flowering plants/Gibbs/
 75n1476
Chen, C/Applications of/77n236/Biomedical,
 scientific/78n1381/Sourcebook on/78n193
Chen, P S/New hndbk/77n1332
Chen, V/Economic conditions/79n799
Chenhall, R G/Nomenclature for/79n269
Chernukhin, A E/English-Russian/78n1206
Chernyi, A I/Publications on/76n229
Cheshier, R G/Principles of/77n1483
Chesman, A/Guide to women's/79n764
Chess: annotated bibliog/Betts/75n767
Chesshyre, D H B/Heraldry of/75n445
Chessick, R D/Technique and/75n1578
Chester, E W/Guide to political/79n519
Chety, S/Research on/79n374
Chi, W-S/Chinese-English/78n1051
Ch'i heavy sword coins & debatable pieces of
 the Chou era/Coole/78n845
Chibnall, B/Organisation of/77n152
Chi-Bonnardel, R V/Atlas of Africa/75n576
Chicago/Furer/75n508
Chicago women's directory/76n790
Chicana: comp bibliographic study/Cabello-
 Argandona/77n440
Chicano perspectives in lit/Lomeli/78n1128
Chicanos/Dunn/76n400
Chickering, C R/Flowers of/75n1474
Chicorel, M/Chicorel abstracts reading/79
 n690/Chicorel bibliog books/76n985/
 Chicorel index abstracting/76n34: Chicorel
 index biographies/76n93/Chicorel index
 crafts/76n954/Chicorel index environ-
 ment/76n1451/Chicorel index poetry/
 76n1212/Chicorel index reading/76n692/
 Chicorel index short/76n1203; 79n1188/
 Chicorel theater/78n937
Chicorel . . .
 abstracts to reading & learning disabilities/
  Chicorel/79n690/Sargent/78n582
 bibliography to bks on music & musicians/
  Chicorel/76n985
 index to abstracting & indexing services:
  humanities & soc sci/Chicorel/76n34

Chicorel . . . (cont'd)
    index to biographies/Chicorel/76n93
    index to environment & ecology/Chicorel/76n1451
    index to poetry in anthologies & collections in print/Chicorel/76n1212
    index to reading disabilities/Chicorel/76n692
    index to short stories in anthologies & collections/Chicorel/76n1203; 79n1188
    index to the crafts/Chicorel/76n954
    theater index to plays in anthologies & collections/Chicorel/78n937
Chielens, E E/Literary journal/76n1218; 78n1109
Child, H/Heraldic design/77n484
Child abuse and neglect/Kalisch/79n748
Child care issues for parents & society/Garoogian/78n656
Child health ency/Feinbloom/76n1543
Child Study Assoc/Family life/78n655
Childers, J W/Tales from/79n1286
Childers, T/Information-poor/76n199
Childhood in poetry, 2nd suppl/Shaw/77n1146
Children and books/Sutherland/79n218
Children using media/Fasick/79n209
Children's authors & illustrators/LaBeau/77n1156/Sarkissian/79n1194
Children's bk review index/Tarbert/76n1196; 77n1147; 79n1196
Children's bk showcase/75n1343; 76n1222
Children's books/Schatzki/75n1322
Children's books: awards & prizes/77n1148; 78n1098
Children's books in print/75n196; 76n154
Children's books in the Rare Book Div of the LC/Library of Congress/76n1197
Children's bks of internat'l interest/Haviland/79n232
Children's bks of the yr/77n1149/Moss/77n1226
Children's bks of yesterday/Holme/77n1155
Children's bks on Africa & their authors/Schmidt/76n1199
Children's dict of occupations/Hopke/75n709
Children's illus'd Bible dict/Beers/78n989
Children's library serv/Burke/75n192
Children's literary almanac/75n1344
Children's literature/Leif/78n1101
Children's literature . . .
    handbook/Wheelbarger/75n1323
    in the elementary school/Huck/77n1153
    issues approach/Rudman/79n1193

Children's literature . . . (cont'd)
    review/Block/77n1150/Riley/77n1151
    selected essays/MacLeod/79n1191
    guide to ref sources, 2nd suppl/Haviland/79n233
Children's media market place/Boyle/79n225
Children's services of public libraries/Richardson/79n216
Children's TV/Clark/79n1177
Childs, B S/Old Testament/78n991
Childs, J F/Encyclopedia of long-/77n821
Chile & Allende/Sobel/75n524
Chilton's . . .
    auto air conditioning manual/Kelly/75n1722
    auto repair manual/77n1573
    basic auto maintenance/77n1574
    complete gd to motorcycles & motorcycling/Koch/75n737
    encyclopedia of gardening/Stangl/77n1560
    guide to emission controls & how they work/75n1723
    more miles per gallon gd/Weiers/75n1739
    motorcycle labor gd/75n1741
    motorcycle repair manual/Kelly/75n1742
    truck repair manual/Kelly/75n1751
Chilton's new repair and tune-up guide . . .
    Hodaka/75n1743
    Kawasaki 900 Z1/75n1744
    Suzuki Triples/75n1745
Chilton's repair and tune-up guide . . .
    Dodge/Plymouth vans/75n1748
    Fiat 2/75n1724
    Gremlin, Hornet/75n1725
    Honda/75n1726
    International Scout/75n1750
    Jaguar 2/75n1727
    Jeep Wagoneer, Commando & Cherokee/75n1749
    Opel 2/75n1728
Chimsky, J/Beginning writer's/79n1169
China: analytical survey of lit/79n368
China & the US/Yim/76n502
China: resource & curriculum gd/Posner/78n297
Chinery, M/Field gd insects/75n1516
Chinese communist materials at the Bureau of Investigation Archives, Taiwan/Donovan/78n473
Chinese-English & English-Chinese dictionaries in the LC/Dunn/79n1131
Chinese-English dict of contemporary usage/Chi/78n1051

Chinese-English dict of modern usage/ Lin/75n1264
Chinese herbs/Keys/77n1505
Chinese historiography on the Revolution of 1911/Hsieh/76n361
Chinese in America 1820-1973/Tung/75n825
Chinese in Hawaii/Young/75n826
Chinese newspapers published in North America/Lo/79n455
Chinese periodicals in the libraries of the Australian National Univ/75n39
Ching, E & N/201 Chinese/79n1130
Chirgwin, F J/Library assistant's/79n321
Chiropractic: internat'l bibliog/Klein/78n1424
Chisholm, L J/Units of/76n1315
Chisholm, M E/Education book/75n643; 76n577/Media personnel/77n219
Chisholm's hndbk of commercial geography/ Stamp/76n832
Cho, S Y/Japanese writings/79n564
Choice: classified cumulation/Gardner/77n198; 79n179
Choosing & using phonograph records for physical educ, recreation, & related activities/79n679
Choral music in print/Nardone/75n1132/ Suppl./77n960
Chou, H/Oracle bone/78n318
Christ Our Lord/Watlington/79n1045
Christenson, S J/Women and/76n791
Christian, P/Agricultural enterprises/79n1512
Christian, R W/Electronic library/79n261/ Librarians and/79n299
Christianity in tropical Africa/Ofori/78n973
Christiano, D/Human rights/76n470; 78n431
Christianson, E/Paraprofessional and/75n203
Christie, G A/Dictionary of drugs/77n1501
Christie, I R/Bibliography of British/78n368
Christina Rossetti/Crump/77n1238
Christopher, J R/C. S. Lewis/75n1390
Chronicles of the Scotch-Irish settlement in Virginia/Chalkley/75n409
Chronological bibliog of English lang fiction in the LC through 1950/Wright/75n1325
Chronological charts of the Old Testament/ Walton/79n1075
Chronology & documentary hndbk of the state of . . . Illinois/Vexler/79n423/ Kentucky/Vexler/79n424/Maryland/Vexler/ 79n425

Chronology & fact bk of the UN/Chamberlin/77n493
Chronology of . . .
African hist/Freeman-Grenville/75n391
music in the Florentine theater 1590-1750/Weaver/79n995
the medieval world/Storey/75n353
the US/Clements/76n333
the war at sea/Rohwer/75n542
world hist/Freeman-Grenville/76n304
Chrystie, F N/Pets/75n1679
Chu, F D/France/75n309
Chu, P/Twentieth-century/78n1185
Chuks-orji, O/Names from/75n447
Chumas, S J/Index of internat'l/75n1719
Chun, K-T/Measures for/76n1486
Church, J O/Mathematical modeling/79n1326
Church cyclopaedia/Benton/76n1080
Church furnishings/Dirsztay/79n912
Church, monastery, cathedral/Whone/79n1046
Church-state relations/Menendez/77n1028
Churchill, C/World of/75n1671
Churchill, R C/Bibliography of Dickensian/ 76n1272
Churgin, B/Thematic catalogue/78n908
Chusid, M/Catalog of Verdi's/75n1165
CIA & the security debate/Buncher/77n510
Cianciolo, P/Adventuring with/78n189
Cifelli, E M/Index of American/79n1217
CILA: problems in the acquisition of Latin American library materials/Clouston/75n210
Cinema booklist/Rehrauer/79n1026
Cinema, the magic vehicle/Garbicz/76n1057
Circles of friends/78n79
Circuit design idea hndbk/Furlow/75n1781
Cirtautas, A M/Nicholas Poppe/79n1088
CIS/Annual/77n511
Cities/Hoover/77n729
Citizen & sci almanac & annotated bibliog/ La Follette/78n1201
Citizen groups in local politics/Hutcheson/ 77n523
Citrus diseases & disorders/Knorr/76n1401
City in print/Bryfogle/77n726/Suppl. 1/ Bryfogle/77n727
Civil aircraft of the world/Taylor/76n1661
Civil rights/Burke/75n796
Clabburn, P/Needleworker's dict/77n890
Clack, D H/Black lit/77n1188
Claghorn, C E/Biographical dict/75n1155
Clair, C/History of European/78n33

Clancy, T H/English Catholic/75n1216
Clapin, S/Dictionnaire Canadien-/76n1140
Clapp, J/Professional ethics/75n79
Clarendon gd to Oxford/Woolley/76n561
Clark, A N/Chisholm's hndbk/76n832
Clark, C E/Maine during/75n378
Clark, C E F/Nathaniel Hawthorne/78n1141; 79n1220
Clark, D S/Index to maps/75n370
Clark, E M/Ohio art/77n857
Clark, H/Introduction to heraldry/75n440
Clark, J/Women/75n856
Clark, J M/Putnam's contemporary/75n1269
Clark, L J/Wild flowers/78n1287
Clark, L L/International catalog/75n1637/ International register/79n1469
Clark, O H/Token coinage/75n1063
Clark, R E/Children's TV/79n1177
Clark, R L/Archive-library/77n153
Clark, S/New century/75n1398
Clark, S/Complete bk baseball/77n930/Illus'd basketball/79n709
Clark, T D/Fifty-year/75n371
Clarke, C B/Edible and/79n1366
Clarke, D/Architecture schools/78n798
Clarke, D/Encyclopedia of how/78n1501
Clarke, D A/Acquisitions from/76n173
Clarke, H/Birds of/77n1375
Clarke, J A/Reader's adviser/78n2
Clarke, J R/Abstracts from/78n410
Clarke, M/Encyclopedia of dance/79n1019
Clarke, M/Essay collections/78n490
Clarke, T/International academic/77n58
Clason, W E/Elsevier's dict library/79n158/ Elsevier's dict measurement/79n1544/ Elsevier's telecommunication/77n1117
Classic guitar, lute & vinhuela discography/ Purcell/78n905
Classical lexicon for Finnegans Wake/O Hehir/ 78n1178
Classical music recordings for home & library/ Halsey/77n965
Classical mythology/Peradotto/75n1240
Classical vocal music in print/Nardone/78 n897
Classical world bibliog of . . .
　Greek & Roman hist/79n402
　Greek drama & poetry/79n1262
　philosophy, religion, & rhetoric/79n1080
　Roman drama & poetry & ancient fiction/ 79n1263
　Vergil/79n1264
Classics illus'd dict/Fuchs/75n1317

Classification & index of the world's languages/Voegelin/78n1022
Classification and indexing in . . .
　science/Vickery/77n263
　the humanities/Langridge/77n256
Classification & subj index for cataloguing & arranging the bks and pamphlets of a library/78n288
Classification in the 1970s/Maltby/78n220
Classification system of Jacques-Charles Brunet/McKeon/78n221
Classified directory of artists' signatures, symbols & monograms/Caplan/78n790
Classified index to persons in the LC classification schedules/Olson/79n279
Classroom cinema/Maynard/79n685
Claude Lévi-Strauss & his critics/Lapointe/ 79n779
Claudio, V S/Nutrition and/76n1525
Clauser, H R/Encyclopedia/hndbk/78n1540/ Materials hndbk/78n1539
Clay, H F/Hawai'i garden tropical exotics/ 78n1488/Hawai'i garden tropical shrubs/ 78n1489
Clay, J W/North Carolina/76n531
Clayton, T/Handbook of wrestling/75n788
Cleartype business control atlas of the US & Canada/77n763
Cleary, F D/Discovering books/78n182
Clegg, P/New low-/76n1458
Clemens, S M/Abstracts of/79n1431
Clemens, W M/American marriage/76n427
Clements, J/Chronology of/76n333
Clements, J F/Birds of/75n1502; 79n1370
Cleminshaw, C H/Beginner's gd/79n1314
Clemoes, P/Anglo-Saxon/77n403
Clergy and laity/Liebard/79n1040
Clergy's fed income tax gd/75n982
Cleveland: chronological & documentary hist/Vexler/78n361
Cleveland Museum of Art/European paintings/76n917
Clifford, H T/Identifying grasses/79n1348
Clifford, M/Security!/75n832
Clift, G G/Kentucky marriages/75n411
Clifton, J A/Computers in/75n274
Climate advisor/Schwartz/79n1417
Climates of the states/Ruffner/79n1413
Climates of the states in two vols/76n1477
Climatic atlas of Nebraska/Lawson/79n1415
Climatic atlas of the tropical Atlantic & Eastern Pacific Oceans/Hastenrath/79 n1414
Climber's sourcebk/Schneider/77n688

Climbing/Bunting/75n755
Cline, G S/Index to criticisms/75n1332
Cline, H F/Guide to ethnohistorical/76n809
Cline, J H/Standing liberty/77n906
Clinical atlas of human chromosomes/ de Grouchy/79n1444
Clinical toxicology of commercial products/ Gosselin/77n1485
Clint, F/Ohio area/78n401
Cloak-and-dagger bibliog/Smith/77n1174
Clock/Erhardt/79n935
Clock book/Nutting/77n901
Clockmakers' library/Bromley/79n934
Close up: contract director/Tuska/78n968
Clotfelter, C F/Hunting and/75n721
Clough, W O/Dutch uncles/78n398
Clouston, J S/CILA/75n210
Cluley, L E/Dictionary catalog/76n293
Clutton, C/Vintage car/78n865
Coakley, R W/War of/76n334
Coal industry in America/Munn/79n846
Coan, E V/World directory/78n1348
Coates, E/Broad system/79n300
Coating equipmt & processes/Weiner/77n1323
Cobb, S/Measures for/76n1486
Coblans, H/Use of/77n1336
COBOL programming: for librarians/Brophy/77n288
Cochran, W/Into print/78n39
Cock-a-hoop: bibliog of the Golden Cockerel Press/Chambers/77n53
Cocker, H/Flowers/76n1599
Cockerell, H A L/British insurance/79n849
Codd, L W/Chemical technology/77n1575
Cody, D T R/Your child's/76n1544
Coe, L C/Folklife and/79n1083
Coelho, J Y/Holdings of/75n1247
Coffey, D J/Dolphins, whales/78n1332
Cogger, H G/Reptiles and/78n1336
Cogswell, H L/Water birds/78n1317
Cohan, L/Readers advisory/76n134
Cohen, D/California experience/79n388
Cohen, D/Multi-ethnic/76n387
Cohen, G A/Summer study/77n590/Teaching abroad/78n572/US college/77n591
Cohen, H L/Official gd/75n66
Cohen, I/Jewish organizations/76n379
Cohen, J/Special bibliog/79n871
Cohen, L/National gd/78n649
Cohen, M D/Selecting educational/77n645
Cohen, R M/Sports ency: baseball/75n733; 78n610/Sports ency: pro football/78n738
Cohen, R M/World series/77n674
Cohn, A A/Bell &/77n1086

COIN: indexed checklist to Colorado state publications/Shaklee/78n95
Coin world almanac/77n907
Coinage of the European continent/Hazlitt/76n968
Coins & paper money of Nicaragua/Stockney/75n1071
Coins of Ecuador/Seppa/75n1070
Coins of the world 1750-1850/Wallace/77n908
Coker, W C/Gasteromycetes of/76n1396
Coldham, P W/English convicts/75n412; 78n399
Cole, J Y/Ainsworth Rand/76n208/LC in/79n237
Cole, K W/Minority organizations/79n444
Cole, W R/Checklist of science-/76n1204
Coleman, A/Epic and/75n1310
Coleman, H/National anthems/77n950
Coleman, J/Writings on/76n411
Coleridge, H/Dictionary of first/77n1072
Colgate, C/Directory of Washington/79n91/National trade/77n87
Colin, P/Craft sources/76n950
Coll, E/Indice informativo/79n1287
Collectible ceramics/Ray/75n1084
Collecting & studying mushrooms, toadstools, & fungi/Major/76n1397
Collecting photographica/Gilbert/77n932
Collecting world sea shells/Major/75n1097
Collection building/79n189
Collection developmt policy/79n193
Collection management/78n156
Collection of upwards of 30,000 names/Rupp/76n440
Collection, use, & care of historical photographs/Weinstein/78n888
Collective bargaining & the academic librarian/Weatherford/77n207
Collective bargaining in higher educ/Abell/78n161/Allen/75n639
Collective bargaining in libraries/Schlipf/76n184
Collective behavior/Morrison/77n707
Collector-investor guidebk & inventory/Durst/78n831
Collectors and collections/Camber/79n878
Collector's Beethoven/Briggs/79n982
Collector's bk of railroadiana/Baker/77n928
Collector's complete dict of American antiques/Phipps/76n964
Collector's encyclopedia of . . . antiques/Phillips/75n1059
Barbie dolls & collectibles/DeWein/78n866

Collector's encyclopedia of . . . (cont'd)
  carnival glass/Hand/79n925
  Depression glass/Florence/78n855
  Fiesta with Harlequin & Riviera/Huxford/
    79n949
  rocks and minerals/Deeson/75n1094
  shells/Dance/78n857
Collector's gd & hist to Lionel trains/McComas/
  77n943
Collector's guide to . . .
  American recordings 1895-1925/Moses/78
    n901
  carnival glass/Klamkin/77n920
  dollhouses and dollhouse miniatures/
    O'Brien/75n1099
  militaria/Johnson/78n871
  19th-century photographs/Welling/77
    n939
  paper money/Berisiner/79n933
  patent & proprietary medicine bottles of
    the 19th cent/Baldwin/75n1078
  relics & memorabilia/Patterson/75n1058
  rocks and minerals/Tindall/77n1440
Collector's Haydn/Burke/79n984
Collector's Verdi & Puccini/de Schauensee/
  79n986
College admissions data serv hndbk/79n651
College charts/76n645
College chemistry faculties/Balser/78n1252
College counseling for transfers & careers/
  75n655
College gd for Jewish youth/Feingold/79n459
College gd for students with disabilities/
  Gollay/78n564
College handbook/Watts/77n613; 79n652
College hndbk index of majors/79n653
College law digest/Blackwell/75n564
College learning resource center/Burlingame/
  79n192
College learning resources programs/78n163
College library/Jefferson/79n196
College on your own/Parker/79n632
College placement & credit by examination/
  77n614; 79n654
College programs for high school students/76
  n646
College programs for paraprofessionals/
  Queens College/76n652
Colleges classified/76n647
Collias, E E/Atlas of physical/75n1576
Collie, M/George Meredith/75n1395/George
  Gissing/77n1233
Collier's encyclopedia/Halsey/79n71
Collins, A F/Radio amateur's/77n1113

Collins, F H/Authors and/75n51
Collins, J L/Women artists/75n1011/Women
  artists America/76n932
Collins, K T/Key words/76n594
Collins, M/Libraries for/79n238
Collins gd to the sea fishes of Britain &
  North-Western Europe/Muus/76n1436
Collins' illus'd atlas of London/76n533
Collins-Robert French-English, English-
  French dict/Atkins/79n1134
Collison, R/Published library/75n17
Colombo, J R/Colombo's Canadian/78n305
Colombo's Canadian refs/Colombo/78n305
Colonial America & the war for independence/
  Eakin/78n343
Colonial and revolutionary families of Penn-
  sylvania/Jordan/79n488
Colonial & state hist of Hartford Cnty, NC/
  Winborne/77n480
Colonial clergy & the colonial churches of
  New England/Weis/78n416
Colonial clergy of Virginia, North Carolina &
  South Carolina/Weis/79n479
Colonial families of the southern states of
  America/Hardy/75n419
Colonial Latin American manuscripts &
  transcripts in the Obadiah Rich collection/
  Brownrigg/79n443
Colonialism in Africa, 1870-1960/Duignan/
  75n288
Color atlas of pediatric dermatology/Wein-
  berg/76n1541
Color dictionary of . . .
  flowers & plants for home & garden/Hay/
    76n1587
  shrubs/Gault/77n1368
Color encyclopedia of . . .
  gemstones/Arem/79n1420
  world art/Jacobs/76n923
Color field gd to common wild edibles/Angier/
  78n1311
Color hndbk of house plants/McDonald/77
  n1558
Color of horses/Green/76n752
Color theory/Buckley/76n914
Color treasury of gemstones/Gübelin/77n1433
Colorado/Walton/75n506
Colorado grubstake/Jones/76n347
Colorado railroads/Wilkins/76n1674
Colorful cacti of the American deserts/Lamb/
  76n1385
Colour atlas of human anatomy/McMinn/
  78n1384
Comay, J/Who's who Jewish/75n397

Combat aircraft of WWII/Weal/78n1567
Combat fleets of the world/Couhat/77n1648; 79n1600
Combined chronology for use with the Mahatma letters to A P Sinnett & the letters of H P Blavatsky to A P Sinnett/Conger/75n1235
Combined glossary: state educat'l records & reports series/US Dept of HEW/76n596
Combined membership list of the AMS, MAA and SIAM/79n1308
Combined retrospective index set to journals in hist 1838-1974/Wile/78n334
Combs, C M/Illustrated family/78n1429
Comic bk price gd/Overstreet/77n1171
Coming of the book/Febvre/78n34
Comitas, L/Complete Caribbeana/79n377
Commager, H S/Documents of/75n354
Commire, A/Something about/77n1162; 77n1163/Yesterday's authors/78n1102
Committee for a New England Bibliography/Massachusetts/77n391
Committees & commissions in India/Kumar/78n484; 79n546
Commodity futures trading/Woy/77n806
Commodity prices/Wasserman/75n920
Common errors in English & how to avoid them/Witherspoon/75n1291
Common fossil plants of western North America/Tidwell/76n1386
Common market/Gurland/76n865
Common plants/Cunningham/78n1279
Common seaweeds of the Pacific coast/Waaland/78n1304
Common symptom gd/Wasson/77n1484
Commonsense cataloging/Piercy/76n192
Commonwealth elections 1945-70/Bloomfield/78n476
Communication abstracts/79n1158
Communication directory/Root/76n1171
Communication knowledge & the librarian/McGarry/76n117
Communication research in library & info science/Waldhart/76n127
Communication studies/McGarry/75n156
Communications & the US Congress/Brightbill/79n1159
Community & jr col directory/75n681
Community college library/Veit/76n140
Community educ bibliog/Schwartz/79n634
Community educ handbook/Berridge/75n654
Community elite & the public library/Wilson/78n177
Community info services in libraries/Turick/79n292
Community market cooperative catalog/75n942
Community power & decision-making/Leif/75n792
Community services/Barefoot/79n1458
Compact ed of the dict of national biog/77n147
Compact photo lab index/Pittaro/78n883
Companion to middle Indo-Aryan literature/Banerji/78n1192
Companion to the ...
    Divine Comedy/Grandgent/76n1296
    Iliad/Willcock/77n1265
    movies/Pickard/75n1199
    opera/May/78n913
    theatre/May/76n1038
Companion to your study of the Book of Mormon/Ludlow/77n1018
Comparative & internat'l library sci/Harvey/79n314
Comparative atlas of America's great cities/77n728
Comparative gd to American colleges/Cass/77n611; 79n650
Comparative gd to two yr colleges & career programs/Cass/78n567
Comparative higher educ abroad/Altbach/77n573
Comparative historical analysis of three associations of prof schools/Davis/75n263
Comparative librarianship/Gidwani/75n256
Comparative survey analysis/Almasy/78n270
Comparative world atlas/76n524
Competency based educ sourcebk/Oregon Competency Based Educ Program/78n577
Complete auto electric handbk/Hallmark/76n1614
Complete book of ...
    baseball cards/Clark/77n930
    bulb gardening/Doerflinger/75n1700
    canoeing & kayaking/Fillingham/76n710
    cooking equipment/Wilkinson/76n1580
    cross-country skiing & ski touring/Liebers/75n784
    herbs/Sanecki/75n1485
    herbs and spices/Loewenfeld/75n1484
    home remodeling/Scharff/76n1641
    houseplants under lights/Fitch/76n1585
    mushrooms/Rinaldi/75n1489
    NASCAR stock car racing/Engel/75n780
    platform tennis/Squires/75n783
    saltwater aquariums/Stevenson/75n1667
    symptoms & what they can mean/Galton/79n1484

Complete book of . . . (cont'd)
   the horse/Edwards/75n1680
   US coin collecting/Davis/77n909
   woodworking & cabinetmaking/Maguire/75n1047
Complete buying gd to photographic equipment/75n1107
Complete Caribbeana/Comitas/79n377
Complete catalogue of . . .
   British cars/Culshaw/75n1826
   sheet music & musical works/Board of Music Trade of the USA/75n1121
Complete color encyclopedia of antiques/Ramsey/76n959
Complete cookery ency/75n1686
Complete dog book/76n1564
Complete encyclopedia of . . .
   horses/Ensminger/78n1463
   ice hockey/Hollander/76n750
   music/Moore/75n1142
   needlework/de Dillmont/79n944
   popular music and jazz/Kinkle/75n1171
   television programs/Terrace/77n1120
Complete fisherman's catalog/Henkin/78n623
Complete food catalogue/Wilson/78n1480
Complete food handbook/Doyle/78n1469
Complete garden/Leggett/76n1594
Complete gd for easy car care/Lien/76n1615
Complete guide to . . .
   acupuncture/Toguchi/75n1634
   bird feeding/Dennis/76n1417
   French-Canadian antiques/Lessard/76n963
   modern dance/McDonagh/77n995
   organizing & documenting research papers/Morse/75n694
   outboard motor serv & repair/Dempsey/77n683
   salt and fresh water fishing equipmt/77n693
   the new copyright law/79n63
   the Soviet Union/Louis/78n533
Complete handbook of . . .
   automotive engines & systems/Evenson/75n1731
   baseball/Hollander/79n708
   cacti & succulents/Innes/78n1286
   locks & locksmithing/Roper/77n1570
   pro basketball/Hollander/77n679
   pro hockey/Hollander/77n698
   soccer/Hollander/79n729
   sports scoring & record keeping/Richards/75n727

Complete home medical gd for cats/Schneck/77n1531
Complete home medical gd for dogs/Schneck/77n1532
Complete hunter's catalog/Strung/79n721
Complete illus'd bk of dyes from natural sources/Krochmal/75n1043
Complete illus'd ency of the world's motorcycles/Tragatsch/78n1515
Complete index for the 6 vols of wild flowers of the US/Rickett/77n1362
Complete layman's gd to the law/Hanna/75n558
Complete manual of criminal forms/Bailey/76n513
Complete motorcycle bk/Engel/75n739
Complete motorcycle nomad/Lovin/75n741
Complete musician/Martin/77n949
Complete official MGB/75n1729
Complete out-of-doors job, business, & prof guide/Joseph/75n977
Complete outdoorsman's gd to birds of Eastern North America/Mackenzie/77n1383
Complete outdoorsman's hndbk/Knap/75n724
Complete secretary's hndbk/Doris/78n714
Complete short wave listener's hndbk/Bennett/75n1202
Complete snowmobile repair hndbk/Dempsey/75n1753
Complete unabridged super trivia ency/Worth/79n104
Completed research in health, physical educ, & recreation/Thomas/78n606
Composite index for CRC hndbks/79n1304
Composite MARC format/US LC/78n216
Composium directory of new music/78n907
Comprehensive annotated bibliog of American black English/Brasch/75n1245
Comprehensive bibliography . . .
   for the study of American minorities/Miller/77n425
   of existing literature on tobacco/Gold/77n1503
   on Delaware Bay/Plunguian/75n1525
   on pregnancy & work/79n1425
Comprehensive catalog of US paper money/Hessler/75n1066
Comprehensive Chicano bibliog/Talbot/75n824
Comprehensive dissertation index/75n688
Comprehensive gd to American colonial coinage/Durst/78n846

Comprehensive index to English-language little magazines/Sader/77n1136
Comprehensive Persian-English dict/Steingass/79n1145
Comprehensive program of user educ for the general libraries, the Univ of Texas at Austin/78n233
Comprehensive virology/Fraenkel-Conrat/76n1361
Compton's ency and fact-index/Lawson/75n74
Compton's precyclopedia/75n75
Computer acronym hndbk/Spencer/75n1775
Computer aided design of digital systems/vanCleemput/77n1587; 78n1528
Computer-assisted research in the humanities/Raben/78n76
Computer dictionary/Sippl/75n1774/Spencer/75n1776
Computer industry review/75n960
Computer-output microfilm/Saffady/79n333
Computer-output-microfilm systems/Gildenberg/75n1770
Computer programs in environmental design/Lee/75n1551
Computer-readable bibliographic data bases/Williams/78n243
Computer review/75n961
Computer security/MacCafferty/78n1525
Computer security hndbk/75n1768
Computers and the UDC/Rigby/76n187
Computers in info data centers/Clifton/75n274
Computext book guides . . .
  business & economics/76n824
  conference publications/76n20
  government publications/76n82
  law/76n509
  medicine/76n1515
  technology/76n1310
Comroe, J H/Annual review physiology/76n1359
Comtois, M E/Contemporary American/79n1013
Conant, R/Field gd reptiles/76n1448
Conant, R/Twentieth-century/75n1120
Concept developmt & the developmt of the God concept in the child/Pitts/79n752
Concert piano repertoire/Faurot/75n1126
Concise atlas of . . .
  the universe/Moore/75n1447
  wine/Born/75n1670

Concise bibliography of . . .
  English-Canadian lit/Gnarowski/79n1260
  French lit/Mahaffey/77n1262
Concise Cambodian-English dict/Jacob/75n1284
Concise Cambridge Italian dict/Reynolds/76n1154
Concise chemical & technical dict/Bennett/76n1342
Concise color ency of sci/Kerrod/76n1314
Concise desk bk of business finance/Moffat/77n775
Concise desk gd to real estate practice & procedure/Gross/77n801
Concise dictionary of . . .
  American biography/78n114
  cats/Bloomfield/79n1522
  English idioms/Freeman/77n1070
  English slang & colloquialisms/Phythian/77n1071
  medicine/Martin/76n1526
  religious quotations/Neil/75n1219
Concise encyclopedia of . . .
  ancient civilizations/Garber/79n404
  antiques/Wills/78n842
  astronomy/Weigert/78n1238
  Jewish music/Nulman/76n997
  management techniques/Finch/78n781
  modern art/Charmet/75n997
  psychology & psychiatry/Small/79n1429
Concise gd to library research/Morse/76n119
Concise herbal ency/Law/75n1482
Concise heritage dict/78n1034
Concise index to English/Ehrlich/75n1287
Concise Manchu-English lexicon/Norman/79n1132
Concise Maori dict/Reed/77n1096
Concise Oxford dictionary of . . .
  ballet/Koegler/78n934
  current English/Sykes/77n1074
  French literature/Reid/78n1188
  the Christian Church/Livingstone/79n1058
Concise Swedish-English glossary of legal terms/Backe/75n552
Concise treasury of Bible quotations/Garvey/76n1099
Concise universal biography/Hammerton/77n121
Concordance to . . .
  Conrad's *Almayer's Folly*/Briggum/79n1237

Concordance to . . . (cont'd)
  Conrad's *Lord Jim*/Parins/77n1231
  F. Scott Fitzgerald's *The Great Gatsby*/
    Crosland/76n1236
  Finnegans Wake/Hart/76n1276
  Juan Ruiz/Mignani/79n1290
  Pascal's *Pensées*/Davidson/77n1261
Concordance to the . . .
  Anglo-Saxon poetic records/Bessinger/
    79n1231
  complete poetry of Stephen Crane/
    Crosland/76n1232
  complete writings of George Herbert/
    Di Cesare/78n1176
  English poems of Andrew Marvell/Guffey/
    75n1393
  fables & tales of Jean de la Fontaine/
    Tyler/75n1418
  oeuvres complètes of Arthur Rimbaud/
    Carter/79n1271
  plays & poems of Federico García Lorca/
    Pollin/76n1305
  poems of Alexander Pope/Bedford/76
    n1282
  poems of Ben Jonson/Bates/79n1243/
    Di Cesare/79n1245
  poems of Dylan Thomas/Lane/77n1246
  poems of Osip Mandelstam/Koubourlis/
    75n1425
  poems of Sir Philip Sidney/Donow/76
    n1288
  poems of Stephen Crane/Baron/76n1231
  poetry of Langston Hughes/Mandelik/76
    n1240
  poetry of Leopoldo Panero/Ruiz-Fornells/
    79n1291
  sayings in Franklin's "Poor Richard"/
    Barbour/75n1356
  Septuagint/Morrish/78n981
  works of Sir Thomas Malory/Kato/75n1392
Concrete construction hndbk/Waddell/75
  n1761
Condensed chemical dict/Hawley/78n1248
Condominium buyer's gd/Karr/75n948
Conely, J/Guide to/76n999
Confederate guns & their current prices/
  Rywell/76n971
Confederate postal hist/Crown/77n923
Confederation, constitution, & early national
  period/Ferguson/76n310
Conger, M/Combined chronology/75n1235
Congress & the nation IV/79n523
Congress investigates/Schlesinger/76n307
Congressional hearings on American defense
  policy/Burt/75n489

Congressional Quarterly's guide to . . .
  Congress/77n512
  1976 elections/78n452
  US elections/76n475
Congressional roll call/76n483; 77n513
Conlin, J R/American radical/75n1293
Conn, S/War of/76n334
Connecticut loyalists/Tyler/78n415
Connell, N/Rape/75n850
Connoly, L W/English drama/79n1007
Connor, B M & J M/Ottemiller's index/77
  n996
Conover, H S/Grounds maintenance/78n1490
Conroy, B/Library staff/79n322
Conscription/Anderson/77n1625
Conseil internat'l de la langue française/
  Glossary of . . . environment/78n1342;
  79n1394
Conservation directory/Decker/77n1412
Conservation ecology/Harrah/76n1465
Considine, D M/Chemical and/75n1755/
  Energy technology/78n1349/Process
  instruments/75n1803/Van Nostrand's/
  79n1292
Consolidated catalog of League of Nations
  publications offered for sale/Birchfield/
  78n429
Consolidated clothbound ed of monthly
  catalog of US gov publications/78n96
Consolidated index to the ILO legislative
  series/Pease/78n772
Constable, G/Medieval monasticism/77n1025
Constitutions of the countries of the world/
  Blaustein/78n427
Construction industry hndbk/Burgess/75
  n1757
Construction info source & ref gd/Ward/75
  n1762
Construction inspection hndbk/O'Brien/
  76n1621
Construction manual/Love/75n1766
Consultants & consulting organizations
  directory/Wasserman/77n789
Consumer complaint gd/Rosenbloom/75n934
Consumer info hndbk/Thorelli/75n936
Consumer protection directory/Osberg/76
  n871
Consumer sourcebk/Wasserman/75n931;
  79n844
Consumer's arsenal/Dorfman/77n814
Consumer's catalog of economy & ecology/
  Bendick/76n882
Consumer's dictionary of . . .
  cosmetic ingredients/Winter/75n940;
  77n818

Consumer's dictionary of ... (cont'd)
  food additives/Winter/79n1535
Consumer's gd to psychotherapy/Wiener/76
  n1502
Consumer's hndbk/Fargis/76n873
Consumers index to product evaluations &
  info sources/Wall/75n943; 77n812
Contact book/76n1041
Contemporary American ...
  composers/Anderson/77n970
  composers based at American colleges &
    universities/Jacobi(y)/76n1005
  literature/Manly/76n1219
  poetry/Davis/76n1223
  theater critics/Comtois/79n1013
Contemporary art & artists/Parry/79n900
Contemporary artists/Naylor/79n909
Contemporary authors/Kinsman/76n97; 76
  n98/Bowden/79n138
Contemporary authors cum index/79n139
Contemporary authors, 1st rev/Kinsman/75
  n119; 76n96/Evory/79n137
Contemporary authors, permanent series/
  Kinsman/76n99/Nasso/79n140
Contemporary British drama/Mikhail/78n928
Contemporary Canadian composers/MacMillan/
  77n971
Contemporary crafts market place/76n951
Contemporary dramatists/Vinson/75n1189;
  78n946
Contemporary fiction in America & England/
  Rosa/78n1105
Contemporary games/Belch/75n697
Contemporary literary criticism/Riley/75
  n1319; 76n1188; 76n1189; 77n1130
Contemporary literary critics/Borklund/79
  n1207
Contemporary Middle East/Atiyeh/77n308
Contemporary Native American lit/Jacobson/
  78n1127
Contemporary novelists/Vinson/77n1182
Contemporary poets/Vinson/76n1214
Contemporary problems in tech library & infor-
  mation center managemt/Rees/76n168
Contemporary sociology/76n776
Contemporary thought on Edmund Spenser/
  Frushell/76n1289
Contento, W/Index to science/79n1203
Continuing education: a guide/78n568
Continuing education opportunities for library,
  info, & media personnel/77n273
Continuing education resource bk/Stone/78
  n254
Continuing library education/Sage/78n252/
  Virgo/78n255

Continuing prof educ in librarianship &
  other fields/Michael/76n222
Controversy over a new Canal treaty between
  the US & Panama/Bray/78n486
Convention decisions & voting records/Bain/
  75n487
Conversion tables for SI metrication/Semioli/
  75n1717
Cook, C/English historical/79n434
Cook, C/European political 1848-1918/79
  n505/1918-1973/76n460/Sources in/
  78n477
Cook, C/Pears cyclopaedia/76n62; 79n78
Cook, G/Bargain hunting/75n953
Cook, G A/How to remodel/76n1637
Cook, M G/New library/76n110
Cook, T D/Stratigraphic atlas/78n513
Cooke, J/Famous kings/78n333
Cooke, J J/France/76n364
Cooking for entertaining/Tudor/77n1551
Cooks' catalogue/Beard/76n1568
Coole, A B/Ch'i heavy/78n845
Coombs, D/Guide to antique/79n911
Coon, N/Dictionary of useful/76n1373
Co-op Handbook Collective/Food co-op/76
  n872
Cooper, A/World of/77n118
Cooper, B/World museums/75n1008
Cooper, C M/Cumulative index/77n1137
Cooper, D E/International bibliog discog-
  raphies/76n986
Cooper, J E/Measurement and/75n1599
Cooper, M/New Oxford/75n1149
Cooperation in library serv to children/
  Dyer/79n208
Copely, U E/Directory of homosexual/78n651
Coppell, W G/World catalogue/79n774
Coptic etymological dict/Černý/78n1053
Copyright and photocopying/Heilprin/79n64
Copyright dilemma/White/79n320
Copyright handbook/Johnston/79n65
Copyright: how to register your copyright/
  Hurst/78n58
Copyright info technology public policy/
  Henry/78n56; 78n57
Copyright law symposium, no. 21/76n41/no.
  22/American Soc of Composers, Authors &
  Publishers/78n54/no. 23/American Soc of
  Composers, Authors & Publishers/78n53
Coral, L/British book/79n60
Corbett, J A/Catalogue of medieval/79n66
Corbett, T/Dreamer's dict/75n1583
Corbetta, F/Health plants/79n1351
Cord Communications Corp/Pro football/76
  n734

Cordasco, F/Bibliography of vocational/78 n538/Immigrant children/78n539/Italian-American experience/76n409/Italian Americans/79n456/Italian community/76n410/Research and/75n693
Cordello, B S/Celebrations/78n1020
Core media collection for secondary schools/Brown/76n156
Corliss, W R/Ancient man/79n394/Strange artifacts/75n401/Strange phenomena/75n91
Cornell, J/Great internat'l/77n98/It happened/75n85
Cornell Center for Improvement in Undergrad Education/Yellow pages/75n682
Cornforth, J/National lifeguard/75n786
Cornwell, P B/Pest control/75n1532
Corporate headings/Verona/77n262
Corporate profiles for executives & investors/77n798
Corpus almanac of Canada/Fawcett/77n335
Corpus delicti of mystery fiction/Herman/76n1207
Corpus Rubenianum Ludwig Burchard/75n990
Corpuscles/Bessis/75n1642
Correll, D S & H B/Aquatic and/76n1382
Correspondence educational directory/Jones/78n569
Correy, T/Library community/79n287
Corrigan, J T/Periodicals for/77n1026
Corrosion of pulp & paper mill equipmt/Pollock/77n1326
Cors, P B/Railroads/76n1670
Cortada, J W/Bibliographic gd Spanish/79n551
Cortes, C E/Mexican American/75n822
Cortes Conde, R/Latin America/79n805
Cortina/Grosset basic . . .
 French dict/Nutting/77n1090
 German dict/Zotter/77n1091
 Italian dict/Berberi/77n1092
 Spanish dict/Laita/77n1099
Corvette service-repair hndbk/Jorgensen/75n1736
Corwin, H G/Second reference/77n1306
Cory, L/Quote unquote/79n95
Cosentino, A F/Paintings of/78n815
Cosmetics/Rinzler/78n1256
Cosminsky, S/Traditional medicine/77n1462
Cosmopolitan world atlas/79n584
Cost analysis of library functions/Mitchell/79n256
Cost of personal borrowing in the US/Gushee/77n802
Cost reduction from A to Z/Higgins/77n774

Costello, R B/Nelson's new/79n1459
Costeloe, M P/Independent Mexico/75n312
Costner, T/Motion picture/77n1005
Costume design in the movies/Leese/78n952
Costume of household servants from the middle ages to 1900/Cunnington/76n979
Cote, N/Directory of business/77n800
Coté, R J/Common plants/78n1279
Cottam, K M/Writer's research/78n102
Cotter, M/Vietnam/78n302
Cotton, H/Typographical gazetteer/77n881
Cotton, I W/Annotated bibliog literature/77n1586
Couch, J N/Gasteromycetes of/76n1396
Coues, E/American ornithological/75n1503
Coughlan, M N/Folklore from/77n1057/Samuel Langhorne/78n1151
Couhat, J L/Combat fleets/77n1648; 79n1600
Coulson, J/Oxford illus'd/76n1146/Pocket Oxford/76n1146/Shorter Oxford/75n1252
Coulson, W D E/Annotated bibliog Greek/77n862
Council of Home Health Agencies & Community Health Services/Directory of/76n1534
Council of State Governments/Book of states/77n519
Council on library resources annual report/78n157
Counselors' comparative gd to American colleges/Cass/77n612
Countries of the world/US Dept of State/75n325
Countries of the world & their leaders/76n461; 78n433
Country antiques companion/D'Imperio/78n834
Country craft tools/Blandford/75n1030
Country inns & back roads/Simpson/77n568; 79n622
Country music ency/Shestack/75n1176
County info systems directory/Matthews/78n464
County year bk/76n494
Court, A/Minerals/76n1480
Court organization & admin/Tompkins/75n549
Courtney, G/Butterick sewing/78n877
Coutumes of France in the LC/Caswell/79n563
Coveney, J/Glossary of German/78n779
Covo, J/Blinking eye/75n1354
Cowan, H J/Dictionary of architectural/75n1016

Cowan, M/Annual review neuroscience/79 n1474
Cowan, S T/Cowan and/76n1360
Cowan and Steel's manual for the identification of medical bacteria/Cowan/76n1360
Cowie, A P/Oxford advanced/75n1260/Oxford dict/77n1069
Cowie, P/Eighty years/78n948/International film/76n1047; 77n999/World filmography/78n964; 79n1032
Cowley, J/Libraries in/77n202
Cowling, E/Cello/76n1014
Cox, G F/Tropical marine/75n1666
Cox, J C/Parish registers/75n436
Cox, W J/Guide to architecture/75n1017
Coxe, A D H/Haunted Britain/75n622
Coyle, W/Roger Williams/78n972
Coyne, J/By hand/75n1031/Getting skilled/77n628
Crabbe, D/World energy/79n1392
Crabtree, J M/Bibliography of aggressive/79n1424
Craft shops/Galleries USA/75n1032
Craft sources/Colin/76n950
Craft suppliers: fiber/75n1041
Craft supplies supermarket/Rosenbloom/76n953
Crafts business ency/Scott/79n941
Crafts for today/Harwell/75n1035
Crafts of the North American Indians/Schneider/75n1037
Craftworker's market/Lapin/79n938
Craig, W/Coins of/77n908
Craig, W/Sweet and/79n985
Cram, M D/Libraries for/79n241
Cramer, N/Museum Council/77n76
Cramp, S/Handbook of birds/79n1371
Crane, J St. C/Robert Frost/75n1357
Crane, R S/English literature 1660-1800/75n1374
Crater, F/Almanac of/78n456
Crawford, C/Handbook of zoning/75n860
Crawford, C L/Guide to middle/76n656; 76n657; 76n658; 76n659
Crawford, H H/Crawford's ency/79n1198
Crawford, M H/Roman republican/76n966
Crawford, S/Directory of health/76n1535
Crawford's ency of comic bks/Crawford/79n1198
CRC hndbk of environmental control/Bond/75n1536
Creating a school media program/Gillespie/75n195
Creative writing in the classroom/Day/79n630
Creativity in human developmt/Arasteh/78n1361
Creativity in the communicative arts/Ceynar/76n1161
Crede, C E/Shock and/77n1607
Creger, W P/Annual review medicine/76n1527
Creighton, J/Discopaedia of/75n1160
Cresswell, D H/American Revolution/77n373
Crews, F/Random House/79n128
Crime & juvenile delinquency/79n574
Crime scene search & physical evidence hndbk/US Dept of Justice/75n835
Criminological bibliographies/Davis/79n575
Criminology & the admin of criminal justice/Radzinowicz/78n499
Criminology index/Wolfgang/76n780
Criminology, law enforcemt & offender treatment/Kinton/75n829
Cripe, H/American manuscripts/78n61
Crisis in copyright/Nasri/77n50
Crisler, J S/Frank Norris/76n1247
Crisp, W/Development and/76n578
Critchfield, S/SHARE/77n183
Critchley, M/Butterworths medical/79n1460
Criteria for planning the college & univ learning resources center/Merrill/78n166
Crites, R/Wastewater management/77n1421
Critical approaches to Rubén Darío/Ellis/76n1299
Critical bibliog of building conservation/Smith/79n892
Critical dict of psychoanalysis/Rycroft/75n1584
Critical hndbk of children's lit/Lukens/77n1158
Critical index: bibliog of articles on film in English/Gerlach/75n1209
Critical lexicon & concordance to the English & Greek New Testament/Bullinger/78n990
Critical reception of Robert Frost/van Egmond/75n1358
Critical writings on Commonwealth literatures/New/76n1182
Crittenden, M/Trees of/79n1359/Wildflowers of/78n1288
Crocker, C/New trade/79n810
Crockett, L J/Wildly successful/78n1310
Cronon, E D/Second world/76n290
Crook, L/Oil terms/77n1410
Crosbie, J S/Crosbie's dict/78n1042
Crosbie's dict of puns/Crosbie/78n1042
Crosby, S S/Early coins/75n1064
Crosland, A T/Concordance to F. Scott/76n1236/Concordance to complete/76n1232

Cross, C A/Atlas of Mercury/78n1235
Cross, F L/Handbook of swimming/75n1758/
   Handbook on environmental/75n1537/
   Marine environmental/76n1668/Oxford
   dict/75n1220
Cross, L/Early childhood/78n595
Cross, R D/Atlas of Mississippi/75n574
Cross, W/Weekend education/77n615
Cross-reference index/Atkins/75n222
Crossword puzzle dict/Swanfeldt/78n1047
Crouch, M/Directory of state/78n351
Crowe, M J/Witchcraft/78n1380
Crowell's hndbk of contemporary American
   poetry/Malkoff/75n1342
Crowell's hndbk of Elizabethan & Stuart
   literature/Ruoff/76n1262
Crowley, E T/Acronyms, initialisms/78n108/
   New acronyms/76n90; 78n109/New trade/
   79n810/Reverse acronyms/77n119/Trade
   names/77n787
Crown, F J/Confederate postal/77n923
Crown treasury of relevant quotations/Murphy/
   79n98
Crows of the world/Goodwin/77n1378
Crump, R W/Christina Rossetti/77n1238
Crumrine, B/Virginia court/75n413
Cruz, G R/Comprehensive Chicano/75n824
Cuadra, C A/Directory of academic/77n209
Cuban revolutionary war/Pérez/77n400
Cuddon, J A/Dictionary of literary/78n1097
Cullinan, B E/Literature and/78n1099
Culshaw, D/Complete catalogue/75n1826
Cultural conformity in bks for children/
   MacCann/78n1120
Cultural revolution in China/Wang/77n320
Culture change/Keesing/75n867
Culver, J B/Atlas of Wisconsin/75n580
Culver, V/Guidebook of Franklin/76n967
Cumberland parish/Bell/75n406
Cummings, C S/Biographical-bibliographical/78
   n154
Cummings, P/Dictionary of contemporary/78
   n823/Fine arts/77n858
Cummings, P/Fairfield County/76n547
Cumulated fict index/Smith/77n1176
Cumulated indexes to the public papers of the
   Presidents of the US . . .
   Dwight D. Eisenhower/79n416
   John F. Kennedy/79n417
   Lyndon B. Johnson/79n418
Cumulative index: Arithmetic Teacher/76
   n588
Cumulative index of hospital lit/Dunlap/78
   n1422

Cumulative index: SAE papers/76n1609
Cumulative index to . . .
   MFS/Cooper/77n1137
   nursing & allied health lit/Grandbois/79
      n1475
   nursing lit/Grandbois/75n1640; 77n1492
   periodical literature/77n38
   the annual catalogues of Her Majesty's
      Stationery Office publications/Black-
      more/77n111
   to the Bulletin of Bibliography & Maga-
      zine Notes/Jones/78n22
Cumulative list and index of treaties & inter-
   nat'l agreements/Vambery/79n560
Cumulative subj gd to US gov bibliographies
   1924-73/Kanely/77n112
Cumulative subj index to the monthly catalog
   of US gov publications, 1900-71/Buchanan/
   75n102
Cumulative subj index to the public affairs
   info serv bulletins 1915-74/78n23
Cunningham, J A/Wildflowers of/75n1478
Cunningham, J J/Common plants/78n1279
Cunningham, P J/Community services/79n1458
Cunningham, W E/Para-legal/75n555
Cunnington, P/Costume of/76n979
Curl, J S/English architecture/78n800
Curley, A/Akers' simple/78n217
Curran, N/National basketball/76n707
Current accounting lit/Baig/77n796
Current bibliog on . . .
   African affairs/Matthews/75n286
   Chicanos, 1960-73/Quintana/76n403
Current bk review citations/77n39
Current coins of the world/Yeoman/75
   n1072; 77n916
Current drug hndbk/Falconer/78n1436
Current index to statistics/Joiner/79n792;
   79n793
Current medical diagnosis & treatment/Krupp/
   75n1609
Current research in comparative communism/
   Whetten/78n468
Currey, L W/Research gd/79n1205
Curriculum alternatives/Case/75n193
Curriculum design for library & info sci/
   Taylor/75n264
Curriculum Information Center/School uni-
   verse/76n660
Curriculum materials exhibited at the 1976
   ASCD annual conf/Dunbar/78n590
Curry, J F/Searching the/76n689
Curry, M M/"Writer's book"/76n1227
Curtis, R H/Medical talk/77n1472

Cut glass price gd/Ehrhardt/75n1079
Cutler, L S & S S/Handbook of housing/75
    n1764
Cutmore, M/Watch collector's/77n898
Cutter, R A/New guide/75n738
Cyr, H W/Filmography of/78n956
Czajka, A F/State laws/76n1449
Czapowskyj, M M/Annotated bibliog on/78
    n1339
Czechoslovakia 1968-69/Hejzlar/76n269

D. W. Griffith/Niver/75n1197
Dahl, N S/International bibliog research/
    76n781/Inventory of/76n784
Dahlberg, M D/Guide to coastal/76n1434
Dahlstrom, L E & W G/MMPI hndbk/76
    n1498
Daily, J E/Cataloging phonorecordings/76
    n188/Encyclopedia of library/76n128;
    78n133; 79n159
Daily planet almanac/Reim/79n1432
Daintith, J/Dictionary of physical/78n1207
Daisne, J/Dictionnaire filmographique: suppl/
    79n1033
Daiute, R J/Library operations/75n261
Dale, D C/Carl Milam/77n278
Dale, E/Living word/77n1066
Dallas, D B/Tool and/77n1611
Dalrymple, M/History preserved/75n607
Dalton, B/Indonesia hndbk/79n372
Damas, G C/Venezuelan history/78n374
Dammann, G H/Encyclopedia of American/
    79n1554/Ford trucks/79n1558/Great
    American/79n1555
Damon, G/Lesbian in/76n1506
Dance, S P/Collector's ency/78n857/World's
    shells/78n858
Dance directory/Norton/79n1017
Dance horizons travel gd to the world's dance
    capitals/Jacobson/79n615
Dance world/Willis/76n1037
Dandurand, G/Directory of health/76n1535
Dangerfield, R J/Documentary source/76
    n476
Dangerous plants/Tampion/78n1282
Dangerous properties of industrial materials/
    Sax/76n1650
Daniel, E H/Process for/79n207/Reader in/76
    n235
Daniel, G/Illustrated ency archaeology/78
    n319
Daniel, T E/Mathematical dict/78n707
Daniells, L M/Business information/77n767

Daniels, H R/Press brake/76n1652
Daniels, L F/International visual/75n652
Daniels, M/French literature/79n1270
Danky, J P/Undergrounds/75n99
Darby, H C/Domesday gazetteer/76n368
Darkest hours/Nash/78n86
Darty, P/Chairs/75n1074
Dasbach, J M/Science for/78n1204
Dasgupta, K/Women on/77n321
Data communications dict/Sippl/77n1583
Data gathering & instruct'l manual for per-
    formance measures in public libraries/
    Altman/78n172
Data processing managemt/Brandon/76n1623
Data-structures & programming/Harrison/75
    n1771
Data systems dict/Schulz/79n1565
D'Attilio, A/Murex shells/77n1395
Daum, E/Dictionary of Russian/78n1065
Davaney, J/Football book/79n717
Davaras, C/Guide to Cretan/77n349
Davenport, T G/Art at/75n1009
David, N/Reference gd for/77n813/TV
    season/77n1116
David Jones/Rees/79n1242
Davids, L E/Dictionary of insurance/79n850
Davidson, A/Handbook of precision/75
    n1804; 75n1805
Davidson, H M/Concordance to Pascal's/77
    n1261
Davidson, J B/Horseman's veterinary/75
    n1661
Davidson, J R/Dictionary of Protestant/76
    n995
Davidson, S/Handbook of modern/78n723
Davies, C W/Dictionary of electrochemistry/
    78n1242
Davies, D W/Public libraries/75n184
Davies, N/Poland, past/78n372
Davies, R A/School library/75n194
Davies, W J K/German army/75n1848
Davinson, D/Bibliographic control/76n197
Davis, A/On-your-/79n612
Davis, A B/Bibliography on women/75n846
Davis, A S/Guide to reprints/79n37
Davis, B J/Information sources/78n1545
Davis, B L/Criminological bibliographies/79
    n575
Davis, B L/Flags and/76n1676
Davis, C/Oral history/78n323
Davis, C H/Illustrative computer/75n275/
    Information retrieval/75n276
Davis, D E/Guide and/77n1366

Davis, D G/American library/79n328/Association of/75n262/Comparative historical/75n263/Reference books/78n4
Davis, D K/Journal of library/79n190
Davis, E/*Liberty Cap*/79n277
Davis, J/Essay collections/78n490
Davis, J S/Guide to literature/79n629
Davis, L/Contemporary American/76n1223
Davis, L G/Black family/79n449/Black woman/76n396/Sickle cell/79n1453
Davis, M D/Winslow Homer/77n863
Davis, N/English language/78n561
Davis, N D/Guide and/77n1366
Davis, N M/Complete bk US/77n909
Davis, R C/North American/78n1482
Davis, R H/Historical dict/78n306
Davis, R M/Donald Barthelme/78n1132
Davis, W H/Mammals of/75n1519
Davis, W R/Purchasing information/78n732
Davis, W T/Genealogical register/76n428
Davis, W W/Boston postmarks/75n1088
Davis, W W H/Genealogical and/76n429
Davison, S E/Bibliography of law-/78n494/Media/77n534
Dawdy, D O/Artists of/75n1012
Dawson, B/Halls of/78n75
Dawson, B/Women's films/76n1055
Dawson, G G/Government and/75n710/Suggestions for/75n200
Dawson, L H/Nicknames and/75n448
Day, A E/Archaeology/79n395/History/78n324
Day, A G/Books about/78n313
Day, H/Occult illustrated/77n1451
Day, M H/Guide to fossil/79n784
Day, M S/Handbook of American/77n1189
Day, R/Creative writing/79n630
Day by day/Leonard/79n403
Dayton, E R/Mission handbook/75n1221
de Anton, G H/Dictionary of agriculture/78n1451/Dictionary of biology/78n1275
de Bary, W T/Guide to Oriental/76n1187
De Bellis, J/Sidney Lanier/79n1210
De Bono, E/Eureka! /76n1307/Wordpower/78n1043
de Callatay, V/Atlas of planets/76n1336
de Dillmont, T/Complete ency needlework/79n944
De Ford, M A/Who was/77n363
de Gámez, T/Simon and/75n1279
de Groote, R/Sports olympiques/77n664
de Grouchy, J/Clinical atlas/79n1444
de Keijzer, A J/China/78n297

de Keyser, E/European offshore/77n1418/Guide to world/78n728
de la Garza, P J/International subscription/75n56
De La Iglesia, M E/Catalogue of American/75n944/New catalogue/77n819; 78n746
de Lerma, D/Igor Stravinsky/75n1157
de Nebrija, E A/Vocabulario de/75n1276
de Padirac, B/SPINES thesaurus/78n1211
de Roberts, E D P/New atlas/79n1445
De Santis, V P/Gilded age/75n357
de Schauensee, M/Collector's Verdi/79n986
De Schauensee, R M/Guide to birds/79n1372
De Sola, R/Abbreviations dict/75n114; 79n105
de Vancouleurs, A & G/Second reference/77n1306
De Ville, W/Acadian church/76n430/Louisiana recruits/75n414
DeVore, R M/Spies and/79n502
de Vries, A/Dictionary of symbols/77n1129
de Vries, L/French-English/77n1290/German-English/79n1295
De Waal, R B/World bibliog/76n1205
Dean, B E/Wildflowers of/75n1475
Dean, D W/World aviation/77n1624
Dean, G C/Science and/75n299
Deans, E/Selecting educational/77n645
Dear faculty: gdbk to the high-school library/Nordling/77n227
DeArmond, R N/Who's who Alaskan/79n540
Death and dying: bibliog/Poteet/78n1427
Death: bibliog'l gd/Miller/78n1426
Death, grief and bereavement/Fulton/78n1425
Deatsman, G/Pianist's resource/76n1019
DeBlase A F/Manual of mammology/75n1520
Deblock, N J I/Elsevier's dict/78n1393
Debons, A/Information sci/75n277
Debrett's peerage & baronetage/Montague-Smith/78n419
Decalo, S/Historical dict Chad/78n283/Historical dict Dahomey/77n313/Historical dict Togo/77n316
DeCarl, L/Hollywood players/77n1015
Decker, G H/Conservation directory/77n1412
Declassified docs quarterly catalog/77n113
Declassified docs retrospective collection/Wile/78n97
Deemer, P/Ecumenical directory/75n1225
Deeson, A F L/Collector's ency/75n1094
Definition & measuremt of poverty/Oster/79n754
Degens, C/Glossary of German/78n779

Deighton, L C/Handbook of American/79n1124
Dejene, T/Experiences in/75n287
DeLancey, M W & V H/Bibliography of Cameroon/76n249
Delaney, J J/Media program/77n220
Delatte, J/Comparative survey/78n270
DeLaura, D J/Victorian prose/75n1372
DeLaurier, N/Slide buyers/75n1003
Delaware papers, English period, 1664-1682/Gehring/79n484
Delfinado, M D/Catalog of Diptera/78n1328
Dell encyclopedia of . . .
    birds/Bruun/75n1501
    cats/Hazen/75n1682
    dogs/Ashworth/75n1678
    tropical fish/Julian/75n1669
Dellantonio, J M/College chemistry/78n1252
Dellar, F/Illustrated ency country/78n917
Dell'Isola, F/Thomas Merton/76n1073
Delly, J G/Particle atlas/75n1433
DeLong, F/DeLong's gd/75n738
DeLong's gd to bicycles & bicycling/DeLong/75n738
Delpar, H/Encyclopedia of Latin/75n316
Delupis, I/Bibliography of internat'l/77n535
Demarco, B/Avocational activities/76n604
deMause, L/Bibliography of psychohistory/76n1487
Democratic republican societies, 1790-1800/Foner/78n439
Demographic atlas of Birmingham/Fussell/77n754
Demographic yearbook/76n814; 77n760
deMoll, L/Rainbook/78n93
Demong, D/How to find/79n467
Dempsey, M W/Purnell's first/78n66
Dempsey, P/Complete gd/77n683/Complete snowmobile/75n1753/Modern guide/75n1730
Demske, R/Furniture repair/75n1795
Denenberg, H S/Shopper's gdbk/75n945
Denham, R D/Northrop Frye/75n1410
Denisoff, R S/Songs of/75n1122
Denmark: official hndbk/76n270
Denney, R C/Dictionary of chromatography/78n1244
Denney, R C/Dictionary of spectroscopy/75n1457
Dennis, J V/Complete gd/76n1417/World gd/77n1349
Denny-Brown, D/Centennial anniversary/76n1510
DeNoyelles, D A/Women in/78n667
Dent, A/World of Shakespeare/75n1397

Denton, L W/Directory of American/75n895
Denver Public Library. Western Hist Dept/Catalog, 1st suppl/76n344
DePauw, L G/Documentary hist/78n453
Depreciation guide/76n911
Depression glass/Klamkin/75n1081
Desai, P B/Survey of research/77n756
Desautels, P E/Rocks and/75n1572
Deschler, L/Deschler's rules/77n494
Deschler's rules of order/Deschler/77n494
Descriptive & annotated bibliog of Thomas Chatterton/Warren/78n1168
Descriptive & bibliographic catalog of the circus & related arts collection at Illinois State Univ/Sokan/78n930
Descriptive cataloging in a new light/Hoffman/78n219
Descriptive gd to the Harvard Univ Archives/Elliott/77n634
Descriptive index to Shakespeare's characters in Shakespeare's words/Jerrold/77n1241
Descriptive inventory of the archives of the State of Illinois/Irons/79n407/Index/79n406
Design of agricul'l settlemts/Yalan/77n732
Designer's gd to OSHA/Hopf/76n1605
Designs: official lit on design protection/Kase/76n1648
Desk-book of errors in English/Vizetelly/76n1132
Desk ref for neuroanatomy/Lockard/79n1462
Deskins, B B/Everyone's gd/76n1570
DeSola, R/Geographic glossary/76n520
Dessauer, J P/Book publishing/75n45
Destenay, A L/Nagel's ency/75n331
Detectionary: detective & mystery fiction/Penzler/78n1104
Detective short story/Mundell/75n1327
Detroit: chronological & documentary hist/Vexler/78n362
Deusch, W R/German painting/75n1027
Deutch, H E/High profits/77n910
Deuterium & heavy water/Vasaru/77n1341
Deutsch, B/Poetry hndbk/75n1333
Deutsch, J A/Sports ency: baseball/75n733/Sports ency: football/76n738/World series/77n674
Deutsch, R R/Northern Ireland/76n276
Deutsches bibliotheksadressbuch/78n135
Devaney, C/Living sea/77n1371
Developing libraries in Brazil/McCarthy/76n216

Developing the library collection in political science/Harmon/77n491
Development & use of the outdoor classrm/Crisp/76n578
Development as if women mattered/Rihani/79n760
Development in the People's Republic of China/Blair/78n296
Development of indices of access to medical care/Aday/77n1453
Developmental tasks resource gd for elementary school children/Harris/77n651
Developments in collection building in univ libraries in Western Europe/Koops/79n197
deVergie, A/Bibliography on/75n546
Devers, C M/Guide to special/77n34
DEVINDEX Canada/Morin-Labatut/79n822
deVore, N/Encyclopedia of astrology/77n1449
DeVore, R M/Arab-Israeli/77n417
DeVries, S J/Yesterday, today/76n1098
DeWein, S/Collectors ency/78n866
DeWitt, H A/Anti-Filipino/77n442
Dexter, H M & M/England and/79n481
Deyl, Z/Bibliography of liquid/78n1239
Di Cesare, M A/Concordance to complete/78n1176/Concordance to poems/79n1245/Concordance to Juan/79n1290
Di Fiori, M S H/New atlas/79n1445
Diagram Group/Musical instruments/77n968/Rules of/75n728/Way to/76n742
Dial: author index/Zingman/76n1221
Diamant, L/Broadcast communications/75n1201; 79n1161
Diaz, A J/Microforms in/76n227
Diccionario del español chicano/Galvan/79n1150
Diccionario escolar Larousse/79n1148
Diccionario moderno español-ingles/Garcia-Pelayo y Gross/78n1068
Diccionario practico Larousse/79n1149
Dichter, H/Handbook of early/79n1001
Dick, T J O/Economic history/79n800
Dick, W P/Dick's ency/76n1638
Dicke, K P/Bibliography of skiing/78n629/Travel research/78n742
Dickens, M/World of/75n1517
Dickens studies annual/Partlow/75n1384
Dickie, J/Who's who Africa/75n131
Dickinson, A/Dictionary of food/77n1545
Dickinson, E C/Field gd birds/76n1423
Dickinson, F/Problems in/76n1181
Dick's ency of practical receipts and processes/Dick/76n1638

Dickson, L E/Law and/75n547
Dictionaries, encyclopedias, & other word-related books/Brewer/76n1114
Dictionary & glossary of the Koran/Penrice/78n982
Dictionary buying gd/Kister/78n1028
Dictionary catalog of the . . .
　Art & Architecture Div/NY Public/76n919
　G. Robert Vincent Voice Library at Michigan State Univ/Cluley/76n293
　Local Hist & Genealogy Div/NY Public/75n382
　Negro collection of the Fisk Univ Library/76n376
　Prints Div/NY Public/76n920
Dictionary: English-Serbocroatian, Serbocroatian-English/78n1067
Dictionary for accountants/Kohler/76n843
Dictionary for calligraphers/Hyde/78n810; 79n896
Dictionary of . . .
　abbreviations/Paxton/75n115
　abbreviations in medicine & the health sciences/Hughes/78n1396
　advertising terms/Urdang/78n726
　agriculture/Haensch/78n1451
　American biography/Drake/75n123; 76n105/suppl 4/Garraty/76n106/suppl 5/Garraty/78n115
　American history/77n384/Martin/79n412
　American library biog/Bobinski/79n185
　American naval fighting ships/US Dept of the Navy/77n1653
　American painters, sculptors & engravers/Fielding/76n921
　American religious biog/Bowden/78n999
　American slang/Wentworth/76n1129
　architectural sci/Cowan/75n1016
　architecture/Pevsner/77n875
　architecture & construction/Harris/76n938
　art/Greenhill/75n998
　Asian philosophies/Nauman/79n1082
　astrology/Wedeck/75n1608
　Australian colloquialisms/Wilkes/79n1117
　aviation/Wragg/75n1824
　ballet/Wilson/75n1181
　basic military terms/US Dept of the Air Force/77n1628
　biblical theology/Léon-Dufour/75n1230
　biochemistry/Stenesh/77n1331
　biographical quotation of British & American subjects/Kenin/79n97
　biographies of authors represented in the authors digest series/Johnson/76n1216

Dictionary of . . . (cont'd)
  biography/Robinson/76n100
  biography, past & present/Vincent/76n103
  biology/Haensch/78n1275
  birds in color/Campbell/76n1416
  black African civilization/Balandier/75n315
  book publishing/Stiehl/79n44
  British antique glass/Ash/77n896
  British surnames/Reaney/77n489; 79n500
  building/Scott/75n1760
  business & economics/Ammer/78n706
  business, finance, & investment/Moore/76n830; 77n777
  butterflies & moths in color/Watson/76n1442
  Canadian biography/Brown/76n109; 78n116
  catch phrases/Partridge/78n1046
  chromatography/Denney/78n1244
  collective nouns & group terms/Sparkes/76n1136
  colonial American printers' ornaments & illustrations/Reilly/77n884
  common fallacies/Ward/79n102
  composers & their music/Gilder/79n963
  computers/Chandor/79n1560
  contemporary American artists/Cummings/78n823
  contemporary music/Vinton/75n1143
  contemporary photography/Stroebel/75n1115
  contemporary quotations/Burke/77n90
  country furniture/Filbee/79n922
  criminal justice/Rush/78n502
  criminal justice data terminology/Search Group/78n503
  data processing/Maynard/77n1581/Wittman/79n1566
  development terminology/Dumouchel/76n799
  diseased English/Hudson/79n1123
  do's and don'ts/Nickles/75n1290
  drugs/Fisher/77n1501
  early Buddhist monastic terms/Upasak/77n1040
  earth sciences/Stiegler/78n1352
  electrochemistry/Davies/78n1242
  English authors/Sharp/79n1232
  English usage in Southern Africa/Beeton/77n1083
  English word-roots/Smith/77n1085
  entomology/Leftwich/77n1390

Dictionary of . . . (cont'd)
  European Economic Community/Paxton/79n809
  famous names in fiction, drama, poetry, history, & art/Johnson/76n1186
  fictional characters/Freeman/75n1326
  food supplements/Fryer/77n1545
  foreign terms/Pei/76n1119/Mawson/76n1118
  genetics/King/76n1356
  geography/Moore/79n581
  geological terms/Amer Geological Inst/77n1425
  geology/Challinor/76n1471
  German synonyms/Farrell/78n1058
  gestures/Bäuml/76n1167
  golf/Adwick/76n747
  house plants/Hay/75n1701
  household hints & helps/Singer/75n1798
  insurance/Davids/79n850
  international biography/78n112
  international law & diplomacy/Gamboa/75n554
  inventions and discoveries/Carter/77n1288
  Japanese artists/Roberts/78n825
  Jewish names & their hist/Kaganoff/78n423
  labour biog/Bellamy/79n547
  life sciences/Martin/78n1276
  linguistics/Pei/77n1061
  literary pseudonyms/Atkinson/78n1096
  literary terms/Cuddon/78n1097
  logical terms & symbols/Greenstein/79n1563
  management/French/76n909
  medical ethics/Duncan/79n1461
  medieval Latin from British sources/Latham/76n1149
  microcomputing/Burton/78n1521
  military terms: Chinese-English/Lowe/79n1595
  military uniform/Carman/78n1556
  Ming biog/Assoc for Asian Studies/77n398
  misinformation/Burnam/77n89
  modern French idioms/Gerber/78n1054
  modern history/Palmer/77n365
  modern revolution/Hyams/75n466
  modern written Arabic/Wehr/78n1050
  Mong Njua: language/Lyman/76n1152
  music/Karp/75n1141
  musical terms/Picerno/78n899
  mythical places/Palmer/77n1054
  naval abbreviations/Wedertz/78n1572

Dictionary of ... (cont'd)
  nutrition/Ashley/77n1469
  nutrition & food tech/Bender/78n1468
  occupational titles/79n855
  onomatopoeic sounds, tones & noises in English & Spanish/Kloe/78n1045
  opera and song themes/Barlow/78n911
  organic compounds, 12th suppl/78n1245/13th suppl/78n1246
  Oriental literatures/Prusek/75n1316; 77n1274
  philosophy/Lacey/78n1006
  physical metallurgy/Tyrkiel/79n1578
  physical sciences/Daintith/78n1207
  physics & allied sciences/Hyman/79n1331
  plants used by man/Usher/76n1374
  political economy/Palgrave/77n778
  politics/Lacqueur/75n467/Raymond/79n504
  problem words & expressions/Shaw/76n1131
  pronunciation/Lass/77n1084
  Protestant church music/Davidson/76n995
  pseudonyms & pen-names/Atkinson/76n1183
  psychology: English-German/Berger/78n1366
  Puget Salish/Hess/77n1097
  radio and TV terms/77n1111
  reading & learning disabilities terms/Bush/75n651
  rubber/Heinisch/76n1647
  Russian verbs/Daum/78n1065
  science & tech: English-German/Dorian/79n1296
  scientific biog/Gillispie/75n1439; 76n1329; 77n1299; 77n1300
  sewing terminology/Carbone/79n943
  sexology/Bustanoby/75n1580
  Slavic word families/Herman/76n1111
  sodium, fats, & cholesterol/Kraus/76n1577
  South African English/Branford/79n1116
  spectroscopy/Denney/75n1457
  speech & hearing, anatomy & physiology/Brown/76n1523; 77n1471
  subjects & symbols in art/Hall/76n922
  symbols & imagery/de Vries/77n1129
  terms in music/Leuchtmann/79n964
  thermodynamics/James/78n1243
  tools used in the woodworking & allied trades/Salaman/77n893
  tropical American crops & their diseases/Wellman/78n1453

Dictionary of ... (cont'd)
  20th century art/Myers/75n999
  Urdū, classical Hindi, & English/Platts/78n1071
  useful & everyday plants & their common names/Howes/75n1463
  useful plants/Coon/76n1373
  water & sewage engineering/Meinck/79n1579
  weapons & military terms/Quick/75n1838
  wit, wisdom, & humor/Prochnow/76n74
  zoology/Leftwich/75n1497
Dictionary of the ...
  characters in George Meredith's fiction/McCullen/78n1179
  Chinese particles/Dobson/75n1263
  dance/Raffe/76n1036
  decorative arts/Fleming/78n828
  environment/Allaby/79n1393
  first, or oldest words in the English language/Coleridge/77n1072
  Hawaiian language/Andrews/75n1280
  history of ideas/Wiener/75n1236
  New Testament/Hastings/75n1229
  occult and paranormal/Chaplin/78n1375
  Old West/Watts/78n350
  social sciences/Reading/79n342
  tarot/Butler/77n1450
Dictionnaire Canadien-Français/Clapin/76n1140
Dictionnaire de bibliographie haitienne/Bissainthe/75n295
Dictionnaire de littérature française contemporaine/Bonnefoy/79n1269
Dictionnaire filmographique de la litterature mondiale: suppl/Daisne/79n1033
Diet food finder/Casale/76n1569
Dieter's checklist/Smith/76n1579
Dieter's companion/Goldbeck/77n1494
Diffor, J C/Educators gd free filmstrips/76n670; 77n649/Educators gd free films/76n669
DiGaspari, V M/Barron's hndbk American/76n635/Barron's hndbk junior/76n637
Digest of educat'l statistics/Grant/76n600
Dikeman, N J/Statistical abstract/79n790
Dilligan, R J/Concordance to Conrad's/77n1231/Concordance to poems/76n1282
Dillon, B/Chaucer dict/75n1383/Malory hndbk/79n1248
Dillon, J/Handbook of internat'l/77n808
Dillon, J M/Classical lexicon/78n1178
Dills, E/Best restaurants/77n1541
Dimitrov, Th. D/Documents of/78n98

Dimmitt, R B/Actor gd/78n953/Title gd/78 n954
D'Imperio, D/Country antiques/78n834
Dining and drinking/Pollack/79n902
Dinkel, J/Road and/78n1511
Diodati, C M/Writings on/76n411
Dionne, N-E/Le parler/76n1141
Directors' & officers' ency'ic manual/Nicolson/77n773
Directorship by objectives/Kemper/78n210
Directory, family planning service sites, US/79n1468
Directory fed state county city governmt consumer offices/US Dept of HEW/77n817
Directory for exceptional children/79n644
Directory: historical societies & agencies in the US & Canada/McDonald/77n386
Directory information serv/79n81
Directory of . . .
   academic library consortia/Black/77n209
   adult day care centers/79n1506
   agencies serving the visually handicapped in the US/77n1480
   agencies: US voluntary, internat'l voluntary, intergovernmental/77n711
   American business periodicals/Ledbetter/75n895
   American fiction writers/77n1193
   American firms operating in foreign countries/Angel/77n779
   American poets/76n1224
   American scholars/75n690; 79n694
   architects for health facilities/78n791
   art & antique restoration/Porter/76n960
   art libraries & visual resource collections in North America/Hoffberg/79n885
   associations in Canada/Land/75n343; 76n65; 79n82
   audiovisual training materials/Wilds/75n699
   blacks in the performing arts/Mapp/79n1016
   British associations & associations in Ireland/75n80/Henderson/78n72
   British photographic collections/Wall/79n955
   business & financial services/Grant/77n800
   business archives in the US & Canada/77n780
   Canadian museums & related institutions/79n83
   college & univ classicists in the US & Canada/Carrubba/75n677

Directory of . . . (cont'd)
   college transfer info/Amer Schools Assoc/75n672
   Colorado manufacturers/77n824
   community resources available in Kalamazoo County/Chapman/75n512
   companies required to file annual reports with the SEC/79n832
   computer software applications: civil & structural engineering/79n1561/Energy/79n1562
   computerized data files & related software/76n1625
   computerized data files, software, & related tech reports/78n1522
   conservative & libertarian serials, publishers, & freelance markets/Murphy/79n88
   consumer protection & environmental agencies/Trzyna/75n932
   continuing educ opportunities for library-info-media personnel/78n256
   corporate affiliations/77n781
   criminal justice info sources/O'Brien/78n506
   data bases in the soc & behavioral sciences/Sessions/76n241
   data sources on racial & ethnic minorities/US Bureau of Labor Statistics/77n429
   economic libraries in Canada/Lackner/79n239
   education associations/Lopez/79n642
   educational statistics/Hamilton/76n579
   engineering educ institutions/77n588
   ethnic publishers & resource organizations/Shapiro/78n378
   ethnic studies librarians/Shapiro/78n136
   European associations/Anderson/76n66; 77n77
   executive recruiters/79n856
   federal agency educ data tapes/US Dept of HEW/77n597
   federal statistics for local areas/79n788
   federal technology/US Natl Sci Foundation/78n1219
   fee-based info services/Warnken/78n138
   fellows 1925-74/77n78
   financial aids for women/Schlachter/79n766
   foreign manufacturers in the US/Arpan/76n894
   foundations in Massachusetts/Fubini/79n92
   foundations in the Commonwealth of Massachusetts/Huber/77n79

Directory of ... (cont'd)
  foundations in the state of Connecticut/ Huber/77n80
  foundations in the state of Maine/Huber/ 77n81
  foundations in the state of New Hampshire/ Huber/77n82
  foundations in the state of Rhode Island/ Huber/77n83
  foundations in the state of Vermont/ McGovern/77n84
  franchising organizations/77n799; 78n709
  genealogical societies in the USA & Canada/ Meyer/79n471
  health sciences libraries in the US/Crawford/ 76n1535
  high-energy radiotherapy centres/78n1403
  historical societies & agencies in the US & Canada/McDonald/79n413
  home health agencies certified as Medicare providers/Council of Home Health Agencies & Community Health Services/76n1534; 78n1404
  homosexual organizations & publications/ Copely/78n651
  homosexual organizations & publications, annotated/76n1507
  information resources in the US fed gov with a suppl of gov sponsored info analysis centers/US Library of Congress/75n483
  institutions offering or planning programs for the training of library tech assts/ Taylor/77n175
  inter-corporate ownership/Angel/76n893
  Jewish archival institutions/Mason/76n383
  juvenile & adult correctional depts, institutions, agencies & paroling authorities, US & Canada/Amer Correctional Assoc/ 77n709
  law-related educ projects/Kelly/79n571
  libraries providing computer-based info services in the NY metro area/79n163
  library associations in Canada/75n160; 78n137
  library reprographic services/Nitecki/75n161; 77n181
  Manhattan office bldgs/Ballard/79n889
  medical libraries in the British Isles/Library Association/78n198
  medical specialists/75n1638
  multiple bkstore owners/75n53; 76n48
  museums in New York/McDarrah/79n93

Directory of ... (cont'd)
  national unions & employee associations/ US Bureau of Labor Statistics/78n775
  New England astrologers/Marks/79n1434
  New Jersey foundations/Mitchell/78n80
  New Jersey newspapers/Wright/79n21
  newspaper libraries in the US & Canada/ Parch/77n182
  non-govmental agricul'l organizations/79n1514
  North and South American universities/ Zils/79n667
  Oklahoma foundations/Broce/75n78
  organizations & personnel in educ'l management/Piele/78n556
  osteopathic specialists 1974/76n1536
  overseas summer jobs/James/77n835
  Pennsylvania library resources/75n162
  post offices/79n84
  postsecondary schools with occupational programs/US Dept of HEW/77n632
  private presses & letterpress printers and publishers/79n51
  public service internships/78n562
  publishing opportunities/Ross/75n54; 76n49
  reference & research library resources systems in NY state/75n163
  registered lobbyists & lobbyist legislation/ 76n477
  religious bodies in the US/Melton/78n984
  religious organizations in the USA/Geisendorfer/79n1060
  research grants/Wilson/76n610; 78n73
  selected instructional materials/VanEtten/ 75n700
  selected resources for the study of English in Japan/Brownell/77n1062
  services for young children/Korkmas/75n799
  shopping centers in the US & Canada/ Paule/75n922
  16mm film collections in colleges & universities in the US/76n206
  small magazine-press editors and publishers/Fulton/75n23; 79n52
  social & health agencies of NY city/75n798; 76n774/McDade/79n1508
  social studies-social sci service organizations/Haley/77n300
  special libraries & info centers/Young/ 75n164; 78n199
  special libraries in Alaska/Schorr/76n171
  special programs for minority group members/Johnson/75n801; 76n389

Directory of . . . (cont'd)
    spoken-voice audio-cassettes/McKee/76
        n681; 77n660
    state & fed funds for business developmt/
        78n710
    state & local hist periodicals/Crouch/
        78n351
    state & provincial archives/Kinney/76n318
    Texas manufacturers/78n755
    Title VII ESEA bilingual educ programs/
        78n557
    Ukrainian publishing houses, periodicals,
        bkstores, libraries & library collections
        of Ukrainica in diaspora/Weres/78n392
    US college & univ degrees for part-time students/Pitchell/75n676
    US gov AV personnel/US Natl AV Center/
        76n630
    US importers/79n833
    unpublished experimental mental measures/
        Goldman/75n1600; 79n1430
    Washington reps of American associations &
        industry/Colgate/79n91
    Western book publishers & production
        services/77n59
    Western book publishing & related suppliers
        and services/75n55
    world museums/Hudson/76n67
Directory of the . . .
    American Baptist churches in the USA/
        79n1061
    college student press in America/Politella/
        75n1299; 78n15
    Education Div of the US Dept of HEW/
        76n618
    European Council of Internat'l Schools/
        76n611; 78n573
Directory: state, county, & city gov consumer
    offices/US Dept of HEW/75n938
Dirsztay, P/Church furnishings/79n912
Disaster tech/Manning/77n705
Discopaedia of the violin/Creighton/75n1160
Discover your ancestors/Peskett/79n468
Discovering bks & libraries/Cleary/78n182
Discursive dict of health care/US Congress/77
    n1477
Disney films/Maltin/75n1195
Disneyana: Disney collectibles/Munsey/75
    n1098
Disraeli's novels reviewed/Stewart/76n1273
Dissertations in English & American lit, suppl 2/
    McNamee/75n1313
Dissertations in philosophy accepted at American universities/Bechtle/79n1078

Dissertations on British hist, 1815-1914/
    Bell/76n366
Dissertations on Iberian & Latin American
    hist/Hanson/77n361
Distin, W H/American clock/78n867
Divien, E/Bibliographie des/77n399
Divilbiss, J L/Economics of/78n241/Negotiating for/79n301
Divoky, D/Rights of/75n560
Divorce & annulment in the 50 states/Mayer/
    77n716
Divorce: selected annotated bibliog/McKenney/
    76n783
Dixon, D/Nineteenth-century/78n1078
Dixon, E L/Franchise annual/79n829
Djuna Barnes/Messerli/77n1198
Do you know what day tomorrow is?/Hopkins/
    77n643
Doak, W A/International index/77n661;
    77n662
Dobson, W A C H/Dictionary of Chinese/
    75n1263
Dobyns, H F/Native American/77n736
Dockstader, F J/Great North/78n381
Dr. David Livingstone & Sir Henry Morton
    Stanley/Casada/77n309
Dr. Taylor's self-help medical gd/Taylor/78
    n1418
Doctoral dissertations in American music:
    classified bibliog/Mead/76n990
Doctoral dissertations in hist/77n360
Doctoral dissertations on Asia/Shulman/76
    n258
Doctoral dissertations on China, 1971-75/
    Shulman/79n369
Doctoral dissertations on Japan & Korea/
    Shulman/77n329
Doctoral research in educ'l media/Kirschner/
    76n581
Doctoral research on Russia & the Soviet
    Union/Dossick/77n346
Doctors and patients hndbk of medicines &
    drugs/Parish/79n1492
Doctor's gd to nonprescription drugs/Rubinstein/79n1503
Doctor's lawyer/Lane/76n1533
Document retrieval systems/Montgomery/76
    n234
Documentary history of . . .
    arms control & disarmament/Dupuy/75
        n1835
    the first fed Congress 1789-91/DePauw/
        78n453
    the Negro people in the US/Aptheker/75
        n810

Documentary history of ... (cont'd)
  the ratification of the Constitution/
  Jensen/77n370; 77n371
Documentary source bk in American gov &
  politics/Ewing/76n476
Documentation on Asia/Kumar/75n300
Documentation stds manual for computer
  systems/Robinson/75n1773
Documents of American hist/Commager/75
  n354
Documents of internat'l organisations/
  Dimitrov/78n98
Documents office classification/Poole/79n123
Documents on India's foreign policy/Kumar/
  76n503
Dodd, D B/Historical atlas Alabama/76n345
Dodd, D B & W S/Historical statistics/77
  n750
Dodge, B J/Audiovisual resources/79n680
Dod's Parliamentary companion/75n469
Dodson, B/Training programs/79n852
Doerflinger, F/Complete bk bulb/75n1700
Doerflinger, W/Magic catalogue/79n722
Dog digest/Bernstein/77n1526
Dog lovers complete gd/Sprung/77n1535
Dog owner's medical manual/Sessions/77
  n1533
Doggett, J/Seventeenth century/78n1126
Dogo, G/Treasures of/78n531
Doherty, E/Antique shops/78n835
Doing business abroad/Joyner/77n782
Dolensek, E P/Practical gd/77n1528
Dollar politics/75n490
Dollfus, A/Atlas of planets/76n1336
Dolmatch, T B/Information please/79n106
Dolphin, D/Tabulation of/79n1321
Dolphins & porpoises/Truitt/75n1521
Dolphins, whales & porpoises/Coffey/78n1332
Domesday gazetteer/Darby/76n368
Domestic & foreign coins manufactured by
  mints of the US/79n919
Donald Barthelme/Klinkowitz/78n1132
Donaldson, G/Who's who Scottish/75n399
Donath, F A/Annual review earth/76n1468
Donelson, K L/Books for/77n232
Donington, R/Interpretation of/75n1145
Donington, R/Performer's gd/75n1146
Donner, G/Pennypincher's wine/75n1672
Donohue, J C/Information for/77n267/Understanding scientific/75n278
Donovan, J/US and Soviet/75n532
Donovan, P/Chinese communist/78n473
Donow, H S/Concordance to poems/76n1288
Donson, T B/Prints and/78n807

Don't ask your waiter/Wasserman/79n1534
Doran, G C/Dictionary of American/76n921
Dorfman, J/Consumer's arsenal/77n814
Dorian, A F/Dictionary of sci/79n1296
Doris, L/Complete secretary's/78n714
Dorland's pocket medical dict/78n1394
Dorling, A R/Use of/78n1223
Dorman, P J/Running Press/77n538
Dorn, G M/Archive of/75n1429/Latin America/77n305
Dorn, S O/Insider's gd/75n1050
Dorner, H/Dictionary of English/77n1083
Dorris, C E/Chinese communist/78n473
Dorst, J/Life of/76n1418
Dosa, M L/Libraries in/75n250
Doskey, J S/Media equipment/77n658
Dossick, J J/Doctoral research/77n346
Double elephant folio/Fries/75n46
Doubleday dict for home, school, & office/
  Landau/76n1120
Doubleday Roget's thesaurus in dict form/
  Landau/78n1040
Douchant, M/Football register/76n735
Dougherty, J J/Writings on/76n309; 78n342
Dougherty, R M/Impriving access/75n234
Douglas, A/Sourcebk of electronic/77n1590
Douglas, J D/New internat'l/75n1218; 79
  n1056
Douth, G/Leaders in/76n484
Dover Historical Society/Vital records/79
  n482
Dow, S T/Maine postal/77n924
Dow Jones-Irwin business almanac/Levine/78
  n715
Dow Jones-Irwin gd to ...
  commodities trading/Gould/75n914
  convertible securities/Noddings/75n917
  tax planning/Sommerfeld/75n986
Dowd, M D/World directory/75n1552
Dowd, M J/Index to American/76n330
Dowell, A T/Cataloging with/77n253
Dowell, R W/Theodore Dreiser/76n1233
Dowley, T/Eerdman's hndbk/78n985
Dowling, L C/Aestheticism and/78n1089
Downbeat music gd/Hopkins/79n957
Downes, E/NY Philharmonic/78n922
Downey, D W/New standard/76n61
Downey, J A/US federal/79n115
Downs, L H/Essentials of/75n1309
Downs, R B/Books and/75n136/British library/
  75n148/Famous books/76n133/Guide to
  Illinois/75n18/How to do/76n133
Doyle, H A/Instructional tech/75n698
Doyle, J M/Reference resources/77n266

Doyle, K O/Education-psychology/76n584
Doyle, P A/Guide to basic/77n1220
Doyle, R P/Complete food/78n1469
Drabek, A G/Politics of/78n470
Dracula book/Glut/76n1046
Drager, M/Most glorious/76n751
Drake, F S/Dictionary of American/75n123; 76n105
Drake, G L/Fire resistant/76n1649
Drake, G R/Everyone's book/75n1792
Drama scholars' index to plays and filmscripts/Samples/75n1187
Dranov, P/Automated library/79n288/Microfilm/77n285
Drazniowsky, R/Map librarianship/76n167
Dreamer's dictionary/Robinson/75n1583
Dreisbach, R H/Handbook of poisoning/75n1628
Dressel, P L/Handbook of academic/77n633
Dressler, C P/Bibliography of creative/77n1251
Dressler, H/Introduction to medieval/79n1091
Dreyer, S S/Bookfinder/78n1100
Dried grasses, grains, gourds, pods, & cones/Karel/76n1590
Driscoll, W G/Handbook of optics/79n1333
Drob, H A/Criteria for/78n166
Drone, J M/Index to opera/79n979
Drossman, E/Watergate and/75n501
Drug abuse bibliog/Advena/75n1652; 76n1547
Drug abuse films/75n1654
Drug abuse law review/Wales/75n1658
Drug-induced ocular side effects & drug interactions/Fraunfelder/77n1502
Drug info for patients/Griffith/79n1497
Drug use & abuse among US minorities/Iiyama/77n1504
Drugs in current use & new drugs/Modell/76n1551
Drury, E/Encyclopedia of Victoriana/76n958
Drury's gd to best plays/Salem/79n1018
Dry strength of paper/Weiner/78n1261
Drying of paper & board/Weiner/78n1262
du Bellet, L P/Some prominent/77n459
Du Mont, R R/Reform and/79n201
Dubé, P H/Concordance to Pascal's/77n1261
Dubin, A D/More classic/75n1832
Dubin, R/Handbook of work/77n792
Dubois, M M/Modern French-/79n1135
DuBois, P Z/Paul Leicester/78n155
Dubuigne, G/Larousse dictionary/78n1454
Ducati service-repair hndbk/75n1746
Duckett, K W/Modern manuscripts/77n352
Duckles, V/Music reference/75n1123

Ducks, geese & swans/Merne/76n1425
Ducks, geese, & swans of the world/Johnsgard/79n1373
Dudas, J L/Energy sourcebook/79n1386
Dugdale, C B/Leaf prints/75n1493/Modern American/79n1352
Duggal, H/Dictionary of nutrition/77n1469
Duggan, M/Tennis catalog/79n730
Duggan, M A/Law and/75n548
Duggan, M M/Fitzgerald/Hemingway/79n1212
Duic, W Z/Europa administration/78n475
Duignan, P/Colonialism in/75n288
Dulin, R O/Battleships/77n1649
Dummer, G W A/Electronic inventions/78n1530
Dumouchel, J R/Dictionary of developmt/76n799
Dun & Bradstreet hndbk of credits & collections/Redding/75n956
Dun & Bradstreet's gd to your investments/Hardy/75n915; 76n855
Dunaway, V/Modern saltwater/76n728
Dunbar, C/Bibliography of Shelley/77n1244
Dunbar, H F/Emotions and/77n1461
Dunbar, H M/Curriculum materials/78n590
Duncan, A S/Dictionary of medical/79n1461
Duncan, R/Encyclopedia of ignorance/79n1297
Duncan, R/Warwick guide/78n768
Duncan, W/Thailand/77n564
Duncan, W H/Wildflowers of/76n1388/Woody vines/76n1383
Dundes, A/Folklore theses/78n1011
Dunkel, P M/Continuing library/78n255
Dunkin, P S/Bibliography/76n198
Dunlap, A/Cumulative index/78n1422/Hospital literature/78n229
Dunmore, C J/Black children/77n715
Dunmore-Leiber, L/Book review/77n37
Dunn, J W/Guide to grading/76n965
Dunn, L P/American Indians/76n412/Asian Americans/76n395/Black Americans/76n397/Chicanos/76n400
Dunn, R/Chinese-English/79n1131
Dunne, T/Gerard Manley/77n1235
Dunnette, M D/Handbook of industrial/77n1448
Dunning, J/Tune in/78n1081
Dunstan, G R/Dictionary of medical/79n1461
Dupuy, R E/Encyclopedia of military/78n331/Outline hist/76n306
Dupuy, T N/Almanac of world/76n1677/Documentary hist/75n1835/Encyclopedia of military/78n331/Online hist/76n306/People and/75n368

Duran, P H/Chicana/77n440
Durand, M/Diccionario moderno/78n1068
Durant, M/Who named/78n1289
Durations/Sandow/79n99
Durey, P/Staff management/77n203
Durkan, M J/Sean O'Casey/79n1279
Durkheimian school/Nandan/78n645
Durnell, J B/Librarian/77n281
Dürr, W T/Urban information/79n734
Durrenberger, R W/California/77n543
Durst, S J/Collector-investor/78n831/Comprehensive guide/78n846
Dusterberg, R B/Official inaugural/77n911
Dutch uncles & New England cousins/Clough/78n398
DuVall, C R/Education and/78n542/Free materials/79n681
Dweck, S/Women/75n843; 76n786
Dwelley, M J/Summer &/79n1342
Dwight, H O/Encyclopedia of missions/76n1081
Dwoskin, R P/Rights of/79n252
Dwyer, F M/Guide for improving/75n711
Dwyer, R E/Labor education/78n765
Dwyer-Shick, S/Study and/77n737
Dye, C M/Directory of college/75n672
Dyer, E R/Cooperation in/79n208
Dyer, L/Project management/78n780
Dyer, N A/Post-liberation/78n474
Dying and death: annotated bibliog/Sell/78n1428
Dykes, J/Fifty great/76n940
Dyment, A R/Literature of/77n1000
Dynamic info and library processing/Salton/77n295
Dyson, A E/English novel/75n1376
Dyson, A J/European drama suppl two/75n1324

E is for everybody/Polette/77n1161
E. M. Forster/McDowell/79n1240
Each in its ordered place/Petersen/76n1235
Eagle, D/Oxford illus'd/76n1117/Oxford literary/78n1159
Eagon, A/Catalog of published/75n1124
Eakin, J L/Colonial America/78n343
Earl of Harewood/New Kobbé's/77n972
Earley, M E/Statistical abstract/79n790
Early American...
  almanacs/Stowell/78n40
  books and printing/Winterich/76n45
  furniture/Kirk/75n1076
    proverbs & proverbial phrases/Whiting/79n103

Early American... (cont'd)
  women printers & publishers/Hudak/79n30
Early childhood curriculum materials/Harbin/78n595
Early children's bks & their illustration/Gottlieb/77n70
Early coins of America/Crosby/75n1064
Early editions of Arthur Hugh Clough/Scott/78n1171
Early editions of Euclid's elements/Thomas-Stanford/78n63
Early Friends families of Upper Bucks/Roberts/76n439
Early Pennsylvania land records/Egle/77n460
Early photographs & early photographers/Mathews/75n1111
Early Puritan writers/Gallagher/77n1185
Early Utah furniture/Morningstar/78n854
Early writings on India/Kaul/77n325
Earned degrees conferred/Baker/76n633
Earney, F C F/Researchers' guide/75n569
Earnings distributions in the US/US Social Security Admin/77n846
East, S K C/Browning music/75n1137
East African community/Howell/78n290
East Asian resources in American libraries/Yang/79n367
East Central & Southeast Europe: library & archival resources in North America/Horecky/77n192
East Central European studies/Blejwas/75n335
East European & Soviet economic affairs/Birkos/76n821
Eastern definitions: religions of the Orient/Rice/79n1059
Eastern North America's wildflowers/Linn/79n1344
Eastlick, J T/Library management/78n212
Eastman, A H/Education for/77n48
Eaton, Q/Opera production/75n1166
Ebert, J & K/Old American/75n1026
Ebony handbook/Saunders/75n812
Echols, J M/English-Indonesian/76n1150
Eckersley-Johnson, A L/Webster's secretarial/78n716
Eckstein, B J/Handicapped funding/79n1507
Ecology field glossary/Lewis/78n1345
Economic & social atlas of Maryland/Thompson/76n491
Economic arithmetic/Palmer/79n807
Economic atlas of Nebraska/Lawson/78n695
Economic conditions of East & Southeast Asia/Chen/79n799

Economic cooperation & regional integration in Africa/75n289
Economic education/Hughes/78n699
Economic hist of Canada/Dick/79n800
Economic hist of milk marketing & pricing/Spencer/75n926
Economic hist of the US prior to 1860/Orsagh/76n826
Economic, social and voting characteristics of Idaho precincts/Rouyer/75n504
Economics & foreign policy/Amstutz/79n796
Economics dictionary/Moffat/77n776
Economics encyclopedia/75n883
Economics of . . .
   academic libraries/Baumol/75n176
   East Africa/Killick/77n770
   library automation/Davilbiss/78n241
   minorities/Gagala/77n423
   technical info systems/Wolfe/75n881
Ecumenical directory of retreat & conf centers/Deemer/75n1225
Eddins, B/Greenberg's price/78n870
Eddleman, F E/American drama/77n987
Eddy, D/Alternative shopping/75n1033
Eddy, R L/What you/75n556
Eddy, S/Northern fishes/75n1513
Edelstein, J M/Wallace Stevens/75n1369
Edgar, N L/History and/76n1162
Edgar, W B/Biographical directory/75n484
Edgar Allan Poe/Hyneman/75n1364
Edgar Lee Masters/Flanagan/76n1246
Edible and useful plants of California/Clarke/79n1366
Edible wild plants of Pennsylvania & New York/Tomikel/75n1470
Edison, M E/Thoreau MacDonald/75n991
Editing by design/White/75n1298
Editing the Middle English manuscript/Moorman/76n1113
L'Edition de langue française catalogue cumulatif/78n8
Editor & publisher internat'l yr bk/78n44
L'Editrice dell'Automobile Lea/World cars/76n1666
Edmond, M/European Parliament/75n471
Edry, C F/Women's yellow/75n847
Edson, J S/Organ preludes/75n1153
Educating the library user/Lubans/75n237
Education and anthropology/Rosenstiel/79n782
Education and education-related serials/Krepel/78n542
Education bk list/Chisholm/75n643; 76n577
Education directory . . .
   colleges & universities/Podolsky/79n664
   higher education/US Dept of HEW/76n655
   public school systems/US Dept of HEW/77n605
   state education agency officials/Porter/79n646
Education for publishing/Eastman/77n48
Education: gd to selected sources/Ralston/78n546
Education in the USSR/Apanasewicz/76n574
Education index/Hewitt/76n609
Education journals, a union list/Hamilton/76n586
Education-psychology journals/Arnold/76n584
Educational games & simulations in economics/Lewis/75n703
Educational market place/Norback/78n555
Educational marketer yellow pages/77n659
Educational media organizations directory/76n619
Educational media resources on Egypt/79n351
Educational media yearbook/Brown/75n656; 76n599; 79n669
Educational programs that work/77n599
Educational tech: definition & glossary of terms/78n578
Educational TV in its cultural & public affairs dimension/Carlson/75n1192
Educators gd to free . . .
   audio & video materials/Berger/78n591
   films/Horkheimer/76n669
   filmstrips/Horkheimer/76n670; 77n649
   guidance materials/Saterstrom/76n671
   health, physical educ & recreation materials/Horkheimer/76n672
   science materials/Saterstrom/76n673
   social studies materials/Suttles/76n674
   tapes, scripts, & transcriptions/Wittich/76n675
Educator's internat'l gd to free & low cost health audio-visual teaching aids/Shugar/79n687
Edwards, E H/Complete bk horse/75n1680
Edwards, I E S/Cambridge ancient/76n357; 79n396
Edwards, J/Guide to world/78n728; 79n831
Edwards, J/Top 10's/76n1023/Suppl/76n1024
Edwards, J D/Modern accountant's/78n721
Edwards, M A/Fair garden/75n185

Authors and Titles—59

Edwards, P/Encyclopedia of philosophy/75 n1237
Edwards, R D/Atlas of Irish/75n396
Edwards, R J/In-service/79n253
Edwards, R M/Role of/77n204
Eckhof-Stork, N/World atlas/77n1543
Een, J D/Women and/79n755
Eerdman's family ency of the Bible/Alexander/ 79n1065
Eerdman's hndbk to the hist of Christianity/ Dowley/78n985
Effecting change in library educ/Hershfield/ 75n264
Effective library/Totterdell/77n215
Efficient electricity use/Smith/77n1600; 79n1389
Egan, E W/Kings, rulers/78n332
Egan, R S/Topics-aids/79n682
Egbert, L D/Multilingual law/79n568
Ege, L/World aircraft/75n1820
Eggenberger, D/New Catholic/76n1085
Eglajs, G E/Birds of/75n1091
Egle, W H/Early Pennsylvania/77n460
Egon Ronay's Lucas gd/79n613
Egon Ronay's 1974 in Britain/Ronay/75n627
Egyptian hieroglyphic dict/Budge/79n1133
Ehlers, R S/Index to Pravda/76n498
Ehresmann, D L/Applied and/78n827/Fine arts/76n915
Ehrhardt, A L/Cut glass/75n1079
Ehrhardt, R/Encyclopedia of old/75n1092
Ehrlich, A/Medical and/78n1398
Ehrlich, E/Concise index/75n1287
Eichelberger, C L/Guide to critical/75n1341/ Harper's lost/77n1184/Published comment/77n1206
Eichman, B/Selective bibliog/78n495
Eidelberg, L/Health sciences/78n1405
18: teenage catalog/Webster/78n661
1815: armies at Waterloo/Pericoli/75n1850
1866 gd to New York City/76n541
Eighteenth century/Bond/76n1257
Eighteenth-century Gothic novel/McNutt/ 76n1209
80 years of American song hits/75n1170
80 years of best sellers 1895-1975/Hackett/ 78n37
Eighty years of cinema/Cowie/78n948
Eimermacher, K/Subject bibliog/78n1025
Ein, M/Whole Washington/76n881
Einhorn, E/Old French/76n1142
Einspahr, B/Index to Brown/77n1042
EIS: key to environmental impact statements/ Herner/79n1395

Eisenberg, A/Rights of/77n504
Eisenberg, B/Practical gd/75n985
Eisenberg, G G/Learning vacations/79n655; 79n656
Eisler, P E/World chronology/75n1139
Ekdahl, J/American sculpture/78n821
Elbert, S H/Place names/75n453/Pocket Hawaiian/76n1153
Elcano, B W/Annotated bibliog homosexuality/78n650
Electoral behavior/Rose/75n474
Electrical engineer's ref bk/Say/76n1632
Electricity, magnetism, & animal magnetism/ Gartrell/77n1591
Electronic databook/Graf/76n1630
Electronic industry telephone directory/77 n825
Electronic inventions 1745-1976/Dummer/ 78n1530
Electronic library/Christian/79n261
Electronic music circuit gdbk/Ward/76n1635
Electronic technician's hndbk of time-savers and shortcuts/Grolle/75n1783
Electronics designers' hndbk/Giacoletto/78 n1531
Electronics dict/Markus/79n1570
Electronics engineers' hndbk/Fink/76n1629
Elementary school library collection/Van Orden/77n233/Suppl/76n157
Elementary teachers gd to free curriculum materials/Suttles/76n676; 79n689
El-Hi textbooks in print/75n701; 76n677
Elie Wiesel/Abramowitz/76n1253
Elizabeth Gaskell/Selig/78n1174/Welch/78 n1175
El-Khawas, M A/American-Southern/77n526
Elkins, E A/Library searching/79n297
Elley, D/International music/77n946/World filmography/79n1032
Elliott, C A/Descriptive guide/77n634
Elliott, H W/Annual review pharmacology/ 76n1548
Elliott, L/Who's who golf/77n696
Elliott, N F/Patterson's American/76n663
Elliott, P/Allied escort/79n1601
Ellis, C/British and/76n1684
Ellis, K/Critical approaches/76n1299
Ellis, K/Word book/78n1039
Ellison, C W/Charles W. Chesnutt/78n1136/ William Wells/79n450
Ellmore, R T/Illustrated dict/79n1162
Ellsworth, D J/Landmarks of/77n279
Ellsworth, R E/Planning manual/75n179
Elmaghraby, S E/Handbook of operations/79 n820

Elman, R/Hunter's field/75n776
Elonka, S M/Standard plant/76n1646
Elrod, J M/Index to LC/76n190
Elsasser, A B/Bibliography of California/78n679
Elsevier's dictionary of . . .
  automobile engineering in five languages/Kondo/78n1512
  food science & tech/Morton/78n1470
  library science, information and documentation in six languages/Clason/79n158
  measurement & control in six languages/Clason/79n1544
  public health/Deblock/78n1393
Elsevier's telecommunication dict in six languages/Clason/77n1117
Elson, A/American composers/75n1117
Elting, J R/Military uniforms/78n1553
Elton, G R/Annual bibliog/77n404; 79n431
Elving, B F/FM atlas/79n1171
Ely, D P/Media personnel/77n219/Process for/79n207
Embleton, G/Military dress/75n1840
Embree, A T/Guide to Oriental/76n1187
Emden, A B/Biographical register/75n691
Emergency medical gd/Henderson/79n1486
Emergency medical services/Noble/75n1617
Emerging field of sociobibliography/Afflerbach/78n214
Emerging trends in library organization/Lee/79n198
Emerson, J P/Provinces of/79n370
Emerson, W K/American museum/77n1394
Emery, R/Staff communication/76n176
Emigrants to Pennsylvania/Tepper/76n443; 78n414
Emily Brontë criticism, 1900-68/Barclay/75n1382
Eminent contributors to psychology/Watson/75n1579; 77n1443
Emmens, C A/Audio-visual/79n1087/Famous people/78n957/Non-theatrical/76n174/Short stories/79n1034
Emmett, K/Perception/78n1362
Emmons, F/Atlantic liners/75n1828; 75n1829
Emotions & bodily changes/Dunbar/77n1461
Employee relations bibliog/Tice/79n857
Employment and earnings, states & areas/77n836
Employment relations in the UK/MacCafferty/77n837
Empresa del libro en America Latina/75n57
Empson, D/Street where/76n548

Encyclopaedia Africana dict of African biog/79n348
Encyclopaedia of . . .
  antibiotics/Glasby/78n1438
  chess/Sunnucks/78n622
  cricket/Golesworthy/76n766
  golf/Evans/75n769
  literary & typographical anecdote/Timperley/78n42
  motor-cycle sport/Carrick/78n635
  mountaineering/Unsworth/76n724
  Southern Africa/Rosenthal/75n319
  swimming/Besford/78n631
Encyclopaedia Sherlockiana/Tracy/78n1172
Encyclopaedic dictionary of . . .
  management & manufacturing terms/Lindemann/75n884
  mathematics for engineers & applied scientists/Sneddon/78n1504
  physics/Thewlis/77n1337
Encyclopaedic hndbk of medical psychology/Krauss/78n1370
Encyclopedia Americana/Cayne/77n72
Encyclopedia and dict of medicine, nursing, & allied health/Miller/79n1463
Encyclopedia buying gd/Kister/77n71; 79n74
Encyclopedia-Handbook of materials, parts & finishes/Clauser/78n1540
Encyclopedia international/77n73
Encyclopedia of . . .
  accounting systems/Pescow/77n797
  ad-libs, crazy jokes, insults & wisecracks/Fechtner/78n1044
  Africa/77n310
  air warfare/Chant/77n1637
  American agricul'l hist/Schapsmeier/77n1516
  American biog/Garraty/75n124
  American cars 1930-42/Moloney/79n1554
  American hist/Kohlmetz/75n366/Morris/77n385
  American Quaker genealogy/Heiss/78n402
  American steam traction engines/Norbeck/78n1550
  animal care/West/78n1462
  animals/Hanzak/76n1408
  anthropology/Hunter/77n748
  antique restoration & maintenance/Richardson/75n1054
  antiques/Bond/77n897
  archaeological excavations in the Holy Land/Avi-Yonah/77n347; 79n393

Encyclopedia of . . . (cont'd)
  associations/Fisk/77n85
  astrology/deVore/77n1449
  aviation/78n1506
  black folklore & humor/Spalding/75n1241
  business info sources/Wasserman/78n705
  cage and aviary birds/Rogers/77n1386
  card tricks/Hugard/76n744
  careers and vocational guidance/76n590
  chemical processing and design/McKetta/78n1247
  comic book heroes/Fleisher/77n1167;77n1168
  common diseases/77n1473
  computer science/Ralston/77n1579
  computer sci & tech/Belzer/76n1626; 78n1523
  contemporary typesetting/Shapiro/79n43
  dance and ballet/Clarke/79n1019
  dogs and puppies/Woodhouse/79n1526
  educational evaluation/Anderson/76n591
  electrochemistry of the elements/Bard/75n1450; 76n1343; 79n1318/Planbeck/78n1249
  energy/Lapedes/77n1411
  energy-efficient building design/Lee/78n1518
  environmental sci & engineering/Pfafflin/78n1343
  fairies/Briggs/78n1009
  fish cookery/McClane/78n1475
  floristry/Stevenson/75n927
  folk, country, and western music/Stambler/76n1031
  food and nutrition/Adams/79n1529
  food science/Peterson/79n1533
  food technology/Johnson/76n1574
  football/Treat/78n626
  geographic info sources/Wasserman/79n813
  German-American genealogical research/Smith/77n478
  golf/Steel/76n748
  governmental advisory organizations/Sullivan/76n481
  graffiti/Reisner/76n63
  hand-weaving/Zielinski/78n882
  health & the human body/Newman/79n1483
  hockey/Styer/75n772
  home building & decorating/Schuler/76n1642
  homonyms/Newhouse/78n1033
  how it works/Clarke/78n1501
  ignorance/Duncan/79n1297
  Indians of the Americas/75n866
  infantry weapons of WWII/Hogg/78n1569

Encyclopedia of . . . (cont'd)
  information systems and services/Kruzas/75n165; 79n166
  jazz in the seventies/Feather/78n915
  knitting and crochet stitch patterns/Mariano/78n879
  knives/Strung/77n894
  land warfare in the 20th century/Bonds/78n1557
  Latin America/Delpar/75n316
  library and info sci/75n152/Kent/76n129; 78n133; 79n159
  long-term financing & capital managemt/Childs/77n821
  military history/Dupuy/78n331
  minerals/Roberts/75n1573
  minerals and gemstones/O'Donoghue/77n1437
  missions/Dwight/76n1081
  modern war/Parkinson/78n1559
  mystery and detection/Steinbrunner/77n1177
  occultism & parapsychology/Shepard/79n1440
  Ohio associations/Alt/79n90
  old pocket knives/Ehrhardt/75n1092
  opera/Orrey/77n974
  organic gardening/79n1539
  PVC/Nass/79n1574
  philosophy/Edwards/75n1237
  physical educ, fitness, & sports/Frost/78n607
  physics/Besançon/75n1456
  political buttons/Hake/75n1095
  pop, rock, & soul/Stambler/76n1030; 78n920
  practical photography/79n951
  quotations about music/Shapiro/79n967
  rhythms/Schillinger/78n900
  sailing/Scharff/79n725
  science fict & fantasy through 1968/Tuck/75n1330; 79n1204
  social work/Turner/78n647
  sociology/75n794
  Soviet law/Feldbrugge/75n553
  sport/Charles/77n670
  sports/Menke/76n698; 79n697; 79n698
  sports talk/Hollander/77n671
  tarot/Kaplan/79n1437
  tennis/Robertson/76n762
  theology/Rahner/76n1082
  US Air Force aircraft and missile systems/Knaack/79n1593
  US gov benefits/Grisham/76n829; 79n96

Encyclopedia of . . . (cont'd)
  urban planning/Whittick/75n862
  Victoriana/Bridgeman/76n958
  women/78n668
  wood/79n1576
  world boxing champions since 1882/
    McCallum/77n686
  world lit in the 20th century/Ungar/76
    n1185
  world regional geology/Fairbridge/77n1426
  world theater/78n933
Encyclopedia of the . . .
  alkaloids/Glasby/79n1319
  American Revolution/Boatner/75n365
  musical theatre/Green/77n992
  Third Reich/Snyder/77n402
  unexplained/Cavendish/75n1604
Encyclopedic dictionary of . . .
  American hist/Hurwitz/75n367
  English usage/Mager/75n1289
  Judaica/Wigoder/75n320
  mathematics/Mathematical Society of
    Japan/78n1227
  school law/Gatti/76n592
Encyclopedic directory of ethnic organizations
  in the US/Wynar/76n394; 77n430
Endres, G G/World airline/79n1583
Energy/Morrison/77n1407
Energy atlas/78n1347
Energy crisis/Sobel/75n1543
Energy demand studies/Basile/77n1398
Energy directory/75n1548
Energy fact book/77n1417
Energy facts/US House/75n1544
Energy guide/Bemis/78n1337
Energy: gd to organizations and info resources/
  75n1547; 79n1382
Energy index/75n1557; 79n1383
Energy info abstracts/77n1401
Energy info locator/77n1413
Energy info resources/Brown/76n1464
Energy: key-phrase dissertation index/78
  n1351
Energy policy-making/Rycroft/79n1384
Energy production & consumption in the paper
  industry/Weiner/79n1327
Energy ref sources/Hsieh/77n1405
Energy-related doctoral scientists & engineers
  in the US/79n1385
Energy–scientific, technical & socioeconomic
  bibliog/Hsieh/78n1340
Energy sourcebook/McRae/79n1386
Energy tech handbook/Considine/78n1349
Energy II: bibliog of social sci & related lit/
  Morrison/79n1387

Engel, L K/Complete bk NASCAR/75n780/
  Complete motorcycle/75n739
Engelbarts, R/Women in/75n485
Engelbrecht, P N/Dictionary catalog/76n293
Engeldinger, E A/Black American/79n1215
Engineering eponyms/Auger/76n1651
Engineering formulas/Gieck/78n1505
Engineering manual/Perry/77n1569
England, C/Children using/79n209
England, G/British directory/75n24
England, P/Favorite operas German/75n1167/
  Favorite operas Italian/75n1168
England and Holland of the pilgrims/Dexter/
  79n481
England: chronology & fact bk, 1485-1973/
  Vexler/75n336
Engle, E/National governments/75n470
English, W E/Complete gd easy/76n1615
English architecture/Curl/78n800
English-Canadian lit to 1900/Moyles/77n1257
English Catholic bks, 1641-1700/Clancy/75
  n1216
English convicts in colonial America/Goldham/
  75n412; 78n399
English drama/Wells/76n1264
English drama and theatre, 1800-1900/Con-
  noly/79n1007
English drama, 1900-50/Mikhail/78n929
English drama, 1660-1800/Link/78n926
English drama to 1660/Penninger/77n988
English fiction, 1660-1800/Beasley/79n1227
English-French glossary/US Dept of State/78
  n1057
English historical facts 1485-1603/Powell/
  79n434
English-Indonesian dict/Echols/76n1150
English-Italian, Italian-English dict/Ragazzini/
  75n1272
English-Khmer dict/Huffman/79n1143
English-Kikuyu dict/Barlow/77n1093
English language & orientation programs in
  the US/75n668/Davis/78n561
English language cookbooks/Axford/77n1539
English literary journal to 1900/White/78n1158
English lit 1660-1800/Crane/75n1374/Fried-
  man/76n1259
English novel/Dyson/75n1376
English novel explication, suppl I/Abernethy/
  77n1227
English novel 1578-1956/Bell/76n1256
English-Persian dict/Wollaston/79n1146
English-Russian dict/Müller/75n1274
English-Russian polytechnical dict/Chernuk-
  hin/78n1206

English-Russian reliability & quality-control dict/Kovalenko/78n1502
English tests and reviews/Buros/76n562
English verse, 1701-50/Foxon/76n1265
Enjoying the summer theatres of New England/Goodrich/75n1184
Enrichment ideas/Carlson/77n642
Enright, J/Official major/75n734
Enser, A G S/Filmed books/77n1001/Subject bibliog/78n330
Ensminger, M E/Complete ency horses/78n1463
Enumeratio pteridophytarum japonicarum/Nakaike/76n1379
Environment abstracts/75n1558; 79n1396
Environment index/75n1559; 79n1397
Environment regulation hndbk/75n1538
Environment USA/Onyx Group/75n1549
Environmental concerns/Burk/78n1338
Environmental engineers' hndbk/Liptak/75n1540; 76n1459; 76n1460
Environmental impact hndbk/Burchell/77n1416
Environmental info sources hndbk/Wolff/75n1553
Environmental law/Schwartz/78n1341
Environmental literature/Bennett/75n1556
Environmental managemt & politics/Sumek/75n1526
Environmental planning/Meshenberg/77n1406
Environmental pollution & mental health/Williams/75n1530
Environmental quality abstracts/77n1402
Environmental-socioeconomic data sources/US Dept of the Air Force/78n1350
Environmental toxicology/Rudd/79n1401
Environmental values/Owings/77n1408
Epic & romance criticism/Coleman/75n1310
Episcopalian's dict/Harper/76n1083
Eponyms dictionaries index/Ruffner/78n111
Eppler, E E/International bibliog Jewish/77n297
Epstein, E M/Barron's gd/79n657
Equal Rights Amendment/Equal Rights Amendments Project/78n496
Equal Rights Amendment Project/Equal Rights/78n496
Equalant I & Equalant II: oceanographic atlas/78n1484
Era of the American Revolution/Smith/76n315
Erhardt, R/Clock/79n935
Eric Dolphy/Simosko/75n1164
Eric Gill/Brady/75n71
Erickson, K V/Aristotle's rhetoric/76n1106
Ericson, C R/Nacogdoches—Texas/75n415

Ericson, V/Amateur navigator's/75n752
Ernest Hemingway/Wagner/78n1143
Ernst, B/Great perpetual/77n648
Ernst, W B/Multitype library/78n120
Eschholz, P A/Contemporary fiction/78n1105
Eshback, O W/Handbook of engineering/77n1566
Esker, K P W/Genealogical department/76n431
Espensahde, E B/Goode's world/79n585
Espina, N/Repertoire for/78n892
Essay collections in internat'l relations/Wright/78n490
Essays for Ralph Shaw/Stevens/76n211
Essays for US adhesive postage stamps/Brazer/78n859
Essays of an info scientist/Garfield/79n302
Essays on Aslib/Taylor/79n317
Essays on bibliography/Brenni/76n196
Essays on info & libraries/Barr/76n207
Essential elements of a copyright clearinghouse/78n55
Essential gd to prescription drugs/Long/78n1441
Essentials of contemporary lit of the Western world/Heiney/75n1309
Essig, K B/700 French/77n1089
Estabrook, L/Libraries in/78n119
Estes, G E/Media center/79n211
Estok, R/Union list/77n1441
Estonians in America/Pennar/76n405
Etched work of Whistler/Kennedy/79n897
Eterovich, A S/Guide and/77n448
Ethiopian perspectives/Brown/79n352
Ethnic American minorities/Johnson/77n424
Ethnic directory of New Jersey/Kipel/79n445
Ethnic groups in Ohio with special emphasis on Cleveland/Wynar/76n393
Ethnic groups of insular Southeast Asia/Lebar/76n810
Ethnic history in Pennsylvania/Bodnar/76n386
Ethnic info sources of the US/Wasserman/77n428
Ethnic serials at selected Univ of California libraries/Bullock/78n379
Ethnic studies/Haley/77n418
Ethnic studies bibliog/78n377
Ethnographic approaches to research in educ/Wolcott/77n747
Ethnographic bibliog of North America/Murdock/77n738
Ethological dictionary/Heymer/79n783
Etymological lexicon of classical Greek/Wharton/76n1145
Eudora Welty/Thompson/77n1215

Eugene O'Neill/Atkinson/75n1362
Eugene O'Neill and the American critic/ Miller/75n1363
Eureka! illust'd hist of inventions/De Bono/ 76n1307
EURIM II: European Conf on the Application of Research in Info Services and Libraries/ 78n267
Euro Wirtschafts Wörterbuch/Zahn/75n887
Europa administration/Duic/78n475
Europa year book/75n322; 76n265
European campgrounds & trailer parks/76 n536
European chemical industries/Charnley/76 n896
European communities yearbook/79n506
European directory of economic & corporate Planning/Lloyd/76n833
European directory of market research surveys/Landau/76n868
European drama criticism 1900-75/Palmer/78 n941/Suppl 2/Palmer/75n1324
European financial almanac/76n886
European historical statistics, 1750-1970/ Mitchell/76n815
European manuscript sources of the American Revolution/Koenig/76n319
European offshore oil & gas yrbk/de Keyser/ 77n1418
European paintings before 1500/Cleveland Museum of Art/76n917
European paintings in the collection of the Worcester Art Museum/75n992
European Parliament digest/Edmond/75n471
European political facts 1848-1918/Cook/ 79n505/1918-73/Cook/76n460
European retail trades/Charnley/77n809
Europe's 5000 largest companies/76n897
Euthanasia controversy/Triche/77n1467
Evaluating library use instruction/Beeler/77 n265
Evaluating media programs/78n183
Evaluation/TenBrink/75n717
Evaluation instruments for bilingual educ/ 77n575
Evaluation of alternative curricula: school library media educ/76n221
Evaluation studies/Glass/77n635
Evaluation techniques for school library- media programs/Woolls/79n221
Evans, A/Glossary of molecular/76n1355
Evans, C F/Cambridge history/76n1097
Evans, E/Weathering the/76n338
Evans, F B/Modern archives/76n291

Evans, G/Women in/76n482
Evans, G E/Introduction to technical/75 n247; 77n269/Management techniques/77 n246
Evans, H/Picture researcher's/76n928
Evans, I O/Book of flags/76n449
Evans, J E/Guide to prose/78n1163
Evans, M/Picture researcher's/76n928
Evans, P/Art pottery/75n1080
Evans, W/Encyclopaedia of golf/75n769
Evans-Pritchard, E E/Bibliography of writings/ 76n803
Evenson, A E/Complete hndbk automotive/ 75n1731
Everett, G A/Select bibliog/75n1419; 76 n1294
Everyman's gd to drugs & medicines/ Massett/76n1550
Everyone has roots/Camp/79n498
Everyone's bk of hand & small power tools/ Drake/75n1792
Everyone's gd to better food & nutrition/ Deskins/76n1570
Everything tenants need to know to get their money's worth/Rejnis/75n933
Everything you can get from the gov for free . . . or almost for free/Norback/76 n84
Everything you wanted to know about drug abuse . . . but were afraid to ask/Winek/ 75n1659
Evolution of the modern presidency/Greenstein/79n524
Evory, A/Contemporary authors/79n137
Ewedemi, S/Bibliography of insurance/79n851
Ewing, C A M/Documentary source/76n476
Ewing, D W/Writing for/75n889
Ewing, K L/Care and/78n1258
Executive & management developmt for business & gov/Hanson/77n849
Executive's digest of financial research/ Buckley/79n825
Exercise equivalents of food/Konishi/75n1690
Exobiology/Sable/79n1337
Expanding media/Boyle/78n246
Experiences in rural developmt/Dejene/75 n287
Explorers Ltd./Explorers source/78n616
Explorers Ltd. gd to lost treasure in the US & Canada/Perrin/79n399
Explorers Ltd source book/Explorers Ltd/ 78n616
Exploring phenomenology/Stewart/75n1238

Exploring the unspoiled West/Society of American Travel Writers/76n555
Exporters directory-US buying gd/79n834
Exporter's financial & marketing hndbk/Jonnard/76n867
Expositor's Bible commentary/78n992
Expository dict of Old Testament words/Vine/79n1074
Eyles, A/Western/76n1068
Eyring, H/Annual review physical/76n1340
Eysenck, H J/Handbook of abnormal/75n1589
Ezell, E C/Small arms/79n1608

FAA historical fact book/US FAA/75n1822
Faber medical dict/Wakeley/76n1524
Fabrics for historic bldgs/Nylander/78n862
Face the nation/76n1156; 76n1157; 76n1158
Facilities & plant engineering hndbk/Lewis/75n1812
Facilities inventory & classification manual/US Office of Education/75n719
Fact bk of US agriculture/US Dept of Agriculture/77n1510
Factors affecting the renewal of periodical subscriptions/Woodward/79n248
Factory store gd to all New England/Miser/75n951
Facts about Alaska/77n520
Facts about the presidents/Kane/75n388; 77n514
Facts & comparisons/Kastrup/79n500
Facts & figures on gov finance/77n823
Facts on file five-yr index 1971-75/Kattleman/77n500
Facts on file yearbook/Hollingsworth/78n84
Faculty alert bulletin/Grant Information System/75n669
Faculty involvemt in library instruction/Rader/78n169
Faculty status for academic librarians/76n136
Fader, D/New hooked/78n586
Fadiman, C/Lifetime reading/79n691/Wine buyers/79n1516
Fahey, W A/Great black/77n434
Fahl, R J/North American/78n1483
Fahy, C/Home remedies/76n1639
Faibisoff, S/Changing times/79n147
Fair, R H/Shell collector's/77n931
Fair garden and the swarm of beasts/Edwards/75n185
Fairbank, J K/Japanese studies/77n319

Fairbanks, C/Black American/79n1215
Fairbridge, R W/Encyclopedia of world/77n1426
Fairchild's dict of fashion/Calasibetta/76n978
Fairchild's dict of home furnishings/Hoffman/75n1105
Fairfield County/Cummings/76n547
Falby, W F/Ontario energy/79n1388
Falconer, M W/Current drug/78n1436
Falge, P/Complete garden/76n1594
Falk, B A/Personal name/77n40
Falk, J D/America/79n415
Falk, V R/Personal name/77n40
Families of ancient New Haven/Jacobus/75n422
Families of early Hartford, CT/Barbour/78n396
Families of flowering plants arranged according to a new system based on their probable phylogeny/Hutchinson/75n1477
Family camping hndbk/Knap/77n687
Family ency of American hist/76n322
Family factbook/Lopata/79n749
Family gd to amusement centers/Hunter/76n550
Family in past time/Milden/79n751
Family legal advisor/Helm/75n557
Family life & child developmt/Child Study Assoc of America/Wel-Met, Inc./78n655
Family records, or genealogies of the first settlers of Passaic Valley/Littell/77n468
Family word finder/77n1081
Famous actors and actresses on the American stage/Young/76n1033
Famous books/Downs/76n133
Famous kings and emperors/Rowland-Entwistle/78n333
Famous people on film/Emmens/78n957
Fang, H-Y/Foundation engineering/76n1622
Fang, J R/International gd library/77n176
Fantini, M D/Alternative educ/77n572; 78n537
FAO production yearbook/79n1515
FAO trade yearbook/79n835
Far East and Australasia/76n267
Farber, E I/Academic library/75n180
Farewell to Alexandria/Gore/77n205
Fargis, P/Consumer's handbook/76n873
Farish, M K/Orchestral music/79n990/String music/75n1125
Farm, ranch & countryside gd/75n594
Farmer, H S/New career/78n773
Farrand, J/Audubon society/78n1315
Farrell, R B/Dictionary of German/78n1058

al Faruqi, I R/Historical atlas religions/76n1091
Farwell's rules of the nautical road/Bassett/78 n1573
Fascism: reader's gd/Laqueur/77n496
Fasick, A M/Children using/79n209
Fassett, N C/Spring flora/77n1352
Fate of drugs in the organism/Société Française des Sciences et Techniques Pharmaceutiques Working Group/78n1437
Faulkner, L L/Handbook of industrial/77n1606
Faulkner, S/L.A. home/75n1102
Faurot, A/Concert piano/75n1126/Team piano/ 77n952
Faust, J L/NY Times bk indoor/76n1584/NY Times bk vegetable/76n1583
Faust, M E/Field gd grasses/79n1349
Favazza, A R/Anthropological and/78n1373
Favorite operas by German and Russian composers/England/75n1167
Favorite operas by Italian and French composers/England/75n1168
Favré, H/Larousse dictionary/79n700
Fawcett, M J/1976 corpus/77n335
Fax & teletext/MacCafferty/78n238
Fay, L C/Getting people/75n715
Fayen, E G/Information retrieval/75n280
Fazal-e-Rab, S/J. P. Movement/79n545
Fazey, C/Aetiology of/79n1454
Fear of the word/Oboler/75n238
Feasibility of maintaining and providing access to data archives through ERIC/Tessier/79 n266
Feather, L G/Encyclopedia of jazz/78n915
Feature films on 8mm and 16mm/Limbacher/ 75n1208; 78n959
Febvre, L/Coming of/78n34
Fechtner, L/Encyclopedia of ad-libs/78n1044
Fedden, R/National Trust/76n556
Federal and state Indian reservations and Indian Trust areas/US Economic Developmt Admin/ 75n809
Federal assistance for programs serving the visually handicapped/McGarry/79n1470
Federal aviation regulations for pilots/79 n1584
Federal career directory/US Civil Service Commission/77n626
Federal Council for Sci and Tech/Federal technology/76n1322
Federal funding gd for elementary and secondary educ/Marshall/78n558
Federal gov libraries in Canada/78n202
Federal info sources and systems/US General Accounting Office/77n110

Federal program evaluations/79n116
Federal Republic of Germany/Price/79n380
Federal statistical directory/US Office of Management and Budget/77n759
Federal tax desk book/77n853
Federal tax return manual/76n912
Federal technology transfer directory of programs, resources, contact points/ Federal Council for Sci and Tech/76n1322
Federico Fellini/Price/79n1025
Federico García Lorca y su mundo/Laurenti/ 75n1427
Fedynskyj, A/Bibliographical index/76n1163
Fee, M/Canadian fiction/77n1255
Feezel, J D/Selected print/77n1121
Fehr, L M/Skiing USA/79n728
Feinbloom, R I/Child health/76n1543
Feineman, G/Handbook of plastics/75n1784
Feingold, M/Scholarships, fellowships/78n566
Feingold, S N/College guide/79n459/Scholarships, fellowships/78n566
Feinman, J/Catalog of food/78n1471/Catalog of free/77n91
Feirer, J L/SI metric/78n1231
Feisenberger, H A/Scientists/76n55
Felber, J E/American's tourist . . . China/77 n565/American's tourist . . . USSR/76 n557; 77n566
Feldbrugge, F J M/Encyclopedia of Soviet/ 75n553
Feldman, S/Handbook of wealth/78n729
Feldzamen, A N/Calculator handbook/75 n1769
Felix, E J/Identify your/79n930
Felkenes, G T/Law enforcement/78n497
Felldin, J R/Index to 1820/77n461
Fellendorf, G W/Bibliography on deafness/79 n1455
Feller, B/Directory of federal/77n597
Fell's gd to coins and money tokens of the world/Angus/75n1061
Fell's internat'l coin bk/Andrews/75n1060; 77n902
Felton, B/Felton & Fowler's best/77n92/ Felton & Fowler's more/77n93
Felton & Fowler's best, worst, and most unusual/Felton/77n92
Felton & Fowler's more best, worst, and most unusual/Felton/77n93
Felzenberg, A S/Evolution of/79n524
Female artists past and present/76n933/ Suppl/76n934
Feminist resources for schools and colleges/ Froschl/78n593

Fenlon, I/Catalogue of printed/77n953
Fennell, J/Black experience/79n448
Ferber, R/Basic bibliography/76n864/
  Handbook of marketing/75n923
Ferguson, A/Annual review English/78n294
Ferguson, E J/Confederation, constitution/76n310
Ferguson, J/Illustrated ency mysticism/79n1057
Ferguson, M A H/Bibliography of English/75n350
Ferguson-Lees, I J/Field gd birds/76n1429
Ferguson-Lees, J/Guide to bird-/77n1376
Fernald, E A/New Florida/75n583
Fernow, B/Records of/77n462
Ferns of Florida/Lakela/78n1284
Ferres, J H/Modern Commonwealth lit/79n1184
Ferris, S P/Information on/78n894
Festivals sourcebook/Wasserman/78n77
Feuereisen, F/Presse in/75n912
ffrench, R/Guide to birds/75n1504
Fiction catalog/Fidell/77n197
FID publications: 80 yr bibliog/77n166
FID yearbook/76n73
Fidell, E A/Fiction catalog/77n197/Short story/77n1134/Suppl 1969-73/76n1210
Field, R/Bibliography and indexes/79n117
Field, S/Professional broadcast/75n1204
Field bk of mountaineering & rock climbing/Lyman/76n718
Field guide to . . .
  animal tracks/Murie/76n1413
  birds' nests of 285 species found breeding in the US East of the Mississippi River/Harrison/76n1422
  edible wild plants/Angier/75n1465
  edible wild plants of eastern and central North America/Peterson/79n1367
  Mexican birds/Peterson/75n1509
  Pacific states wildflowers/Niehaus/77n1361
  reptiles and amphibians of eastern and central North America/Conant/76n1448
  rocks and minerals/Pough/77n1438
  seashells of the world/Lindner/79n929
  western mushrooms/Smith/76n1398
Field guide to the . . .
  birds of Britain and Europe/Peterson/76n1429
  birds of Galapagos/Harris/76n1421
  birds of South-East Asia/King/76n1423
  butterflies of North America, east of the Great Plains/Klots/78n1330

Field guide to the . . . (cont'd)
  butterflies of the West Indies/Kelly/77n1391
  fish of Puget Sound and the Northwest Coast/Somerton/77n1388
  grasses, sedges and rushes of the US/Knobel/79n1349
  insects of Britain and Northern Europe/Chinery/75n1516
  little people/Arrowsmith/78n1008
  mammals/Burt/77n1392
  nests, eggs and nestlings of British and European birds/Harrison/77n1380
  trees of Britain and Northern Europe/Mitchell/75n1492
  vascular plants of Grand Teton Natl Park and Teton County, WY/Shaw/77n1356
Fieldbook of natural hist/Palmer/76n1364
Fielding, M/Dictionary of American/76n921
Fielding, N & T/Fielding's low-cost/75n623/Fielding's selective/76n537
Fielding, T/Fielding's travel/77n567
Fielding's gd to the Caribbean plus the Bahamas/Harman/75n620
Fielding's low-cost Europe/Fielding/75n623
Fielding's selective shopping gd to Europe/Fielding/76n537
Fielding's travel gd to Europe/Fielding/77n567
Fields, D C/College learning/79n192
Fierst, J/Jacob Riis/78n644
Fifteenth century English prayers & meditations/Revell/77n1030
Fifteenth to eighteenth century rare books on education/78n540
Fifth internat'l directory of anthropologists/76n812
Fifty businessmen/Businessman's entertainment/75n593
55 years of recorded country-western music/Osborne/77n980
Fifty great western illustrators/Dykes/76n940
Fifty-year index: Mississippi Valley historical review/Clark/75n371
Fifty years of Indian historical writings/Abidi/76n359
Fighters for independence/White/79n411
Figlio, R M/Criminology index/76n780
Filaseta, K/Bargain hunting/75n954
Filbee, M/Dictionary of country/79n922
Filby, P J/Specialist sports/76n765
Filby, P W/American & British/77n449
Filipinos in Hawaii/Alcantara/78n388

Filler, L/Progressivism and/77n378
Fillingham, P/Complete bk/76n710
Film actors gd/Parish/78n960
Film criticism/Heinzkill/76n1065
Film directors/Parish/76n1058
Film director's gd/Parish/78n961
Film lit index/Aceto/76n1063; 77n1014
Film-makers' cooperative catalogue/76n1056
Film music/Limbacher/75n1147
Film review/Speed/77n998; 79n1039
Film review digest/Brownstone/76n1064
Film user's hndbk/Rehrauer/76n182
Filmarama/Stewart/76n1070; 78n966
Filmed books and plays/Enser/77n1001
Filmgoer's bk of quotes/Halliwell/75n1191
Filmgoer's companion/Halliwell/76n1052; 79n1023
Filmographic dict of world lit: suppl/Daisne/79n1033
Filmography of the Third World/Cyr/78n956
Films for Korean studies/Butler/79n373
Films: for schools, colleges and libraries/77n1008
Films of Howard Hawks/Willis/76n1060
Films of Robert Redford/Spada/78n963
Films on art/79n1035
Films: public domain films/Minus/75n1196
Filosa, G F R/Surfer's almanac/78n632
Filsinger, C/Locus/77n869/National radio/76n1176
Final report on 'databases suitable for users of environmental info'/Yska/79n304
Financial aids for higher educ/Kesslar/75n678; 78n563
Financial analyst's hndbk/Levine/76n887
Financial capitalization rate tables based on mortage-equity relationships for use in the real estate appraisal both before and after tax/76n854
Finch, C/Art of/75n1190
Finch, F/Concise ency/78n781
Finch, V/British directory/75n24
Finding a job/Sprague/79n865
Finding info in the library/Gibson/77n223
Finding list of journals indexed in *Current Index to Journals in Education*/METRO/78n583
Finding our fathers/Rottenberg/78n408
Finding your roots/Westin/78n395
Findley, J S/Mammals of/77n1393
Fine, M/American Jewish/75n321
Fine arts/Ehresmann/76n915
Fine arts marketplace/Cummings/77n858
Fine books/Pollard/75n65
Fine prints/Shapiro/78n814
Fink, D G/Electronics engineers'/76n1629/Standard hndbk/79n1546
Fink, G M/Biographical dict/75n975/Labor unions/78n766/State labor/78n767
Fink, J W/Indices to/77n1191
Fink, R/Language of/76n996
Finlay, P/Jane's freight/78n1546
Finley, M I/Atlas of classical/78n317
Finneran, R J/Anglo-Irish/78n1193
Fintel, M/Handbook of concrete/75n1759
Fire and crash vehicles from 1950/Vanderveen/77n1622
Fire protection for the design profession/Jensen/77n1578
Fire protection gd on hazardous materials/75n1714
Fire resistant textiles hndbk/Reeves/76n1649
Fire sciences dict/Kuvshinoff/78n1503
Firearms price gd/Byron/78n849
Fireman, J/Cat catalog/77n1527
Firsoff, G I & V A/Rockhound's hndbk/76n1481
First complete home decorating catalogue/Wilson/77n942
First edition?/Zempel/79n57
First French dict/Henstock/75n1265
First London catalogue/Lucie-Smith/75n949
First printings of American authors/Bruccoli/78n1110
First sci dict/Lucas/78n1209
Fischler, S/Fischlers' hockey/76n749
Fischlers' hockey ency/Fischler/76n749
Fish, B/Water publications/77n1428
Fishbein, M/Handy home/75n1648/Modern home/77n1474
Fisher, J/Thorburn's birds/77n1377
Fisher, M/Who's who children's/76n1198
Fisher, P G/Materials for/76n800
Fisher, R/Heroes of/75n1156
Fisher, R B/Dictionary of drugs/77n1501
Fisher, T N/Ganley's Catholic/75n683
Fisher, W H/Free at/78n444
Fisheries of the US/US Natl Marine Fisheries Service/75n969; 78n761
Fishes of the Gulf of Mexico/Hoese/78n1326
Fishes of the Red River drainage, eastern Kentucky/Branson/75n1512
Fishes of the world/Lindberg/75n1514/Wheeler/76n1437
Fishing/Bates/75n759
Fishing in print/Gingrich/75n760
Fishman, S Z/College gd/79n459
Fisk, M/Encyclopedia of associations/77n85

Fitch, C M/Complete bk houseplants/76n1585
Fitter, A & R/Wild flowers/76n1389
Fitzgerald, G/Metropolitan opera/79n994
Fitzgerald, M G/Universal pictures/78n949
Fitzgerald/Hemingway annual/Duggan/79n1212
Fitzgibbon, D S/Processors of/75n968/Wholesale dealers/75n928
Fitzgibbon, R H/Argentina/75n339/Brazil/75n340
Fitzgibbon, T/Food of/77n1544
Five centuries of tapestry/Bennett/78n861
Five hundred years of printing/Steinberg/75n49
5,000 questions answered abt maintaining, repairing, & improving your home/Schuler/78n1535
Five-year index, *The Alaska Journal*/79n387
Fjällbrant, N/User educ/79n312
Flack, M J/World's students/77n582
Flags and standards of the Third Reich/Davis/76n1676
Flags through the ages and across the world/Smith/77n486
Flake, C J/Mormon bibliog/79n1048
Flammability hndbk for plastics/Hilado/76n1656
Flanagan, C D/American folklore/78n1012
Flanagan, J T/American folklore/78n1012/Edgar Lee/76n1246
Flanders, P/Thematic index/76n1007
Flannery O'Connor and Caroline Gordon/Golden/78n1123
Flanz, G H/Constitutions of/78n427
Flaste, R/NY Times/77n559
Flavell, C W/Ohio area/78n401/Ohio genealogical gd/79n483/Ohio genealogical periodical/78n400
Flaxman, A/National directory/79n645
Flayderman, N/Flayderman's guide/78n851
Flayderman's gd to antique American firearms and their values/Flayderman/78n851
Fleischer, E B/Bibliographic citations/76n87/Style manual/79n129
Fleisher, M L/Encyclopedia of comic/77n1167; 77n1168
Fleiss, R/Museum companion/75n1004
Fleming, G/Wild flowers/78n1290
Fleming, J/Dictionary of architecture/77n875/Dictionary of decorative/78n828
Fleming-Mitchell, L/Running Press/78n1376
Flesch, R/Look it/78n103
Flexner, S B/Dictionary of American/76n1129/I hear/78n1031
Flight instructor's manual/Kershner/76n731

Flood damage prevention/Tennessee Valley/75n1756
Flora, G B/Directory of college/75n672
Flora of . . .
 eastern Himalaya/Ohashi/77n1355
 Manila/Merrill/77n1353
 Okinawa & the southern Ryukyu Islands/Walter/77n1358
Florence, G/Collectors ency/78n855
Flores, A/Kafka bibliography/78n1189
Florida place names/Morris/75n452
Flowering shrubs and small trees/Hersey/75n1702
Flowers, S/Mosses/75n1487
Flowers/Pizzetti/76n1599
Flowers and plants/Shosteck/75n1464
Flowers of Greece and the Aegean/Huxley/79n1343
Flowers of Guatemala/Chickering/75n1474
Flowers of the southwest mesas/Patraw/79n1345
Floyd, M K/Abortion bibliog/76n1516/Bibliography of noise/76n1452
Fluk, L R/Jews in/76n380
Fly dressers' guide/Veniard/75n762
Fly tackle/Henkin/77n692
FM atlas and station directory/Elving/79n1171
Foam and foam control/Louden/79n1324
Fodell, B/Cesar Chavez/75n976
Fogden, M & P/Animals and/75n1495
Fogel, E/Concordance to poems/79n1245
Fogg, H G W/History of popular/78n1491
Fokker, N/Oriental carpets/75n1103
Folk, E L/Securities law/76n518
Folk, K R/Indians of/78n682
Folk music sourcebk/Sandberg/77n982
Folk schools in soc change/Paulston/75n647
Folklife and the fed gov/Coe/79n1083
Folklore/Brunvand/78n1010
Folklore from Africa to the US/US Library of Congress/77n1057
Folklore theses and dissertations in the US/Dundes/78n1011
Folktale/Thompson/78n1015
Follett, W/Modern American/75n1288
Follett vest-pocket . . .
 50,000 words/Sharp/79n1127
 French dict/Switzer/79n1136
 Italian dict/Bocchetta/79n1142
Foner, P S/Democratic Republican/78n439
Food and Agriculture Organization of the UN/International directory/78n757
Food and nutrition/75n1687

Food catalog/Woodward/79n1536
Food composition tables updated annotated bibliog/78n1472
Food co-op directory/78n711
Food co-op hndbk/Co-op Handbook Collective/76n872
Food co-ops for small groups/Vellela/76n880
Food of the Western world/Fitzgibbon/77n1544
Foot-loose in the Swiss Alps/Reifsnyder/75n626
Football book/Lorimer/79n717
Football register/Douchant/76n735
Foote, L E/Wildflowers of/76n1388
Footnotes to American hist/Sharp/78n346
For good measure/Johnstone/76n1316
For younger readers/79n338
Foray, C P/Historical dict/78n288
Forbes, E/Opera from/78n912
Ford, B/Pelican gd/75n1373
Ford, C/Guide to black/79n600
Ford, G H/Victorian fiction/79n1228
Ford trucks since 1905/Wagner/79n1558
Fordney, M T/Insurance hndbk/78n1410
Ford-Smith, J/Dictionary of rubber/76n1647
Fordyce, R/Caroline drama/79n1008
Foreign affairs bibliog/Kreslins/77n528
Foreign lang tests and reviews/Buros/76n563
Foreign trade marketplace/Schultz/78n734
Foreign versions, variations, and diminutives of English names and foreign equivalents of US military and civilian titles/US Immigration and Naturalization Service/75n450
Foreman, L/Systematic discography/75n1135
Forest fertilization/Sykes/77n1321
Forest service organizational directory/79n1537
Forest tree seed directory/77n1367
Forestry, 1967-73/76n845
Forestry theses accepted by colleges and universities in the US/Kinch/79n1538
Forinash, M R/Reader development/78n592
Forman, N/Serials updating/76n23
Forman, R E/Medical abbreviations/78n1415
Formula book/Stark/76n1645/Book 2/77n1313
Formulary of cosmetic preparations/Ash/78n1253
Formulary of paints and other coatings/Ash/79n1320
Forney, M N/Railroad car/76n1671
Forsman, J/Recipe index/75n1694
Forster, R A/Checklist of world's/77n1379

FORTRAN to PL/1 dict, PL/1 to FORTRAN dict/Brown/76n1624
Foseco foundryman's hndbk/77n1612
Foskett, A C/Subject approach/79n270
Foskett, D J/National library/78n125/Reader in/78n249
Foss, C F/Armoured fighting/78n1562/Artillery of/77n1642/Infantry weapons/78n1568/Military vehicles/77n1643
Fossett, R O/Screen printing/75n1108
Foster, C O/Organic flower/76n1586
Foster, D L/Managing the/77n254
Foster, D W/Manual of Hispanic/78n1200/Modern Latin/76n1301/20th century/76n1300
Foster, L/NY Times/75n1688
Foster, L T/Annotated bibliog Canadian/77n1420
Foster, V R/Manual of Hispanic/78n1200/Modern Latin/76n1301
Foster, W M/Homeowner's gd/77n1419
Fothergill, R/Non-book materials/79n148
Found, P/International literary/77n60
Foundation Center/Foundation directory/78n74
Foundation Center source bk/Beck/76n571
Foundation directory/Lewis/76n620/Foundation Center/78n74
Foundation engineering hndbk/Winterkorn/76n1622
Foundation grants index/Noe/79n85
Foundations of the public library/Shera/75n190
Founders: portraits of persons born abroad/Bolton/77n456
Four French dramatists/SantaVicca/75n1417
Fournier, R/Illustrated dict/78n881
Fourth directory of periodicals publishing articles on English and Amer lit and lang/Gerstenberger/76n1193
Fout, J C/German history/75n395
Fowler, H S/Fieldbk of natural/76n1364
Fowler, H W/Shorter Oxford/75n1252
Fowler, M/Felton & Fowler's best/77n92/Felton & Fowler's reader/77n93
Fowler, N/German wine/78n1455
Fowler, W B/American diplomatic/76n311
Fox, E/Santa Clara/75n605
Fox, H N/Index to periodical/78n1103
Fox, J J/Profiles of/79n542
Fox, N/Santa Clara/75n605
Fox, S/Jewish films/77n1009
Foxley, C H/Locating, recruiting/77n793
Foxon, D F/English verse/76n1265

Foy, F A/Catholic almanac/76n1086
Fraenkel, O K/Rights we/75n481
Fraenkel-Conrat, H/Comprehensive virology/76n1361
Fraizer, D W/Alain Robbe-Grillet/75n1415
France: especially for women/Tully/76n560
France: events of May-June 1968/Wylie/75n309
France: Illustrated gd to textile collections/Lubell/79n950
France, 1789-1962/Cooke/76n364
Franchise annual/Dixon/79n829
Franchise index-profile/US Small Business Admin/75n919
Franchise opportunities hndbk/US Dept of Commerce/77n804; 79n830
Francis, E/Lost links/76n432
Francis, G A/Whitman at/79n1225
Francis, J J/New English/79n1433
Francis Cotes/Johnson/78n817
Franck, I M/Film review/76n1064
Franck, M/Emerging field/78n214
Frank, H T/Hammond's atlas/79n1066
Frank, R/Plan for/75n1248
Frank, S/Sweet home/75n602
Frank Norris/Crisler/76n1247
Frank Schoonmaker's ency of wine/Schoonmaker/75n1676; 76n1563; 79n1521
Franke, D/America's 50/75n833
Franklin, A C/J&P transformer/75n1790
Franklin, B V/Anaïs Nin/75n1416
Franklin, D A/Guide to medical/75n1629
Franklin, J L/Human resources/79n858
Franklin, L C/Antiques and/79n913
Franko, L G/Petroleum industry/77n1404
Frase, R W/Library funding/75n137
Fraser, B J & S E/Scandinavian educ/75n644
Fraunfelder, F T/Drug-induced/77n1502
Frautschi, R/Bibliographie du/78n1186
Frazer, J M/Resource bk/77n1312
Free and inexpensive . . .
    learning materials/77n650
    materials for preschool and early childhood/Monahan/78n597
Free at last: bibliog of Martin Luther King, Jr./Fisher/78n444
Free earth gd to gardening/Kramer/75n1704
Free materials and educ/DuVall/79n681
Freedman, R/Sociology of/76n771
Freedom's voice in poetry and song/Anderson/79n958
Freeman, P/Index to research/78n184/Pathfinder/77n221
Freeman, R B/Works of/78n1272

Freeman, T W/Geographers biobibliographical/78n536; 79n626
Freeman, W/Concise dict/77n1070/Dictionary of fictional/75n1326
Freeman-Grenville, G S P/Chronology of African/75n391/Chronology of world/76n304/Modern atlas/77n397
Freethought in the US/Brown/79n1079
Freewheeling: bicycle camping/Bridge/75n735
Freidel, F/Harvard guide/75n355
Freides, T K/Literature and/75n170
Freinkel, N/Year in/78n1421
Freitus, J/160 edible/76n1384
French, D/Dictionary of managemt/76n909
French, H/Ceramic, furniture/78n830
French, J R P/Measures for/76n1486
French, R M/Guide to diagnostic/76n1529
French, S R/People's yellow/76n80
French bilingual dict/Lipton/75n1266
French bks in print/79n14
French-English sci and tech dict/de Vries/77n1290
French fifth republic/Heinz/75n519
French in America, 1488-1974/Pula/76n406
French lit in early Amer translation/Bowe/79n1270
French periodical index/Ponchie/77n45; 79n25
French XX bibliog/Alden/79n1266
French's index of differential diagnosis/Hart/75n1630
Freshman's friend/Johnson/77n585
Freudenthal, J R & P M/Index to anthologies/78n1194
Freundlich, I/Music for/75n1127
Frey, R L/Official ency/78n615
Frick collection/78n868
Fried, L/Jacob Riis/78n644
Friedman, A/English lit/76n1259
Friedman, B/Women's work/77n717
Friedman, L J/Sex role/78n1075
Friedman, M P/Biology of/75n1588
Friedman, P/Guide to Jewish/75n398
Fries, J F/Take care/78n1432
Fries, W H/Double elephant/75n46
Frisbee/Johnson/76n767
Frisbie, C J/Music and/78n890
Friskin, J/Music for/75n1127
Frison, T H/Stoneflies, or/76n1440
Fritsch, A J/Household pollutants/79n1400
Fritschler, A L/Urban affairs/76n802
From abacus to Zeus/Pierce/79n882
From Diatyas to Devatas in Hindu mythology/Gupta/75n1239

From protest to challenge/Karis/75n520; 78 n471
From radical left to extreme right/Spahn/77 n506
Frontier claims in the lower South/Lackey/78 n404
Froschl, M/Feminist resources/78n593
Frost, J M/World radio/77n1112
Frost, R B/Encyclopedia of physical/78n607
Frushell, R C/Contemporary thought/76n1289
Fry, B M/Publishers and/78n35
Fry, R/Black genealogy/78n397
Fryer, L/Dictionary of food/77n1545
Fubini, C/Directory of foundations/79n92
Fuchs, J W/Classics illustrated/75n1317
Fuhr, J R/Bibliography on atomic/79n1330
Fujioka, J Y/Japanese in/77n445
Fullard, H/Nelson Philip/79n592
Fuller, F/Handbook for translators/75n1249
Fulmer, C M/George Eliot/79n1239
Fulton, L/Access index/78n19/Directory of small/75n23; 79n52/International directory/75n26; 78n46/Small press/76n11; 79n39
Fulton, R/Dealth, grief/78n1425
Fun land USA/Onosko/79n713
Fundaburk, E L/Art at/75n1009/Pocket guide/79n884
Fundamentals of ornithology/Van Tyne/78 n1324
Fundamentals of quantity food preparation/ Hardwick/76n1572
Funeral service/Harrah/77n704
Funk & Wagnalls . . .
  comprehensive std internat'l dict/75n1251
  crossword puzzle word finder/Schwartz/75 n1262
  guide to the world of stamp collecting/Ilma/79n931
  standard college dict/78n1035
  standard desk dict/78n1036
Fur trade in Minnesota/White/79n409
Furer, H B/Chicago/75n508/New York/75 n509
Furlough from prison/Tompkins/75n840
Furlow, B/Circuit design/75n1781
Furniture repair and refinishing/Meyers/75n1795
Furth, S E/Survey of/75n283
Fussell, R/Demographic atlas/77n754
Fussler, H H/Management educ/75n215
Fussler, H H/Prospects for/78n215/Research libraries/75n181
Futas, E/Library acquisition/78n204
Future: gd to info sources/79n112

Future of card catalogs/76n189
Futures directory/McHale/79n113
Futurism and the arts/Andreoli-deVillers/77 n861

Gable, M/Market segmentation/79n838/ Marketing channel/77n810
Gabriel, A L/Summary bibliog/75n645
Gabriel, I/Herb identifier/77n1348
Gabriel Marcel and his critics/Lapointe/78 n1001
Gaddy, D/Microform handbook/76n226
Gaffney, M/More films/79n1024
Gagala, K L/Economics of/77n423
Gager, N/Women's rights/75n848
Gagnebin, B/Manuscrits et/75n68
Gaherty, S/Library Lit/75n142
Gailey, H A/Historical dict/76n251
Gaines, E/Woman's Day/75n1075
Gaines, L/Working press/75n1305
Galaxies and the universe/Sandage/77n1311
Galbraith, I C J/Life of/76n1418
Gale, R L/Plots and/75n1370
Gales, R L/Bicentennial Philadelphia/75n606
Gall, J/Layman's English-/76n1144
Gallagher, E J/Early Puritan/77n1185
Galler, M/Soviet prison/78n1066
Gallup, G H/Gallup poll/79n507
Gallup poll/Gallup/79n507
Galton, L/Complete bk symptoms/79n1484
Galván, R A/Diccionario del/79n1150
Gamboa, M J/Dictionary of international/75 n554
Game birds of North America/Rue/75n779
Games of the world/Grunfeld/76n743
Gander, T J/Infantry weapons/78n1568
Gandhi, H N D/Indian periodicals/75n40
Gandhiana 1962-76/Satyaprakash/78n298
Ganley, C/NCEA/Ganley's/77n600
Ganley's Catholic schools in America/Fisher/75n683
Gann, L H/Colonialism in/75n288
Gannett, H/Gazetteer of Maryland/77n463/ Gazetteer of Virginia/76n455/Geographic dict of Connecticut/79n596/Geographic dict of Massachusetts/79n594/Geographic dict of New/79n595
Ganz, A/Literary terms/76n1184
Garb, S/Abbreviations and/77n1475/Undesirable drug/75n1655
Garber, J S/Concise ency ancient/79n404
Garber, M B/Modern military/77n1627
Garbicz, A/Cinema, the/76n1057

Garcia-Pelayo y Gross, R/Diccionario moderno/ 78n1068/Pequeño Larousse/79n1151
Garden spice and wild pot-herbs/Muenscher/ 79n1353
Gardener's catalogue/Riker/75n1707
Gardener's gd to plant names/Healty/76n1588
Gardenhour, N D/Developmental tasks/77n651
Gardening in colour/Perry/77n1559
Gardening indoors with house plants/Poincelot/ 76n1600
Gardening with perennials month by month/ Hudak/77n1555
Gardner, A W/Good Housekeeping/77n1493
Gardner, J B/Illustrated soccer/78n630
Gardner, K A/LC Main/77n32
Gardner, M A/Press of/75n1294
Gardner, R/Alternative America/78n92
Gardner, R K/Choice/77n198; 79n179
Garfield, A M/Information on/78n894
Garfield, E/Essays of/79n302
Gargal, B/Magazines for/75n171
Garland, H/Oxford companion/77n1263
Garland, J D/National electrical/78n1532
Garland, M/Oxford companion/77n1263
Garner, S/Bibliography of writings/76n1238
Garoogian, A & R/Child care/78n656
Garraty, J A/Dictionary of American/76n106; 78n115/Encyclopedia of American/75 n124/New guide/75n663; 79n641
Garrison, L W/ABC pol sci/78n436
Garry, C & L S/Canadian libraries/79n313
Gartrell, E G/Electricity, magnetism/77n1591
Garvey, R/Concise treasury/76n1099
Garzke, W H/Battleships/77n1649
Gassan, A/Handbook for contemporary/75 n1109
Gaster, A/International authors/79n1208/International who's/79n1002
Gasteromycetae of Ohio/Johnson/76n1396
Gasteromycetes of the eastern US & Canada/ Coker/76n1396
Gateley, J J/Register of/76n339
Gates, J K/Guide to use/75n138/Introduction to librarianship/77n154
Gateways to readable bks, 5th ed/Withrow/77 n1166
Gatland, K/Missiles and/77n1647
Gatner, E S M/Research and/75n693
Gatrell, S/Bibliography of George/79n1238
Gatti, D J & R D/Encyclopedic dict/76n592
Gault, S M/Color dict/77n1368
Gaustad, E S/Historical atlas/77n1019
Gay, R M/Words into/75n113
Gay American hist/Katz/78n652

Gay source/Sanders/79n741
Gaylor/SIRS Bicentennial special program package for the American issues forum/ Goldstein/76n325
Gaynor, F/Dictionary of linguistics/77n1061
Gazdar, G/Bibliography of contemporary/ 79n1089
Gazetteer of . . .
  India/76n261
  Kashmir and Ladak/75n332
  Maryland and Delaware/Gannett/77n463
  Scotland/Munro/75n572
  Sikhim/75n333
  the state of Pennsylvania/Gordon/76 n456
  Virginia and West Virginia/Gannett/76 n455
Gearhart, L/Museum Council/77n76
Gebbie House magazine directory/76n24
Gebhard, D/Guide to architecture/79n890
Gebhardt, W/Special collections/78n194
Gechman, M/Survey of/75n283
Geddes, C/Complete bk horse/75n1680
Geddes, C L/Analytical gd . . . Arab/76n253/ Analytical gd . . . Arabian/75n291/Analytical gd . . . Islam/75n290
Geelan, P J M/Times atlas/76n535
Gehm, H W/Handbook of water/77n1422
Gehring, C T/Delaware papers/79n484
Geis, D/Wine buyers/79n1516
Geisendorfer, J V/Directory of religious/79 n1060
Geiser, E/Book publishers/78n43
Gelber, L/Dictionary of American/79n412
Gellatly, P/Guide to magazine/77n199
Gellert, W/VNR concise/78n1228
Gems/Webster/76n1483
Gems, minerals, crystals, and ores/Pearl/78 n1360
Gemstones and minerals/Villiard/75n1101
Gemstones of the world/Schumann/79n1422
Genealogical and heraldic hist of the commoners of Great Britain and Ireland/Burke/ 78n393
Genealogical and personal hist of Bucks County, PA/Davis/76n429
Genealogical bks in print/Schreiner-Yantis/76 n421
Genealogical data from colonial NY newspapers/Scott/78n409
Genealogical dept: source records from the DAR magazine/Esker/76n431
Genealogical dict of Rhode Island/Austin/79 n475

Genealogical periodical annual index/Towle/ 79n473
Genealogical reader: northeastern US & Canada/Wright/75n434
Genealogical records of Utah/Jaussi/75n423
Genealogical register of Plymouth families/ Davis/76n428
Genealogies in the LC; suppl 1972-76/Kaminkow/78n394
Genealogies of the descendants of the first settlers of the patent and city of Schenectady/Pearson/77n473
Genealogies of the first settlers of the ancient county of Albany/Pearson/77n474
Genealogist's guide/Barrow/79n466
Genelle, P/Wild flowers/78n1290
General armory of England, Scotland, Ireland, and Wales/Burke/77n483
General armory two/Morant/75n442
General Assembly of Virginia/Leonard/79n533
General bibliog for music research/Mixter/76n991
General censuses and vital statistics in the Americas/US Library of Congress/75n875
General classification systems in a changing world/79n271
General index to the reports from committees of the House of Commons, 1715-1801/ Brooke/75n476
General sources of statistics/Lock/77n751
Generic book/Shores/79n155
Genesis/Owens/79n1072
Gentle, E J/Aviation and/75n1721
Geographers biobibliographical studies/Freeman/78n536; 79n626
Geographic dictionary of . . .
    Connecticut and Rhode Island/Gannett/79n596
    Massachusetts/Gannett/79n594
    New Jersey/Gannett/79n595
Geographic glossary & traveller's gd/DeSola/76n520
Geographical lit on Nigeria/Aiyepeku/75n567
Geographical name index to the LC classification schedules/Olson/79n280
Geography and cartography/Lock/77n555
Geography and earth sciences publications/Van Balen/79n579; 79n580
Geology fld gd to northern Calif/Harbaugh/75n1564
George Eliot/Fulmer/79n1239
George Eliot-George Henry Lewes library/ Baker/78n1160

George Gershwin/Schwartz/76n1010
George Gissing/Collie/77n1233
George Gissing/Wolff/75n1386
George Gordon, Lord Byron/Santucho/78n1167
George Meredith/Collie/75n1395/Olmsted/79n1249
George Orwell/Meyers/78n1180
Georges Simenon/Young/77n1179
Georgia history/Simpson/77n395
Geothermal world directory/Tratner/79n1403
Geraghty, J J/Water atlas/75n1567
Gerald R. Ford/Lankevich/79n414
Gerard Manley Hopkins/Dunne/77n1235
Gerber, B L/Dictionary of modern/78n1054
Gerber, P L/Plots and/78n1137
Gerhart, G M/From protest/78n471
Gerlach, J C & L/Critical index/75n1209
German-American lit/Tolzmann/78n1191
German-Americana/Tolzmann/76n407
German army handbook, 1939-1945/Davies/ 75n1848
German bks in print/79n15
German-English sci dict/De Vries/79n1295
German expressionism in the fine arts/Spalek/ 78n786
German hist and civilization 1806-1914/ Fout/75n395
German lang press of the Americas/Arndt/77n444
German literature/76n1295
German new river settlement/Heavener/77n464
German painting of the 16th century/Deusch/ 75n1027
German warships of the 2nd WW/Lenton/77n1650
German wine atlas and vineyard register/ Fowler/78n1455
German word family dict/Keller/79n1137
Gershator, P/Bibliographic guide/77n1195
Gerstenberger, D/Fourth directory/76n1193
Gersumky, A T/Foundation Center/76n571
Gertrude Stein/Wilson/76n1248
Gerulaitis, L V/Printing and/78n36
Getchell, D R/Mariner's catalog/75n748; 76n711
Getting into medical school/Brown/75n1636; 77n610
Getting people to read/Fay/75n715
Getting skilled/Hebert/77n628
Getting the bks off the shelves/Smith/77n241
Getting yours: for the working woman/Pogrebin/76n796

Gettleson, L/Official world/76n705
Ghetto and suburbia/Antinoro-Polizzi/75n859
Ghosh, A & R/Indian political/78n483
Ghost towns of Montana/Miller/76n552
Ghosts' who's who/Hallam/78n1377
Giacoletto, L J/Electronics designers'/78n1531
Gianakos, L J/Television drama/79n1178
Gibbney, H J/Labor in/76n903
Gibbons, F/Catalogue of Italian/78n808
Gibbs, D A/Bibliography of studies/76n1293
Gibbs, J M/University of/76n823
Gibbs, R D/Chemotaxonomy of/75n1476
Gibson, A H/Artists of/76n935
Gibson, G D/Bibliography of discographies/79n970
Gibson, J/Wills and/75n437
Gibson, M J/Finding information/77n223
Gibson, P R/Yearbook of higher/75n661
Gibson, R/Jefferson Davis/79n420/Name and/79n419
Gidwani, N N/Comparative librarianship/75n256/Guide to reference/77n322
Gieck, K/Engineering formulas/78n1505
Giefer, G J/Sources of/77n1429/Water publications/77n1428
Giese, J/Multicultural educ/78n598
Giesecke, J/Health organizations/76n1539
Gifford, D/British comic/77n1169
Gifford, D/Notes for/75n1388
Gifis, S H/Law dictionary/76n511
Gifted student/Laubenfels/79n631
Gil de Montes, C/Cortina/Grosset/77n1099
Gilbert, C B/Best books/79n230
Gilbert, G/Collecting photographica/77n932
Gilbert, K D/Picture indexing/75n224
Gilbert, M/Atlas of Arab-/76n358/Jerusalem history/79n440/Jewish history/78n371
Gilded age, 1877-96/De Santis/75n357
Gildenberg, R F/Computer-output-/75n1770
Gilder, E/Dictionary of composers/79n963
Gildersleeve, T R/Organizing and/78n1524
Giles, H A/Glossary of reference/75n317
Gill, B/Motor sport/75n781
Gill, E R/Bibliography of Eric/75n72
Gill, J M/International register/79n1469
Gill, R/Magic as/78n637
Gillespie, G T/Catalogue of persons/75n1420
Gillespie, J T/Best books/79n230/Creating a/75n195/Model school/78n185/More junior-plots/79n229/Paperback books/79n229
Gillett, C/Rock almanac/77n979
Gillie, C/Longman companion/76n1261
Gillingham, A/Arms traffic/78n1555

Gillis, E J/Purchasing information/78n732
Gillis, F J/African music/77n962
Gillispie, C C/Dictionary of scientific/75n1439; 76n1329; 77n1299; 77n1300
Gilreath, C L/CAIN online/77n255
Ginger, A F/Human rights/75n475
Gingerich, M E/W H Auden/78n1165
Gingrich, A/Fishing in/75n760
Girls series books/79n1213
Gitler, I/Encyclopedia of jazz/78n915/Ice hockey/79n719/Jazz masters/75n1162
Give me yesterday: hist in song/Levy/76n1028
Gladstone, B/NY Times/75n1793
Gladstone, J/Air conditioning/75n1806
Glare, P G W/Oxford Latin/77n1095; 79n1144
Glasby, J S/Encyclopaedia of antibiotics/78n1438/Encyclopedia of alkaloids/79n1319
Glasheen, A/Third census/78n1177
Glass, G V/Evaluation studies/77n635
Glassman, J/National gd/76n952/New new/75n1034
Glassman, L/Utilizing resources/75n687
Glenn, L/Charles W./77n1249
Glenn, R W/Black rhetoric/77n1122
Glick, N B/Bowker annual/79n172
Glossaire de météorologie et de climatologie/Villeneuve/75n1570
Glossary hndbk for law enforcemt educ/Gunn/75n831
Glossary of . . .
  applied managemt and financial statistics/Broster/76n908
  art, architecture and design since 1945/Walker/78n789
  astronomy and astrophysics/Hopkins/77n1307
  automotive terminology/79n1552
  chemical terms/Hampel/77n1330
  conference terms: English, French, Arabic/76n1138
  environmental terms (terrestrial)/US Army/75n1534
  Faulkner's South/Brown/77n1202
  German and English managmt terms/Coveney/78n779
  indexing terms/Buchanan/77n170
  modern sailing terms/Rousmaniere/77n685
  molecular biology/Evans/76n1355
  reference on subjects connected with the Far East/Giles/75n317
  the environment/Brace/78n1342; 79n1394

Glossary of . . . (cont'd)
   transformational grammar/Ambrose-Grillet/
      79n1094
   words used in the dialect of Cheshire/
      Leigh/75n1258
Glover, H/Standard guide/79n1523
Glut, D F/Dracula book/76n1046
Gnarowski, M/Concise bibliog/79n1260
Gnirss, C/International bibliog reprints/78n41
GO, PEP, and POP! /Baeckler/77n211
Gocek, M A/Benedict Arnold/75n358/Orange County/75n379
Gochberg, H S/Follett vest-/79n1136
Godden, G A/British pottery/77n919
Godel, J B/Sources of construction/78n1517
Gods and heroes/Harnsberger/78n1016
Goeldner, C R/Bibliography of skiing/78n629/Travel research/78n742
Goetzman, R/James Anthony/79n432
Goff, F R/Incunabula in/75n64
Gohdes, C/Bibliographical gd study/77n1186
Gohn, J B/Kingsley Amis/77n1228
Going out in New York/Shepard/75n615
Goins, C R/Historical atlas/78n356
Gold, M J/Multicultural educ/78n598
Gold, R S/Comprehensive bibliog/77n1503
Gold, R S/Jazz talk/76n1025
Goldbeck, D & N/Dieter's companion/77n1494
Goldberg, L/Goldberg's diet/78n1473
Goldberg, R L/Systems approach/78n207
Goldberg's diet catalog/Goldberg/78n1473
Goldblatt, B/Baseball's best/79n706
Golden, R E/Flannery O'Connor/78n1123
Golden goodies/Propes/77n981
Golden oldies/Propes/75n1173
Golden picture dict/Ogle/78n1030
Goldfien, A/Review of medical/75n1657; 79n1502
Goldman, B/Reading and/79n887
Goldman, B A/Directory of unpublished/75n1600; 79n1420
Goldman, D & J J/Nothing new/75n946
Goldsack, P J/Jane's world/78n1548
Goldsmith, V F/Titles of/77n333; 78n9
Goldsmiths'-Kress Library of Economic Lit/77n768; 79n801
Goldstein, E/Gaylor/SIRS/76n325
Goldstein, G/Biological indicators/75n1528
Goldstein, H/Milestones to/79n327
Goldstein, R M/Movies for/75n1200
Goldstein, S/Library networks/75n139
Goldstein, S/Video in/78n248
Goldstein, S/Oldies but/78n916

Goldstein, W L/Teaching English/76n678
Goldstone, A/Bibliography of Arthur/75n1391/John Steinbeck/76n1249
Goldstone, H H/History preserved/75n607
Golesworthy, M/Encyclopaedia of cricket/76n766
Gollay, E/College guide/78n564
Gollnick, D M/Multicultural educ/78n541
Gomer's guides from the Atlantic to the Mississippi/Lewis/77n560
Gomer's guides from the Mississippi to the Pacific/Lewis/78n525
Gomez-Quinones, J/Chicana/77n440
González Ollé, F/Manual bibliográfico/79n1288
Gonzalez-Paz, E E/Héroes de/75n374
Gooch, B N S/Musical settings/77n954
Good, P K-E/Practical gd/76n1499
Good earth almanac/Balfour/76n1567
Good earth almanac survival bk/Gregory/75n723
Good Housekeeping . . .
   basic gardening techniques/Bailey/75n1697
   dictionary of symptoms/Gardner/77n1493
   guide to fixing things around the house/Liles/75n1794
   guide to medicines and drugs/Jones/79n1488
   woman's almanac/McDowell/78n670
Good reading/Weber/79n693
Good reading for poor readers/Spache/75n707
Goodall, D M/Horses of/75n1681
Goode, S H/Index to American/76n1191/Index to Commonwealth/77n1138; 77n1139/Population and/75n872; 76n813/Venereal disease/75n1614; 76n1517
Goodell, J S/Libraries and/76n112
Gooders, J/Great book/76n1419/Wildlife photography/75n1110
Goode's world atlas/Espenshade/79n585
Goodfellow catalog of wonderful things/Weills/78n875
Goodman, A H/Instrumental music/78n891
Goodman, E/Canadian writer's/79n1167
Goodman, F/Thesaurus of/76n593
Goodman, H G/Aspects of/76n381
Goodman, M B/William Burroughs/77n1201
Goodman, M M/Catalogue of history/77n1281
Goodman, R L/Indexed guide/75n1782
Goodman, R M/Lawyers desk/76n517
Goodman, S E/Handbook on contemporary/77n636
Goodrich, A/Enjoying the/75n1184

Goodrich, L C/Dictionary of Ming/77n398
Goodrum, C A/Library of/75n204
Goodwater, L/Women in/76n792
Goodwin, D/Crows of/77n1378/Pigeons and/78n1318
Gordan, J/Margaret Mead/78n678
Gordon, A J/Cumulated fiction/77n1176
Gordon, B L/Guide book/76n1435
Gordon, C/Atlantic alliance/79n552
Gordon, C/Dictionary of household/75n1798
Gordon, E/Pacific historical/77n388
Gordon, F S/Legal word/79n569
Gordon, J B/New gospel/77n955
Gordon, L W/On-campus/77n616
Gordon, T F/Gazetteer of/76n456
Gore, D/Bibliography for/75n244/Farewell to/77n205/Management problems/75n217/To know/79n194
Goren, C H/Goren's bridge/75n768
Goren's bridge complete/Goren/75n768
Gorer, R/Trees and/78n1492
Gorman, K A/Library operations/75n261
Gosselin, R E/Clinical toxicology/77n1485
Gotsick, P/Information for/77n815
Gottlieb, G/Early children's/77n70
Gottlieb, R/Publishing children's/79n1214
Gottschalk, L/Lafayette/76n317
Goudzwaard, M B/Treasurer's hndbk/78n722
Gough, C/Systems analysis/79n254
Gould, B G/Dow Jones-/75n914
Gould, F W/Grasses of/77n1364
Gould, K F/Popular names/77n115
Gould, S H/Russian-English/76n1333
Goulden, S L/Day by/79n403
Goulet, G/Women's yellow/75n847
Gourmet's dict of cheeses/77n1546
Government and the economy/Dawson/75n710
Government & the media in conflict/Knappman/75n494
Government contracts and grants for research/Scurlock/76n653
Government docs in the library lit 1909-74/Schorr/78n131
Government of Northern Ireland/Maltby/75n521
Government production prime contractors directory/77n824
Government publications: gd to bibliographic tools/Palic/77n108
Government ref books/Schorr/77n106; 79n125/Wynkoop/75n108
Government Studies and Systems, Inc./Improving state/78n173
Governors of Tennessee/Phillips/79n534

Governors of the states/Solomon/75n505
GPO sales publications ref file/US Superintendent of Documents/78n100
Graduate assistantship directory in the computer sciences/Assoc for Computing Machinery/75n673
Graduate programs and faculty in reading/Guthrie/77n618
Graduate thesis/Sugden/75n696
Grae, I/Nature's colors/75n1042
Graedon, J/People's pharmacy/78n1439
Graf, R F/Electronic databk/76n1630/Modern dictionary/79n1568/Reston ency/78n1395
Graff, H F/Modern researcher/78n322
Graham, J/Dictionary of computers/79n1560
Grammar of the film lang/Arijon/78n947
Grandbois, M/Cumulative index nursing/75n1640; 77n1492; 79n1479
Grandgent, C H/Companion to/76n1296
Granger's index to poetry, 1970-77/Smith/79n1201
Grannis, C B/Banned books/79n310
Grant, C A/Multicultural educ/78n598
Grant, F J/Manual of heraldry/77n485
Grant, M B/Indexes to/79n451
Grant, M McN/Directory of business/77n800
Grant, S/Trees of/79n1363/Wild flowers/79n1346
Grant, S A/Scholars' gd/78n309
Grant, W V/Digest of/76n600
Grant info system/Faculty alert/75n669
Grants/White/78n78
Grant's atlas of anatomy/Anderson/79n1443
Grants register/Turner/76n612
Graphic Artists Guild, directory/78n809
Grasses of Texas/Gould/77n1364
Graves, E B/Bibliography of English/77n408
Graves, J/Film literature/76n1063; 77n1014
Graviss, J D/Documentation standards/75n1773
Gray, B A/Uganda/79n362
Gray, D A/Science and/77n1286
Gray, E/New pronouncing/75n1277
Gray, H/Anatomy, descriptive/76n1530
Gray, H J/New dictionary/76n1350
Gray, L M/Access to/75n230
Gray, M H/Bibliography of discographies/79n970
Gray, R A/Science and/77n1286
Grayson, C T/Impeachment Congress/75n491/State info/78n461/Washington IV/76n478
Great American woodies and wagons/Narus/79n1555

Great black Americans/Richardson/77n434
Great bk of birds/Gooders/76n1419
Great Britain/Wiener/76n372
Great contemporary issues: black Africa/ Lynch/75n329
Great escape/Yee/75n722
Great gangster pictures/Parish/77n1011
Great internat'l disaster bk/Cornell/77n98
Great North American Indians/Dockstader/78n381
Great outdoors catalog/Oberrecht/78n621
Great perpetual learning machine/Blake/77n648
Great Pets!/Stein/77n1536
Great Plains Flora Assoc/Atlas of flora/78n1283
Great science fict pictures/Parish/78n962
Great Soviet encyclopedia/75n76
Great spy pictures/Parish/75n1198
Great treasury of Western thought/Adler/78n85
Great Western pictures/Parish/77n1012
Great world encyclopedia/77n74
Greek-English lexicon to the New Testament/ Hickie/79n1068
Greek-English lexicon of the New Testament/ Thayer/78n998
Greek experience/Melas/75n1020
Green, B K/Color of/76n752
Green, D B/Illustrated ency country/78n917
Green, E/British insurance/79n849
Green, J/Dictionary of golf/76n747
Green, J C/Minnesota birds/76n1420
Green, M I/Sigh of/79n1485
Green, S/Encyclopedia of musical/77n992
Green, T M/Historic families/76n443
Green, W/Observer's bk/76n1659/Observer's Soviet/77n1638/Observer's world/76n1660
Green thumb directory/Schroeder/78n1496
Green world/Stone Soup/77n1561
Greenberg, B/Index of scientific/76n94; 77n1296
Greenberg, B C/Greenberg's price/78n869; 78n870
Greenberg, D S/Science and gov/78n435
Greenberg, M/American political/77n507
Greenberg, R M/National register/77n387
Greenberg's price gd to Lionel trains/Greenberg/78n869; 78n870
Greene, D G/Bibliographia Oziana/77n1187
Greene, E/Multi-media approach/79n231/Storytelling/79n205
Greene, J S/Standard educ/75n658/Yearbook of higher/75n661

Greene, R E/Black defenders/75n813
Greenfeld, H/Books/77n49
Greenfield, E/Penguin stereo/79n971
Greenfield, S R/National directory/79n86
Greenhill, E S/Dictionary of art/75n998
Greenstein, C H/Dictionary of logical/79n1563
Greenstein, F I/Evolution of/79n524/Handbook of political/76n466
Greenwood, L L/KWIC index/75n1665
Greenwood, N N/Index of vibrational/79n1323
Greenwood, V D/Researcher's gd/75n416
Gregg, D W/Life and/75n972
Gregg ref manual/Sabin/78n718
Gregory, M/Good earth/75n723
Gregory, R W/Anniversaries and/76n1108
Greisman, B/How to run/75n891
Grenville, J A S/Major internat'l/75n533
Grieb, L/Operas of/76n1008
Grieder, T/Acquisitions/79n245
Grier, B/Lesbiana/78n674
Grieve, B J/How to know/76n1387
Grieves, F L/International law/76n1453
Griffin, A/Motorcycles/75n740
Griffin, T K/Pelican gd/75n608
Griffith, H W/Drug information/79n1497
Griffiths, J F & M J/Bibliography of urban/75n1529
Grimes, G H/Reference resources/77n266
Grimwade, A G/London goldsmiths/77n899
Grimwood-Jones, D/Arab Islamic/78n278
Grinstein, A/Index of psychoanalytic/76n1503/Sigmund Freud's/78n1363
Grisham, R A/Encyclopedia of US/76n829; 79n96
Grobani, A/Guide to baseball/76n702/Guide to football/76n736
Grogan, D/Science and/77n1282
Grogg, S L/American film/77n1004; 79n1029
Grolle, C G/Electronic technician's/75n1783
Grollenberg, L H/Penguin shorter/79n1067
Grollig, F X/Serial publications/75n869
Grommon, A H/Reviews of/77n653
Groom, A J R/International relations/79n553
Gropp, A E/Bibliography of Latin/77n339
Gross, C/Bibliography of English/77n408
Gross, D C/1,001 questions/79n1062
Gross, J S/Concise desk/77n801
Gross, R W F/Handbook of chemical/78n1255
Gross, W/Market segmentation/79n838
Grosser, P E/Causes and/79n437
Grosset and Dunlap's all-sports world record book/Neft/77n665
Grosset starter picture dict/77n1076

Grossfeld, B/Bibliography of Targum/79n1049
Grossinger, T/Book of gadgets/75n92
Grossman, H J/Grossman's gd/75n1673; 78
  n1456/Manual on terminology/75n1590
Grossman, M/Quick reference/75n1632
Grossman's gd to wines, spirits, and beers/
  Grossman/75n1673; 78n1456
Grotpeter, J J/Historical dictionary/76n255
Grotz, G/Antique restorer's/78n836
Ground water/van der Leeden/76n1475
Ground water pollution/Summers/75n1527
Grounds maintenance hndbk/Conover/78
  n1490
Group for the Advancement of Psychiatry/
  Index of publications/75n1602
Group work in the helping professions/Zimpfer/77n1444
Grove, P S/New Mexico/76n22/Nonprint
  media/76n137
Grover, P/Wyndham Lewis/79n1247
Grow, L/Old house/78n852
Growing exotic plants indoors/Menage/76
  n1596
Growing wildflowers/Sperka/75n1708
Grumm, P/Choice/77n198; 79n179
Grun, B/Timetables of/76n305
Grundman, C/NY Times/76n1135
Grunfeld, F V/Games of/76n743
Gruson, E S/Checklist of world's/77n1379
Grzegorczyk, D/Handbook of plastics/75n1784
Grzimek, B/Grzimek's animal/75n1523; 76
  n1403; 76n1404; 76n1405; 76n1406;
  76n1407/Grzimek's encyclopedia ecology/
  78n1344/Grzimek's ency ethology/78
  n1313/Grzimek's ency evolution/78n1274
Grzimek's animal life encyclopedia . . .
  insects/Grzimek/76n1404
  lower animals/Grzimek/76n1403
  mammals II/Grzimek/76n1406
  mammals III/Grzimek/76n1407
  mollusks and echinoderms/Grzimek/75n1523
  reptiles/Grzimek/76n1405
Grzimek's encyclopedia of . . .
  ecology/Grzimek/78n1344
  ethology/Grzimek/78n1313
  evolution/Grzimek/78n1274
Guardian directory of pressure groups and representative associations/78n478
Gübelin, E/Color treasury/77n1433
Guenther, P/Book review/79n346
Guerry, H/Bibliography of philosophical/78
  n1000
Gueulette, D/Media and/77n577
Guffey, G R/Concordance to English/75n1393

Guiana Maroons/Price/78n677
Guide and bibliog to research on Yugoslavs in
  the US & Canada/Eterovich/77n448
Guide and key to Alabama trees/Davis/77
  n1366
Guide bk of . . .
  English coins/Bressett/77n904
  Mexican coins/Buttrey/78n843
  US coins/Yeoman/78n848
Guide bk to the marine fishes of Rhode
  Island/Gordon/76n1435
Guide-bk to the missions of Calif/Camphouse/
  76n545
Guide des sources de l'histoire des etats-unis
  dans les archives françaises/78n367
Guide for . . .
  dating early published music/Krummel/
    75n1118
  improving visualized instruction/Dwyer/
    75n711
  the conversion of school libraries into
    media centres/79n210
Guide to . . .
  all Mexico/Wilhelm/75n631
  alternative colleges and universities/Blaze/
    76n643
  alternative periodicals/Carnahan/79n111
  American educ'l directories/Klein/76
    n582
  American Indian docs in the Congressional
    Serial Set/Johnson/78n382
  American lit from Emily Dickinson to the
    present/Callow/78n1115
  American lit from its beginnings through
    Walt Whitman/Callow/78n1116
  American scientific and technical directories/Klein/77n1284
  American trade catalogs 1744-1900/
    Romaine/78n703
America's Indians, ceremonies, reservations, and museums/Marquis/75n806
Anthony Trollope/Hardwick/75n1405
antique collecting/Coombs/79n911
aquarium fishes/76n1559
art resources in Los Angeles/Hugo/78n792
atlases suppl/Alexander/78n510
backpacking in the US/Meves/78n620
Barsoom/Roy/78n1135
baseball literature/Grobani/76n702
basic info sources in engineering/Mount/
  78n1500
basic info sources in English lit/Doyle/
  77n1220
basic info sources in the visual arts/
  Muehsam/79n888

Guide to ... (cont'd)
- basic ref materials for Canadian libraries/ Henderson/79n180
- bird finding east of the Mississippi/Pettingill/78n1320
- bird-watching in Europe/Ferguson-Lees/ 77n1376
- buying or selling a business/Hansen/76 n866
- buying plants/Rottenberg/78n1495
- California wines/Melville/77n1520
- career education/Lederer/75n657; 77n629
- Chinese poetry and drama/Bailey/75n1413
- Chinese prose/Paper/75n1414
- coastal fishes of Georgia and nearby states/ Dahlberg/76n1434
- consumer services/78n747
- Cretan antiquities/Davaras/77n349
- critical reviews of US fiction, 1870-1910/ Eichelberger/75n1341
- critical reviews, pt II: the musical/Salem/ 78n940
- current British journals/Woodworth/75n28
- dance in film/Parker/78n1038
- diagnostic procedures/French/76n1529
- drug information/Sewell/78n1443
- ecology info and organizations/Burke/77 n1403
- educational and learning aids/Meyer/78 n594
- educational programs in noncollegiate organizations/77n617
- English and Amer lit/Bateson/78n1088
- ethnic museums, libraries, and archives in the US/Wynar/79n446
- ethnohistorical sources/Cline/76n809
- federal archives relating to Africa/79n349
- federal career lit/US Civil Serv Commission/ 77n596
- federal funds for elementary and secondary education/Hoffman/76n662
- federal programs for historic preservation, 1976 suppl/National Trust for Historic Preservation/78n352
- fishes of the temperate Atlantic Coast/Ursin/ 79n1378
- fluorescence literature/Passwater/76n1352
- football literature/Grobani/76n736
- foreign genealogical research/Wellauer/77 n452
- foreign language courses and dictionaries/ Walford/79n1092
- fossil man/Day/79n784

Guide to ... (cont'd)
- four-year college majors/76n613
- gas chromatography lit/Signeur/76n1346
- geographical bibliographies & ref wks in Russian or on the Soviet Union/Harris/ 76n522
- global giving/Berryman/77n712
- graduate studies in Great Britain/Tomlinson/76n665
- graduate study in economics and agric'l economics/Owen/79n661
- Hungarian studies/Bakó/75n304
- Illinois library resources/Downs/75n18
- improvisation: for church organists/Conely/ 76n999
- independent study through correspondence instruction/76n621
- indexed periodicals in religion/Regazzi/ 76n1075
- Indian periodical lit (soc sci & humanities)/ Jain/76n35
- Jane Austen/Hardwick/75n1381
- Japanese drama/Pronko/75n1178
- Japanese poetry/Rimer/77n1272
- Jewish hist under Nazi impact/Robinson/ 75n398
- library research in public admin/Simpson/ 77n852
- local historical material in the libraries of South Central NY state/77n392
- local occupational info/US Dept of Labor/ 77n845
- Long Island news media/Meyer/75n1301
- magazine and serial agents/Katz/77n199
- manuscripts/Harris/75n380
- marine coastal plankton and marine invertebrate larvae/Smith/79n1381
- medical mathematics/Franklin/75n1629
- microforms in print/Walsh/79n36
- middle states schools in Delaware, District of Columbia, Maryland, Puerto Rico, Canal Zone, Virgin Islands, overseas/ Crawford/76n656
- middle states schools in New Jersey/ Crawford/76n657
- middle states schools in New York/Crawford/76n658
- middle states schools in Pennsylvania/ Crawford/76n659
- mineral identification/Kohland/79n1421
- Mormon diaries and autobiographies/ Bitton/78n971
- national practices in Western Europe/75 n890

Guide to . . . (cont'd)
   natural cosmetics/Krochmal/75n1677
   newspaper indexes in New England/79n22
   non-sexist children's bks/Adell/77n1142
   North American passenger ships/Miller/79n1586
   Oriental classics/de Bary/76n1187
   periodicals in educ and its academic disciplines/Camp/76n585
   personal finance/Stillman/76n878
   play selection/Mersand/76n1034
   Polish libraries and archives/Lewanski/76n215
   political platforms/Chester/79n519
   professional developmt opportunities for college and univ administrators/Irwin/76n648
   programs in linguistics/77n1063
   prose fiction in the *Tatler* and the *Spectator*/Evans/78n1163
   psychologists and their concepts/Nordby/76n1504
   public gardens/78n526
   recurrent and special governmental statistics/US Bureau of the Census/77n752
   reference books/Sheehy/77n14
   reference books for school media centers/1974-75 suppl/Wynar/77n234
   reference material/Walford/77n15; 79n4
   reference materials on India/Gidwani/77n322
   reference sources in the computer sciences/Carter/75n273
   reprints/Davis/79n37
   research collections in microform in the Univ of Toronto Library/Wagle/76n143
   research in American library hist/Harris/76n223
   resources for the study of the recent hist of the US in the libraries of the Univ of Iowa, the State Historical Soc of Iowa & in the Herbert Hoover Presidential Library/Swigger/78n354
   restaurants of greater Miami/Steiman/78n530
   reviews of bks from and abt Hispanic America/Matos/77n341; 77n342
   selected manuscript collections in the Univ of Arkansas Library/Sizer/77n355
   selected ref materials: Russia and East Europe/Zalewski/75n310
   self-sufficiency/Seymour/78n1447
   selling a business/Rubel/78n739

Guide to . . . (cont'd)
   shells/Oliver/76n974
   social sci resources in women's studies/Oakes/79n758
   sources in educ'l media and tech/Taggart/76n686
   sources of consumer info/Thomas/75n935
   sources of educ'l info/Woodbury/77n584
   special issues and indexes of periodicals/Devers/77n34
   state historic preservation programs/Abel/78n353
   subjects & concepts in picture bk format/Yonkers Public Library/75n1348
   summer camps and summer schools/76n661
   teaching abt computers in secondary schools/Spencer/75n716
   the architecture of Minnesota/Gebhard/79n890
   theses and dissertations/Reynolds/76n583
   trade and securities statistics/Balachandran/78n727
   two-year college majors and careers/76n649
   UN organization, documentation, & publishing/Hajnal/79n554
   US Army museums and historic sites/US Dept of the Army/77n1646
   US gov maps/Andriot/78n1355
   venture capital sources/Rubel/75n957; 78n753
   Virginia military organizations in the American Revolution/Sanchez-Saavedra/79n1596
   women's publishing/Joan/79n764
   world commodity markets/Reidy/78n728; 79n831
   Yugoslav libraries and archives/Jovanović/76n214
Guide to the . . .
   architecture of Washington, D.C./Cox/75n1017
   archives of labor hist and urban affairs/Pflug/75n979
   birds of Panama/Ridgely/77n1385
   birds of Trinidad and Tobago/ffrench/75n1504
   birds of Venezuela/De Schauensee/79n1372
   black apple/Ford/79n600
   British cathedrals/Houghton/75n1018
   craft world/Brabec/76n949

Guide to the ... (cont'd)
- Dag Hammarskjold Collection on developing nations/Kamenetsky/78n273
- Edward Christopher Weatherly papers/Mitterling/76n349
- evaluation of educ'l experiences in the armed services/Miller/76n650
- genera of native and commonly introduced ferns and seed plants of eastern North America/Batson/79n1341
- grading of US coins/Brown/76n965
- Harper M. Orahood papers/Mitterling/76n350
- Henry Moore Teller papers/Mitterling/76n351
- historic places of the American Revolution/US Natl Park Service/75n601
- holdings of the Stanford Univ libraries on middle American anthropology/Breedlove/75n864
- life of Horace Walpole/Lewis/75n1407
- literature for the industrial microbiologist/Hahn/75n1459
- literature of astronomy/Seal/78n1236
- literature of soc change/Bundy/78n646
- literature of student financial aid/Davis/79n629
- manuscript collection of the Tamiment Library/79n517
- manuscripts in the National Maritime Museum/Knight/79n408
- medicinal plants of the US/Korchmal/75n1466
- National Archives of the US/US Natl Archives and Records Service/75n363
- National Trust in Devon & Cornwall/Laws/79n616
- official publications of the European communities/Jeffries/79n119
- recommended country inns of New England/Chapin/75n604
- research collections of the NY Public Library/Williams/77n194
- sources of US military history/Higham/76n1675
- Soviet navy/Breyer/79n1599
- study of the USA/US Library of Congress/77n338
- use of books & libraries/Gates/75n138
- vascular flora of Illinois/Mohlenbrock/77n1354
- work of Greene and Greene/Makinson/76n939

Guidebook of electronic circuits/Markus/75n1785
Guidebook of Franklin Mint issues/Culver/76n967
Guidebook to historic western Pennsylvania/Swetnam/78n360
Guidebook to pension planning/78n748
Guidelines for AV materials and services for large public libraries/American Library Association/76n144
Guides to educ'l media/Rufsvold/78n600
Guido, M/Sicily/78n320
Guild, B/Alaskan mushroom/78n1300
Guilford, N/Oregon biog/77n390
Guillot, G/Book of ballet/77n994
Guinea-Bissau and Cape Verde Islands/McCarthy/79n353
Guinness book of ...
- Olympic records/McWhirter/76n697
- phenomenal happenings/McWhirter/77n99
- world records/McWhirter/77n100
- young recordbreakers/McWhirter/77n101

Guinness sports record book/McWhirter/77n666
Gulf handbook/79n614
Gulf Publishing Co dict of business and sci/Tver/75n886
Gullans, C/Bibliography of published/75n1353
Gun collector's fact bk/Steinwedel/76n972
Gun collector's hndbk of values/Chapel/78n850
Gun trader's guide/Wahl/76n759
Gunn, C R/World gd/77n1349
Gunn, D W/American and/75n1308/Mexico in/75n1311
Gunn, R S/Glossary handbook/75n831
Gunn, W W/Bibliography of naval/75n1524
Guns and ammo/75n777
Guns illustrated/Murtz/77n690
Gunter, P A Y/Henri Bergson/76n1107
Günter Grass/O'Neill/77n1264
Gupta, S M/From Daityas/75n1239
Guralnik, D B/Webster's new world dict/76n1125; 76n1126; 79n1105/Webster's new world large/79n1106
Gurland, R/Common market/76n865
Gushee, C H/Cost of/77n822
Gustafson, E A/Current drug/78n1436
Gustafson, W E/Pakistan and/77n330/Sources on/76n360
Gutgesell, H P/Atlas of pediatric/79n1446

Guth, D J/Late-medieval/77n409
Guthrie, J T/Graduate programs/77n618
Guthrie, K M/Process plant/75n1810
Guttag, J/Julius Guttag/75n1065
Guyton, T L/Unionization/76n177

H. P. Lovecraft companion/Shreffler/78n1145
Habig, M A/Saints of/76n1092
Habitat gd to birding/McElroy/75n1506
Hackett, A P/80 years/78n37
Hadlock, R/Jazz masters/75n1163
Haensch, G/Dictionary of agriculture/78n1451/ Dictionary of biology/78n1275
Hagan, L/Bibliography on atomic/78n1267
Hagendorf, S/Tax guide/77n854
Hager, A M/Pacific historical/77n388
Hahn, P A/Guide to literature/75n1459
Haiek, J R/Mideast business/79n818
Haight, A L/Banned books/79n310
Haight, T R/Mass media/79n1166
Hail, Columbia/Larkin/76n1048
Haimes, N/Helping others/75n841
Hajducki, S M/Railway atlas/76n1672
Hajnal, P I/Guide to UN/79n554
Hake, T/Encyclopedia of political/75n1095
Halberstadt, A/Guide to Long/75n1301
Hale, G/World atlas/75n1695
Hale, W S/Films/75n1196/Your introduction/ 78n59
Halevy, R/Knitting and/78n878
Haley, F/Directory of social/77n300/Ethnic studies/77n418
Haliburton, G/Historical dict Lesotho/78n286
Hall, A/Wild food/77n1350
Hall, C M/Atlantic bridge/75n417
Hall, C S/Guide to psychologists/76n1504
Hall, H W/Science fict/76n1206/SFBRI: science fict/78n1106
Hall, J/Dictionary of subjects/76n922
Hall, J L/On-line information/78n242
Hall, P/Penguin world/76n528
Hallam, J/Ghosts' who's/78n1377
Haller, M/Book collector's/77n63
Halliwell, L/Filmgoer's book/75n1191/Filmgoer's companion/76n1052; 79n1023/Halliwell's film/78n958
Halliwell's film guide/Halliwell/78n958
Hallmark, C L/Auto electronics/76n1613/Complete auto/76n1614
Halls of fame/Jones/78n75
Hallucinogenic and poisonous mushroom fld guide/Menser/78n1301
Hallucinogenic plants/Schultes/78n1281

Halpenny, F G/Dictionary of Canadian/76 n109
Halperin, E G/Causes and/79n437
Halperin, J/Plots and/77n1229
Halpern, F M/International classified/76n50
Halsey, R S/Classical music/77n965
Halsey, W D/Collier's ency/79n71/Macmillan dictionary/76n1121/Magic world/79 n1111/Merit students/79n75
Halstead, B W/Poisonous and/79n1380/ Tropical fish/76n1558
Hamburg, M/Library planning/75n213
Hamburger, R/Illustrated gd international/ 77n259/Index of festschriften/75n1217
Hamer, F/Potter's dict/77n891
Hamilton, B/Popular and/79n999/Record albums/79n974
Hamilton, B A/Multitype library/78n120
Hamilton, C/Big name/75n1096
Hamilton, D/Big name/75n1096
Hamilton, G E/Catalogue of translator's/77 n766
Hamilton, M C/Directory of educ'l/76n579/ Education journals/76n586
Hamilton, R W/Oxford Bible/75n1232
Hamilton, W B/Macmillan book/79n625
Hamilton, W R/Larousse guide/78n1359
Hamilton-Edwards, G/In search/75n438
Hamlin, C H/They went/75n418
Hamlin, M/Celebrating with/78n191
Hamlin Garland and the critics/Bryer/75 n1359
Hamlyn French dictionary/78n1055
Hamlyn German dictionary/78n1059
Hamlyn Italian dictionary/78n1061
Hamlyn Spanish dictionary/78n1069
Hammelmann, H/Book illustrators/77n66
Hammer, D P/Information age/77n155
Hammerman, G M/Documentary hist/75n1835/ People and/75n368
Hammerton, J A/Concise universal/77n121
Hammond, D/Pictorial price/79n914
Hammond, J R/Herbert George/79n1256
Hammond, W K/What's in/75n449
Hammond ambassador world atlas/79n586
Hammond Bicentennial road atlas/76n549
Hammond internat'l world atlas/75n577; 77 n544
Hammond medallion world atlas/79n587
Hammond new contemporary world atlas/78 n514
Hammond's atlas of the Bible lands/Frank/ 79n1066
Hampel, C A/Glossary of chemical/77n1330

Hamsa, C F/Bookman's guide/78n49
Hanchey, M M/Abstracts and/75n1432
Hand, S/Collector's ency/79n925
Handbook for . . .
  chemical technicians/Strauss/77n1335
  contemporary photography/Gassan/75n1109
  electronics engineering technicians/Kaufman/77n1593
  professional divers/Titcombe/75n787
  recreation/US Children's Bureau/77n667
  recruiting at the traditional black colleges/Beaumont/75n653
  scholars/van Leunen/79n132
  storytellers/Bauer/78n180
  translators/Fuller/75n1249
Handbook in diagnostic teaching/Mann/76n690
Handbook of . . .
  abnormal psychology/Eysenck/75n1589
  academic evaluation/Dressel/77n633
  adhesives/Skeist/78n1541
  African names/Madubuike/78n424
  aging and the soc sciences/Binstock/78n648
  American English spelling/Deighton/79n1124
  American literature/Day/77n1189
  American minorities/Miller/77n419
  attic red-figured vases/Hoppin/75n403
  biblical criticism/Soulen/78n997
  black librarianship/Josey/78n142
  chemical lasers/Gross/78n1255
  chemistry and physics/Weast/76n1344
  circuit analysis languages and techniques/Jensen/77n1592
  comparative librarianship/Simsova/76n217
  common poisonings in children/US Food and Drug Admin/78n1431
  components for electronics/Harper/78n1533
  concrete engineering/Fintel/75n1759
  corporate soc responsibility/76n898
  cross-national MMPI research/Butcher/77n1447
  data processing for libraries/Hayes/76n230
  denominations in the US/Mead/76n1087
  distinctively American coats of arms/Johnson/75n441
  early American sheet music/Dichter/79n1001
  educational admin/Stoops/77n639
  electronic circuit designs/Lenk/77n1595
  electronic instrumentation, testing, and troubleshooting/Robinson/75n1788

Handbook of . . . (cont'd)
  engineering fundamentals/Eshback/77n1566
  English/Stratton/77n1088
  English-German idioms and useful expressions/Stern/75n1271
  environmental civil engineering/Zilly/76n1619
  environmental data on organic chemicals/Verschueren/79n1322
  food preparation/76n1571
  freshwater fishery biology, Centrarchid fishes/Carlander/78n1325
  Gilbert and Sullivan/Moore/76n1009
  highway engineering/Baker/76n1662
  housing systems for designers and developers/Cutler/75n1764
  hydraulics for the solution of hydraulic engineering problems/Brater/77n1604
  industrial and organizational psychology/Dunnette/77n1448
  industrial noise control/Faulkner/77n1606
  international data on women/Boulding/78n669
  international direct marketing/Dillon/77n808
  iron meteorites/Buchwald/77n1432
  Japanese art/Tsuda/78n797
  labor statistics/US Bureau of Labor Statistics/77n843
  Latin American studies no. 35/Stewart/75n296
  leadership/Stogdill/75n797
  library regulations/Murphy/78n146
  literature for the flute/Pellerite/79n993
  major Soviet nationalities/Katz/76n385
  manpower statistics for South Dakota/Bergman/75n974
  marine science/Smith/76n1470
  marketing research/Ferber/75n923
  mathematical calculations for sci students and researchers/Assaf/75n1440
  medical specialties/Wechsler/77n1490
  medical treatment/Chatton/75n1627
  micromethods for the biological sciences/Keleti/75n1462
  middle American Indians/Harrison/77n749
  modern accounting/Davidson/78n723
  non-prescription drugs/78n1440
  North American birds/Palmer/77n1384
  obstetrics and gynecology/Benson/75n1626
  ocular pharmacology/Smith/76n1554
  operational amplifier circuit design/Stout/77n1601

Handbook of ... (cont'd)
  operations research/Moder/79n820
  optics/Driscoll/79n1333
  pediatrics/Silver/77n1486
  pictorial symbols/Modley/78n812
  plastics and elastomers/Harper/77n1614
  plastics in electronics/Grzegorczyk/75n1784
  poisoning/Dreisbach/75n1628
  political sci/Greenstein/76n466
  precision engineering: forming processes/Davidson/75n1804
  precision engineering: production engineering/Davidson/75n1805
  private schools/77n601
  pseudonyms and personal nicknames: 1st suppl/Sharp/76n451
  psychiatric therapies/Masserman/75n1593
  psychiatry/Solomon/75n1597
  sampling for auditing and accounting/Arkin/75n904
  solar and wind energy/Hickok/76n1461
  stainless steels/Peckner/78n1544
  swimming pool construction, maintenance, and sanitation/Cross/75n1758
  symbols in Christian art/Sill/76n926
  tables for applied engineering sci/Bolz/75n1713
  tables of functions for applied optics/Levi/76n1351
  the birds of Europe, the Middle East, and North Africa/Cramp/79n1371
  the birds of India and Pakistan, Bangladesh, Nepal, Sikkim, Bhutan and Sri Lanka/Ali/77n1373
  the Indians of Calif/Kroeber/78n683
  the martial arts and self-defense/Logan/76n768
  the nutritional content of foods/Watt/77n1552
  thick film hybrid microelectronics/Harper/75n1786
  20th century opera/Teasdale/78n914
  US coins/Yeoman/77n917; 79n921
  veterinary drugs/Rossoff/76n1553
  veterinary surgical instruments and glossary of surgical terms/Hurov/79n1543
  water resources and pollution control/Gehm/77n1422
  wealth management/Barnes/78n729
  work, organization, and society/Dubin/77n792
  wrestling terms and holds/Clayton/75n788
  zoning and land use ordinances/Crawford/75n860

Handbook on ...
  contemporary educ/Goodman/77n636
  environmental monitoring/Cross/75n1537
  international study for US nationals/Lowenstein/78n574
  international study for US nationals/Young/77n589
  the 1970 fed drug act/Bogomolny/76n1549
  the primary identification of revolvers and semiautomatic pistols/Millard/76n756
Handbook to plants in Victoria/Willis/75n1472
Handbuch der musikalischen Litteratur: reprint of 1817 ed and 10 suppls, 1818-1827/Whistling/76n987
Handel, B/National directory/75n1185; 76n1043; 79n1014; 79n1015
Handicapped funding directory/Eckstein/79n1507
Handley, W/Industrial safety/78n1538
Handling special materials in libraries/Kaiser/75n248
Handloader's digest/Amber/76n754
Handsfield, H & L/Dick's ency/76n1638
Handy, W J/Twentieth century/75n1320
Handy home medical adviser and concise medical ency/Fishbein/75n1648
Handy key to your "National Geographics"/Underhill/78n1278
Handyman's ency, American ed/Waugh/78n1536
Hanff, P E/Bibliographica Oziana/77n1187
Hanham, H J/Bibliography of British/77n410
Hanifi, M J/Historical and/77n317
Hanna, J P/Complete layman's/75n558
Hanna, P B/People make/79n289
Hannaford, C/Promotion planning/76n200
Hannah, H W/Beuscher's law/76n1557
Hanneman, A/Supplement to Ernest/76n1239
Hanney, P W/Rodents/76n1444
Hannigan, J A/Media center/79n211
Hansen, J M/Guide to buying/76n866
Hansen, S J/New Mexico/76n22
Hanson, A O/Executive and/77n849
Hanson, C A/Dissertations on/77n361
Hanzak, J/Encyclopedia of animals/76n1408
Happy bookers/Armour/77n149
Harbaugh, J W/Geology field/75n1564
Harbin, E/Blue and/79n948
Harbin, G/Early childhood/78n595
Harburn, G/Atlas of optical/77n1338
Hardaway, M C/Central America/76n558
Harder, K B/Illustrated dict place/77n551
Hardesty, L L/Use of/79n195

Hardgrove, C E/Mathematics library/79n1311
Harding, A/Vintage car/78n865
Harding, C/Latin America/76n280
Harding, E/Hamlin Garland/75n1359
Harding, M/Make it/79n945
Hardwick, G B/Fundamentals of/76n1572
Hardwick, M/Bernard Shaw/75n1401/Guide to Anthony/75n1405/Guide to Jane/75n1381
Hardy, C C/Dun &/75n915; 76n855
Hardy, D E/Catalog of Diptera/78n1328
Hardy, S P/Colonial families/75n419
Harf, M A/Encyclopedia of Ohio/79n90
Hargreaves, V B/Tropical marine/79n701
Hargreaves-Mawdsley, R/Bristol and/79n485
Harkness Collection in the LC/US Library of Congress/75n313
Harleston, R M/Administration of/75n214
Harman, G S/Politics of/76n580
Harman, H E/Fielding's guide/75n620
Harman, J/Fielding's guide/75n620
Harmon, G L/Scholar's market/76n1194
Harmon, K R/National prison/76n778
Harmon, M/Select bibliog/79n1280
Harmon, R B/Annotated gd works/78n1181/Developing the/77n491/Political sci/75n460/Political science/77n492/Understanding Ernest/78n1142
Harmon, S M/Scholar's market/76n1194
Harnsberger, C T/Gods and/78n1016
Harper, C A/Handbook of components/78n1533/Handbook of plastics/77n1614/Handbook of thick/75n1786
Harper, H/Episcopalian's dict/76n1083
Harper dict of contemporary usage/Morris/76n1130
Harper dict of modern thought/Bullock/78n83
Harper's dict of Hinduism/Stutley/78n983
Harper's ency of US history, 458 A.D. to 1915/Lossing/76n323
Harper's lost reviews/Eichelberger/77n1184
Harrah, B K & D F/Alternate sources/76n1454/Conservation-ecology/76n1465/Funeral service/77n704
Harrar, E S/How to know/75n1467
Harriet Beecher Stowe/Ahston/78n1149/Hildreth/77n1214
Harris, A/Biographical history/75n420
Harris, C D/Bibliography of geography/77n548/Guide to geographical/76n522
Harris, C M/Developmental tasks/77n651
Harris, C M/Dictionary of architecture/76n938/Historic architecture/78n801/Shock and/77n1607

Harris, E E/Music education/79n959
Harris, K/Guide to manuscripts/75n380
Harris, K H/Notes from/78n179/Special child/77n216
Harris, M/Field gd to birds/76n1421
Harris, M H/Advances in/78n140/Age of/76n209/American library/79n328/Guide to research/76n223/History of libraries/77n280
Harris, W H/New Columbia/76n60
Harris Michigan manufacturers industrial directory/77n827
Harrison, C/Field gd to nests/77n1380
Harrison, C E/Women's movement/76n793
Harrison, F L/New college/77n969; 79n968
Harrison, H H/Field gd birds'/76n1422
Harrison, H S/Houses/75n1765
Harrison, I E/Traditional medicine/77n1462
Harrison, J H/Settlers by/76n434
Harrison, L H/Hollywood on/79n975
Harrison, M A L/Handbook of middle/77n749
Harrison, M C/Data-structures/75n1771
Harrison, R/Warwick guide/78n768
Harrison, S P/Mokilese-English/78n1063
Harrod, L M/Indexers on/79n331/Librarians' glossary/79n160
Harryman, E/Terminology of/79n1175
Ḥarsūsi lexicon and English-Ḥarsūsi word list/Johnstone/79n1139
Hart, C/Concordance to Finnegans/76n1276
Hart, D V/Thailand/78n301
Hart, F D/French's index/75n1630
Hart, H H/Animal kingdom/79n901/Catalog of unusual/75n100/Chairs/79n923/Dining and/79n902/Picture ref/77n883; 78n813/Weather/79n1416
Hart, J/Walking softly/78n617
Hart, M H/100/79n397
Hart, T L/Instruction in/79n212/Multi-media indexes/76n679
Hartdegen, S J/Nelson's complete/78n994
Harte, B/Contemporary literary/75n1319
Harting, E C/Literary tour . . . England/77n1223/Literary tour . . . US/79n601
Hartnoll, P/Who's who George/78n1173/Who's who Shaw/76n1287
Hartsuch, P J/Think metric/75n1715
Hartung, A E/Manual of writings/77n1224
Hartwig, G W/Student Africanist's/76n246
Harvard College Library/Catalogue of books/76n58
Harvard concise dict of music/Randel/79n966
Harvard concordance to Shakespeare/Spevack/75n1400

Authors and Titles—87

Harvard gd to American hist/Freidel/75n355
Harvard University. Library/Ancient hist/76n295/British hist/76n369
Harvard Univ dict catalogue of the Byzantine Collection of the Dumbarton Oaks Research Library/76n294
Harvey, A F/Bibliography of microwave/78n1266
Harvey, J F/Comparative and/79n314
Harvey, J M/Specialised info/77n237/Statistics Africa/79n789
Harvey, M G/Marketing and/77n807
Harvey, S/Information economics/77n292/Online age/77n293
Harwell, A J & R M/Crafts for/75n1035
Harzfeld, L A/Periodical indexes/79n345
Haskell, J D/Massachusetts/77n391
Haskin, L L/Wild flowers/78n1291
Haslam, M/Marks and/78n829
Hassall, A G & W O/Treasures from/77n29
Hastenrath, S/Climatic atlas/79n1414
Hastings, J/Dictionary of New/75n1229
Hatch, J V/Black playwrights/79n1009
Hatje, G/1601 decorating/75n1104
Haunted Britain/Coxe/75n622
Haushalter, M M/Stories to/75n198
Haven, R/Samuel Taylor/77n1230
Havighurst, A F/Modern England/77n411
Haviland, V/Children's books/79n232/Children's lit/79n233/Samuel Langhorne/78n1151
Havlice, P P/Index to literary/76n1192/Popular song/76n1026/Suppl/79n980/World painting/78n816
Hawai'i garden tropical exotics/Clay/78n1488
Hawai'i garden tropical shrubs/Clay/78n1489
Hawaiian lang imprints, 1822-99/Judd/79n389
Hawes, G R/College on/79n632/New American/78n565
Hawkes, J/Atlas of ancient/75n402/Atlas of early/78n327
Hawkin, M/Who's who UN/76n471
Hawkins, D T/Auger electron/79n1316/Physical and/78n1240
Hawkins, J N/Teacher's resource/77n340
Hawley, G G/Condensed chemical/78n1248/Glossary of chemical/77n1330
Hay, D/New Cambridge/76n288
Hay, R/Color dict/76n1587/Dictionary of house/75n1701/Practical gardening/79n1540
Hayashi, T/Index to Arthur/77n1210/John Steinbeck/77n1213/Study gd Steinbeck/75n1368

Haycox, B J & S W/Melvin Ricks'/79n390
Haycox, S W/Melvin Ricks'/79n390
Hayes, G P/Almanac of world/76n1677/World military/75n1844
Hayes, R M/Handbook of data/76n230/System for/75n232
Hayes, S/Environmental concerns/78n1338
Hayne, D M/Dictionary of Canadian/76n109
Hays, T E/Anthropology in/77n739
Hazeltine, M E/Anniversaries and/76n1108
Hazen, A T/Bibliography of Horace/75n1406
Hazen, B S/Dell encyclopedia/75n1682
Hazlitt, W C/Coinage of/76n968
HBJ school dictionary/79n1109
Head, S W/Bibliography of African/76n1164
Headley, R K/Cambodian-English/79n1129
Headstrom, R/Beetles of/78n1329
Healey, B J/Gardener's guide/76n1588
Healey, J S/John E/75n251
Health/Ash/77n1454
Health and medical economics/Ackroyd/79n795
Health manpower/American Hospital Assn/75n1613; 77n1463
Health organizations of the US, Canada and internationally/Wasserman/76n1539; 79n1472
Health plants of the world/Bianchini/79n1351
Health resources statistics/US Natl Center for Health Statistics/78n1419
Health sciences AV resource list/Brantz/79n1451
Health sciences librarianship/Basler/78n197
Health sciences video directory 1977/Eidelberg/78n1405
Health technology/78n1411
Heard, J N/Bookman's guide/78n49
Hearing, speech, and communication disorders/Information Center for Hearing, Speech, and Disorders of Human Communication/76n1518
Heasley, J/Production figure/78n756
Heath, G L/Mutiny does/77n502/Vandals in/77n503
Heavener, U S A/German New/77n464
Hebb, R L/Low maintenance/76n1589
Hebert, T/By hand/75n1031/Getting skilled/77n628
Hebrew-English lexicon of the Bible/76n1100
Hebrew printing and bibliog/78n38
Hecht, M/Alternatives to/76n622
Hechtlinger, A/Pelican guide/77n561
Hedberg, H D/International stratigraphic/78n1356

Hede, A A/Reference readiness/78n152
Hedgecoe, J/Photographer's hndbk/79n952
Heffner, R/Spenser allusions/75n1402
Hegener, K C/Architecture schools/78n798/
  Peterson's annual/77n623; 79n662; 79
  n663/Peterson's guide/77n627
Heiliger, W S/Bibliography of Soviet/79n385
Heilprin, L B/Copyright and/79n64
Heim, R D/Reader's companion/76n1101
Hein, I N & W S/Hein's legal/79n565
Heiney, D/Essentials of/75n1309
Heinisch, K F/Dictionary of rubber/76n1647
Hein's legal periodical check list/Hein/79
  n565
Heinz, G/French fifth/75n519
Heinzkill, R/Film criticism/76n1065
Heise, J O/Travel guidebks/79n598
Heisley, M/Annotated bibliog Chicano/78
  n1013
Heiss, W/Encyclopedia of American/78n402
Heizer, R F/Bibliography of California/78
  n679/California/79n785/California Indian/
  76n804/Indians of/77n740
Hejzlar, Z/Czechoslovakia/76n269
Held, R E/Rise of/75n186
Helgeson, D/Computers in/75n274
Helicopter directory/Brown/77n1619
Helicopters of the world/Taylor/78n1508
Heller, M/Black names/77n488
Hellicar, E/Prime ministers/79n548
Helm, A K/Family legal/75n557
Helm, J/Indians of/77n741
Helmbold, F W/Tracing your/77n450; 77n451
Helmreich, W B/Afro-Americans/78n386
Helms, H D/Literature in/77n1580
Help/Rowse/79n107
Helping others: selected soc serv agencies and
  occupations/Haimes/75n841
Hemnes, T M S/Legal word/79n569
Hemperley, M R/Placenames of/76n459
Hendershot, C H/Programmed learning/75n702
Henderson, D/Guide to basic/79n180
Henderson, G P/Directory of British/78n72
Henderson, J/Emergency medical/79n1486
Henderson, K L/Major classification/78n218
Henderson, R/Encyclopedia of sailing/79n725
Henderson, R W/Checklist and/77n1397
Henderson, S P A/Directory of British/78n72
Hendin, D/World almanac/79n1487
Hendrick, G/Fourth directory/76n1193
Hendry, J D/Social history/76n224
Henke, D/California legal/76n516
Henkin, H/Complete fisherman's/78n623/Fly
  tackle/77n692

Henle, F/Calculator hndbk/75n1769
Hennessee, D/Women in/76n1002
Hennessee, D A/Nineteenth-century/78n938
Henning, B/Milepost: travel gd/75n634
Henri Bergson/Gunter/76n1107
Henriksen, L/Karen Blixen/79n1265
Henry, N/Copyright information/78n56; 78
  n57
Henry Blake Fuller and Hamlin Garland/
  Silet/78n1125
Henry James/Ricks/76n1242
Henstock, C/First French/75n1265
Hepple, B A/Bibliography of lit/76n904
Her way: biographies of women/Kulkin/77
  n719
Heraldic design/Child/77n484
Heraldry of the world/von Volborth/75n445
Herb identifier and hndbk/Gabriel/77n1348
Herbal body bk/Rose/77n1524
Herbert, I/Who's who theatre/78n943
Herbert, M E/How to know/75n1467
Herbert, T T/Management educ/79n870
Herbert George Wells/Hammond/79n1256
Herbert Hoover/Tracey/78n448
Herbs and spices/Morton/78n1299
Herbst, J/History of American/75n646
Herdeck, D E/African authors/76n1215
Here was the revolution/US Natl Park Service/
  78n336
Herickes, S/Audio-visual/79n677
Hering's dict of classical and modern cookery
  for the hotel, restaurant and catering trade/
  Bickel/76n1573
Heriteau, J/Color handbook/77n1558
Herling, E B/Century of/77n157
Herman, E/Festivals sourcebk/78n77/Museum
  media/75n83
Herman, L/Corpus delicti/76n1207
Herman, L J/Dictionary of Slavic/76n1111
Herman, M/Japanese in/75n818
Herman, V/Parliaments of/77n495
Hermann Hesse/Mileck/78n1190
Hernandez, M J/Winnipeg/75n393
Herner, S/EIS: key/79n1395
Hernes, H/Multinational corp/78n698
Hernon, P/Municipal government/79n537
Héroes de Puerto Rico/Tuck/75n374
Heroes of music/Fisher/75n1156
Herrick, C N/Oscilloscope hndbk/75n1787
Hersey, J/Flowering shrubs/75n1702/Woman's
  Day/77n1360
Hershfield, A F/Effecting change/75n264
Herskowitz, I H/Bibliography on genetics/75
  n1460

Hertzberg, R/Radio amateur's/77n1113
Hertzendorf, M S/Air pollution/75n1539
Herwig, R/Treasury of/77n1554
Hess, S W/Directory of art/79n885
Hess, T/Dictionary of Puget/77n1097
Hessler, G/Comprehensive catalog/75n1066
Hewitt, M/Education index/76n609
Hey miss! you got a book for me?/Chambers/79n226
Heymer, A/Ethological dict/79n783
Hiatt, D/Kliatt paperback/75n199
Hickie, W J/Greek-English/79n1068
Hickin, N E/Wood preservation/75n1046
Hickok, F/Handbook of solar/76n1461
Hickok, R/New encyclopedia/78n608
Hicks, W B/Managing multimedia/78n208
Hidaru, A/Short guide/77n314
Hiers, R H/Reader's guide/79n1069
Higginbotham, D/Atlas of American/75n364
Higgins, D/Whole COSMEP/75n25
Higgins, J L/Metric handbook/75n712
Higgins, L R/Cost reduction/77n774/Maintenance engineering/78n1542
High Middle Ages in England 1154-1377/Wilkinson/79n435
High profits without risk/Deutch/77n910
High school math library/Schaaf/77n1305
Higham, R/Guide to sources/76n1675
Higher educ in developing nations/Altbach/76n573
Higher educ in the United Kingdom/78n575
Highfill, P H/Biographical dict/75n1188; 76n1045; 79n1022
Highsmith, R M/Atlas of Pacific/75n578
Highway statistics/US Fed Highway Admin/78n1552
Hilado, C J/Flammability hndbk/76n1656
Hilbert, S/Barron's how/76n597
Hilburn, J L/Manual of active/75n1807
Hildreth, M H/Harriet Beecher/77n1214
Hilgemann, W/Anchor atlas/76n297; 79n401
Hill, A/Visual dictionary/75n1000
Hill, C R/Trademarks and/78n741
Hill, D/Complete hndbk sports/75n727
Hill, E E/Office of/75n804
Hill, J P A/History of Henry/77n465
Hill, M/Into print/78n39
Hill, M D/Puerto Rican/75n1424
Hill, T E/Hill's manual/77n794
Hillard, J M/Where to find more/78n239/Where to find what/76n130
Hillman, B J/Writer's market/79n1168
Hills, L C/History and/76n435
Hill's manual of soc and business forms/Hill/77n794

Hills of faraway: fantasy/Waggoner/79n1206
Hillson, C J/Seaweeds/78n1303
Hinckley, C/Peterson's travel/79n658
Hindelang, M J/Sourcebook of criminal/75n837; 78n491
Hines, D M/Index of archived/78n1014
Hines, T C/Guide to indexed/76n1075
Hinson, M/Piano in/79n991/Piano teacher's/76n1015
Hinton, D A/Catalogue of Anglo-/75n994
Hintz, C B/Kings, rulers/78n332
Hirsch, J/Super catalog/75n1732
Hirsch, R O/Political campaign/75n462
Hirsch, Y/Mutual funds/78n730/Stock trader's/76n856
Hirschfelder, A B/American Indian/75n805
Hirschman, R/Encyclopedia of Ohio/79n90
Hirtz, J/Fate of/78n1437
Hirzel, B M/Gateways to/77n1166
Hisamatsu, S/Biographical dict Japanese/77n1271
Historic American engineering record catalog/US Natl Park Service/78n1499
Historic architecture sourcebk/Harris/78n801
Historic buildings of Massachusetts/77n874
Historic docs of 1974/76n485
Historic families of Kentucky/Green/76n433
Historic heraldry of Britain/Wagner/76n450
Historic preservation/Rath/77n381
Historic preservation grants-in-aid catalog/US Natl Park Service/77n877
Historic preservation law/Kettler/77n536
Historic preservation plans/National Trust for Historic Preservation in the US/78n344
Historical account of the settlements of Scotch Highlanders prior to the peace of 1783/MacLean/79n489
Historical accounting lit/76n842
Historical and cultural dict of . . .
  Afghanistan/Hanifi/77n317
  India/Kurian/77n326
  Thailand/Smith/77n331
  the Sultanate of Oman and the Emirates of Eastern Arabia/Anthony/77n315
  Vietnam/Whitfield/77n332
Historical atlas of . . .
  Alabama/Dodd/76n345
  Jerusalem/Bahat/76n356
  Oklahoma/Morris/78n356
  religion in America/Gaustad/77n1019
  the religions of the world/al Faruqi/76n1091
Historical dictionary of . . .
  Burundi/Weinstein/77n312
  Cameroon/LeVine/75n318
  Chad/Decalo/78n283

Historical dictionary of . . . (cont'd)
  Colombia/Davis/78n306
  Dahomey/Decalo/77n313
  Guinea/O'Toole/79n354
  Haiti/Perusse/78n308
  Honduras/Meyer/77n344
  Lesotho/Haliburton/78n286
  Mali/Imperato/78n287
  Sierra Leone/Foray/78n288
  Somalia/Castagno/76n254
  Swaziland/Grotpeter/76n255
  Tanzania/Kurtz/79n361
  the British Caribbean/Lux/76n282
  the Gambia/Gailey/76n251
  the People's Republic of the Congo (Congo-Brazzaville)/Thompson/76n250
  the Republic of Botswana/Stevens/76n248
  the Sudan/Voll/79n360
  Togo/Decalo/77n316
  Upper Volta (Haute Volta)/McFarland/79n363
  Uruguay/Willis/76n283
Historical intro to library educ/White/77n275
Historical statistics of the US: colonial times to 1970/US Bureau of the Census/77n753
Historical statistics of the US, 1790-1970/Dodd/77n750
Historiography/Stephens/76n292
Historiography, method, history teaching/Birkos/76n284
Historiography of Latin America/Wilgus/76n373
History/Day/78n324
History and bibliog of American magazines, 1810-20/Edgar/76n1162
History and bibliog of American newspapers, 1690-1820/Brigham/77n1110
History and genealogy of Fenwick's Colony/Shourds/77n476
History and genealogy of the families of Old Fairfield/Jacobus/77n466
History and genealogy of the Mayflower planters, and first comers to ye olde colonie/Hills/76n435
History and gd to Judaic bibliog/Brisman/79n458
History atlas of our country/77n376
History of . . .
  American educ/Herbst/75n646
  anthropology/Kemper/79n776
  book publishing in the US, 1865-1919/Tebbel/76n43
  book publishing in the US, 1920-1940/Tebbel/79n31

History of . . . (cont'd)
  economic analysis/Hutchinson/77n769
  European printing/Clair/78n33
  Henry County, VA/Hill/77n465
  libraries in the Western world/Johnson/77n280
  popular garden plants from A to Z/Fogg/78n1491
  psychology and the behavioral sciences/Watson/79n1426
  scientific and tech periodicals/Kronick/77n1278
  the American Library Assoc/Thomison/79n329
  the life sciences/Smit/76n1354
  the principles of librarianship/Thompson/79n156
  the USA/Cassara/78n341
  war at sea/Pemsel/79n1604
History preserved: NY city landmarks & historic districts/Goldstone/75n607
Hitchcock, H-R/American architectural/78n802
Hixon, D L/Nineteenth-century/78n938/Women in/76n1002
Hobbs, J L/Local history/75n265
Hobson, B/Catalogue of world's/78n844
Hoch, A D/Canadian tokens/75n1067
Hochman, S/American film/75n1210/French-English/77n1290
Hockenhull, D J D/Progress in/76n1365
Hockett, C F/Menomini lexicon/76n1148
Hockey encyclopedia/Ronberg/75n771
Hockey register/Spink/78n627
Hockliffe, Q/Guide to bird-/77n1376
Hodge, W H/Bibliography of contemporary/77n742
Hodgson, J/Music titles/77n956
Hodson, H V/Annual register/75n84/International foundation/75n82
Hodupp, S/Shopper's guide/79n842
Hoebel, E A/Plains Indians/79n775
Hoedeman, J J/Naturalists' guide/75n1668
Hoehn, R P/Union list/78n764
Hoese, H D/Fishes of/78n1326
Hoevers, L G/Checklist and/77n1397
Hoffberg, J A/Directory of art/79n885
Hoffman, D B/Schistosomiasis III/78n1392; 79n1442
Hoffman, E/Fairchild's dict/75n1105
Hoffman, H H/Alphanumeric filing/79n819/Bibliography without/78n104/Descriptive cataloging/78n219/Introduction to quantitative/78n268/Small library/79n272/What happens/77n270

Hoffman, J/Guide to federal/76n662
Hoffmann, A/Lives of/78n369
Hoffmann, F/Analytical survey/75n1321
Hofmeister, F/Handbuch der/76n987
Hofstadter, D/Mexico 1946-73/75n341
Hogan, E/Rivers of/76n521
Hogarth, G A/Illustrators of/79n898
Hogg, G/Museums of/75n81
Hogg, I V/Encyclopedia of infantry/78n1569/ Military small/78n1558
Holderness, G/Who's who D. H./77n1237
Holdings of the Stanford Univ libraries on Latin American languages and linguistics/ Coelho/75n1247
Hole thing: pinhole fotografy/Shull/75n1114
Hollander, J M/Annual review energy/77n1415
Hollander, Z/Complete ency ice/76n750/ Complete hndbk baseball/79n708/Complete hndbk pro basketball/77n679/Complete hndbk pro hockey/77n698/Complete hndbk soccer/79n729/Encyclopedia sports/ 77n671/Pro basketball/78n614
Hollenberg, G J/Marine algae/77n1365
Holler, F L/Information sources/76n463
Hollingsworth, B/Facts on/78n84
Hollom, P A D/Field gd birds/76n1429
Hollowak, T L/Index to marriages/79n487/ Index to marriages and deaths/79n486
Hollowell, J S/Bibliotherapy in/79n309
Hollywood character actors/Parish/79n1037
Hollywood on record/Pitts/79n975
Hollywood players: forties/Parish/77n1015/ Thirties/Parish/77n1016
Holme, C G/Children's books/77n1155
Holmes, M Z/Super dictionary/79n1110
Holmgren, A/Mosses/75n1487
Holocaust/Cargas/79n436
Holroyd, G/Studies in/76n178; 77n247; 78n209
Holstrom, J E/Analytical index publications/ 78n1516
Holt, R M/Architectural strategy/77n214
Holtje, H F/National directory/79n845
Holum, J R/Topics and/79n1398
Holzman, A G/Encyclopedia of computer/76 n1626; 78n1523
Holzman, R S/Take it/75n983
Home computer hndbk/Schlossberg/79n1564
Home gardener's gd to bulb flowers/Vance/75 n1709
Home gardener's gd to trees and shrubs/ Brimer/77n1553
Home office officials, 1782-1870/Sainty/ 76n499

Home remedies/Fahy/76n1639
Home renovation/Schuler/75n1797
Home repair and improvement/Schipf/75 n1796
Homegrown energy/Wade/76n1466
Homeowner's compl gd/Treves/75n1800
Homeowner's directory/Schuler/79n1573
Homeowner's ency of house construction/ Krieger/79n1571
Homeowner's gd to solar heating and cooling/ Foster/77n1419
Homosexuality bibliog/Parker/78n653
Homstead, K C/National directory/79n645
Hong, A/Marketing economics gd/79n837/ Marketing economics key/77n783/MEI marketing/76n869
Honigfeld, G/Psychiatric drugs/79n1498
Honkala, B H/Trees and/78n1306
Honolulu index to plastic surgery/79n1480
Honour, H/Dictionary of architecture/77 n875/Dictionary of decorative/78n828
Hony, H C/Oxford English-/79n1153
Hood, R/Criminology and/78n499
Hoover, D W/Cities/77n729
Hoover, J H/Bookman's guide/78n49
Hoover, K H/Professional teacher's/75n713
Hopf, P S/Designer's guide/76n1605
Hopi bibliography/Laird/79n777
Hopke, W E/Children's dict/75n709
Hopkins, A/Downbeat music/79n957
Hopkins, I/Organized crime/75n827
Hopkins, J/Glossary of astronomy/77n1307
Hopkins, J R/James Jones/76n1244
Hopkins, L B/More books/75n1345
Hopkins, L B/Do you/77n643
Hopkins, S J/Principal drugs/79n1499
Hoppin, J C/Handbook of attic/75n403
Hopwood, D/Arab Islamic/78n278
Horak, S M/Russia, the/79n378
Horan, M/Index to parachuting/79n724
Horchler, G F/Hungarian economic/79n802
Horecky, P L/East Central/77n192
Horkheimer, M F/Educators gd films/76n669/ Educators gd filmstrips/76n670; 77n649
Horkheimer, F A/Educators gd free/76n672
Horn, D/Literature of American/78n893
Horn, M/World ency/77n1170
Hornback, K E/Collective behavior/77n707
Hornby, A S/Oxford advanced/75n1260/ Oxford student's/79n1098
Horne, E C/Javanese-English/75n1283
Hornstein, L H/Reader's companion/75n1307
Horowitz, F D/Review of child/76n1501
Horrobin, P/Complete catalogue British/75 n1826

Horse owner's hndbk/McKibbin/78n1464
Horse world catalog/Roberts/78n1465
Horseman's veterinary advisor/Davidson/75n1661
Horses and horsemanship/Pady/75n1684
Horse's health from A to Z/Rossdale/75n1663
Horses of the world/Goodall/75n1681
Horsley, E M/New Hutchinson/79n72
Horton, H L/Machinery's hndbk/76n1653
Horton, J J/Yugoslavia/79n392
Horton, L/Home computer/79n1564
Hortus third/Bailey/78n1485
Horwitz, O/Index of suspicion/76n1531
Horwitz, T/Sweet home/75n602
Hoskin, B M/California experience/79n388
Hosking, E/Wildlife photography/75n1110
Hospital/health care training media profiles/76n1532
Hospital lit subj headings/Dunlap/78n229
Hotchkiss, J F/Limited edition/75n1085
Hotchkiss, J/African-Asian/77n1152
Hotel and travel index/75n584
Hotline! /Hyde/77n105
Hotten, J C/Original lists/75n421
Houart, V/Buttons/79n936
Houghton, B/Scientific periodicals/76n1308
Houghton, L/Guide to British/75n1018
Houlgate, D/Complete motorcycle/75n739
House & Garden's antiques/Boger/75n1053
Housebuilding book/Browne/75n1763
Household pollutants gd/Fritsch/79n1400
Houser, L/Search for/79n323
Houses/Harrison/75n1765
Housing/Paulus/75n1767
Houston, D/MGA-MGB/75n1733
Hovemeyer, G A/Bibliography on taxation/78n783
Hovet, E/Chronology and fact/77n493
Hovet, T/Chronology and fact/77n493
How it works/78n1208
How the experts buy and sell gold bullion, gold stocks and gold coins/Sinclair/76n862
How to . . .
  achieve competence in English/Johnson/77n1087
  buy food for economy and quality/76n883
  clean everything/Moore/79n1572
  decipher and study old docs/Thoyts/76n287

How to . . . (cont'd)
  distinguish the saints in art by their costumes, symbols, and attributes/Bles/76n925
  do library research/Downs/76n111
  eat better and spend less/Rice/75n1706
  find out/Chandler/75n3
  find out about the soc sciences/Burrington/76n238
  find your family roots/Beard/79n467
  fix almost everything/Schuler/76n1643
  get money for: arts and humanities, drug and alcohol abuse, and health/Human Resources Network/76n623
  get money for: conservation and community developmt/Human Resources Network/76n624
  get money for: education, fellowships, and scholarships/Human Resources Network/76n625
  get money for: youth, the elderly, the handicapped, women, and civil liberties/Human Resources Network/76n626
  get things changed/Strauss/75n515
  grow house plants/75n1703
  identify and care for houseplants/Kramer/76n1591
  identify and collect American first editions/Tannen/77n65
  know American antique furniture/Bishop/75n1073
  know the grasses/Pohl/79n1350
  know the insects/Bland/79n1379
  know Western Australian wildflowers/Blackall/76n1387
  know wild fruits/Peterson/75n1467
  live better on less/Jurgensen/76n874
  live in Britain/78n576
  obtain money for college/Lever/77n620
  pronounce the names in Shakespeare/Irvine/76n1035
  remodel your kitchen and save $$$$/Cook/76n1637
  run a small business/Greisman/75n891
  start an AV collection/Nadler/79n306
  tie freshwater flies/Bay/76n727
  trace your family tree/American Genealogical Research Institute Staff/76n420
  use WISC scores in reading diagnosis/Searls/76n691
Howard, A/Psychiatric drugs/79n1498
Howard, E N/Local power/79n255

Howard, N E/Telescope hndbk/76n1337
Howard, P F/Wife beating/79n746
Howard Univ bibliog of African and Afro-American religious studies/Williams/78n979
Howat, G/Who did/75n121
Howden, R/Anatomy, descriptive/76n1530
Howe, A/International yearbk educ'l/77n637
Howell, B/Sports olympiques/77n664
Howell, J B/Special collections/79n164
Howell, J B/East African/78n290/Tanganyika African/78n293
Howes, C A/Canadian postage/75n1090
Howes, D/American women/75n849
Howes, F N/Dictionary of useful/75n1463
Hoy, P C/French XX/79n1266
Hoyle, N/Indexing terms/79n674/Physical education/79n676
Hrvatske knjige i knjizice u iseljenistvu/Prpić/75n823
Hryciw, C A/John Hawkes/78n1140
Hsiao, T C/Who's who computer/77n1588
Hsieh, K/Energy/78n1340/Energy reference/77n1405
Hsieh, W/Chinese historiography/76n361
Hu, T-W/Benefit-cost/77n248
Hubbard, C/Guide bk Mexican/78n843
Hubbard, J C/Hawai'i garden tropical exotics/78n1488/Hawai'i garden tropical shrubs/78n1489
Huber, J P/Directory of foundations Connecticut/77n80/Directory of foundations Massachusetts/77n79/Directory of foundations Maine/77n81/Directory of foundations New Hampshire/77n82/Directory of foundations Rhode Island/77n83
Huck, C S/Children's literature/77n1153
Huck-Tee, L/Barefoot librarian/76n218
Hudak, J/Gardening with/77n1555
Hudak, L M/Early American/79n30
Hudman, H L/Analysis and/78n735
Hudman, L E/Analysis and/78n735
Hudson, H P/Hudson's Washington/76n1169/Newsletter yrbook/78n16
Hudson, K/Dictionary of diseased/79n1123/Directory of world/76n67
Hudson, M E/Hudson's Washington/76n1169
Hudson, N/Antiques, illustrated/79n915
Hudson, R/Brownings' correspondence/79n1233
Hudson's Washington news media contacts directory/Hudson/76n1169
Huffman, F E/English-Khmer/79n1143
Hüfner, K/UN system/78n430; 79n555; 79n556

Hug, W E/Instructional design/77n224/Strategies for/75n140
Hugard, J/Encyclopedia of card/76n744
Huggins, R A/Annual review materials/77n1564; 77n1565
Hugh Johnson's pocket ency of wine/Johnson/79n1518
Hughes, A/Medieval music/76n988
Hughes, C/New York/79n1020
Hughes, C A/Economic educ/78n699
Hughes, H K/Dictionary of abbreviations/78n1396
Hughes, L/Pictorial history/75n814
Hughes, M M/Sexual barrier/79n756
Hughes, R/American composers/75n1117
Hugo, J/Guide to art/78n792
Hull, C R/Pickup camper/75n1752
Human (and anti-human) values in children's books/77n1154
Human resources developmt in the organization/Franklin/79n858
Human Resources Network/How to get money for . . . arts and humanities/76n623/conservation and/76n624/Education, fellowships/76n625/Youth, the/76n626/User's guide funding/76n627
Human rights organizations & periodicals directory/Christiano/76n470; 78n431/Ginger/75n475
Human settlements: annotated bibliog/International Institute for Environment and Development/77n730
Human settlements: national reports/International Institute for Environment and Development/77n731
Humanities/Rogers/75n174
Humanities: doctoral dissertations accepted by Indian universities/77n323
Humanities index/75n35/Pingree/76n36
Humes, J C/Speaker's treasury/79n1174
Humfrey, M/Sea shells/76n973
Hummel, C F/Winterthur gd/78n853
Hummel, R O/More Virginia/76n346/Portraits and/79n879
Hümmelchen, G/Chronology of war/75n542
Humphrey, P/Popular names/77n115
Humphreys, C/Popular dict/77n1038
Hundsdörfer, V/Bibliographie zur/76n256
Hungarian economic reforms/Horchler/79n802
Hungarian hist and lit/76n274
Hungarians in America, 1583-1974/Széplaki/76n408
Hunsberger, I/Quintessential dict/79n1125
Hunt, G N S/Oxford Bible/75n1232

Hunt, M A/Multi-media/76n679
Hunt, P/Marshall Cavendish/79n1541
Hunter, B/Soviet-Yugoslav/77n527
Hunter, D E/Encyclopedia of anthropology/77n748
Hunter, S/Family gd/76n550
Hunter, W B/Milton ency/79n1250
Hunter's fld gd to the game birds and animals of North America/Elman/75n776
Hunting and fishing/Clotfelter/75n721
Hunting with a camera/Bauer/75n775
Huq, A M/Librarianship and/78n251
Hurd, B/Oceans of/75n550
Hurlbut, C S/Planet we/77n1424
Hurov, L/Handbook of veterinary/79n1543
Hurrell, R/Van Nostrand/75n1205
Hurst, W E/Copyright/78n58/Your introduction/78n59
Hurwitz, H L/Encyclopedic dict/75n367
Hutcheson, J D/Citizen groups/77n523
Hutchings, R T/Colour atlas/78n1384
Hutchinson, J/Families of/75n1477
Hutchinson, W K/History of economics/77n769
Hutchison, J W/ISA hndbk/77n1608
Huts and hikes in the Dolomites/Rudner/75n628
Huxford, B & S/Collectors ency/79n949
Huxley, A/Flowers of/79n1343
Hyams, E/Dictionary of modern/75n466
Hyde, D C/Dictionary for/78n810
Hyde, M O/Hotline! /77n105
Hyde, R C/Dictionary for/79n896
Hylton, W H/Rodale herb/75n1481
Hyman, C J/Dictionary of physics/79n1331
Hyman, R J/Analytical access/79n262
Hymn and scripture selection gd/Spencer/79n1063
Hymn-tunes of Lowell Mason/Mason/77n959
Hyneman, E F/Edgar Allan/75n1364
Hyperactive child/Archuleta/75n1645
Hyperkinetic child/Winchell/76n1490

I can be anything: careers and colleges for young women/Mitchell/76n651; 79n660
I hear America talking/Flexner/78n1031
Iacone, S J/Pleasures of/77n64
Ice hockey A to Z/Gitler/79n719
Ichiko, C/Japanese studies/77n319
Ichioka, Y/Buried past/75n819
Icolari, D/Reference ency/75n808
Idaho local history/Nelson/78n357
Ideas and the university library/Oboler/78n167

Identification guide to . . .
    cage and aviary birds/Stringer/79n710
    freshwater tropical aquarium fish/79n702
    marine tropical aquarium fish/79n703
Identify your stamps/Felix/79n930
Identifying American architecture/Blumenson/78n799
Identifying grasses/Clifford/79n1348
Idlin, R/Dictionary of physics/79n1331
IEEE standard dict of electrical and electronics terms/Jay/79n1569
IFLA annual/79n315
IFLA's first fifty years/Koops/79n316
Igor Fedorovitch Stravinsky, 1882-1971/de Lerma/75n1157
Iiyama, P/Drug use/77n1504
Illinois women's directory/Ligare/79n765
Illuminated manuscripts and bks in the Bodleian Library/Ohlgren/79n68
Illustrated auto racing dict for young people/Olney/79n705
Illustrated basketball dict for young people/Clark/79n709
Illustrated biog ency of artists of the American West/Samuels/77n872
Illustrated bk of table games/Arnold/76n741
Illustrated dictionary of . . .
    broadcast-CATV-telecommunications/Ellmore/79n1162
    ceramics/Savage/75n1040
    chess/Brace/79n715
    glass/Newman/79n926
    ornament/Stafford/76n924
    place names, US and Canada/Harder/77n551
    practical pottery/Fournier/78n881
Illustrated encyclopedia of . . .
    archaeology/Daniel/78n319
    astronomy and space/Ridpath/78n1237
    country music/Dellar/78n917
    crafts and how to master them/Rose/79n940
    indoor plants/Beckett/78n1487
    jazz/Case/79n996
    mysticism and the mystery religions/Ferguson/79n1057
    rock/Logan/78n918
    ships, boats, vessels, and other water-borne craft/Blackburn/79n1582
    the classical world/Avi-Yonah/77n364
    the mineral kingdom/Woolley/79n1423
    woodworking handtools, instruments, and devices/Blackburn/75n1045

Illustrated ency'ic dict of building and construction terms/Brooks/77n1577
Illustrated family medical ency/Combs/78n1429
Illustrated football dict for young people/Olgin/77n695
Illustrated football rules/Nelson/77n694
Illustrated glossary of horse equipment/77n1529
Illustrated gd to . . .
 collecting bottles/Munsey/77n921
 common rocks and their minerals/Brown/77n1431
 the international std bibliographic description for monographs/Sayre/77n259
 the treasures of America/75n595
Illustrated hndbk of electronic tables, symbols, measurements and values/Ludwig/78n1534
Illustrated heritage dict and info book/78n1027
Illustrated hockey dict for young people/Walker/78n628
Illustrated inventory of famous dismembered works of art with a section on dismembered tombs in France: European painting/76n945
Illustrated Mexico vacation gd/McCready/75n630
Illustrated soccer dict for young people/Gardner/78n630
Illustrated sourcebk on the Holocaust/Szajkowski/79n438
Illustrative computer programming for libraries/Davis/75n275
Illustrator and the bk in England from 1790 to 1914/Ray/77n67
Illustrators of books for young people/Ward/76n944
Illustrators of children's books/78n811
Illustrators of children's books, 1967-76/Kingman/79n898
Ilma, V/Funk &/79n931
Image interpretation equipment catalog/US Naval Air Systems Command/75n971
Image of pluralism in American lit/Inglehart/76n388
Imhof, T A/Alabama birds/78n1319
Immigrant children in American schools/Cordasco/78n539
Immigrants to the middle colonies/Tepper/79n497
Immigration and ethnicity/Buenker/78n375
Immroth, J P/Introduction to cataloging/77n264/Intro to classification/77n250/Ronald B. McKerrow: his essays/75n266

Impeachment/US House Committee on Judiciary/75n499
Impeachment and the US Congress/75n492
Impeachment Congress, 93rd US Congress/Grayson/75n491
Imperato, P J/Historical dict Mali/78n287
Implementation & admin of development activities in Africa/75n292
Improving access to library resources/Dougherty/75n234
Improving library services to the blind, partially sighted, and physically handicapped in NY state/Prentiss/75n240
Improving medical practice and health care/Williamson/79n1457
Improving state aid to public libraries/Government Studies and Systems, Inc./78n173
In black and white/Spradling/77n436
In other words/Schiller/79n1120
In pursuit of educ'l opportunity/Quay/79n633
In pursuit of values/Kelley/75n1346
In search of British ancestry/Hamilton-Edwards/75n438
Ina Coolbrith/Rhodehamel/75n252
Inaugural addresses of the Presidents of the US/US House of Representatives/75n389
Income & employment generation in Africa/75n293
Incunabula in American libraries/Goff/75n64
Independence docs of the world/Blaustein/79n518
Independent Mexico/Steele/75n312
Independent reading grades 1 thru 3/Jacob/76n158; 77n652
Index Africanus/Asamani/76n245
Index Islamicus, 4th suppl/Pearson/75n345; 77n303; 79n383
Index of . . .
 administrative publications/US Dept of the Army/79n1597
 American periodical verse/Zulauf/75n1340; 76n1225; 77n1196; 79n1217
 archived resources for a folklife and cultural hist of the inland Pacific Northwest frontier/Hines/78n1014
 festschriften in religion/Sayre/75n1217
 human ecology/Jones/75n1560
 international stds/US Natl Bureau of Standards/75n1719
 mathematical papers/76n1332
 model periodicals/Cardwell/78n876
 names in *Pearl, Purity, Patience*, and *Gawain*/Chapman/79n1251

Index of ... (cont'd)
  paramedical vocabulary/Schmidt/75n1624
  proper names in French Arthurian prose
    romances/West/79n1275
  psychoanalytic writings/Grinstein/76n1503
  publications, Sept 1947-June 1971/Group
    for the Advancemt of Psychiatry/75
    n1602
  scientific writings on creativity: creative
    men and women/Rothenberg/76n94
  scientific writings on creativity: general/
    Rothenberg/77n1296
  SNAME publications/76n1655
  suspicion in treatable diseases/Horwitz/76
    n1531
  the source records of Maryland/Passano/
    75n429
  tissue culture/Stahl/78n1423
  US nuclear stds/Slattery/79n1406
  vibrational spectra of inorganic and
    organometallic compounds/Greenwood/
    79n1323
Index to ...
  abstracts on crime and juvenile delinquency
    1968-75/79n576
  accounting and auditing technical pro-
    nouncements/79n826
  all bks on the physical sciences in English
    1967-74/75n1438
  America/Ireland/77n389
  American little magazines 1900-19/Goode/
    76n1191
  American ref bks annual, 1970-74/Sprug/
    75n38
  anthologies of Latin American lit in English
    translation/Freudenthal/78n1194
  art reproductions in books/75n1010
  Arthur Miller criticism/Hayashi/77n1210
  Asian educ'l periodicals/76n589
  bank letters, bulletins, and reviews/78
    n751; 78n752
  biographical fragments in unspecialized
    scientific journals/Barr/75n1437
  biographies of contemporary composers/
    Bull/75n1152
  biographies of Englishmen 1000-1485
    found in dissertations and theses/Reel/
    76n370
  black poetry/Chapman/76n1211
  book reviews in historical periodicals/Brew-
    ster/76n303; 77n368; 79n405
  Brown, Drive & Briggs Hebrew lexicon/
    Einspahr/77n1042

Index to ... (cont'd)
  children's plays in collections/Kreider/78
    n939
  Civil Serv Commission info/77n114
  Commonwealth little magazines/Goode/
    77n1138; 77n1139
  critical film reviews in British and Ameri-
    can film periodicals/Bowles/76n1062
  criticisms of British and American poetry/
    Cline/75n1332
  educational records/76n693
  1820 North Carolina census/Potter/79
    n493
  free periodicals/Rzepecki/77n41
  handicrafts, model making, and workshop
    projects/Turner/76n955
  how to do it information/78n24
  IEEE publications/75n1718
  illustrations of the natural world/Thomp-
    son/78n1277
  inspiration/Ireland/77n94
  instructional media catalogs/75n689
  legal periodicals/Sahanek/78n508
  literary biography/Havlice/76n1192
  literature in the New Yorker/Johnson/77
    n42
  maps of the American Revolution in bks
    and periodicals/Clark/75n370
  marriages and deaths in the (Baltimore)
    Sun, 1837-50/Hallowak/79n486
  marriages in the (Baltimore) Sun, 1851-
    60/Hollowak/79n487
  New England periodicals/79n23
  Nineteenth-Century Fiction, Summer
    1945-March 1976/Tennyson/78n1107
  opera, operetta and musical comedy
    synopses in collections and periodicals/
    Drone/79n979
  outdoor sports, games, and activities/
    Turner/79n699
  parachuting 1900-75/Horan/79n724
  periodical fict in English/Messerli/78n1103
  poetry for children and young people/
    Brewton/79n1189
  Pravda/Ehlers/76n498; 79n515
  record and tape reviews/Maleady/79n973
  reproductions of American paintings appear-
    ing in more than 400 bks/Smith/78
    n820
  research in school librarianship, 1960-74/
    Freeman/78n184
  science fict anthologies and collections/
    Contento/79n1203

Index to ... (cont'd)
  scientific and tech proceedings/79n1305
  scientific reviews/76n1326
  16mm educ'l films/76n694
  Southeast Asian journals, 1960-74/ Johnson/78n295
  statistics and probability: citation index/ Tukey/75n878
  statistics and probability: locations and authors/Ross/75n877
  statistics and probability: permuted titles/ Ross/76n819
  35mm educ'l filmstrips/76n695
  US gov periodicals/Carpenter/75n103; 76n37
  users studies/76n124
  young readers' collective biographies/Silverman/76n1200
Index to the ...
  American Archivist, 1958-67/Dowd/76n330
  Argonauts of California, Charles Warren Haskins/Spinazze/76n441
  contemporary scene/Brunton/76n21
  correspondence of the Foreign Office, 1946/ 79n557/1947/79n558
  1850 census of Delaware/Olmsted/78n407
  1800 census of Massachusetts/Bentley/79n478
  1830 census of Georgia/Register/75n430
  1820 census of Virginia/Felldin/77n461
  formal sources of Rembrandt's art/Broos/ 79n904
  James A. Garfield papers/US Library of Congress/75n372
  letters and papers of Frederick Temple, Archbishop of Canterbury 1896-1902/ Barber/77n1041
  LC cataloging service bulletin, June 1945-Winter 1977/Olson/78n223
  LC classification/Elrod/76n190
  picture collection of the American Jewish Archives/Marcus/79n460
  Thomas Jefferson papers/78n441
  Waverley novels/Bradley/76n1283
  Wilson authors series/77n1140
Index translationum 26/79n3
Indexed bibliog of Office of Research and Development reports, to Jan 1975/US Environmental Protection Agency/76n1456
Indexed gd to modern electronic circuits/ Goodman/75n1782
Indexed periodicals: 170 yrs of coverage in 33 indexing services/Marconi/77n43
Indexers on indexing/Harrod/79n331
Indexes to *The Competitor*/Grant/79n451
Indexes to the NY State Museum bulletins, 1888-1973/Liebe/76n930
Indexing concepts and methods/Borko/79n330
Indexing languages and thesauri/Soergel/76n194
Indexing terms for physical educ and allied fields/Hoyle/79n674
India/76n262; 77n324
India and Indians/Sharma/75n301
India votes two/Chandidas/75n518
Indian bks in print/Singh/75n10
Indian bks 1973-74/Prasher/75n12
Indian land tenure/Sutton/76n806
Indian names in Connecticut/Trumbull/75n457
Indian Ocean atlas/US Central Intelligence Agency/78n519
Indian periodicals in print/Gandhi/75n40
Indian political movement 1919-71/Ghosh/ 78n483
Indian response to lit in English/Naqvi/75n1422
Indian sci index/Satyaprakash/78n1221
Indiana authors and their bks, 1917-66/ Thompson/76n354
Indiana place names/Baker/76n453
Indians of ...
  California/Heizer/77n740
  Maine and the Atlantic provinces/Ray/78n681
  North and South America/Wolf/78n682
  the Subarctic/Helm/77n741
  the US and Canada/Smith/76n414
Indice informativo de la novela hispano-americana/Coll/79n1287
Indices to American literary annuals and gift books 1825-65/Kirkham/77n1191
Indigenous trees of the Hawaiian Islands/ Rock/75n1494
Indonesia/Tairas/77n327
Indonesia handbook/Dalton/79n372
Indonesian manuscripts in Great Britain/ Ricklefs/79n69
Indoor garden/Wickham/78n1497
Indoor trees/Kramer/76n1592
Industrial marketing/Pingry/78n737
Industrial pollution/Sax/76n1463
Industrial research labs of the US/76n1323; 78n1218
Industrial safety hndbk/Handley/78n1538

Industrial wastewater mgmt hndbk/Azad/77n1605
Industry statistics/Association of American Publishers/77n46
Ineson, F A/Brazil 1980/75n1224
Inexpensive wine/Lee/75n1674
Infantry weapons of the world/Foss/78n1568
Infinite riches: adventures of a rare bk dealer/Magee/75n67
Inflation and the Nixon Admin/Sobel/75n495; 76n820
Inflation in the United Kingdom/MacCafferty/78n702
Influencing students toward media center use/Blazek/77n217
Information age/Hammer/77n155
Information Center for Hearing, Speech, and Disorders of Human Communication/Hearing, speech/76n1518
Information economics: Europe/Pratt/77n292
Information for everyday survival/Gotsick/77n815
Information for sci and tech/Adams/75n134
Information for the community/Kochen/77n267
Information mgmt in the 1980's/79n303
Information on music: the Americas/Marco/78n894/Basic and universal sources/Marco/76n989
Information please almanac, atlas & yrbk/Dolmatch/79n106
Information-poor in America/Childers/76n199
Information retrieval/van Rijsbergen/77n296
Information retrieval and documentation in chemistry/Davis/75n276
Information retrieval, British & American/Metcalfe/77n291
Information retrieval on-line/Lancaster/75n280
Information science/Debons/75n277
Information society/Josey/79n149
Information sources in . . .
  children's lit/Meacham/79n234
  power engineering/Metz/77n1400
  science and tech/Parker/77n1287
  transportation, material mgmt, and physical distribution/Davis/78n1545
Information sources: membership directory . . . Information Industry Assoc/78n45
Information sources of pol sci/Holler/76n463
Information systems and networks: symposium 1974/Sherrod/76n236
Information systems, COINS IV/Tou/76n237
Information through cooperative action: library serv in metro Washington/77n156
Information worker/Raffin/78n127
Informational interviews and questions/Slavens/79n298
Ingbar, S H/Year in/78n1420
Inglehart, B F/Image of/76n388
Inglis, C M/Konkordanz zu/79n1278
Ingram, K E/Libraries and/76n213
INIS atomindex/77n1339
INIS: authority list for corp entries and report no. prefixes/79n273
INIS: descriptive cataloguing samples/79n274
INIS: thesaurus/79n1298
Inkeles, A/Annual review sociology/76n775
Inn book/Neuer/75n612
Innes, C/Complete hndbk cacti/78n1286
Innovative grad programs directory/79n619
Inouye, J/Index to Library/76n190
Insects that feed on trees and shrubs/Johnson/77n1389
In-service training in British libraries/Edwards/79n253
Inside the world of miniatures & dollhouses/Rosner/77n938
Insider's gd to antiques, art, and collectibles/Dorn/75n1050
Insiders' gd to the colleges/79n665
Instruction in school media center use/Hart/79n212
Instructional design and the media program/Hug/77n224
Instructional materials for the handicapped/Thorum/77n644
Instructional technology/Cantwell/75n698
Instrument catalogs of Leopoldo Franciolini/Ripin/76n1020
Instrument pilot's gd/Reithmaier/76n733
Instrumental music gd/Goodman/78n891
Insurance hndbk for the medical office/Fordney/78n1410
Insurance manual for libraries/Meyers/78n145
Integral geometry and geometric probability/Santalo/78n1229
Integrative mechanisms in lit growth/Kochen/76n114
Intellectual freedom manual/Office for Intellectual Freedom of the American Library Assoc/75n154
Intellectual freedom primer/Busha/78n266
Intelligence, espionage, counterespionage, and covert operations/Blackstock/79n501

Intelligence tests and reviews/Buros/76n564
Inter-American Statistical Institute/Bibliography of selected/75n873
Interdisciplinary glossary on child abuse and neglect/79n747
Interdisciplinary studies in the humanities/Bayerl/78n560
InterDok directory of published proceedings: science/engineering/medicine/technology/75n1435
Interior painting, wallpapering, and paneling/Wheeler/75n1106
Interlibrary loan policies directory/Thomson/76n202
Intermediate world atlas/76n525
International academic and specialist publishers directory/Clarke/77n58
International almanac of electoral history/Mackie/75n473
International and area studies librarianship/Sable/75n258
International and regional politics in the Middle East and North Africa/Schulz/78n488
International art & antiques yrbk/Smith/79n916
International Atomic Energy Agency/Manual on radiation/75n1461
International authors and writers who's who/Kay/77n1180/Gaster/79n1208
International bibliog, info, documentation: publications of internat'l organizations/79n118
International bibliography of . . .
  comics lit/Kempkes/75n1312
  discographies; classical music and jazz and blues, 1962-72/Cooper/76n986
  economics/75n882; 78n700
  Jewish affairs/Eppler/77n297
  political sci/75n461
  reprints, books and serials/Gnirss/78n41
  research in marriage and the family/Aldous/76n781
  sociology/75n791
  the book trade and librarianship/77n54
  translation/Van Hoff/75n1246
  works by and abt Mikhail Bulgakov/Proffer/78n1197
International book of trees/Johnson/75n1491
International businessman's gd to official Washington/Joyner/75n894
International butterfly book/Smart/76n1441
International catalog, aids and appliances for blind & visually impaired persons/Clark/75n1637

International catalogue of commercial vehicles/76n1665
International classified directory of dealers in sci fict and fantasy bks/Halpern/76n50
International cook's catalogue/79n1530
International dictionaries of sci and tech: sound/Stephens/76n1353
International dict of building construction/Schwicker/76n1618
International dict of educ/Page/79n639
International dict of food and cooking/Martin/75n1693
International directory of . . .
  archives/77n353
  behavior and design research/Beckman/75n1550
  certified radioactive materials/77n1340
  computer and info system services/75n1772
  executive recruiters/76n834; 79n859
  fish tech institutes/Food and Agriculture Organization of the UN/78n757
  little magazines & small presses/Fulton/75n26; 78n46
  occupational safety and health services & institutions/79n860
  scholarly publishers/79n53
International education: American experience/Tysse/75n649; 78n549
International educ: directory of resource materials on comparative educ and study in another country/von Klemperer/75n666
International encyclopedia of . . .
  aviation/Mondey/79n1587
  higher educ/Knowles/79n638
  psychiatry, psychology, psychoanalysis & neurology/Wolman/78n1367
International family-planning programs, 1966-75/Lyle/79n750
International Federation of Library Associations/Standards for/75n187
International film gd/Cowie/76n1047; 77n999
International foundation directory/Hodson/75n82
International glossary of hydrology/76n1472
International gd to . . .
  aids and appliances for blind and visually impaired persons/78n1406
  library, archival, and info sci associations/Fang/77n176
  the academic market place/76n572
International horseman's dict/Stratton/76n1566

International index to film periodicals/Jones/ 76n1066/Moulds/75n1211
International index to multi-media info/Doak/ 77n661; 77n662
International Institute for Environment and Developmt/Human settlements: annotated bibliog/77n730/Human settlements: national/77n731
International ISBN publishers' index/79n54
International law of pollution/Barros/75n1535
International law, organization, and the environment/Grieves/76n1453
International list of articles on the hist of educ published in non-educ'l serials, 1965-74/McCarthy/78n584
International literary marketplace/Found/77n60
International maps and atlases in print/Winch/ 78n512
International microfilm source bk/77n61
International microforms in print/Veaner/75n16
International migration review cumulative index/79n794
International mimes and pantomimists directory/75n1177
International motor racing/Nye/75n782
International music guide/Elley/77n946
International organizations/Atherton/78n428
International patents digest of foamed plastics/ 76n1657
International publications/75n13; 76n4
International register of research on blindness and visual impairment/Gill/79n1469
International relations theory/Groom/79n553
International resource directory/79n861
International riding/Johnson/75n773
International scholars directory/Montgomery/ 76n666
International sourcebk of paper hist/Leif/79 n38
International stock & commodity exchange directory/Wyckoff/76n863
International subscription agents/de la Garza/75 n56/Buckeye/79n49
International stratigraphic guide/IUGS Commission on Stratigraphy/78n1356
International visual dict/Daniels/75n652
International who's who/76n101; 76n102
International who's who in community service/ Watkins/75n800
International who's who in music and musicians' directory/Gaster/79n1002/Kay/76n1004
International who's who in poetry/Kay/79 n1199
International Wine and Food Society's gd to the wines of Germany/Meinhard/78n1457
International women's yr world conf docs index/78n672
International yrbk of educ'l and instruct'l technology/Howe/77n637
Internationale bibliographie zur geschichter der deutschen literatur von den anfängen bis zur gegenwart/Albrecht/79n1276
Interpretation/Rath/79n400
Interpretation of early music/Donington/75 n1145
Interpreter's dict of the Bible/77n1044
Interstate gd to good listening/Lay/79n1172
Into print/Hill/78n39
Introducing more books/Spirt/79n235
Introduction to . . .
  cataloging/Boll/75n223
  cataloging and classification/Wynar/77 n264
  classification and number bldg in Dewey/ Bloomberg/77n250
  heraldry/Clark/75n440
  index lang construction/Ramsden/75n228
  librarianship/Gates/77n154
  library research in French literature/ Baker/79n1268
  library science/Shera/77n165
  library services for library media technical assistants/Wisdom/75n147
  medieval Latin studies/McGuire/79n1091
  public services for library technicians/ Bloomberg/78n231
  quantitative research methods for librarians/Srikantaiah/78n268
  reference work/Katz/75n245; 79n294
  subject indexing: programmed text, subj analysis and practical classification/ Brown/77n251
  subject indexing: programmed text. UDC and chain procedure in subj cataloguing/ Brown/77n252
  technical services for library technicians/ Bloomberg/75n247; 77n269
  the literature of vertebrate zoology/ Wood/75n1496
  the SEC/Skousen/78n731
  US public documents/Morehead/76n83; 79n120
  university library administration/Thompson/75n182
Introductory bibliog for Japanese studies/ 76n263

Introductory gd to Midwest antiques/Semple/ 78n840
Inventory of info resources and services available to the US House of Representatives/ US House of Representatives/78n99
Inventory of major research facilities in the European community/79n87
Inventory of marriage and family literature/ Olson/76n784
Inventory of power plants in the US/79 n1408
Inventory of recent US research in geographic education/Saveland/77n549
Inverted medical dictionary/Rigal/78n1399
Investigative methods for info specialists/ Bundy/75n243
Investment companies/76n857
Investor relations hndbk/Roalman/75n918
Investor's ency of gold, silver & other precious metals/Persons/76n860
IRA directory/75n670
Ireland, B/Warships of/78n1574
Ireland, N O/Index to America/77n389/Index to inspiration/77n94
Iribas, J L/New pronouncing/75n1277
Iris Murdoch and Muriel Spark/Tominaga/77 n1221
Irish family names/Kelly/77n487
Irish literature, 1800-1875/McKenna/79n1281
Irish pedigrees/O'Hart/77n481
Irons, V/Descriptive inventory/79n407
Irregular serials & annuals/77n35
Irvine, B J/Slide libraries/75n205
Irvine, T U/How to pronounce/76n1035
Irwin, J T/Guide to professional/76n648
Irwin, R/Contemporary American/76n1223
ISA hndbk of control valves/Hutchison/77 n1608
Isaacs, A/New dict physics/76n1350
Isenberg, I/South America/76n281
ISIS cumulative bibliog/Whitrow/77n1283
ISI's who is publishing in science/77n1294
Islam in Africa South of the Sahara/Ofori/79 n1051
Islam in Sub-Saharan Africa/Zoghby/79n1055
Islamic Jesus/Wismer/78n980
Islamic Near East and North Africa/Littlefield/ 78n281
Isotopes of water/Summers/77n1430
Israel, S/Bibliography on divorce/76n782
Israel & the Arabs/Sobel/75n525
Israel, 2500 B.C.-1972/Litvinoff/75n328
Israeli periodicals & serials in English and other Western languages/Tronik/75n20

Issues in library admin/Tsuneishi/75n218
It happened last year! /Cornell/75n85
Italian-American experience/Cordasco/76 n409
Italian Americans/Cordasco/79n456
Italian baroque solo sonatas for the recorder and the flute/McGowan/79n992
Italian community and its lang in the US/ Cordasco/76n410
Italian hist and lit/76n275
Italian paintings in the Walters Art Gallery/ Zeri/77n888
Italy A to Z/Kane/78n532
IUGS Commission on Stratigraphy/International stratigraphic gd/78n1356
Iverson, P/Navajos/77n743
İz, F/Oxford English-/79n1153

J&P transformer book/Stigant/75n1790
J. M. Synge/Levitt/75n1404/Mikhail/76 n1291
J.P. movemt and the emergence of Janata Party/Fazal-e-Rab/79n545
Jaber, W/Cadillac modern/75n73
Jack, A/New age/78n1007
Jack and Jill: study in our Christian names/ Weekley/76n452
Jack London/Woodbridge/75n1360/Sherman/ 78n1144
Jack the ripper/Kelly/75n828
Jackson, A/Best musicals/79n1036
Jackson, C O/Building a/76n1195
Jackson, D/What every/75n1734
Jackson, D W/Marketing profitability/79n836
Jackson, J S/Who was when?/77n363
Jackson, K T/Atlas of American/79n410
Jackson, M/World gd/79n1517
Jackson, R/US music/75n1128
Jackson, S L/Century of/77n157/Libraries and/75n267
Jacob, G S/Independent reading/76n158; 77n652
Jacob, J M/Concise Cambodian-/75n1284
Jacob A. Riis/Fried/78n644
Jacobi(y), H W/Contemporary American/76 n1005
Jacobs, A/British music/76n998/New dict/ 75n1140
Jacobs, B C L/Musica/77n947
Jacobs, D M/Antebellum black/77n432/Significant American/77n127
Jacobs, H E/Annotated bibliog Shakespearean/ 77n1240

Jacobs, J/Color encyclopedia/76n923
Jacobs, S-E/Women in/76n794
Jacobson, A/Contemporary native/78n1127
Jacobson, A/Oldies but/78n916
Jacobson, E & S/Dance horizons/79n615
Jacobson, I D/Plumbing dict/77n1616
Jacobson, M K/American Museum/77n1394
Jacobus, D L/Families of/75n422/History and/77n466
Jacques, J W/Leisure reading/78n596
Jaffe, E D/Barron's how/76n597
Jaffe, J/Cost analysis/79n256
Jahn, J/Bibliography of creative/77n1251
Jain, M K/Bibliography of bibliographies/76n5
Jain, V K/Guide to Indian/76n35
Jamaica/Sangster/75n621
James, A M/Dictionary of electrochemistry/78n1242/Dictionary of thermodynamics/78n1243
James, C J/Directory of overseas/77n835
James, E T/Dictionary of American/76n106
James, G/Mathematics dict/77n1302
James, H I/First science/78n1209
James, P/Children's books/77n1155
James, R/Mathematics dict/77n1302
James Anthony Froude/Goetzman/79n432
James Jones/Hopkins/76n1244
James Thomson/Campbell/77n1247
Jane's all the world's aircraft/Taylor/79n1589
Jane's fighting ships/Moore/78n1575
Jane's freight containers/Finlay/78n1546
Jane's infantry weapons/Archer/78n1570
Jane's major companies of Europe/Love/78n758
Jane's ocean technology/Trillo/79n1545
Jane's pocket book of . . .
  commercial transport aircraft/Taylor/75n1821
  home-built aircraft/Taylor/79n1550
  major combat aircraft/Taylor/75n1845
  remotely piloted vehicles/Taylor/79n1594
  rifles and light machine guns/Archer/79n1607
  space exploration/Wilding-White/78n1510
Jane's surface skimmers/McLeavy/78n1547
Jane's weapon systems/Pretty/79n1609
Jane's world railways/Goldsack/79n1548
Janssen, R B/Minnesota birds/76n1420
Japanese and US research libraries at the turning point/Stevens/78n250
Japanese in America 1843-1973/Herman/75n818
Japanese in Hawaii/Matsuda/77n445
Japanese research on mass communication/Kato/75n1295

Japanese studies of modern China since 1953/Kamachi/77n319
Japanese writings on communist Chinese law/Cho/79n564
Japan's foreign policy, 1868-1941/Morley/75n540
Jaques, H E/How to know/79n1397
Jacquet, C H/Yearbook of American/76n1089
Jarman, L/Canadian music/77n957
Jarrett, F/Stamps of/76n975
Jarvi, E/Canadian selection/79n181
Jarvis, L P/Social responsibility/78n744
JASA: Journal of the American Statistical Assoc, index 1966-77/78n694
Jaussi, L R/Genealogical records/75n423
Javanese-English dictionary/Horne/75n1283
Jawetz, E/Review of medical microbiology/79n1475/Review of medical pharmacology/75n1657; 79n1502
Jay, F/IEEE std/79n1569
Jazz in the movies/Meeker/78n919
Jazz masters of the forties/Gitler/75n1162
Jazz masters of the twenties/Hadlock/75n1163
Jazz records 1897-1942/Rust/79n1000
Jazz talk/Gold/76n1025
Jean Charlot's prints/Morse/77n882
Jean-Paul Sartre and his critics/Lapointe/77n1051
Jefferson, A A/Libraries and/76n213
Jefferson, G/College library/79n196
Jefferson Davis and the Confederacy and treaties concluded by the Confederate states with Indian tribes/Gibson/79n420
Jeffreys, A/Art of/75n141
Jeffries, J/Guide to official/79n119
Jelenko, M/American Jewish/75n321
Jenkins, D H/Woman's Day/75n1075
Jenkins, J H/Works of/76n53
Jenkins, N/Thematic catalogue/78n908
Jenkins, W A/In other/79n1120/Junior thesaurus/79n1121/My first/78n1029
Jenkinson, M/Wild rivers/75n632
Jensen, J T/Yapese-English/78n1073/Yapese reference/79n1154
Jensen, M/Documentary history/77n370; 77n371
Jensen, M C/America in/78n349
Jensen, R/Fire protection/77n1578
Jensen, R W/Handbook of circuit/77n1592
Jentschura, H/Warships of/79n1602
Jerrold, W/Descriptive index/77n1241
Jerusalem hist atlas/Gilbert/79n440
Jesse Hill Ford/White/76n1237
Jeuck, J E/Management educ/75n215

Jewell, B/Veteran sewing/77n933
Jewish and Hebrew onomastics/Singerman/78n425
Jewish bk annual/75n323; 76n382
Jewish community in America/Brickman/78n389
Jewish films in the US/Fox/77n1009
Jewish hist atlas/Gilbert/78n371
Jewish landmarks of NY/Postal/79n609
Jewish organizations/Cohen/76n379
Jewish yellow pages/Rockland/77n820
Jews in Spain and Portugal/Singerman/76n384
Jews in the Soviet Union/Fluk/76n380
Joan, P/Guide to women's/79n764
Job hunter's gd to 8 great Amer cities/Salmon/79n864
Jobbers directory/78n205
Jobs '77/Yeomans/78n778
Jochum, K P S/W. B. Yeats/79n1258
Joekes, R/National trust/76n556
Joetta Community Library/Brown/76n146
John Ashbery/Kermani/77n864
John Barth/Vine/78n1131/Weixlmann/77n1199
John Berryman/Arpin/77n1200/Stefanik/76n1228
John Dryden/Latt/77n1232
John Dunton and the English bk trade/Parks/77n55
John E. Fogarty/Healey/75n251
John F. Kennedy/Newcomb/78n446
John Gay/Klein/75n1385
John Hawkes/Hryciw/78n1140
John Osborne/Northouse/76n1280
John Peabody Harrington/Walsh/77n734
John Ruskin/Beetz/77n1239
John Steinbeck/Goldstone/76n1249/Hayashi/77n1213
John Updike/Sokoloff/75n1371
Johns, C J/Handbook of library/78n146
Johns Hopkins atlas of human fundamental anatomy/Zuidema/78n1383
Johnsgard, P A/Ducks, geese/79n1373/Waterfowl of/77n1381
Johnsich, J R/Modern real/77n802
Johnson, A H/Encyclopedia of food/79n1533/Encyclopedia of food technology/76n1574
Johnson, C B/New English-/76n1143
Johnson, C D/Annotated bibliog Shakespearean/77n1240
Johnson, C R/Plots and/78n1164; 79n1229
Johnson, D B/National party/75n493; 79n520
Johnson, D C/Index to Southeast/78n295
Johnson, D E/Collector's gd/78n871

Johnson, D E/Manual of active/75n1807
Johnson, D E/Survey of/78n1026
Johnson, D P/Handbook of distinctively/75n441
Johnson, E/International riding/75n773
Johnson, E D/History of libraries/77n280
Johnson, E M/Francis Cotes/78n817
Johnson, E W/How to achieve/77n1087
Johnson, F/Start early/77n225
Johnson, G W/American political/79n521
Johnson, H/Hugh Johnson's/79n1518/International book/75n1491/Wine/76n1561
Johnson, H A/Ethnic American/77n424
Johnson, M M/Gasteromycetae of/76n1396
Johnson, P/Boating facts/77n684/Yachting world/75n747
Johnson, R/Dictionary of biographies/76n1216/Dictionary of famous/76n1186
Johnson, R B/California/77n543
Johnson, R D/Libraries for/78n261
Johnson, R E/Handbook of educ'l/77n639
Johnson, R O/Index to literature/77n42
Johnson, R T/Sports encyclopedia: baseball/75n733; 78n610/Sports ency: pro football/76n738
Johnson, S E D/Frisbee/76n767
Johnson, S L/Guide to American/78n382
Johnson, S W/Freshman's friend/77n585
Johnson, W L/Directory of special/75n80; 76n389
Johnson, W T/Insects that/77n1389
Johnston, D F/Copyright hndbk/79n65
Johnston, D M/International law/75n1535
Johnston, G S/Atlas of gallium-67/75n1643
Johnston, M T/Amelia Gayle/79n186
Johnston, R B/West Virginians/78n403
Johnston, R F/Annual review ecology/76n1357
Johnston, W B/Minorities in/76n391
Johnstone, W D/For good/76n1316
Johnstone, T M/Ḥarsūsi lexicon/79n1139
Johnston's gazetteer of Scotland/Munro/76n457
Joiner, B L/Current index statistics/79n792/v2/79n793
Joklik, W K/Zinsser microbiology/77n1491
Joncich, M J/Measurement and/78n121
Jones, A E/Atlas of gallium-67/75n1643
Jones, C/British children's/77n1225
Jones, D/Songwriter's market/79n978
Jones, D G/Bibliography of business/78n701
Jones, D L/Books in English/76n278
Jones, E/World of/77n1547
Jones, E A/Index of human/75n1560

Jones, E C/Cumulative index (1897-1975)/78n22
Jones, F D/Machinery's hndbk/76n1653
Jones, G F/Concordance to Juan/79n1290
Jones, J E/Reference gd handbooks/78n1372
Jones, J H/Correspondence educ'l/78n569
Jones, J K/Good Housekeeping/79n1488
Jones, J O/Index of human/75n1560
Jones, K/International index/76n1066
Jones, K/Year bk social/75n337
Jones, K W/Sources on/76n360
Jones, L A/Parker directory/77n539
Jones, L S/US bombers/76n1682
Jones, M L/Survey of/79n670
Jones, R/Atlas of world/79n786
Jones, T/Oxford-Harrap/79n1138
Jones, T A/Soviet sociology/79n732
Jones, T C/Halls of/78n75
Jones, V A/North American/76n1170
Jones, W/Colorado grubstake/76n347
Jonnard, C M/Caribbean investment/75n916/Exporter's financial/76n867
Jordan, A H/Cannons' bibliog/77n167
Jordan, J W/Colonial and/79n488
Jordan, L/NY Times/77n116
Jordan, M/Cannons' bibliog/77n167
Jordan, R/Lesbian in/76n1506
Jordan, W B/Maine in/77n393
Jorgensen, E/Audi service/75n1735/Corvette service/75n1736
Jorgensen, N/Sierra Club/79n1338
Jorstad, D/Creativity in/76n1161
Joseph, J/Complete out-/75n977
Joseph, T/Bibliography of Ismāʿīlī/79n1052
Josey, E J/Century of/77n157/Handbook of black/78n142/Information society/79n149/New dimensions/76n138/Opportunities for/78n257
Journal index (AAUW) 1882-1975/American Assoc of Univ Women/79n673
Journal of documentation retrospective index/Anthony/78n158
Journal of library hist index/Davis/79n190
Jovanović, S/Guide to Yugoslav/76n214
Joy, J/Development as/79n760
Joyner, N T/Doing business/77n782/International businessman's/75n894
Judd, B/Hawaiian language/79n389/Voyages to/75n424
Jugs/Paton/78n872
Juhl, M/B-J paperback/77n195
Julian, T W/Dell ency/75n1669
Julius Guttag Collection of Latin American coins/Guttag/75n1065
Jung, D/Warships of/79n1602
Junior high school library catalog/Schechter/76n159
Junior pears ency/Blishen/79n73
Junior thesaurus/Schiller/79n1121
Juran, J M/Quality control/75n1811
Jurgensen, B/How to live/76n874
Justice, C/Abbreviations and/77n1475
Justice for the California consumer/Silva/77n816
Juvenile rights since 1967/von Pfeil/76n510

K. T. Maclay's total beauty catalog/Maclay/79n1491
Kaczmarek, M/Finding information/77n223
Kadish, F/London on/76n559
Kaganoff, B C/Dictionary of Jewish/78n423
Kahn, G/Word book/76n1133
Kaid, L L/Political campaign/75n462
Kail, J/Who was/78n365
Kaiser, F E/Handling special/75n248
Kaiser, J F/Literature in/77n1580
Kafka bibliog 1908-1976/Flores/78n1189
Kalber, F A/Handbook of marine/76n1470
Kalia, D R/Bibliography of bibliographies/76n5
Kalidasa bibliog/Narang/77n1268
Kalinsky, G/Ballparks/76n706
Kalisch, B J/Child abuse/79n748
Kallenbach, J E & J S/American state/78n458
Kaltreider, L W/Benefit-cost/77n248
Kamachi, N/Japanese studies/77n319
Kamenetsky, I/Guide to Dag/78n273
Kaminkow, M J/Genealogies in/78n394/United States local/76n348
Kaminsky, L J/Nonprofit repertory/78n923
Kammerer, K L/Writer's gd/76n1537
Kane, J N/Facts about/75n388; 77n514/Kane book/75n93; 75n388; 77n95
Kane, R S/Italy A to Z/78n532
Kane bk of famous first facts and records in the US/Kane/75n93; 77n95
Kanely, E A/Cumulative subj gd/77n112/Cumulative subj index/75n102
Kanet, R E/Soviet and/75n534
Kansas territorial settlers of 1860 who were born in Tennessee, Virginia, North Carolina and South Carolina/Robertson/77n475
Kaplan, D F/Selected bibliog nutrition/75n1689
Kaplan, S R/Encyclopedia of tarot/79n1437

Kaprelian, M H/Aesthetics for/78n924
Karan, P P/Atlas of Kentucky/78n520
Karassik, I J/Pump hndbk/77n1610
Karel, L/Dried grasses/76n1590
Karel Boleslav Jirák/Tischler/76n1011
Karen Blixen-Isak Dinesen/Henriksen/79n1265
Kari, J M/Navajo reading/76n413
Karis, T/From protest/75n520; 78n471
Karkala, J A & L/Bibliography of Indo-/77n1267
Karklis, M/Latvians in/75n820
Karlgren, B/Analytic dict/76n1151
Karlgren, H/Natural language/79n337
Karnaookh, G I/Shortage survival/75n947
Karnataka/Satyaprakash/79n371
Karp, T/Dictionary of music/75n1141
Karpinski, L M/Religious life/79n1050
Karr, J N/Condominium buyer's/75n948
Kasbeer, T/Bibliography of continental/75n1565
Kase, F J/Designs/76n1648/Trademarks/75n962
Kaspar, P/1601 decorating/75n1104
Kastlemusick directory for collectors of recordings/79n972
Kastrup, E K/Facts and/79n1500
Kate Greenaway: catalogue of the Collection, Detroit Public Library/Thomson/78n1161
Katherine Anne Porter and Carson McCullers/Kiernan/77n1211
Kato, H/Japanese research/75n1295
Kato, T/Concordance to works/75n1392
Kattleman, D/Facts on/77n500
Katz, B/Guide to magazine/77n199/Library Lit/75n142; 76n113; 77n158; 79n173/Magazines for/75n171; 79n17/Reference and/79n295
Katz, D B/Guide to special/77n34
Katz, J/Concordance to poems/76n1231
Katz, J/Gay American/78n652
Katz, W A/Introduction to reference/75n245; 79n294
Katz, Z/Handbook of major/76n385
Katzner, K/Languages of/76n1110
Kauffman, D T/Baker's pocket/76n1084
Kaufman, M/Handbook for electronics/77n1593/Handbook of operational/77n1601
Kaufman, W I/Whole-world/79n1519
Kaufmann, W/Musical references/77n948
Kaufrufe und strabenhandler/Beall/78n806
Kaul, H K/Early writings/77n325/Periodicals in/75n44
Kavaliunas, J/Environmental-socioeconomic/78n1350

Kay, E/International authors/77n1180/International who's who music/76n1004/International who's who poetry/79n1199/Men of/78n113/World who's who/77n124
Kay, E R/Directory of postsecondary/77n632
Kay, M/Natural language/79n337
Kay, M A/Southwestern medical/78n1397
Kaye, G W C/Tables of/75n1458
Kaye, M/Catalog of music/79n723
Kaye, P J/National playwrights/78n944
Kaylor, P C/Abstract of/77n467
Kaysing, B/Robin Hood/75n756
Kazickas, J/American woman's/77n724
Kazmer, D R & V/Russian economic/79n803
Keane, C B/Encyclopedia and/79n1463
Keaveney, S S/American painting/75n1028
Keckeissen, R G/Guide to reference/77n14
Keegan, J/Rand McNally/78n1560/Who's who military/77n1635
Keeling, D F/British library/76n225
Keesey, R E/Modern parliamentary/75n472
Keesing, F M/Culture change/75n867
Keeslar, O/Financial aids/75n678; 78n563
Keeton, G W/Year bk world/75n90; 76n507; 79n513
Kehde, N/Access/76n28/Access index/78n19/American left/77n505
Kehler, D/Problems in/76n1181
Keleti, G/Handbook of micromethods/75n1462
Keller, C D/How to do/76n111/Union catalogs/75n249
Keller, H H/German word/79n1137
Kelley, A P/Anatomy of/76n961
Kelley, M E/In pursuit/75n1346
Kelley, P/Brownings' correspondence/79n1233
Kelly, A/Jack the Ripper/75n828
Kelly, B/Who's who golf/77n696
Kelly, C A/Directory of law-/79n571
Kelly, D H/Higher educ/76n573
Kelly, J/Bibliography in history/77n401
Kelly, J/Chilton's auto/75n1722
Kelly, J D/Chilton's motorcycle/75n1742/Chilton's truck/75n1751
Kelly, P/AA guide/79n711
Kelly, P/Irish family/77n487
Kemmer, E J/Rape and/78n675
Kemmerling, D/Commodity prices/75n920
Kemp, D A/Nature of/77n159
Kemp, E C/Manuscript solicitation/79n246
Kemp, G/Congressional hearings/75n489
Kemp, P/Oxford companion/78n1549

Kempe, C H/Handbook of pediatrics/77n1486
Kempe, H K/Louisiana almanac/76n490
Kemper, R E/Directorship by/78n210
Kemper, R V/History of anthropology/79n776
Kempkes, W/International bibliog comics/75n1312
Kempton, R/Art nouveau/78n785
Ken Russell/Rosenfeldt/79n1027
Kendall, A/Art of/75n988
Kenin, R/Dictionary of biographical/79n97
Kennedy, C/Buying antiques/78n837
Kennedy, E G/Etched work/79n897
Kennedy, R L/Fundamentals of/76n1572
Kenneson, C/Bibliography of cello/76n1016
Kent, A/Encyclopedia of computer/76n1626; 78n1523/Encyclopedia of library/76n129; 78n133; 79n159/Resource sharing/75n211
Kent, F L/Retrospective index/79n1306
Kent, J A/Riegel's hndbk/75n1452
Kent, R/Reading the/75n155
Kentucky marriages/Clift/75n411
Keown, I/Lovers' guide/75n596
Kerfoot, J B/American pewter/77n900
Kermani, D K/John Ashbery/77n864
Kern, K/Owner-built/76n1640
Kerr, J A/Miguéis/79n1289
Kerrod, R/Concise color/76n1314
Kershner, W K/Flight instructor's/76n731
Kersnowski, F L/Bibliography of modern/77n1269
Kertis, J/English language/78n561
Kess, S/Practical gd individual/75n985/Practical tax/75n984
Ketchum, W C/Catalog of American/79n917
Kettler, E L/Historic preservation/77n536
Key, J D/Library automation/77n289
Key, K/ABC of/75n1698
Key, M R/Nonverbal communication/78n1074
Key influences in the American right/Solara/75n482
Key resources in career educ/Tiedeman/78n570
Key to the publications of the US census, 1790-1887/Lunt/78n685
Key words in educ/Collins/76n594
Keyes, K/Master guide/75n1605
Keynes, G/Bibliography of George/77n1027
Keys, J D/Chinese herbs/77n1505
Keys to the marine invertebrates of Puget Sound, the San Juan Archipelago/Kozloff/76n1412
Keywords/Williams/77n1065

Khadduri, J/Palestine and/75n535
Khalidi, W/Palestine and/75n535
Khalsa, P S/Spiritual community/79n1087
Khan, S A/Sources for/76n362
Kibbey, R A/Picasso/79n906
Kibler, J E/Pseudonymous publications/77n1212
Kidd, D A/Microcomputer dict/77n1584
Kidney, W C/Nelson's new/79n1099
Kiernan, R F/Katherine Anne/77n1211
Kiernan, T/Shrinks, etc./75n1591
Kies, C/Problems in/75n235
Kilgour, F G/Library and/78n147
Killeen, J/Best restaurants/77n1542
Killick, T/Economies of/77n770
Kim, C H/Books by/78n143
Kim, H/Koreans in/75n821
Kim, U C/Policies of/77n177; 79n247
Kimber, R T/Automation in/76n231
Kincaid, E B/Bird life/76n1427
Kinch, M P/Forestry theses/79n1538
Kinder, H/Anchor atlas/76n297; 79n401
Kinert, R/Racing planes/76n732
King, B F/Field gd birds/76n1423
King, C L/Ramon J. Sender/77n1275
King, C S/Psychic and/79n1438
King, D A/Underground buying/78n749
King, H W/Handbook of hydraulics/77n1604
King, J D/Women's studies/77n718
King, R C/Dictionary of genetics/76n1356
King Research, Inc./Library photocopying/79n318
Kingman, L/Illustrators of/79n898/Newbery and/77n1192
Kings and queens of England/Murray/75n624
Kings, rulers and statesmen/Egan/78n332
Kingsley Amis/Gohn/77n1228
Kinkade, R G/Thesaurus of/76n1495
Kinkle, R D/Complete ency popular/75n1171
Kinney, J M/Directory of state/76n318
Kinsman, C D/Contemporary authors/75n119; 76n96; 76n97; 76n98; 76n99
Kintner, E W/Primer on/75n892
Kinton, J F/American ethnic/76n390/Criminology, law/75n829
Kipel, Z/Ethnic directory/79n445
Kipling primer/Knowles/75n1389
Kirby, D K/American fiction/77n1194
Kirby, R F/Physical education/79n675
Kirby-Smith, H T/US observatories/77n1308
Kirk, J T/Early American/75n1076
Kirk, R/Washington state/75n609

Kirk, T G/Library research/79n1335
Kirkendall, C A/Putting library/79n290
Kirkham, E B/Indices to/77n1191
Kirschenbaum, D M/Atlas of protein/75n1451
Kirschner, C D/Doctoral research/76n581
Kirshenblatt-Gimblett, B/Speech play/77n1123
Kirshner, G/Teachers guides/79n1180
Kirtisinghe, P/Sea shells/79n928
Kirtland, K/London on/76n559
Kislia, J A/Let's see/76n680
Kismaric, C/Photography catalog/78n887
Kissinger, W S/Sermon on/77n1045
Kister, K F/Dictionary buying/78n1028/Encyclopedia buying/77n71; 79n74
Kitchen wisdom/Arkin/78n1467
Kitching, J/Birdwatcher's guide/77n1382
Kits and plans/Rosenbloom/75n1036
Kitter, A/US and/75n924
Klaber, D/Violets of/78n1292
Klaits, B/When you/77n1434
Klamkin, C/Railroadiana/77n934
Klamkin, M/Collector's guide/77n920/Depression glass/75n1081/Old sheet/76n1027
Klassen, F H/Multicultural educ/78n541
Klawans, Z H/Reading and/78n847
Kleeberg, I C/Butterick fabric/76n875/Butterick home/77n941
Klein, B/Bibliography of American/77n422/Guide to American educ'l/76n582/Guide to American scientific/77n1284/Reference ency . . . American Indian/75n808; 79n463/Reference ency . . . American psychology/76n1500
Klein, C/Kliatt paperback/75n199
Klein, E/Bibliography of contemporary/79n1089
Klein, F J/Administration of/77n537
Klein, H D/Guide to non-sexist/77n1142
Klein, J E/Tennis player's/75n585
Klein, J T/John Gay/75n1385
Klein, L/Chiropractic/78n1424
Klema, E D/Public regulation/79n1409
Klemp, E/America in/77n542
Klempner, I M/Audiovisual materials/79n305
Kliatt paperback bk gd/Hiatt/75n199
Klimas, J E/Wild flowers Connecticut/76n1390/Wildflowers of eastern/75n1478/Wild flowers Massachusetts/76n1394/Wild flowers New Hampshire/76n1391/Wild flowers New Jersey/76n1392/Wild flowers New York/76n1393/Wild flowers Pennsylvania/76n1395
Kline, N S/Psychotropic drugs/75n1656

Klink, W/Maxwell Anderson/78n925
Klinkowitz, J/Donald Barthelme/78n1132/Kurt Vonnegut/76n1251
Klinowski, J/Cinema, the/76n1057
Kloe, D R/Dictionary of onomatopoeic/78n1045
Kloesel, C J W/English novel/77n1227
Klos, J/Dictionary of data/79n1566
Kloss, H/Linguistic composition/76n1112
Klots, A B/Field gd butterflies/78n1330
Klyne, W/Atlas of stereochemistry/76n1345
Knaack, M S/Encyclopedia of US/79n1593
Knap, A/Family camping/77n687
Knap, J J/Complete outdoorsman's/75n724/Family camping/77n687/Where to fish/76n729
Knapp, W/Politics of/78n470
Knappman, E W/Government and/75n494/South Vietnam/75n530/Watergate and/75n501
Knatz, H/Finding a/79n865
Knauer, K/Handbook of veterinary/79n1543
Knees, D/Butterick kitchen/78n1474
Knight, D/Sources for/76n1309
Knight, G H/Dun &/75n956
Knight, H M/1-2-3 guide/77n160
Knight, J/Guide to graduate/76n665
Knight, L L/Biographical dict/79n1219
Knight, R J B/Guide to manuscripts/79n408
Knitting and crocheting pattern index/Halevy/78n878
Knives and knifemakers/Latham/75n1093
Knobel, E/Field gd grasses/79n1349
Knorr, L C/Citrus diseases/76n1401
Knott, D/University of London/76n823
Know & claim your African name/Sanyika/77n490
Knowledge and its organization/Batty/77n150
Knowles, A S/International ency higher/79n638
Knowles, F L/Kipling primer/75n1389
Knutsen, K/Wild plants/76n1575
Kobetz, R W/Law enforcement/76n779
Koch, D/Chilton's complete/75n737
Kochen, M/Information for/77n267/Integrative mechanisms/76n114/Principles of/75n279
Koegler, H/Concise Oxford/78n934
Koehler, S R/US art/78n795
Koenig, W J/European manuscript/76n319/Two world/78n326
Koester, J/Writer's market/76n1175; 77n1132
Kohland, W F/Guide to mineral/79n1421
Kohler, E L/Dictionary for/76n843

Kohlmetz, E/Encyclopedia of American/75n366
Kolesar, A/Bibliography of Colorado/78n12
Kolman, R/Health sciences/79n1451
Kondo, K/Elsevier's dictionary/78n1512
Konishi, F/Exercise equivalents/75n1690
Konkordanz zu den gedichten Hugo von Hofmannsthals/Sondrup/79n1278
Koops, W R H/Developments in/79n197/IFLA's first/79n316
Kopecky, J/Bibliography of liquid/78n1239
Koppman, L/American Jewish/78n528/Jewish landmarks/79n609
Koreans in America 1882-1974/Kim/75n821
Korkie, B M/Mathematical dict/78n707
Korkmas, A/Directory of services/75n799
Kornegay, F A/American-Southern/77n526
Korsant, P B/World travel/75n591
Kostka, S M/Bibliography of computer/75n1129
Kosut, H/South Vietnam/75n529; 75n530
Koubourlis, D J/Concordance to poems/75n1425
Kovalenko, E G/English-Russian/78n1502
Kovel, R & T/Kovels' collector's... American/75n1082/Kovels' collector's... limited/75n1086
Kovel, R & T/Kovels' complete antiques/75n1055/Official bottle/75n1083
Kovels' collector's gd to American art pottery/Kovel/75n1082
Kovels' collector's gd to limited editions/Kovel/75n1086
Kovels' complete antiques price list/Kovel/75n1055
Kowalik, J/Polish press/79n465
Kowalski, R R/Women and/77n1002
Kozloff, E N/Keys to/76n1412/Plants and/77n1346
Kraay, C M/Archaic and/77n912
Kraemer, K L/Municipal information/78n463
Krafsun, R P/American film/77n1006
Krakauer, E/Abbreviations and/77n1475
Kramer, J/Encyclopedia of tennis/76n762/Free earth/75n1704/How to identify/76n1591/Indoor trees/76n1592/Picture ency/79n1339/Pit n'pot/76n1593/Seasonal gd/77n1556
Kranz, J L/American nautical/76n962
Kraus, B/Barbara Kraus/76n1576/Basic food/75n1691; 75n1692/Dictionary of sodium/76n1577
Kraus, D H/American bibliography/76n272; 78n307
Krause, C L/Guidebk of Franklin/76n967/Standard catalog/75n1068; 76n969

Krauskopf, F J/Fifty-year/75n371
Krauskopf, R W/World War/77n362
Krauss, R E/Sculpture of/78n822
Krauss, S/Encyclopaedic hndbk/78n1370
Kravitz, D/Who's who Greek/78n1017
Krawczyk, C/Mountaineering/78n618
Kreider, B A/Index to children's/78n939
Kreitzman, R/Teachers' centers/78n559
Krepel, W J/Education and/78n542/Free materials/79n681
Kresheck, J/Terminology of/79n1175
Kreslins, J A/Foreign affairs/77n528
Krichmar, A/Women's movement/78n663/Women's studies/76n142
Krieger, M/Homeowner's ency/79n1571
Kristian, J/Galaxies and/77n1311
Krivinyi, N/World military/75n1846
Krochmal, A & C/Complete illus'd/75n1043/Guide to medicinal/75n1466/Making it/76n876
Krochmal, C/Guide to natural/75n1677
Kroeber, A L/Handbook of Indians/78n683
Krommer-Benz, M/World guide/79n1095
Krompotich/Traveling F.M./78n1082
Kronick, D A/History of scientific/77n1278/Manual on medical/75n1610
Kruger, A N/Argumentation and/76n1177
Krummel, D W/Guide for dating/75n1118
Krupp, M A/Current medical/75n1609/Physician's handbook/77n1488
Kruzas, A T/Directory of special/75n164; 78n199/Encyclopedia of governmental/76n481/Encyclopedia of info/75n165; 79n166/Medical and/78n1407/New special/78n200/Subject directory/76n172; 78n201
Kryszak, W D/Small business/79n823
Kubat, J/Accountants' index/78n719; 78n720; 79n827
Kubo, S/Reader's Greek-/77n1046
Kuda, M J/Women loving/77n1127
Kuehn, J/Feasibility of/79n266
Kuhn, R/Annotated bibliog Aspen/78n543
Kuhn, R A/Woman's almanac/77n723
Kujoth, J S/Boys' and/76n696/Subject gd humor/77n1141
Kulkarni, H B/Stephen Spender/78n1182
Kulkin, M-E/Her way/77n719
Kumar, G/Documentation on/75n300
Kumar, K/Research libraries/75n257
Kumar, S/Documents on/76n503
Kumar, V/Committees and/78n484; 79n546
Kunert, J/Plots and/77n1229
Kunz, V/Collector's book/77n928
Kunz, W/Methods of/79n263

Kuo, T C/East Asian/79n367
Küper, W/Bibliographie zur/76n256
Kurds in Iran/Behn/78n284
Kurian, G T/Historical and/77n326
Kurt Vonnegut, Jr./Pieratt/76n1251
Kurtz, E/Lineman's and/77n1594
Kurtz, L S/Historical dict Tanzania/79n361
Kurtz, S/World guide/76n299
Kusaiean-English dictionary/Lee/77n1094
Kusin, V V/Czechoslovakia/76n269
Kutler, S I/Reviews in/76n316
Kuvshinoff, B W/Fire sciences/78n1503
Kuwayama, Y/Trademarks &/75n963
Kverneland, K O/World metric/79n1547
KWIC index to the Commonwealth Bureau of Soils/Greenwood/75n1665
Kyed, J M/Scientific, technical/75n1430; 77n1285

L.A. home furnishing, decorating & accessory buying gd/Faulkner/75n1102
La Beau, D/Author biographies/79n135/Biographical dictionaries/76n91; 77n120/Children's authors/77n1156
La Follette, M C/Citizen and/78n1201
LaBarr, D F/Study of/77n529
Labor arbitration gd/Baer/75n973
Labor economics/Azvedo/79n853
Labor educ in the US/Dwyer/78n765
Labor in print: Australia 1850-1939/Gibbney/76n903
Labor unions/Fink/78n766
Laby, T H/Tables of/75n1458
Lacey, A R/Dictionary of philosophy/78n1006
Lackey, R S/Frontier claims/78n404
Lackmann, R/TV soap/77n1118
Lackner, I/Directory of economic/79n239
Ladd, B/National inventory/78n124
Ladendorf, J M/Changing role/75n206
Ladenson, A/American library/79n174
Ladies' Home Journal family medical gd/Nourse/75n1650
Lady laureates/Opfell/79n770
Lafayette: letters, docs, manuscripts/Gottschalk/76n317
LaFleur, L/Library programs/77n163
Lafourcade, B/Bibliography of writings/79n1246
Lagoon info source bk/Middlebrooks/79n1580
Lagua, R T/Nutrition and/76n1525
LaHood, C G/Reprographic services/77n286
Lai, H M/Chinese newspapers/79n455
Laird, C/Webster's new/76n1134
Laird, H/Rainbow dict/79n1113

Laird, W D/Hopi bibliog/79n777
Laita, L M/Cortina/Grosset/77n1099
Lake, E E/Definition and/79n754
Lakela, O/Ferns of/78n1284
Lal, P/Annotated Mahabharata/75n1421
Lamar, H R/Reader's ency/78n314
Lamb, B & E/Colorful cacti/76n1385
Lamb, P J/Climatic atlas/79n1414
Lambert, C M/Village studies/79n778
Lambert, E/World of/77n940
Lancaster, F W/Applications of/76n232/Information retrieval/75n280/Measurement and/78n121/Proceedings of/75n282/Use of/77n290
Lance, J/Teachers' centers/78n559
Lancour, H/Encyclopedia of library/76n129; 78n133; 79n159
Land, B/Directory of associations/75n343; 76n65; 79n82
Land tenure and agrarian reform in Africa and the Near East/Land Tenure Center Library Staff/77n1514
Land Tenure Center Library Staff/Land tenure/77n1514
Land use planning abstracts/76n1462; 79n1404
Landa, B L/Tropical fish/76n1558
Landau, S I/Doubleday dictionary/76n1120/Doubleday Roget's/78n1040
Landau, T/European directory/76n868/Who's who librarianship/75n253
Landi, V/Bantam great/79n712
Landmarks of library lit/Ellsworth/77n279
Landmarks of Rochester and Monroe County/Malo/75n1019
Landmarks of the American Revolution/Boatner/76n326
Landon, G/Encyclopedia of folk/76n1031
Landovitz, L F/Funk &/75n1262
Landrum, P W/Who's who graphology/78n1378
Landsat index atlas of the developing countries of the world/78n515
Landwehr, L J/Student's gd/76n25
Lane, G/Concordance to poems/77n1246/Sylvia Plath/79n1222
Lane, J T/Bibliography: books/75n1347
Lane, M J/Doctor's lawyer/76n1533
Lane, N D/Writer's guide/76n1537
Lang, V/Bliss bibliographic: class J/78n225/Bliss bibliographic: class P/78n226/Bliss bibliographic: class Q/78n227
Langer, W L/New illustrated/76n300
Langhans, E A/Biographical dict actors/75n1188; 76n1045; 79n1022

Langman, J/Atlas of medical/79n1447
Langridge, D W/Classification and/77n256/
  Introduction to/77n252
Langs, R J/Technique of/75n1592
Langston, A L/Pedigrees of/75n425
Language and sentiment of flowers/75n1244
Language of . . .
  business/McCaffrey/75n885
  psychoanalysis/Laplanche/75n1581
  show biz/Sergel/75n1180
  the foreign bk trade/Orne/77n57
  the railroader/Adams/79n1114
  twentieth century music/Fink/76n996
Languages of the world/Katzner/76n1110
Lankevich, G J/Atlanta/79n426/Boston/75
  n507/Gerald R. Ford/79n414/Milwaukee/
  78n355
Lann, J H/Who's who arts/75n1014
Lanzing, G/Library, documentation/77n36
Lapedes, D N/Encyclopedia of energy/77n1411/
  McGraw-Hill dict . . . life/77n1347/McGraw-
  Hill dict physics/79n1332/McGraw-Hill
  dict scientific/75n1434; 78n1210; 79n1299/
  McGraw-Hill ency food/78n1452/McGraw-
  Hill ency geological/79n1418
Lapin, L/Art and/78n874/Artist's and/77n856/
  Craftworker's market/79n938
Lapin, N/Fairfield County/76n547
Laplanche, J/Language of/75n1581
Lapointe, C & F/Claude Lévi-Strauss/79n779/
  Gabriel Marcel/78n1001/Jean-Paul/77n1051/
  Maurice Merleau-Ponty/78n1002
Laqueur, W/Dictionary of politics/75n467/
  Fascism/77n496
Large type books in print/77n18
Larkin, R/Hail, Columbia/76n1048
Larousse dict of the freshwater aquarium/
  Favré/79n700
Larousse dict of wines of the world/Dubuigne/
  78n1454
Larousse ency of the animal world/77n1372
Larousse gd to birds of Britain and Europe/
  Bruun/79n1369
Larousse gd to minerals, rocks and fossils/
  Hamilton/78n1359
Larrick, N/Parent's guide/77n1157
Larsgaard, M/Map librarianship/79n240
Larson, K A/Public relations/79n804
Larson, L/GO, PEP/77n211
Larson, L & P/Sierra Club/78n1270
Laska, L L/Tennessee legal/79n573
Lass, A & B/Dictionary of pronunciation/77
  n1084
Lass-Woodfin, M J/Books on American/79n464

Last Celt/Lord/79n1218
Last whole film catalog/77n1010
Late-medieval England/Guth/77n409
Latham, R E/Dictionary of medieval/76n1149
Latham, S/Knives and/75n1093
Lathrop, J/Willa Cather/76n1230
Latin, H A/Privacy/78n271
Latin America/Sobel/75n342
Latin America books/Wilgus/75n297
Latin America: economic hist, 1830-1930/
  Cortes Conde/79n805
Latin America review 1 of books/Harding/
  76n280
Latin America, Spain and Portugal/Wilgus/
  79n384
Latin America, Spain, and Portugal: paper-
  back books/Dorn/77n305
Latin American initialisms and acronyms/UN
  Economic Commission for Latin America/
  75n344
Latin American Jewry/Sable/79n461
Latin American lit in English translation/
  Shaw/77n1273
Latin American serial docs . . . Venezuela/
  Quintero-Mesa/79n26
Latt, D J/John Dryden/77n1232
Latvians in America 1640-1973/Karklis/75
  n820
Laubenfels, J/Gifted student/79n631
Laufe, A/Broadway's greatest/79n1004
Laugher, C T/Thomas Bray's/75n268
Laurence Urdang Associates/Lives of/77n412
Laurenti, J L/Federico García/75n1427
Lavin, M A/Seventeenth-century/77n866
Law, D/Concise herbal/75n1482
Law, S/Rights of/75n559
Law & legal lit of Peru/Valderrama/78n493
Law and the computer/Duggan/75n548
Law and the environment/Dickson/75n547
Law and the writer/Polking/79n561
Law dictionary/Gifis/76n511
Law enforcement/Felkenes/78n497
Law enforcement/Prostano/75n830
Law enforcement and criminal justice educ
  directory/Kobetz/76n779
Law schools of the world/Tseng/79n572
Lawall, D B/Asher B. Durand/79n907
Lawlor, R/Bicentennial book/76n551
Laws, P/Guide to national/79n616
Lawson, A/Australian literature/79n1259/
  Patrick White/75n1409
Lawson, D E/Compton's ency/75n74

Lawson, M P/Agricultural atlas/78n1448/ Climatic atlas/79n1415/Economic atlas/78n695
Lawyer's desk book/Casey/76n515
Lawyers desk reference/Philo/76n517
Lay, R/Interstate guide/79n1172
Layman, R/Fitzgerald-Hemingway/79n1212/ Ring Lardner/77n1209
Layman's English-Greek concordance/Gall/76n1144
Layman's gd to AV jargon/76n595
Layton, R/Penguin stereo/79n971
Layzer, D/Annual review astronomy/75n1444
Leaders in educ/Jaques Cattell/75n692
Leaders in profile: US Senate/Douth/76n484
Leaf prints of American trees and shrubs/Marx/75n1493
League of Nations documents 1919-46/Reno/75n112; 77n501
Leaman, A/Complete food/78n1480/First complete/77n942
Leamer, L E/Suggestions for/75n200
Learning centers/Bennie/79n206
Learning disabilities with emphasis on reading/Lee/79n692
Learning resource centers/Pearson/75n216
Learning resource centers in community colleges/Thomson/77n206
Learning vacations/Eisenberg/79n656
Learning vacations: college seminars/Eisenberg/79n655
Leary, L/American literature/78n1111
Leathart, S/Trees of/79n1360
Leather, J/World warships/78n1576
Leavy, H T/Recreational vehicles/78n619
Lebar, F M/Ethnic groups/76n810
Leblanc, J Y/Pelican guide/75n610
Leck, C/Birds of/76n1424
Lector's gd to biblical pronunciations/Staudacher/76n1102
Ledbetter, W/Directory of American/75n895
Lederer, M/Guide to career/75n657; 77n629
Lederer, W H/Handbook of micromethods/75n1462
Lederman, D B/Russian-English/76n1147
Ledgard, H F/Programming proverbs/76n1627/ Programming proverbs FORTRAN/76n1628
Lee, E J/Lee of/75n426
Lee, G/Education for/77n48
Lee, G E/Learning disabilities/79n692
Lee, H F/Modern parents'/75n1647
Lee, J A/Reference manual/78n717

Lee, K/Bibliography of energy/78n803/Computer programs/75n1551/Encyclopedia of energy/78n1518
Lee, K-D/Kusaiean-English/77n1094
Lee, K S/Dictionary of rubber/76n1647
Lee, S/Inexpensive wine/75n1674
Lee, S H/Emerging trends/79n198/Library budgeting/78n211
Lee, T F/Seaweed handbook/79n1357
Lee, W/Reference gd fantastic/75n1194
Lee of Virginia/Lee/75n426
Leek, S/Sybil Leek's/75n1483
Leekley, J & S/Moments: Pulitzer Prize/79n953
Leeming, G/Who's who Henry/77n1207/ Who's who Jane/75n1377
Leeming, G/Who's who Thomas/76n1275
Leese, E/Costume design/78n952
Leftwich, A W/Dictionary of entomology/77n1390/Dictionary of zoology/75n1497
Legal first aid/Shain/76n508
Legal medicine annual/Wecht/78n1412
Legal secretary's encyclopedic dict/Thomae/78n501
Legal secretary's word finder and desk book/Reilly/75n561
Legal word bk/Gordon/79n569
Legg, W D/Annotated bibliog homosexuality/78n650
Leggett, A/Complete garden/76n1594
Leggett, G/Prentice-Hall/79n130
Legum, C/Africa contemporary/75n326/ Middle East/79n355
Lehnus, D J/Milestones in/75n225
Leider, M/Color atlas/76n1541
Leidy, W P/Popular guide/77n107
Leif, I P/Children's literature/78n1101/Community power/75n792/International sourcebk/79n38
Leigh, E/Glossary of words/75n1258
Leisure reading for adults/Jacques/78n596
Leita, C/SHARE: directory/77n183
Leitch, A/Princeton companion/79n671
Leitenberg, M/Vietnam conflict/75n463
Leith, M A/Summer employment/77n842
Lembeck, H/Grossman's guide/78n1456
Lemke, A/Museum companion/75n1004
Len Buckwalter's CB channel directory/78n1083
Lenk, J D/Handbook of electronic/77n1595
Lennette, E H/Manual of clinical/76n1362
Lenton, H T/German warships/77n1650
Lentricchia, F & M C/Robert Frost/77n1204
Leon, P W/William Styron/79n1224

Leonard, C M/General Assembly/79n533
Leonard, J W/Woman's who's/77n122
Leonard, T M/Day by/79n403
Leonard, W T/Hollywood players/77n1016
Léon-Dufour, X/Dictionary of biblical/75n1230
Lerner, G/Bibliography in history/77n720
Lerro, J P/Basic mathematics/77n1303
Lesbian in literature/Damon/76n1506
Lesbiana/Grier/78n674
Leslie, L A/20,000 words/78n1048
Lessard, M/Complete gd French-/76n963
Lesser, C H/Fighters for/79n411/Sinews of/77n372
Let it rot! /Campbell/76n1582
Let's go: Europe/Brown/79n617
Let's see it again/Kislia/76n680
Leuchtmann, H/Dictionary of terms/79n964
Leuz, C A/Leuz index/79n1481
Leuz index of plastic surgery/Leuz/79n1481
Levenston, E A/New Bantam-/78n1060
Lever, W E/How to obtain/77n620
Levey, J S/New Columbia/76n60
Levi, L/Handbook of tables/76n1351
Levi-Setti, R/Trilobites/76n1363
Levine, A/Rights of/75n560
Levine, C/Mansions, mills/76n554
Levine, E/Political dict/75n523
Levine, H M/American guide/77n301
Levine, S N/Dow Jones-/78n715/Financial analyst's/76n887
LeVine, V T/Historical dict Cameroon/75n318
Levinson, L/Medical risks/78n1416
Levitan, S A/Minorities in/76n391
Levite, C G/Business media: Africa/75n905/Business media: Asia/75n906
Levith, M J/What's in/79n1252
Levitt, P M/J. M. Synge/75n1404
Levy, L S/Give me/76n1028
Lewanski, R C/Guide to Polish/76n215
Lewchuk, R C/National register/75n679
Lewis, A L/Automobiles of/79n1553
Lewis, B T/Facilities and/75n1812
Lewis, D R/Educational games/75n703
Lewis, G/Gomer's guides/77n560; 78n525
Lewis, G/Sporting heritage/75n725
Lewis, G E D/Metric and/75n1716
Lewis, J W/Oxford advanced/75n1260
Lewis, M O/Foundation directory/76n620; 78n74
Lewis, R/NY book/77n1523
Lewis, R H/Book browser's/76n54
Lewis, W H/Ecology field/78n1345
Lewis, W S/Guide to life/75n1407

Lewytzkyj, B/Who's who socialist/79n143
Li, C/Political participation/78n447
Li-H-C/Social work/79n731
Li, Y/Bibliography of studies/76n1293
Liao, A Y/Acupuncture/77n1464
Liber, G/Nonconformity and/79n549
Liberty cap/Davis/79n227
Librarian and the patient/Phinney/78n196
"Librarian": selections/Pearson/77n281
Librarians and online services/Atherton/79n299
Librarians' glossary of terms/Harrod/79n160
Librarian's handbook/Taylor/79n175
Librarianship/Atkinson/75n135/Maidment/76n115
Librarianship and the Third World/Huq/78n251
Libraries and librarianship in the West/Jackson/75n267
Libraries and library services in the Southeast/Anders/77n148
Libraries and the arts & humanities/Bolté/79n146
Libraries and the challenge of change/Ingram/76n213
Libraries and the life of the mind in America/78n122
Libraries and work sampling/Goodell/76n112
Libraries as communication systems/Orr/78n126
Libraries for small museums/Collins/79n238
Libraries for teaching, libraries for research/Johnson/78n261
Libraries for the blind/Schauder/79n241
Libraries for today and tomorrow/Mathews/77n162
Libraries in higher educ/Cowley/77n202
Libraries in post-industrial society/Estabrook/78n119
Libraries in the political scene/Dosa/75n250
Library acquisition policies and procedures/Futas/78n204
Library acquisitions: practice and theory/78n159
Library and information CumIndex/Kilgour/78n147
Library and info services for special groups/Smith/75n236
Library and info studies in the United Kingdom and Ireland/Taylor/78n132
Library & media/Burlingame/79n251
Library and resource center in Christian educ/McMichael/78n195

Library as a learning serv center/Penland/79n153
Library assistant's manual/Chirgwin/79n321
Library Association/Directory of medical/78n198
Library at Mount Vernon/Carroll/79n326
Library automation: Orient/Key/77n289
Library automation: state of the art/Martin/76n233
Library automation systems/Salmon/77n294
Library bibliographies and indexes/Wasserman/76n128
Library budgeting/Lee/78n211
Library-centered approach to learning/Schuster/79n325
Library community services/Correy/79n287
Library connection: essays/Public Library Assoc/78n174
Library, documentation and archives serials/Lanzing/77n36
Library funding and public support/Frase/75n137
Library guiding/Carey/75n233
Library-information sci/MacCafferty/78n129
Library instruction gd/Peterson/75n239
Library instruction in the seventies/Rader/78n236
Library instruction programs: Wisconsin/76n132
Library Journal bk review/77n200; 79n182
Library life—American style/Plotnik/76n121
Library Lit/Katz/75n142; 76n113; 77n158; 79n173
Library literature 1974-75/Rentschler/78n148
Library management/Stueart/78n212
Library management: bibliog/Shonyo/78n213
Library management cases/Lowell/76n179
Library networks/Goldstein/75n139/Martin/77n161; 79n150
Library of Congress/Goodrum/75n204
LC as the national bibliographic center/77n238
LC Classification schedules/Savage/77n257
LC in perspective/Cole/79n237
LC Main Reading Room ref collection subj catalog/US Library of Congress/77n32
LC subj headings/Chan/79n268
Library operations research/Daiute/75n261
Library photocopying and the US Copyright Law of 1976/79n319
Library photocopying in the US/King Research/79n318
Library planning and decision-making systems/Hamburg/75n213

Library power/Thompson/75n146
Library programs/Robotham/77n163
Library research gd to biology/Kirk/79n1335
Library resources in Scotland/Smith/75n166
Library sci dissertations, 1925-72/Schlachter/75n150
Library searching/Morris/79n297
Library serv to children/Ray/79n215
Library serv to the Spanish speaking/Peterson/79n202
Library services for the institutionalised, the elderly, and the physically handicapped/Bramley/79n285
Library services to the blind and physically handicapped/Strom/78n237
Library services to the disadvantaged/Martin/76n201
Library staff developmt and continuing educ/Conroy/79n322
Library statistics of colleges and universities/Smith/78n170
Library tech assistant's hndbk/Borkowski/77n151
Library tech services/Magrill/78n244
Library telecommunications directory Canada-US/Bird/78n134
Library trustee/Young/79n204
Library work with children/Broderick/78n181
Library's public/Berelson/77n213
Libros en español/79n1190
Libros en Venta/76n16/Waldhüter/79n13
Lichine, A/Alexis Lichine's/76n1562
Lichtenstein, N/Political profiles/78n440
Liddell Hart, B/World War/79n398
Liebard, O M/Clergy and/79n1040/Love and/79n1041
Liebe, J/Indexes to NY/76n930
Liebers, A/Complete bk cross-/75n784
Lieberthal, K/Research gd central/77n524
Liederbach, C A/America's thousand/75n1226
Lien, D A/Complete gd for/76n1615
Liesener, J W/Systematic process/78n186
Life and health insur hndbk/Gregg/75n972
Life in and around freshwater wetlands/Ursin/76n1367
Life insurance desk book/Casey/76n901
Life of birds/Dorst/76n1418
Lifetime reading plan/Fadiman/79n691
Lifton, S/Call for/76n884
Ligare, K M/Illinois women's/79n765
Light lists/US Coast Guard/78n1551
Liles, M D & R M/Good Housekeeping/75n1794

Lilley, G P/Bibliography of John/76n1279
Limbacher, J L/Feature films/75n1208; 78n959/Film music/75n1147/Song list/75n1130
Limited edition collectibles/Hotchkiss/75n1085
Lin, Y/Chinese-English/75n1264
Lincoln, C E/Pictorial history/75n814
Lincoln, J E/Encyclopedia of comic . . . Batman/77n1167/ . . . Wonder Woman/77n1168
Lind, C G/Digest of/76n600
Lind, H Y/Voyages to/75n424
Lind, M/California catalogue/78n529
Lindberg, G U/Fishes of/75n1514
Linde, S/Whole health/79n1489
Lindemann, A J/Encyclopaedic dict/75n884
Lindner, G/Field gd seashells/79n929
Line, M/Essays on/76n207
Lineage & ancestry of H.R.H. Prince Charles/Paget/78n420
Lineman's and cableman's hndbk/Kurtz/77n1594
Lingfelter, M R/Vocations in/76n1208
Linguistic atlas of Scotland/Mather/76n1116; 78n1023
Linguistic atlas of the upper Midwest in three volumes/Allen/76n1115; 77n1058
Linguistic composition of the nations of the world: South Asia/Kloss/76n1112
Linguistic key to the Greek New Testament/Rienecker/78n996
Linguistics and English linguistics/Allen/78n1024
Link, C B/Whole seed/77n1557
Link, F M/English drama/78n926
Linn, J B/Annals of Buffalo/76n436
Linn, L C/Eastern North/79n1344
Linn's world stamp almanac/79n932
Linton, C D/American almanac/78n348/Bicentennial almanac/76n331
Linton, G E/Modern textile/75n964
Lippincott, L/Bibliography of writings/75n1366
Lippman, D/Craft sources/76n950
Lipscomb, E J/Amelia Gayle/79n186
Liptak, B G/Environmental engineers'/75n1540; 76n1459; 76n1460
Lipton, G C/French bilingual/75n1266/Spanish bilingual/77n1100
LIST: library and info services today/Wasserman/75n149; 76n125

List of . . .
  Admiralty records/78n479
  available publications of the US Dept of Agri/US Dept of Agriculture/78n1450
  Colonial Office records/78n480; 78n481
  nineteenth century maps of the state of Alabama/75n571
  theses and dissertations on tobacco and tobacco related research/Cheek/75n959
  worthwhile life and health insur bks/77n833
Listokin, D/Environmental impact/77n1416
Literacy and the nation's libraries/Lyman/78n144
Literary and library prizes/Weber/77n178
Literary hist of the US/Spiller/75n1339
Literary journal in America, 1900-50/Chielens/78n1109
Literary journal in America to 1900/Chielens/76n1218
Literary market place, with names & numbers/76n51
Literary research gd/Patterson/77n1126
Literary reviews in British periodicals 1821-1826/Ward/78n1157
Literary terms/Beckson/76n1184
Literary tour gd to England and Scotland/Harting/77n1223
Literary tour gd to the US: Northeast/Harting/79n601
Literary writings in America/78n1112
Literature and bibliog of the social sciences/Freides/75n170
Literature and young people/Cullinan/78n1099
Literature in digital signal processing/Helms/77n1580
Literature of . . .
  American music in bks and folk music collections/Horn/78n893
  Spain in English translation/Rudder/77n1276
  the Filipino-American in the US/Norell/77n443
  the film/Dyment/77n1000
Literature on Byzantine art 1892-1967/Allen/77n860
Literature survey of communication satellite systems and technology/Unger/78n1509
Lithographs of George Bellows/Mason/79n899

Litman, T J/Sociology of/78n1388
Littell, F H/Macmillan atlas/77n1020
Littell, J/Family records/77n468
Littérature occitane du moyen age/Taylor/
  79n1274
Little, E L/Atlas of US/78n1305/Trees and/
  78n1306
Little, W/Shorter Oxford/75n1252
Little red bk: metric conversion tables/Nelson/
  76n769
Littlefield, D W/Islamic Near/78n281
Litvinoff, B/Israel, 2500/75n328
Liu, A J/American sporting/77n935
Livermore, M A/American women/75n853
Lives of the Stuart age/Laurence Urdang
  Associates/77n412
Lives of the Tudor age 1485-1603/Hoffmann/
  78n369
Living black American authors/Shockley/75
  n1349
Living sea/Burton/77n1371
Living word vocabulary/Dale/77n1066
Livingstone, E A/Concise Oxford/79n1058/
  Oxford dictionary/75n1220
Livingstone's dict for nurses/Roper/75n1622
Livingstone's pocket medical dict/Roper/75
  n1623
Livres disponibles/79n14
Lloyd, C/Atlas of maritime/76n1688; 78
  n328/Catalogue of earlier/78n818
Lloyd, G/Broad system/79n300
Lloyd, P/European directory/76n833
Lloyd's calendar/76n902
Lo, K/Chinese newspapers/79n455
Local hist and the library/Hobbs/75n265
Local hist collections/Thompson/79n176
Local power and the community library/
  Howard/79n255
Locating, recruiting, and employing women/
  Foxley/77n793
Locational analysis and economic geography/
  Muller/79n578
Lock, C B M/Geography and/77n555
Lock, F/Australian lit/79n1259
Lock, G F/General sources/77n751
Lock, R N/Manual of library/78n123
Lockard, I/Desk reference/79n1462
Locke, D/Virus diseases/79n1490
Lockwood, L V/Ceramic, furniture/78n830
Lockwood, T/Motorcycle repair/75n1747
Lockwood, Y R/Yugoslav folklore/77n1053
Locock, F/Biographical gd Divina/76n1297
Locus: directory of NY galleries/Filsinger/
  77n869

Lodewijk, T/Way things/75n1712
Lodwick, K L/Quien es/77n185
Loebl, S/Nurse's drug/79n1501
Loertscher, D V/Budgeting for/77n226/Evaluation techniques/79n221
Loewenfeld, C/Complete bk herbs/75n1484
Loewenson, D F/Bicentennial Philadelphia/75
  n606
Logan, H B/Traveller's gd/75n633
Logan, N/Illustrated ency rock/78n918
Logan, T P/New intellectuals/78n927/Popular school/76n1032
Logan, W/Handbook of martial/76n768
Login new title abstracts/75n1615
Lohwater, A J/Russian-English/76n1333
Lolley, J/Your library/75n143
Lombardi, J V/Venezuelan hist/78n374
Lombardi, M/Brazilian serial/75n109
Lomeli, F A/Chicano perspectives/78n1128
London bibliog of the soc sciences, suppl/
  77n298; 78n272; 79n341
London goldsmiths 1697-1837/Grimwade/77
  n899
London on $500 a day/Kadish/76n559
London stage 1890-99/Wearing/77n990
Loney, G/Shakespeare complex/76n1042
Long, J W/Essential gd/78n1441
Long, R P/Castle hotels/79n618
Long, R W/Ferns of/78n1284/Wild flowers/
  78n1290
Long, T/Living sea/77n1371
Long, W A/Catalogue of steam/75n1833
Long Island genealogies/Bunker/77n457
Longman companion to English lit/Gillie/76
  n1261
Longman companion to 20th century lit/Ward/
  76n1190
Longman illus'd companion to world history/
  Uden/77n356
Look it up: spelling and style/Flesch/78n103
Loomis, L/Bibliography of modern/77n1269
Looper, T/Byron and/79n1234
Lopata, H Z/Family factbook/79n749
Lopez, L V/Directory of educ/79n642
Lord, G/Last Celt/79n1218
Lord, S/American travelers'/78n527
Loré, J M/Atlas of head/75n1644
Lorimer, L/Football book/79n717
Loring, D W/Monographs on/77n913
Loring, R K/New life/77n721
Los Angeles/Mayer/79n427
Los Angeles and its environs in the 20th cent/
  Nunis/75n381
Lossing, B J/Harper's ency/76n323

Lost links/Francis/76n432
Lost mines and buried treasures of the West/ Probert/78n358
Louden, L/Mathematical modeling/79n1326/ Odors and/77n1315/Paper mill/77n1316/ Permanence/79n1325/Pulping of/77n1314/ Short rotation/78n1484/Wet pressing/77n1317
Louis, J & V/Complete gd Soviet/78n533
Louis Auchincloss and his critics/Bryer/78n1130
Louis Kossuth "The Nation's Guest"/Szeplaki/77n382
Louisiana almanac/Calhoun/76n490
Louisiana birds/Lowery/75n1505
Louisiana recruits 1752-58/De Ville/75n414
Louisiana sports ency/Remy/78n609
Love, J/Jane's major/78n758
Love, T W/Construction manual/75n1766
Love and sexuality/Liebard/79n1041
Lovejoy, C E/Lovejoy's career/79n666/Lovejoy's college/77n621
Lovejoy's career and vocational school gd/Lovejoy/79n666
Lovejoy's college gd/Lovejoy/77n621
Lovell, H/Annotated bibliog Chinese/75n989
Lovers' gd to America/Keown/75n596
Lovin, R/Complete motorcycle/75n741
Low, J G-M/Acquisition of/77n245
Low maintenance perennials/Hebb/76n1589
Lowe, J D/Dictionary of military/79n1595
Lowell, M H/Library management/76n179
Lowens, I/Bibliography of songsters/77n958/ Music and/79n987
Lowenstein, J/Handbook on international/78n574
Lowery, G H/Louisiana birds/75n1505
Lowery, L/Backyard treasure/75n1051
Lowrey, A M/Curriculum alternatives/75n193
Loy, W G/Atlas of Oregon/78n521
Loyd, L C/Origins of/76n445
Lozynsky, A/Whitman at/79n1225
Lu, D J/Sources of/75n392
Lu, J K/US government/76n240
Lubans, J/Educating the/75n237/Progress in/79n291/Reader in/76n180
Lubell, C/France/79n950/United Kingdom-/78n863/US/78n864
Lucas, D J/First science/78n1209
Lucas, S T/Bibliography of water/78n819
Lucas, V B/Life and/75n972
Lucas-Phillips, C E/Trees around/76n1400
Lucie-Smith, E/First London/75n949
Ludlow, D H/Companion to/77n1018
Ludman, J/Lithographs of/79n899

Ludwig, R H/Illustrated hndbk electronic/78n1534
Lueker, E L/Lutheran cyclopedia/77n1039
Lui, A J/American sporting/78n832
Lukenbill, W B/Media and/78n190
Lukens, R J/Critical hndbk/77n1158
Lukowski, S/Impeachment Congress/75n491/ State information/78n461/Washington IV/76n478
Lunati, R/Book selection/76n186
Lund, H/Encyclopedia of electrochemistry/79n1318
Lundberg, D E/Tourist business/77n828
Lundeen, M/Thin-layer/75n1453
Lundgren, E F/Encyclopaedic dictionary/75n884
Lunt, E C/Key to/78n685
Lutheran cyclopedia/Lueker/77n1039
Lux, W/Historical dict British/76n282
Lyday, L F/Bibliography of Latin/79n1010
Lyle, G R/Administration of/76n139
Lyle, K C/International family-/79n750
Lyles, W H/Mary Shelley/77n1243
Lyman, H H/Literacy and/78n144/Reading and/78n234
Lyman, T/Field book/76n718
Lyman, T A/Dictionary of Mong/76n1152
Lynch, H/Great contemporary/75n329
Lynch, M/All-Asia/79n619
Lynn, N B/Research guide/76n795
Lyon, H H/Insects that/77n1389
Lyon, L J/Basic electrocardiography/78n1413
Lyons, D C/Whole world/75n950
Lyons, J L/Lyons' ency/77n1609
Lyons' ency of valves/Lyons/77n1609
Lytle, M-J/Book of successful/76n1636
Lytle, R J/American metric/77n1567

Maas, G S/Symbolism/77n1124
MacArdle, D W/Beethoven abstracts/75n1158
MacBride, D D/Bibliography of appraisal/76n858
MacCafferty, M/Annotated bibliog automation/77n168/Computer security/78n1525/ Employment relations/77n837/Fax &/78n238/Inflation in/78n702/Library-info/78n129/Right to/77n1104/Thesauri &/79n1090/User education/78n235
MacCann, D/Cultural conformity/78n1120
MacCann, R D/New film/76n1067
Macdonald, A/Art at/75n1002
Macdonald, J R & L/Sabretooth cats/75n1577
Macek, K/Bibliography of paper/77n1324

Authors and Titles—117

MacFall, R P/Minerals and/77n1435
MacGregor, M J/Blacks in/79n452
Mach, R/Catalogue of Arabic/78n60
Machamer, P/Perception/78n1362
Machinery's handbk/Oberg/76n1653
Machinists' ready ref/Weingartner/75n1808; 79n1575
Machwe, V/Documentation on/75n300
Mackay, A L/Scientific quotations/79n1302
Mackay, J/Turn-of-/75n1056
MacKay, P/Shakespeare complex/76n1042
MacKee, M/Handbook of comparative/76 n217
MacKeigan, H/American library/75n158
MacKenzie, C/Canadian selection/79n181
Mackenzie, J P S/Complete outdoorsman's/77n1383
Mackenzie, K/Wild flowers Midwest/78n1293/ Wild flowers North/75n1480/Wild flowers South/78n1294
Mackie, T T/International almanac/75n473
Mackin, R/Oxford dict/77n1069
Macksey, J & K/Book of women's/77 n722; 78n671
Macksey, K/Tank facts/76n1685
Maclay, K T/K. T. Maclay's/79n1491
MacLean, A/Common market/76n865
MacLean, J P/Historical account/79n489
MacLean, K/Oral history/78n323
MacLeod, A S/Children's lit/79n1191
MacMillan, K/Contemporary Canadian/77 n971
MacMillan, L J/Serials in/79n19
Macmillan atlas hist of Christianity/Littell/77n1020
Macmillan Bible atlas/Aharoni/78n988
Macmillan bk of Canadian place names/Hamilton/79n625
Macmillan dict for children/Halsey/76n1121
Macmillan dict of historical slang/Partridge/76n1128
MacMurray, J V A/Treaties and/75n536
Madden, D M/Religious guide/76n1071
Madden, J F/My first/76n526/Wonderful world/79n588
Madden, L/Nineteenth-century/78n1078
Madmen and geniuses/Barzman/75n488
Madubuike, I/Handbook of African/78n424
Maeroff, G I/NY Times/77n602
Magazines for libraries/Katz/75n171; 79n17
Magee, D/Infinite riches/75n67
Magee, J H/Index of suspicion/76n1531
Mager, N H & S K/Encyclopedic dict/75n1289
Magic as a performing art/Gill/78n637

Magic catalogue/Doerflinger/79n722
Magic world of words/Halsey/79n1111
Magill, F N/Magill's literary/79n1185
Magill's literary annual/Magill/79n1185
Magnotti, S/Master's theses/76n126; 78n130
Magrill, R M/Building library/75n219/Library technical/78n244
Maguire, B W/Complete bk woodworking/75 n1047
Magyary-Kossa, I/Medical librarian?/75n207
Mahaffey, D/Concise bibliog French/77n1262
Maher, A/Schools abroad/76n614
Mai, L H/Men and/76n840; 79n876
Maidment, W R/Librarianship/76n115
Mail-order crafts catalogue/Boyd/76n948
Mail order food gd/Tilson/78n1478
Maine bibliographies/Ring/75n386
Maine during the colonial period/Clark/75 n378
Maine during the federal and Jeffersonian period/Banks/76n343
Maine in the Civil War/Jordan/77n393
Maine postal hist and postmarks/Dow/77 n924
Maine shipbuilding/Baker/75n376
Maine union list of serials/Campo/78n27
Mainelli, V P/Social justice/79n1042
Mainiero, L/Encyclopedia of world/76n1185
Maintenance engineering hndbk/Higgins/78 n1542
Major, A/Collecting and/76n1397/Collecting world/75n1097
Major acquisitions of the Pierpont Morgan Library 1924-74/Pierpont Morgan Library/75n19
Major classification systems/Henderson/78 n218
Major internat'l treaties/Grenville/75n533
Major libraries of the world/Steele/77n184
Majumdar, R/Virginia Woolf/78n1184
Make it/Shields/76n956
Make it yourself/Harding/79n945
Makers of the harpsichord and clavichord 1440-1840/Boalch/76n1012
Making it/Krochmal/76n876
Makinson, R L/Guide to work/76n939
Makower, J W/Help/79n107
Male homosexual in lit/Young/77n1128
Maleady, A O/Index to record/79n973/ Record and/75n1154; 76n1003
Malinowsky, H R/Science and/77n1286
Malins, E/Preface to/76n1292
Malkoff, K/Crowell's hndbk/75n1342
Malo, P/Landmarks of/75n1019

Malory handbook/Dillon/79n1248
Maltby, A/Classification in/78n220/Government of/75n521
Maltin, L/Disney films/75n1195
Mammals of Canada/Banfield/76n1443
Mammals of Kentucky/Barbour/75n1519
Mammals of New Mexico/Findley/77n1393
Mammals of the world/Walker/76n1446
Mammals of trans-Pecos Texas/Schmidly/78n1333
Man and the beasts within/Walker/78n1379
Management & control of growth/Scott/76n801
Management and economics journals/Tega/78n704
Management educ/Fussler/75n215
Management educ and developmt/Herbert/79n870
Management of the info dept/Arnold/79n249
Management practice in soc welfare/Patti/77n708
Management principles and practices/Bakewell/79n869
Management problems in serials work/Spyers-Duran/75n217
Management techniques for librarians/Evans/77n246
Managing multimedia libraries/Hicks/78n208
Managing the catalog dept/Foster/77n254
Managing the library fire risk/Morris/76n118
Managing the modern school library/Marshall/77n222
Manahan, P/Exploring the/76n555
Mancini, R E/New atlas/79n1445
Mandel, J K/Significant American historians/77n131/Significant American Indians/77n132/Significant American sport/77n139
Mandelik, P/Concordance to poetry/76n1240
Mandeville, M S/Used book/75n62/suppl/79n58
Mangi, J/Who's who and/76n787
Mangione, A R/Image of/76n388
Manheim, J B/Political violence/76n472
Manly, J M/Contemporary American/76n1219
Mann, P H/Handbook in diagnostic/76n690
Manning, D H/Disaster technology/77n705
Manpower research and developmt projects/77n838
Man's domain: thematic atlas/76n527
Mansions, mills, and main streets/Rifkind/76n554
Manual bibliográfico de estudios españoles/ González Ollé/79n1288

Manual de bibliografiá de la literatura española/75n1428
Manual for dialect research in the southern states/Pederson/75n1250
Manual for prison law libraries/Werner/77n242
Manual of . . .
    active filter design/Hilburn/75n1807
    business library practice/Campbell/76n166
    clinical microbiology/Lennette/76n1362
    European languages for librarians/Allen/77n189
    heraldry/Grant/77n485
    Hispanic bibliog/Foster/78n1200
    library economy/Lock/78n123
    mammology with keys to families of the world/DeBlase/75n1520
    neotropical birds, Spheniscidae to Laridae/Blake/78n1316
    practical homesteading/Vivian/76n849
    the writings in middle English, 1050-1500/Hartung/77n1224
Manual on . . .
    bookselling/Anderson/75n47
    medical lit for law librarians/Mersky/75n1610
    radiation sterilization of medical and biological materials/International Atomic Energy Agency/75n1461
    terminology and classification in mental retardation/Grossman/75n1590
Manuscript catalogue of the Library of the Royal Commonwealth Society/Simpson/77n413
Manuscript solicitation/Kemp/79n246
Manuscript sources in the LC for research on the American Revolution/76n320
Manuscripts collections of the Minnesota Historical Society/78n339
Manuscripts gd to collections at the Univ of Illinois at Urbana-Champaign/Brichford/77n28
Manuscrits et autographes français/Gagnebin/75n68
Manuscrits français du Moyen Age/76n59
Many faces of info sci/Weiss/79n157
Map abstract of trends in calls for police serv/Sumrall/79n742
Map collections in the US and Canada/Carrington/79n236
Map librarianship/Larsgaard/79n240
Map librarianship/Nichols/77n240
Map librarianship: readings/Drazniowsky/76n167

Mapes, J L/Doctoral research/76n581
Mapp, E/Directory of blacks/79n1016
Maquet, J/Dictionary of black/75n315
Marcan, P/Poetry themes/79n1200
March, I/Penguin stereo/79n971
Marchant, M P/Participative management/78n164
Marcin, J/Football register/76n735/Sporting News'/76n737
Marco, G A/Information on music: The Americas/78n894/ . . . Basic & universal/76n989
Marconi, J V/Indexed periodicals/77n43
Marcus, J R/Index to picture/79n460
Marcus, M/Directory of criminal/78n506
Marcus, M/Economics of/75n176
Marcuse, S/Survey of musical/76n1017
Marcy, M/Cortina-Grosset/77n1090
Margaret Fuller/Myerson/79n757
Margaret Mead/Gordon/78n678
Margolin, J-C/Neuf années/78n1003
Marianne Moore/Abbott/78n1147
Mariano, L/Encyclopedia of knitting/78n879
Marien, M/Societal directions/77n299
Marietta College crafts directory USA/77n895
Marihuana/Waller/77n1507
Marine, W M/British invasion/78n405
Marine algae of California/Abbott/77n1365
Marine environmental engineering hndbk/Cross/76n1668
Mariner's catalog/Getchell/75n748; 76n711/Putz/76n713
Marines in Vietnam, 1954-73/US Marine Corps/75n1855
Marino, S J/Your library/75n143
Marion, J F/Bicentennial city/75n611
Mark, C/Sociology of/77n706
Mark, L/Reference sources/78n26
Mark Twain/Tenney/78n1152
Market segmentation/Michman/79n838
Market structure and the business of book publishing/Vanier/75n50
Marketing and the black consumer/Barry/77n807
Marketing channel strategy/Michman/77n810
Marketing doctoral dissertation abstracts/Shawver/78n736
Marketing economics guide/Hong/79n837
Marketing economics key plants/Hong/77n783
Marketing of info services/Raffin/79n154
Marketing profitability analysis/Jackson/79n836
Marketing terms/Shapiro/75n925

Markey, K/ONTAP/79n264
Markle, A/Author's guide/78n1369
Marks, G A/New English-/76n1143
Marks, H S/Who was who/75n125
Marks, T/Directory of New/79n1434
Marks and monograms of the modern movmt 1875-1930/Haslam/78n829
Marks' std hndbk for mechanical engineers/Baumeister/79n1577
Markun, P M/Bibliog: books/75n1347
Markus, J/Electronics dict/79n1570/Guide-bk of electronic/75n1785
Marmion, K M/Hein's legal/79n565
Marquardt, D A/Illustrators of/76n944
Marquis, A/Guide to America's/75n806
Marquis who's who publications index to all books/76n92
Marr, W/Negro almanac/77n433
Marriages and deaths from Baltimore newspapers, 1796-1816/Barnes/79n477
Marriages of Isle of Wight County, VA, 1628-1800/Chapman/77n458
Marron, J P/Facilities and/75n1812
Marshall, D W/Campaigns of/77n377
Marshall, F D/Managing the/77n222
Marshall, J/Biographical dict/79n1585/Rail facts/75n1834
Marshall, J D/Of, by/75n144
Marshall, J J/Federal funding/78n558
Marshall, J K/On equal/79n275
Marshall, M/Micronesia/77n744
Marshall Cavendish illus'd ency of gardening/Hunt/79n1541
Marshallese-English dict/Abo/78n1062
Martell, P/World military/75n1844
Martells, J/Beer can/77n936
Martenhoff, J/Powerboat hndbk/76n712
Martens, G R/African trade/78n769
Martial arts ency/Winderbaum/78n639
Martial law in the Philippines/Walsh/75n551
Martin, A/Bibliographie du/78n1186
Martin, B/Principal's hndbk/79n213
Martin, D P/Turfgrass bibliog/79n1347
Martin, E A/Dictionary of life/78n1276
Martin, G A/Bibliography on atomic/79n1330
Martin, H-J/Coming of/78n34
Martin, J/Complete musician/77n949
Martin, L A/Adults and/75n188
Martin, M/Dictionary of American/79n412
Martin, M S/Budgetary control/79n199
Martin, M W/Concise dict medicine/76n1526
Martin, R/International dict food/75n1693
Martin, R A/Syntactical and/79n1070
Martin, R E/Manual of mammology/75n1520

Martin, S K/Library automation/76n233/Library networks/77n161; 79n150
Martin, T J/North American/79n382
Martin, W/Library services/76n201
Martinson, T/Guide to architecture/79n890
Martna, M/Arctic bibliog/77n1343
Martyn, J/Final report/79n304
Martz, C W/Solar energy/79n1410
Marvin, K/Specification book/79n1556
Marx, A/Bibliographical studies/79n67
Marx, D S/Leaf prints/75n1493
Mary Shelley/Lyles/77n1243
Mary Wollstonecraft/Todd/77n1250
Maryland marriages, 1634-1777/Barnes/76n423/1778-1800/79n476
Maryland records: colonial, revolutionary, county and church/Brumbaugh/76n424
Maryland rent rolls/77n469
Marzio, P C/Nation of/77n420
Mason, A/Wildflowers of/75n1475
Mason, A/World of/77n1436
Mason, A T/American constitutional/78n445
Mason, H L/Hymn-tunes/77n959
Mason, L/Fine prints/78n814/Lithographs of/79n899/Print reference/76n941
Mason, P R/Directory of Jewish/76n383
Mass communication and journalism in the Pacific Islands/Richstad/79n1160
Mass media/Sterling/79n1166
Massachusetts/Committee for a New England Bibliography/77n391
Masserman, J H/Hndbk of psychiatric/75n1593
Massett, L/Everyman's guide/76n1550
Master gd to preparing your natal horoscope/Keyes/75n1605
Master hndbk of 1001 practical electronic circuits/Sessions/77n1599
Masters, D/Chronology of war/75n542
Masters' theses in anthropology/McDonald/79n780
Master's theses in library sci 1960-69/Magnotti/76n126/1970-74/78n130
Matarazzo, J M/Scientific, technical/75n1430; 77n1285
Matasar, A B/Research gd/76n795
Materials and techniques of painting/Wehlte/77n887
Materials for the study of Washington/Fisher/76n800
Materials hndbk/Brady/78n1539
Materials on creative arts . . . for persons with handicapping conditions/79n684
Mathai, A/Library as/79n153
Mathematical dict for economics & business admin/Skrapek/78n707

Mathematical economics and operations research/Zaremba/79n808
Mathematical modeling/Louden/79n1326
Mathematical sciences administrative directory/79n1309
Mathematical Society of Japan/Encyclopedic dict/78n1227
Mathematics dict/James/77n1302
Mathematics ency/Shapiro/78n1230
Mathematics library/Wheeler/79n1311
Mathematics teacher cum index/78n1233
Mathematics tests and reviews/Buros/76n565
Mather, C/Atlas of Kentucky/78n520
Mather, F L/Who's who of/77n439
Mather, J Y/Linguistic atlas/76n1116; 78n1023
Matheson, M/World museums/75n1008
Mathews, M/Soviet government/75n522
Mathews, O/Early photographs/75n1111
Mathews, V H/Libraries for/77n162
Mathieson, T J/Bibliography of sources/75n1131
Matney, W C/Who's who among/77n438
Matos, A/Guide to reviews/77n341; 77n342
Matson, K/Psychology Today/79n1428
Matsuda, M/Japanese in/77n445
Matter of life and death/Schwab/78n826
Matthes, H/Bibliography of African/75n1515
Matthews, D/Almanac of American/75n480; 76n474
Matthews, D G/Current bibliog/75n286
Matthews, G O/Black American/76n398
Matthews, J L/Bibliography on common/75n546
Matthews, J R/County information/78n464
Matthews, M/Soviet sociology/79n732
Matthews, R J/Who's who in/78n987
Matthews, W/American diaries/75n361
Matthews, W H/Resource materials/77n1399
Mattson, C/Organized crime/75n827
Maurice Falcolm Tauber/Szigethy/75n151
Maurice Merleau-Ponty and his critics/Lapointe/78n1002
Mauser, A J/Assessing the/79n672
Mawson, C O S/Dictionary of foreign/76n1118
Max Planck/78n1268
Maxwell, J K/Organized crime/75n827
Maxwell Anderson and S. N. Behrman/Klink/78n925
May, H G/Oxford Bible/75n1232
May, J D/Avant-garde/78n895
May, R/Companion to opera/78n913/Companion to theatre/76n1038
May, W E/Badges and/76n1678

Authors and Titles—121

May Sarton/Blouin/79n1223
Mayer, M F/Divorce and/77n716
Mayer, R/Los Angeles/79n427/San Diego/ 79n428/San Francisco/75n511
Mayer, S L/European manuscript/76n319/ Two world/78n326
Mayes, P/Periodicals admin/79n265
Mayflies, or Ephemeroptera, of Illinois/ Burks/76n1439
Mayflower families through five generations/ 77n470
Maylor, M/National Academy/75n993
Maynard, J/Dictionary of data/77n1581
Maynard, R A/Classroom cinema/79n685
Mayr, E/Birds of/79n1374
Mazour, A G/Modern Russian/77n414
McArthur, L L/Oregon geographic/76n458
McBride, R/World energy/79n1392
McCabe, D/PCC's reference/79n1548
McCaffrey, B/Language of/75n885
McCallum, H/Research collections/75n1179
McCallum, J D/Encyclopedia of world/77n686
McCarthy, C/Developing libraries/76n216
McCarthy, J F X/Record of/76n324
McCarthy, J M/Guinea-Bissau/79n353/International list/78n584
McCauley, M/Russian revolution/76n374
McCavitt, W E/Radio and/79n1173
McClane, A J/Encyclopedia of fish/78n1475/ McClane's field gd freshwater/79n1376/ McClane's field gd saltwater/79n1377/ McClane's new/75n761
McClane's field gd to freshwater fishes of North America/McClane/79n1376
McClane's field gd to saltwater fishes of North America/McClane/79n1377
McClane's new std fishing ency and international angling gd/McClane/75n761
McClean, C D/McClean gd/75n1683
McClean gd to kennels of America/McClean/ 75n1683
McClure, E/British place-/75n451
McCollum, K G/Nelson Algren/75n1351
McComas, T/Collector's gd and/77n943
McConaughy, P D/Encyclopedia of US/76 n829; 79n96
McCormick, M/Primary education/77n576
McCormick, M G/Williams &/76n42
McCormick, R/Directory of social/77n300
McCoy, F N/Researching and/75n347
McCoy, R E/Theodore Schroeder/75n1296
McCready, R N/Illustrated Mexico/75n630
McCrimmon, B/American library/76n116

McCrone, W C/Particle atlas/75n1433
McCullen, M/Dictionary of characters/78 n1179
McCullough, K/Approval plans/78n165
McDade, R/Directory of social/79n1508
McDarrah, F W/Museums in/79n93/Photography market/76n980/Stock photo/78 n884
McDermott, T J/Sailboat racing/75n749
McDonagh, D/Complete gd modern/77n995
McDonald, D/Directory: historical/77n386; 79n413
McDonald, D R/Masters' theses/79n780
McDonald, E/Color hndbk/77n1558/Good Housekeeping/75n1697/World book/76 n1595
McDonald, P J/Moody's handbook/76n859
McDonough, I/Canadian bks children/77 n1256/Canadian bks young/79n1192/ Profiles/77n1258
McDowell, B/Good Housekeeping/78n670
McDowell, F P W/E. M. Forster/79n1240
McDowell, J & R/Asian-Pacific/79n364
McDowell, R/Bibliography of lit/76n1302
McDowell, R & J/Asian-Pacific/79n364
McEliece, R J/Theory of/78n1225
McElrath, J R/Frank Norris/76n1247
McElroy, T P/Habitat guide/75n1506
McEvedy, C/Atlas of world/79n786/Penguin atlas/77n357
McFarland, D M/Historical dict Upper Volta/ 79n363
McFerrin, T/Cumulative index MFS/77n1137
McGarry, B D/Federal assistance/79n1470
McGarry, K J/Communication knowledge/76 n117/Communication studies/75n156
McGary, N/Atlas of physical/75n1576
McGill, M E/Marketing and/77n807
McGillivray, A V/America votes/78n449
McGlenen, E W/Boston marriages/78n406
McGlynn, E A/Middle American/77n733
McGovern, D M/Directory of foundations/77 n84
McGovern, J P/Annotated checklist Osleriana/ 78n1389
McGowan, R A/Italian baroque/79n922
McGrath, D F/Bookman's price/78n48; 79 n59
McGraw-Hill dict of physics and math/Lapedes/ 79n1332/Scientific and tech terms/Lapedes/ 75n1434; 79n1299/The life sciences/ Lapedes/77n1347

McGraw-Hill ency of environmental science/ 75n1533/Food, agri & nutrition/Lapedes/ 78n1452/Science and tech/Lapedes/78 n1210/The geological sciences/Lapedes/ 79n1418
McGraw-Hill yearbk of science and technology/76n1317
McGregor, M/Army uniforms/75n1849
McGuffie, H L/Samuel Johnson/77n1236
McGuire, M R P/Introduction to medieval/ 79n1091
McHale, J & M/Futures directory/79n113
McHaney, T L/William Faulkner/77n1203
McIlvaine, B/Aging/79n1456
McIlvaine, E/Guide to reference/77n14
McInnis, R G/New Perspectives/79n296/ Social science/76n239
McIntyre, P K/American students/76n616
McKee, G/Directory of spoken-/76n681; 77n660
McKee, K B/Women's studies/78n664
McKenna, B/Irish literature/79n1281
McKenney, M/Divorce/76n783/SHARE/77 n183
McKeon, D B/Classification system/78n221
McKetta, J J/Encyclopedia of chemical/78 n1247
McKibbin, L S/Horse owner's/78n1464
McKinney, F M/Black experience/79n448
McKinven, J G/Bradford bk/77n918
McKirahan, R D/Plato and/79n1081
McLachlan, J/Princetonians 1748-68/78n601
McLane, C B/Soviet-Asian/75n537/Soviet-Middle/75n538
McLaren, D/Ontario ethno-/75n1300
McLaughlin, C J/Black parents'/77n1495
McLean, I/Canadian selection/79n181
McLean, J/New consultants/77n790/Who's who in consulting/75n902
McLean, M/Annotated bibliog oceanic/79n960
McLeavy, R/Jane's surface/78n1547
McLeod, J A/Index to book/76n303; 77n368; 79n405
McMahan, V E/Washington, D.C./78n824
McManaway, J G/Selective bibliog Shakespeare/76n1285
McManus, E G/Palauan-English/78n1064
McMichael, B/Library and/78n195
McMillen, M/Mass communication/79n1160/ Pacific Islands/75n1303
McMillan, K S/Texas trade/78n712
McMinn, R M H/Colour atlas/78n1384
McMullin, R/Oral history/76n302
McNamee, L F/Dissertations in/75n1313

McNamee, L P/Handbook of circuit/77n1592
McNaughton, A/Book of kings/76n446
McNulty, D E O/Polluted groundwater/77 n1423
McNutt, D J/Eighteenth-century/76n1209
McPherson, A & S/Wild food/78n1312
McPherson, C/Guide to black/79n600
McRae, A/Energy sourcebk/79n1386
McReynolds, E C/Historical atlas Oklahoma/ 78n356
McShean, G/Running a/79n311
McWhirter, N D & R/Guinness book Olympic/ 76n697/Guinness bk phenomenal/77 n99/Guinness bk world/77n100/Guinness bk young/77n101/Guinness sports/77 n666
Meacham, M/Information sources/79n234/ Library at/79n326
Mead, C D/Prentice-Hall/79n130
Mead, F S/Handbook of denominations/76 n1087
Mead, R H/Doctoral dissertations/76n990
Meade, W W/Old churches/79n490
Meadow, C T/Analysis of/75n281
Measurement and classification of psychiatric symptoms/Wing/75n1599
Measurement and evaluation of library services/Lancaster/78n121
Measures for psychological assessment/Chun/ 76n1486
Meckler, A M/International microforms/75 n16/Microform market/75n60/Oral hist/ 76n302
Medals and plaquettes from the Molinari Collection at Bowdoin College/Norris/ 77n914
Media and adult learning/Ohliger/77n577
Media and the young adult/Lukenbill/78n190
Media: annotated catalogue of law-related AV materials/Davison/78n534
Media center facilities design/Hannigan/79 n211
Media equipment/Rosenberg/77n658
Media for the Bicentennial/77n379
Media gd international . . .
  business-professional: Asia, Australasia and USSR/77n784; 77n785; 78n724; 78n725
  newspapers and newsmagazines/77n786
Media personnel in educ/Chisholm/77n219
Media program in the elementary and middle schools/Delaney/77n220
Media programs: district and school/76 n149

Authors and Titles—123

Media report to women/Allen/77n1107
Media review digest/Wall/78n585
Medical abbreviations and acronyms/Roody/ 78n1415
Medical and health annual/78n1414
Medical and health information directory/ Kruzas/78n1407
Medical & health sciences word bk/Ehrlich/ 78n1398
Medical bks for the layperson/Philbrook/77 n1466
Medical librarian?/Magyary-Kossa/75n207
Medical risks/Singer/78n1416
Medical school admission/Nelson/75n1639
Medical socioeconomic research sources/75 n1616
Medical talk for beginners/Curtis/77n1472
Medical terminology from Greek and Latin/ Patterson/79n1464
Medical word finder/Willeford/78n1401
Medication gd for patient counseling/Smith/ 78n1444
Medicine show/75n1649
Medicines from the earth/Thomson/79n1354
Medieval Celtic lit/Bromwich/76n1258
Medieval health hndbk (Tacuinum sanitatis)/ Arano/77n69
Medieval monasticism/Constable/77n1025
Medieval music/Hughes/76n988
Medieval studies/Powell/78n325
Medi-KWOC index/76n1540
Meditation hndbk/Alibrandi/77n1446
Medley, D J/Bibliography of British/78n370
Meeker, D/Jazz in/78n919
Meeker, T A/Military-industrial/75n464/Proliferation of/75n1836/SALT II/75n541
Meggett, J M/Music periodical/79n961
Megivern, J J/Bible interpretation/79n1043/ Worship and/79n1044
Mehr, L H/Motion pictures/79n1165
MEI marketing economics gd/Hong/76n869
Meinck, F/Dictionary of water/79n1579
Meinhard, H/International wine/78n1457
Melas, E/Greek experience/75n1020
Mellott, D W/New product/78n738
Melnick, J L/Review of medical/79n1475
Melody, M E/Apaches/79n781
Melton, J G/Directory of religious/78n984
Meltzer, I S/Significant American authors/77 n126/Significant American musicians/ 77n135/Significant American women/77 n140
Meltzer, M/Pictorial history/75n814
Melvil Dewey/Vann/79n188

Melvin Ricks' Alaska bibliog/Ricks/79n390
Melville, J/Guide to California/77n1520
Members of Congress since 1789/78n454
Men and ideas in economics/Mai/76n840; 79n876
Men of achievement/Kay/78n113
Menage, R H/Growing exotic/76n1596
Mendel, F/Parliaments of/77n495
Mendell, R L/Who's who football/75n765
Mendelson, P C/Contemporary literary/77 n1130/Twentieth-century/79n1183
Menendez, A J/Church-state/77n1028
Menke, F G/Encyclopedia of sports/76 n698; 79n697; 79n698
Menomini lexicon/Bloomfield/76n1148
Menser, G P/Hallucinogenic and/78n1301
Mental health almanac/Allen/79n1435
Mental health directory/US Natl Institute of Mental Health/78n1374
Mental retardation dict/Tymchuk/75n1585
Menze, E A/Anchor atlas/76n297
Meranus, L S/Law and/79n561
Merck veterinary manual/75n1662
Meridian hndbk of classical mythology/ Tripp/75n1242
Merit students ency/Halsey/79n75
Merne, O J/Ducks, geese/76n1425
Merriam-Webster dictionary/77n1077
Merriam-Webster dict for large print users/ 78n1037
Merrill, A L/Handbook of nutritional/77 n1552
Merrill, E D/Flora of/77n1353
Merrill, I R/Criteria for/78n166
Merriman, L/Woodwind solo/77n963
Merritt, A J & R/Politics, economics/79 n379
Merritt, F S/Building construction/76n1620/ Standard handbook civil/77n1576
Merritt, R L/Politics, economics/79n379
Mersand, J/Guide to play/76n1034
Mersky, R M/Manual on medical/75n1610
Meserole, H T/Guide to English/78n1088
Meshenberg, M J/Environmental planning/ 77n1406
Mesozoic and Cenozoic paleocontinental maps/Smith/78n1357
Messerli, D/Djuna Barnes/77n1198/Index to periodical/78n1103
Meta Systems, Inc./Systems analysis/76n1473
Metalcrafting ency/Morgenstern/77n892
Metals ref book/Smithells/77n1613
Metcalf, E W/Charles W. Chesnutt/78n1136/ Paul Laurence/76n1234/William Wells/ 79n450

Metcalfe, J/Information retrieval/77n291
Methodist union catalog: pre-1976 imprints/ Rowe/76n1078; 77n1032; 79n1054
Methods of analysis and evaluation of info needs/Kunz/79n263
Methods of financing interlibrary loan services/ Assoc of Research Libraries/75n231
Metric and other conversion tables/Lewis/75n1716
Metric hndbk for teachers/Higgins/75n712
Metric manual/76n1318
Metric system guide/76n1319
Metric system guide bulletins/76n1320
Metric yearbook/78n1232
Metrication handbook/77n1304
METRO CAP catalog/78n149
METRO directory of members/77n179
METRO Educ and Psychology Librarians Discussion Group/Finding list journals/78n583
Metropolitan area guide to serials/78n28
Metropolitan NY AYH Council/American youth/77n681
Metropolitan opera annals, 3rd suppl/Pelz/79n994
Metz, K S/Information sources/77n1400
Meves, E/Guide to backpacking/78n620
Mexican American bibliographies/Cortes/75n822
Mexican Americans: research bibliog/Pino/76n402
Mexican-Americans: selected bibliog/76n401
Mexican political biographies 1935-75/Camp/78n485
Mexico: especially for women/Tully/77n569
Mexico in American and British letters/Gunn/75n1311
Mexico 1946-73/Hofstadter/75n341
Meyer, H K/Historical dict Honduras/77n344
Meyer, L/World traveler's/76n538
Meyer, M/Centeno Collection/79n1285
Meyer, M H/Ornamental grasses/76n1597
Meyer, M K/Directory of genealogical/79n471
Meyer, M K/Guide to educ'l/78n594
Meyer, N/World traveler's/76n538
Meyer, P/Guide to Long/75n1301
Meyer, S/Chiropractic/78n1424
Meyer, S E/Business media/75n909
Meyers, F H/Review of medical/75n1657; 79n1502
Meyers, G E/Insurance manual/78n145
Meyers, J/George Orwell/78n1180/T. E. Lawrence/76n1277

Meyers, L D/Furniture repair/75n1795
Meyers, V/George Orwell/78n1180
MGA-MGB service-repair hndbk/Houston/75n1733
Miami/Buchanan/79n421
Michael, G/Basic book/75n1057
Michael, J R/Working on/75n104
Michael, M E/Continuing professional/76n222
Michael Morcombe's Australian marsupials and other native mammals/Morcombe/76n1445
Michaelides, S/Music of/79n965
Michigan legal literature/Beer/75n545
Michigan place names/Romig/75n454
Michigan statistical abstract/Verway/78n688
Michman, R D/Market segmentation/79n838/ Marketing channel/77n810
Mickel, P/Warships of/79n1602
Mickelson, A R/Yearbook of American/76n1090
Mickunas, A/Exploring phenomenology/75n1238
Microanatomy of cell and tissue surfaces/ Motta/79n1336
Microcomputer dict and gd/Sippl/77n1584
Microfilm: Librarians' view/Dranov/77n285
Microfilm source bk/75n58
Microform hndbk/American Assoc of Community and Jr. Colleges/76n226
Microform librarianship/Teague/79n335
Microform market place/Veaner/75n60
Microforms in libraries/Diaz/76n227
Microforms: librarians' view/Bahr/79n332
Micrographics/Saffady/79n334
Micronesia, 1944-74/Marshall/77n744
Microorganism control/Weiner/78n1263
Microprocessor applications manual/Motorola Semiconductor Products Inc./77n1598
Microprocessors and microcomputers/Soucek/77n1585
Microscopy of pulp and paper/Weiner/77n1328
Middle American anthropology/McGlynn/77n733
Middle East and North Africa/76n266; 77n311
Middle East conflict/Rubner/79n358
Middle East contemporary survey/Legum/79n355
Middle East Libraries Committee/Union catalogue/78n29
Middle East: US policy/75n539
Middle East yearbook/79n356
Middlebrooks, E J/Lagoon info/79n1580
Mideast business gd/Haiek/79n818

Miekina, G/Significant American gov/77n130/
   Significant American military/77n134/
   Significant American social/77n138
Miele, M/Bowker annual/77n190
Mignani, R/Concordance to complete/78
   n1176/Concordance to Juan/79n1290
Migration theory and fact/Shaw/77n757
Miguéis—To the seventh decade/Kerr/79
   n1289
Mihailovich, V D/Modern Slavic/78n1199
Mikhail, E H/Contemporary British/78n928/
   English drama/78n929/J. M. Synge/76
   n1291
Miksa, F L/Charles Ammi/78n153
Milar, M/Photographer's market/79n954
Milden, J W/Family in/79n751
Mildren, K W/Use of/77n1568
Mileck, J/Hermann Hesse/78n1190
Milepost: all-the-North travel gd/Henning/75
   n634
Miles, W D/American chemists/78n1257
Milestones in cataloging/Lehnus/75n225
Milestones to the present/Goldstein/79n327
Milgram, G G/Alcohol educ/77n1465
Military aircraft of the world/Taylor/77n1640
Military atlas of the first world war/Banks/
   76n296
Military balance 1975-76/77n1630
Military dress of North America, 1665-1970/
   Windrow/75n1840
Military-industrial complex/Meeker/75n464
Military small arms of the 20th century/
   Hogg/78n1558
Military uniforms in America, 1796-1851/
   Elting/78n1553
Military vehicles of the world/Foss/77n1643
Millard, J T/Handbook on primary/76n756
Miller, A/Arnold Bennett/78n1166
Miller, A B/Shaker herbs/78n1298
Miller, A J/Death/78n1426
Miller, B F/Encyclopedia and dict/79n1463
Miller, B J/Bibliography on atomic/79n1330
Miller, B L/Bible-related/77n1049
Miller, B M/Complete secretary's/78n714
Miller, C G/Tables and/76n1607
Miller, D C/Ghost towns/76n552
Miller, D E/Occupational safety/78n770
Miller, D M/Topical Bible/78n993
Miller, E/Barron's guide/79n659
Miller, J D/700 French/77n1089
Miller, J Y/Eugene O'Neill/75n1363
Miller, J W/Guide to evaluation/76n650
Miller, L F/Contemporary American/79n1013
Miller, M M/Bows and/76n763

Miller, M R/Library networks/75n139
Miller, O K/Mushrooms of/78n1302
Miller, R A/Atlas of central/79n1448
Miller, R H/Root anatomy/76n1372
Miller, R W/Wallace-Homestead flea/78n833/
   Wallace-Homestead price/78n838
Miller, S E/Thesaurus of terms/79n872
Miller, S S/Symptoms/77n1496
Miller, S T/Visual approach/75n458
Miller, W/Symmetry and/78n1226
Miller, W C/Comprehensive bibliog/77n425/
   Handbook of American/77n419
Miller, W H/Guide to North/79n1586
Millet, S/South Vietnam/75n527; 75n528
Millett, S M/Selected bibliog American/76n312
Millets and minor cereals/Rachie/75n1696
Millgate, L/Almanac of dates/78n88
Millon, R/Urbanization at/75n404
Mills, J/Bliss bibliographic/78n224; 78n225;
   78n226; 78n227/Introduction to subj/
   77n252
Mills, J W/Black world/76n160; 77n1159
Mills, M/State labor/78n767
Millsaps, D/National directory/77n86
Millspaugh, C F/American medicinal/76n1377
Milner, A C/Newspaper indexes/78n1079
Milt, H/Basic handbook/75n1594
Milton ency/Hunter/79n1250
Milton's library/Boswell/76n1278
Milwaukee: chronological & documentary
   history/Lankevich/78n355
Miner, D D/Management &/76n801
Minerals/Court/76n1480
Minerals and gems/MacFall/77n1435
Minerals of the world/Sorrell/75n1574
Minicomputer review/75n965
Minister's library/Barber/75n1213; 77n235/
   suppl 2/79n1047
Minneapolis. Public Library. Environmental
   Conservation Library/Book catalog/75
   n1531
Minnelfarb, M/American Jewish/75n321
Minnesota birds/Green/76n1420
Minnesota multiphasic personality inventory
   (MMPI)/Taulbee/77n1364
Minor, B B/Alternative careers/79n324/Pro-
   ceedings of/78n258
Minorities and women/Schlachter/79n762
Minorities in the US/Levitan/76n391
Minority group media gd/78n1076
Minority organizations/Cole/79n444
Minority studies/Oaks/77n426
Minus, J/Films/75n1196
Misch, R J/Quick guide/78n1458

Mischler, C/Standard catalog/75n1068
Miser, A/Factory store/75n951
Mishler, C/Standard catalog/76n969
Missiles and rockets/Gatland/77n1647
Missiles of the world/Taylor/78n1571
Mission handbook/Dayton/75n1221
Mission handbk: North American Protestant ministries overseas/Missions Advanced Research & Communication Center/78n986
Misspeller's dict/Norback/75n1259
Mitchell, A/Field gd to trees/75n1492
Mitchell, B J/Cost analysis/79n256
Mitchell, B R/European historical/76n815
Mitchell, C/Speech index: suppl/78n1085
Mitchell, C R/International relations/79n553
Mitchell, J/Random House/78n68
Mitchell, J A/Directory of New/78n80
Mitchell, J S/I can/76n651; 79n660/Stopout! working ways to learn/79n643
Mitchell, P M/Bibliography of modern/77n1266
Mitchell, T W/Norton on/77n354
Mitterling, D/Guide to Edward/76n349/Guide to Harper/76n350/Guide to Henry/76n351
Mittler, T E/Annual review entomology/76n1409
Mitton, S/Cambridge ency/79n1313
Mixter, K E/General bibliog music/76n991
MLA handbook/79n131
MMPI hndbk/Dahlstrom/76n1498
Mobil city vacation & business gd/76n553
Mobil travel guide ...
    California and the West/79n602
    Great Lakes area/79n603
    Middle Atlantic states/79n604
    Northeastern states/79n605
    Northwest and Great Plains states/79n606
    Southeastern states/79n607
    Southwest and South Central area/79n608
Mocker, D W/Urban educ/79n635
Model railroading hndbk/Schleicher/77n944
Model school dist media program/Gillespie/78n185
Modell, W/Drugs in/76n1551
Moder, J J/Handbook of operations/79n820
Modern accountant's hndbk/Edwards/78n721
Modern American herbal/Dugdale/79n1352
Modern American usage/Follett/75n1288
Modern Arabic lit/Altoma/77n1252
Modern archives and manuscripts/Evans/76n291
Modern atlas of African history/Freeman-Grenville/77n397

Modern black writers/Popkin/79n1186
Modern British lit, vol. 4 suppl/Tucker/76n1263
Modern Chinese society/Skinner/75n302
Modern Commonwealth lit/Ferres/79n1184
Modern dict of electronics/Graf/79n1568
Modern ency of Russian and Soviet history/Wieczynski/77n415; 79n442
Modern ency of Russian and Soviet lit/Weber/79n1283
Modern England/Havighurst/77n411
Modern English-Canadian poetry/Stevens/79n1261
Modern English painters/Rothenstein/76n937
Modern English-Yiddish, Yiddish-English dict/Weinreich/79n1156
Modern French-English dict/Dubois/79n1135
Modern French lit/Popkin/78n1187
Modern gd to auto tuneup and emission control servicing/Dempsey/75n1730
Modern home dict of medical words/Fishbein/77n1474
Modern Latin American lit/Foster/76n1301
Modern manuscripts/Duckett/77n352
Modern Middle East/Simon/79n359
Modern military dict/Garber/77n1627
Modern news library/Whatmore/79n243
Modern parents' gd to baby and child care/Broadribb/75n1647
Modern parliamentary procedure/Keesey/75n472
Modern real estate dict/Johnsich/77n802
Modern researcher/Barzun/78n322
Modern revolutions and revolutionists/Blackey/77n359
Modern rifle/Carmichel/76n755
Modern Russian historiography/Mazour/77n414
Modern saltwater fishing/Dunaway/76n728
Modern school library/Saunders/76n151
Modern Slavic literatures/Mihailovich/78n1199
Modern textile and apparel dict/Linton/75n964
Modern woman's fix it yourself hndbk of home repair/Zarchy/75n1802
Modglin, N/Rhymer and/79n1126
Modley, R/Handbook of pictorial/78n812
Modules in security studies/Williams/75n459
Moerman, D E/American medical/78n1280
Moffat, D W/Concise desk/77n775/Economics dict/77n776/Plant engineer's/75n1813
Möhle, H/Dictionary of water/79n1579
Mohlenbrock, R H/Guide to vascular/77n1354

Mojares, R B/Cebuano literature/78n1195
Mokilese-English dict/Harrison/78n1063
Mokres, J A/Ski America/75n785
Moldon, D/Bibliography of Russian/78n896
Moller, E V/Original world-/75n952
Mollo, A/Army uniforms/75n1849/Naval, marine/77n1631
Mollo, J/Uniforms of/76n1679
Moloney, J/Encyclopedia of American/79n1554
Moments: Pulitzer Prize photographs/Leekley/79n953
Monahan, R/Free and/78n597
Monastic manuscript microfilm project/Plante/75n15
Mondey, D/Air facts/76n1683; 79n1590/International ency aviation/79n1587
Money and politics/Sobel/75n496
Money, banking, and macroeconomics/Rock/79n873
Monk, S H/John Dryden/77n1232
Monmouth County, NJ: bibliog of published works, 1676-1973/Van Benthuysen/76n355
Monographic series/US Library of Congress/76n12
Monographs on varieties of US large cents 1795-1803/Loring/77n913
Monser, H E/Topical index/75n1231
Monson, D L/Research in/77n1160
Montagne, P/New Larousse/78n1476
Montague-Smith, P/Debrett's peerage/78n419
Montgomery, F H/Seeds and/78n1285
Montgomery, J W/International scholars/76n666
Montgomery, K L/Document retrieval/76n234
Montgomery, P K/Teaching media/78n188
Monthan, D & G/Art and/76n936
Monthly labor review: index/US Bureau of Labor Statistics/78n776
Monthly periodical index/79n24
Moody, F/10 bibliographies/79n1284
Moody's hndbk of common stocks/McDonald/76n859
Mookini, E T/Place names/75n453/Pocket Hawaiian/76n1153
Moon, H/Simplified guide/77n1596
Moon-shiners manual/Barleycorn/76n1560
Moore, A C/How to clean/79n1572
Moore, E S/Lost links/76n432
Moore, F L/Handbook of Giblert/76n1009
Moore, G/Utah plants/75n1471
Moore, J E/Jane's fighting/78n1575
Moore, J W/Complete ency music/75n1142
Moore, N D/Dictionary of business/76n830; 77n777

Moore, P/A-Z of/78n1234/Atlas of Mercury/78n1235/Concise atlas/75n1447/Patrick Moore's/75n1448/Yearbook of astronomy/77n1309
Moore, R/Bowker annual/77n190
Moore, R A/Current bibliog/76n403
Moore, R H/Fishes of/78n1326
Moore, W G/Dictionary of geography/79n581
Moorman, C/Editing the/76n1113
Móra, I/Worterbuch des/75n52
Morales-Macedo, F/Multilingual law/79n568
Moran, J/Bilingual bicultural/78n548
Morant, A/General armory/75n442
Morcombe, I & M K/Australian bush/76n1426
Morcombe, M K/Michael Morcombe's/76n1445
More bks by more people/Hopkins/75n1345
More classic trains/Dubin/75n1832
More films kids like/Gaffney/79n1024
More juniorplots/Gillespie/79n228
More miles . . . less gas with your recreation vehicle/Nulsen/76n770
More Virginia broadsides before 1877/Hummel/76n346
Morehead, J/Introduction to US/76n83; 79n120
Morehouse, L G/Mycotoxic fungi/79n1477
Morehouse, W/India votes/75n518
Morgan, J/Consumer sourcebook/75n931; 79n844
Morgan, J/Guide to California/77n1520
Morgenstern, S/Dictionary of opera/78n911
Morgenstern, S/Metalcrafting ency/77n892
Morin-Labatut, G/DEVINDEX Canada/79n822
Morini, S/Simona Morini's/77n1497
Morison, S L/Ships & aircraft/77n1651
Morley, J W/Japan's foreign/75n540
Morley, W F E/Ontario and/79n376
Mormon bibliog 1830-1930/Flake/79n1048
Morningstar, C/Early Utah/78n854
Morpeth, R S/Who's who Scottish/75n399
Morrell, R E/Guide to Japanese/77n1272
Morris, A/Florida place/75n452
Morris, C G/Macmillan dict/76n1121
Morris, D/Who was who/75n486
Morris, D H/Stephane Mallarmé/79n1272
Morris, F/Color handbook/77n1558
Morris, I/Who was who/75n486
Morris, J/Managing the/76n118
Morris, J B/Encyclopedia of American/77n385
Morris, J D/Research in/75n1606
Morris, J M/Library searching/79n297

Morris, J O/Bibliography of industrial/76n905
Morris, J W/Historical atlas Oklahoma/78n356
Morris, M/Harper dict/76n1130/Morris dict/78n1032
Morris, P C/American sailing/75n1830
Morris, R B/Encyclopedia of American/77n385
Morris, R J B/Parliament and/78n175
Morris, R L/Research in/75n1606
Morris, W/Harper dict/76n1130/Morris dict/78n1032
Morris, W/Xerox intermediate/75n1255
Morris, W P/Searching the/76n689
Morris dict of word and phrase origins/Morris/78n1032
Morrish, G/Concordance of Septuagint/78n981
Morrison, D E/Collective behavior/77n707/Energy/77n1407/Energy II/79n1387
Morrison, J L/Goode's world/79n585
Morrow, B/Bibliography of writings/79n1246
Morrow, L C/Maintenance engineering/78n1542
Morse, G W/Complete gd organizing/75n694/Concise gd library/76n119
Morse, P/Jean Charlot's/77n882
Mortimer, R/Catalogue of books/76n58
Morton, C & I D/Elsevier's dict/78n1470
Morton, J F/Herbs and/78n1299
Morton, L T/Use of medical/75n1611; 79n1441
Mosak, B & H H/Bibliography for Adlerian/76n1488
Moses, A J/Practicing scientist's/79n1303
Moses, H A/Bibliotherapy in/79n309
Moses, J M/Collectors' gd/78n901
Moses, K J/Aids to/77n657
Mosher, F C/Basic documents/78n438
Moskowitz, L R/Permanent magnet/77n1597
Moss, C/Bibliographical gd/79n1425
Moss, E/Children's books/77n1226
Moss, W W/Oral hist/75n348
Mosses: Utah and the West/Flowers/75n1487
Most glorious crown/Drager/76n751
Mostovych, A/Nonconformity and/79n549
Mothers' and fathers' medical ency/Pomeranz/78n1430
Mothers of achievement in American hist/77n396
Motif-index of the Italian novella in prose/Rotunda/75n1423
Motion picture film editor/Ash/75n1207
Motion picture market place/Costner/77n1005
Motion picture performers ... suppl/Schuster/77n1003
Motion pictures/78n951
Motion pictures, TV, and radio/Mehr/79n1165

Motor sport yearbook/Gill/75n781
Motorboat, yacht or canoe—you name it/Taggart/75n1831
Motorcycle repair ency/Lockwood/75n1747
Motorcycles/Griffin/75n740
Motorcycles to 1945/Vanderveen/77n1623
Motorcyclopedia/Radlauer/75n743
Motorola Semiconductor Products Inc./Microprocessor applications/77n1598
Mott, R C/Total book/76n1598
Motta, P/Microanatomy of/79n1336
Mottelay, P F/Bibliographical history/76n1631
Mottoes and badges of families, regiments, schools, colleges, states, towns, livery companies, societies/Anson/77n482
Moul, K R/Theodore Roethke's/78n1148
Moulds, M/International index/75n1211
Mount, E/Guide to basic/78n1500/University science/77n239
Mountaineering/Krawczyk/78n618
Mountfort, G/Field gd birds/76n1429
Moure, N D W/Index to reproductions/78n820
Movies for kids/Zornow/75n1200
Moving pictures: bibliography/Sheahan/75n1193
Moyer, K E/Bibliography of aggressive/79n1424
Moyle, E W & J B/Northland wild/78n1295
Moyles, R G/English-Canadian/77n1257
Mrs. Byrne's dict of unusual, obscure, and preposterous words/Byrne/75n1257
Muehsam, G/Guide to basic/79n888
Muenscher, W C/Garden spice/79n1353/Poisonous plants/76n1378
Mugs and tankards/Stratton/78n873
Muir, K/Shakespeare survey/76n1286; 77n1242
Muirden, J/Amateur astronomer's/75n1445
Mulkerne, D J D/Word book/76n1133
Mullenix, D/Antiques/78n839
Muller, P O/Locational analysis/79n578
Müller, V K/English-Russian/75n1274
Müller-Hayes, B/Bibliography of Criollo/79n1524
Mulligan, B O/Woody plants/79n1361
Mullins, L J/Annual review biophysics/76n1348
Mullins, M D/Republic of/75n427
Multicultural educ, a functional bibliog for teachers/Giese/78n598
Multicultural educ and ethnic studies in the US/Gollnick/78n541
Multi-ethnic media/Cohen/76n387

Multilingual law dict/Egbert/79n568
Multi-media approach to children's lit/ Greene/79n231
Multi-media indexes, lists, and review sources/ Hart/76n679
Multimedia library/Cabeceiras/79n244
Multinational corporation/Hernes/78n698
Multitype library cooperation/Hamilton/78n120
Multivariate analysis/Subrahmaniam/75n874
Mumby, F A/Publishing and/75n48
Munby, A N L/British book/79n60
Mundell, E H/Detective short/75n1327
Mundkur, M/Aging/79n1456
Mundo de los negocios/Renty/79n1152
Municipal gov ref sources/Hernon/79n537
Municipal info systems directory/Kraemer/78n463
Municipal year bk/76n495; 79n538
Munn, R F/Coal industry/79n846/Strip mining/ 75n1814
Munoz, O/Spanish bilingual/77n1100
Munro, R W/Gazetteer of Scotland/75n572/ Johnston's gazetteer/76n457
Munsey, C/Disneyana/75n1098/Illustrated guide/77n921
Munson, K/Bombers in/77n1639/Jane's all/ 79n1589/Jane's pocket bk commercial/ 75n1821/Jane's pocket bk major/75n1845/ Jane's pocket bk remotely/79n1594
Murdoch, C G/Hawaiian language/79n389
Murdock, G P/Ethnographic bibliog/77n738
Murex shells of the world/Radwin/77n1395
Murfin, J V/Guide to historic/75n601
Murfin, M E/Reference service/78n240
Murie, O J/Field gd animal/76n1413
Murphy, D/Concise index/75n1287
Murphy, D D/Directory of conservative/79n88
Murphy, E F/Crown treasury/79n98
Murphy, H J/Where's what/77n839
Murphy, M/Handbook of library/78n146
Murphy, T P/Urban politics/79n539
Murr, L E/Atlas of binary/75n1454
Murray, C/Field gd fish/77n1388
Murray, J/Kings and/75n624
Murray, M A/Atlas of Atlanta/75n880/Atlas of metro-Atlanta/77n545
Murrell, K L/Bibliography of sources/76n910
Murrin, M R/Directory of New/78n80
Murtz, H A/Guns illustrated/77n690
Musciano, W A/Automobiles of/79n1553
Muse and the librarian/Basler/75n260
Museum companion: art terms/Lemke/75n1004

Museum Council of Philadelphia gd to museums in the Delaware Valley/Cramer/ 77n76
Museum media/Wasserman/75n83
Museums of England/Hogg/75n81
Museums of the world/76n68
Museums USA/National Endowment for the Arts/76n69
Mushroom pocket fld gd/Bigelow/75n1486
Mushrooms in the wild/Tribe/79n1356
Mushrooms of North America/Miller/78n1302
Music and dance research of Southwestern US Indians/Frisbie/78n890
Music bks of Ruebush & Kieffer, 1866-1942/ Showalter/76n992
Music education/Harris/79n959
Music for Shelley's poetry/Pollin/75n1133
Music for the piano/Friskin/75n1127
Music gd to . . .
   Austria and Germany/Brody/77n945
   Belgium, Luxembourg, Holland and Switzerland/Brody/78n889
   Italy/Brody/79n956
Music in America and American music/Lowens/ 79n987
Music in the modern age/Sternfeld/75n1151
Music Library Assoc catalog of cards for printed music 1953-72/Olmsted/75n1138
Music of ancient Greece/Michaelides/79n968
Music periodical lit/Meggett/79n961
Music ref and research materials/Duckles/75n1123
Music titles in translation/Hodgson/77n956
Musica: first gd to classical music on American radio stations/Jacobs/77n947
Musical biography/Parker/76n1006
Musical Europe/Adelmann/75n1144
Musical instruments of the world/Diagram Group/77n968
Musical manual or tech directory/Busby/78n898
Musical references in the Chinese classics/ Kaufmann/77n948
Musical settings of late Victorian and modern British literature/Gooch/77n954
MusiCatalog, suppl/78n902
Muslim peoples/Weekes/79n772
Muster, B/Rand McNally traveler's/79n621
Muster rolls of the soldiers of the War of 1812/ North Carolina. Adjutant-General's Office/ 77n472
Mutiny does not happen lightly/Heath/77n502
Mutual funds almanac/Hirsch/78n730

Muus, B J/Collins guide/76n1436
My first atlas/Madden/76n526
My first picture dict/Jenkins/78n1029
My first world hist atlas/77n358
Mycological Society of America/Mycology guidebook/75n1488
Mycology guidebook/Mycological Society of America/78n1488
Mycotoxic fungi, mycotoxins, mycotoxicoses/Wyllie/79n1477
Myers, A B/World of/76n1241
Myers, B S/Dictionary of 20th/75n999
Myers, C F/Black American/76n1226/Women in/77n1125
Myers, M/Women in/76n120
Myers, R/Radio amateur's/75n1206
Myers, S D/Dictionary of 20th/75n999
Myerson, J/Margaret Fuller/79n757
Mylne, V G/Bibliographie du/78n1186
Mynchenberg, G C/Official catalog/76n977
Myra Waldo's travel and motoring gd to Europe/Waldo/75n629
Myra Waldo's travel gd to South America/Waldo/77n570
Myrus, D/Photography catalog/78n887
Myths and legends of all nations/Robinson/77n1055

Nachbar, J G/Western films/76n1050
Nacogdoches—gateway to Texas/Ericson/75n415
Nadarajah, R/Barefoot librarian/76n218
Nadler, M/How to start/79n306
NAEB public telecommunications directory/79n1163
Nagel's encyclopedia-gd: China/Destenay/75n331
Nakaike, T/Enumeratio pteridophytarum/76n1379
Nalty, B C/Blacks in/79n452
Name and subj index to the presidential chronology series/Gibson/79n419
Name, title, and place index to the critical writings of Henry James/Stafford/76n1243
Names and numbers/Nordland/79n1164
Names from Africa, their origin, meaning, and pronunciation/Chuks-orji/75n447
Names in the hist of psychology/Zusne/76n1505
Nanassy, L C/Reference manual/78n717
Nandan, Y/Durkheimian School/78n645
Nantucket: gd with tours/Burroughs/75n603
Naqvi, R A/Indian response/75n1422

Narang, S P/Kalidasa bibliog/77n1268
Nardone, T R/Choral music/75n1132/1976 suppl/77n960/Classical vocal/78n897/Organ music/76n1018
Nariai, K/Atlas of representative/79n1315
Narratives of captivity among the Indians of North America/Smith/75n807
Narus, D J/Great American/79n1555
NASA factbook/76n1608
NASA thesaurus/US Natl Aeronautics and Space Admin/77n1563
Nash, J R/Darkest hours/78n86
Nason, J D/Micronesia/77n744
Nasri, W Z/Crisis in/77n50
Nass, L I/Encyclopedia of PVC/79n1574
Nasso, C/Contemporary authors/79n140
NASW register of clinical social workers/79n735/1977 suppl/79n736
Natella, A A/Spanish in/76n419
Nathan, H/William Billings/78n909
Nathan, R/Businessman's gd/76n836
Nathanael West/Vannatta/77n1216/White/76n1252
Nathaniel Hawthorne/Clark/78n1141; 79n1220
Nation, E F/Annotated checklist/78n1389
Nation of nations/Marzio/77n420
National Academy of Design exhibition record: 1861-1900/Naylor/75n993
National and international library planning/Vosper/77n271
National anthems of the world/Shaw/77n950
National Assoc of Housing and Redevelopment officials/Urban careers/75n680
National atlas of Canada/76n534
National basic intelligence factbk/US Central Intelligence Agency/78n274; 79n508
National Basketball Assoc official gd/Curran/76n707/Winick/77n680
National children's directory/Bundy/78n659
National Commission on Libraries and Info Science/Annual report/79n151
National comparison local school costs/76n601
National Council of Teachers of English/Adventuring with/78n189
National criminal justice thesaurus/US Natl Criminal Justice Ref Service/78n504
National directory for the performing arts and civic centers/Handel/76n1043; 79n1014
National directory for the performing arts—educational/Handel/79n1015

National directory of ...
    addresses and telephone numbers/Greenfield/79n86
    arts support by private foundations/78n793
    grants and aid to individuals in the arts, international/Millsaps/77n86
    manufacturers' reps/Holtje/79n845
    newsletters and reporting services/79n18
    public alternative schools/Flaxman/79n645
    runaway programs/78n660
    state agencies/Vellucci/76n70
    the performing arts and civic centers/Handel/75n1185
National drug code directory/79n1505
National electrical code ref bk/Garland/78n1532
National Endowment for the Arts/Museums USA/76n69
National Endowment for the Arts: gd to programs/76n628
National faculty directory/77n622
National Football League/NFL's official/75n766
National formulary/National Formulary Board/76n1552
National Gallery, London/Potterton/79n880
National governments around the world/Engle/75n470
National gd to craft supplies/Glassman/76n952
National gd to gov and foundation funding sources in the field of aging/Cohen/78n649
National health directory/78n1408
National heraldry of the world/Briggs/75n439; 76n448
National Institute for Automotive Service Excellence/Where to find/76n1616
National inventory of library needs/Ladd/78n124
National library and info services/Penna/78n125
National Library of Medicine classification/79n276
National library serv cum book review index 1905-74/77n44
National lifeguard manual/Cornforth/75n786
National medical AV center catalog/78n1390
National outdoorsmen's ency/Bergaust/76n715
National party conventions/77n515
National party platforms: 1840-1972/Johnson/75n493; 79n520
National periodicals center/79n152

National playwrights directory/Kaye/78n944
National prison directory/Bundy/76n778; 77n710/suppl 2/78n505
National radio publicity directory/Filsinger/76n1176
National referral services for industry/76n899
National register of historic places/US Natl Park Service/77n387
National register of internships and experiential education/Lewchuk/75n679
National school directory/75n684
National school market index/76n602
National trade and prof associations of the US and Canada and labor unions/Colgate/77n87
National Trust for Historic Preservation/Gd to federal/78n352/Historic preservation/78n344
National Trust gd to England, Wales and Northern Ireland/Fedden/76n556
National union catalog of US gov publications received by depository libraries/75n105
Native American historical demography/Dobyns/77n736
Native Americans of North America/Perkins/76n805
Native trees of the Sierra Nevada/Peterson/76n1402
Natkiel, R/Atlas of Second/75n1843
NATTS directory of accredited private trade and tech schools/77n630
Natural lang in info sci/Walker/79n337
Naturalist's color gd/Smithe/76n1366
Naturalists' directory internat'l/Baetzenr/76n1368
Naturalists' gd to fresh-water aquarium fish/Hoedeman/75n1668
Nature of knowledge/Kemp/77n159
Nature-Science annual/76n1321
Nature's colors/Grae/75n1042
Naul, G M/Specification book/79n1556
Nault, M/Saul Bellow/78n1133
Nault, W H/World bk ency/78n70
Nauman, St. E/Dictionary of Asian/79n1082
Naumann, J/UN system/78n430; 79n555; 79n556
Navajo reading bibliog/Kari/76n413
Navajos: critical bibliog/Iverson/77n743
Naval, marine and air force uniforms of WWII/Mollo/77n1631
Naval terms dict/Noel/79n1603
Navalani, K/Guide to reference/77n322

Navon, A R/American bibliog/76n272
Naylor, C/Contemporary artists/79n909
Naylor, K E/American bibliog/75n303
NCEA-Ganley's Catholic schools in America/ Ganley/77n600
NCTE gd to teaching materials for English/ 75n704/suppl/76n682
Nead, D W/Pennsylvania-German/76n437
Neal, V L/NY library/77n180
Near East studies hndbk/Bacharach/78n280
Nebenzahl, K/Atlas of American/75n364/ Bibliography of printed/76n313
Neblette's hndbk of photography and reprography/Sturge/78n885
Needleworker's dict/Clabburn/77n890
Neeson, J M/Bibliography of literature/76n904
Neft, D S/Grosset and/77n665
Neft, D S/Sports ency: baseball/75n733; 78 n610/Sports ency: pro/76n738
Negley, G/Utopian literature/79n1181
Negotiating for computer services/Divilbiss/79 n301
Negro almanac/Ploski/77n433
Negro in American history/75n815
Nehmer, K S/Elementary teachers/79n689
Neil, W/Concise dictionary/75n1219
Neill, W A/Butterflies afield/78n1331
Neiswender, R/Russia, the/79n378
Nelki, A/Picture researcher's/76n928
Nelli, H O/Bibliography of insurance/79n851
Nelson, B/Little red/76n769
Nelson, D M/Illustrated football/77n694
Nelson, J/Poorperson's gd/79n1520
Nelson, J S/Medical school/75n1639
Nelson, M G/Idaho local/78n357
Nelson, W/Patents and/77n471
Nelson Algren/McCollum/75n1351
Nelson Philip American compact atlas/Fullard/ 79n592
Nelson's complete concordance of the new American Bible/Hartdegen/78n994
Nelson's new compact . . .
    illustrated Bible dict/79n1071
    medical dict/Brace/79n1459
    Roget's thesaurus/Boyer/79n1118
    Webster's dict/Kidney/79n1099
Nemeth, B A/Chemical tables/77n1333
Netzorg, M J/Philippines in/78n299
Neuberg, V E/Thomas Frognall/79n187
Neuborne, B/Rights of/77n504
Neuer, K/Inn book/75n612
Neuf années de bibliographie Erasmienne (1962-70)/Margolin/78n1003
Neumann, A J/Technical gd/75n1778

Neuropsychiatry and the war/Brown/77n1459
Nevada place names/Carlson/76n454
Neveling, U/Terminology of/77n172
Neville, B/Real steel/77n937
New, P G/Reprography for/76n228
New, W H/Critical writings/76n1182
New acronyms and initialisms: suppl/Crowley/76n90
New acronyms, initialisms, and abbreviations/ Crowley/78n109
New African yearbk/Rake/79n350
New age baby name bk/Browder/75n446
New age dictionary/Jack/78n1007
New American . . .
    guide to colleges/Hawes/78n565
    medical dict and health manual/Rothenberg/76n1546
    pocket medical dict/Roper/79n1465
New atlas of histology/Di Fiori/79n1445
New Bantam-Megiddo Hebrew & English dict/ Sivan/78n1060
New bk of knowledge/77n75
New Cambridge bibliog of English lit: 600-1660/Watson/76n1260/Pickles/78n1156
New Cambridge modern hist: 1493-1520/ Hay/76n288
New career options for women/Phelps/78 n773
New catalogue of catalogues/de la Iglesia/77 n819; 78n746
New Catholic ency/Eggenberger/76n1085
New Caxton ency/79n76
New color-picture dict for children/Bennett/ 79n1108
New Columbia ency/Harris/76n60
New complete bk of bicycling/Sloane/75 n744
New consciousness/Biteaux/76n1508
New consultants/Wasserman/77n790
New contemporary French/English, English/ French dict/75n1267
New century Shakespeare hndbk/Clark/75 n1398
New college ency of music/Westrup/77n969; 79n968
New dictionary of . . .
    music/Jacobs/75n1140
    physics/Gray/76n1350
    statistics/Webb/75n876
New dimensions for academic library service/ Josey/76n138
New directions in transport sources of information/Aslib Transport and Planning Group and Library Assoc/77n1617

New Emily Post's etiquette/Post/76n1109
New ency Britannica/77n75; 79n77
New ency of little known, highly profitable business opportunities/Payne/75n896
New ency of sports/Hickok/78n608
New ency'ic dict of business law/Ross/76n831
New England beach bk/Bryfonski/76n544
New England records/Bongartz/79n386
New English astrological thesaurus/Francis/79n1433
New English-French dict of slang and colloquialisms/Marks/76n1143
New environment-heredity controversy/Rosenfield/75n793
New film index/McCann/76n1067
New Florida atlas/Wood/75n583
New gospel treasure select-a-song/Gordon/77n955
New governance structure for OCLC/79n257
New gd to motorcycling/Cutter/75n738
New gd to popular gov publications/Newsome/79n121
New gd to study abroad/Garraty/75n663; 79n641
New Hampshire's role in the American Revolution/76n352
New hndbk of chemistry/Chen/77n1332
New hooked on books/Fader/78n586
New Hutchinson 20th cent ency/Horsley/79n72
New illus'd ency of world history/Langer/76n300
New illus'd medical ency for home use/Rothenberg/76n1545
New intellectuals/Logan/78n927
New internat'l dict of New Testament theology/Brown/77n1043; 78n995
New internat'l dict of the Christian church/Douglas/75n1218; 79n1056
New Jersey/Newberry/78n315
New Kobbé's complete opera bk/Earl of Harewood/77n972
New Larousse gastronomique/Montagne/78n1476
New library buildings/Ward/76n204
New library key/Cook/76n110
New life options: working woman's resource bk/Loring/77n721
New low-cost sources of energy for the home/Clegg/76n1458
New Mexico newspapers/Grove/76n22
New music vocabulary/Risatti/76n1001
New New York gd to craft supplies/Glassman/75n1034

New Oxford hist of music/Wellesz/75n1148/ Cooper/75n1149
New periodicals index/78n25
New perspectives for ref serv in academic libraries/McInnis/79n296
New product planning mgmt of the marketing-R&D interface/Rothberg/78n738
New pronouncing dict of the Spanish and English languages/Velázquez de la Cadena/75n1277
New revised gd to the recommended country inns of New England/Chapin/76n546
New Sabin/Thompson/75n5; 77n20; 77n21
New Schöffler-Weis German & English dict/Schöffler/75n1270
New serial titles/75n41
New serial titles 1950-70 subj gd/76n26
New space encyclopaedia/75n1443
New special libraries/Young/78n200
New spiritual community gd for North America/75n1222
New std ency/Downey/76n61
New std Jewish ency/Wigoder/78n285
New Testament words/Barclay/75n1228
New trade names/Crowley/79n810
New Unesco source bk for sci teaching/75n714
New Walt Whitman hndbk/Allen/77n1217
New yacht racing rules/Bavier/75n750
New York art yearbk/Tannenbaum/78n796
New York bk of bars, pubs & taverns/Yeadon/77n1523
New York: chronological & documentary hist/Furer/75n509
New York for children/Shaw/75n614
New York: gd to the metropolis/Wolfe/77n563
New York library instruction programs/Neal/77n180
New York manuscripts: Dutch/Van Laer/75n428
New York Philharmonic gd to the symphony/Downes/78n922
New York Public Library/Catalog of theatre/77n989
New York Public Library. Astor, Lenox & Tilden Foundations/Dictionary catalog Art/76n919/Dictionary catalog Prints/76n920
New York Public Library. Local Hist and Genealogy Div/Dictionary catalog local/75n382/US local/75n383
New York Radical Feminists/Rape/75n850
New York theatre annual/Hughes/79n1020

New York Times . . .
  atlas of the world/79n589
  biographical service/79n141
  book of baseball history/76n703
  book of indoor & outdoor gardening questions/Faust/76n1584
  book of vegetable gardening/Faust/76n1583
  book review index, 1896-1970/75n172
  correspondents' choice: restaurants and recipes from arnd the world/Foster/75n1688
  crossword puzzle dict/Pulliam/76n1135
  cumulative subj & personal name index: environment/79n1399
  cumulative subj & personal name index: women/79n769
  directory of the theatre/75n1186
  encyclopedia of television/Brown/79n1176
  guide to children's entertainment, in NY, NJ, and CT/Flaste/77n559
  guide to home repairs without a man/Gladstone/75n1793
  guide to student adventures and studies abroad/Rowland/75n664
  guide to suburban public schools/Maeroff/77n602
  manual of style and usage/Jordan/77n116
New York women's directory/Womanpower Project/75n854
New York women's yellow pages/79n767
New Zealand atlas/Wards/78n524
New Zealand bks in print/Wilson/76n17
New Zealand in maps/Anderson/79n597
Newark: chronological & documentary hist/Rice/78n359
Newberry, L/New Jersey/78n315
Newbery and Caldecott medal bks, 1966-75/Kingman/77n1192
Newby, E/Rand McNally/76n298
Newcomb, J I/John F. Kennedy/78n446
Newcomb, L/Newcomb's wildflower/78n1296
Newcomb's wildflower gd/Newcomb/78n1296
Newhouse, D/Encyclopedia of homonyms/78n1033
Newkirk, L I/National and/77n271
Newland, M R/Resource gd adult/75n1214
Newman, G/Encyclopedia of health/79n1483
Newman, G B/Guide to medical/75n1629
Newman, H/Illustrated dict ceramics/75n1040/Illustrated dict glass/79n926
Newman, R M/Rock on/79n998
News bureaus in the US/Weiner/75n1304; 78n1077

News dictionary/Trotsky/76n467; 77n498
Newsletter yrbk-directory/Hudson/78n16
Newsome, W L/New gd popular/79n121
Newspaper indexes/Milner/78n1079
Newspaper indexing for historical societies, colleges and high schools/Perica/76n191
Newsprint/Pollock/78n1260
NFL's official ency'ic hist of prof football/National Football League/75n766/Bennett/78n624
NFPA hndbk of the National Electrical Code/Summers/76n1634
Nguyễn P-K/Vietnamese legal/79n566
Nicholas, I D/Managing the/76n118
Nicholas Poppe/Cirtautas/79n1088
Nicholls, A/Directory of world/76n67
Nicholls, D/Nineteenth-century/79n433
Nicholls, R E/Plant buyer's/78n1493
Nichols, H/Map librarianship/77n240
Nicholsen, M E/People in/78n110
Nicholson, J/Australian books/75n6; 79n9
Nickel, M L/Steps to/76n150
Nickerson, C B/Accounting hndbk/76n844
Nickerson, M/State laws/76n1449
Nickles, H G/Dictionary of do's/75n1290
Nicknames and pseudonyms/Dawson/75n448
Nicolosi, L/Terminology of/79n1175
Nicolson, M S/Directors' and/77n773
Niehaus, T F/Field gd Pacific/77n1361
Nigeria: comp bibliog in the humanities and social sciences/Aguolu/75n285
Nigerian civil war/Aguolu/75n390
NIH factbook/77n1481
1909 checklist, correlation index as indicated in "Deptmental publication" part, serial number to classification number/Poole/75n107
1974 directory of gov doc collections & librarians/American Library Assoc/75n157
Nineteenth-century . . .
  American drama/Hixon/78n938
  Britain 1815-1914/Nicholls/79n433
  painters and painting/Norman/79n908
  periodical press in Britain/Madden/78n1078
Nippon: charted survey of Japan/77n328
Nissen, K M/California Indian/76n804
Nite, N N/Rock on/76n1029; 79n998
Nitecki, J Z/Directory of library/75n161; 77n181
Niver, K R/D. W. Griffith/75n1197
Noble, G W/Noble official/76n976
Noble, J H/Emergency medical/75n1617

Noble official catalog of bureau precancels/ Noble/76n976
Nock, O S/Railways in/76n1673
Noddings, T C/Dow Jones-Irwin/75n917
Noe, L/Foundation grants/79n85/Travel marketing/79n847
Noe, S P/Silver coinage/75n1069
Noel, J V/Naval terms/79n1603
Nolan, P B/Wright brothers/78n1507
Nolan, W F/Ray Bradbury/76n1229
Nomenclature for museum cataloging/Chenhall/79n269
Nominated for survival/75n173
Non-book materials in libraries/Fothergill/79n148
Nonconformity and dissent in the Ukrainian SSR/Liber/79n549
Non-ferrous metal data/76n900
Nonformal educ in Latin America/Poston/77n580
Nonnenman, V/Official meeting/75n586
Nonprint materials on communication/Buteau/77n1103
Nonprint media in academic libraries/Grove/76n137
Nonprint media information networking/Brown/78n247
Nonprofit repertory theatre in North America, 1958-75/Kaminsky/78n923
Nonsulfur pulping/Weiner/78n1265
Nonte, G C/Pistol and/76n757
Non-theatrical film distributors/Emmens/76n174
Nonverbal communication/Key/78n1074
Norback, C T & P G/Educational market/78n555/Everything you/76n84/Misspeller's dictionary/75n1259/Older American's/79n738
Norbeck, J/Encyclopedia of American/78n1550
Nordby, V J/Guide to psychologists/76n1504
Nordland, R/Names and/79n1164
Nordling, J A/Dear faculty/77n227
Noreault, T/Feasibility of/79n266
Norell, I P/Literature of Filipino-/77n443
Norimoto, Y/Atlas of representative/79n1315
Norman, G/Nineteenth-century/79n908
Norman, J/Concise Manchu-/79n1132
Norman, J/Romanian phrase/75n1286/Turkish phrase/75n1285
Norman Mailer/Adams/76n1245
Norman people/76n447
Norrie, I/Publishing and/75n48
Norris, A S/Medals and/77n914
Norris, N/Complete home ... cats/77n1531/ Complete home ... dogs/77n1532

North, W J/Underwater California/77n699
North American ...
  collections of Islamic manuscripts/Martin/79n382
  film and video directory/Weber/77n186
  forest and conservation hist/Fahl/78n1483
  forest history/Davis/78n1482
  Indians/78n383
  radio-TV station gd/Jones/76n1170
  trees/Preston/77n1370
North Carolina. Adjutant-General's Office/ Muster rolls/77n472
North Carolina atlas/Clay/76n531
Northern fishes/Eddy/75n1513
Northern Ireland 1921-74/Deutsch/76n276
Northland wild flowers/Moyle/78n1295
Northouse, C/John Osborne/76n1280/ Twentieth century/77n973
Northrop Frye/Denham/75n1410
Northwest foraging/Benoliel/76n1381
Northwest trees/Arno/79n1358
Norton, C/Dance directory/79n1017
Norton, M C/Norton on/77n354
Norton on archives/Norton/77n354
Norwegian-Americans/Andersen/76n415
Notable children's bks 1940-70/78n1121
Notable names in American hist/75n126
Notable names in the American theatre/78n945
Notary public practices & glossary/Rothman/79n562
Notes for Joyce/Gifford/75n1388
Notes from a different drummer: juvenile fict portraying the handicapped/Baskin/78n179
Nothing new: second-hand shopping in L.A./ Goldman/75n946
Nourse, A E/Ladies' Home/75n1650
Nova, sci adventures on TV/75n1431; 76n1311
Novak, G/Running out/79n258
Novak, R/Handbook of English-/75n1271
Novak, S R/Accounting desk/79n824
Novalis, P N/New American/78n565
Novello, J R/Practical handbook/75n1595
Novotny, A/Picture sources/76n942
Nowlan, S E/How to get/76n623; 76n624; 76n625; 76n626/User's gd funding/76n627
NPT: current issues in nuclear proliferation/ Ridgeway/79n559
NSF factbook/76n603
NTIS subj classification/78n1526

Nuclear proliferation factbk/79n1407
Nuclear weapons and NATO/US Dept of Defense/77n1626
Nueckel, S/Selected gd sports/75n726/Selected gd travel/75n587
Nugent, N M/Cavaliers and/79n491
Nugent, S/Rock almanac/77n979
Nukuoro lexicon/Carroll/75n1282
Nulman, M/Concise ency Jewish/76n997
Nulsen, D R & R H/More miles/76n770
Nunis, D B/L.A. and/75n381
Nunn, G R/Southeast Asian/79n365
Nunn, M E/Sports/77n668
Nurse's drug hndbk/Loebl/79n1501
Nursing care of the alcoholic and drug abuser/Burkhalter/76n1528
Nussbaum, F/Annotated bibliog 20th/78n1154
Nutrition almanac/Nutrition Search, Inc./77n1498
Nutrition and diet therapy ref dict/Lagua/76n1525
Nutrition Policy and Programmes Serv Food Policy and Nutrition Div FAO/Food composition/78n1472
Nutrition Search, Inc./Nutrition almanac/77n1498
Nutritive value of American foods/Adams/77n1548
Nutting, T/Cortina-Grosset/77n1090
Nutting, W/Clock book/77n901
NYCLU gd to women's rights in NY state/Cary/79n763
Nye, D/International motor/75n782
Nye, J H/Choral music/75n1132
Nye, R P/Historical dict Cameroon/75n318
Nyhus, L M/Surgery annual/77n1489
Nykoruk, B/Authors in/77n1108/Biography news/75n117/Business people/77n795
Nylander, J C/Fabrics for/78n862
Nyrop, R F/Area hndbk Persian/79n357

O Hehir, B/Classical lexicon/78n1178
Oak from an acorn: American Philosophical Soc Library 1770-1803/Smith/78n262
Oakes, E H/Guide to social/79n758
Oakes, L/Livingstone's pocket/75n1623
Oaks, P/Minority studies/77n426
O'Barr, W M/Student Africanist's/76n246
Ober, K H/Bibliography of modern/77n1266
Oberg, E/Machinery's hndbk/76n1653
Oberholser, H C/Bird life/76n1427
Oberrecht, K & P/Great outdoors/78n621
Oboler, E M/Fear of/75n238/Ideas and/78n167

O'Brien, B/Summer employmt/79n867
O'Brien, B A & E J/Bibliography of festschriften/76n1074
O'Brien, J J/Construction inspection/76n1621
O'Brien, K E/Directory of criminal/78n506/Terrorism/78n642
O'Brien, M M/Collector's gd/75n1099
O'Brien, R/Basic gd research/77n13
Observer's army vehicles directory to 1940/Vanderveen/76n1681
Observer's book of . . .
    aircraft/Green/76n1659
    automobiles/Turner/78n1513
    British steam locomotives/Casserley/76n1669
    commercial vehicles/Baldwin/76n1663
Observer's Soviet aircraft directory/Green/77n1638
Observer's world airlines and airliners directory/Green/76n1660
Obstetrics and gynecology annual/Wynn/77n1487
Obudho, C E/Black-white racial/77n427
Occult illus'd dict/Day/77n1451
Occultism update/Shepard/79n1439
Occupational outlook for college graduates/78n771; 79n862
Occupational outlook hndbk/US Bureau of Labor Statistics/77n844
Occupational safety and health/Peck/75n978
Occupational safety, health and fire index/Miller/78n770
Ocean engineering and oceanography tech lit collection, Water Resources Center Archives, Univ of Calif, Berkeley/US Natl Oceanic and Atmospheric Admin/75n1817
Oceans of the world/US Natl Oceanic and Atmospheric Admin/75n550
Ockerman, H W/Source bk food/79n1531
O'Connell, J A/List/75n149
O'Connell, M R/Care and/78n321/Historic preservation/77n381/Interpretation/79n400
O'Connor, E/Avocational activities/76n604
Ocran, E B/Ocran's acronyms/79n79/Transportation costs/76n825
Ocran's acronyms/Ocran/79n1300
Odeh, R E/Pocket bk statistical/78n689
O'Donnell, T F/Bibliography of writings/76n1238
O'Donoghue, M/Encyclopedia of minerals/77n1437

Odors and odor control/Louden/77n1315
O'Driscoll, J/English language/78n561
Of books and men/Wright/78n265
Of, by and for librarians/Marshall/75n144
Office for Intellectual Freedom of the American Library Assoc/Intellectual freedom/75n154
Office of Indian Affairs, 1824-1880/Hill/75n804
Official Associated Press sports almanac/76n699
Official baseball dope book/Spink/78n611
Official baseball guide/Spink/78n612
Official baseball register/Balzer/79n707
Official baseball rules/75n730; 76n704
Official bottle price list/Kovel/75n1083
Official catalog of Canada precancels/Walburn/76n977; 78n860
Official congressional directory/US Congress/76n486; 77n517/Suppl 1978/79n122
Official ency of baseball/Turkin/77n678
Official ency of bridge/Frey/78n615
Official gd to comic bks and big little bks/Cohen/75n66
Official gd to historic places/76n327
Official hotel & resort gd/Rubin/75n588
Official inaugural medals of the Presidents of the US/Dusterberg/77n911
Official major league baseball playbk/Tanner/75n734
Official meeting facilities gd/Nonnenman/75n586
Official rules of chess/US Chess Federation/76n746
Official rules of sports & games/76n700; 78n604
Official Scrabble players dict/79n727
Official world series records/75n731/Gettleson/76n705; 77n675
Ofori, P E/Black African/77n1029/Christianity in/78n973/Islam in/79n1051
Ogawa, D M/Japanese in/77n445
Ogle, L/Golden picture/78n1030
O'Hart, J/Irish pedigrees/77n481
Ohashi, H/Flora of/77n1355
O'Higgins, P/Bibliography of literature/76n904
Ohio area key/Flavell/78n401
Ohio art and artists/Clark/77n857
Ohio College Library Center/On-line cataloging/75n226
Ohio genealogical gd/Flavell/79n483
Ohio genealogical periodical index/Flavell/78n400

Ohio manufacturers industrial directory/78n759
Ohio Valley history/Bolin/77n455
Ohles, J F/Biographical dict American/79n695
Ohlgren, T H/Illuminated manuscripts/79n68
Ohliger, J/Media and/77n577
Oikonomides, A N/Abbreviations in/76n285
Oil terms/Crook/77n1410
Oilfields of the world/Titratsoo/75n1566
Ojibwas: critical bibliog/Tanner/77n745
Ojo-Ade, F/Analytic index/78n276
O'Keefe, D/Cheese buyer's/79n1532
Okinshevich, L/US history/77n380
Oklahoma place names/Shirk/75n456
Oksman, C G/Definition and/79n754
Old American prints for collectors/Ebert/75n1026
Old and middle English poetry to 1500/Beale/77n1219
Old and new Monongahela/Van Voorhis/75n433
Old churches, ministers and families of VA/Meade/79n490
Old French: concise hndbk/Einhorn/76n1142
Old house catalogue/Grow/78n852
Old sheet music/Klamkin/76n1027
Old Testament bks for pastor and teacher/Childs/78n991
Oldenburg, L/NY Times/76n1584
Older American's handbk/Norback/79n738
Oldfield, P/Library assistant's/79n321
Oldies but goodies/Goldstein/78n916
O'Leary, T J/Ethnographic bibliog North/77n738
Olgin, J/Illustrated football/77n695
Oliu, W E/Business writer's/79n816
Olivas, M A/Annotated bibliog John/76n1250
Oliver, A P H/Guide to shells/76n974
Oliver, E/American antique/78n856
Olmsted, E H/Music Library/75n1138
Olmsted, J C/George Meredith/79n1249/Reputation of/79n1255/Thackeray and/78n1183
Olmsted, V L/Index to 1850/78n407
Olney, R R/Illustrated auto/79n705
-Ologies & -isms/Zettler/79n1128
Olsen, U G/Preparing the/77n117
Olson, D H L/Inventory of/76n784
Olson, E E/Methods of/75n231
Olson, J/Shooter's bible/77n691

Olson, M E/German language/77n444
Olson, N B/Author-number/79n277/Biographical subj/79n278/Classified index persons/79n279/Geographical name/79n280/Index to LC/78n223/Subject keyword/79n281
Oman, M&Anthropological and/78n1373
On-campus/off-campus degree programs for part-time students/Gordon/77n616
On equal terms/Marshall/79n275
On-line age: info retrieval/Pratt/77n293
On-line bibliographic services/Watson/79n267
On-line cataloging/Ohio College Library Center/75n226
On-line information retrieval/Hall/78n242
On-your-own gd to Asia/Davis/79n612
100/Hart/79n397
100 years of national league baseball/Reidenbaugh/77n676
160 edible plants commonly found in the Eastern USA/Freitus/76n1384
1000 largest companies in . . .
 Denmark/76n889
 Norway/76n890
 Sweden/76n891
1500 largest companies in Finland/Thilman/76n892
1,001 questions and answers about Judaism/Gross/79n1062
1601 decorating ideas for modern living/Hatje/75n1104
1-2-3 gd to libraries/Knight/77n160
O'Neall, J B/Annals of Newberry/75n410
O'Neill, J E/WW II/77n362
O'Neill, P/Günter Grass/77n1264
Onions, C T/Shorter Oxford/75n1252
Onosko, T/Fun land/79n713
ONTAP/Markey/79n264
Ontario and the Canadian North/Morley/79n376
Ontario energy catalogue/Powell/79n1388
Ontario ethno-cultural newspapers, 1835-1972/McLaren/75n1300
Open admissions and the academic library/Breivik/78n162
Open Dallas/75n613/Warren/78n81
Opera from A to Z/Forbes/78n912
Opera production II/Eaton/75n1166
Operanatomy/Alexander/76n1021
Operas of Gian Carlo Menotti, 1937-72/Grieb/76n1008
Opfell, O S/Lady laureates/79n770
Oppedisano-Reich, M/National gd gov/78n649
Oppelt, N T/Southwestern pottery/78n680
Opportunities for minorities in librarianship/Josey/78n257

Opportunities in library and info sci/Sullivan/78n259
Oracle bone collections in the US/Chou/78n318
Oral antecedents of Greek librarianship/Wright/78n264
Oral history/Davis/78n323
Oral history collections/Meckler/76n302
Oral history program manual/Moss/75n348
Oram, R/Transportation system/77n1620
Orchestral music in print/Farish/79n990
Oregon biog index/Brandt/77n390
Oregon Competency Based Educ Program/Competency based/78n577
Oregon geographic names/McArthur/76n458
Oregon Historical Soc microfilm gd/75n384
O'Reilly, A M/Data processing/76n1623
O'Relley, Z E/Soviet-type/79n806
Organ music in print/Nardone/76n1018
Organ preludes/Edson/75n1153
Organic directory/Stoner/76n885
Organic flower gardening/Foster/76n1586
Organic gardening under glass/Abraham/76n1581
Organisation of media/Chibnall/77n152
Organization and staffing of the libraries of Columbia Univ/Booz, Allen & Hamilton, Inc./75n117
Organization of the library profession/Chaplin/75n255
Organized crime/Hopkins/75n827
Organizing and documenting data processing information/Gildersleeve/78n524
Organizing for health care/Source Collective/75n1631
Oriental carpets for today/Fokker/75n1103
Original lists of persons of quality/Hotten/75n421
Original manuscript music for wind and percussion instruments/Weerts/75n1134
Original world-wide mail order shoppers' gd/Moller/75n952
Origins of some Anglo-Norman families/Loyd/76n445
Orimoloye, S A/Biographia Nigeriana/78n117
Ormond, C/Outdoorsman's hndbk/76n719
Ornamental conifers/77n1369
Ornamental grasses/Meyer/76n1597
Orne, J/Language of/77n57
O'Rourke, J/Living word/77n1066
Orr, D M/North Carolina/76n531
Orr, J M/Libraries as/78n126
Orr, M C & R T/Wildflowers of/75n1479
Orr, S D/Concordance to poems/79n1243

Orrey, L/Encyclopedia of opera/77n974
Orsagh, T/Economic history/76n826
Osberg, S R/Consumer protection/76n871
Osborn, M/Translations of/76n1267
Osborne, H/Oxford companion/76n946
Osborne, J/55 years/77n980/Popular & rock/ 79n999/Record album/78n903/Record albums/79n974/Record collector's/78 n904
Oscar movies from A-Z/Pickard/79n1030
Oscilloscope hndbk/Herrick/75n1787
OSHA compliance manual/Petersen/76n906
Oster, D/Dictionnaire de/79n1269
Oster, S M/Definition and/79n754
Ostling, J K/C. S. Lewis/75n1390
Ostrander, R E/Directorship by/78n210
Ostrom, L L/Marketing profitability/79n836
O'Toole, T E/Historical dict Guinea/79n354
Ottemiller's index to plays in collections/ Connor/77n996
Otto, H A/New life/77n721
Oughton, M/Geographers biobibliographical/ 78n536
Our American artists 1879/Benjamin/78n794
Our Quaker friends of ye olden time/Bell/ 77n454
Outdoor life gun data book/Rice/76n758
Outdoor recreation/Schipf/77n669
Outdoorsman's hndbk/Ormond/76n719
Outline hist of the American Revolution/ Dupuy/76n306
Outlines of Chinese symbolism and art motives/ Williams/75n1001; 78n1018
Overs, R P/Avocational activities/76n604
Overstreet, R M/Comic bk/77n1171
Ovington, R/Wildlife illust'd/76n1414
Owen, B M/Smorgasbord of/76n161
Owen, D B/Abstracts and/75n1432/American gd/77n301
Owen, W F/Guide to graduate/79n661
Owen D. Young/Szladits/75n69
Owens, E A/Bibliography on taxation/78n783
Owens, J J/Genesis/79n1072
Owings, L C/Environmental values/77n1408
Owls of the world/Burton/75n1507
Owner-built home/Kern/76n1640
Oxbridge omnibus of holiday observances arnd the world/78n1021
Oxford advanced learner's dict of current English/Hornby/75n1260
Oxford Bible atlas/May/75n1232
Oxford children's dict in color/Weston/77n1080

Oxford companion to . . .
  film/Bawden/77n997
  German literature/Garland/77n1263
  ships & the sea/Kemp/78n1549
  the decorative arts/Osborne/76n946
  world sports and games/Arlott/76n701
Oxford dictionary of . . .
  current idiomatic English/Cowie/77n1069
  English Christian names/Withycombe/78 n426
  the Christian church/Cross/75n1220
Oxford English-Turkish dict/İz/79n1153
Oxford-Harrap std German-English dict/ Jones/79n1138
Oxford illust'd dict/Coulson/76n1117
Oxford Latin dict/Glare/77n1095; 79n1144
Oxford literary gd to the British Isles/Eagle/ 78n1159
Oxford picture dict of American English/ Parnwell/Spanish/79n1100/French/79 n1101/Monolingual English/79n1102
Oxford regional economic atlas/77n764
Oxford student's dict of current English/ Hornby/79n1098
Oxford University. Ashmolean Museum/ Catalogue of Anglo-Saxon/75n994

Pacey, P/Art library/78n260
Pacific historical review/Hager/77n388
Pacific Islands press/Richstad/75n1303
Pacific liners, 1927-72/Emmons/75n1829
Pady, D S/Horses and/75n1684
Page, G T/Internat'l dict/79n639
Page, N M/Wild plants/76n1380
Paget, G/Lineage & ancestry/78n420
Painting and sculpture in the Museum of Modern Art/Barr/79n877
Paintings of Charles Bird King (1785-1862)/ Cosentino/78n815
Pakistan and Bangladesh: bibliographic essays in soc sci/Gustafson/77n330
Pakistan: selected, annotated bibliog/Abernethy/76n264
Palauan-English dict/McManus/78n1064
Palestine and the Arab-Israeli conflict/Khalidi/ 75n535
Palestine question/79n503
Paley, H/Antebellum black/77n432
Palgrave, R H I/Dictionary of political/77 n778
Palic, V M/Government publications/77n108

Palley, A D/Data processing/76n1623
Palley, R/Porcelain art/77n889
Palmegiano, E M/Women and/78n665
Palmer, A/Military atlas/76n296/Quotations in/77n366
Palmer, A M/Research centers/76n629
Palmer, A W/Dictionary of modern/77n365
Palmer, E L/Fieldbook of natural/76n1364
Palmer, G/Western treebook/79n1362
Palmer, H H/European drama/75n1324; 78n941
Palmer, M A/Training and/79n814
Palmer, R/Dictionary of mythical/77n1054
Palmer, R C/Reader in/78n232
Palmer, R S/Handbook of North/77n1384
Palmer, S H/Economic arithmetic/79n807
Palmer, V/Quotations in/77n366
Palmour, V E/Access to/75n230/Methods of/75n231
Palumbo, J/Terrorism/78n642
Pan Am's world guide/75n589; 79n620
Pancheri, P/Handbook of cross-/77n1447
Pannell, C W/Inventory of/77n549
Panofsky, H E/Bibliography of Africana/76n247
Pap, L/Portuguese in/78n391
Paper, J D/Guide to Chinese/75n1414
Paper mill sludge characteristics, utilization and disposal/Louden/77n1316
Paperbound bks in print/76n9
Paperback bks for young people/Gillespie/79n229
Papers of Woodrow Wilson/78n442
Paperweights for collectors/Selman/77n922
Paquet, M/Atlas of pediatric/79n1446
Paradis, A A/Research hndbk/75n695
Paradis, R/Language of/75n885
Paradiso, J L/Mammals of/76n1446
Para-legal and the lawyer's library/Cunningham/75n555
Paraprofessional and nonprofessional staff in special libraries/Christianson/75n203
Parch, G D/Directory of newspaper/77n182
Parent's gd to children's reading/Larrick/77n1157
Parents' yellow pages/Caplan/79n745
Pargellis, S/Bibliography of British/78n370
Parins, J W/Concordance to Conrad's/77n1231
Parish, D W/State government/75n106
Parish, J R/Actors' TV/79n1179/Film actors/78n960/Film directors/76n1058/Film director's guide/78n961/Great gangster/77n1011/Great science/78n962/Great spy/75n1198/Great western/77n1012/Hollywood

Parish, J R (cont'd) ... character/79n1037/Hollywood players/77n1015; 77n1016
Parish, P/Doctors and/79n1492
Parish registers of England/Cox/75n436
Parisi, N/Sources of national/79n577
Parker, B J & F/American dissertations/77n578; 77n579; 78n544
Parker, C C/Information sources/77n1287
Parker, D L/Guide to dance/79n1038
Parker, G T/College on/79n632
Parker, J/SALT II/75n541
Parker, J C/Personal name/79n492
Parker, J R/Musical biography/76n1006
Parker, S/Antebellum black/77n432
Parker, T F/Violence in/75n834
Parker, W/Homosexuality bibliog/78n653
Parker directory of attorneys/Jones/77n539
Parkinson, R/Encyclopedia of modern/78n1559
Parks, S/John Cunton/77n55
Parlapiano, K/Health sciences/79n1451
Parlato, S J/Superfilms/77n1013
Parler populaire des Canadiens Français/Dionne/76n1141
Parliament and the public libraries/Morris/78n175
Parliamentary procedures simplified/Place/77n497
Parliaments of the world/Herman/77n495
Parming, M R & T/Bibliography of English-/75n305; 76n273
Parnwell, E C/Oxford picture dictionary/79n1100; 79n1101; 79n1102
Parramore, B M/Children's dictionary/75n709
Parrin, K C/Business media/75n907; 75n908; 75n910
Parris, J H/Convention decisions/75n487
Parry, P J/Contemporary art/79n900
Participative mgmt in academic libraries/Marchant/78n164
Particle atlas/McCrone/75n1433
Partington, P G/W. E. B. DuBois/78n387
Partlow, R B/Dickens studies/75n1384
Partnow, E/Quotable woman/79n768
Partridge, B/Bargain hunting/75n953
Partridge, E/Dictionary of catch/78n1046/Macmillan dict/76n1128
Paschal, D I/Penny whimsy/77n915
Pascoe, D J/Quick reference/75n1632
Paskar, J/Statistics sources/75n879
Passano, E P/Index of source/75n429
Passel, P/Best, encore/78n89
Passengers to America/Tepper/78n413
Passero, B/Oceans of/75n550

Passmore, R/Information worker/78n127
Passwater, R A/Guide to fluorescence/76n1352
Pastman, R A/Randax graduate/77n625
Paszek, L J/US Air/75n1847
Patch, V D/Handbook of psychiatry/75n1597
Patents and deeds and other early records of New Jersey/Nelson/77n471
Pater, A F & J R/What they/77n96
Pathfinder: operational gd for the school librarian/Freeman/77n221
Paton, J/Jugs/78n872
Paton, J/Rand McNally's children's/78n67
Patraw, P M/Flowers of/79n1345
Patrick Moore's color star atlas/Moore/75n1448
Patrick White/Lawson/75n1409
Patten, D J/Art index/76n929
Patten, M/Books for cooks/77n1549
Patterson, G J/Plastics book/77n1615
Patterson, H R/Current drug/78n1436
Patterson, J A/Study gd/75n1633
Patterson, J E/Autographs/75n1100/Collector's gd/75n1058
Patterson, M C/Literary research/77n1126
Patterson, M L P/South Asian/77n243; 77n244
Patterson, S R/Medical terminology/79n1464
Patterson, T J S/Zeis index/79n1482
Patterson, W/Koreans in/75n821
Patterson's American educ/Elliott/76n663
Patti, R J/Management practice/77n708
Patton, C P/Atlas of Oregon/78n521
Paul Felix Warburg union catalog of arbitration/Seide/75n980
Paul Laurence Dunbar/Metcalf/76n1234
Paul Leicester Ford/DuBois/78n155
Paule, M/Working press/75n1305
Paule, M A/Directory of shopping/75n922
Paulsen, K/Woman's almanac/77n723
Paulson, G D/Project mgmt/78n780
Paulson, G L/Environment USA/75n1549
Paulston, R G/Folk schools/75n647
Paulus, V/Housing/75n1767
Pavlakis, C/American music/75n1150
Paxton, J/Dictionary of abbreviations/75n115/ Dictionary of European/79n809/European political/76n460; 79n505/Statesman's year-book/75n87; 76n77/World legislatures/76n465
Paylore, P/Arid lands/79n1405
Payne, J/New encyclopedia/75n896
Payne, J R/John Steinbeck/76n1249/W. H. Hudson/78n1273
Paysan, K/Guide to aquarium/76n1559

PCC's ref bk of personal and home computing/McCabe/79n1548
Pearl, I A/Annual review lignin/77n1334
Pearl, R M/Gems, minerals/78n1360
Pears cyclopaedia/Barker/76n62; 79n78
Pears' shilling cyclopaedia/79n79
Pearson, E L/Librarian/77n281
Pearson, J/Genealogies of . . . Albany/77n474/ Genealogies of . . . Schenectady/77n473
Pearson, J D/Arab Islamic/78n278/Index Islamicus/75n345; 77n303; 79n383/ World bibliography African/76n2/World bibliography Oriental/76n3
Pearson, N P/Learning resource/75n216
Pease, M/Consolidated index/78n772
Peck, H/Encyclopedia of sport/77n670
Peck, T P/Occupational safety/75n978
Peckham, H H/Campaigns of/77n377/Toll of/76n335
Peckner, D/Handbook of stainless/78n1544
Pederson, L/Manual for/75n1250
Pederson, V L/Checklist of American/78n498
Pediatric drug hndbk/Shirkey/79n1504
Pedigrees of some of the Emperor Charlemagne's descendants/Langston/75n425
Peebles, J D/Rates of/77n574
Peeples, K E/Opportunities for/78n257
Peer, L H/Terms of/75n1318
Pei, M A/Dictionary of foreign/76n1119/ Dictionary of linguistics/77n1061
Pelican guide to . . .
  English literature/Ford/75n1373
  gardens of Louisiana/Leblanc/75n610
  historic homes and sites of revolutionary America/Hechtlinger/77n561
  New Orleans/Griffin/75n608
Pell, A R/Women's gd/77n850
Pellerite, J J/Handbook of literature/79n993
Pellowski, A/World of/79n214
Pelto, G H & P J/Reviews in anthropology/75n868; 76n807
Peltola, B J/Research in/77n1160
Pelton, R W/Writer's research/78n102
Peltz, M E/Metropolitan Opera/79n994
Pemberton, J E/British official/75n110
Pemsel, H/History of war/79n1604
Penguin atlas of ancient hist/McEvedy/77n357
Penguin bk of tables/75n1441
Penguin dict of . . .
  Archaeology/Bray/77n348
  geology/Whitten/77n1427
  physics/Pitt/78n1269
Penguin gd to London/Banks/79n611

Penguin medical ency/Wingate/77n1478
Penguin shorter atlas of the Bible/Grollenberg/79n1067
Penguin stereo record gd/Greenfield/79n971
Penguin world atlas/Hall/76n528
Penitente bibliog/Weigle/77n1035
Penland, P R/Library as/79n153
Penna, C V/National library/78n125
Pennar, J/Estonians in/76n405
Penninger, F E/English drama/77n988
Pennsylvania-German in the Revolutionary War/Richards/79n495
Pennsylvania-German in the settlement of Maryland/Nead/76n437
Pennsylvania German pioneers/Strassburger/76n442
Penny, M/Birds of/76n1428
Penny whimsy/Sheldon/77n915
Pennypincher, A/Factory store/75n951
Pennypincher's wine gd/Donner/75n1672
Penrice, J/Dictionary and/78n982
Penrose graphic arts internat'l annual/Smith/76n943
Penzler, O/ABC's wide/75n720/Detectionary/78n1104/Encyclopedia of mystery/77n1177
People and events of the American Revolution/Dupuy/75n368
People in books/Nicholsen/78n110
People make it happen/Hanna/79n289
People's almanac/Wallechinsky/77n102; 79n109
People's almanac presents the book of lists/Wallechinsky/78n94
Peoples Bicentennial Commission/America's birthday/75n1243
People's pharmacy/Graedon/78n1439
Peoples Republic of China/78n523
People's yellow pages of America/French/76n80
Pequeño Larousse ilustrado/Garcia-Pelayo y Gross/79n1151
Peradotto, J/Classical mythology/75n1240
Perception: annotated bibliog/Emmett/78n1362
Pérez, L A/Cuban revolutionary/77n400
Performer's gd to baroque music/Donington/75n1146
Performing arts research/Whalon/77n991
Performing arts resources/Perry/76n1039; 78n936; 79n1005
Perica, E/Newspaper indexing/76n191
Pericoli, U/1815/75n1850

Periodical indexes in the soc sciences and humanities/Harzfeld/79n345
Periodical title abbreviations/Alkire/78n13
Periodicals admin in libraries/Mayes/79n265
Periodicals and newspapers currently received in the Ohio State Univ Libraries/75n42
Periodicals for religious educ resource centers and parish libraries/Corrigan/77n1026
Periodicals for school media programs/Richardson/79n184
Periodicals from Africa/Travis/78n277
Periodicals in humanities/Wajid/75n44
Periodicals on the socialist countries and on Marxism/Shaffer/78n467
Peripherals review/75n966
Perkins, D/Native Americans/76n805
Perkins, J W/Branch library/79n259
Perkins, R M/Fire resistant/76n1649
Perkinson, H J/Review of/76n587
Permanence/Louden/79n1325
Permanent magnet design and application hndbk/Moskowitz/77n1597
Perrin, A T/Explorers Ltd./78n616
Perrin, R D/Explorers Ltd./79n399
Perry, E S/New film/76n1067
Perry, F/Gardening in/77n1559/Simon and/77n1351
Perry, R/Road rider/75n742
Perry, R H/Engineering manual/77n1569
Perry, T/Performing arts/76n1039; 78n936; 79n1005
Personal filmmaking/Piper/76n1049
Personal name index to Orton's "Records of the California Men in the War of the Rebellion, 1861-1867"/Parker/79n492
Personal name index to 'The NY Times Index' 1851-1974/Falk/77n40
Personality research in marketing/Twedt/78n743
Personality tests and reviews II/Buros/76n566
Personnel utilization in libraries/Ricking/76n183
Persons, R H/Investor's ency/76n860
Perusse, R I/Historical dict Haiti/78n308
Pescow, J K/Encyclopedia of accounting/77n797
Peskett, H/Discover your/79n468
Pesko, C/Solar directory/77n1414
Pest control in buildings/Cornwell/75n1532
Pestieau, P S/Lafayette/76n317
Peter, L J/Peter's quotations/78n87

Peters, J/Book collecting/78n50/Bookman's glossary/76n46
Peter's quotations/Peter/78n87
Petersen, C/Each in/76n1235
Petersen, D/OSHA compliance/76n906
Petersen's hunting annual/75n778
Peterson, A F/French fifth/75n519
Peterson, A R/Library service/79n202
Peterson, C S/Reference bks/76n162
Peterson, L/Field gd edible/79n1367
Peterson, M G/How to know/75n1467
Peterson, M S/Encyclopedia of food science/79n1533/Encyclopedia of food technology/76n1574
Peterson, P V/Native trees/76n1402
Peterson, R T/Field gd birds/76n1429/Field gd Mexican/75n1509
Peterson, V E/Library instruction/75n239
Peterson's annual gd to undergrad study/Hegener/79n663
Peterson's annual guides to grad study/Hegener/79n662
Peterson's annual guides to undergrad & grad study/Hegener/77n623
Peterson's gd to college admissions/Zuker/77n627
Peterson's travel gd to colleges/Hinckley/79n658
Petit Larousse illustré/78n1056
Petite encyclopédie Larousse/78n65
Petrarch: catalogue of the Petrarch collection in Cornell Univ Library/76n1298
Petras, H/Handbook of martial/76n768
Petroleum industry in Western Europe/Franko/77n1404
Petrovich, M B/Yugoslavia/75n307
Pets/Chrystie/75n1679
Pettingill, O S/Guide to bird/78n1320
Petzoldt, P/Wilderness hndbk/75n757
Pevsner, N/Dictionary of architecture/77n875
Pfafflin, J R/Encyclopedia of environmental/78n1343
Pfaltzgraff, R L/Study of/78n487
Pfeiffer, C F/Baker's pocket/75n1233/Wycliffe Bible/77n1050
Pfeiffer, J W/Reference guide/78n1372
Pflug, W W/Guide to archives/75n979
Phaidon dict of 20th-century art/79n881
Phair, J T/Bibliography of William/76n314
Phan, T C/Vietnamese communism/77n525
Phares, T B/Who's who football/75n765
Pharmaceutical manufacturers of the US/78n1442
Phelps, A T/New career/78n773

Phelps, W H/Guide to birds/79n1372
Philadelphia. Library Company/Afro-Americana/75n816
Philbrook, M M/Medical books/77n1466
Philip Roth/Rodgers/75n1367
Philippine research materials and library resources/Saito/75n311
Philippine retrospective natl bibliog: 1523-1699/Bernardo/76n14
Philippines in WW II and to independence/Netzorg/78n299
Phillips, D/Selected bibliog music/76n170
Phillips, J G/Annual review astronomy/75n1444
Phillips, J W/Washington state/77n552
Phillips, K/Catalogue of South/75n98
Phillips, K/Southeastern bibliographic/79n169
Phillips, M I/Governors of/79n534
Phillips, P/Collectors' ency/75n1059
Phillips, R/Trees of/79n1363/Wild flowers/79n1346
Phillipson, J S/Thomas Wolfe/78n1153
Philo, H M/Lawyers desk/76n517
Phinney, E/Librarian and/78n196
Phinney, J F S/History of anthropology/79n776
Phipps, F/Collector's complete/76n964
Phoenix/Buchannan/79n422
Photo-atlas of the US/76n532
Photo lab index/Pittaro/76n982
Photocopying in libraries/Whitestone/79n293
Photographer's hndbk/Hedgecoe/79n952
Photographer's market/Milar/79n954
Photographic Magazine equipmt buyer's gd/75n1112
Photographs: Sheldon Memorial Art Gallery collections, Univ of Nebraska/78n886
Photography catalog/Snyder/78n887
Photography: history, materials, and processes/Swedlund/75n1116
Photography market place/McDarrah/76n980
Photography year/76n981
Photography year bk/Sanders/75n1113
Physical and chemical properties of water/Hawkins/78n1240
Physical educ index/Kirby/79n675
Physical education-sports index/Hoyle/79n676
Physical sciences: doctoral dissertations accepted by Indian universities 1857-1970/76n1312
Physician's hndbk/Krupp/77n1488

Physics and astronomy classification scheme/ 79n1334
Physiology of physical stress/Chapman/76n1514
Phythian, B/Concise dict English/77n1070/Concise dict English slang/77n1071
Pianist's resource gd/Rezits/76n1019
Piano in chamber ensemble/Hinson/79n991
Piano owner's guide/Schmeckel/75n1161
Piano teacher's source bk/Hinson/76n1015
Picasso/Kibbey/79n906
Piccirillo, M L/Law enforcement/75n830
Picerno, V J/Dictionary of musical/78n899
Pick, A/Standard catalog/76n970
Pick, T P/Anatomy, descriptive/76n1530
Pickard, R/Oscar movies/79n1030
Pickard, R A E/Companion to/75n1199
Pickett, D C/Approval plans/78n165
Pickles, J D/New Cambridge/78n1156
Pickup camper manual/Hull/75n1752
Pictorial hist of black Americans/Hughes/75n814
Pictorial price gd to American antiques and objects made for the American market/Hammond/79n914
Picture ency of small plants/Kramer/79n1339
Picture indexing for local hist materials/Gilbert/75n224
Picture ref file/Hart/77n883; 78n813
Picture researcher's hndbk/Evans/76n928
Picture sources 3/Novotny/76n942
Pidhainy, O I & O S/Ukrainian Republic/76n375
Piele, P K/Directory of organizations/78n556
Piepkorn, A C/Profiles in/78n970
Pieratt, A B/Donald Barthelme/78n1132/Kurt Vonnegut/76n1251
Pierce, J S/From abacus/79n882
Piercy, E J/Commonsense cataloging/76n192
Pierpont Morgan Library/Major acquisitions/75n19
Pigeons and doves of the world/Goodwin/78n1318
Pike, L J/Lafayette/76n317
Pilgrim's gd to planet earth/75n1223
Pilkington, R/Waterways in/75n625
Piloting, seamanship and small boat handling/Chapman/76n709
Pinchemel, P/Geographers biobibliographical/78n536; 79n626
Pinches, J H & R V/Royal heraldry/75n443
Pingree, E E/Humanities index/76n36
Pingry, J R/Industrial marketing/78n737
Pinion, F G/Brontë companion/76n1269
Pino, F/Mexican Americans/76n402

Pioneer miner and the pack mule express/Wiltsee/77n925
Piper, J/Personal filmmaking/76n1049
Pistol and revolver gd/Nonte/76n757
Pit n'pot grower's bk/Kramer/76n1593
Pitch/Pollock/77n1327
Pitchell, R J/Directory of US/75n676
Pitkin, G M/Serials automation/77n169
Pitkin, R E/Theological dict/77n1048
Pitt, B/World War II/79n398
Pitt, V H/Penguin dict/78n1269
Pittaro, E M/Compact photo/78n883/Photo lab/76n982
Pitts, M R/Film directors/76n1058/Great gangster/77n1011/Great science/78n962/Great spy/75n1198/Great western/77n1012/Hollywood on/79n975/Radio soundtracks/77n1114
Pitts, V P/Concept development/79n752
Pittsburgh: chronological & documentary hist/Vexler/78n363
Pizer, D/Theodore Dreiser/76n1233
Pizzetti, I/Flowers/76n1599
Place, L/Parliamentary procedures/77n497
Place names of Hawaii/Pukui/75n453
Place-names of the world/Room/75n455
Placenames of Georgia/Utley/76n459
Plains Indians/Hoebel/79n775
Plambeck, J A/Encyclopedia of electrochemistry/78n1249
Plan for the dict of Old English/Frank/75n1248
Planché, J R/Introduction to heraldry/75n440
Planet we live on/Hurlbut/77n1424
Planning and design of library bldgs/Thompson/75n145; 79n260
Planning and operating media centers/77n228
Planning library workshops and institutes/Warncke/77n274
Planning manual for academic library bldgs/Ellsworth/75n179
Planning, programming, budgeting systems in academic libraries/Young/77n208
Plano, J C/American political/77n507/Political science/75n468
Plant buyer's hndbk/Nicholls/78n1493
Plant engineer's hndbk of formulas, charts and tables/Moffat/75n1813
Plant manager's hndbk/Becker/75n1809
Plantagenet ancestry/Turton/76n444
Plante, J G/Monastic manuscript/75n15
Plants and animals of the Pacific Northwest/Kozloff/77n1346

Plants & flowers/75n1705
Plastics bk list/Patterson/77n1615
Plato and Socrates/McKirahan/79n1081
Platts, J T/Dictionary of Urdū/79n1071
Plea bargaining and guilty pleas/Bond/76n514
Pleasures of book collecting/Iacone/77n64
Ploski, H A/Negro almanac/77n433
Plotnik, A/Library life/76n121
Plots and characters in major Russian fiction/Berry/78n1196; 79n1282
Plots and characters in the . . .
    fiction of 18th-century English authors/Johnson/78n1164; 79n1229
    fiction of Jane Austen, the Brontës, and George Eliot/Halperin/77n1229
    fiction of Theodore Dreiser/Gerber/78n1137
    fiction of William Dean Howells/Carrington/77n1205
    works of Mark Twain/Gale/75n1370
Plumbing dict/Jacobson/77n1616
Plunguian, M/Comprehensive bibliog/75n1525
Pluscauskas, M/Canadian bks/77n23; 77n24; 79n11/Canadian serials/78n14/Subject gd/75n9
Plymouth church records, 1620-1859/76n438
Pocket bk of statistical tables/Odeh/78n689
Pocket data bk, USA/US Bureau of the Census/78n693
Pocket dictionary/79n1103
Pocket ency of dogs/Swedrup/77n1538
Pocket gd to the location of art in the US/Fundaburk/79n884
Pocket Hawaiian dict with a concise Hawaiian grammar/Pukui/76n1153
Pocket Oxford Russian-English dict/Coulson/76n1146
Podolsky, A/Education directory/79n664
Podrazik, W J/All together/77n978/Beatles Again?/79n997
Poe, creator of words/Pollin/75n1365
Poetry hndbk/Deutsch/75n1333
Poetry themes/Marcan/79n1200
Poets & Writers, Inc. 1977 suppl/78n1113
Pogrebin, L C/Getting yours/76n796
Pohl, R W/How to know/79n1350
Poincelot, R P/Gardening indoors/76n1600
Poisonous and venomous marine animals of the world/Halstead/79n1380
Poisonous plants of the US/Muenscher/76n1378
Poland, past and present/Davies/78n372
Polette, N/Celebrating with/78n191/E is/77n1161/Modern school/76n151
Policies of publishers/Kim/77n177; 79n247

Polish American hist and culture/Zurawski/76n416
Polish press in America/Kowalik/79n465
Politella, D/Directory of college/75n1299; 78n15
Political campaign communication/Kaid/75n462
Political dict of the Middle East in the 20th century/Shimoni/75n523
Political events annual/79n509
Political hndbk of the world/Banks/76n468; 79n510
Political participation of women in the US/Stanwick/78n447
Political profiles . . .
    the Eisenhower years/Schoenebaum/79n527
    the Kennedy years/Lichtenstein/78n440
Political science/Harmon/75n460
Political sci bibliographies/Harmon/77n492
Political sci dict/Plano/75n468
Political sci thesaurus/Beck/76n464
Political terrorism/Sobel/76n462
Political violence in the US, 1875-1974/Manheim/76n472
Politics, economics, and society in the two Germanies/Merritt/79n379
Politics of African and Middle Eastern states/Drabek/78n470
Politics of educ/Harman/76n580
Polking, K/Artists and/77n856/Artist's market/76n927/Beginning writer's/79n1169/Law and/79n561/Private pilot's/75n763
Pollack, P/Animal kingdom/79n901/Chairs/79n923/Dining and/79n902/Picture reference/78n813/Weather/79n1416
Pollak, K & O B/Rhodesia-Zimbabwe/78n291
Pollard, A/Webster's new/77n1311
Pollard, A W/Fine books/75n65/Short-title/77n27
Pollard, M L/Cumulative index/78n22
Pollin, A M/Concordance to plays/76n1305
Pollin, B R/Music for/75n1133/Poe, creator/75n1365
Pollock, V/Analytical methods/77n1325/Corrosion of/77n1326/Newsprint/78n1260/Nonsulfur pulping/78n1265/Pitch/77n1327/Retention of/77n1318/Runnability of/77n1319/Tall oil/78n1259/Wood waste/77n1320
Pollutant removal hndbk/Sittig/75n1542
Polluted groundwater/Todd/77n1423
Polmar, N/Guide to Soviet/79n1599/Ships and/79n1605/World combat/78n1565

Polsby, N W/Handbook of political/76n466
Polunin, O/Trees and/78n1307
Pomeranz, V E/Mothers' and/78n1430
Pommery, J/What to do/77n1530
Ponchie, J-P/French periodical/77n45; 79n25
Poniatowski, M/Ocean engineering/75n1817
Pontalis, J-B/Language of/75n1581
Poole, H/Academic libraries/78n168
Poole, M E/Documents office/79n123/1909 checklist/75n107
Poonawala, I K/Bibliography of Ismāʻīlī/79n1052
Poorperson's gd to great cheap wines/Nelson/79n1520
Pope, E/Simulation activities/78n128
Pope, M/Sex and/75n269
Popenoe, C/Wellness/79n1493
Pope-Selman, L/Paperweights for/77n922
Popkin, D & M/Modern French/78n1187
Popkin, M/Modern black/79n1186
Popovich, E/Libros en venta/79n13
Popular & rock records 1948-78/Osborne/79n999
Popular dict of Buddhism/Humphreys/77n1038
"Popular dogs"/Sprug/76n1565
Popular gd to gov publications/Leidy/77n107
Popular music/Shapiro/75n1175
Popular music periodicals index/Tudor/75n1172; 77n983
Popular names of US gov reports/US Library of Congress/77n115
Popular periodical index/Bottorff/75n34
Popular school: English renaissance drama/Logan/76n1032
Popular song index/Havlice/76n1026/Suppl/79n980
Popular titles and subtitles of musical compositions/Berkowitz/76n983
Population activist's hndbk/75n514
Population and demography/78n686
Population and the population explosion/Goode/75n872/Triche/75n813
Population in development planning/Bilsborrow/78n684
Population: organizations and info resources/Trzyna/77n713
Population problems in Africa/75n294
Porcelain art of Edward Marshall Boehm/Palley/77n889
P-Orridge, G/Contemporary artists/79n909
Port, J G/Dictionary of composers/79n963
Porter, A/Directory of art/76n960
Porter, J/Education directory/79n646
Porter, K H/National party/75n493

Porter, K R/Microanatomy of/79n1336
Porter, L W/Annual review psychology/76n1496
Porter, R E/Writer's manual/78n106
Porter, S/Sylvia Porter's/76n877
Portnov, L & V/US guide/79n469
Portraits and statuary of Virginians owned by the Virginia State Library/Hummel/79n879
Portuguese in the US/Pap/78n391
Posey, E D/Approval plans/78n165
Positive images: non-sexist films for young people/Artel/78n995
Posner, A/China/78n297
Posner, M E/Saul Bellow/75n1352
Post, E L/New Emily/76n1109
Post, J A/Information-poor/76n199
Post, J B/Atlas of fantasy/75n1328
Postage stamps and postal hist of Canada/Boggs/75n1089
Postal, B/American Jewish/78n528/Jewish landmarks/79n609
Post-liberation works of Mao Zedong/Starr/78n474
Poston, S L/Nonformal educ/77n580
Poteet, G H/Death and/78n1427/Published radio/76n1165/Tom Swift/75n708
Potter, D W/Index to 1820/79n493
Potter's complete bk of clay and glazes/Chappell/79n947
Potter's dict of materials and techniques/Hamer/77n891
Potterton, H/National Gallery/79n880
Pottery and ceramics/Campbell/79n946
Potts, D H/Association of/77n700
Pough, F H/Field gd rocks/77n1438
Poulos, K/Checklist of writings/75n642
Pound, O S/Wyndham Lewis/79n1247
Powell, B/Avant gardener/76n1601
Powell, D M/Arizona gathering II/75n385
Powell, J M/Medieval studies/78n325
Powell, K/English historical/79n434
Powell, M/Treasury of/77n1554
Powell, T/Avant gardener/76n1601
Powell, W L/Ontario energy/79n1388
Power, J/Camper's hndbk/75n635
Powerboat hndbk/Martenhoff/76n712
Powers, A/Blacks in/76n1051
PR for pennies/Baeckler/79n284
Practical approach to serials cataloging/Smith/79n283
Practical ency of natural healing/Bricklin/78n1433
Practical gardening ency/Hay/79n1540

Practical guide to . . .
   flexible working hours/Baum/75n981
   impractical pets/Dolensek/77n1528
   individual income tax return preparation/ Kess/75n985
   tax planning/Kess/75n984
   the MMPI/Good/76n1499
   psychiatry/Novello/75n1595
Practicing scientist's hndbk/Moses/79n1303
Prakken, S L/Bowker annual/77n190/Reader's adviser/75n1314
Prasher, R G/Indian bks/75n12/Supplement to reference/76n18
Pratt, G/Information economics/77n292/ On-line age/77n293
Pratt gd to planning and renewal for New Yorkers/Alpern/75n857
PRECIS index system/Wellisch/78n222
Preface to Yeats/Malins/76n1292
Pre-law handbook/78n507
Premier world atlas/79n509
Preminger, A/Princeton ency/76n1213
Prenis, J/Running Press/78n1527
Prentice, A E/Public library/78n176/Suicide/ 76n772
Prentice-Hall hndbk for writers/Leggett/79 n130
Prentiss, S/Improving library/75n240
Preparing the manuscript/Olsen/77n117
Prescription drugs and their side effects/ Stern/77n1506
Presidency/76n487
Presidential elections since 1789/77n516
Presidential succession/Sobel/76n488
Presidential vetoes, 1789-1976/79n525
Presidents from the inauguration of Washington to the inauguration of Ford/US Natl Park Service/78n337
Presley, J W/Robert Graves/77n1234
Press brake and shear hndbk/Daniels/76 n1652
Press directory of Pakistan/Siddiqi/76n1172
Press of Latin America/Gardner/75n1294
Presse in Afrika/Feuereisen/75n912
Preston, R J/North American/77n1370
Preston, W/American biographies/75n373
Pretty, R T/Jane's weapon/79n1609
Price, A H/Federal republic/79n380
Price, B A/Federico Fellini/79n1025
Price, R/Guiana Maroons/78n677
Price, S D/Whole horse/79n1525
Price, T/Federico Fellini/79n1025
Prières en ancien français/Sinclair/79n1273
Priestley, B/British qualifications/76n664

Primary educ for the disadvantaged/ McCormick/77n576
Primary prevention in drug abuse/US Natl Institute on Drug Abuse/78n1446
Prime ministers of Britain/Hellicar/79n548
Primer on the law of mergers/Kintner/75n892
Princeton companion/Leitch/79n671
Princeton ency of classical sites/Stillwell/77 n350
Princeton ency of poetry and poetics/Preminger/76n1213
Princetonians 1748-68/McLachlan/78n601
Principal drugs/Hopkins/79n1499
Principal legislative staff offices/79n535
Principal's hndbk on the school library media center/Martin/79n213
Principles of info retrieval/Kochen/75n279
Principles of medical librarianship/Cheshier/ 77n1483
Print ref sources/Mason/76n941
Printed bk in America/Blumenthal/78n32
Printing and publishing in 15th-cent Venice/ Gerulaitis/78n36
Prints and the print market/Donson/78n807
Prison group directory/75n839/Bundy/76 n777
Privacy and public disclosures under the Freedom of Info Act/Anderson/77n531
Privacy: selected bibliog/Latin/78n271
Private elementary and secondary educ/ Zeidner/78n552
Private independent schools/75n685
Private pilot's dict and hndbk/Polking/75 n763
Private press work/Anderson/79n28
Private schools illus'd/77n603
Pro and amateur hockey gd/75n770
Pro basketball ency/Hollander/78n614
Pro football/Cord Communications Corp/ 76n734
Pro football A to Z/Sullivan/76n739
Probert, T/Lost mines/78n358
Problems in developing academic library collections/Schad/75n212
Problems in intellectual freedom and censorship/Anderson/75n229
Problems in library public relations/Kies/75 n235
Problems in literary research/Kehler/76 n1181
Proceedings: innovative developmts in info systems/American Soc for Info Sci/75 n272

Proceedings of the Hague Peace Conferences: The conferences of 1899 and 1907, index/Scott/78n437
Proceedings of the information broker/free lance librarian—new careers—new library services workshop/Minor/78n258
Proceedings of the 1973 clinic on library applications of data processing/Lancaster/75n282
Process control/Weiner/79n1328
Process for developing a competency based educational program for media professionals/Daniel/79n207
Process instruments and controls hndbk/Considine/75n1803
Process plant estimating eval and control/Guthrie/75n1810
Processors of fishery products/US Natl Marine Fisheries Service/75n968
Prochnow, H V/Dictionary of wit/76n74
Prodrick, G/Directory of economic/79n239
Production figure bk for US cars/Heasley/78n756
Production yearbook/76n846
Productivity: selected, annotated bibliog/US Bureau of Labor Statistics/78n777
Professional and non-prof duties in libraries/76n181
Professional broadcast writer's hndbk/Field/75n1204
Professional directory of writers/75n1302
Professional ethics and insignia/Clapp/75n79
Professional organizations in the Commonwealth/Tett/77n88
Professional teacher's hndbk/Hoover/75n713
Professional's gd to public relations services/Weiner/76n1159
Proffer, E/International bibliog works/78n1197
ProFile: prof file architectural firms/Schirmer/79n891
Profiles/McDonough/77n1258
Profiles and portraits of Amer presidents/Bassett/77n509
Profiles in belief/Piepkorn/78n970
Profiles of black mayors in America/Fox/79n542
Profiles of financial assistance programs/79n1509
Programmed learning and individually paced instruction/Hendershot/75n702
Programming proverbs/Ledgard/76n1627
Programming proverbs for FORTRAN programmers/Ledgard/76n1628

Progress in educating the library user/Lubans/79n291
Progress in industrial microbiology/Hockenhull/76n1365
Progressive educ movement/Winick/79n637
Progressivism and muckraking/Filler/77n378
Proia, N C/Barron's hndbk American/76n635/Barron's hndbk college/76n636/Barron's hndbk jr./76n637
Project management/Dyer/78n780
Proliferation of nuclear weapons and the nonproliferation treaty/Meeker/75n1836
Promotion planning/Hannaford/76n200
Pronko, L C/Guide to Japanese/75n1178
Propes, S/Golden goodies/77n981/Golden oldies/75n1173
Prospects for change in bibliographic control/Bookstein/78n215
Prostaglandin abstracts/Sparks/75n1641
Prostano, E T/Law enforcement/75n830
Prostano, E T & J S/School library/78n187
Protecting your right to privacy/US Office of the Fed Register/78n492
Protective and decorative coatings for paper/Weiner/77n1329
Proum, I/English-Khmer/79n1143
Proverbial comparisons and related expressions in Spanish/Arora/79n1147
Provinces of the People's Republic of China/Emerson/79n370
Provisional world list of periodicals dealing with sci and tech policies/76n1324
Prpić, G J & M/Hrvatske Knjige/75n823
Prucha, F P/Bibliographical gd history/78n345/US Indian/79n526
Prudhommeau, G/Book of ballet/77n994
Prusek, J/Dictionary of Oriental/75n1316; 77n1274
Pseudonymous pubs of William Gilmore Simms/Kibler/77n1212
PSI: Other world catalog/Regush/76n1509
Psilocybe mushrooms & their allies/Stamets/79n1355
Psychedelics ency/Stafford/78n1445
Psychiatric drugs/Honigfeld/79n1498
Psychiatric glossary/American Psychiatric Assoc/76n1494
Psychic and religious phenomena limited/King/79n1438
Psychological abstracts info services/78n1371
Psychology almanac/Wilkening/75n1598
Psychology ency/75n1582
Psychology of religion/Capps, D/77n1024

Psychology Today omnibk of personal development/Matson/79n1428
Psychotropic drugs/Kline/75n1656
PTFE seals in reciprocating compressors/76n1654
Public, academic & special library serv record/Wisconsin. Div of Library Services/75n167
Public admin in English-speaking West Africa/Asiedu/78n469
Public affairs info serv/Wilson/75n477
Public affairs info serv bulletin/Wall/75n37
Public educ directory/79n647
Public land statistics/US Bureau of Land Mgmt/78n692
Public libraries as culture and social centers/Davies/75n184
Public library and federal policy/Wellisch/75n191
Public Library Assoc/Library connection/78n174
Public library finance/Prentice/78n176
Public library in non-traditional educ/Brooks/75n183
Public library subj headings for 16mm motion pictures/75n227
Public regulation of site selection for nuclear power plants/Klema/79n1409
Public relations, the Edward L. Bernayses and the American scene/Larson/79n804
Public works/Szykitka/75n96
Publications and services of the Natl Marine Fisheries Serv/US Natl Marine Fisheries Service/75n970
Publications on theoretical foundations of info science/Basova/76n229
Published comment on William Dean Howells through 1920/Eichelberger/77n1206
Published library catalogues/Collison/75n17
Published radio, TV, and film scripts/Poteet/76n1165
Publishers and libraries/Fry/78n35
Publishers' internat'l directory/75n59; 79n55
Publishers' trade list annual/76n10; 79n7
Publishing and bookselling/Mumby/75n48
Puckett, N N/Black names/77n488
Puerto Rican authors/Hill/75n1424
Puerto Ricans: migration and gen bibliog/76n417
Puerto Rico: materials in the Univ of Conn Library/Brown/77n336
Pugh, E/Second dictionary/75n116
Pukui, M K/Place names/75n453/Pocket Hawaiian/76n1153
Pula, J S/French in/76n406
Pulliam, T/NY Times/76n1135
Pullum, G K/Bibliography of contemporary/79n1089
Pulping of bagasse and other papermaking fibers/Louden/77n1314
Pump handbook/Karassik/77n1610
Purcell, R C/Classic guitar/78n905
Purchasing info sources/Basil/78n732
Purdy, R L/Thomas Hardy/79n1241
Purnell's first ency in colour/Dempsey/78n66
Purnell's first ency of animals/Burton/78n1314
Purnell's illus'd world atlas/Tunney/78n516
Putnam, R E/Architectural and/75n1021
Putnam's contemporary . . .
    French dictionary/Rudler/75n1268
    German dictionary/Clark/75n1269
    Spanish dictionary/Brown/75n1278
Putting library instruction in its place/Kirkendall/79n290
Putz, G/Mariner's catalog/76n713
Pyle, C/Bibliography of finance/75n955

Quadrupeds of North America/Audubon/77n1410
Quality control hndbk/Juran/75n1811
Quay, R H/In pursuit/79n633/Research in/78n545
Queens College, New Human Services Institute/College programs/76n652
Quick, J/Artists' and/78n788/Dictionary of weapons/75n1838
Quick gd to the wines of all the Americas/Misch/78n1458
Quick ref ency/78n90
Quick ref to pediatric emergencies/Pascoe/75n1632
Quien es quien: Spanish heritage librarians in the US/Trejo/77n185
Quiet world/Shores/76n210
Quimby, H B/Building a/76n1195/Illustrators of/79n898
Quimme, P/Signet bk/78n1459
Quinly, W J/Standards for/77n261
Quinn, A W/Significant American inventors/77n133/Significant American scientists/77n137
Quinn, B/Readings for/76n1072
Quintana, H/Current bibliog/76n403
Quintero-Mesa, R/Latin American/79n26
Quintessential dict/Hunsberger/79n1125

Quotable woman 1800-1975/Partnow/79n768
Quotations in history/Palmer/77n366
Quote unquote/Cory/79n95
Quotoons/Battista/79n94

R. J. Unstead's dict of hist/Unstead/77n367
R.U.S.I. and Brassey's defence yearbk/76n1680
Raben, J/Computer-assisted/78n76
Rabeneck, M/Clock/79n935
Rabiner, L R/Literature in/77n1580
Rachie, K O/Millets and/75n1696
Racing motorcycles/Rivola/79n1557
Racing planes and air races/Kinert/76n732
Rader, H B/Faculty involvement/78n236/Library instruction/78n236
Radio amateur's hndbk/Myers/75n1206; 77n1113; 78n1084
Radio and TV/McCavitt/79n1173
Radio contacts/77n1115
Radio soundtracks/Pitts/77n1114
Radio, TV & audio tech ref bk/Amos/79n1567
Radlauer, E/Motorcyclopedia/75n743
Radwin, G E/Murex shells/77n1395
Radzinowicz, L/Criminology and/78n499
Raffe, W G/Dictionary of dance/76n1036
Rafferty, M/Handbook of educ'l/77n639
Raffin, M R/Information worker/78n127/Marketing of/79n154
Ragan, D/Who's who Hollywood/78n965
Ragazzini, G/English-Italian/75n1272
Rahmato, D/Short gd/77n314
Rahner, K/Encyclopedia of theology/76n1082
Rail facts and feats/Marshall/75n1834
Rail talk/Beck/79n1115
Railroad car builder's pictorial dict/Forney/76n1671
Railroadiana/Klamkin/77n934
Railroads/Cors/76n1670
Rails of the world: family Rallidae/Ripley/79n1375
Railway atlas of Ireland/Hajducki/76n1672
Railways in the transition from steam 1940-65/Nock/76n1673
Raimo, J/Biographical directory Governors/79n543
Rainbook: resources for appropriate technology/deMoll/78n93
Rainbow dict/Wright/79n1113
Rainey, B/Shoot-em-ups/79n1031
Rajec, E M/Study of names/79n1182
Rake, A/New African/79n350/Who's who Africa/75n131

Rakowski, C A/Women in/79n761
Rakowski, J P/Transportation economics/77n771
Ralston, A/Encyclopedia of computer/77n1579
Ralston, V H/Education/78n546/Water resources/76n1474
Rambo, L/Psychology of/77n1024
Ramon J. Sender/King/77n1275
Ramondino, S/Dictionary of foreign/76n1119
Ramsden, M J/Introduction to index/75n228
Ramsey, L G G/Complete color/76n959
Rana, M S/Writings on/75n565
Rand McNally . . .
  auto road atlas of the US/75n597
  campground and trailer park gd/79n714
  concise atlas of the earth/77n546
  encyclopedia of transportation/77n1621
  encyclopedia of WWII/Keegan/78n1560
  grand atlas and picture bk of the world/78n518
  guide to travel by train/Wojtas/75n590
  road atlas/75n636
  traveler's almanac/Muster/79n621
Rand McNally atlas of . . .
  exploration/Newby/76n298
  the body and mind/77n1456
  the oceans/78n517
Rand McNally's children's ency/Paton/78n67
Randall, R G/Women's gd/75n855
Randax educ guide/77n624
Randax grad school directory/Pastman/77n625
Randel, D M/Harvard concise/79n966
Random House . . .
  dictionary/Stein/79n1104
  encyclopedia/Mitchell/78n68
  handbook/Crews/79n128
Ranganathan, S R/Cataloguing practice/76n193
Ransohoff, P/Psychology of/77n1024
Rape and rape-related issues/Kemmer/78n675
Rape: bibliography/Barnes/78n673
Rape: first sourcebk for women/NY Radical Feminists/75n850
Raphael, L J/Biographical dict/79n1157
Rapoport, R/California catalogue/78n529
Rapp, G R/Encyclopedia of minerals/75n1573
Rare bk librarianship/Cave/77n191
Rates of comprehension/Berger/77n574
Rath, F L/Care and/78n321/Historic preservation/77n381/Interpretation/79n400

Rathbauer-Vincie, M/C. G. Jung/78n1365
Rationale, developmt and standardization of a basic word vocabulary test/US Natl Center for Health Statistics/75n718
Raum, H/Directory of state/78n351
Rausch, G J/Detective short/75n1327
Ray, C/Library service/79n215
Ray, G N/Illustrator and/77n67
Ray, M/Collectible ceramics/75n1084
Ray, R B/Indians of/78n681
Ray, S/Youth library/77n212
Ray Bradbury companion/Nolan/76n1229
Raymond, W J/Dictionary of politics/79n504
Rayward, W B/Universe of/77n258
Rea, J/Wycliffe Bible/77n1050
Read, J/Wines of/75n1675
Read, W R/Brazil 1980/75n1224
Reader developmt bibliog/76n683/Forinash/78n592/Suppl 1975/76n684
Reader in . . .
   comparative librarianship/Foskett/78n249
   library and info services/Reynolds/76n235
   library communication/Cassata/78n232
   library management/Shimmon/77n249
   library systems analysis/Lubans/76n180
   library technology/Adamovich/76n175
   music librarianship/Bradley/75n201
Reader on the library bldg/Schell/76n205
Reader's adviser/Prakken/75n1314/Sypher/78n1090/Clarke/78n2
Readers advisory serv/Cohan/76n134
Reader's companion to the Bible/Heim/76n1101
Reader's companion to world lit/Brown/75n1307
Reader's Digest . . .
   almanac and yearbk/78n91
   encyclopaedia of garden plants and flowers/78n1494
   illustrated gd to gardening/Calkins/79n1542
   treasury of modern quotations/76n75
Reader's ency of the American West/Lamar/78n314
Reader's Greek-English lexicon of the New Testament and a beginner's gd for the translation of New Testament Greek/Kubo/77n1046
Reader's guide to . . .
   Shakespeare's plays/Berman/75n1396
   the Bible/Hiers/79n1069
   the great religions/Adams/78n969
Reading, H F/Dictionary of social/79n342

Reading and dating Roman imperial coins/Klawans/78n847
Reading and language arts/79n683
Reading and the adult new reader/Lyman/78n234
Reading and writing in the arts/Goldman/79n887
Reading tests and reviews/Buros/76n567
Reading the Russian lang/Kent/75n155
Readings for town & country church workers/Byers/76n1072
Real estate appraisal terminology/Boyce/76n851
Real estate investmt tables/Casey/76n853
Real estate investmts and how to make them/76n861
Real founders of New England/Bolton/75n408
Real steel/Neville/77n937
Reams, B D/Historic preservation/77n536
Reaney, P H/Dictionary of British/77n489; 79n500
Rechcigl, M/World food/76n847
Recipe index/Forsman/75n1694
Recipes for home repair/Ubell/75n1801
Recommendations for AV materials and services for small & medium-sized public libraries/American Library Assoc. Public Library Assoc/76n145
Recommended East Asian core collections for children's, high school, public, community college, and undergrad college libraries/Scott/76n259
Record album price gd/Osborne/78n903
Record albums 1948-78/Osborne/79n974
Record and tape reviews index/Maleady/75n1154; 76n1003
Record collector's price gd/Osborne/78n904
Record of America: ref hist of the US/McCarthy/76n324
Records in review/Carter/76n1000; 78n1000
Records of New Amsterdam from 1653-74/Fernow/77n462
Records of Plymouth colony/Shurtleff/77n477
Recreational vehicles/Leavy/78n619
Recurring reports to the Congress/US Gen Accounting Office/77n518
Reddig, J S/Guide to ecology/77n1403
Redding, H T/Dun & Bradstreet/75n956
Redding, J L/Complete food/78n1469
Redfern, M/Effective library/77n215
Redgrave, G R/Short-title/77n27
Redmond, G/Sporting heritage/75n725

Redmond, J/Year's work/79n1187
Reed, A W/Concise Maori/77n1096
Reed's nautical almanac and tide tables/Watts/79n726
Reel, J V/Index to biographies/76n370
Rees, A/Contemporary problems/76n168
Rees, S/David Jones/79n1242
Reese, R S/Care and/78n321/Interpretation/79n400
Reeves, P/Thomas Wolfe/76n1254
Reeves, W A/Fire resistant/76n1649
Reference aids to South Asia/Wagle/79n366
Reference and info services/Katz/79n295
Reference and subscription bks review/76n135; 78n150; 78n151; 79n183
Reference as the promotion of free inquiry/Shores/77n268
Reference books/Bell/79n178
Reference bks for elementary and jr high school libraries/Peterson/76n162
Reference bks in paperback/Wynar/77n17
Reference bks in the soc sciences and humanities/Stevens/78n4
Reference catalogue of Indian bks in print/75n11
Reference ency of American psychology and psychiatry/Klein/76n1500
Reference ency of the American Indian/Klein/75n808; 79n463
Reference gd for consumers/David/77n813
Reference guide to . . .
   fantastic films/Lee/75n1194
   handbooks and annuals/Pfeiffer/78n1372
   Minnesota history/Brook/75n377
   Texas law and legal hist/Boner/77n532
Reference list of AV materials produced by the US gov/79n124
Reference manual for office workers/Nanassy/78n717
Reference materials on Mexican Americans/Woods/77n441
Reference readiness/Ziskind/78n152
Reference resources/Doyle/77n266
Reference service/Murfin/78n240
Reference sources/Mark/78n26
Reference sources in English and American lit/Schweik/78n1093
Reform and reaction/Du Mont/79n201
Reforming metropolitan governments/White/76n496
Regan, M/Serials/76n38
Regan, M M/Guide to special/77n34
Regazzi, J J/Guide to indexed/76n1075

Regional dict of Chicano slang/Vasquez/76n1155
Register, A K/Index to 1830/75n430/State census/79n494
Register: American Assoc of Marriage & Family Counselors/79n753
Register of . . .
   commissioned and warrant officers of the US Navy/79n1606
   reporting labor organizations/79n863
   Salomon Lachaire/Scott/79n496
   the governors of the states of the USA, 1776-1974/Gateley/76n339
Regush, J & N/PSI/76n1509
Rehder, A/Bibliography of cultivated/79n1364
Rehrauer, G/Cinema booklist/79n1026/Film user's/76n182/Short film/76n1059
Reich, D L/Public library/75n183
Reid, J M H/Concise Oxford/78n1188
Reid, S/Verb synonyms/75n1253/Writer's cue/75n1261
Reidenbaugh, L/100 years/77n676
Reidy, B/Guide to workd/78n728; 79n831
Reifsnyder, W E/Foot-loose/75n626
Reigel, E R/Riegel's hndbk/75n1452
Reilly, E C/Dictionary of colonial/77n884
Reilly, R J/Guide to American/78n1115; 78n1116
Reilly, R P/Selected and/79n686
Reilly, T M/Legal secretary's/75n561
Reim, T/Daily Planet/79n1432
Reincke, M/American bench/79n570
Reinecke, J E/Bibliography of Pidgin/77n1060
Reinfeld, F/Catalogue of world's/78n844
Reinhart, B/Vocational-technical/75n705
Reinmiller, E C/Physiology of/76n1514
Reisner, R/Encyclopedia of graffiti/76n63
Reiss, A H/Arts mgmt/75n1005
Reithmaier, L W/Aviation and/75n1721/Instrument pilot's/76n733
Rejnis, R/Everything tenants/75n933
Relegation and stock control in libraries/Urquhart/78n171
Religions of America/Rosten/76n1088
Religious bks and serials in print/79n1053
Religious gd to Europe/Madden/76n1071
Religious life of man/Karpinski/79n1050
Religious reading/76n1076; 78n974; 78n975
Reluctant weekend gardener/Wallach/75n1710
Remmling, G W/Sociology of/76n773

Remy, B/Louisiana sports/78n609
Reno, E A/League of/75n112; 77n501
Rentschler, C/Library lit/78n148
Renty, I/El mundo/79n1152
Répertoire des livres de langue française disponibles/77n26
Repertoire for the solo voice/Espina/78n892
Reprographic services in libraries/LaHood/77n286
Reprography for librarians/New/76n228
Reptiles and amphibians of Australia/Cogger/78n1336
Reptiles & amphibians of the West/Brown/76n1447
Republic of Texas: poll lists for 1846/Mullins/75n427
Reputation of Trollope/Olmsted/79n1255
Requirements for certification/Woellner/75n660; 76n631
Requirements for certification for elementary schools, secondary schools, jr colleges/Woellner/77n638; 78n579
Research & developmt directory/76n835
Research and report writing/Cordasco/75n693
Research centers directory/Palmer/76n629
Research collections in Canadian libraries/McCallum/75n1179; 76n169
Research guide in . . .
  history/Wilson/75n349
  journalism/Anderson/75n1292
  speech/Tandberg/76n1178
  women's studies/Lynn/76n795
Research guide to central party and gov meetings in China/Lieberthal/77n524
Research guide to sci fict studies/Tymm/79n1205
Research handbk/Paradis/75n695
Research in . . .
  children's lit/Monson/77n1160
  higher education/Quay/78n545
  outdoor education/Swan/79n636
  parapsychology, abstracts and papers from the 16th Annual Conv of the Parapsychological Assn/Rolls/75n1606
  progress in English and hist in Britain, Ireland, Canada, Australia, and New Zealand/Bindoff/77n406
Research libraries and technology/Fussler/75n181
Research libraries in developing countries/Kumar/75n257
Research on Thailand in the Philippines/Chety/79n374

Researcher's guide to . . .
  American genealogy/Greenwood/75n416
  iron ore/Earney/75n569
  Washington/78n82
Researching and writing in hist/McCoy/75n347
Resnick, M/Choral music/75n1132
Resnick, R P/World gd social/75n665
Resource bk on chemical educ in the United Kingdom/Frazer/77n1312
Resource gd for adult religious educ/Newland/75n1214/Thomson/76n1077
Resource materials for environmt'l mgmt and educ/Matthews/77n1399
Resource sharing in libraries/Kent/75n211
Resources in women's educ'l equity/79n759
Restaurants of NY/Britchky/75n1685; 79n599
Reston ency of biomedical engineering terms/Graf/78n1395
Retention of fillers by papermaking fibers/Pollock/77n1318
Retirement hndbk/Buckley/75n930; 79n841
Retrospective index to film periodicals 1930-71/Batty/76n1061
Retrospective index to theses of Great Britain and Ireland 1716-1950/Turner/78n1222/Bilboul/79n1306
Revell, P/Fifteenth century/77n1030
Reverse acronyms, initialisms, & abbreviations dict/Crowley/77n119
Review of . . .
  child developmt research/Horowitz/76n1501
  education/Perkinson/76n587
  medical microbiology/Jawetz/79n1475
  medical pharmacology/Meyers/75n1657; 79n1502
Reviews in . . .
  American history/Kutler/76n316
  anthropology/Pelto/75n868; 76n807
  European history/Rowen/76n363
Reviews of selected published tests in English/Grommon/77n653
Revised, annotated bibliog of the Chumash and their predecessors/Anderson/79n773
Revised new gen catalogue of nonstellar astronomical objects/Sulentic/75n1446
Reynolds, B/Concise Cambridge Italian/76n1154
Reynolds, M M/Guide to theses/76n583/Reader in library/76n235

Reynolds, R P/Bookhunter's guide Northeast/ 78n47/Bookhunter's gd West/79n56
Rezits, J/Pianist's resource/76n1019
Rhodehamel, J D/Ina Coolbrith/75n252
Rhodesia-Zimbabwe: internat'l bibliog/Pollak/ 78n291
Rhymer, J/Bible in/77n1047
Rhymer and other helps for poets/Modglin/ 79n1126
Rhythm: annotated bibliog/Winick/76n993
Ricci, R/Language of/76n996
Rice, A S/Newark/78n359
Rice, E/Eastern definitions/79n1059
Rice, E/How to eat/75n1706
Rice, F P/Outdoor life/76n758
Rice, M A/Garden spice/79n1353
Rice, W/Where to/78n1477
Rich, M F/Who's who opera/77n975
Richard Lester/Rosenfeldt/79n1028
Richard M. Nixon, 1913- /Bremer/76n332
Richards, B G/Magazines for/79n17
Richards, H M/Pennsylvania-German/79n495
Richards, J/Complete hndbk/75n727
Richards, J M/Who's who architecture/78 n804
Richardson, B A/Great black/77n434
Richardson, J/Encyclopedia of antique/75 n1054
Richardson, R C/British economic/77n407
Richardson, S K/Children's services/79 n216/Periodicals for/79n184
Richmond, M L/Shaker lit/77n1031; 78n976
Richstad, J/Mass communication/79n1160/ Pacific Islands/75n1303
Rickenbacker, W F/William Rickenbacker's/77 n803
Rickert, E/Contemporary American/76 n1219
Rickett, H W/Complete index/77n1362
Ricking, M/Personnel utilization/76n183
Ricklefs, M C/Indonesian manuscripts/79 n69
Ricks, B/Henry James/76n1242
Ricks, D A/Directory of foreign/76n894
Ricks, M/Melvin Ricks'/79n390
Riddell, E/Lives of/77n412
Rider, A D/Story of books/77n282
Ridge, J D/Annotated bibliographies mineral/ 77n1439
Ridgely, B S/Birds of/75n1091
Ridgely, R S/Guide to birds/77n1385
Ridgeway, S/NPT/79n559
Ridgway, R/Water birds/75n1499
Ridpath, I/Illustrated ency astronomy/78 n1237

Riegel's hndbk of industrial chemistry/Reigel/ 75n1452
Rienecker, F/Linguistic key/78n996
Riesch, M/Bibliographical notes military/76 n497/ . . . transnational/76n828
Riesner, D/Reference sources/78n1093
Rifkind, C/Mansions, mills/76n554
Rigal, W A/Inverted mecical/78n1399
Rigby, M/Computers and/76n187
Right to know/MacCafferty/77n1104
Right to read and the nation's libraries/75 n241
Right word: thesaurus/79n1119
Rights of . . .
 candidates and voters/Neuborne/77n504
 students/Levine/75n560
 suspects/Rosengart/75n562
 the poor/Law/75n559
 the public employee/Dwoskin/79n252
 women/Ross/75n563
Rights we have/Fraenkel/75n481
Rihani, M/Development as/79n760
Riker, T/Gardener's catalogue/75n1707/ Guide to buying/78n1495
Riley, C/Children's lit/77n1150; 77n1151/ Contemporary literary/75n1319; 76n1188; 76n1189; 77n1130
Riley, M F/Dissertations in/79n1078
Riley, N D/Field gd butterflies/77n1391
Rimer, J T/Guide to Japanese/77n1272
Rinaldi, A/Complete bk/75n1489
Rinehart, C/Library technical/78n244
Ring, E/Maine bibliographies/75n386
Ring W. Lardner/Bruccoli/77n1209
Ringgren, H/Theological dict/76n1096; 79 n1064
Ringquist, D/Guide to Dag/78n273
Rinn, R C/Author's gd/78n1369
Rinzler, C A/Cosmetics/78n1256
Rioux, J W/Durations/79n99
Ripin, E M/Instrument catalogs/76n1020
Ripley, S D/Handbook of birds/77n1373/ Rails of/79n1375
Risatti, H/New music/76n1001
Rise of the public library in Calif/Held/75 n186
Riseborough, D J/Canada &/76n504
Rising, T L/Songbirds of/78n1321
Ristow, W W/World directory/77n554
Rittel, H W J/Methods of/79n263
Rivers, W L/Aspen hndbk/77n1102
Rivers of the West/Hogan/76n521
Riviere, B/Field bk mountaineering/76n718
Rivkin, S R/Cable TV/76n1179
Rivola, L/Racing motorcycles/79n1557

Rizzitiello, T G/Annotated bibliog movement/78n547
Road & Track illus'd dict/Dinkel/78n1511
Road atlas of Great Britain/75n579
Road rider: gd to on-the-road motorcycling/Perry/75n742
Roalman, A R/Investor relations/75n918
Robb, D A/Lawyers desk/76n517
Robbins, J A/American literary manuscripts/78n1118/American literary scholarship/75n1337
Robert Frost/Crane/75n1357/Lentricchia/77n1204
Robert Graves manuscripts and letters at So Illinois Univ/Presley/77n1234
Robert Loftin Newman/US Smithsonian Institution/75n995
Robert Louis Stevenson/Slater/75n1403
Roberts, C V/Early Friends/76n439
Roberts, E/Horse world/78n1465
Roberts, G/Atlas of discovery/75n351
Roberts, J/Map abstract/79n742
Roberts, J A/Selective bibliog Shakespeare/76n1285
Roberts, J C/Born in/78n1297
Roberts, L P/Dictionary of Japanese/78n825
Roberts, N/Use of social/78n269
Roberts, P/Theatre in/75n1183
Roberts, W L/Encyclopedia of minerals/75n1573
Robertson, C H/Kansas territorial/77n475
Robertson, C J R/Birds in/76n1430
Robertson, M/Encyclopedia of tennis/76n762
Robertson, P/Book of firsts/75n94
Robertson, R/Spices, condiments/76n1578
Robin Hood hndbk/Kaysing/75n756
Robinson, A H/Atlas of Wisconsin/75n580
Robinson, H S/Dictionary of biog/76n100/Myths and/77n1055
Robinson, J/Guide to Jewish/75n398
Robinson, J P/Documentation stds/75n1773
Robinson, J W/San Bernardino/76n720
Robinson, R E/Buy books/79n61
Robinson, S/Dreamer's dict/75n1583
Robinson, V/Handbook of electronic/75n1788
Robotham, J S/Library programs/77n163
Roccograndi, A J/Handbook on 1970/76n1549
Rock, J F/Indigenous trees/75n1494
Rock, J M/Money, banking/79n873
Rock almanac/Gillett/77n979
Rock on/Nite/76n1029; 79n998
Rockhound's hndbk/Firsoff/76n1481
Rockland, M A & M S/Jewish yellow/77n820

Rocks and minerals/Desautels/75n1572
Rocky Mountain flora/Weber/77n1359
Rocq, M M/California local/77n394
Rodale herb bk/Hylton/75n1481
Rodents: their lives and habits/Hanney/76n1444
Roderer, N K/Methods of/75n231
Rodgers, B F/Philip Roth/75n1367
Rogalin, W C/Women's guide/77n850
Roger Williams/Coyle/78n972
Rogers, A R/Humanities/75n174
Rogers, C H/Encyclopedia of cage/77n1386
Rogers, D G/Sherwood Anderson/77n1197
Rogers, F/Story of/75n270
Roget's internat'l thesaurus/Chapman/78n1041
Rohn, P H/Treaty profiles/77n530/World treaty/76n506
Rohrer, R L/KWIC index/75n1665
Rohwer, J/Chronology of/75n542
Rojnić, M/Guide to Yugoslav/76n214
Rokkan, S/Scandinavian political/79n511
Roland, C G/Annotated checklist/78n1389
Role of the beginning librarian in univ libraries/Edwards/77n204
Roller, D H D/Catalogue of history/77n1281
Rolling Stone record review/75n1174
Rollinson, M/Source gd borrowing/78n754
Rollock, B/Black experience/76n163
Rolls, W G/Research in/75n1606
Romaine, L B/Guide to American/78n703
Roman, H L/Annual review/77n1342
Roman baroque painting/Waterhouse/77n886
Roman Republican coinage/Crawford/76n966
Romanian phrase bk/Vorvoreanu/75n1286
Romanians in America, 1748-1974/Wertsman/76n418
Romanofsky, P/Social service/79n733
Romig, W/Michigan place/75n454
Romiszowski, A J/International yrbk/77n637
Ronald Brunlees McKerrow/Immroth/75n266
Ronay, E/Egon Ronay's/75n627
Ronberg, G/Hockey ency/75n771
Roody, P/Medical abbreviations/78n1415
Room, A/Place-names/75n455
Root, V M/Communication directory/76n1171
Root anatomy and morphology/Miller/76n1372
Roper, C/Latin America/76n280
Roper, C A/Complete hndbk/77n1570
Roper, F W/Alfred William/77n283

Roper, N/Livingstone's dict/75n1622/Livingstone's pocket/75n1623/New American/79n1465
Rosa, A F/Contemporary fiction/78n1105
Rose, G B/Illustrated ency/79n940
Rose, J/Herbal body/77n1524
Rose, M/Spenser's art/76n1290
Rose, R/Electoral behavior/75n474/Internat'l almanac/75n473
Rose-Innes, A/Beginners' dict/78n1052
Rose-lover's gd/Browne/75n1699
Rosenbaum, B E/Chronological bibliog English/75n1325
Rosenbaum, S/Yiddish word/79n1155
Rosenberg, J K/Watergate/76n473/Young people's/78n1122
Rosenberg, K C/Media equipment/77n658/Watergate/76n473
Rosenberg, M B/Research gd/76n795/Women and/76n797
Rosenberg, P M/Urban information/79n734
Rosenberg-Dishman, M B/Women and/79n755
Rosenbloom, J/Consumer complaint/75n934/Craft supplies/76n953/Kits and/75n1036
Roseneder, J M/Winnipeg/75n393
Rosenfeldt, D/Ken Russell/79n1027/Richard Lester/79n1028
Rosenfelt, D S/Strong women/78n599
Rosenfield, G/New environment-/75n793
Rosengart, O/Rights of/75n562
Rosenof, T/Second World/76n290
Rosenstiel, A/Education and/79n782
Rosenthal, E/Encyclopaedia of Southern/75n319
Rosenzweig, M R/Annual review psychology/76n1496
Rosenzweig, P D/Thomas Eakins/78n787
Rosichan, R H/Stamps and/75n1052
Rosignoli, G/Army badges/77n1644; 77n1645
Roskies, D K/Teaching the/76n685
Rosner, B/Inside the/77n938
Ross, B H/Urban affairs/76n802
Ross, C T/Bibliography of Southern/78n312
Ross, E J F/Index of vibrational/79n1323
Ross, I C/Index to statistics/75n877; 76n819
Ross, M B/Directory of publishing/75n54
Ross, M J/New encyclopedic/76n831
Ross, S C/Rights of/75n563
Rossano, A T/Air pollution/75n1541
Rossdale, P D/Horse's health/75n1663
Rossoff, I S/Handbook of veterinary/76n1553

Rosten, L/Religions of/76n1088
Roswell, J/Arms control/75n1837
Roth, A/Allergy in/79n1476
Roth, G D/Astronomy/77n1310
Roth, L/Forest fertilization/77n1321/Protective and/77n1329
Rothberg, R R/New product/78n738
Rothblatt, H B/Complete manual/76n513
Rothenberg, A/Index of scientific/76n94; 77n1296
Rothenberg, R E/New American/76n1546/New illus'd/76n1545
Rothenstein, J/Modern English/76n937
Rothgeb, C L/Abstracts of collected/79n1431/Abstracts of std/75n1596
Rothman, R C/Notary public/79n562
Rothman, W A/Bibliography of collective/77n840
Rotoli, N J/Black American/77n986
Rottenberg, D/Finding our/78n408
Rottenberg, H/Gardener's catalogue/75n1707/Guide to buying/78n1495
Rotunda, D P/Motif-index/75n1423
Rouse, S H/Computer-readable/78n243
Rousmaniere, J/Glossary of modern/77n685
Rouyer, A R/Economic, social/75n504
Rowe, J S/Ships and/77n1651
Rowe, K E/Methodist union/76n1078; 77n1032; 79n1054
Rowell, L/American organ/77n966
Rowen, H H/Reviews in/76n363
Rowland, B L & H S/NY Times/75n664/Student adventure/77n562
Rowland-Entwistle, T/Famous kings/78n333
Rowley, I/Bird life/76n1431
Rowse, A E/Help/79n107
Roy, J F/Guide to Barsoom/78n1135
Roy Harris/Strassburg/75n1159
Royal heraldry of England/Pinches/75n443
Rubel, S M/Guide to selling/78n739/Guide to venture/75n957; 78n753/Source gd/78n754
Rubén Darío/Woodbridge/76n1303
Rubinstein, M K/Doctor's gd/79n1503
Rubin, D H/Official hotel/75n588
Rubin, R J/Bibliotherapy sourcebk/79n307/US prison/75n208/Using bibliotherapy/79n308
Rubner, M/Middle East/79n358
Rudd, R L/Environmental toxicology/79n1401
Rudder, R S/Literature of Spain/77n1276
Ruder, W/Businessman's gd/76n836
Rudler, G/Putnam's contemporary/75n1268

Rudman, M K/Children's lit/79n1193
Rudner, R/Huts and/75n628
Rue, L L/Game birds/75n779
Ruffner, J A/Climates of/79n1413/Eponyms dictionaries/78n111/Weather almanac/75n1568; 78n1353
Rufsvold, M I/Guides to/78n600
Ruggles, J/World food/78n1481
Ruiz-Fornells, E/Concordance to poetry/79n1291
Rule, L R/What's in/75n449
Rulers and governments of the world/Spuler/78n434; 79n512
Rules of the game/Diagram Group/75n728
Rumsey, S/Annotated bibliog Aspen/78n543
Runnability of printing papers/Pollock/77n1319
Running a message parlor/McShean/79n311
Running out of space—What are the alternatives?/Novak/79n258
Running Press dict of law/Dorman/77n538
Running Press glossary of . . .
    astrology terms/Fleming-Mitchell/78n1376
    banking language/Batz/78n750
    baseball language/Scholl/78n613
    computer terms/Prenis/78n1527
    real estate language/Volpe/78n782
    sailing language/Shuwall/78n633
Ruoff, J E/Crowell's hndbk/76n1262
Rupp, I D/Collection of upwards/76n440
Rural-development literature/US Dept of Agriculture/77n1515
Rusch, F E/Theodore Dreiser/76n1233
Ruse, C/Oxford student's/79n1098
Rush, G E/Dictionary of criminal/78n502
Rush, J E/Information retrieval/75n276
Rush, T G/Black American/76n1226
Russell, V A/Stories to/75n198
Russia, the USSR, and Eastern Europe/Horak/79n378
Russian and Soviet studies/Bezer/75n334
Russian economic history/Kazmer/79n803
Russian-English . . .
    chemical and polytechnical dict/Callaham/76n1341
    dictionary/Smirnitsky/75n1275
    dictionary of suppositional names/Lederman/76n1147
    dictionary of the mathematical sciences/Lohwater/76n1333
Russian ref aids in the Univ of Toronto Library/Skoric/75n306
Russian revolution and the Soviet state/McCauley/76n374
Russian revolutionary lit collection Houghton Library, Harvard Univ/77n416
Russians in America/Wertsman/77n44
Rust, B/American dance/76n994/Jazz records/79n1000
Ruzicka, R/Dictionary of Russian/78n1065
Rycroft, C/Critical dict/75n1584
Rycroft, R W/Energy policy-/79n1384
Ryde, P/Encyclopedia of golf/76n748
Ryder, D E/Canadian reference/76n6
Rywell, M/Afro-American/76n377/Confederate guns/76n971
Rzepecki, A M/Book review/79n346/Index to free/77n41

Sabin, W A/Gregg reference/78n718
Sable, M H/Exobiology/79n1337/Internat'l and/75n258/Latin American/79n461
Sabretooth cats and imperial mammoths/Macdonald/75n1577
Sachs engine serv, repair hndbook/Bishop/75n1740
Sackheim, D E/Historic American/78n1499
Sader, M/Comprehensive index/77n1136
Sadhu, S N/Indian books/75n10
SAE hndbk/76n1610
SAE motor vehicle, safety and environmental terminology/78n1514
SAE transactions and lit/76n1611
Safadi, Y H/Union catalogue/78n29
Saffady, W/Computer-output/79n333/Micrographics/79n334
Sage, M/Continuing library/78n252
Sahanek, T/Index to legal/78n508
Sailboat racing rules/McDermott/75n749
Sailing/Somerville/75n751
Sailing boats of the world/Budd/75n746
St. Louis: chronological & doc hist/Vexler/75n510
Saints of the Americas/Habig/76n1092
Sainty, J C/Home office/76n499
Saito, S/Philippine research/75n311
Salad, M K/Somalia/78n289
Salaman, R A/Dictionary of tools/77n893
Salem, J M/Drury's gd/79n1018/Guide to critical/78n940
Salley, H E/Selected sound/78n1091
Salmon, R D/Job hunter's/79n864
Salmon, S R/Library automation/77n294
Saloon/Thompson/77n1521
SALT II: selected research bibliog/Parker/75n541
Salton, G/Dynamic information/77n295

Samples, G/Drama scholars'/75n1187
Sampson, H T/Blacks in/78n950
Samudio, J/Book review/76n30
Samuel, E R/Sources for/78n421
Samuel Johnson in the British press, 1749-84/McGuffie/77n1236
Samuel Langhorne Clemens/Haviland/78n1151
Samuel Taylor Coleridge/Caskey/79n1235/ Haven/77n1230
Samuels, H/Illustrated biographical/77n872
Samuels, P/Illustrated biographical/77n872
San Bernardino mountain trails/Robinson/76n720
San Diego: chronological & doc hist/Mayer/79n428
San Francisco: chronological & doc hist/Mayer/75n511
Sanchez-Saavedra, E M/Guide to Virginia/79n1596
Sandage, A & M/Galaxies and/77n1311
Sandberg, L/Folk music/77n982
Sandberg, W/Annual of new/75n1006
Sandeau, G/Selective mgmt/77n851
Sanderlin, D/Writing the/76n286
Sanders, D/Canadian Indian/75n863
Sanders, D/Gay source/79n741
Sanders, E T & J/Encyclopedia of geographic/79n813
Sanders, J/Photography year/75n1113
Sanders, K R/Political campaign/75n462
Sanders, W B/Sociologist as/75n789
Sanderson, M/Sea battles/76n301
Sandford, C/Cock-A-Hoop/77n53
Sandhage, P A/Artist's and/77n856/Writer's market/77n1132
Sandow, S A/Durations/79n99
Sanecki, K N/Complete bk of herbs/75n1485
Sangster, I/Jamaica/75n621
Sanjian, A K/Catalogue of medieval/78n62
Sanner, M/Commonsense cataloging/76n192
Sanskrit-Hindi-English dict/Suryakanta/77n1098
Santa Clara County bk/Fox/75n605
Santalo, L A/Integral geometry/78n1229
Santals: classified & annotated bibliog/Troisi/77n746
SantaVicca, E F/Four French/75n1417
Santucho, O J/George Gordon/78n1167
Sanyika, B/Know and/77n490
Sanyo's tri-lingual glossary of chemical terms/Yamada/78n1250
Sarber, M A/Charles F. Lummis/79n1221
Sargent, E/Chicorel abstracts/78n582
Sarkissian, A/Children's authors/79n1194

Sartorius, N/Measurement and/75n1599
Saterstrom, M H/Educators gd guidance/76n671/Educators gd science/76n673
Saturday morning gardener/Wyman/75n1711
Satyaprakash/Agriculture/79n1513/ Gandhiana/78n298/Indian science/78n1221/Karnataka/79n371
Saul Bellow/Nault/78n1133/Sokoloff/75n1352
Saulniers, S S/Women in/79n761
Saunders, D E/Ebony hndbk/75n812
Saunders, H E/Modern school/76n151
Saunders, J L/Directory of unpublished/75n1600
Saunders, N/Rulers and/79n512
Savage, G/Illustrated dict/75n1040
Savage, H/LC classification/77n257
Savaiano, E/2001 Spanish/77n1101
Saveland, R N/Inventory of/77n549
Saville, J/Dictionary of labour/79n547
Savoye, D-M/Symbolism/77n1124
Saward, H/Dictionary of mgmt/76n909
Sawin, L/Dictionary of characters/78n1179
Sax, N I/Dangerous properties/76n1650/ Industrial pollution/76n1463
Say, M G/Electrical engineer's/76n1632
Sayers, J E/Calendar of/77n1033
Sayre, J L/Illustrated gd internat'l/77n259/ Index of festschriften/75n1217
Saywell, J/Canadian annual/75n338; 76n500
Scammon, R M/America votes/78n449
Scandinavian education/Fraser/75n644
Scandinavian political studies/Rokkan/76n501; 79n511
Scanlan, J P/American bibliog/76n271
Scarborough, M/Women in/76n120
Scarne's new complete gd to gambling/ Scarne/76n745
Schaaf, W L/Bibliography of recreational/79n1310/High school/77n1305
Schad, J G/Problems in/75n212
Schaf, F L/Intelligence, espionage/79n501
Schaffer, J P/Tahoe Sierra/76n721
Schapsmeier, E L & F H/Encyclopedia of American/77n1516
Scharff, R/Complete bk home/76n1641/Encyclopedia of sailing/79n725
Schatt, S/Concordance to poetry/76n1240
Schatzki, W/Children's books/75n1322
Schauder, D E/Libraries for/79n241
Schechter, I R/Jr high/76n159
Scheick, W J/Seventeenth century/78n1126
Schell, H B/Reader on/76n205
Schemmer, B F/Almanac of liberty/76n336

Schenk, W/Dictionary of Russian/78n1065
Scherf, W/Die Besten/77n1144
Schertel, A/Abbreviations in/79n1466
Schiffer, H & N & P/Brass book/79n937
Schiller, A/In other/79n1120/Junior thesaurus/79n1121/My first/78n1029
Schillinger, J/Encyclopedia of rhythms/78n900
Schipf, R G/Home repair/75n1796/Outdoor recreation/77n669
Schirmer, H W/ProFile/79n891
Schistosomiasis III/Warren/78n1392
Schistosomiasis IV/Hoffman/79n1442
Schlachter, G A/Directory of financial/79n766/Library science/75n150/Minorities and/79n762
Schleicher, R/Model railroading/77n944
Schleifer, H B/Puerto Rican/75n1424
Schlesinger, A M/Congress investigates/76n307
Schlipf, F A/Collective bargaining/76n184
Schlobin, R C/Research gd science/79n1205
Schlossberg, E/Home computer/79n1564
Schmacke, E/Presse in Afrika/75n912
Schmeckel, C D/Piano owner's/75n1161
Schmidly, D J/Mammals of/78n1333
Schmidt, H/Retirement hndbk/75n930; 79n841
Schmidt, J E/Index of paramedical/75n1624
Schmidt, N J/Children's books/76n1199
Schmierer, H F/Prospects for/78n215
Schnapper, M B/American symbols/75n444
Schneck, S/Complete home . . . cats/77n1531/Complete home . . .dogs/77n1532
Schneider, A & S/Climber's sourcebk/77n688
Schneider, B/Whole grains/75n95
Schneider, J H/Survey of commercially/75n283
Schneider, R C/Crafts of/75n1037
Schneidermeyer, W/Iris Murdoch/77n1221
Schoenebaum, E W/Political profiles/79n527
Schoenfeld, M/Multi-media approach/79n231
Schöffler, H/New Schöffler-/75n1270
Scholars' gd to Washington, D.C. for Russian-Soviet studies/Grant/78n309
Scholar's market/Harmon/76n1194
Scholarships, fellowships and loans/Feingold/78n566
Scholberg, H/Bibliographie des français/77n399
Scholl, R/Running Press/78n613
Schon, I/Bicultural heritage/79n462/Books in Spanish/79n1292

School & public library media programs for children & young adults/Baker/78n178
School librarian as educator/Wehmeyer/77n229
School library media center/Davies/75n194/Prostano/78n187
School library volunteer/Wehmeyer/76n153
School music program/75n1119
School universe data bk/Curriculum Info Center/76n660; 77n604
Schools abroad of interest to Americans/Maher/76n614
Schoonmaker, F/Frank Schoonmaker's/75n1676; 76n1563; 79n1521
Schorr, A E/Directory of special/76n171/Government docs/78n131/Government reference/77n106; 79n125
Schrader, A M/Search for/79n323
Schrank, J/Seed catalog/75n706
Schreiber, M/Key resources/78n570
Schreiner-Yantis, N/Archives of/75n362/Genealogical books/76n421
Schroeder, M/Green thumb/78n496
Schub, J H/On-campus/77n616
Schubert, M/Treasury of/77n1554
Schubert, P B/Conversion tables/75n1717
Schuler, S/Encyclopedia of home/76n1642/5,000 questions/78n1535/Home renovation/75n1797/Homeowner's directory/79n1573/How to fix/76n1643
Schultes, R E/Hallucinogenic plants/78n1281
Schultz, C K/Thesaurus of/79n161
Schultz, D/Mothers' and/78n1430
Schultz, G J/Foreign trade/78n734
Schultz, H D/How the/76n862
Schultz, N D/Guide to federal/78n352
Schultz, V/Bibliography of quantitative/77n1409
Schulz, A/International and/78n488
Schulz, J/Data systems/79n1565
Schulzetenberg, A C/College learning/79n192
Schuman, P G/Social responsibilities/77n164
Schumann, W/Gemstones of/79n1422
Schuster, M/Library-centered/79n325
Schuster, M/Motion picture/77n1003
Schwab, A T/Matter of/78n826
Schwark, B L/Guide to periodicals/76n585
Schwartz, B/Aging bibliog/79n739/Community education/79n634/Leisure reading/78n596
Schwartz, C/George Gershwin/76n1010
Schwartz, E I/Funk &/75n1262

Schwartz, G/Climate advisor/79n1417
Schwartz, M D/Environmental law/78n1341
Schwartz, N L/Articles on/78n1092
Schwarzenberger, G/Year bk world/75n90; 76n507; 79n513
Schweik, R C/Reference sources/78n1093
Schweitzer, H B/Medical abbreviations/78n1415
Schwenke, K/Sierra South/76n725
Schwerin, K/Bibliography of German/79n567
Schwicker, A C/International dict/76n1618
Schwinn bicycle serv manual/75n1754
Schwuchow, W/Methods of/79n263
Science and engineering lit/Malinowsky/77n1286
Science & gov report internat'l almanac/Greenberg/78n435
Science and tech/Grogan/77n1282
Science and tech/Stonehouse/75n175; 76n148
Science and tech in the developmt of modern China/Dean/75n299
Science citation index/76n1327
Science fair project index 1960-72/Stoffer/76n1328
Science fict bk review index, 1923-73/Hall/76n1206
Science for society/Dasbach/78n1204
Science of fingerprints/US Dept of Justice/75n836
Science policy: working glossary/US Congress/77n1291
Science tests and reviews/Buros/76n568
Scientific and technical bks and serials in print/78n1205
Scientific and technical pubs of the Environmental Research Laboratories/US Natl Oceanic and Atmospheric Admin/75n1561
Scientific, engineering, and medical societies pubs in print/Kyed/77n1285
Scientific instruments/Wynter/77n1279
Scientific periodicals/Houghton/76n1308
Scientific quotations/Mackay/79n1302
Scientific, technical, and engineering societies pubs in print/Kyed/75n1430
Scientists/Feisenberger/76n55
Sclar, D/Annual register/75n667
Scott, A F/Who's who Chaucer/76n1270
Scott, E L/Tennis catalog/79n730
Scott, J B/Proceedings of Hague/78n437
Scott, J S/Dictionary of building/75n1760
Scott, J W/Social science/76n239
Scott, K/Abstracts from/78n410/Buried genealogical/78n411/Genealogical data/78n409/NY manuscripts/75n428/Register of/79n496

Scott, M/Crafts business/79n941
Scott, P/World atlas/75n1511
Scott, P G/Early editions/78n1171
Scott, R M/Thin-layer/75n1453
Scott, R W/Management and/76n801
Scott, W H O/Recommended East/76n259
Scott, Foresman beginning dict/Thorndike/77n1078
Scottish family hist/Stuart/79n499
Scotto, R M/Three contemporary/78n1124
Screen, J E O/Guide to foreign/79n1092
Screen printing photographic techniques/Fossett/75n1108
Scribner-Bantam English dict/Williams/78n1038
Scully, B/Handyman's ency/78n1536
Sculpture of David Smith/Krauss/78n822
Scurlock, R/Government contracts/76n653
Sea battles/Sanderson/76n301
Sea fiction guide/Smith/77n1175
Sea shells of Sri Lanka/Kirtisinghe/79n928
Sea shells of the West Indies/Humfrey/76n973
Seal, R A/Guide to lit/78n1236
Sean O'Casey/Ayling/79n1279
Search and research/Stevenson/79n470
Search for a scientific profession/Houser/79n323
Search Group, Inc./Dictionary of criminal/78n503
Searching the prof lit in reading/Curry/76n689
Searls, E F/How to use/76n691
Sears list of subj headings/Westby/78n230
Seas and their shells/Angeletti/79n927
Seashore life of Florida and the Caribbean/Voss/78n1335
Seasonal gd to indoor gardening/Kramer/77n1556
Seaweed handbook/Lee/79n1357
Seaweeds/Hillson/78n1303
Second dict of acronyms & abbreviations/Pugh/76n116
Second Jewish catalog/Strassfeld/78n390
Second ref catalogue of bright galaxies/de Vaucouleurs/77n1306
Second World War and the atomic age, 1940-73/Cronon/76n260
Secrets from the super spas/Wilkens/77n1525
Securities law review/Folk/76n518
Securities Reform Act of 1975/76n888
Security! how to protect yourself, your home, your office, and your car/Clifford/75n832

Seed catalog/Schrank/75n706
Seeds and fruits of plants of eastern Canada & northeastern US/Montgomery/78n1285
Segal, S J/International family/79n750
Segrè, E/Annual review nuclear/76n1349
Seibel, H/Barron's how/77n608
Seide, K/Paul Felix/75n980
Seidman, A H/Handbook for electronics/77n1593
Seidman, R J/Notes for/75n1388
Selden, W/Reference manual/78n717
Select bibliog for the study of Anglo-Irish lit and its backgrounds/Harmon/79n1280
Select bibliography of . . .
  Günter Grass/Everett/75n1419; 76n1294
  the principal modern presses public & private in Great Britain and Ireland/Tomkinson/77n56
Select bibliog to Calif Catholic lit, 1856-1974/Weber/76n1079
Selected and annotated bibliog of bicultural classroom materials for Mexican American studies/Reilly/79n686
Selected, annotated bibliog of Caribbean bibliographies in English/Chang/77n337
Selected bibliog and abstracts for ambulatory health care computer applications/76n1519
Selected bibliography of . . .
  American constitutional hist/Millett/76n312
  music librarianship/Phillips/76n170
  nutrition materials/Kaplan/75n1689
Selected discography of solo song, suppl 1971-74/Stahl/77n967
Selected free materials for classroom teachers/Aubrey/77n647
Selected gd to sports and recreation books/Nueckel/75n726
Selected gd to travel books/Nueckel/75n587
Selected print & nonprint resources in speech communication/Feezel/77n1121
Selected sound recordings of American, British, & European lit in English/Salley/78n1091
Selected titles in chemistry/79n1317
Selected US gov series/Van Zant/79n126
Selecting educ'l equipmt and materials for school and home/Deans/77n645
Selecting instructional media/Sive/79n688
Selection of the vice president/Tompkins/75n497
Selective bibliog for the study of English and American lit/Altick/76n1180
Selective bibliography of . . .
  audio-visual materials reflecting a civil liberties theme/Eichman/78n495
  Shakespeare editions, textual studies, commentary/McManaway/76n1285
Selective gd to materials for mental health and family life educ/77n1442
Selective mgmt bibliog/Sandeau/77n851
Selective music lists: vocal solos, vocal ensembles/77n961
Selfridge-Field, E/Venetian instrumental/76n984
Selig, R L/Elizabeth Gaskell/78n1174
Selim, G D/American doctoral/78n282
Selim, S/Turkish phrase/75n1285
Sell, I L/Dying and/78n1428
Sellers, R C/Armed forces/78n1561
Selling your crafts and art in L.A./Weingarten/75n1038
Selman, L H/Paperweights for/77n922
Seltz-Petrash, A/AAAS science/77n1280
Semioli, W J/Conversion tables/75n1717
Semple, M/Introductory gd Midwest/78n840
Senate campaign information/79n528
Senior citizens/Tripp/79n843
Senkevitch, A/Soviet architecture/75n1022
Seppa, D/Coins of/75n1070
Sergel, S L/Language of/75n1180
Serial pubs in anthropology/Tax/75n869
Serials: advertising, business, finance, marketing, social sci in libraries in the NY area/Regan/76n38
Serials automation in the US/Pitkin/77n169
Serials in psychology and allied fields/Tompkins/77n1445
Serials in transition/MacMillan/79n19
Serials librarian/78n160
Serials updating service annual/Forman/76n23/Sweeney/79n191
Sermon on the Mount/Kissinger/77n1045
Service etiquette/Swartz/78n1563
Serving youth: high school library/Shapiro/76n152
Sessions, B/Dog owner's/77n1533
Sessions, K W/Master handbk/77n1599
Sessions, V S/Directory of data/76n241
Settel, B/Subject description/79n282
Settlers by the long grey trail/Harrison/76n434
700 French idioms/Miller/77n1089
7000 old books: current values/78n51
Seventeenth century American poetry/Scheick/78n1126

Seventeenth-century Barberini docs & inventories of art/Lavin/77n866
78 RPM records & prices/Soderbergh/79n976
Sewell, P H/National library/78n125
Sewell, W/Guide to drug/78n1443
Sewell's dog's medical dict/White/78n1466
Sex and the handicapped/78n1391
Sex and the undecided librarian/Pope/75n269
Sex differences and reading/Sheridan/77n581
Sex role stereotyping in the mass media/Friedman/78n1075
Sexual barrier/Hughes/79n756
Seymour, J/Guide to self-sufficiency/78n1447
Seymour Britchky's new, revised gd to the restaurants of NY/Britchky/77n1540
Seymour-Smith, M/Who's who twentieth/77n1181
SFBRI: sci fict bk review index/Hall/78n1106
Shaaber, M A/Sixteenth-century/77n30
Shabecoff, A/Whole Washington/76n881
Shadily, H/English-Indonesian/76n1150
Shadwell, W J/Catalogue of American/76n918
Shaffer, D E/Career educ/77n654/Sources of free/77n655
Shaffer, H G/Periodicals on/78n467
Shaheen, N/Biblical references/77n1245
Shain, H/Legal first/76n508
Shaker herbs/Miller/78n1298
Shaker lit/Richmond/77n1031; 78n976
Shakespeare: dict/Wells/79n1254
Shakespeare: study and research gd/Bergeron/76n1284
Shakespeare complex/Loney/76n1042
Shakespeare survey/75n1399/Muir/76n1286; 77n1242
Shaklee, R/COIN/78n95
Shanas, E/Handbook of aging/78n648
Shane, J/All-in-one/75n1789
Shank, W/California hndbk/76n492
Shannon, B/Ballparks/76n706
Shapiro, B J/Directory of ethnic publishers/78n378/Directory of ethnic studies/78n136
Shapiro, C/Encyclopedia of contemporary/79n43
Shapiro, C/Fine prints/78n814
Shapiro, E/Handbook of early/79n1001
Shapiro, I J/Marketing terms/75n925
Shapiro, L/Color atlas/76n1541

Shapiro, L L/Children's media/79n225/Serving youth/76n152/Teaching yourself/79n217
Shapiro, M S/Cadillac modern/75n73/Mathematics ency/78n1230
Shapiro, N/Encyclopedia of quotations/79n967/Popular music/75n1175
SHARE: Directory of feminist library workers/Leita/77n183; 79n167
Sharff, L E/Uniformed services/77n1632; 77n1633; 77n1634
Sharma, H S/Agriculture/79n1513/Indian science/78n1221
Sharma, R N/India and/75n301
Sharma, S K/Fifty years/76n359
Sharp, H/Follett vest-/79n1127
Sharp, H S/Footnotes to/78n346/Handbk of pseudonyms/76n451
Sharp, R F/Dictionary of English/79n1232
Shatzman, I/Illustrated ency classical/77n364
Shaub, B M/Treasures from/76n1482
Shaw, B A/Latin American/77n1273
Shaw, H/Dictionary of problem/76n1131
Shaw, J M/Childhood in/77n1146
Shaw, M/National anthems/77n950
Shaw, R/NY for/75n614
Shaw, R J/Field gd vascular/77n1356
Shaw, R P/Migration theory/77n757
Shawcross, J T/Milton ency/79n1250
Shawver, D L/Marketing doctoral/78n736
Shea, P/Language of/75n885
Sheahan, E/Moving pictures/75n1193
Sheehy, E P/Guide to ref/77n14
Sheldon, K E/Guide to social/79n758
Sheldon, R/Viktor Shklovsky/78n1198
Sheldon, W H/Penny whimsy/77n915
Shell collector's gd/Fair/77n931
Shells and shores of Texas/Andrews/78n1334
Shelton, C S/South Dakota/75n43
Shepard, L/Encyclopedia of occultism/79n1440/Occultism update/79n1439
Shepard, R F/Going out/75n615
Shepard's federal tax locator/76n913
Shepherd, W R/Shepherd's historical/75n352
Shepherd's historical atlas/Shepherd/75n352
Sheppard, J/Social work/75n842
Shera, J H/Dictionary of American/79n185/Foundations of/75n190/Introduction to library/77n165
Sheridan, E M/Sex differences/77n581
Sheridan, L W/Manual on medical/75n1610
Sherman, J/Arab-Israeli/79n439

Sherman, J R/Jack London/78n1144
Sherman, M/Amnesty in/75n478
Sherr, L/American woman's/77n724
Sherrod, J/Information systems/76n236
Sherwood Anderson/Rogers/77n1197/White/78n1129
Shestack, M/Country music/75n1176
Shevin, J/Citizen groups/77n523
Shields, G R/Children's library/75n192
Shields, J F/Make it/76n956
Shilling, C W/Underwater medicine/75n1618
Shimmon, R/Reader in/77n249
Shimoni, Y/Political dict/75n523
Ship passenger lists: Natl and New England, 1600-1825/Boyer/79n479/New York & New Jersey, 1600-1825/Boyer/79n480
Ships & aircraft of the US fleet/Morison/77n1651/Polmar/79n1605
Shipton, C K/Sibley's Harvard/76n667
Shirey, D/Evaluation techniques/79n221
Shirk, G H/Oklahoma place/75n456
Shirkey, H C/Pediatric drug/79n1504
Shirley, N/Serials in/77n1445
Shishkoff, S/Subject bibliog/78n1025
Shock and vibration hndbk/Harris/77n1607
Shockley, A A/Handbook of black/78n1142/Living black/75n1349
Shoemaker, T M/Lineman's and/77n1594
Sholtys, P/World directory/75n1552
Shonyo, C/Library mgmt/78n213
Shoot-em-ups/Adams/79n1031
Shooter's bible/Olson/77n691
Shopper's gd to museum stores/Hodupp/79n842
Shopper's gdbk to life insurance, health insur, auto insur, homeowner's insur, doctors, dentists, lawyers, pensions, etc/Denenberg/75n945
Shopping round the mountains/Camblos/75n941
Shore protection manual/US Corps of Engineers/75n1816
Shores, L/Collier's ency/79n71/Generic bk/79n155/Merit students/79n75/Quiet world/76n210/Reference as/77n268
Short, L L/Birds of/77n1387
Short film/Rehrauer/76n1059
Short gd to the study of Ethiopia/Hidaru/77n314
Short rotation trees/Louden/78n1484
Short stories on film/Emmens/79n1034
Short story index/Bogart/77n1134/Suppl 1969-73/Fidell/76n1210

Short-title catalogue of bks printed in England, Scotland, & Ireland and of English bks printed abroad 1475-1640/Pollard/77n27
Shortage survival hndbk/Karnaookh/75n947
Shorter Oxford English dict on historical principles/Little/75n1252
Shostak, J/Barron's guide/79n657
Shosteck, R/Flowers and/75n1464/Weekender's guide/75n616
Shourds, T/History and/77n476
Showalter, G I/Music books/76n992
Showers, V/World in/75n86
Showman, R K/Harvard guide/75n355
Shreffler, P A/H. P. Lovecraft/78n1145
Shrinks, etc: consumer's gd to psychotherapies/Kiernan/75n1591
Shtohryn, D M/Ukrainians in/76n107
Shugar, G/Educator's internat'l/79n687
Shull, J/Hole thing/75n1114
Shulman, D/Annotated bibliog cryptography/77n1105
Shulman, F J/Allied occupation/75n544/Doctoral dissertations Asia/76n258/Doctoral dissertations China/79n369/Doctoral dissertations Japan/77n329/East Asian/79n367
Shurtleff, N B/Records of/77n477
Shuwall, M/Running Press/78n633
Shy, J/American Revolution/75n359
SI metric hndbk/Feirer/78n1231
Sibley's Harvard graduates/Shipton/76n667
Sicily: archaeological gd/Guido/78n320
Sickle cell anemia/Davis/79n1453
Sickle cell hemoglobinopathies/Triche/75n1620; 77n1468
Siddiqi, A R/Press directory/76n1172
Sidney Lanier, Henry Timrod, and Paul Hamilton Hayne/De Bellis/79n1210
Siegel, B J/Annual review anthropology/76n808
Siegel, E/Guide to dance/79n1038
Sierra Club naturalist's guide to . . .
   Southern New England/Jorgensen/79n1338
   the deserts of the Southwest/Larson/78n1270
Sierra South/Winnett/76n725
Sigh of relief: first-aid hndbk/Green/79n1485
Sigler, J/Independence documents/79n518
Sigmund Freud's writings/Grinstein/78n1363
Signers of the Constitution/US Natl Park Service/78n338

Signers of the Declaration/US Natl Park
 Service/75n375
Signet bk of American wine/Quimme/78n1459
Signet-Hammond world atlas/79n591
Signet Hebrew-English, English-Hebrew dict/
 Ben Abba/79n1140
Signeur, A V/Guide to gas/76n1346
Significant American . . .
 artists and architects/Tegland/77n125
 authors, poets, & playwrights/Meltzer/77
  n126
 blacks/Jacobs/77n127
 colonial leaders/Buske/77n128
 entertainers/Tegland/77n129
 government leaders/Miekina/77n130
 historians and educators/Mandel/77n131
 Indians/Mandel/77n132
 inventors/Quinn/77n133
 military leaders/Miekina/77n134
 musicians, composers, and singers/Meltzer/
  77n135
 Presidents of the US/Buske/77n136
 scientists/Quinn/77n137
 social reformers and humanitarians/Miekina/
  77n138
 sport champions/Mandel/77n139
 women/Meltzer/77n140
Significant Americans/77n141
Silet, C L P/Henry Blake/78n1125
Sill, G G/Handbook of symbols/76n926
Silva, F/Film literature/76n1063; 77n1014
Silva, J/Justice for/77n816
Silver, H K/Handbook of pediatrics/77n1486
Silver coinage of MA/Noe/75n1069
Silverman, D/Antebellum black/77n432
Silverman, J/Index to young/76n1200
Silverstone, P H/Stamp collector's/75n1087
Simandl, D/Broad system/79n300
Simmler, O/World directory/77n187
Simms, G/World of golf/79n718
Simon, R S/Modern Middle/79n359
Simon and Schuster's . . .
 complete gd to freshwater and marine
  aquarium fishes/79n704
 complete gd to plants and flowers/Perry/
  77n1351
 guide to trees/79n1365
 international dict: English-Spanish, Span-
  ish-English/de Gámez/75n1279
Simona Morini's ency of health and beauty/
 Morini/77n1497
Simons' list bk/Simons/79n610
Simonsgaard, S/Antique collecting/78n841
Simora, F/Bowker annual/79n172

Simosko, V/Eric Dolphy/75n1164
Simplified gd to electronic circuits, test pro-
 cedures and troubleshooting/Moon/77
 n1596
Simpson, A E/Guide to library/77n852
Simpson, D B/State library/79n168
Simpson, D H/Manuscript catalogue/77n413
Simpson, I S/Basic statistics/76n122
Simpson, J/First science/78n1209
Simpson, J/Macmillan dict/76n1128
Simpson, J E/Georgia history/77n395
Simpson, M G/Tested secretarial/75n893
Simpson, N T/Country inns/77n568; 79n622
Sims, T/Marketing channel/77n810
Simsova, S/Handbook of comparative/76
 n217
Simulation activities in library, communica-
 tion and info sci/Williams/78n128
Simulation teaching of library admin/Zachert/
 76n185
Sinclair, J E/How the/76n862
Sinclair, K V/Prières en/79n1273
Sinews of independence/Lesser/77n372
Singer, J D/Study of internat'l/77n529
Singer, K/Dictionary of household/75n1798
Singer, R B/Medical risks/78n1416
Singerman, R/Jewish and/78n425/Jews in/
 76n384
Singh, S/Indian books/75n10
Singleton, C S/Companion to/76n1296
Sipkov, I/Coutumes of/79n563
Sippl, C J/Calculator user's/77n1582/Com-
 puter dictionary/75n1774/Data communi-
 cations/77n1583/Microcomputer dict/
 77n1584
SIPRI yrbk, world armaments and disarma-
 ment/Stockholm Internat'l Peace Research
 Institute/76n505
Sir John Betjeman/Stapleton/76n1268
Siracusa, J/Federico García/75n1427
Sisson, J D/Storia dell'arte/77n871
Sittig, M/Pollutant removal/75n1542
Sittler, C J/Isotopes of/77n1430
Sivan, R/New Bantam-/78n1060
Sive, M R/Selecting instructional/79n688
6,000 words/77n1068
Sixteen modern American authors/Bryer/75
 n1338
Sixteenth-century imprints in the libraries of
 the Univ of PA/Shaaber/77n30
Sizer, S A/Guide to selected/77n355
Skalka, L M/Tracing, charting/76n422
Skallerup, H R/Books afloat/75n271
Skateboarder's bible/Cassorla/78n636

Skeist, I/Handbook of adhesives/78n1541
Ski America cheap/Mokres/75n785
Skiing USA/Fehr/79n728
Skillin, M E/Words into/75n113
Skinner, G W/Modern Chinese/75n302
Skluth, B/Performing arts/79n1005
Skoric, S/Russian reference/75n306
Skousen, K F/Introduction to SEC/78n731
Skowronski, J/Women in/79n962
Skrapek, W A/Mathematical dict/78n707
Skrupskelis, I K/William James/78n1004
Skurnik, W A E/Sub-Saharan Africa/78n292
Skuse, G/Sub-aqua illust'd/78n634
Slater, C/Things your/75n1799
Slater, J H/Robert Louis/75n1403
Slater, M/Assessing the/78n253
Slater, W T/Aspen hndbk/77n1102
Slattery, W J/Index of US/79n1406
Slavens, T P/Informational interviews/79n298
Sleet, R J/Resource book/77n1312
Sletwold, E/Sletwold's manual/77n533
Sletwold's manual of docs and forms for the legal secretary/Sletwold/77n533
Slide buyers gd/DeLaurier/75n1003
Slide libraries/Irvine/75n205
Sloane, D L/Winnipeg/75n393
Sloane, E A/New complete bk/75n744
Slocum, R B/Biographical dictionaries/79n134
Slote, S J/Weeding library/76n203
Small, A/Birds of California/75n1510; 76n1432/Birds of West/77n1375
Small, A/Concise ency/79n1429
Small arms of the world/Smith/75n1839/Ezell/79n1608
Small business index/Kryszak/79n823
Small college/Askew/75n640
Small library cataloging/Hoffman/79n272
Small press record of bks/Fulton/76n11
Small press record of bks in print/Fulton/79n39
Small tech libraries/Campbell/75n202
Smart, P/International butterfly/76n1441
Smirnitsky, A I/Russian-English/75n1275
Smit, P/History of life/76n1354
Smith, A G/Mesozoic and/78n1357
Smith, A H/Field gd western/76n1398
Smith, A P-C/American genealogical/78n412/Encyclopedia of German-/77n478
Smith, B/Penrose graphic/76n943
Smith, C/Library resources/75n166
Smith, C A/Narratives of/75n807
Smith, C B/Efficient electricity/77n1600; 79n1389
Smith, C B/Getting people/75n715

Smith, C H/Marketing profitability/79n836
Smith, C N/American genealogical/78n412/Encyclopedia of German-/77n478
Smith, C N/Annual review entomology/76n1409
Smith, C R/Education directory/79n664
Smith, D A/Dictionary of rubber/76n1647
Smith, D B F/Subject index/79n1195
Smith, D L/Afro-American/75n360/Era of/76n315/Indians of/76n414
Smith, D L/Guide to marine/79n1381
Smith, D L/Medication gd/78n1444
Smith, D S/New intellectuals/78n927/Popular school/76n1032
Smith, E W/Dieter's checklist/76n1579
Smith, F G W/Handbook of marine/76n1470
Smith, G R/Manual on bookselling/75n47
Smith, H/Guidebook to/78n360
Smith, H E/Historical and/77n331
Smith, J D/California hndbk/76n492/Population/77n713/World food/78n1481
Smith, J E/Small arms/75n1839
Smith, J F/Critical bibliog/79n892
Smith, J I/Library and/75n236
Smith, J M/World ency/76n1053
Smith, K M/Portraits and/79n879
Smith, L S/Practical approach/79n283
Smith, L W/Index to reproductions/78n820
Smith, M/International art/79n916
Smith, M B/Handbook of ocular/76n1554
Smith, M D/Oak from/78n262
Smith, M J/American Navy/75n1851; 75n1852; 75n1853/Cloak-and-/77n1174/Sea fiction/77n1175/World War I/78n1566/World War II/77n1652
Smith, R/Wastewater mgmt/77n1421
Smith, R A/Farwell's rules/78n1573
Smith, R C/Biographical index American/77n870
Smith, R F/Annual review entomology/76n1409
Smith, R F/Cumulated fiction/77n1176
Smith, R S/Getting the/77n241/Promotion planning/76n200
Smith, R W L/Dictionary of English/77n1085
Smith, S/Women who/76n1069
Smith, S B/Tennessee history/76n353
Smith, S C/Directory of organizations/78n556
Smith, S E/Experiences in/75n287
Smith, S V/Library statistics/78n170
Smith, V C/Women's movement/78n663
Smith, W/Flags through/77n486
Smith, W H B/Small arms/75n1839

Smith, W J/Directory of social/79n1508/ Granger's index/79n1201
Smith-Burnett, G C K/College library/79n196
Smithe, F B/Naturalist's color/76n1366
Smithells, C J/Metals reference/77n1613
Smollen, L E/Source guide/78n754
Smorgasbord of books/Owen/76n161
Smythe, M M/Black American/77n435
Snakes of the world/Stidworthy/76n1450
Snaster, M/Women in/78n373
Sneddon, I N/Encyclopaedic dict/78n1504
Snell, E E/Annual review biochemistry/76n1339
Snyder, L L/Encyclopedia of Third/77n402
Snyder, N/Photography catalog/78n887
Soaring directory/78n638
Sobel, L A/Chile & Allende/75n524/Energy crisis/75n1543/Inflation and/75n495; 76n820/Israel &/75n525/Latin America/75n342/Money and/75n496/Political terrorism/76n462/Presidential succession/76n488/South Vietnam/75n529/World food/76n848
Sobel, R/Biographical directory governors/79n543/Biographical directory US/78n451; 79n541
Social hist of branch library developmt with special ref to the city of Glasgow/Hendry/76n224
Social justice/Mainelli/79n1042
Social policy and admin in Britain/Blackstone/77n703
Social responsibilities and libraries/Schuman/77n164
Social responsibility in marketing/Uhr/78n744
Social sci research hndbk/McInnis/76n239
Social sciences citation index/76n242
Social sciences index/75n36/Bloomfield/77n304
Social security programs throughout the world/79n875
Social serv organizations/Romanofsky/79n733
Social studies curriculum materials data bk/77n656
Social studies tests and reviews/Buros/76n569
Social system and culture of modern India/Chekki/76n260
Social work educ/Li/79n731
Social work ref aids in the Univ of Toronto libraries/Sheppard/75n842

Societal directions and alternatives/Marien/77n299
Society of American Travel Writers/Exploring the/76n555
Society of Automotive Engineers/Unified numbering/76n1612
Sociologist as detective/Sanders/75n789
Sociology of . . .
  America/Mark/77n706
  human fertility/Freedman/76n771
  Karl Mannheim/Remmling/76n773
  medicine and health care/Litman/78n1388
Socolich, S/Bargain hunting/75n954
Soderberg, P/Big book/78n603
Soderbergh, P A/78 RPM/79n976
Soderman, J/Basic gd/77n13
Soergel, D/Indexing languages/76n194
Sohmer, M/Call for/76n884
Sohn, H/Woleaian-English/78n1072
Sokan, R/Descriptive and/78n930
Sokol, D M/American architecture/77n876
Sokoloff, B A/Bibliography of Norman/75n1361/John Updike/75n1371/Saul Bellow/75n1352
Solar age catalog/79n1411
Solar directory/Pesko/77n1414
Solar energy & research directory/79n1412
Solar energy source book/Martz/79n1410
Solara, F V/Key influences/75n482
Solomon, P/Handbook of psychiatry/75n1597
Solomon, S R/Governors of/75n505
Soltow, M J/American women/77n841
Somalia: bibliographical survey/Salad/78n289
Some prominent Virginia families/du Bellet/77n459
Somerton, D/Field gd fish/77n1388
Somerville, H/Sailing/75n751
Something about the author/Commire/77n1162; 77n1163
Sommerfeld, R M/Dow Jones-Irwin/75n986
Sommers, L M/Atlas of Michigan/78n522
Son of young adult reviewers/77n1164
Sondrup, S P/Konkordanz zu/79n1278
Song list/Limbacher/75n1130
Songbirds of the Eastern and Central states/Rising/78n1321
Songe, A H/American universities/79n640/International guide/77n176
Songs from Hollywood musical comedies/Woll/77n984

Songs of protest, war & peace/Denisoff/75 n1122
Songwriter's market/Brohaugh/79n978
Songwriters' rhyming dict/Whitfield/76n1137
Sonnenreich, M R/Handbook on 1970/76 n1549
Sopher, D E/Historical atlas religions/76 n1091
Sorrell, C A/Minerals of/75n1574
Soucek, B/Microprocessors and/77n1585
Souders, M/Handbook of engineering/77 n1566
Soulen, R N/Handbook of biblical/78n997
Soulik, T/Nukuoro lexicon/75n1282
Source bk for food scientists/Ockerman/ 79n1531
Source Collective/Organizing for/75n1631
Source gd for borrowing capital/Smollen/78 n754
Sourcebook for Hispanic lit and language/ Bleznick/75n1426
Sourcebook of criminal justice statistics/US Dept of Justice/75n837; 78n491
Sourcebook of electronic organ circuits/Douglas/77n1590
Sourcebook of equal educ'l opportunity/78 n580
Sourcebook of library technology/77n193
Sourcebook on aging/79n740
Sourcebook on health sciences librarianship/ Chen/78n193
Sources: print and nonprint materials/78 n3; 79n40
Sources and docs of US Constitutions/Swindler/75n566; 79n536
Sources for Roman Catholic and Jewish genealogy and family history/Steel/78n421
Sources for the hist of British India in the 17th century/Khan/76n362
Sources for the history of sci 1660-1914/Knight/ 76n1309
Sources in British political hist 1900-51/Cook/ 78n477
Sources of . . .
    construction information/Godel/78n1517
    European economic info/76n827; 79n798
    free teaching materials/Shaffer/77n655
    information in the soc sciences/White/75 n284
    information in water resources/Giefer/77 n1429
    Japanese history/Lu/75n392
    national criminal justice statistics/Parisi/79 n577

Sources of . . . (cont'd)
    serials/78n17
    support for training and research on Russia and the USSR/Boisture/76 n277
    Punjab history/Gustafson/76n360
Sources, organization, utilization of international documentation/75n259
South African political materials/Wynne/78 n472
South America: problems and prospects/ Isenberg/76n281
South American markets review/Walsh/77 n811
South Asia: systematic geographic bibliog/ Sukhwal/76n523
South Asian library resources in North America/Assoc for Asian Studies/77n243; 77n244
South Carolina Baptists/Townsend/75n431
South Dakota union list of serials/Shelton/75 n43
South Vietnam: US-Communist confrontation in Southeast Asia/Millet/75n527; 75n528/Sobel/75n529/Knappman/75 n530
Southeast Asian periodicals/Nunn/79n365
Southeastern bibliog'ic instruction directory/ Ward/79n169
Southern almanac/Stevens/79n391
Southwestern medical dict/Kay/78n1397
Southwestern pottery/Oppelt/78n680
Soviet and East European foreign policy/ Kanet/75n534
Soviet architecture, 1917-62/Senkevitch/75 n1022
Soviet Asia/Allworth/77n345
Soviet-Asian relations/McLane/75n537
Soviet cinema/Birkos/77n1007
Soviet government/Mathews/75n522
Soviet-Middle East relations/McLane/75n538
Soviet prison camp speech/Galler/78n1066
Soviet sociology/Matthews/79n732
Soviet-type economic systems/O'Relley/79 n806
Soviet-Yugoslav relations/Hunter/77n527
Spache, G D/Good reading/75n707
Spada, J/Films of/78n963
Spahn, J P & T J/From radical/77n506
Spalding, H D/Encyclopedia of black/75 n1241
Spalek, J M/German expressionism/78n786
Spanish bilingual dict/Lipton/77n1100
Spanish in America, 1513-1974/Natella/76 n419

Spanish-speaking groups in the US/Burma/75 n817; 76n392
Sparkes, I G/Dictionary of collective/76n1136
Sparks, R M/Prostaglandin abstracts/75n1641
Sparrow, C J/Annotated bibliog Canadian/77 n1420
Sparrow, W S/Women painters/77n859
Spaulding, C E/Veterinary guide/77n1534
Spaulding, S/World's students/77n582
Speaker's treasury of anecdotes about the famous/Humes/79n1174
Spear, G E/Urban education/79n635
Special bibliog in monetary economics and finance/Cohen/79n871
Special child in the library/Baskin/77n216
Special collections in German libraries/Gebhardt/78n194
Special collections in libraries of the Southeast/Howell/79n164
Special librarian as a supervisor or middle mgr/Bailey/78n192
Special libraries: gd for mgmt/Aufdenkamp/76n165
Special libraries directory/78n203
Specialised information centres/Harvey/77 n237
Specialist sports cars/Filby/76n765
Specialized communications techniques for the radio amateur/76n1633
Specification bk for US cars 1920-29/Naul/79n1556
Spectre, P H/Mariner's catalog/76n713
Speech index/Mitchell/78n1085
Speech play/Kirshenblatt-Gimblett/77n1123
Speed, F M/Film review/77n998; 79n1039
Speed, W J/International index/77n661; 77n662
Speitel, H H/Linguistic atlas/76n1116; 78 n1023
Spencer, D A/Hymn and/79n1063
Spencer, D D/Computer acronym/75n1775/Computer dictionary/75n1776/Guide to teaching/75n716
Spencer, J/National directory/75n1185; 76 n1043; 79n1014; 79n1015
Spencer, L/Economic history/75n926
Spenser allusions in the 16th and 17th centuries/Heffner/75n1402
Spenser's art/Rose/76n1290
Sperka, M/Growing wildflowers/75n1708
Sperry, K/Survey of American/79n472
Spevack, M/Harvard concordance/75n1400
Spices, condiments, teas, coffees and other delicacies/Robertson/76n1578

Spiegel, Z/Ground water/75n1527
Spiegelman, A/Whole grains/75n95
Spies and all that/DeVore/79n502
Spiller, D/Book selection/75n220
Spiller, R E/Literary history/75n1339
Spinazze, L M/Index to Argonauts/76n441
Spinelli, D C/Annotated bibliog French/77 n1260
Spinelli, F M/Community educ/79n634
SPINES thesaurus/Unesco Secretariat/78 n1211
Spink, C C J/Hockey register/78n627/Official baseball dope/78n611/Official baseball gd/78n612/Sporting News'/78n625
Spinks, C W/Bibliography of modern/77n1269
Spiritual community gd/Khalsa/79n1085
Spirt, D L/Creating a/75n195/Introducing more/79n235
Spock, B/Baby and/77n1499
Spooner, A/Oxford children's/77n1080
Sporting heritage/Lewis/75n725
Sporting News' natl football gd/Marcin/76 n737/Spink/78n625
Sporting News official baseball record bk/75n732; 77n677
Sports/Nunn/77n668
Sports collectors bible/Sugar/79n696
Sports encyclopedia:
 baseball/Neft/75n733; 78n610
 pro football/Neft/76n738
Sports olympiques album officiel/de Groote/77n664
SportSource/Anderson/77n663
Spradling, M M/In black/77n436
Sprague, N/Finding a/79n865
Spratto, G/Nurse's drug/79n1501
Spring flora of Wisconsin/Fassett/77n1352
Springer, H S/Washington Irving/77n1208
Sprug, J W/Index to ARBA/78n38/Time research/76n1491
Sprung, D B/Dog lovers/77n1535/"Popular dogs"/76n1565
Spuler, B/Rulers and/78n434; 79n512
Spyers-Duran, P/Management problems/75 n217
Squeglia, M/All about/76n1644
Squier, E/Guide to recommended/75n604/New revised gd/76n546
Squires, D/Complete bk platform/75n783
Srikantaiah, T/Introduction to quantitative/78 n268/Systems analysis/79n254
Staar, R F/Yearbook on international/75n531
Stachura, P D/Weimar era/79n430
Staff communication in libraries/Emery/76 n176

Staff mgmt in univ and college libraries/ Durey/77n203
Stafford, M/Illustrated dictionary/76n924
Stafford, P/Psychedelics ency/78n1445
Stafford, W T/Name, title/76n1243
Stage mgmt/Stern/75n1182
Stage scenery, machinery, and lighting/ Stoddard/78n931
Stahl, D/Selected discography/77n967
Stahl, J N/Index of tissue/78n1423
Stallybrass, O/Harper dictionary/78n83
Stam, D H/Wordsworthian criticism/75n1408
Stambler, I/Encyclopedia of folk/76n1031/ Encyclopedia of pop/76n1030; 78n920
Stamets, P/Psilocybe mushrooms/79n1355
Stamp, D/Chisholm's hndbk/76n832
Stamp collector's gd to Europe/Allen/75 n1087
Stamps and coins/Rosichan/75n1052
Stamps of British North America/Jarrett/76 n975
Standard & Poor's register of corporations, directors and executives/79n811
Standard catalog of . . .
    Mexican coins, paper money and medals/ Vogt/79n920
    world coins/Krause/75n1068; 76n969
    world paper money/Pick/76n970
Standard catalogue of Canadian coins, tokens and paper money/Charlton/75n1062
Standard dict of computers and info processing/Weik/78n1529
Standard educ almanac/Greene/75n658
Standard gd to pure-bred dogs/Glover/79 n1523
Standard hndbk for civil engineers/Merritt/ 77n1576
Standard hndbk for electrical engineers/ Fink/79n1546
Standard medical almanac/78n1417
Standard occupational classification manual/ 79n868/Index/79n866
Standard old book value gd/79n62
Standard periodical directory/78n18
Standard plant operators' manual/Elonka/76 n1646
Standard terms of the energy economy/79 n1390
Standards and practices for instrumentation/ Yothers/78n1543
Standards for . . .
    cataloging nonprint materials/Tillin/77 n261
    library service/Withers/76n123

Standards for . . . (cont'd)
    public libraries/75n187; 79n203
Standing liberty quarters/Cline/77n906
Stangl, M/Chilton's ency/77n1560
Stanley, W F/Birds of/75n1091
Stanley, W T/Broadway in/79n1021
Stanton, R J/Bibliography of modern/79 n1230
Stanwick, K/Political participation/78n447
Stapleton, M L/Sir John/76n1268
Stapper, M M/Samuel Taylor/79n1235
Star Trek concordance/Trimble/78n1087
Stark, F C/Whole seed/77n1557
Stark, N/Formula book/76n1645; 77n1313
Starr, J B/Post-liberation works/78n474
Starr, M P/Annual review microbiology/76 n1358
Starr, S F/Sources of/76n277
Start early for an early start/Johnson/77 n225
State administrative officials/78n459
State-approved schools of nursing L.P.N.- L.V.N./77n631
State-approved schools of nursing—R.N./76 n1538
State-by-state gd to women's legal rights/ Alexander/76n512
State census of North Carolina 1784-87/ Register/79n494
State constitutional conventions/Yarger/77 n522
State constitutional conventions, revisions, and amendments, 1959-76/Canning/78 n457
State consumer action/US Consumer Affairs Office/75n937
State elective officials and the legislatures/ 78n460
State government ref publications/Parish/75 n106
State information bk/Lukowski/78n461
State labor proceedings/Fink/78n767
State laws regulating the collecting of reptiles and amphibians in the US/Czajka/76 n1449
State library agencies/Simpson/79n168
Statesman's year-book/Paxton/75n87; 76 n77
Statistical abstract of Oklahoma/Dikeman/ 79n790
Statistical hist of the US/78n690
Statistical methods for librarians/Carpenter/ 79n336

Statistical survey of museums in the US and Canada/American Assoc of Museums/78n71
Statistical yearbook/77n761
Statistical yearbk of the US Dept of Housing and Urban Development/77n829
Statistics Africa/Harvey/79n789
Statistics sources/Wasserman/75n879; 78n687
Status of the world's nations/US Dept of State/75n324
Status of women/78n666
Staudacher, J M/Lector's gd/76n1102
Staudhammer, K P/Atlas of binary/75n1454
Steadman, J M/Milton ency/79n1250
Steady-state, zero growth and the academic library/Steele/79n200
Stedman's medical dict/77n1476
Steel, D/Encyclopedia of golf/76n748
Steel, D J/Sources for Roman/78n421
Steele, C/Independent Mexico/75n312/Major libraries/77n184/Steady-state/79n200
Stefanik, E C/John Berryman/76n1228
Steffek, E F/Marshall Cavendish/79n1541
Steiman, H/Guide to restaurants/78n530
Stein, G/Freethought in/79n1079
Stein, J/Random House/79n1104
Stein, R/Modern British/76n1263
Stein, S/Great pets! /77n1536
Stein, S J/Latin America/79n805
Steinberg, H/Angry buyer's/75n939
Steinberg, J/Camper's favorite/75n598
Steinberg, S H/Five hundred/75n49
Steinbrunner, C/Encyclopedia of mystery/77n1177
Steiner, R/Yearbook of Association/77n556; 79n582
Steingass, F A/Comprehensive Persian-/79n1145
Steinwedel, L W/Gun collector's/76n972
Stellhorn, P A/Directory of New/79n21
Stellingwerff, J/Developments in/79n197
Stember, S/Bicentennial guide/75n599
Stenesh, J/Dictionary of biochemistry/77n1331
Stenmark, D E/Minnesota multiphasic/78n1364
Stenton, M/Who's who British/78n482
Steph, J A/Educators guide/76n671
Stephane Mallarmé/Morris/79n1272
Stephans, H/Thomas Paine/78n443
Stephen, D/Encyclopedia of animals/76n1408
Stephen Spender, works and criticism/Kulkarni/78n1182
Stephens, H A/Woody plants/75n1469
Stephens, L D/Historiography/76n292
Stephens, R W B/International dictionaries/76n1353
Stephenson, D G/American constitutional/78n445
Stephenson, R W/Map collections/79n236
Steps to service: procedures for the school library media center/Nickel/76n150
Sterling, C H/Mass media/79n1166
Stern, E/Encyclopedia of archaeological/79n393
Stern, E L/Prescription drugs/77n1506
Stern, H R/Handbook of English-/75n1271
Stern, L/Stage mgmt/75n1182
Stern, S/Women composers/79n988
Sternfeld, F/Music in/75n1151/New Oxford/75n1148
Steven Caney's play book/Caney/76n764
Stevens, C/Biographical dict of phonetic/79n1157
Stevens, H/Southern almanac/79n391
Stevens, M/Sylvia Plath/79n1222
Stevens, N D/Essays for/76n211/Landmarks of/77n279/Librarian/77n281
Stevens, P/Modern English-/79n1261
Stevens, R B/Mycology guidebook/75n1488
Stevens, R D/Japanese and/78n250
Stevens, R E/Reference books/78n4
Stevens, R P/Historical dict Republic/76n248
Stevenson, I/Tony Award/77n985
Stevenson, M/Health/77n1454
Stevenson, M/User education/79n312
Stevenson, N C/Search &/79n470
Stevenson, R A/Complete book/75n1667
Stevenson, V/Encyclopedia of floristry/75n927
Stewart, C D/Taylors of/76n1201
Stewart, D/Exploring phenomenology/75n1238
Stewart, D E J/Handbook of Latin/75n296
Stewart, J/Filmarama/76n1070; 78n966
Stewart, R W/Disraeli's novels/76n1273
Stichting Druckwerk in de Marge/Bibliografie/79n41
Stickney, P J/World guide/75n665
Stidger, R W/Cost reduction/77n774
Stidworthy, J/Snakes of/76n1450
Stiegler, S E/Dictionary of earth/78n1352
Stiehl, U/Dictionary of book/79n44
Stiel, B/Corpus delicti/76n1207
Stigant, S A/J & P transformer/75n1790
Stillman, F/Songwriters' rhyming/76n1137
Stillman, R J/Guide to personal/76n878

Stillwell, R/Princeton ency/77n350
Stock, K F, & M/Bibliography of programming/75n1777
Stock photo and assignment source bk/McDarrah/78n884
Stock trader's almanac 1976/Hirsch/76n856
Stockholm International Peace Research Institute/Arms trade/76n870/SIPRI yearbook/76n505
Stockney, B/Coins and/75n1071
Stoddard, R/Stage scenery/78n931/Theatre and/79n1011
Stoffer, J Y/Science fair/76n1328
Stoffle, C J/Administration of/75n214
Stogdill, R M/Handbook of leadership/75n797
Stone, E W/American library/78n263/Continuing education/78n254
Stone, R M/African music/77n962
Stone Soup, a Collective/Green world/77n1561
Stoneflies, or Plecoptera, of Illinois/Frison/76n1440
Stonehouse, M L/Science and/75n175; 76n148
Stoner, C/Organic directory/76n885
Stoops, E/Handbook of educat'l/77n639
Stopout! /Mitchell/79n643
Storey, E/World of/77n436
Storey, J/AAAS science/79n1294
Storey, R L/Chronology of/75n353
Storia dell'arte italiana: index/Venturi/77n871
Stories to tell to children/Cathon/75n198
Storrer, W A/Architecture of/79n893
Story key to geographic names/von Engeln/77n553
Story of a small town library/Rogers/75n270
Story of books and libraries/Rider/77n282
Storytelling/Baker/79n205
Storzer, G H/Dictionary of modern/78n1054
Stout, A M & J H/Backpacking with/76n722
Stout, D F/Handbook of operational/77n1601
Stowe, M E/How to get/75n515
Stowell, M B/Early American/78n40
Strable, E G/Special libraries/76n165
Strange artifacts/Corliss/75n401
Strange phenomena/Corliss/75n91
Strassburg, R/Roy Harris/75n1159
Strassburger, R B/Pennsylvania German/76n442
Strassfeld, M & S/Second Jewish/78n390
Strategies for change in info programs/Hug/75n140
Stratigraphic atlas of North and Central America/Cook/78n513

Stratton, C/Handbook of English/77n1088
Stratton, C/International horseman's/76n1566
Stratton, D/Mugs and/78n873
Straub, C P/CRC handbook/75n1536
Strauss, B/How to get/75n515
Strauss, H J/Handbook for chemical/77n1335
Street where you live: St. Paul/Empson/76n548
Streips, L/Latvians in/75n820
Strharsky, H/Bibliographical notes military/76n497/Bibliographical notes transnational/76n828
String music in print/Farish/75n1125
Stringer, M/Identification guide/79n710
Strip mining/Munn/75n1814
Strip-mining for coal/Tompkins/75n1815
Stroebel, L/Dictionary of contemporary/75n1115
Strom, M G/Library services/78n237
Strong women/Rosenfelt/78n599
Stroynowski, J/Who's who socialist/79n143
Strugnell, C/Adjustment to/75n852
Strung, N/Complete hunter's/79n721/Encyclopedia of knives/77n894
Strunsky, R/Catalogue of American/76n918
Stryker-Rodda, K/Buried genealogical/78n411/NY manuscripts/75n428/Register of/79n496
Stuart, A W/North Carolina/76n531
Stuart, M/Scottish family/79n499
Stuart, S L/Who won/79n100
Stuckey, M/Western treebook/79n1362
Student activities in secondary schools/75n648
Student adventure travel & study, USA/Rowland/77n562
Student Africanist's hndbk/Hartwig/76n246
Student aid—annual/76n654
Student teaching/Tittle/75n659
Student's English-Sanskrit dict/Apte/75n1281
Student's gd for writing college papers/Turabian/78n105
Student's gd to leftist periodicals/Landwehr/76n25
Studer, J H/Studer's popular/78n1322
Studer's popular ornithology/Studer/78n1322
Studies in library mgmt/Holroyd/76n178; 77n247; 78n209
Studies of Chinese religion/Thompson/77n1034

Studio dict of design and decoration/75n1023
Study abroad/76n615
Study and teaching of anthropology within academic institutions/Dwyer-Shick/77n737
Study gd for emergency medical and drug abuse technicians/Patterson/75n1633
Study gd to Steinbeck/Hayashi/75n1368
Study of international politics/LaBarr/77n529
Study of internat'l relations/Pfaltzgraff/78n487
Study of names in lit/Rajec/79n1182
Stueart, R D/Library mgmt/78n212
Sturge, J M/Neblette's handbook/78n885
Stutley, J & M/Harper's dict/78n983
Styer, R A/Encyclopedia of hockey/75n772
Style manual for citing microform and nonprint media/Fleischer/79n129
Stylebook-editorial manual/78n1382
Su, P Y/Random House/79n1104
Sub-aqua illust'd dict/Zanelli/78n634
Subject approach to info/Foskett/79n270
Subject bibliog of Soviet semiotics/Eimermacher/78n1025
Subject bibliog of the Second World War/Enser/78n330
Subject collections/Ash/76n131
Subject cross ref guide/77n260
Subject description of books/Settel/79n282
Subject directory of special libraries and info centers/Young/76n172; 78n201
Subject guide to . . .
    books in print/77n19; 79n8
    Canadian books in print/Bohne/75n9
    children's books in print/75n197; 76n155
    humor/Kujoth/77n1141
    microforms in print/Walsh/79n42
Subject index to poetry for children and young people/Smith/79n1195
Subject keyword index to LC classification schedules/Olson/79n281
Submarines, diving, and the underwater world/Anderson/76n1687
Submarines of World War Two/Bagnasco/79n1598
Subrahmaniam, K/Multivariate analysis/75n874
Sub-Saharan Africa/Skurnik/78n292
Sudden infant death syndrome/Archuleta/76n1512
Suffolk parochial libraries/79n177
Sugar, B R/Sports collectors/79n696
Sugden, V M/Graduate thesis/75n696

Sugerman, A/Horse owner's/78n1464
Suggestions for a basic economics library/Leamer/75n200
Suicide: selective bibliog/Prentice/76n772
Suit your spirit: travel guidebks/76n540
Suitable for children?/Tucker/77n1165
Suiter, P/Handbook in diagnostic/76n690
Sukhwal, B L/South Asia/76n523
Sulentic, J W/Revised new/75n1446
Sullivan, E J/Guide to evaluation/76n650
Sullivan, G/Pro football/76n739
Sullivan, L E/Encyclopedia of governmental/76n481
Sullivan, L R/Chinese communist/78n473
Sullivan, M C/Flannery O'Connor/78n1123
Sullivan, P/Carl H. Milam/77n284/Opportunities in/78n259
Sullivan, R C/Reprographic services/77n286
Sumek, L/Environmental mgmt/75n1526
Summary bibliog of the hist of the universities of Great Britain and Ireland up to 1800/Gabriel/75n645
Summary of school statistics by county/75n686
Summer & fall wildflowers of New England/Dwelley/79n1342
Summer employment directory of the US/Leith/77n842/O'Brien/79n867
Summer study abroad/Cohen/77n590
Summerhays' ency for horsemen/Summerhays/77n1537
Summers, W I/NFPA hndbk/76n1634
Summers, W K/Ground water/75n1527/Isotopes of/77n1430
Sumrall, R O/Map abstract/79n742
Sun, N & R Q/Asian animal/75n1607
Suniewick, N/Women/75n843; 76n786
Sunlight on the southside/Bell/75n407
Sunnucks, A/Encyclopaedia of chess/78n622
Sunrise and sunset tables for key cities and weather stations of the US/78n1354
Sunset travel gd to Southern Calif/75n617
Super catalog of car parts and accessories/Hirsch/75n1732
Super dict/Holmes/79n1110
Superfilms/Parlato/77n1013
Superka, D P/Values education/77n646
Supplement to . . .
    Ernest Hemingway/Hanneman/76n1239
    reference catalogue of Indian bks in print in English/Prasher/76n18
    the directory of community resources available in Kalamazoo County/Chapman/75n513

Supplement to . . . (cont'd)
   the Oxford companion to Canadian hist
     and literature/Toye/75n1412
   the Oxford English dict/Burchfield/77
     n1073
   top 10's and trivia of rock & roll and
     rhythm & blues 1950-73/Edwards/76
     n1024
Surfer's almanac/Filosa/78n632
Surgery annual/Nyhus/77n1489
Survey of . . .
   American genealogical periodicals and periodical indexes/Sperry/79n472
   commercially available computer-readable bibliographic data bases/Schneider/75n283
   materials for the study of the uncommonly taught languages/Johnson/78n1026
   musical instruments/Marcuse/76n1017
   research in demography/Desai/77n756
   research in sociology and social anthropology/77n701; 77n702
   school media standards/Jones/79n670
Surveys in parapsychology/White/77n1452
Survival themes in fict for children and young people/Wilkin/79n1197
Suryakanta/Sanskrit-Hindi-/77n1098
Sussman, J/US info/75n209
Sussman, M B/Author's guide/79n737
Sutherland, E W/Everyman's guide/76n1550
Sutherland, Z/Children and/79n218
Suttles, P H/Elementary teachers/76n676; 79n689
Suttles, S A/Educators guide/76n674
Sutton, A/Wilderness areas/75n637
Sutton, I/Indian land/76n806
Sutton, M/Wilderness areas/75n637
Sutton, R M/Manuscripts guide/77n28
Suzuki, Y/Issues in/75n218
Sviridov, F A/Publications on/76n229
Swan, H/Who's who fiction?/77n1178
Swan, M/Research in/79n636
Swan, S B/Winterthur guide/78n880
Swanborough, G/Civil aircraft/76n1661/Military aircraft/77n1640/Observer's Soviet/77n1638/Observer's world/76n1660/US Navy/78n1577
Swanfeldt, A/Crossword puzzle/78n1047
Swank, R C/Japanese and/78n250
Swans of the world/Wilmore/76n1433
Swanson, A Q/Women and/76n791
Swanson, D R/Management education/75n215
Swartz, O D/Service etiquette/78n1563
Swedlund, C/Photography/75n1116

Swedrup, I/Pocket ency/77n1538
Sween, R D/Bibliography of science/75n1329
Sweeney, M J/Serials updating/79n191
Sweet and lowdown: pop song writers/Craig/79n985
Sweet home Chicago/Banes/75n602
Sweetser, W/Bibliography of Arthur/75n1391
Swetnam, G/Guidebook to historic/78n360
Swidan, E A/Reference books/79n178
Swift, E M/Vermont place-names/78n535
Swift, L H/Botanical classifications/76n1371
Swigger, B K/Guide to resources/78n354
Swindler, W F/Sources and/75n566; 79n536
Switzer, R/Follett vest-/79n1136
Sybil Leek's bk of herbs/Leek/75n1483
Sykes, J/Forest fertilization/77n1321/White water-/77n1322
Sykes, J B/Concise Oxford/77n1074
Sylvia Plath/Lane/79n1222
Sylvia Porter's money book/Porter/76n877
Symbolism/Anderson/77n1124
Symmetry and separation of variables/Miller/78n1226
Symptoms /Miller/77n1496
Syndicated columnists/Weiner/76n1173
Synerjy: energy alternatives/79n1391
Synge, P M/Color dictionary/76n1587
Syntactical and critical concordance to the Greek text of Baruch and the Epistle of Jeremiah/Martin/79n1070
Sypher, F J/Reader's adviser/78n1090
System for inter-library communication/Association of Research Libraries/75n232
Systematic discography/Foreman/75n1135
Systematic process for planning media programs/Liesener/78n186
Systems analysis in libraries/Gough/79n254
Systems analysis in water resources planning/Meta Systems/76n1473
Systems approach to library program development/Goldberg/78n207
Szajkowski, Z/Illustrated sourcebk/79n438
Széplaki, J/Hungarians in/76n408/Louis Kossuth/77n382
Szigethy, M C/Maurice Falcolm/75n151
Szladits, L L/Owen D. Young/75n69
Szwed, J F/Afro-American folk/79n453
Szykitka, W/Public works/75n96

T. E. Lawrence/Meyers/76n1277
T. L. Yuan bibliog of Western writings on Chinese art and archaeology/Vanderstappen/77n865

Taber's cyclopedic medical dict/Thomas/78 n1400
Tables and charts of equilibrium normal shock & shock-tube solutions for helium-hydrodgen [sic] mixtures with velocities to 70 km./sec./Miller/76n1607
Tables of physical and chemical constants and some math functions/Kaye/75n1458
Tabulation of infrared spectral data/Dolphin/79n1321
Taggart, D T/Guide to sources/76n686
Taggart, J E/Motorboat, yacht/75n1831
Taggart, R/Minorities in/76n391
Tahoe Sierra/Schaffer/76n721
Tairas, J N B/Indonesia/77n327
Taiwan demography 1946-71/Chang/75n871
Take care of yourself/Vickery/78n1432
Take it off! tax deductions/Holzman/75 n983
Talbot, J M/Comprehensive Chicano/75 n824
Talbot-Booth, E C/Talbot-Booth's/79n1588
Talbot-Booth's merchant ships/Talbot-Booth/79n1588
Tales from Spanish picaresque novels/Childers/79n1286
Talking book topics/79n339
Talking books adult/79n340
Tall oil/Pollock/78n1259
Tambs, L A/African and/77n431/East European/76n821/Historiography, method/76n284
Tampion, J/Dangerous plants/78n1282
Tandberg, G/Research guide/76n1178
Tanganyika African national union/Howell/78 n293
Tanis, N E/Cost analysis/79n256/Native Americans/76n805/Problems in/75n212
Tank facts and feats/Macksey/76n1685
Tanks & transport vehicles: WWII/Vanderveen/76n1686
Tannen, J/How to identify/77n65
Tannenbaum, J/NY art/78n796
Tanner, C/Official major/75n734
Tanner, H H/Ojibwas/77n745
Tanner, J/Badges and/76n1678
Tanselle, G T/Checklist of editions/78n1146
Tarbert, G C/Biographical dictionaries/76 n91; 77n120/Book review/75n32; 76n31; 76n32; 76n33; 78n21/Children's book/76 n1196; 77n1147; 79n1196
Tarr, A/Reference and/79n295
Tarr, D W/Modules in/75n459
Tarr, Y/Up-with-/77n1550

Taster's gd to beer/Weiner/78n1461
Taubert, S/Book trade/77n51
Taulbee, E S/Minnesota multiphasic/78n1364
Tawerilmang, A F/Woleaian-English/78n1072
Tax, S/Serial publications/75n869
Tax desk bk for farming and ranching/Wheeler/77n855
Tax gd for buying and selling a business/Hagendorf/77n854
Tayler, A/Theatre in/75n1183
Tayleur, B/Encyclopedia of antique/75 n1054
Taylor, C A/Atlas of optical/77n1338
Taylor, C J H/New guide/79n641
Taylor, D V/Blacks in/77n437
Taylor, E/Directory of art/76n960
Taylor, G/Trees and/75n1490
Taylor, J/Directory of foundations/79n92
Taylor, J W R/Air facts/76n1683; 79n1590/Civil aircraft/76n1661/Helicopters of/78 n1508/Jane's all/79n1589/Jane's pocket book combat/75n1845/Jane's pocket book commercial/75n1821/Jane's pocket book home-/79n1550/Jane's pocket book remotely/79n1594/Military aircraft/77 n1640/Missiles of/78n1571
Taylor, K/Selling your/75n1038
Taylor, L J/Librarian's handbook/79n175
Taylor, M/Basic reference/75n246
Taylor, M J H/Air facts/76n1683; 79n1590/Helicopters of/78n1508/Jane's pocket book combat/75n1845/Jane's pocket book commercial/75n1821/Jane's pocket book home-/79n1550/Missiles of/78n1571
Taylor, M L/Handbook on internat'l/77 n589; 78n574
Taylor, P J/Essays on/79n317/Library and/78n132
Taylor, R A/Littérature occitane/79n1274
Taylor, R B/Dr. Taylor's/78n1418
Taylor, R L/Directory of institutions/77 n175
Taylor, R S/Curriculum design/75n264
Taylor, T A/Great spy/75n1198
Taylor, T F/Thematic catalog/78n910
Taylor, W/Flowers of/79n1343
Taylors of Ongar/Stewart/76n1201
Tchen, M D/Guide to holdings/75n864
Tchobanoglous, G/Wastewater mgmt/77n1421
Teacher brothers' modern-day almanac/79 n108
Teacher training bibliog/77n583
Teachers' centers exchange directory/Lance/78n559

Teachers guides to TV/Kirschner/79n1180
Teacher's resource hndbk for Latin American studies/Hawkins/77n340
Teacher's word bk of the 20,000 words found most frequently and widely in general reading for children & young people/Thorndike/77n586
Teaching abroad/Cohen/78n572
Teaching English as a second language/ Goldstein/76n678
Teaching media skills/Walker/78n188
Teaching the Holocaust to children/Roskies/ 76n685
Teaching with books/Branscomb/75n178
Teaching yourself in libraries/Shapiro/79 n217
Teague, S J/Microform librarianship/79n335
Team piano repertoire/Chang/77n952
Teasdale, M S/Handbook of 20th/78n914
Tebbel, J/History of book/76n43; 79n31
Technical gd to computer-communications interface stds/US Natl Bureau of Stds/75 n1778
Technician educ yearbk/76n605
Technique and practice of intensive psychotherapy/Chessick/75n1578
Technique of psychoanalytic psychotherapy/ Langs/75n1592
Technology math handbk/Tuma/76n1334
Tega, V G/Management and/78n704
Tegland, J/Significant American artists/77 n125/Significant American entertainers/ 77n129
Telescope hndbk and star atlas/Howard/76 n1337
Television contacts/77n1119
Television drama series programming/Gianakos/ 79n1178
Television factbook/78n1086
Telfer, D/Wildflowers of/78n1288
Telling stories to children/Ziskind/77n230
10 bibliographies of 20th cent Russian lit/ Moody/79n1284
TenBrink, T D/Evaluation: gd for teachers/ 75n717
Tennenhouse, M A/Contemporary authors/75 n119
Tennessee history/Smith/76n353
Tennessee legal research hndbk/Laska/79n573
Tennessee records/Acklen/75n405
Tennessee Valley Authority/Flood damage/75 n1756
Tenney, M C/Zondervan pictorial/76n1104
Tenney, T A/Mark Twain/78n1152

Tennill, C/Uniformed services/77n1633
Tennis catalog/Duggan/79n730
Tennis player's vacation gd/Klein/75n585
Tennyson, E J & G B/Index to 19th-/78 n1107
Tepper, M/Emigrants to/76n443; 78n414/ Immigrants to/79n497/Passengers to/78 n413
Tepperman, B/Eric Dolphy/75n1164
Terminals review/75n967
Terminology of communication disorders/ Nicolosi/79n1175
Terminology of documentation/Wersig/77 n172
Terms of literary study/Peer/75n1318
Terrace, V/Complete ency TV/77n1120
Terrace gardener's hndbk/Yang/76n1602
Terrall, M/France/75n309
Terrell, E E/Checklist of names/79n1340
Terrell, J U/American Indian/76n811
Terrorism: selected bibliog/Boston/78n642
Terry, W/Ballet guide/76n1040; 78n935
Teschner, R V/Diccionario del/79n1150
Tessier, J A/Feasibility of/79n266
Tested secretarial techniques for getting things done/Simpson/75n893
Tests in print II/Buros/75n1601
Tett, N/Professional organizations/77n88
Texas collection of comedias sueltas/Boyer/ 79n1006
Texas ref sources/77n521
Texas sources/Wright/78n316
Texas trade and prof associations and other selected organizations/Wright/78n712
Text-atlas of hematology/Block/77n1455
Textile hndbk/76n879
Thackeray and his 20th-cent critics/Olmsted/78n1183
Thailand: annotated bibliog of bibliographies/ Hart/78n301
Thailand: complete guide/Duncan/77n564
Thatcher, D S/Musical settings/77n954
Thayer, J H/Greek-English/78n998
Theatre and cinema architecture/Stoddard/ 79n1011
Theatre-drama & speech index/76n1044
Theatre in Britain/Roberts/75n1183
Theatre lighting/Wehlburg/77n993
Thematic catalogue of the works of Giovanni Battista Sammartini/Jenkins/78n908
Thematic catalog of the works of Jeremiah Clarke/Taylor/78n910
Thematic index to the works of Benedetto Pallavicino/Flanders/76n1007

Theodore Dreiser/Pizer/76n1233
Theodore Roethke's career/Moul/78n1148
Theodore Schroeder/McCoy/75n1296
Theological dict of the Old Testament/ Botterweck/76n1096; 79n1064/Pitkin/ 77n1048
Theory of info and coding/McEliece/78n1225
Theory of partitions/Andrews/78n1224
Theosophical glossary/Blavatsky/75n1234
Thesauri & thesauri construction/MacCafferty/ 79n1090
Thesaurus of . . .
    agricultural terms as used in the bibliog of agriculture from data provided by the Natl Agricul'l Library, US Dept of Agriculture/77n1517
    descriptors used for info processing in the ILO Library/77n171
    ERIC descriptors/Goodman/76n593
    information sci terminology/Schultz/79 n161
    psychological index terms/Kinkade/76 n1495
    sociological research terminology/van de Merwe/75n795
    terms in mortgage and consumer credit/ Miller/79n872
Thevet, A/Vrais pourtraits/75n120
Thewlis, J/Encyclopaedic dict/77n1337
They went thataway/Hamlin/75n418
Thibault, C/Bibliographia Canadiana/75n394
Thiele, V F/Nutrition and/76n1525
Thiers, HD/California mushrooms/76n1399
Thilman, B/1500 largest/76n892
Thin-layer chromatography abstracts/Scott/ 75n1453
Things your mother never taught you/Slater/ 75n1799
Think metric now! /Hartsuch/75n1715
Third, B J/Business periodicals/76n839
Third census of Finnegans Wake/Glasheen/78 n1177
Thoburn, T/Golden picture/78n1030
Thomae, B K/Legal secretary's/78n501
Thomas, C L/Taber's cyclopedic/78n1400
Thomas, J/Universal pronouncing/77n1056
Thomas, J B/International dict/79n639
Thomas, J L/Turning kids/79n219
Thomas, J L/Wildflowers of/75n1475
Thomas, J R/Completed research/78n606
Thomas, R C/Book review/75n33
Thomas, S M/Guide to sources/75n935
Thomas, W A/Biological indicators/75n1528
Thomas-Stanford, C/Early editions/78n63

Thomas Bray's grand design/Laugher/75 n268
Thomas Eakins collection of the Hirshhorn Museum and Sculpture Garden/Rosenzweig/78n787
Thomas Frognall Dibdin/Neuberg/79n187
Thomas grocery register/77n830
Thomas Hardy/Purdy/79n1241
Thomas Merton/Breit/75n1215/Dell'Isola/76 n1073
Thomas Paine collection of Richard Gimbel in the Library of the Amer Philosophical Soc/ Stephans/78n443
Thomas Wolfe/Phillipson/78n1153/Reeves/76 n1254
Thomassen, C E/CATV and/75n242
Thomison, D/History of American/79n329/ Library science/75n150
Thompson, A M C/Bibliography of nursing/ 75n1619
Thompson, B G/Fisheries of/75n969
Thompson, D/Atlas of Maryland/79n593/ Economic and/76n491
Thompson, D E/Indiana authors/76n354
Thompson, E T/Local history/79n176
Thompson, G/Planning and/75n145; 79 n260
Thompson, J/History of principles/79n156/ Introduction to university/75n182/Library power/75n146
Thompson, J W/Index to illustrations/78n1277
Thompson, L G/Studies of Chinese/77n1034
Thompson, L S/Bibliography of dissertations/ 78n551/Bibliography of French/76n365/ Medical terminology/79n1464/New Sabin/ 75n5; 77n20; 77n21
Thompson, R/Illustrated ency country/78 n917
Thompson, S/Folktale/78n1015
Thompson, S C/Official ency/77n678
Thompson, T/Saloon/77n1521
Thompson, V/Historical dict/76n250
Thompson, V H/Eudora Welty/77n1215
Thomson, C W/Resource gd/76n1077
Thomson, D/Biographical dict/77n1017
Thomson, O S/Spring flora/77n1352
Thomson, S R/Kate Greenaway/78n1161
Thomson, S K/Interlibrary loan/76n202/ Learning resource/77n206
Thomson, T R/Catalogue of British/78 n422
Thomson, W A R/Black's medical/76n1522; 77n1470/Medicines from/79n1354/Thomson's concise/75n1625

Thomson's concise medical dict/Thomson/75 n1625
Thorburn's birds/Fisher/77n1377
Thoreau MacDonald/Edison/75n991
Thorelli, H B & S V/Consumer information/ 75n936
Thornberry, T P/Criminology index/76n780
Thorndike, D/Thorndike ency/75n958
Thorndike, E L/Scott, Foresman/77n1078/ Teacher's word/77n586/Thorndike Barnhart/ 76n1122
Thorndike Barnhart intermediate dict/Thorndike/76n1122
Thorndike ency of banking & financial tables/ Thorndike/75n958
Thornhill, R/Collector's guide rocks/77n1440
Thorny paradise/Blishen/77n1145
Thorum, A R/Instructional materials/77n644
Thoyts, E E/How to decipher/77n287
Three contemporary novelists/Scotto/78 n1124
300 most abused drugs/Bludworth/75n1653
Thrill sports catalog/78n605
Thuronyi, G T/Antarctic bibliog/78n1203; 79 n1307
Tice, T N/Employee relations/79n857
Tidwell, W D/Common fossil/76n1386
Tiedeman, D V/Key resources/78n570
Tifft, W G/Revised new/75n1446
Tillin, A M/Managing multimedia/78n208/ Standards for/77n261
Tilson, A/Mail order/78n1478
Time-Life bk of the family car/75n1737
Time research/Zelkind/76n1491
Time-saver stds for architectural design data/ Callender/75n1015
Times atlas of . . .
China/Geelan/76n535
the world/76n529
world history/Barraclough/79n583
Timetables of history/Grun/76n305
Timperley, C H/Encyclopaedia of literary/78 n42
Tindale, N B/Aboriginal tribes/75n870
Tindall, J R/Collector's guide/77n1440
Tinker, C B/Translations of/76n1267
Tischler, A/Karel Boleslav/76n1011
Titcombe, R M/Handbook for professional/75 n787
Title gd to the talkies/Aros/78n954
Titles in series/Baer/75n2
Titles of English books/Allison/77n333; 78n9
Titratsoo, E N/Oilfields of/75n1566
Tittle, C K/Student teaching/75n659

To know a library/Gore/79n194
Todd, D K/Polluted groundwater/77n1423/ Water publications/77n1428
Todd, H N/Dictionary of contemporary/75 n1115
Todd, J M/Mary Wollstonecraft/77n1250
Toguchi, M/Complete gd acupuncture/75 n1634
Token coinage of Guatemala/Clark/75n1063
Tolkien companion/Tyler/77n1248
Toll of independence/Peckham/76n335
Tollers, V L/Bibliography of Matthew/76 n1266
Tolzmann, D H/German-American/78n1191/ German-Americana/76n407
Tom Swift and his electric English teacher/ Poteet/75n708
Tomikel, J/Edible wild/75n1470
Tominaga, T T/Iris Murdoch/77n1221
Tomkinson, G S/Select bibliog/77n56
Tomlinson, J C/Guide to graduate/76n665
Tompkins, D C/Court organization/75n549/ Furlough from/75n840/Selection of/75 n497/Strip-mining/75n1815
Tompkins, M/Serials in/77n1445
Tony Award/Stevenson/77n985
Tool and mfg'ing engineers hndbk/Dallas/77 n1611
Toom, E/Applied science/76n1325
Toomey, A F/World bibliog/78n5
Top 10's and trivia of rock & roll and rhythm & blues 1950-73/Edwards/76n1023
Topical Bible concordance/Miller/78n993
Topical gd to the Scriptures of the Church of Jesus Christ of Latter-Day Saints/79 n1073
Topical index and digest of the Bible/Monser/ 75n1231
Topics-aids: biology/Egan/79n682
Topics and terms in environmental problems/ Holum/79n1398
Torbert, E C/Cervantes' place-/79n1293
Toshokan/Welch/77n272
Total bk of house plants/Mott/76n1598
Totten, H L/Administrative aspects/76n220
Totterdell, B/Effective library/77n215
Tou, J T/Advances in/78n1520/Information systems/76n237
Tougas, G/Checklist of printed/75n1411
Tourguide to the Rocky Mtn wilderness/ Bridge/76n716
Tourist business/Lundberg/77n828
Tourist gd to Mount McKinley/Washburn/75 n618

Tourville, E A/Alaska/75n387
Towle, L C/Genealogical periodical/79n473
Townsend, L/South Carolina/75n431
Townsend, S/Amateur navigator's/75n752
Township atlas of the US/Andriot/78n462
Toxic substances sourcebook/79n1402
Toye, W/Supplement to/75n1412
Tracey, K/Herbert Hoover/78n448
Tracing, charting and writing your family history/Skalka/76n422
Tracing your ancestry: logbook/Helmbold/77n451/Tracing your ancestry: step-by-step gd/Helmbold/77n450
Tracy, J/Encyclopaedia Sherlockiana/78n1172
Trade names dict/Crowley/77n787
Trade yearbook/78n740
Trademarks and brand mgmt/Hill/78n741
Trademarks & symbols/Kuwayama/75n963
Trademarks: official trademark lit/Kase/75n962
Traditional medicine/Harrison/77n1462
Tragatsch, E/Complete illust'd/78n1515
Tragedy of Julius Caesar/Velz/79n1253
Trailer Life's recreational vehicle campground & services guide/75n600
Trailer Life's RV campground & services directory/76n723; 77n689
Training and developmt organizations directory/Wasserman/79n814
Training film profiles/76n687
Training programs and placement services: severely handicapped/Appleby/79n852
Transistor ignition systems/Brant/77n1572
Translations of Beowulf/Tinker/76n1267
Translator referral directory/77n1064
Transportation and traffic engineering hndbk/Baerwald/77n1618
Transportation costs and costing/Ocran/76n825
Transportation economics/Rakowski/77n771
Transportation libraries in the US & Canada/79n242
Transportation system mgmt/Oram/77n1620
Tratner, A A/Geothermal world/79n1403
Traub, L/Alternatives to/76n622
Traue, J E/Who's who New/79n144
Travel guidebks in review/Heise/79n598
Travel market yearbk/77n831
Travel marketing/Noe/79n847
Travel research bibliog/Goeldner/78n742
Travelers' gd to US-certified doctors abroad/77n1482
Traveling F.M. radio gd/Krompotich/78n1082
Traveller's gd to North American gardens/Logan/75n633
Travis, C/Periodicals from/78n277
Traylor, C T/Atlas ofsMississippi/75n574
Treasure, G R R/Who's who history/76n371
Treasure trove: bks concerning sunken gold, lost mines, & buried treasure/Underbrink/76n957
Treasurer's hndbk/Weston/78n722
Treasures from the Bodleian Library/Hassall/77n29
Treasures from the earth/Shaub/76n1482
Treasures of Britain and treasures of Ireland/78n534
Treasures of Italy/Dogo/78n531
Treasury of houseplants/Herwig/77n1554
Treat, R/Encyclopedia of football/78n626
Treaties & agreements with and concerning China/MacMurray/75n536
Treaties and alliances of the world/75n543
Treaties in force/US Dept of State/78n489
Treaty profiles/Rohn/77n530
Trees and bushes of Europe/Polunin/78n1307
Trees & shrubs/Gorer/78n1492
Trees and shrubs hardy in the British Isles/Bean/75n1490
Trees and shrubs of the US/Little/78n1306
Trees around us/Barber/76n1400
Trees of ...
  East Texas/Vines/78n1308
  North America and Europe/Phillips/79n1363
  the West/Crittenden/79n1359
  the world/Leathart/79n1360
Trejo, A D/Bibliografia Chicana/76n404/Quien es/75n185
Treves, R/Homeowner's complete/75n1800
Tribe, I/Mushrooms in/79n1356
Tribune almanac & political register for 1876/76n308
Triche, C W & D S/Euthanasia controversy/77n1467/Population and/76n813/Sickle cell/75n1620; 77n1468
Trigg, M G/Dance directory/79n1017
Trillo, R L/Jane's ocean/79n1545
Trilobites: photographic atlas/Levi-Setti/76n1363
Trimble, B/Star Trek/78n1087
Tripp, E/Meridian hndbk/75n1242
Tripp, M J/Senior citizens/79n843
Troisi, J/Santals/77n746
Tronik, R/Israeli periodicals/75n20
Tropical fish/Halstead/76n1558
Tropical marine aquaria/Cox/75n1666
Tropical marine aquarium/Hargreaves/79n701

Tropical marine fishes/Zeiller/76n1438
Trotsky, J/News dictionary/76n467; 77n498
Troy, L M/Barron's guide law/79n657
Trueba, H T/Bilingual bicultural/78n548
Truitt, D/Dolphins and/75n1521
Truitt, E M/Who was who/75n1212; 78n967
Trumbull, J H/Indian names/75n457
Trump, D/Penguin dictionary/77n348
Trustee$ of wealth/Brodsky/77n595
Try us, 1975: natl minority business directory/76n837
Trzyna, T C/California hndbk/76n492/Consumer protection/76n871/Directory of consumer/75n932/Population/77n713/World directory/78n1348/World food/78n1481
Tseng, H P/Law schools/79n572
Tsuda, N/Handbook of Japanese/78n797
Tsuneishi, W M/Issues in/75n218
Tubangui, H R/Catalog of Filipiniana/76n279
Tubesing, R/Architectural preservation/79n894
Tuck, D H/Encyclopedia of sci-fict/75n1330; 79n1204
Tuck, J N/Héroes de/75n374
Tucker, B/Who's who graphology/78n1378
Tucker, K/Bibliography of writings/78n932
Tucker, M/Modern British/76n1263/Modern Commonwealth/79n1184
Tucker, N/Suitable for/77n1165
Tudor, D/Annual index/75n1169; 77n976; 77n977/Canadian book/77n196/Cooking for/77n1551/Popular music/75n1172; 77n983/Wine, beer/77n1522
Tudor, N/Canadian book/77n196/Canadian essay/77n1135/Cooking for/77n1551/Popular music/75n1172
Tukey, J W/Index to statistics/75n877; 75n878; 76n819
Tully, G/France/76n560/Mexico/77n569
Tuma, J J/Technology math/76n1334
Tune in yesterday: old-time radio/Dunning/78n1081
Tung, W L/Chinese in/75n825
Tunney, C/Purnell's illus'd/78n516
Tuohy, J/Collector's guide/77n943
Tupper, H A/Encyclopedia of missions/76n1081
Turabian, K L/Student's guide/78n105
Turfgrass bibliog from 1672 to 1972/Beard/79n1347
Turgeon, C/New Larousse/78n1476
Turick, D/Community information/79n292

Turkin, H/Official ency/77n678
Turkish phrase book/Selim/75n1285
Turleau, C/Clinical atlas/79n1444
Turley, R V/Information sources/77n1287
Turn-of-the-century antiques/Mackay/75n1056
Turner, A/Scientific instruments/77n1279
Turner, A C/Index to LC/76n190
Turner, E G/Typology of/79n70
Turner, H W/Bibliography of new/78n977
Turner, J B/Encyclopedia of social/78n647
Turner, M/Observer's book/78n1513
Turner, N/National directory/75n1185; 76n1043
Turner, P/Afro-American singers/79n977
Turner, P/Index to handicrafts/76n955/Index to outdoor/79n699
Turner, R/Grants register/76n612
Turner, R/Retrospective index/78n1222
Turning kids on to print using nonprint/Thomas/79n219
Turton, W H/Plantagenet ancestry/76n444
Tuska, J/Close up/78n968
Tussing, R-E/French XX/79n1266
Tuve, G L/Handbook of tables/75n1713
TV season/David/77n1116
TV soap opera almanac/Lackmann/77n1118
Tver, D F/Gulf Publishing/75n886
Twedt, D W/Personality research/78n745
Tweedie, M/Atlas of insects/75n1518
Tweney, G H/Jack London/75n1360
Twentieth-century . . .
 Chinese writers and their pen names/Chu/78n1185
 criticism/Handy/75n1320
 English novel/Cassis/78n1162
 harpsichord music/Bedford/75n1120
 literary criticism/Bryfonski/79n1183
 music for trumpet & orchestra/Carnovale/76n1013
 opera in England and the US/Northouse/77n973
 short story explication/Walker/75n1331; 78n1108
 Spanish-American novel/Foster/76n1300
20,000 words: spelled & divided for quick ref/Leslie/78n1048
Twitchett, D C/Times atlas/76n535
201 Chinese verbs/Ching/79n1130
2001 Spanish and English idioms/Savaiano/77n1101
Two world wars/Mayer/78n326
Tyler, J A/Concordance to fables/75n1418
Tyler, J E A/Tolkien companion/77n1248

Tyler, J W/Connecticut loyalists/78n415
Tymchuk, A J/Mental retardation/75n1585
Tymm, M B/Research gd science/79n1205
Tyndalo, V/Complete bk mushrooms/75 n1489
Type for books/77n885
Type specimen book/76n44
Typographical gazetteer/Cotton/77n881
Typology of the early Codex/Turner/79 n70
Tyrkiel, E F/Dictionary of physical/79n1578
Tysse, A/International educ/75n649; 78 n549

Ubell, A/Recipes for/75n1801
Uden, G/Longman illust'd/77n356
Udvardy, M D F/Audubon Society/78n1323
Uganda, G/79n362
Uhr, E B/Social responsibility/78n744
Ujifusa, G/Almanac of American/75n480; 76 n474
Ukraine: selected refs in the English language/ Weres/75n308
Ukrainian Republic in the great East-European Revolution/Pidhainy/76n375
Ukrainians in America/Wertsman/77n447
Ukrainians in North America/Shtohryn/76 n107
Ulrich's internat'l periodicals directory/ 75n27; 76n27; 79n20
Umlauf, H/Good Housekeeping/78n670
Underbrink, R L/Treasure trove/76n957
Underground buying gd for hams, CBers, experimenters and computer hobbyists/ King/78n749
Undergrounds: union list of alternative periodicals in libraries of the US & Canada/ Danky/75n99
Underhill, C S/Handy key/78n1278
Underhill, J C/Northern fishes/75n1513
Understanding Ernest Hemingway/Harmon/78 n1142
Understanding scientific literatures/Donohue/ 75n278
Underwater Calif/North/77n699
Underwater medicine and related sciences/ Shilling/75n1618
Undesirable drug interactions/Garb/75n1655
UNESCO: IBE educ thesaurus/77n587
Unesco, records of the Gen Conf, Nov 1974/ 79n516
Unesco Secretariat/SPINES thesaurus/78 n1211

Unesco statistical yearbk/76n816
Unesco thesaurus/Aitchison/79n344
Ungar, F/Encyclopedia of world/76n1185
Unger, J H W/Literature survey/78n1509
Unger, L/American writers/75n1350
Unger, M F/Unger's guide/76n1103
Unger, S G/Bibliography of water/76n1455
Unger's gd to the Bible/Unger/76n1103
Unified numbering system for metals and alloys/Society of Automotive Engineers/ 76n1612
Uniformed services almanac/Sharff/77n1632; 77n1633; 77n1634
Uniforms of the American Revolution/ Mollo/76n1679
Union catalogs and lists/Keller/75n249
Union catalogue of Arabic serials and newspapers in British libraries/Middle East Libraries Committee/78n29
Union catalogue of scientific libraries in the Univ of Cambridge/76n1313
Union list of . . .
  conference proceedings in libraries of Germany/79n27
  German lang serials in libraries of Germany/79n381
  oceanographic expeditions/Estok/77n1441
  Sanborn Fire Insurance maps held by institutions in the US and Canada/ Hoehn/78n764
  selected microforms in libraries in the NY metropolitan area/77n31
  serials holdings/76n39
  serials in libraries of Germany/78n30
  serials indexed by Public Affairs Info Service Bulletin held by Canadian libraries/78n31
USSR agri atlas/77n1511
USSR: analytical survey of lit/US Dept of the Army/78n310
Unionization: viewpoint of librarians/Guyton/ 76n177
United Kingdom—Ireland: illust'd gd to textile collections/Lubell/78n863
United Nations docs index/76n85
United Nations Economic Commission for Latin America, Library/Latin American/ 75n344
United Nations system—internat'l bibliog/ Hüfner/78n430; 79n555; 79n556
US Air Force history/US Dept of the Air Force/75n1847
US and Canada: illust'd gd to the textile collections/Lubell/78n864

US and EEC: American reaction to and involvemt in the "Common Market"/Kitter/75n924
US & Soviet policy in the Middle East/Donovan/75n532
US Arms Control and Disarmament Agency/World military/78n1564
US art directory and year-book/Koehler/78n795
US bombers/Jones/76n1682
US Bureau of Drugs/National drug/79n1505
US Bureau of Economic Analysis/Provinces of/79n370
US Bureau of Labor Statistics/BLS hndbk/78n691/Directory of data/77n429/Directory of natl/78n775/Handbook of labor/77n843/Monthly labor/77n776/Occupational outlook/77n844/Productivity/78n777
US Bureau of Land Mgmt/Public land/78n692
US Bureau of the Census/Environmental-socioeconomic/78n1350/Guide to recurrent/77n752/Historical stats/77n753/Pocket data/78n693/Women-owned/77n788
US-Canadian range mgmt, 1935-77/Vallentine/79n1527
US Central Intelligence Agency/Atlas of issues/75n330/Indian Ocean/78n519/National basic/78n274
US Chess Federation/Official rules/76n746
US Civil Service Commission/Federal career/77n626/Guide to federal/77n596
US Coast Guard/Light lists/78n1551
US college sponsored programs abroad/Cohen/77n591
US Congress/Art in/77n867/Astronauts and/77n1571/Catalog of federal/79n874/Discursive dictionary/77n1477/Energy facts/75n1544/Impeachment/75n499/Inaugural addresses/75n389/Inventory of/78n99/Official congressional/77n517/Science policy/77n1291/US Senate/78n455
US Consumer Affairs Office/State consumer/75n937
US Corps of Engineers/Shore protection/75n1816
US court directory/US Courts/79n529
US Dept of Agriculture/Fact bk/77n1510/List of available/78n1450/Rural development/77n1515

US Dept of Commerce/Annotated bibliog literature/77n1586/Franchise opportunities/77n804
US Dept of Defense/Nuclear weapons/77n1626
US Dept of HEW/American students/76n616/Combined glossary/76n596/Directory: federal/77n817/Directory of federal agency/77n597/Directory of post-secondary/77n632/Directory: state/75n938/Education directory/76n655; 77n605/Handbook for recreation/77n667
US Dept of Justice/Crime scene/75n835/Science of/75n836/Sourcebook of criminal/75n837
US Dept of Labor/Guide to local/77n845
US Dept of Labor library catalog/76n907
US Dept of State/Census of/75n432/Countries of/75n325/English-French/78n1057/Status of/75n324/Treaties in/78n489
US Dept of the Air Force/Dictionary of basic/77n1628/Environmental-socioeconomic/78n1350/US Air/75n1847
US Dept of the Army/Glossary of environmental/75n1534/Guide to US/77n1646/Index of administrative/79n1597/USSR/78n310
US Dept of the Navy/Dictionary of American/77n1653/US Navy/75n1854
US Economic Developmt Admin/Federal and/75n809
US Environmental Data Service/Bibliography of urban/75n1529
US Environmental Protection Agency/Indexed bibliog/76n1456
US facilities and programs for children with severe mental illnesses/79n1436
US fact bk/76n817
US Federal Aviation Admin/FAA historical/75n1822
US Federal Highway Admin/Highway stats/78n1552
US federal official publications/Downey/79n115
US foamed plastics markets & directory/76n1658; 78n760
US Food and Drug Admin/Handbook of common/78n1431
US General Accounting Office/Alphabetical listing/75n498/Federal information/77n110/Recurring reports/77n518
US gov manual/76n86; 79n530
US gov pubs relating to the soc sciences/Lu/76n240

US gov purchasing & sales directory/79n821
US gov scientific & tech periodicals/Yannarella/77n1295
US gd to family records/Portnov/79n469
US history and historiography in postwar Soviet writings/Okinshevich/77n380
US Immigration and Naturalization Service/Foreign versions/75n450
US Indian policy/Prucha/79n526
US industrial outlook/79n848
US information serv libraries/Sussman/75n209
US Library of Congress/American Revolution/77n373/Archive of/75n1429/Ataturk and/75n526/Children's bks/76n1197/Composite MARC/78n216/Directory of info/75n483/Folklore from/77n1057/General censuses/75n875/Guide to study/77n338/Harkness Collection/75n313/Index to James/75n372/LC Main/77n32/Monographic series/76n12/Nuclear proliferation/79n1407/Popular names/77n115/Yugoslavia/75n307
US local histories in the LC/Kaminkow/76n348
US local history catalog/NY Public Library/75n383
US Marine Corps/Marines in/75n1855
US medical directory/Alperin/79n1471
US Military Academy, West Point/Atlas of landforms/75n581
US military shoulder patches of the US Armed Forces/Britton/77n1629
US music/Jackson/75n1128
US National Aeronautics and Space Admin/NASA thesaurus/77n1563
US Natl Archives and Records Service/Guide to National/75n363/Written word/78n340
US National AV Center/Directory of US/76n630
US Natl Bureau of Stds/Building technology/78n1519/Index of internat'l/75n1719/Technical gd computer-/75n1778/Vibrationally excited/75n1455
US Natl Center for Health Statistics/Health resources/78n1419/Rationale, developmt/75n718
US Natl Criminal Justice Information and Statistics Service/Sourcebook of criminal/78n491/National criminal/78n504
US Natl Institute of Mental Health/Mental health/78n1374

US Natl Institute on Drug Abuse/Primary prevention/78n1446
US Natl Marine Fisheries Service/Fisheries of/75n969; 78n761/Processors of/75n968/Publications and/75n970/Wholesale dealers/75n928
US Natl Oceanic and Atmospheric Admin/Bibliography of NY/75n1563/Ocean engineering/75n1817/Oceans of/75n550/Scientific and/75n1561
US Natl Park Service/Guide to historic/75n601/Here was/78n336/Historic American/78n1499/Historic preservation/77n877/National register/77n387/Presidents from/78n337/Signers of Constitution/78n338/Signers of Declaration/75n375
US Natl Science Foundation/Directory of federal/78n1219
US Naval Air Systems Command/Image interpretation/75n971
US Naval Weather Service Command/Worldwide marine/75n1569
US Navy aircraft since 1911/Swanborough/78n1577
US Navy chaplains, 1957-70/US Dept of the Navy/75n1854
US observatories/Kirby-Smith/77n1308
US Office of Education/Aids to/77n657/American students/76n616/Bibliography of research/75n650/Catalog of federal/78n571/Facilities inventory/75n719
US Office of Mgmt and Budget/Federal statistical/77n759/Standard occupational/79n868
US Office of the Federal Register/Protecting your/78n492
US political sci docs/78n450; 79n522
US prison library services & their theoretical basis/Rubin/78n208
US Securities and Exchange Commission/Directory of companies/79n832
US Senate/US Congress/78n455
US Small Business Admin/Franchise index/75n919/US government/79n821
US Smithsonian Institution/Art of/75n1013/Robert Loftin/75n995
US Social Security Admin/Earnings distributions/77n846
US Superintendent of Documents/GPO sales/78n100
US Supreme Court decisions/Anderman/77n540
US Travel Service/USA plant/78n762

Units of weight and measure/Chisholm/76 n1315
Universal bibliographic control/Anderson/76 n195
Universal dict of the English lang/Wyld/79 n1097
Universal pictures: panoramic hist/Fitzgerald/78n949
Universal pronouncing dict of biog and mythology/Thomas/77n1056
Universal ref system: suppl/75n465
Universe of info/Rayward/77n258
University desk ency/78n69
University libraries in Britain/Bryan/77n201
University of California, Water Resources Center Archives/Sources of info/77n1429
University of Chicago Spanish dict/Castillo/78n1070
University of Delaware. Hugh M. Morris Library/Bibliog of Delaware/78n311
University of London library catalogue of the Goldsmiths' Library of Economic Lit/Canney/76n823
University of Toronto doctoral theses 1968-75/78n550
University press bks for secondary school libraries/76n164
University sci and engineering libraries/Mount/77n239
Unrau, H D/Here was/78n336
Unstead, R J/R. J. Unstead's/77n367
Unsworth, W/Encyclopaedia of mountaineering/76n724
Up-with-wholesome, down-with-store-bought book of recipes and household formulas/Tarr/77n1550
Upasak, C S/Dictionary of early/77n1040
(Updated) last whole earth catalog/76n81
Urban affairs abstracts: 1972 cumulation/75n861
Urban affairs bibliog/Ross/76n802
Urban careers guide/National Assoc of Housing and Redevelopmt Officials/75n680
Urban education/Spear/79n635
Urban information thesaurus/Rosenberg/79n734
Urban politics/Murphy/79n539
Urbanization at Teotihuacan, Mexico/Millon/75n404
Urdang, L/CBS News/76n76/Dictionary of advertising/78n726
Urioste, D W/Chicano perspectives/78n1128
Urquhart, F/Dictionary of fictional/75n1326
Urquhart, J A/Relegation and/78n171
Urquhart, J M/Story key/77n553
Urquhart, N C/Relegation and/78n171
Ursin, M J/Guide to fishes/79n1378/Life in/76n1367
USA plant visits/US Travel Service/78n762
Use of . . .
  computers in libraries and info centres/Bidmead/77n287
  computers in lit searching and related ref activities in libraries/Lancaster/77n290
  criminology literature/Wright/75n838
  engineering literature/Mildren/77n1568
  management and business lit/Vernon/77n772
  mathematical lit/Dorling/78n1223
  medical lit/Morton/75n1611; 79n1441
  physics lit/Coblans/77n1336
  reports lit/Auger/76n1306
  slide-tape presentations in academic libraries/Hardesty/79n195
  social sciences lit/Roberts/78n269
Used book price gd/Mandeville/75n62/1977 suppl/79n58
User educ in libraries/Fjällbrant/79n312
User educ: towards a better use of info resources/MacCafferty/78n235
User's gd to funding resources/Human Resources Network/76n627
Usher, G/Dictionary of plants/76n1374
Using bibliotherapy/Rubin/79n308
Using the chemical lit/Woodburn/76n1347
Utah plants: tracheophyta/Welsh/75n1471
Utilizing resources in the handicapped services field/Glassman/75n687
Utley, F L/Placenames of/76n459
Utopian literature/Negley/79n1181

Vaill, P B/Bibliography of sources/76n910
Valderrama, D M/Law & legal/78n493
Vallentine, J F/US-Canadian/79n1527
Valletutti, J F/Writings on/76n411
Values educ sourcebk/Superka/77n646
Vambery, J T/Annual review UN/78n432
Vambery, J T & R V/Cumulative list/79n560
Van Auken, H E/Annotated bibliog interorganizational/78n640
Van Balen, J/Geography and/79n579; 79n580
Van Benthuysen, R F/Monmouth County/76n355
Van Bruggen, T/Vascular plants/77n1357
van de Merwe, C/Thesaurus of sociological/75n795

van der Leeden, F/Ground water/76n1475/ Water resources/76n1476
Van Doren, C/Great treasury/78n85/Webster's American/75n127
Van Dusen, W D/Guide to literature/79n629
Van Dyke, M/Annual review fluid/77n1602; 77n1603
van Egmond, P/Critical reception/75n1358
Van Hoof, H/International bibliog translation/ 75n1246
Van Laer, A J F/NY manuscripts/75n428
van Leunen, M-C/Handbook for scholars/79 n132
Van Nostrand Reinhold manual of film-making/Callaghan/75n1203/TV graphics/ Hurrell/75n1205
Van Nostrand's scientific ency/Considine/77 n1292
Van Orden, P/Elementary school/76n157; 77 n233
van Rijsbergen, C J/Information retrieval/77 n296
Van Tyne, J/Fundamentals of/78n1324
Van Voorhis, J S/Old and/75n433
Van Why, E W/Adoption bibliog/78n657
Van Wyck Brooks/Vitelli/78n1134
Van Zant, N P/Selected US/79n126
Vance, R/Home gardener's/75n1709
vanCleemput, W M/Computer aided/77 n1587; 78n1528
Vandals in the bomb factory/Heath/77n503
Vander Velde, J J/Cavalry journal/75n1841
Vanderstappen, H A/T. L. Yuan/77n865
Vanderveen, B H/American trucks/76n1667/ Fire and/77n1622/Motorcycles to/77 n1623/Observer's Army/76n1681/Tanks & transport/76n1686
Vane, S B/California Indians/78n676
VanEtten, C/Directory of selected/75n700
Vanier, D J/Market structure/75n50
Vann, S K/Melvil Dewey/79n188
Vannatta, D P/Nathanael West/77n1216
Varlejs, J/Akers' simple/78n217/Young adult/ 79n220
Varney, C/Carleton Varney/79n942
Vasaru, G/Deuterium and/77n1341
Vascular plants of South Dakota/Van Bruggen/ 77n1357
Vasquez, L K & M E/Regional dictionary/76 n1155
Vasu, E S/Statistical methods/79n336
Vaughan, D/Encyclopedia of dance/79n1019
Vaughan, W/Handbook of optics/79n1333

Veaner, A B/International microforms/75 n16/Microform market/75n60
Veit, F/Community college/76n140
Velázquez de la Cadena, M/New pronouncing dict/75n1277
Veley, C/Catching up/79n101
Vellela, T/Food co-ops/76n880
Vellucci, M J/National directory/76n70
Velz, J W/Tragedy of/79n1253
Venereal disease bibliog/Goode/75n1614; 76n1517
Venetian instrumental music from Gabrieli to Vivaldi/Selfridge-Field/76n984
Venezuelan history/Lombardi/78n374
Veniard, J/Fly dressers'/75n762
Venker, V A/American film/77n1004
Venomous animals of the world/Caras/76 n1411
Venomous arthropod hndbk/Biery/78n1327
Venturi, A/Storia dell'arte/77n871
Verb synonyms and related words/Reid/75 n1253
Verbände und Gesellschaften der Wissenschaft/75n1436
Vergara, N C/Héroes de/75n374
Vergil concordance/Warwick/76n1304
Verkler, L A/First edition?/79n57
Vermont place-names/Swift/78n535
Vernon, K D C/Use of management/77n772
Verona, E/Corporate headings/77n262
Versage, J V/Ghetto and/75n859
Verschueren, K/Handbook of environmental/ 79n1322
Versey, G R/Domesday gazetteer/76n368
Verway, D I/Michigan statistical/78n688
Verzeichnis lieferbarer bücher/79n15
Veselovsky, Z/Encyclopedia of animals/76 n1408
Vessie, P A/Zen Buddhism/78n978
Veteran sewing machines/Jewell/77n933
Veterinary gd for animal owners/Spaulding/ 77n1534
Vexler, R I/Chronology ... Illinois/79n423/ Chronology ... Kentucky/79n424/ Chronology ... Maryland/79n425/ Cleveland: chronological/78n361/Detroit/ 78n362/England/75n336/Pittsburgh/78 n363/St. Louis/75n510/Vice-presidents and/76n340
Vibrationally excited hydrogen halides/ US Natl Bureau of Stds/75n1455
Vice-presidents and cabinet members/Vexler/ 76n340

Vickery, B C/Classification and/77n263
Vickery, D M/Take care/78n1432
Victorian fiction/Ford/79n1228
Victorian periodicals/Bennett/79n1226
Victorian poets and prose writers/Buckley/78n1155
Victorian prose/DeLaura/75n1372
Video in libraries/Goldstein/78n248
Vietnam conflict/Leitenberg/75n463
Vietnam: gd to ref sources/Cotter/78n302
Vietnamese communism/Phan Tien/77n525
Vietnamese legal materials/Nguyễn/79n566
Viktor Shklovsky/Sheldon/78n1198
Village studies/Lambert/79n778
Villeneuve, G-O/Glossaire de/75n1570
Villiard, P/Gemstones and/75n1101
Vincent, B/Dictionary of biog/76n103
Vincenti, W G/Annual review fluid/77n1602; 77n1603
Vincie, J F/C. G. Jung/78n1365
Vine, R A/John Barth/78n1131
Vine, W E/Expository dict/79n1074
Vines, P/Social policy/77n703
Vines, R A/Trees of/77n1308
Vines, R F/Concordance to oeuvres/79n1271
Vinson, J/Contemporary dramatists/75n1189; 78n946/Contemporary novelists/77n1182/Contemporary poets/76n1214
Vintage car gd/Clutton/78n865
Vinton, J/Dictionary of contemporary/75n1143
Viola/Barrett/79n989
Violence in the US/Parker/75n834
Violets of the US/Klaber/78n1292
Virginia court records in Southwestern PA/Crumrine/75n413
Virginia Woolf/Majumdar/78n1184
Virgo, J A/Continuing library/78n255
Virus diseases/Locke/79n1490
Visser-Fuchs, L/Classics illust'd/75n1317
Visual approach to British and American gov/Wates/75n458
Visual dict of art/Hill/75n1000
Visual ency of sci fiction/Ash/79n1202
Vital records of Dover, NH 1686-1850/Dover Historical Society/79n482
Vitale, P H/Basic tools/78n1094
Vitelli, J R/Van Wyck Brooks/78n1134
Vivian, J/Manual of practical/76n849
Vizetelly, F H/Desk-book of/76n1132
VNR concise ency of math/Gellert/78n1228
Vocabulario de romance en Latín/de Nebrija/75n1276

Vocational-technical learning materials/Reinhart/75n705
Vocational-technical periodicals for community college libraries/77n210
Vocational tests and reviews/Buros/76n570
Vocations in fiction/Lingfelter/76n1208
Voegelin, C F & F M/Classification and/78n1022
Vogel, M/Chicorel abstracts/78n582
Vogt, G W/Standard catalog/79n920
Voigt, M J/Advances in/75n153; 78n140
Volkswagen beetle, super beetle, karmann ghia/Volkswagen of America/75n1738
Voll, J O/Historical dict Sudan/79n360
Volpe, C C/Running Press/78n782
von Engeln, O D/Story key/77n553
von Frank, A J/Whittier/77n1218
von Kaas, H K/Encyclopaedic dict management/75n884
von Klemperer, L/International educ/75n666/New gd study/75n663; 79n641
von Pfeil, H P/Juvenile rights/76n510
von Volborth, C A/Heraldry of/75n445
Vondersmith, B J/Contemporary thought/76n1289
Voorhoeve, P/Indonesian manuscripts/79n69
Vorvoreanu, G/Romanian phrase/75n1286
Vos, H F/Wycliffe Bible/77n1050
Vosper, R/National and/77n271
Voss, G L/Seashore life/78n1335
Voss, T M/Antique American/79n924
Vowell, F N/Comprehensive bibliog study/77n425
Voxman, H/Woodwind solo/77n963
Voyages to Hawaii before 1860/Judd/75n424
Vrais pourtraits et vies des hommes illustres/Thevet/75n120
Vreeland, N/Area hndbk Philippines/78n300

W. B. Yeats/Jochum/79n1258
W. E. B. DuBois/Partington/78n387
W. H. Auden/Gingerich/78n1165
W. H. Hudson/Payne/78n1273
Waaland, J R/Common seaweeds/78n1304
Waddell, J J/Concrete construction/75n1761
Wade, C/Brand-name/78n1479
Wade, G/Homegrown energy/76n1466
Waggoner, D/Hills of/79n1206
Wagle, I/Guide to research/76n143/Reference aids/79n366
Wagner, A/Historic heraldry/76n450
Wagner, J/Bernstein's reverse/76n88

Wagner, J K/Ford trucks/79n1558
Wagner, L W/Ernest Hemingway/78n1143
Wagner, R R/Comprehensive virology/76n1361
Wahl, P/Gun trader's/76n759
Wajid, J A/Periodicals in/75n44
Wakeley, C/Faber medical/76n1524
Wakelyn, J L/Biographical dict/78n364
Wakeman, J/World authors/76n1217
Walburn, H G/Official catalog/76n977; 78n860
Waldhart, E S & T J/Communication research/76n127
Waldhüter, D/Libros en/79n13
Waldo, M/Myra Waldo's Europe/75n629/Myra Waldo's South America/77n570
Wales, H W/Drug abuse/75n1658
Wales, R W/Atlas of Mississippi/75n574
Walford, A J/Guide to foreign/79n1092/Guide to reference/77n15; 79n4
Walker, B/Man and/78n1379
Walker, D E/Natural language/79n337
Walker, E H/Flora of/77n1358
Walker, E P/Mammals of/76n1446
Walker, G/CFL yearbk/75n764
Walker, H/Illustrated hockey/78n628
Walker, H T/Teaching media/78n188
Walker, J A/Glossary of art/78n789
Walker, L W/Book of owls/75n1508
Walker, R H/American studies/77n334
Walker, R S/Library resources/75n166
Walker, S A/Summerhays' ency/77n1537
Walker, W S/20th-century short/75n1331; 78n1108
Walker's manual of Western corporations/79n812
Walking softly in the wilderness/Hart/78n617
Wall, C E/Consumers index/75n943; 77n812/Media review/78n585/Public affairs/75n37
Wall, J/Directory of British/79n955
Wall, J N/Guide to prose/78n1163
Wallace, A/People's almanac/78n94
Wallace, D I M/Field gd birds/76n1429
Wallace, H/Coins of/77n908
Wallace, I/People's almanac/77n102; 79n109/People's almanac presents/78n94
Wallace, M/Political violence/76n472
Wallace-Homestead flea market price gd/Miller/78n833
Wallace-Homestead price gd to antiques and pattern glass/Miller/78n838
Wallace Stevens/Edelstein/75n1369
Wallach, C/Reluctant weekend/75n1710
Walle, D F/Manuscripts guide/77n28

Wallechinsky, D/People's almanac/77n102; 79n109/People's almanac presents/78n94
Waller, C W/Marihuana/77n1507
Walling, R/Academic library/75n180
Walsh, A/Index Islamicus/75n345; 77n303
Walsh, J J/Guide to microforms/79n36/Subject gd microforms/79n42
Walsh, J M/John Peabody/77n734
Walsh, R A/South American/77n811
Walsh, T/Martial law/75n551
Walsh, T P/John Osborne/76n1280
Walter Breen's ency of US and Colonial proof coins 1722-1977/Breen/79n918
Walters, L/Bibliography of bioethics/76n1520; 78n1385; 78n1386
Walters, S/Canadian almanac/78n304
Walton, J H/Chronological charts/79n1075
Walton, R A/Colorado/75n506
Wang, J C F/Cultural revolution/77n320
Wangstedt, E/Concise Swedish-/75n552
War of the American Revolution/Coakley/76n334; 77n374
Ward, A C/Longman companion/76n1190
Ward, B/Electronic music/76n1635
Ward, H/New library/76n204
Ward, J E/Southeastern bibliographic/79n169
Ward, J W/Construction info/75n1762
Ward, M E/Illustrators of/76n944
Ward, P/Dictionary of common/79n102
Ward, R E/Allied occupation/75n544
Ward, W S/Literary reviews/78n1157
Ward-Thomas, P/World atlas golf/77n697
Warden, J/Annual of/76n519
Wards, I M/New Zealand/78n524
Ware, D/Illustrated dict ornament/76n924
Warf, S L/Education directory/77n605
Warmke, G L/Caribbean seashells/77n1396
Warncke, R/Planning library/77n274
Warner, E J/Biographical register/76n341
Warnken, K/Directory of fee-based/78n138
Warren, K S/Schistosomiasis III/78n1392; 79n1442
Warren, M/Descriptive and/78n1168
Warren, M/Open Dallas/78n81
Warshaw, T S/Bible-related/77n1049
Warships of the Imperial Japanese Navy/Jentschura/79n1602
Warships of the world/Ireland/78n1574
Warwick, H H/Vergil concordance/76n1304
Warwick gd to British labour periodicals 1790-1970/Harrison/78n768
Waserman, M/Bibliography on oral/77n383

Washburn, B/Tourist guide/75n618
Washburn, W E/American Indian/75n369
Washington, G/US military/77n1629
Washington, H/Big bk/78n603
Washington, D.C. artists born before 1900/ McMahan/78n824
Washington educ directory/75n671
Washington IV: comp directory of the nation's capital/Grayson/76n478
Washington info directory/76n479
Washington Irving/Springer/77n1208
Washington lobbyists-lawyers directory/79n531
Washington lobby/75n500
Washington Post deskbook on style/Webb/79n133
Washington Post gd to Washington/Babb/77n558
Washington state national parks, historic sites, recreation areas, and natl landmarks/Kirk/75n609
Washington state place names/Phillips/77n552
Wasserman, P/Awards, honors/76n71; 76n72/Commodity prices/75n920/Consultants and/77n789/Consumer sourcebk/75n931; 79n844/Encyclopedia of business/78n705/Encyclopedia of geographic/79n813/Ethnic info/77n428/Festivals sourcebook/78n77/Health organizations/76n1539; 79n1472/Library bibliographies/76n128/List/75n149; 75n125/Museum media/75n83/New consultants/77n790/Statistics sources/75n879; 78n687/Training and/79n814/Who's who consulting/75n902
Wasserman, P & S/Don't ask/79n1534
Wasserman, S/Wines of/78n1460
Wasson, J/Common symptom/77n1484
Wastewater mgmt/Tchobanoglous/77n1421
Watch collector's hndbk/Cutmore/77n898
Water atlas of the US/Geraghty/75n1567
Water birds of Calif/Cogswell/78n1317
Water birds of North America/Baird/75n1499
Water for agriculture/75n1664
Water publications of state agencies, 1st suppl/Giefer/77n1428
Water quality abstracts/75n1562
Water resources/Ralston/76n1474
Water resources of the world/van der Leeden/76n1476
Waterfowl of North America/Johnsgard/77n1381
Watergate and the White House/Drossman/75n501

Watergate: annotated bibliog/Rosenberg/76n473
Watergate: chronology of a crisis/75n502; 76n489
Waterhouse, E/Roman baroque/77n886
Waters, M B/Worldwide directory/75n898
Waterways in Europe/Pilkington/75n625
Wates, C J/Visual approach/75n458
Watkins, N/International who's/75n800
Watkins, S W/Annotated bibliog literature/77n1586
Watlington, A G/Christ our/79n1045
Watson, A/Dictionary of butterflies/76n1442
Watson, G/New Cambridge/75n1375; 76n1260
Watson, J/Lesbian in/76n1506
Watson, L/Identifying grasses/79n1348
Watson, P G/On-line bibliographic/79n267
Watson, R I/Eminent contributors/75n1579; 77n1443/History of psychology/79n1426
Watt, B K/Handbook of nutritional/77n1552
Watt, D E R/Biographical dict/79n441
Watt, I/British novel/75n1378
Watt, L B/Aids to/77n657
Watts, O M/Reed's nautical/79n726
Watts, P/Dictionary of Old/78n350
Watts, S/College handbook/77n613; 79n652
Waugh, A/Handyman's ency/78n1536
Waverman, L/Pennypincher's wine/75n1672
Way, O R/British children's/77n1225
Way things work/Lodewijk/75n1712
Way things work bk of the computer/75n1779
Way to play: games of the world/Diagram Group/76n742
Weal, E C/Combat aircraft/78n1567
Wearing, J P/English drama/79n1007/London stage/77n990
Weast, R C/Handbook of chemistry/76n1344
Weather/Pollack/79n1416
Weather almanac/Ruffner/75n1568; 78n1353
Weather atlas of the US/Baldwin/76n1479
Weatherford, J W/Collective bargaining/77n207
Weathering the storm: women of the American Revolution/Evans/76n338
Weaver, G C/Creative writing/79n630
Weaver, N & R/Chronology of music/79n995
Weaver, R E/Wild plants/76n1380
Weaver, S M/Canadian Indian/75n863

Weaving, spinning, and dyeing/Axford/76n947
Webb, A D/New dict/75n876
Webb, J S/Wolfson geochemical/79n1419
Webb, R A/Washington Post/79n133
Webber, R/World list/78n1080
Webber, W L/Books about/75n70; 76n56
Webbert, C A/Idaho local/78n357
Weber, F J/Select bibliog/76n1079
Weber, H B/Modern ency/79n1283
Weber, H H/Introduction to classification/77n250/World War II/76n289
Weber, I/Medals and/77n914
Weber, J/Encyclopedia of minerals/75n1573
Weber, J S/Good reading/79n693
Weber, O S/Literary and/77n178/North American/77n186
Weber, R/Building a/76n1195
Weber, W A/Rocky Mountain/77n1359
Webster, H & J/18: teenage/78n661
Webster, R/Gems/76n1483
Webster, V R/Tropical fish/76n1558
Webster's American biographies/Van Doren/75n127
Webster's American military biographies/79n1592
Webster's atlas and zip code directory/75n582
Webster's collegiate thesaurus/77n1082
Webster's concise family dictionary/77n1079
Webster's intermediate dict/79n1112
Webster's new dict of synonyms/75n1254
Webster's new elementary dict/76n1123
Webster's new students dict/76n1124
Webster's new 20th cent dict/79n1096
Webster's new world companion to English and American lit/Pollard/77n1131
Webster's new world crossword puzzle dict/Whitfield/78n1049
Webster's new world dict/Guralnik/76n1125; 76n1126; 79n1105
Webster's new world large print dict/Guralnik/79n1106
Webster's new world thesaurus/Laird/76n1134
Webster's secretarial hndbk/Eckersley-Johnson/78n716
Webster's sports dict/77n672
Wechsler, H/Handbook of medical/77n1490
Wechsler, L/Encyclopedia of graffiti/76n63
Wecht, C H/Legal medicine/78n1412
Weddington, B/Guide to sources/75n935
Wedeck, H E/Dictionary of astrology/75n1608
Wedertz, B/Dictionary of naval/78n1572

Wedgeworth, R/ALA yearbook/77n188
Weeding library collections/Slote/76n203
Weeds in winter/Brown/78n1309
Weedend educ source bk/Cross/77n615
Weekender's guide/Shosteck/75n616
Weekes, R V/Muslim peoples/79n772
Weekley, E/Jack and/76n452
Weeks, E H/Bibliography of 17th cent/79n5
Weeks, J/Military small/78n1558
Weerts, R K/Original manuscript/75n1134
Wehausen, J V/Annual review fluid/77n1602; 77n1603
Wehlburg, A F C/Theatre lighting/77n993
Wehlte, K/Materials and/77n887
Wehmeyer, L B/School librarian/77n229/School library/76n153
Wehr, H/Dictionary of modern/78n1050
Weiers, R M/Chilton's more/75n1739
Weigert, A/Concise ency/78n1238
Weigle, M/Penitente bibliog/77n1035
Weik, M H/Standard dict/78n1529
Weills, C/Goodfellow catalog/78n875
Weimar era and Hitler/Stachura/79n430
Weinberg, S/Color atlas/76n1541
Weiner, J/Analytical methods/77n1325/Coating equipmt/77n1323/Corrosion of/77n1326/Dry strength/78n1261/Drying of/78n1262/Energy production/79n1327/Microorganism control/78n1263/Microscopy of/77n1328/Newsprint/78n1260/Nonsulfur pulping/78n1265/Odors and/77n1315/Paper mill/77n1316/Pitch/77n1327/Process control/79n1328/Protective and/77n1329/Retention of/77n1318/Runnability of/77n1319/Wet pressing/77n1317/Wet strength/78n1264/White water-/77n1322/Wood waste/77n1320
Weiner, M A/Taster's guide/78n1461
Weiner, R/News bureaus/75n1304; 78n1077/Professional's guide/76n1159/Syndicated columnists/76n1173
Weingarten, L/Selling your/75n1038
Weingartner, C/Machinists' ready/75n1808; 79n1575
Weinheimer, G/Rights of/75n562
Weinreich, U/Modern English-/79n1156
Weinstein, R A/Collection, use/78n888
Weinstein, W/Historical dict Burundi/77n312
Weird America: places of mystery/Brandon/79n1085
Weis, E/New Schöffler-/75n1270

Weis, F L/Colonial clergy & colonial/78n416/ Colonial clergy of VA/77n479
Weiser, I H/Index of American/75n1340; 76n1225; 77n1196
Weiss, C H/Mail order/78n1478
Weiss, E C/Many faces/79n157
Weiss, L/Access to/79n623
Weiss, M/Catalog of free/77n91
Weiss, R A/Completed research/78n606
Weissman, D/Folk music/77n982
Weixlmann, J/John Barth/77n1199
Welberry, T R/Atlas of optical/77n1338
Welbourn, R B/Dictionary of medical/79n1461
Welch, J E/Elizabeth Gaskell/78n1175/ Reputation of/79n1255
Welch, T F/Japanese and/78n250/Toshokan/77n272
Weld, W C/World directory/75n1227
Wellauer, M A/Guide to foreign/77n452
Weller, R C/Sea fiction/77n1175
Wellesz, E/New Oxford/75n1148
Welling, W/Collectors' guide/77n939
Wellisch, H H/PRECIS index/78n222
Wellisch, J B/Public library/75n191
Wellman, F L/Dictionary of tropical/78n1453
Wellness/Popenoe/79n1493
Wells, A Q/Earned degrees/76n633
Wells, S/English drama/76n1264/Shakespeare/79n1254
Wellsted, T/Wild flowers/79n1346
Welsh, G S/MMPI hndbk/76n1498
Welsh, J M/Ben Jonson/75n1387
Welsh, S L/Utah plants/75n1471
Wengraf, S/Positive images/78n955
Wennrich, P/Anglo-American and/78n1202; 79n1301
Wentworth, H/Dictionary of American/76n1129
Weres, R/Directory of Ukrainian/78n392/ Ukraine/75n308
Werge, T/Early Puritan/77n1185
Werner, O J/Manual for prison/77n242
Wersig, G/Terminology of/77n172
Wertheimer, L/Books in other/78n206
Werts, M F/Underwater medicine/75n1618
Wertsman, V/Armenians in/79n447/Romanians in/76n418/Russians in/77n446/ Ukrainians in/77n447
Wery, M K/American women/77n841
Wessell, T R/Key resources/78n570
West, G D/Index of proper/79n1275
West, G P/Encyclopedia of animal/78n1462
West, J L W/William Styron/78n1150

West, R L/Public regulation/79n1409
West African travels/Boone/75n638
West Virginians in the American Revolution/Johnston/78n403
Westbrook, M/Twentieth century/75n1320
Westby, B M/Sears list/78n230
Westerman, S/CBS news/76n76; 77n97
Western/Eyles/76n1068
Western Canada since 1870/Artibise/79n375
Western films/Nachbar/76n1050
Western treebook/Palmer/79n1362
Westin, J E/Finding your/78n395
Westley, F/Chemical kinetics/78n1241/ Vibrationally excited/75n1455
Westmoreland, G T/Annotated gd basic/76n399
Weston, J/Oxford children's/77n1080
Weston, J F/Treasurer's hndbk/78n722
Weston-Smith, M/Encyclopedia of ignorance/79n1297
Westrup, J A/New college/77n969; 79n968
Wet pressing/Louden/77n1317
Wet strength of paper/Weiner/78n1264
Whalen, G J/Reston ency/78n1395
Whaley, R G/National children's/78n659/ National prison/77n710
Whalley, P E S/Dictionary of butterflies/76n1442
Whalon, M K/Performing arts/77n991
Wharton, E R/Etymological lexicon/76n1145
What every woman should know . . . about her car/Jackson/75n1734
What happens in library filing?/Hoffman/77n270
What they said in 1975/Pater/77n96
What to do till the veterinarian comes/ Pommery/77n1530
What you should know about marriage, divorce, annulment, separation and community property in Louisiana/Eddy/75n556
Whatmore, G/Modern news/79n243
What's in a name?/Rule/75n449
What's in Shakespeare's names/Levith/79n1252
Wheatcroft, A/Who's who military/77n1635
Wheelbarger, J J/Children's literature/75n1323
Wheeler, A/Fishes of/76n1437
Wheeler, G J/Interior painting/75n1106
Wheeler, H R/Womanhood media/76n798
Wheeler, J D/Tax desk/77n855
Wheeler, J O/Bibliography on geographic/77n550

Wheeler, M M/Mathematics library/79n1311
When you find a rock/Klaits/77n1434
Where are their papers?/Akeroyd/78n1117
Where the great German wines grow/ Ambrosi/77n1518
Where to . . .
    eat in America/Rice/78n1477
    find certified mechanics for your car/ National Institute for Automotive Serv Excellence/76n1616
    find more/Hillard/78n239
    find what/Hillard/76n130
    fish & hunt in North America/Knap/76n729
Where's what: sources of info for fed investigators/Murphy/77n839
Whetten, L L/Current research/78n468
Whistler, A E/California experience/79n388
Whistling, C F/Handbuch der/76n987
Whitaker, J/Almanack for/75n88
Whitaker's five-yr cumulative bk list 1968-72/ 75n14
Whitaker's three-yr cumulative bk list 1973-75/ 78n10
White, A G/Reforming metropolitan/76n496
White, B A/American women/79n1211
White, B M/Fur trade/79n409
White, C L/Aelfric/75n1380
White, C M/Historical introduction/77n275/ Sources of info/75n284
White, H/Architecture bk/77n878
White, H/Jesse Hill Ford/76n1237
White, H A/Alaska-Yukon/75n1473
White, H S/Copyright dilemma/79n320/Publishers and/78n35
White, J/Angry buyer's/75n939
White, J T/Fighters for/79n411
White, J V/Editing by/75n1298
White, O/Australia/75n619
White, R A/Surveys in/77n1452
White, R B/English literary/78n1158
White, R C/Sewell's dog's/78n1466
White, R L/Sherwood Anderson/78n1129
White, V P/Grants/78n78
White, W/Nathanael West/76n1252
White House record library/75n1136
White water-savealls/Sykes/77n1322
Whiteford, A H/US and/78n864
Whitehouse, D & R/Archaeological atlas/77 n351
Whiteman, J R/Bibliography for finite/76 n1603; 77n1562
Whitestone, P/Photocopying in/79n293
Whitfield, D J/Historical and/77n332
Whitfield, J S/Songwriters' rhyming/76n1137/ Webster's new/78n1049

Whiting, B J/Early American/79n103
Whitlow, R/Black American/75n1336
Whitman, J/Whitman's off/77n571
Whitman at auction/Francis/77n1225
Whitman's off season travel gd to Europe/ Whitman/77n571
Whitney, C A/Whitney's star/75n1442
Whitney's star finder/Whitney/75n1442
Whitrow, M/ISIS cumulative/77n1283
Whitten, D G A/Penguin dict/77n1427
Whitten, P/Encyclopedia of anthropology/77 n748
Whittick, A/Encyclopedia of urban/75n862
Whittier/von Frank/77n1218
Who did what/Howat/75n121
Who named the daisy? who named the rose?/ Durant/78n1289
Who was when? dict of contemporaries/ De Ford/77n363
Who was who among North American authors 1921-39/77n1183/Eng & European authors 1931-49/79n1209
Who was who during the American Revolution/Kail/78n365
Who was who in . . .
    America/77n142
    American history: arts and letters/77 n143
    American history: science and tech/ 77n1301
    American history: military/77n1636
    American politics/Morris/75n486
    Florida/Marks/75n125
    journalism, 1925-28/79n1170
Who was who on screen/Truitt/75n1212; 78n967
Who won what when/Stuart/79n100
Whole car catalog/79n1559
Whole COSMEP catalog/Higgins/75n25
Whole earth atlas/76n530
Whole earth epilog/75n101
Whole fishing catalog/79n716
Whole grains: bk of quotations/Spiegelman/ 75n95
Whole health catalog/Linde/79n1489
Whole horse catalog/Price/79n1525
Whole house catalog/78n1537
Whole oil world oil directory/78n763
Whole seed catalog/Link/77n1557
Whole Washington handbk/Ein/76n881
Whole world catalog/Lyons/75n950
Whole-world wine catalog/Kaufman/79 n1519
Wholesale dealers of fishery products/US Natl Marine Fisheries Service/75n928

Whone, H/Church, monastery/79n1046
Who's who/75n132; 79n145
Who's who among...
  Black Americans/Matney/77n438
  innkeepers/75n901
  Latin Americans in Washington/77n343
Who's who and where in women's studies/Berkowitz/76n787
Who's who biographical record—child development professionals/77n606
Who's who biographical record—school dist officials/78n602
Who's who in...
  Africa/Dickie/75n131
  Alaskan politics/Atwood/79n540
  America/77n144
  American art/77n873; 79n910
  American law/78n509
  American politics/76n480; 78n465
  architecture from 1400 to the present/Richards/78n804
  aviation/75n1823
  boxing/Burrill/75n753
  Chaucer/Scott/76n1270
  children's books/Fisher/76n1198
  church history/Barker/79n1076
  computer educ and research/Hsiao/77n1588
  consulting/Wasserman/75n902
  D. H. Lawrence/Holderness/77n1237
  electronics/77n832
  fiction?/Swan/77n1178
  finance and industry/75n903
  football/Mandell/75n765
  George Eliot/Hartnoll/78n1173
  golf/Elliott/77n696
  government/78n466
  graphology and questioned documents world-wide/Landrum/78n1378
  Greek and Roman mythology/Kravitz/78n1017
  health care/79n1473
  Henry James/Leeming/77n1207
  history, England 1789-1837/Treasure/76n371
  Hollywood 1900-76/Ragan/78n965
  Jane Austen and the Brontës/Leeming/75n1377
  Jewish history after the period of the Old Testament/Comay/75n397
  labor/77n847
  librarianship and info sci/Landau/75n253
  military history/Keegan/77n1635
  modern Japanese prints/Blakemore/76n931
  new thought/Beebe/79n1077

Who's who in... (cont'd)
  New Zealand/Traue/79n144
  opera/Rich/77n975
  public relations/Barbour/77n1109
  religion/76n1093
  rock music/York/79n1003
  Saudi Arabia/78n118
  science fiction/Ash/77n1172
  Scottish history/Donaldson/75n399
  Shaw/Hartnoll/76n1287
  Thomas Hardy/Leeming/76n1275
  twentieth-century lit/Seymour-Smith/77n1181
Who's who in the...
  arts/Lann/75n1014
  Bible/Barr/76n1094
  book of Mormon/Matthews/78n987
  East/75n128
  Midwest/77n145
  socialist countries/Lewytzkyj/79n143
  South and Southwest/75n129; 77n146
  theatre/Herbert/78n943
  UN and related agencies/Hawkin/76n471
  West/75n130
  world/77n123; 79n142
Who's who of...
  American women/79n771
  British engineers/Baynton/75n1720
  British members of Parliament/Stenton/78n482
  the colored race/Mather/77n439
Who's who, what's what and where in Ireland/75n133
Wick, A/Tabulation of/79n1321
Wickham, C/Indoor garden/78n1497
Wieczynski, J/Modern ency/77n415; 79n442
Wieder, J/IFLA's first/79n316
Wiederrecht, A E/Women's movement/78n663
Wiener, D N/Consumer's guide/76n1502
Wiener, J H/Great Britain/76n372
Wiener, P P/Dictionary of history/75n1236
Wiesenberger Investment Company service investment companies/77n805
Wife beating/Howard/79n746
Wigge, L/Sporting News'/76n737
Wigoder, G/Encyclopedic dictionary Judaica/75n320
Wigoder, G/New std/78n285
Wijasuriya, D E K/Barefoot librarian/76n218
Wilcox, W H/Biological indicators/75n1528
Wild flowers of...
  Britain/Phillips/79n1346
  Britain and Northern Europe/Fitter/76n1389

Wild flowers of ... (cont'd)
    Connecticut/Klimas/76n1390
    Florida/Fleming/78n1290
    Massachusetts/Klimas/76n1394
    New Hampshire and Vermont/Klimas/76n1391
    New Jersey/Klimas/76n1392
    New York/Klimas/76n1393
    Pennsylvania/Klimas/76n1395
Wild flowers of the ...
    Midwest/Mackenzie/78n1293
    North country/Mackenzie/75n1480
    Pacific Coast/Haskin/78n1291
    Pacific Northwest/Clark/78n1287
    South/Mackenzie/78n1294
Wild food plants of Indiana and adjacent states/McPherson/78n1312
Wild food trailguide/Hall/77n1350
Wild plants in the city/Page/76n1380
Wild plants you can eat/Knutsen/76n1575
Wild rivers of North America/Jenkinson/75n632
Wilder, S E/Tables and/76n1607
Wilderness areas of North America/Sutton/75n637
Wilderness handbk/Petzoldt/75n757
Wildflowers of ...
    Alabama and adjoining states/Dean/75n1475
    Eastern America/Klimas/75n1478
    the East/Crittenden/78n1288
    the redwood empire/Young/77n1363
    the Southeastern US/Duncan/76n1388
    Western America/Orr/75n1479
Wilding-White, T M/Jane's pocket/78n1510
Wildlife illust'd/Ovington/76n1414
Wildlife photography/Hosking/75n1110
Wildly successful plants/Crockett/78n1310
Wilds, T/Directory of AV/75n699
Wildwater touring/Arighi/75n745
Wile, A N/Combined retrospective/78n334/Declassified documents/78n97
Wile, J/Frank Schoonmaker's/79n1521
Wiley, P L/British novel/75n1379
Wilgus, A C/Historiography of/76n373/Latin America/79n384
Wilgus, K S/Latin America/75n297
Wilhelm, C, J, & L/Wilhelms' guide/79n624
Wilhelm, J/Guide to all/75n631
Wilhelms' gd to all Mexico/Wilhelm/79n624
Wilkening, H E/Psychology almanac/75n1598
Wilkens, E/Secrets from/77n1525
Wilkes, G A/Dictionary of Australian/79n1117

Wilkie Collins/Beetz/79n1236
Wilkin, B T/Survival themes/79n1197
Wilkins, T E/Colorado railroads/76n1674
Wilkinson, B/High middle/79n435
Wilkinson, J/Complete bk cooking/76n1580/Tourist business/77n828
Wilkinson, J P/Canadian juvenile/77n1259
Willa Cather/Lathrop/76n1230
Willard, F E/American women/75n853
Willcock, M M/Companion to/77n1265
Willeford, G/Medical word/78n1401
Willett, H P/Zinsser microbiology/77n1491
William Beebe/Berra/78n1271
William Billings/Nathan/78n909
William Everson/Bartlett/78n1138
William Faulkner/McHaney/77n1203
William James/Skrupskelis/78n1004
William Rickenbacker's savings and investment guide/Rickenbacker/77n803
William S. Burroughs/Goodman/77n1201
William Styron/Leon/79n1224/West/78n1150
William Wells Brown and Martin R. Delany/Ellison/79n450
William Wordsworth/Bauer/79n1257
Williams, A/Modules in/75n459
Williams, C A S/Outlines of/75n1001; 78n1018
Williams, E B/Scribner-Bantam/78n1038
Williams, E L/Howard University/78n979
Williams, F E/Neuropsychiatry and/77n1459
Williams, J/Atlas of weapons/78n1554
Williams, J G/Simulation activities/78n128
Williams, J S/Environmental pollution/75n1530
Williams, J W/Education directory/77n605
Williams, L H/Allende years/78n11
Williams, M/Almanac of Virginia/78n456
Williams, M E/Annual review information/78n141; 79n171/Computer-readable/78n243
Williams, O/American black/79n454
Williams, R/Keywords/77n1065
Williams, S P/Guide to research/77n194
Williams, T I/Biographical dict/76n1330
Williams & Wilkins case/McCormick/76n42
Williamsburg collection of antique furnishings/75n1077
Williamson, J/Feminist resources/78n593/Who's who and/76n787
Williamson, J W/Improving medical/79n1457
Williamson, R/Dictionary of computers/79n1560
Willis, D/Annotated bibliog Aspen/78n543

Willis, D C/Films of/76n1060
Willis, J/Dance world/76n1037
Willis, J H/Handbook to plants/75n1472
Willis, J L/Historical dict Uruguay/76n283
Wills, G/Concise ency antiques/78n842
Wills and where to find them/Gibson/75n437
Wilmeth, D B/American stage/79n1012
Wilmore, S B/Swans of/76n1433
Wilson, B L/Directory of research/76n610; 78n73
Wilson, C/New college/77n969; 79n968
Wilson, C/Rape/75n850
Wilson, G B L/Dictionary of ballet/75n1181
Wilson, J/Complete food/78n1480/First complete/77n942
Wilson, J/New Zealand/76n17
Wilson, J R M/Research gd history/75n349
Wilson, K/Myths and/77n1055
Wilson, L N/Bibliography of child/76n1489
Wilson, M C/Women in/76n482
Wilson, P/Art at/75n1002
Wilson, P/Community elite/78n177
Wilson, R A/Ben K. Green/78n1139/Gertrude Stein/76n1248
Wilson, R S/Public affairs/75n477
Wilson, W K/Directory of research/76n610; 78n73/World directory/75n1552
Wiltsee, E A/Pioneer miner/77n925
Wimmer, W/Catalogue of vocal/79n969
Winborne, B B/Colonial and/77n480
Winch, K L/International maps/78n512
Winchell, C A/Hyperkinetic child/76n1490
Wind, H W/Encyclopedia of golf/76n748
Winderbaum, L/Martial arts/78n639
Windrow, M/Military dress/75n1840
Wine/Johnson/76n1561
Wine, beer and spirits/Tudor/77n1522
Wine buyers guide/Fadiman/79n1516
Winek, C L/Everything you/75n1659
Wines of Italy/Wasserman/78n1460
Wines of Spain and Portugal/Read/75n1675
Wing, J K/Measurement and/75n1599
Wingate, P/Penguin medical/77n1478
Winger, V/Shopping round/75n941
Winget, L W/2001 Spanish/77n1101
Winick, M/National Basketball/77n680
Winick, M P/Progressive educ/79n637
Winick, S D/Rhythm/76n993
Winnett, T/Sierra South/76n725
Winnipeg: centennial bibliog/Sloane/75n393
Winslow Homer/Davis/77n863
Winston, M/Call for/76n884

Winter, R/Consumer's dict cosmetic/75n940; 77n818/Consumer's dict food/79n1535
Winterich, J T/Early American/76n45
Winterkorn, H F/Foundation engineering/76n1622
Winterthur gd to . . .
    American Chippendale furniture/Hummel/78n853
    American needlework/Swan/78n880
Wintle, J/Dictionary of biographical/79n97
Wischnitzer, S/Barron's guide/75n1635; 78n1409
Wisconsin. Div of Library Services/Public, academic/75n167
Wisdom, A C/Introduction to library/75n147
Wisdom, B/Recipe index/75n1694
Wise, L F/Kings, rulers/78n332
Wismer, D/Islamic Jesus/78n980
Wisner, B/Complete gd salt/77n693
Wit, A/Nurse's drug/79n1501
Witchcraft: catalogue of the collection in Cornell Univ Library/Crowe/78n1380
Withers, F N/Standards for/76n123
Withers, S/Biographical dict scientists/76n1330
Witherspoon, A M/Common errors/75n1291
Withrow, D E/Gateways to/77n1166
Withycombe, E G/Oxford dictionary/78n426
Wittich, W A/Educators guide/76n675
Wittman, A/Dictionary of data/79n1566
Wodehouse, L/American architects/77n879; 78n805/British architects/79n895
Woellner, E H/Requirements for/75n660; 76n631; 77n638; 78n579
Woerdeman, M W/Atlas of medical/79n1447
Woffinden, B/Illustrated ency rock/78n918
Wojtas, E J/Rand McNally/75n590
Wolcott, H F/Ethnographic approaches/77n747
Woleaian-English dict/Sohn/78n1072
Wolf, B/Where to/78n1477
Wolf, C E/Indians of/78n682
Wolf, T P/Bibliography of NM/76n493
Wolfe, G R/New York/77n563
Wolfe, J N/Economics of/75n881
Wolff, G R/Environmental information/75n1553
Wolff, J J/George Gissing/75n1386
Wolff, K/AAAS science/79n1294
Wolfgang, M E/Criminology index/76n780

Wolfson geochemical atlas of England and Wales/Webb/79n1419
Woll, A L/Songs from/77n984
Wollaston, A N/English-Persian/79n1146
Wolman, B B/International ency/78n1367
Womanhood media suppl/Wheeler/76n798
Womanpower project/NY women's/75n854
Woman's almanac/Paulsen/77n723
Woman's body/79n1494
Woman's Day bk of wildflowers/Hersey/77n1360
Woman's Day dict of antique furniture/Gaines/75n1075
Woman's who's who of America/Leonard/77n122
Women and British periodicals 1832-67/Palmegiano/78n665
Women and drug use/Christenson/76n791
Women and film/Kowalski/77n1002
Women and literature/78n1095
Women and society/Een/79n755/Rosenberg/76n797
Women and world development/Buvinic/78n662
Women artists in America/Collins/75n1011; 76n932
Women at work/Bickner/75n845
Women: bibliographic sources in the Univ of Toronto libraries/Woodsworth/75n856
Women: bibliog on their educ and careers/Astin/75n843; 76n786
Women composers/Stern/79n988
Women in . . .
   American music/Skowronski/79n962
   antiquity/Goodwater/76n792
   California/DeNoyelles/78n667
   early Texas/Carrington/76n337
   federal politics/Evans/76n482
   focus/Betancourt/76n1054
   librarianship/Myers/76n120
   literature/Myers/77n1125
   medicine/Chaff/78n1387
   music/Hixon/76n1002
   perspective/Jacobs/76n794
   public office/77n508; 79n544
   Spanish America/Snaster/78n373
   the development process/Saulniers/79n761
   the Middle East and North Africa/al-Qazzaz/78n279
   the US Congress/Engelbarts/75n485
   transition: separation and divorce/Women in Transition, Inc./76n785
   US history/78n347

Women in Transition, Inc./Women in/76n785
Women loving women/Kuda/77n1127
Women on the Indian scene/Dasgupta/77n321
Women-owned businesses/US Bureau of the Census/77n788
Women painters of the world/Sparrow/77n859
Women who make movies/Smith/76n1069
Women's films in print/Dawson/76n1055
Women's gd to books/Randall/75n855; 77n725
Women's gd to mgmt positions/Rogalin/77n850
Women's movement in the seventies/Krichmar/78n663
Women's movement media/Harrison/76n793
Women's rights almanac/Gager/75n848
Women's studies/McKee/78n664
Women's studies: publications and services available in the library of the Univ of California/Krichmar/76n142
Women's studies sourcebk/King/77n718
Women's work and women's studies/Friedman/77n717
Women's yellow pages/Edry/75n847
Wonderful world of maps/Madden/79n588
Wones, B/Art and/78n874/Artist's market/79n886
Wood, C A/Introduction to lit/75n1496
Wood, D/New trade/79n810
Wood, G L/Animal facts/79n1368
Wood, R/New Florida/75n583
Wood, R F/Ina Coolbrith/75n252
Wood preservation/Hickin/75n1046
Wood waste/Pollock/77n1320
Woodard, G/Cultural conformity/78n1120
Woodbridge, B A/Alfred North/78n1005
Woodbridge, H C/Benito Pérez/77n1277/Jack London/75n1360/Rubén Darío/76n1303
Woodbridge, M E/American Federation/78n774
Woodburn, H M/Using the/76n1347
Woodbury, M/Guide to sources/77n584
Woodhouse, B/Encyclopedia of dogs/79n1526
Woodress, J/American fiction/76n1220/American literary/78n1114
Woods, H M/Annotated bibliog lit/77n1586
Woods, R D/Reference materials/77n441
Woodsworth, A/Women: bibliographic/75n856
Woodward, A M/Factors affecting/79n248
Woodward, N H/Food catalog/79n1536

Woodward, R H/Bibliography of writings/76n1238
Woodwind solo and study material music gd/Voxman/77n963
Woodworth, D P/Guide to current/75n28
Woody plants in the Univ of Washington arboretum/Mulligan/79n1361
Woody plants of the north central plains/Stephens/75n1469
Woody vines of the southeastern US/Duncan/76n1383
Woodyard, G W/Bibliography of Latin/79n1010
Wooley, D/Advertising law/75n913
Woolley, A/Illustrated ency mineral/79n1423
Woolley, A R/Clarendon gd/76n561/Larousse gd minerals/78n1359
Woolls, B/Evaluation techniques/79n221/Multi-media indexes/76n679
Woolmer, J H/Checklist of Hogarth/77n1222
Woolven, G B/Warwick guide/78n768
Word book/Ellis/78n1039/Kahn/76n1131
Word index to Rainer Maria Rilke's German lyrical poetry/Bartlett/79n1277
Wordpower: dict of vital words/De Bono/78n1043
Words into type/Skillin/75n113
Wordsworthian criticism 1964-73/Stam/75n1408
Working on the system/Michael/75n104
Working press of the nation/Paule/75n1305
Works of Charles Darwin/Freeman/78n1272
Works of genius/Jenkins/76n53
World aircraft in color/Ege/75n1820
World airline fleets/Endres/79n1583
World almanac & bk of facts/77n103
World almanac whole health gd/Hendin/79n1487
World atlas of . . .
 birds/Scott/75n1511
 cheese/Eekhof-Stork/77n1543
 food/Hale/75n1695
 golf/Ward-Thomas/77n697
 military history/Banks/75n1842
World authors 1950-70/Wakeman/76n1217
World aviation directory/Dean/77n1624
World bibliography of . . .
 African bibliographies/Besterman/76n2
 bibliographies, 1964-74/Toomey/78n5
 Oriental bibliographies/Besterman/76n3
 Sherlock Holmes and Dr. Watson/De Waal/76n1205
World book dict/Barnhart/77n1075
World bk ency/Nault/78n70

World bk of house plants/McDonald/76n1595
World cars/75n1827; 76n1666
World catalogue of theses and dissertations about the Australian Aborigines and Torres Strait Islanders/Coppell/79n774
World catalogue of very large floods/78n1358
World chronology of music history/Eisler/75n1139
World combat aircraft directory/Polmar/78n1565
World communications/76n1160
World countermarks on medieval and modern coins/Brunk/77n905
World directory of . . .
 administrative libraries/Simmler/77n187
 environmental organizations/Trzyna/78n1348
 environmental research centers/Wilson/75n1552
 map collections/Ristow/77n554
 social sci institutions/79n343
 theological educ by extension/Weld/75n1227
World encyclopedia of . . .
 comics/Horn/77n1170
 the film/Smith/76n1053
World energy book/Crabbe/79n1392
World environmental directory/76n1467
World factbook/75n89
World filmography/Cowie/78n964; 79n1032
World food crisis/Sobel/76n848/Trzyna/78n1481
World food problem/Rechcigl/76n847
World guide to . . .
 abbreviations of organizations/Buttress/76n89
 antiquities/Kurtz/76n299
 beer/Jackson/79n1517
 higher education/77n592
 libraries/75n168
 scientific associations/75n1436
 scientific associations and learned societies/79n89
 social work educ/Stickney/75n665
 terminological activities/Krommer-Benz/79n1095
 trade associations/75n897
 tropical drift seeds and fruits/Gunn/77n1349
 universities/Zils/77n593; 79n668
World in figures/Showers/75n86
World legislatures/Paxton/76n465

World list of . . .
- aquatic sciences and fisheries serial titles/ Suppl 2/79n1528
- national newspapers/Webber/78n1080
- social sci periodicals/77n302
- universities/77n594

World Meteorological Organization/Annotated bibliog precipitation/75n1571
World metric stds for engineering/Kverneland/79n1547
World military aviation/Krivinyi/75n1846
World military expenditures and arms transfers, 1966-75/US Arms Control and Disarmament Agency/78n1564
World military leaders/Martell/75n1844
World museums guide/Cooper/75n1008
World of . . .
- automobiles/79n1591
- cheese/Jones/77n1547
- fashion/Lambert/77n940
- golf/Simms/79n718
- learning/76n617
- logotypes/Cooper/77n118
- moths/Dickens/75n1517
- rocks and minerals/Mason/77n1436
- Shakespeare: sports & pastimes/Dent/75n1397
- storytelling/Pellowski/79n214
- wines/Churchill/75n1671

World painting index/Havlice/78n816
World radio and TV hndbk/Frost/77n1112
World series/Cohen/77n674
World statistics in brief/79n791
World travel directory/Korsant/75n591
World traveler's almanac/Meyer/76n538
World treaty index/Rohn/76n506
World trends in library educ/Bramley/76n219
World War I in the air/Smith/78n1566
World War II/Liddell Hart/79n398
World War II: account of its docs/O'Neill/77n362
World War II and its origins/Bloomberg/76n289
World War II at sea/Smith/77n1652
World warships in review 1860-1906/Leather/78n1576
World who's who of women/Kay/77n124
Worldmark ency of the nations/77n306
World's languages catalog/79n1093
Worlds of Washington Irving/Myers/76n1241
World's shells/Dance/78n858
World's students in the US/Spaulding/77n582
Worldwide directory of computer companies/Waters/75n898

Worldwide directory of federal libraries/Bettelheim/75n169
Worldwide marine weather broadcasts/US Naval Weather Service Command/75n1569
Worship and liturgy/Megivern/79n1044
Wörterbuch des verlagswesens in 20 sprachen/Móra/75n52
Worth, F L/Complete unabridged/79n104
Woy, J B/Commodity futures/77n806
Wragg, D W/Dictionary of aviation/75n1824
Wreford, S M/Horse's health/75n1663
Wright, A H/Selective bibliog/76n1180
Wright, H C/Oral antecedents/78n264
Wright, H W/Minnesota multiphasic/78n1364
Wright, L B/Of books/78n265
Wright, M/Essay collections/78n490
Wright, M/Use of criminology/75n838
Wright, N D/National directory/76n70
Wright, N E/Genealogical reader/75n434
Wright, R G/Chronological bibliog/75n1325
Wright, R J/Texas sources/78n316/Texas trade/78n712
Wright, S/Bibliography of writings/76n1281
Wright, W C/Directory of NJ/79n21
Wright, W W/Rainbow dict/79n1113
Wright brothers collection/Nolan/78n1507
Writers' and artists' year bk/76n1174
"Writer's book" by Sherwood Anderson/Curry/76n1227
Writer's cue/Reid/75n1261
Writers directory/75n1306
Writer's gd to medical journals/Lane/76n1537
Writer's hndbk/Burack/76n1168/Porter/78n106
Writer's market/Hillman/79n1168/Koester/76n1175; 77n1132
Writer's research hndbk/Cottam/78n102
Writing for results in business, gov, and the professions/Ewing/75n889
Writing in subj-matter fields/Burkett/78n101
Writing the history paper/Sanderlin/76n286
Writings of Marshall McLuhan/77n1106
Writings on American history/Dougherty/76n309; 78n342
Writings on Indian Constitution 1861-1972/Rana/75n565
Writings on Italian-Americans/Diodati/76n411
Written word endures/US Natl Archives and Records Service/78n340
Wyckoff, P/International stock/76n863
Wycliffe Bible ency/Pfeiffer/77n1050
Wycoco, C/Filipinos in/78n388

Wyld, H C/Universal dictionary/79n1097
Wylie, L/France/75n309
Wyllie, T D/Mycotoxic fungi/79n1477
Wyman, D/Saturday morning/75n1711/ Wyman's gardening/78n1498
Wyman's gardening ency/Wyman/78n1498
Wynar, A T/Encyclopedic directory ethnic/ 77n430/Encyclopedic directory ethnic organizations/76n394
Wynar, B S/American reference/75n1; 76n1/ Best reference/77n16/Dictionary of American/79n185/Introduction to cataloging/77n264/Reference books/77 n17
Wynar, C L/Guide to reference/77n234
Wynar, L R/Building ethnic/78n376/Encyclopedic directory ethnic newspapers/77 n430/Encyclopedic directory ethnic organizations/76n394/Ethnic groups/76 n393/Guide to ethnic/79n446/Reference service/78n240
Wyndham Lewis/Pound/79n1247
Wynkoop, S/Government reference/75n108
Wynn, R M/Obstetrics and/77n1487
Wynne, S G/South African/78n472
Wynter, H/Scientific instruments/77n1279

Xerox intermediate dictionary/Morris/75 n1255

Yachting world hndbk/Johnson/75n747
Yagerman, H/New environment-/75n793
Yalan, E/Design of/77n732
Yamada, H/Sanyo's tri-lingual/78n1250
Yamashita, Y/Atlas of representative/79 n1315
Yang, L/Terrace gardener's/76n1602
Yang, T S/East Asian/79n367
Yanker, G/Angry buyer's/75n939
Yannarella, P A/US government/77n1295
Yanuck, M/South Asian/77n244
Yapese-English dictionary/Jensen/78n1073
Yapese ref grammar/Jensen/79n1154
Yarger, S R/State constitutional/77n522
Yeadon, D/NY book/77n1523
Year book of . . .
 labour statistics/77n848
 social policy in Britain/Jones/75n337
 world affairs/Keeton/75n90; 76n507; 79n513
Year in endocrinology/Ingbar/78n1420
Year in metabolism/Freinkel/78n1421

Yearbook Association for Childhood Educ International/76n688
Yearbook of . . .
 adult and continuing educ/76n606; 78 n581
 American and Canadian churches/Jacquet/ 76n1089
 astronomy/Moore/77n1309
 consumer electronics/Belt/75n1791
 equal educational opportunity/76n607
 forest products/76n850
 higher education/Greene/75n661
 national accounts statistics/77n762
 science and the future/78n1220
 special education/76n608; 77n640
 the American Lutheran Church/Mickelson/76n1090
 the Assoc of Pacific Coast Geographers/ Steiner/77n556; 79n582
 the United Nations/76n469; 77n499; 79 n514
Yearbook on international communist affairs/ Staar/75n531
Yearns, W B/Biographical register/76n341
Year's work in English studies/Redmond/79 n1187
Yee, M S/Great escape/75n722
Yellow pages of undergrad innovations/Cornell Center for Improvement in Undergrad Education/75n682
Yeoman, R S/Current coins/75n1072; 76n916/ Guide book US/78n848/Handbook of US/ 77n917; 79n921
Yeomans, W N/Jobs '77/78n778
Yesterday, today and tomorrow: time and hist in the Old Testament/DeVries/76 n1098
Yesterday's authors of bks for children/ Commire/78n1102
Yff, J/Multicultural education/78n541
Yiddish word bk for English-speaking people/ Rosenbaum/79n1155
Yim, K H/China &/76n502
Yonkers Public Library/Guide to subjects/75 n1348
Yoo, Y/Books on/77n1036
York, W/Who's who rock/79n1003
Yoruba of Southwestern Nigeria/Baldwin/ 77n735
Yost, E B/Management educ/79n870
Yost, S K/Specification book/79n1556
Yothers, M T/Standards and/78n1543
Young, D K/Wildflowers of/77n1363

Young, H C/Directory of special/75n164; 78n199/New special/78n200/Planning, programming/77n208/Subject directory/76n172; 78n201
Young, I/Male homosexual/77n1128
Young, M L/Directory of special/75n164; 78n199/New special/78n200/Subject directory/76n172; 78n201
Young, N/Handbook on internat'l/77n589
Young, N F/Chinese in/75n826
Young, P/Atlas of Second/75n1843
Young, R E/Follett vest-pocket Italian/79n1142
Young, T/Georges Simenon/77n1179
Young, V G/Library trustee/79n204
Young, W C/Famous actors/76n1033
Young, W E/Cavalry journal/75n1841
Young, W M/Practical guide/75n981
Young adult lit in the seventies/Varlejs/79n220
Young people's lit in series/Rosenberg/78n1122
Youngs, C T/Films for/79n373
Your child's ears, nose, and throat/Cody/76n1544
Your intro to music-record copyright, contracts and other business and law/Hurst/78n59
Your Irish ancestors/Black/75n435
Your library/Lolley/75n143
Your teeth, your dentist, and your health/Zebooker/75n1651
Youth library work/Barnes/77n212
Yska, G/Final report/79n304
Yugoslav folklore/Lockwood/77n1053
Yugoslavia/Horton/79n392
Yugoslavia: bibliographic gd/US Library of Congress/75n307

Zaccaria, J S/Bibliotherapy in/79n309
Zachert, M J K/Simulation teaching/76n185
Zahn, H E/Euro wirtschafts/75n887
Zakanycz, J P/Map abstract/79n742
Zalewski, W/Guide to selected/75n310
Zamonski, J A/Annotated bibliog John/76n1274/Wright brothers/78n1507
Zanelli, L/Sub-aqua illust'd/78n634
Zarchy, H/Modern woman's/75n1802
Zaremba, J/Mathematical economics/79n808
Zaugg, A-M V/Guide to holdings/75n864/Holdings of/75n1247
Zebooker, E P/Your teeth/75n1651
Zeidner, N I/Private elementary/78n552

Zeiller, W/Tropical marine/76n1438
Zeis index and history of plastic surgery/Patterson/79n1482
Zelinsky, W/Bibliographic gd population/77n758
Zelkind, I/Time research/76n1491
Zell, H M/African book world/79n45/African books/76n13
Zempel, E N/First edition?/79n57
Zen Buddhism/Vessie/78n978
Zeri, F/Italian paintings/77n888
Zettler, H G/-Ologies &/79n1128
Ziegler, E N/Encyclopedia of environmental/78n1343
Zielinski, S A/Encyclopedia of hand-weaving/78n882
Zilly, R G/Handbook of environmental/76n1619
Zils, M/Directory of North/79n667/World guide/79n668
Zimmerli, W H/Comprehensive bibliog/77n1503
Zimmermann, A/Concise encyclopedia/78n1238
Zimpfer, D G/Group work/77n1444
Zingman, B/Dial/76n1221
Zinsser microbiology/Joklik/77n1491
Ziskind, S/Reference readiness/78n152/Telling stories/77n230
Zoghby, S M/Islam in/79n1055
Zogner, L/Bibliographia cartographica/78n511
Zondervan manual of style/78n107
Zondervan pictorial ency of the Bible/Tenney/76n1104
Zornow, E/Movies for/75n1200
Zotter, J/Cortina-Grosset/77n1091
Zubkoff, H/Bibliography of audiotapes/75n1621
Zuidema, G D/Johns Hopkins/78n1383
Zuker, R F/Peterson's guide/77n627
Zulauf, S W/Index of American/75n1340; 76n1225; 77n1196; 79n1217
Zurawski, J W/Polish American/76n416
Zurick, T/Air conditioning/79n1549
Zusne, L/Names in/76n1505
Zweeres, K/Guide to bird-watching/77n1376

SUBJECTS

ABBREVIATIONS AND ACRONYMS
Acronyms, initialisms, & abbreviations dict/ 78n108
Alkire/Periodical title abbreviations/78n13
Buttress/World gd to abbreviations of organizations 5th ed/76n89
De Sola/Abbreviations dict 4th ed/75n114/ 5th ed/79n105
Garb/Abbreviations in medicine/77n1475
New acronyms & initialisms: suppl/76n90; 78n109
Ocran/Ocran's acronyms . . . in scientific writing/79n1300
Paxton/Dictionary of abbreviations/75n115
Pugh/2nd dict of acronyms/75n116
Reverse acronyms, initialisms & abbreviations dict/77n119
Schertel/Abbreviations in medicine/79n1466
Spencer/Computer acronym hndbk/75n1775
UN/Latin American initialisms/75n344
Wennrich/Anglo-American & German abbreviations in science/78n1202; 79n1301

ABORTION
Floyd/Abortion bibliog/76n1516

ACADEMIC LIBRARIES
See College and university libraries

ACADIANS
De Ville/Acadian church records/76n430

ACCOUNTING
Accounting desk bk/76n841; 79n824
Accountants' index/Kubat/78n719; 78n720
Arkin/Handbook of sampling for auditing/75n904
Current Accounting Literature/77n796
Encyclopedia of accounting systems/Pescow/ 77n797
Edwards/Modern accountant's hndbk/78n721
Handbook of modern accounting/Davidson/ 78n723
Historical accounting lit: catalogue/76n842
Index to accounting pronouncements/79n826
Kohler/Dictionary for accountants/76n843
Kubat/Accountant's index/79n827
Nickerson/Accounting hndbk for non-accountants/76n844

ACQUISITIONS (libraries)
See Libraries—acquisitions
See also Book selection

ACRONYMS
See Abbreviations and acronyms

ACTORS AND ACTRESSES
See also Film actors and actresses
Highfill/Biographical dict of actors London 1660-1800/79n1022
Mapp/Directory of blacks in performing arts/ 79n1016
Young/Famous actors & actresses on American stage/76n1033

ACUPUNCTURE
Liao/Acupuncture: bibliog/77n1464
Toguchi/Complete gd/75n1634

ADHESIVES
Skeist/Handbook of adhesives/78n1541

ADLERIAN PSYCHOLOGY
Mosak/Bibliography/76n1488

ADOPTION
Van Why/Adoption bibliog & multi-ethnic sourcebook/78n657

ADULT EDUCATION
See also Continuing education; Industry training; Management training; Vocational education
Berridge/Community educ hndbk/75n654
Catalog of resource matl on community educ/79n678
Cross/Weekend educ source bk/77n615
Guide to educ'l programs in noncollegiate organizations/77n617
Ohliger/Media and adult learning/77n577
Yearbook of adult & continuing educ/76 n606; 78n581

ADVANCED PLACEMENT PROGRAM
College placemt & credit by exam/77n614

ADVERTISING
Ayer glossary of advertising/79n828
Business media gd international:
 Africa & Middle East/75n905
 Asia & Russia/75n906
 Europe/75n907; 75n908
 Latin America/75n909
 Newspaper/newsmagazines/75n910
 North America & Oceania/75n911
Dillon/Handbook of internat'l marketing/77 n808
Feuerisen/Press in Africa/75n912
Media guide international:
 Asia, Australasia & USSR/78n724
 Europe/77n784
 Latin America/78n725
 Middle East & Africa/77n785
 Newspapers and newsmagazines/77n786

200–Subjects

ADVERTISING (cont'd)
Minority group media gd/78n1076
Urdang/Dictionary of advertising terms/78n726
Wooley/Advertising law hndbk/75n913

AEGEAN REGION
Cambridge ancient hist: Middle East & Aegean/Edwards/76n357

AELFRIC
White/Aelfric/75n1380

AERONAUTICAL AND SPACE MUSEUMS
Allen/Aviation & space museums/76n64

AERONAUTICS
America's soaring book/76n730
Encyclopedia of aviation/78n1506
FAA historical fact book/75n1822
Federal aviation regulations for pilots/79n1584
Gentle/Aviation & space dict/75n1721
Miller/Tables of equilibrium shock for helium-hydrogen mixtures/76n1607
Mondey/International ency of aviation/79n1587
NASA factbook/76n1608
Soaring directory/78n638
Taylor/Air facts/76n1683; 79n1590
Who's who in aviation/75n1823
Wragg/Dictionary of aviation/75n1824

AEROSPACE
See Astronautics
See also Aeronautics

AFGHANISTAN
Hanifi/Historical dict of Afghanistan/77n317

AFL
Fink/State labor proceedings, 1885-1974/78n767
Woodbridge/AFL & CIO pamphlets 1889-1955/78n774

AFRICA
African bk world & press/Zell/79n45
African bks in print/76n13
Africa contemporary record/75n326; 76n243
African encyclopedia/75n314
Africa/Africa magazine/75n327; 76n244
Africa yr bk & who's who/Africa Journal/78n275
Asamani/Index Africanus/76n245
Balandier/Dictionary of black African civilization/75n315
Besterman/World bibliog of African bibliographies/76n2
Birkos/African & black American studies/77n431
Current bibliog on African affairs/75n286
Dickie/Who's who in Africa/75n131

AFRICA (cont'd)
Drabek/Politics of African & Middle Eastern states/78n470
Duignan/Colonialism in Africa/75n288
Encyclopedia of Africa/77n310
Feuerisen/Press in Africa/75n912
Encyclopedia Africana dict of biog/79n348
Guide to federal archives/79n349
Hartwig/Student Africanist's hndbk/76n246
Harvey/Statistics Africa/79n789
Hotchkiss/African-Asian reading gd for children/77n1152
Lynch/Great contemporary issues/75n329
Ojo-Ade/Analytic index of *Présence Africaine*/78n276
Population problems in Africa/75n294
Public Record Office/List of colonial office records, v1, Africa/78n480
Rake/New African yearbk/79n350
Schmidt/Children's bks on Africa/76n1199
Travis/Periodicals from Africa/78n277
ECONOMICS
Dejene/Experiences in rural developmt/75n287
Economic cooperation in Africa/75n289
Implementation of developmt activities in Africa/75n292
Income & employment in Africa/75n293
Land tenure & agrarian reform in Africa & Near East/77n1514
Martens/African trade unionism/78n769
GEOGRAPHY
Bederman/Africa: bibliog/75n568
Chi-Bonnardel/Atlas of Africa/75n576
Ridge/Annotated bibliographies of mineral deposits/77n1439
HISTORY
Casada/David Livingstone & Stanley/77n309
Freeman-Grenville/Chronology of African history/75n391
Freeman-Grenville/Modern atlas of African history/77n397
RELIGION
Ofori/Black African traditional religions: bibliog/77n1029
Ofori/Christianity in tropical Africa: bibliog/78n973
Turner/Bibliography of new religious movements, v1, black Africa/78n977
Williams/Howard Univ bibliog of African & Afro-American religious studies/78n979

AFRICA, NORTH
Middle East & North Africa/77n311

AFRICA, SUBSAHARAN
Africa south of Sahara/76n268; 77n307
Ofori/Islam in Africa/79n1051
Saulniers/Women in developmt process/79n761

Subjects—201

AFRICA, SUB-SAHARAN (cont'd)
Skurnik/Sub-Saharan Africa/78n292
Zoghby/Islam in Sub-Saharan Africa/79n1055

AFRICAN AUTHORS
Herdeck/African authors, 1300-1973/76 n1215

AFRICAN LIBERATION MOVEMENTS
Skurnik/Sub-Saharan Africa/78n292

AFRICAN LITERATURE
Jahn/Bibliography of creative African writing/77n1251

AFRICAN NAMES
Chuks-orji/Names from Africa/75n447
Puckett/Black names in America/77n488
Madubuike/Handbook of African names/78n424
Sanyika/Know & claim your African name/77n490

AFRIKAANS LANGUAGE
Beeton/Dictionary of English usage in Southern Africa/77n1083

AFRO-AMERICANS
See Blacks

AGGRESSIVENESS (psychology)
Crabtree/Bibliography of aggressive behavior/79n1424

AGING
See also Elderly; Old age assistance
Binstock/Handbook of aging & soc sciences/78n648
Cohen/National gd to sources in aging/78n649
McIlvaine/Aging/79n1456
Norback/Older American's hndbk/79n738
Sourcebook on aging/79n740

AGRICULTURE
Agricultural credit/78n1449
Agricultural outlook/US Dept of Agri/77n1508
Agricultural sci in Netherlands/76n1556
Agricultural statistics/77n1509
Agriculture terms/79n1510
Agrindex/77n1512
American men & women of sci: agriculture/75n1660
Beuscher's law & the farmer/Hannah/76n1557
Bibliography of food & agricul'l marketing/79n1511
Biological & agric'l index/Brooks/76n1370
Christian/Agricultural enterprises mgmt/79n1512
Directory of non-governmental organizations/79n1514
FAO production yrbk/79n1515
Greenwood/KWIC index to Commonwealth Bureau of Soils/75n1665
Haensch/Dictionary of agriculture/78n1451

AGRICULTURE (cont'd)
Lawson/Agricultural atlas of Nebraska/78n1448
List of pubs of US Dept of Agri/78n1450
McGraw-Hill ency of food, agriculture/78n1452
Owen/Guide to grad study/79n661
Production yrbk/FAO/76n846
Satyaprakash/Agriculture/79n1513
Schapsmeier/Encyclopedia of American agric'l history/77n1516
Thesaurus of agric'l terms . . . bibliog/77n1517
Trade yearbook/78n740
USSR agri atlas/77n1511
US Dept of Agri/Fact bk/77n1510
Vivian/Manual of practical homesteading/76n849
Water for agriculture/75n1664
Wheeler/Tax desk bk for farming/77n855

AIR CONDITIONING
Gladstone/Air conditioning testing/75n1806
Zurick/Air conditioning, heating dict/79n1549

AIR-CUSHION VEHICLES
Jane's surface skimmers/McLeavy/78n1547

AIR FORCES
Chant/Encyclopedia of air warfare/77n1637
Green/Observer's Soviet aircraft directory/77n1638
Munson/Bombers in service/77n1639
Polmar/World combat aircraft directory/78n1565
Taylor/Military aircraft of the world/77n1640

AIR PILOTS
See also Flight training
Airman's info manual/75n1818; 79n1581
Federal aviation regulations for pilots/79n1584
Kershner/Flight instructor's manual/76n731
Polking/Private pilot's dict & hndbk/75n763
Reithmaier/Instrument pilot's gd/76n733

AIR POLLUTION
Air quality abstracts/75n1554
Environmental engineers' hndbk, v2/76n1459
Hertzendorf/Air pollution control/75n1539
Rossano/Air pollution control/75n1541
Sparrow/Annotated bibliog of Canadian air pollution lit/77n1420
US Environmental Data Service/Bibliography of urban modification of atmosphere/75n1529

AIR WARFARE
Smith/World War I in the air/78n1566

AIRLINE INDUSTRY
Endres/World airline fleets/79n1583
Green/Observer's world airlines & airlines directory/76n1660
World aviation directory/Dean/77n1624

AIRPLANE RACES
Racing planes & air races/Kinert/76n732

AIRPLANES
Angelucci/Airplanes/75n1819
Ege/World aircraft in color/75n1820
Endres/World airline fleets/79n1583
Green/Observer's bk of aircraft/76n1659
Jane's pocket bk of commercial transport craft/Taylor/75n1821
Racing planes/Kinert/76n732
Taylor/Civil aircraft of the world/76n1661
Taylor/Jane's all the world's aircraft/79n1589
Taylor/Jane's pocket bk of home-built aircraft/79n1550

AIRPLANES, MILITARY
Chant/Encyclopedia of air warfare/77n1637
Green/Observer's Soviet aircraft/77n1638
Jane's pocket bk of major combat aircraft/75n1845
Jones/US bombers/76n1682
Knaack/Encyclopedia of US Air Force aircraft/79n1593
Krivinyi/World military aviation/75n1846
Munson/Bombers in service/77n1639
Polmar/World combat aircraft/78n1565
Ships and aircraft of US fleet/Morison/77n651/Polmar/79n1605
Swanborough/US Navy aircraft/78n1577
Taylor/Military aircraft of the world/77n1640
Weal/Combat aircraft of World War 2/78n1567

ALABAMA
Dodd/Historical atlas/76n345
List of 19th cent maps/75n571

ALASKA
Alaska fishing guide/75n758
Alaska hunting guide/75n774
Alaska-Yukon wild flowers gd/White/75n1473
Atwood/Who's who in Alaskan politics/79n540
Facts about Alaska/77n520
Five-year index/Alaska Journal/79n387
Helm/Indians of the SubArctic: bibliog/77n741
Melvin Ricks' Alaska bibliog/79n390
Milepost travel guide/75n634
Schorr/Directory of special libraries/76n171
Tourville/Alaska, bibliog 1570-1970/75n387

ALBANY COUNTY, NY
Pearson/Genealogies of the first settlers/77n474

ALCOHOL
Fazey/Aetiology of psychoactive substance use/79n1454

ALCOHOLIC BEVERAGES
Grossman/Grossman's gd to wines, beers, & spirits/78n1456
Thompson/Saloon/77n1521
Tudor/Wine, beer & spirits/77n1522

ALCOHOLISM
Alcoholism digest annual/75n1586
Andrews/Bibliography of drug abuse/78n1435
Burkhalter/Nursing care of the alcoholic/76n1528
Milgram/Alcohol educ matls: bibliog/77n1465

ALEUT LANGUAGE
Survey of materials for uncommonly taught languages/Johnson/78n1026

ALEXANDER'S MAGAZINE
Analytical guide 1905-09/75n29

ALGAE
Algae abstracts/75n1555

ALGREN, NELSON
McCollum/N. Algren/75n1351

ALKALOIDS
Glasby/Encyclopedia of alkaloids/79n1319

ALLERGY
Roth/Allergy in the world/79n1476

ALLOYS
Staudhammer/Atlas of binary alloys/75n1454
Unified numbering system for metals & alloys/76n1612

ALMANACS
CBS news almanac/Westerman/76n76; 77n97
Corliss/Strange phenomena/75n91
Information please almanac/79n106
Kane bk of famous first facts.../75n93; 77n95
McWhirter/Guinness bk of world records/77n100
Millgate/Almanac of dates/78n88
Passel/Best, encore/78n89
Quick ref encyclopedia/78n90
Reader's Digest almanac/78n91
Rowse/Help/79n107
Showers/World in figures/75n86
Statesman's year-book/Paxton/76n77
Stowell/Early American almanacs/78n40
Szykitka/Public works/75n96
Teacher brothers' modern-day almanac/79n108
Tribune almanac for 1876/76n308
Wallechinsky/People's almanac/77n102; 79n109

ALMANACS (cont'd)
Whitaker/Almanack for 1974/75n88
World almanac/77n103

ALMAYER'S FOLLY
Briggum/Concordance to Conrad's .../79n1237

ALTAIC LANGUAGES
Cirtautas/Nicholas Poppe/79n1088

ALTERNATIVE CULTURE
Alternative press index/76n78
Alternatives: gd to newspapers.../Akeroyd/77n104
Alternatives in print/75n97; 76n79; 79n110
Bundy/Alternatives to trad library services/79n286
Carnahan/Guide to alternative periodicals/79n111
Catalogue of South/Phillips/75n98
Danky/Undergrounds/75n99
Gardner/Alternative America/78n92
Hart/Catalog of the unusual/75n100
Hyde/Hotline!/77n105
Murphy/Directory of conservative & libertarian serials/79n88
New periodicals index/78n25
People's yellow pages/French/76n80
Rainbook/78n93
(Updated) last whole earth catalog/76n81
Webster/18: teenage catalog/78n661
Whole earth epilog/75n101
Szykitka/Public works/75n96

ALTERNATIVE EDUCATION
Eisenberg/Learning vacations/79n656
Eisenberg/Learning vacations: educ'l tours/79n655
Fantini/Alternative educ/77n572; 78n537
Flaxman/National directory alternative schools/79n645
Mitchell/Stopout!/79n643
Zeidner/Private elementary & secondary educ/78n552

AMERICA
America in maps/Klemp/77n542
Inter-American Statistical Institute/Bibliog of statistical sources of American nations/75n873
US Library of Congress/General censuses & vital stats in Americas/75n875

AMERICA: HISTORY AND LIFE
Five-year index/79n415

AMERICAN ANNALS OF THE DEAF
Fellendorf/Bibliography on deafness/79n1455

AMERICAN ARCHIVIST
Dowd/Index, vols 21-30/76n330

AMERICAN ART
American art directory/75n1007; 79n883
Britannica ency of American art/75n996
Clark/Ohio art & artists/77n857
Fielding/Dictionary of American painters, sculptors & engravers, enl. ed by Genevieve C. Doran/76n921
Keaveney/American painting/75n1028
Kranz/American nautical art & antiques/76n962
Monthan/Art & Indian individualists/76n936
Sokol/American architecture & art/77n876
US Smithsonian Institution/Art of the Pacific NW from 1930s/75n1013

AMERICAN ARTISTS
Benjamin/Our American artists 1879/78n794
Clark/Ohio art & artists/77n857
Collins/Women artists in America/75n1011; 76n932
Cummings/Dictionary of contemp American artists/78n823
Dawdy/Artists of American West/75n1012
Gibson/Artists of early Michigan/76n935
Koehler/US art directory & yr-bk/78n795
Locus: directory of NY galleries/77n869
McMahan/Washington, DC artists born before 1900/78n824
New York art yrbk/78n796
Samuels/Illustrated biographical ency of artists of American West/77n872
Schwab/Matter of life & death: American artists/78n826
Significant American artists & architects/Tegland/77n125
Smith/Biographical index of American artists/77n870
Smithsonian Institution/Art of Pacific NW from the 1930s/75n1013
Who's who in American art/77n873

AMERICAN ASSOCIATION OF UNIVERSITY WOMEN
Journal index 1882-1975/79n673

AMERICAN AUTHORS
Akeroyd/Where are their papers?/78n1117
Directory of fiction writers/77n1193
Fairbanks/Black American fiction/79n1215
First printings of American authors/Bruccoli/78n1110
Gallagher/Early Puritan writers/77n1185
Hirschfelder/American Indian and Eskimo authors/75n805
Knight/Biographical dict of Southern authors/79n1219
Matthews/Black American writers/76n398
Poets & Writers/suppl/78n1113

AMERICAN AUTHORS (cont'd)
Robbins/American literary manuscripts/78 n1118
Rush/Black American writers/76n1226
Shockley/Living black American authors/75 n1349
Significant American authors/Meltzer/77 n126
Thompson/Indiana authors/76n354
White/American women writers/79n1211
Who was who among North American authors/77n1183
Who was who in American history: arts & letters/77n143
Zingman/Dial: author index/76n1221

AMERICAN BAR ASSOCIATION
Pederson/Checklist of Assoc matls/78n498

AMERICAN CHEMICAL SOCIETY
Abstracts: 169th natl meeting/76n1338

AMERICAN DRAMA
Hixon/19th cent American drama/78n938
Reader's adviser, v2/Sypher/78n1090

AMERICAN DRAMATISTS
Arata/Black American playwrights, 1800 to present: bibliog/77n986
Hatch/Black playwrights 1823-1977/79n1009
Klink/Maxwell Anderson & S. N. Behrman: ref gd/78n925
Kaye/National playwrights directory/78n944

AMERICAN FICTION
Directory of fiction writers/77n1193
Eichelberger/Guide to critical reviews, 1870-1910/75n1341
Fairbanks/Black American fiction/79n1215
Golden/Flannery O'Connor & Caroline Gordon: ref gd/78n1123
Kirby/American fiction to 1900/77n1194
Reader's advisor: v1/75n1314
Rosa/Contemporary fiction in America & England, 1950-70/78n1105
Scotto/Three contemporary novelists/78n1124
Woodress/American fiction 1900-50/76n1220

AMERICAN INDIANS
See Native Americans

AMERICAN INSTITUTE OF ARCHITECTS
Schirmer/ProFile/79n891

AMERICAN ISSUES FORUM
Gaylord–SIRS Bicentennial program/Goldstein/76n325

AMERICAN JEWISH ARCHIVES
Marcus/Index to picture collection/79n460

AMERICAN LIBRARY ASSOCIATION
ALA yearbook/77n188; 78n139; 79n170
Libraries & life of the mind/78n122
Sullivan/Carl H. Milam/77n284
Thomison/History of ALA/79n329

AMERICAN LITERATURE
See also American drama; American fiction; Chicano literature
Also names of authors
Altick/Bibliography for English & Amer lit/76n1180
American book review/79n1216
American literary scholarship/75n1337; 78n1114
Bateson/Guide to English & Amer lit/78 n1088
Blanck/Bibliography of Amer lit/75n1335
Bryer/Sixteen modern Amer authors/75 n1338
Callow/Guide to Amer lit/from beginnings/78 n1116/from Dickinson/78n1115
Chielens/Literary journal in America/76n1218
Day/Handbook of Amer lit/77n1189
De Bellis/S. Lanier, H. Timrod, & P. H. Hayne/79n1210
Duggan/Fitzgerald-Hemingway annual/79 n1212
Fairbanks/Black Amer fiction/79n1215
Gallagher/Early Puritan writers/77n1185
Gohdes/Bibliographical gd to lit of the USA/77n1186
Gunn/American & British writers in Mexico/75n1308
Gunn/Mexico in American & British letters/75n1311
Harting/Literary tour gd: Northeast/79 n601
Kirkham/Indices to literary annuals/77 n1191
Leary/American lit: guide/78n1111
Literary writings in America: bibliog/78n1112
Magill's literary annual/79n1185
Manly/Contemporary Amer lit/76n1219
McNamee/Dissertations in English & Amer lit, suppl/75n1313
Patterson/Literary research gd/77n1126
Reader's advisor, v1/75n1314
Robbins/American literary manuscripts/78 n1118
Salley/Selected sound recordings of Amer lit/78n1091
Schweik/Reference sources in English & Amer lit/78n1093
Scotto/Three contemp novelists/78n1124
Spiller/Literary hist of the US/76n1339
Unger/American writers/75n1350
Webster's companion to English & Amer lit/77n1131
Year's work in English studies, v55/Redmond/79n1187
  MINORITIES
Bailey/Broadside authors & artists/75n1334
Clack/Black lit resources/77n1188
Inglehart/Image of pluralism in Amer lit/76 n388

AMERICAN LITERATURE (cont'd)
  MINORITIES (cont'd)
Jacobson/Contemporary Native Amer lit/
  78n1127
Lomeli/Chicano perspectives in lit/78n1128
Matthews/Black Amer writers/76n398
Tolzmann/German-Amer lit/78n1191
Whitlow/Black Amer lit/75n1336

AMERICAN MATHEMATICAL SOCIETY
Combined membership list of AMS, Mathematical Assoc, & Soc for Industrial & Applied Math/79n1308

AMERICAN NEUROLOGICAL ASSOCIATION
Centennial anniversary volume/Denny-Brown/
  76n1510

AMERICAN NEWSPAPERS
Brigham/History & bibliog 1690-1820/77n1110
Wynar/Encyclopedic directory of ethnic newspapers & periodicals/77n430

AMERICAN PHILOSOPHICAL SOCIETY
Smith/Oak from an acorn/78n262

AMERICAN POETRY
Cline/Index to criticisms/75n1332
Childhood in poetry, 2nd suppl/77n1146
Davis/Contemporary Amer poetry/76n1223
Gershator/Bibliographic gd to the lit of contemp Amer poetry/77n1195
Malkoff/Crowell's hndbk of contemp poetry/
  75n1342
Scheick/Seventeenth cent poetry/78n1126
Zulauf/Index of periodical verse/75n1340;
  76n1225; 77n1196; 79n1217

AMERICAN POETS
Akeroyd/Where are their papers?: 42 contemp Amer poets & writers/78n1117
Directory of Amer poets/76n1224/Suppl/78n1113
Significant Amer authors, poets, & playwrights/Meltzer/77n126

AMERICAN PSYCHIATRIC ASSOCIATION
Biographical directory/75n1603; 78n1368

AMERICAN REPUBLICS
  See America

AMERICAN SOCIETY FOR INFORMATION SCIENCE
Information mgmt in the 1980s/79n303

AMERICAN SONGS
Anderson/Freedom's voice in poetry & song/
  79n958
80 yrs of Amer song hits, 1892-1972/75n1170
Levy/Give me yesterday: Amer hist in song, 1890-1920/76n1028

AMERICAN SONGS (cont'd)
Lowens/Bibliography of songsters printed in Amer before 1821/77n958
Woll/Songs from Hollywood music comedies, 1927 to present/77n984

AMERICAN STUDIES
LC/Guide to study of the USA, suppl/77n338
Walker/American studies/77n334

AMERICANISMS
Flexner/I hear America talking/78n1031

AMIS, KINGSLEY
Gohn/K. Amis: checklist/77n1228

AMNESTY
Sherman/Amnesty in America/75n478

AMPHIBIANS
Brown/Reptiles & amphibians of the West/
  76n1447
Cogger/Reptiles & amphibians of Australia/
  78n1336
Conant/Field gd to reptiles & amphibians of North America/76n1448
Czajka/State laws regulating the collection of reptiles & amphibians, US/76n1449
Henderson/Checklist and key to amphibians & reptiles of Central America/77n1397

AMUSEMENTS
Flaste/NY Times gd to children's entertainment/77n559
Hunter/Family gd to amusement centers/76n550
Onosko/Fun land USA/79n713

ANATOMY, HUMAN
Anderson/Grant's atlas of anatomy/79n1443
Gray/Anatomy: 1901 ed/76n1530
Johns Hopkins atlas/78n1383
Langman/Atlas of medical anatomy/79n1447
McMinn/Colour atlas/78n1384
Rand McNally atlas of the body & mind/77n1456

ANCIENT HISTORY
  See History

ANDERSON, MAXWELL
Klink/M. Anderson & S. N. Behrman/78n925

ANDERSON, SHERWOOD
Curry/"Writer's Book" by S. Anderson/76n1227
Rogers/S. Anderson: bibliog/77n1197
White/S. Anderson: ref gd/78n1129

ANGLO-SAXON POETRY
Bessinger/Concordance to Anglo-Saxon poetic records/79n1231

206 – Subjects

ANIMAL BEHAVIOR
Grzimek's ency of ethology/Grzimek/78n1313
Heymer/Ethological dict/79n783

ANIMAL MAGNETISM
Gartrell/Electricity & animal magnetism, chklist, 1600-1850/77n1591

ANIMAL TRACKS
Murie/Field gd to animal tracks/76n1413

ANIMALS
Audubon/Quadrupeds of North Amer/76n1410
Fogden/Animals & thr colors/75n1495
Grzimek's animal life encyclopedia:
  v1 lower animals/76n1403
  v2 insects/76n1404
  v6 reptiles/76n1405
  v11 mammals/76n1406
  v12 mammals/76n1407
Kosloff/Plants & animals Pacific NW/77n1346
Larousse ency of animal world/77n1372
Purnell's first ency of animals/Burton/78n1314
Thompson/Index to illus of natural world/78n1277
Wood/Animal facts & feats/79n1368

ANIMALS IN ART
Pollack/Animal kingdom/79n901

ANNE ARUNDEL COUNTY, MD
Maryland rent rolls, 1705-42/77n469

ANNIVERSARIES
Emmens/AV gd to Amer holidays/79n1086
Gregory/Anniversaries & holidays/76n1108

ANONYMS AND PSEUDONYMS
See Pseudonyms

ANTARCTIC
Thuronyi/Antarctic bibliog/78n1203/Indexes/79n1307

ANTHROPOLOGISTS
Evans-Pritchard/Bibliography of writings of Evans-Pritchard/76n803
Fifth internat'l directory/76n812
Gordan/Margaret Mead: bibliog/78n678
Lapointe/Claude Levi-Strauss/79n779

ANTHROPOLOGY
Anderson/Revised, bibliog of the Chumash/79n773
Annual review of anthropology/Siegel/76n808
Breedlove/Guide to holdings of Stanford Univ libraries/75n864
Burnett/Anthropology & educ/75n865
Coppell/World catalogue of theses about Aborigines/79n774
Dwyer-Shick/Study & teaching of anthropology/77n737
Encyclopedia of Indians of the Americas/75n866

ANTHROPOLOGY (cont'd)
Favazza/Anthropological themes in mental health/78n1373
Handbook of Middle Amer Indians/77n749
Hays/Anthropology in New Guinea/77n739
Hunter/Encyclopedia of anthropology/77n748
Keesing/Culture change/75n867
Kemper/History of anthropology/79n776
Lambert/Village studies, v2/79n778
Lebar/Ethnic groups of Southeast Asia, v2/76n810
Marshall/Micronesia/77n744
McDonald/Master's theses in anthropology/79n780
McGlynn/Middle Amer anthropology/77n733
Reviews in anthropology/75n868; 76n807
Rosentiel/Education & anthropology/79n782
Survey of research in soc anthropology/77n701; 77n702
Tax/Serial publications/75n869

ANTIBIOTICS
Glasby/Encyclopedia of antibiotics/78n1438

ANTIQUARIAN BOOKSELLERS
Robinson/Buy books where/79n61

ANTIQUES
See also Furniture; Glass; etc.
Boger/House & Garden's antiques/75n1053
Bond/Encyclopedia of antiques/77n897
Bridgeman/Encyclopedia of Victoriana/76n958
Coombs/Guide to antique collecting/79n911
D'Imperio/Country antiques companion/78n834
Doherty/Antique shops USA/78n835
Franklin/Antiques & collectibles/79n913
Erick collection, illus catalogue, v8/78n868
Grotz/Antique restorer's hndbk/78n836
Hammond/Pictorial price gd to Amer antiques/79n914
Hudson/Antiques, illus'd & priced/79n915
Kelley/Anatomy of antiques/76n961
Kennedy/Buying antiques in Europe/78n837
Ketchum/Catalog of Amer antiques/79n917
Kovel/Kovel's complete antique price list/75n1055
Kranz/American nautical art/76n962
Lessard/Complete gd to French-Canadian antiques/76n963
Mackay/Turn-of-the-century antiques/75n1056
Michael/Basic bk of antiques/75n1057
Mullenix/Antiques: hndbk/78n839
Phillips/Collectors' ency of antiques/75n1059

ANTIQUES (cont'd)
Phipps/Collector's dict of Amer antiques/ 76n964
Porter/Directory of art restoration/76n960
Ramsey/Complete color ency of antiques/76n959
Richardson/Encyclopedia of antique restoration/75n1054
Schiffer/Brass book/79n937
Semple/Introductory gd to Midwest antiques/ 78n840
Simonsgaard/Antique collecting in the Midwest/78n841
Smith/International art yrbk/79n916
Voss/Antique Amer country furn/79n924
Wills/Concise ency of antiques/78n842

ANTI-SEMITISM
Grosser/Causes and effects/79n437

ANTI-WAR MOVEMENT
Heath/Mutiny does not happen lightly: Vietnam war/77n502
Melody/Apaches/79n781

APPALACHIA
Bibliography of southern Appalachia/Ross/ 78n312

APPLIED ARTS
See Art industries and trade
See also Crafts

APPRAISAL (valuation)
MacBride/Bibliography of appraisal lit/76n858

AQUARIUMS
Favre/Larousse dict of freshwater aquarium/79n700
Halstead/Tropical fish/76n1558
Hoedeman/Naturalists' gd to fresh-water aquarium fish/75n1668
Paysan/Guide to aquarium fishes/76n1559
Simon & Schuster's gd to aquarium fishes/ 79n704

AQUATIC PLANTS
Ashton/Aquatic plants of Australia/75n1468

ARAB COUNTRIES
Abdulrazak/Arabic historical writing/78n366
Arab Islamic bibliog/Grimwood-Jones/78n278
Bidwell's gd to gov ministers—Arab world/75n516
Selim/American doctoral dissertations on Arab world/78n282

ARAB-ISRAELI CONFLICT
Arab-Israeli conflict 1945-71/79n439
DeVore/Arab-Israeli conflict: bibliog/77n417
Gilbert/Atlas of Arab-Israeli conflict/76n358
Khaliki/Palestine & Arab-Israeli conflict/75n535
Sobel/Israel & the Arabs/75n525

ARABIA
Geddes/Analytical gd to bibliographies on: Arabian peninsula/75n291
Islam, Muhammad/75n290
Gulf handbook/79n614
Nyrop/Area hndbk for Persian Gulf states/ 79n357

ARABIC LANGUAGE
Bakalla/Bibliography of Arabic linguistics/ 77n1059
Wehr/Dictionary of modern written Arabic/ 78n1050

ARABIC LITERATURE
Altoma/Modern Arabic lit/77n1252

ARABIC PERIODICALS
Union catalogue of Arabic serials/78n29

ARBITRATION
Baer/Labor arbitration gd/75n973
Seide/Warburg union catalog of arbitration/ 75n980

ARCHAEOLOGY
Archaeologists' year bk/75n400
Atlas of classical archaeology/Finley/78n317
Avi-Yonah/Encyclopedia of excavations in the Holy Land/79n393
Bray/Penguin dict of archaeology/77n348
Chou/Oracle bone collections/78n318
Corliss/Ancient man/79n394
Corliss/Strange artifacts/75n401
Daniel/Illustrated ency of archaeology/78n319
Day/Archaeology: hndbk/79n395
Guido/Sicily: prehistoric & Roman remains/ 78n320
Hawkes/Atlas of ancient archaeology/75n402
Hawkes/Atlas of early man/78n327
Hoppin/Handbook of attic red-figured vases/ 75n403
Millon/Urbanization at Teotihuacan, Mexico/ 75n404
Oppelt/Southwestern pottery/78n680
Stillwell/Princeton ency of classical sites/77n350
Whitehouse/Archaeological atlas of the world/77n351

ARCHERY
Bobbs/Bows & arrows: bibliog/76n763

ARCHITECTS
Directory of architects for health facilities/ 78n791
Schirmer/ProFile/79n891
Significant Amer artists & architects/Tegland/77n125
Who's who in architecture, 1400 to the present/Richards/78n804

ARCHITECTS (cont'd)
Wodehouse/American architects to WWI/77n879/to the present/78n805/British architects/79n895

ARCHITECTURAL PRESERVATION
Smith/Critical bibliog of bldg conservation/79n892
Tubesing/Architectural preservation in the US/79n894

ARCHITECTURE
Ballard/Directory of Manhattan office bldgs/79n889
Bibliographic gd to art & architecture/77n1
Blumenson/Identifying Amer architecture/78n799
Callender/Time saver stds for arch'l design/75n1015
Coulson/Annotated bibliog of Greek & Roman architecture/77n862
Cowan/Dictionary of architectural sci/75n1016
Curl/English architecture/78n800
Gebhard/Guide to architecture of Minnesota/79n890
Guide to architecture of Washington, DC/75n1017
Harris/Dictionary of architecture/76n938
Harris/Historic architecture sourcebk/78n801
Historic bldgs of Massachusetts/77n874
Hitchcock/American architec'l bks/78n802
Houghton/Guide to British cathedrals/75n1018
Lee/Bibliography of energy conservation/78n803
Lee/Encyclopedia of energy-efficient bldg design/78n1518
Makinson/Guide to work of Greene & Greene/76n939
Malo/Landmarks of Rochester & Monroe County/75n1019
Melas/Greek experience/75n1020
Pevsner/Dictionary of architecture/77n875
Putnam/Architectural & bldg dict/75n1021
Schwicker/International dict of bldg construction/76n1618
Senkevitch/Soviet architecture/75n1022
Sokol/American architecture & art/77n876
Studio dict of design & decoration/75n1023
Walker/Glossary of art, architecture & design/78n789
White/Architecture book/77n878

ARCHITECTURE SCHOOLS
Architecture schools in N. America/Hegener/78n798

ARCHIVAL ASSOCIATIONS
Fang/International gd to library, archival & info sci assocs/77n176

ARCHIVES
Brichford/Manuscripts gd to collections at Univ of Illinois/77n28
Clark/Archive-library relations/77n153
Descriptive inventory of archives of state of Illinois: index/79n406
Dowd/Index to Amer Archivist/76n330
Duckett/Modern manuscripts/77n352
East central and SE Europe: library & archival resources/Horecky/77n192
Elliot/Descriptive gd to Harvard Univ archives/77n634
Evans/Modern archives & manuscripts/76n291
Guide des sources de l'histoire des états-unis dans les archives françaises/78n367
Harris/Guide to manuscripts (Iowa)/75n380
International directory of archives/77n353
Kinney/Directory of state & provincial archives (US & Canada)/76n318
Lanzing/Library, documentation & archives serials/77n36
Manuscripts collections of MN Historical Society, no. 3/78n339
Matthews/American diaries in manuscript, 1580-1954/75n361
Norton/Norton on archives/77n354
Rath/Care & conservation of collections/78n321
Schreiner-Yantis/Archives of pioneers of Tazewell County, VA/75n362
US National Archives & Records Service/Gd to national archives of the US/75n363
US National Archives & Records Service/Written word endures/78n340

ARCHIVES NATIONALES
Guide des sources de l'histoire des états-unis dans les archives françaises/78n367

ARCTIC
Arctic bibliog, v XVI/77n1343
Gunn/Bibliography of naval Arctic research/75n1524

ARGENTINA
Fitzgibbon/Argentina/75n339

ARID LANDS
Paylore/Arid lands research institutions/79n1405

ARISTOTLE
Erickson/Aristotle's rhetoric/76n1106

ARITHMETIC TEACHER
Cumulative index, 1954-73/76n588

ARIZONA
Arizona blue book/75n503
Powell/Arizona gathering II/75n385

ARMAMENTS
See Arms and armor
See also Armed forces; Arms trade; Disarmament; Weapon systems

ARMED FORCES
Armed forces of the world/Sellers/78n1561
Dupuy/Almanac of world military power/76n1677
Military balance/77n1630
Miller/Guide to evaluation of educ'l experiences in the armed services/76n650
RUSI & Brassey's defence yrbk/76n1680
US Arms Control & Disarmament Agency/World military expenditures & arms transfers 1966-75/78n1564

ARMENIAN AMERICANS
Wertsman/Armenians in America/79n447

ARMENIAN LITERATURE
Sanjian/Catalogue of medieval Armenian manuscripts in the US/78n62

ARMORED VEHICLES, MILITARY
Chamberlain/British & Amer tanks of WWII/76n1684
Foss/Armoured fighting vehicles of the world/78n1562

ARMS AND ARMOR
See also Weapon systems; and specific types of weapons, e.g., Firearms; Infantry weapons; Nuclear weapons; Tanks
Foss/Infantry weapons of the world/78n1568
Hogg/Encyclopedia of infantry weapons of WWII/78n1569
Hogg/Military small arms of the 20th cent/78n1558
Jane's infantry weapons/Archer/78n1570
Quick/Dictionary of weapons & military terms/75n1838
Williams/Atlas of weapons & war/78n1554

ARMS CONTROL
See Disarmament; SALT II

ARMS TRADE
Gillingham/Arms traffic/78n1555
Stockholm Internat'l Peace Research Institute/Arms trade with the Third World/76n870
US Arms Control & Disarmament Agency/World military expenditures & arms transfers 1966-75/78n1564

ARNOLD, BENEDICT
Gocek/Benedict Arnold/75n358

ARNOLD, MATTHEW
Tollers/Bibliography of M. Arnold, 1932-70/76n1266

ART
See also American art; Baroque art, Decorative art, etc.
Art at auction/75n1002
Art Index/Patten/76n929
Art Kunst 1/75n987
Bibliographic gd to art & architecture/77n1
Films on art/79n1035

ART (cont'd)
Goldman/Reading & writing in the arts/79n887
Greenhill/Dictionary of art/75n998
Grotz/Antique restorer's hndbk/78n836
Jacobs/Color ency of world art/76n923
Lemke/Museum companion/75n1004
Muehsam/Guide to basic info sources/79n888
Myers/Dictionary of 20th cent art/75n999
National directory of art support by private foundations/78n793
NY Public Library/Dictionary catalog of art & architecture division/76n919
Phaidon dict of 20th cent art/79n881
Quick/Artists' & illustrators' ency/78n788
Unesco/Illustrated inventory of famous dismembered works of art/76n945
Visual dict of art/Hill/75n1000
Walker/Glossary of art, architecture & design since 1945/78n789
Wones/Artist's market/79n886

ART, AMERICAN
See American art

ART, DECORATIVE
See Decorative art

ART, MODERN
See Modern art

ART DEALERS
International art & antiques yrbk/Smith/79n916

ART EDUCATION
Bunch/Art educ/79n627

ART GALLERIES AND MUSEUMS
Abse/Art galleries of Britain & Ireland/77n868
Collectors & collections/Camber/79n878
Cooper/World museums guide/75n1008
Fundaburk/Art at educ'l institutions in the US/75n1009
Fundaburk/Pocket gd to location of art in the US/79n884
Potterton/National Gallery, London/79n880
Hugo/Guide to art resources in LA/78n792
Lemke/Museum companion/75n1004
Locus: directory of NY galleries & art sources.../77n869
US Congress/Art in the US Capitol/77n867

ART HISTORY
Pierce/From abacus to Zeus/79n882

ART INDUSTRIES AND TRADE
Art & crafts market/Lapin/78n874
Ehresmann/Applied & decorative arts: bibliog/78n827
Wones/Artist's market/79n886

210—Subjects

ART LIBRARIES
Hoffberg/Directory of art libraries in North America/79n885
Hugo/Guide to art resources in Los Angeles/78n792
Irvine/Slide libraries/75n205
Pacey/Art library manual/78n260

ART METAL-WORK
Oxford Univ/Catalogue of Anglo-Saxon ornamental metalwork/75n994

ART SOCIETIES
Koehler/US art directory & yr-bk/78n795
Reiss/Arts mgmt handbk/75n1005

ART NOUVEAU
Kempton/Art nouveau: bibliog/78n785

ART REPRODUCTIONS
Index to art reproductions in books/75n1010
Parry/Contemporary art & artists/79n900

ARTHROPODS
Biery/Venemous arthropod hndbk/78n1327

ARTHURIAN LEGENDS
West/Index of proper names in French Arthurian prose romances/79n1275

ARTIFACTS
Chenhall/Nomenclature for museum cataloging/79n269

ARTIFICIAL SATELLITES
Unger/Literature survey of communication satellite systems/78n1509

ARTILLERY
Foss/Artillery of the world/77n1642

ARTISTS
See also by nationality, e.g., American artists
Artist's & photographer's market/77n856
Artist's market/Polking/76n927
Contemporary artists/Naylor/79n909
Graphic artists guild/78n809
Parry/Contemporary art & artists/79n900
Who's who in American art/79n910
Who's who in the arts/75n1014
Writers' & artists' yr bk/76n1174
Women's Hist Research Center/Female artists past and present/76n933; 76n934

ARTISTS' MARKS
Caplan/Classified directory of artists' signatures/78n790
Haslam/Marks & monograms of modern movement 1875-1930/78n829

ARTS
See also Art; Performing arts; etc.
Andreoli-deVillers/Futurism and the arts/77n861
Bibliographic gd to art & architecture/77n1

ARTS (cont'd)
Bibliography-1: ref books/78n784
Bolte/Libraries and the arts & humanities/79n146
Ehresmann/Fine arts: gd to ref works/76n915
Fine arts marketplace/77n858
Index to art reproductions in books/75n1010
National directory of grants to individuals in the arts/Millsaps/77n86
National Endowment for the Arts/76n628
Spalek/German expressionism in the fine arts/78n786
Who was who in Amer hist: arts & letters/77n143

ARTS FOR HANDICAPPED
Materials on creative arts . . . for persons with handicapping conditions/79n684

ASHBERY, JOHN
Kermani/J. Ashbery: bibliog/77n864

ASHMOLEAN MUSEUM
Lloyd/Catalogue of earlier Italian paintings/78n818

ASIA
See also East Asia; Pacific Islands; South Asia; Southeast Asia
Annual review of English bks on Asia/Ferguson/78n294
Association for Asian Studies/South Asian library resources in N. Amer/77n243
Besterman/World bibliog of Oriental bibliog/76n3
Bibliography of Asian studies/76n257
Chang/Asia & Pacific planning bibliog/75n298
Chen/Economic conditions of East & SE Asia/79n799
Davis/On-your-own gd to Asia/79n612
Doctoral dissertations on Asia/76n258
Far East & Australasia/76n267
Hotchkiss/African-Asian reading gd for children & young adults/77n1152
Index to Asian educ'l periodicals/76n589
Kumar/Documentation on Asia, v IV/75n300
Lynch/All-Asia guide/79n619
McDowell/Asian-Pacific literatures in English/79n364
McLane/Soviet-Asian relations/75n537
Parker/American dissertations on foreign educ, v VI, Far East/77n578
Ridge/Annotated bibliogs of mineral deposits in Africa, Asia (exclusive of USSR) and Australasia/77n1439

ASIAN AMERICANS
Asian Americans: bibliog/78n384
Dunn/Asian Americans: gd/76n395

Subjects—211

ASLIB
Taylor/Essays on Aslib/79n317

ASPEN INSTITUTE
Kuhn/Annotated bibliog of publications/78n543

ASSOCIATION FOR CHILDHOOD EDUCATION INTERNATIONAL
ACEI/Yearbook/76n688

ASSOCIATION OF AMERICAN LIBRARY SCHOOLS
Davis/AALS, 1915-68/75n262

ASSOCIATION OF PACIFIC COAST GEOGRAPHERS
Yearbook/77n556; 79n582

ASSOCIATIONS
See also Trade and professional associations
Alt/Encyclopedia of Ohio assocs/79n90
Buttress/World gd to abbreviations of organizations/76n89
Circle of Friends/78n79
Directory of assocs in Canada/76n65; 79n82
Directory of info service/79n81
Gardner/Alternative America/78n92

ASTROLOGERS
Marks/Directory of New England astrologers/79n1434

ASTROLOGY
Daily planet almanac/Reim/79n1432
deVore/Encyclopedia of astrology/77n1449
Fleming-Mitchell/Running Press glossary of astrology terms/78n1376
Francis/New English astrological thesaurus/79n1433
Keyes/Master gd to preparing your natal horoscope/75n1605
Sun/Asian animal zodiac/75n1607
Wedeck/Dictionary of astrology/75n1608

ASTRONAUTICS
See also Space craft
Gentle/Aviation & space dict/75n1751
NASA factbook/76n1608
New space ency/75n1443
Ridpath/Illustrated ency of astronomy & space/78n1237

ASTRONAUTS
US Congress/Astronauts & cosmonauts biographical & statistical data/77n1571

ASTRONOMERS
American men & women of sci: physics, astronomy, math, stats, & computer sci/78n1216

ASTRONOMICAL OBSERVATORIES
Kirby-Smith/US observatories/77n1308

ASTRONOMY
Annual review of astronomy & astrophysics/75n1444; 76n1335
Burnham's celestial hndbk/79n1312
Cambridge ency of astronomy/Mitton/79n1313
Cleminshaw/Beginner's gd to the skies/79n1314
de Callatay/Atlas of the planets/76n1336
de Vaucouleurs/Second ref catalogue of bright galaxies/77n1306
Encyclopaedic dict of physics/77n1337
Hopkins/Glossary of astronomy & astrophysics/77n1307
Howard/Telescope hndbk & star atlas/76n1337
Moore/A-Z of astronomy/78n1234
Moore/Color star atlas/75n1448
Moore/Concise atlas of the universe/75n1447
Moore/1976 yearbk of astronomy/77n1309
Muirden/Amateur astronomer's hndbk/75n1445
New space ency/75n1443
Physics & astronomy classification scheme/79n1334
Ridpath/Illustrated ency of astronomy & space/78n1237
Roth/Astronomy/77n1310
Sandage/Galaxies & universe/77n1311
Seal/Guide to lit of astronomy/78n1236
Sulentic/Revised catalogue of nonstellar astronomical objects/75n1446
Weigert/Concise ency of astronomy/78n1238
Whitney/Star finder/75n1442
Yamashita/Atlas of stellar spectra/79n1315

ASTROPHYSICS
Annual review of astronomy & astrophysics/75n1444; 76n1335
Hopkins/Glossary of astronomy & astrophysics/77n1307

ATKINSON REPORT
Steele/Steady-state, zero growth & academic library/79n200

ATLANTA, GA
Lankevich/Atlanta: hist 1813-1976/79n426
Murray/Atlas of Atlanta/75n880
Murray/Atlas of metro-Atlanta/77n545

ATLANTIC ALLIANCE
Gordon/Atlantic alliance/79n552

ATLANTIC OCEAN
Hastenrath/Climatic atlas of tropical Atlantic & Pacific Oceans/79n1414

ATLASES
See also under individual countries, regions, places
Alexander/Guide to atlases suppl/78n510
International maps & atlases in print/75n570
Winch/International maps & atlases in print/78n512

GENERAL
Black/Blathwayt atlas, commentary/76n367
Comparative world atlas/76n524
Cosmopolitan world atlas/79n584
Espenshade/Goode's world atlas/79n585
Hammond ambassador world atlas/79n586
Hammond internat'l world atlas/75n577; 77n544
Hammond medallion world atlas/79n587
Hammond new contemp world atlas/78n514
Intermediate world atlas/76n525
Landsat index atlas of developing countries/World Bank/78n515
Madden/My first atlas/76n526
Man's domain/76n527
New York Times atlas of the world/79n589
Penguin world atlas/76n528
Premier world atlas/79n590
Purnell's illust'd world atlas/Tunney/78n516
Rand McNally atlas of the oceans/78n517
Rand McNally concise atlas of the earth/77n546
Rand McNally grand atlas & pic book of the world/78n517
Signet-Hammond world atlas/79n591
Times atlas of the world/76n529
US Military Academy, West Point/Atlas of landforms/75n581
Webster's atlas & zip code/75n582
Whole earth atlas/76n530

HISTORICAL
Atlas of discovery/Roberts/75n351
Barraclough/Times atlas of world hist/79n583
Hawkes/Atlas of early man/78n327
Kinder/Anchor atlas of world hist/76n297; 79n401
Lloyd/Atlas of maritime hist/78n328
Pemsel/History of war at sea/79n1604
Shepherd's historical atlas/75n352

ATOMIC ENERGY
See Nuclear energy

ATOMIC TRANSITION PROBABILITIES
Fuhr/Bibliography/79n1330

AUCHINCLOSS, LOUIS
Bryer/L. Auchincloss & his critics/78n1130

AUCTIONS
American bk prices current/77n68
Art at auction/75n1002

AUCTIONS (cont'd)
Francis/Whitman at auction 1899-1972/79n1225
Munby/British bk sale catalogues 1676-1800/79n60

AUDEN, W. H.
Gingerich/W. H. Auden: guide/78n1165

AUDIO CASSETTES
See Phonotapes

AUDIO ENGINEERING
Amos/Radio, TV & audio tech'l ref bk/79n1567

AUDIOVISUAL EQUIPMENT
Audio-visual eqpmt directory/79n677
Audiovisual market place/78n553
Layman's gd to AV jargon/76n595
Norback/Educational market place/78n555
Rosenberg/Media eqpmt: gd & dict/77n658
Selecting educ'l eqpmt & matls/Deans/77n645

AUDIOVISUAL INDUSTRY
Audiovisual market place/78n553
Norback/Educational market place/78n555

AUDIOVISUAL MEDIA
See also Instructional media; specific media formats, e.g., Filmstrips; and under specific subjects
Audiovisual market place/78n553
BAMEG reviews/79n222
Brown/Core media collection for secondary schools/76n156
Burlingame/Library & media/79n251
Cabeceiras/Multimedia library/79n244
Catalog of US gov produced AV matls/76n668
Educators gd to free tapes, scripts/Wittich/76n675
Elementary school library collection/Van Orden/77n233
Fleischer/Style manual for citing microform & nonprint media/79n129
Fothergill/Non-book matls in libraries/79n148
Hart/Multi-media indexes/76n679
International index to multi-media info/77n661; 77n662
Media review digest/Wall/78n585
Nadler/How to start an AV collection/79n306
Norback/Educational market place/78n555
Reference list of AV matls produced by the US gov/79n124
Rufsvold/Guides to educ'l media/78n600
Sive/Selecting instructional media/79n688
Thomas/Turning kids on to print using non-print/79n219
US Natl AV Center/Directory of US gov AV personnel/76n630

AUDIOVISUAL SERVICES (libraries)
See also Film libraries
A-V connection: gd to federal funds/78n245
ALA/Guidelines for AV matls & services for large public libraries/76n144
ALA/Recommendations for AV matls & services for small & medium-sized public libraries/76n145
Baker/School & public library media programs/78n178
Boyle/Expanding media/78n246
Brown/Nonprint media info networking/78n247
Directory of 16mm film collections in colleges in the US/76n206
Goldstein/Video in libraries/78n248
Nadler/How to start an AV collection/79n306
Grove/Nonprint media in academic libraries/76n137
Weber/North Amer film & video directory/77n186

AUDITING
Index to accounting & auditing pronouncements/79n826

AUDUBON, JOHN JAMES
Fries/Double elephant folio/75n46

AUGER EFFECT
Hawkins/Auger electron spectroscopy/79n1316

AUGUSTA COUNTY, VA
Kaylor/Abstracts of land grant surveys, 1761-1791/77n467

AUSTEN, JANE
Halperin/Plots & characters in fiction of J. Austen, Brontës and G. Eliot/77n1129
Hardwick/Guide to J. Austen/75n1381
Leeming/Who's who in J. Austen & the Brontës/75n1377

AUSTRALASIA
Far East & Australasia/76n267
Ridge/Annotated bibliogs of mineral deposits in Africa, Asia, & Australasia/77n1439

AUSTRALIA
Australian bks in print/75n6; 79n9
Australian dict of biog, v5/76n108
Balnaves/Australian libraries/76n212
Borchardt/Australian bibliog/77n22
Castles/Australia: fact bk 1606-1976/79n429
Cogger/Reptiles & amphibians of Australia/78n1336
Gibbney/Labor in print, 1850 and 1939/76n903
Taubert/Book trade of the world. V II, Americas, Australia, New Zealand/77n51
White/Australia/75n619
Willis/Handbook to plants in Victoria/75n1472

AUSTRALIAN ABORIGINES
Coppell/World catalogue of theses/79n774
Tindale/Aboriginal tribes of Australia/75n870

AUSTRALIAN LITERATURE
Lock/Australian literature/79n1259

AUTHORS
See also American authors; Black authors; Women authors; Children's literature; individual authors, by name
Author biogs master index/La Beau/79n135
Authors in the news/77n1108
Contemporary authors:
  V 9-12/75n119
  V 13-16/76n96
  V 29-32/79n137
  V 49-52/76n97
  V 53-56/76n98
  V 69-72/79n138
Contemporary authors cum index/79n139
Contemporary authors, permanent series:
  v1/76n99
  v2/79n140
Havlice/Index to literary biog/76n1192
Index to Wilson author series/77n1140
International authors & writers who's who/77n1180; 79n1208
Johnson/Biographies of authors represented in authors digest series/76n1216
Professional directory of writers/75n1302
Schwartz/Articles on women writers:bibliog/78n1092
Seymour-Smith/Who's who in 20th cent lit/77n1181
Vinson/Contemporary novelists/77n1182
Wakeman/World authors, 1950-70/Kunitz/76n1217
Who was who among English & European authors 1931-49/79n1209
Women & literature/78n1095

AUTHORSHIP
See also Editing; Publishers and publishing; Report writing; Style manuals
Burack/Writers handbook/76n1168
Burkett/Writing in subj-matter fields/78n101
Cottam/Writer's research hndbk/78n102
Directory of publishing opportunities/75n54; 76n49
Flesch/Look it up: spelling & style/78n103
Goodman/Canadian writer's market/79n1167
Hill/Into print/78n39
Leggett/Prentice-Hall hndbk for writers/79n130
NY Times manual of style & usage/Jordan/77n116
Olsen/Preparing the manuscript/77n117
Polking/Beginning writer's answer bk/79n1169

AUTHORSHIP (cont'd)
Polking/Law & the writer/79n561
Turabian/Student's gd for writing research papers/78n105
Writers' & artists' year bk/76n1174
Writers directory/75n1306
Writer's manual/78n106
Writer's market/76n1175; 77n1132; 79n1168
Zondervan manual of style/78n107

AUTOGRAPHS
Hamilton/Big name hunting/75n1096
Patterson/Autographs/75n1100

AUTOMATIC CONTROL
Clason/Elsevier's dict of measuremt & control in six languages/79n1544
Considine/Process instruments & controls handbook/75n1803
Standards & practices for instrumentation/Yothers/78n1543

AUTOMOBILE INDUSTRY
Glossary of automotive terminology: French-English, English-French/79n1552
Heasley/Production figure bk for US cars/78n756

AUTOMOBILE MAINTENANCE AND REPAIR
Brant/Transistor ignition systems/77n1572
Chilton's:
   Auto air conditioning manual/75n1722
   Auto repair manual/77n1573
   Basic auto maintenance/77n1574
   Guide to emission controls/75n1723
   More miles per gallon gd/75n1739
Chilton's repair & tune-up guide:
   Fiat 2/75n1724
   Gremlin, Hornet/75n1725
   Honda/75n1726
   International Scout/75n1750
   Jaguar 2/75n1727
   Opel 2/75n1728
Complete official MGB/75n1729
Dempsey/Modern gd to auto tuneup & emission control servicing/75n1730
Evenson/Complete hndbk of automotive engines & systems/75n1731
Hallmark/Auto electronics simplified/76n1613
Hallmark/Complete auto electric hndbk/76n1614
Hirsch/Super catalog of car parts & accessories/75n1732
Houston/MGA-MGB service-repair hndbk/75n1733
Jackson/What every woman should know abt her car/75n1734
Jorgensen/Audi service: Fox series/75n1735
Jorgensen/Corvette service/75n1736

AUTOMOBILE MAINTENANCE AND REPAIR (cont'd)
Lien/Complete gd for easy car care/76n1615
Time-Life book of the family car/75n1737
Volkswagen Beetle, Super Beetle, Karmann Ghia/75n1738

AUTOMOBILE MECHANICS
National Institute for Auto Service/Where to find certified mechanics for your car/76n1616

AUTOMOBILE RACING
Complete bk of NASCAR stock car racing/75n780
Motor sport yrbk/Gill/75n781
Nye/International motor racing/75n782
Olney/Illustrated auto racing dict for young people/79n705

AUTOMOBILES
Auto enthusiast directory/77n926; 77n927
Burness/American car spotter's guide:
   1940-65/75n1825
   1920-39/76n1664
   1940-65/79n1551
Clutton/Vintage car guide/78n865
Culshaw/Complete catalogue of British cars/75n1826
Filby/Specialist sports cars/76n765
Lewis/Automobiles of the world/79n1553
Moloney/Encyclopedia of Amer cars/79n1554
Narus/Great Amer woodies & wagons/79n1555
Naul/Specification bk for US cars/79n1556
Neville/Real steel: investor's gd to the Amer auto/77n937
Observer's bk of automobiles/Olyslager Organization/78n1513
Whole car catalog/79n1559
World cars 1974/75n1827; 76n1666
World of automobiles/79n1591

AUTOMOTIVE ENGINEERING
Dinkel/Road & Track illust'd dict/78n1511
Kondo/Elsevier's dict of auto engineering in five languages/78n1512
SAE handbook/76n1610
SAE motor vehicle, safety & environmen'l terminology/78n1514
Society of Auto Engineers/Cumulative index: SAE papers, 1965-73/76n1609
SAE transactions & lit/76n1611

AVIATION
See Aeronautics

AVIATION INDUSTRY
World aviation directory/Dean/77n1624

AWARDS, PRIZES, ETC.
Awards, honors, & prizes: v1/76n71; 76n2
Stuart/Who won what when/79n100

BACKPACKING
See also Camping; Hiking; Outdoor Life
Bridge/America's backpacking bk/75n754
Hart/Walking softly in the wilderness/78 n617
Meves/Guide to backpacking in the US/78 n620
Stout/Backpacking with small children/76 n722

BACTERIOLOGY
Cowan & Steel's manual for the identification of medical bacteria/Cowan/76n1360

BAEDEKER'S HANDBOOKS
Baedeker's hndbks for travellers/76n539

BAHAMA ISLANDS
Fielding's gd to the Caribbean plus the Bahamas/Harman/75n620

BALLET
Clarke/Encyclopedia of dance & ballet/79 n1019
Guillot/Book of ballet/77n994
Koegler/Concise Oxford dict of ballet/78 n934
Terry/Ballet gd/76n1040; 78n935
Wilson/Dictionary of ballet/75n1181

BALTIMORE
Barnes/Marriages & deaths from Baltimore newspapers 1796-1816/78n477
Hollowak/Index to marriages & deaths in the Sun 1837-50/1851-60/79n486
Shosteck/Weekender's guide/75n616

BALTIMORE COUNTY, MD
Maryland rent rolls, 1700-07/77n469

BAND MUSIC
Band music guide/77n951

BANGLADESH
Gustafson/Pakistan & Bangladesh/77n330

BANGS, JOHN KENDRICK
Harper's lost reviews/77n1184

BANK LOANS
Catalog of fed loan guarantee programs/79 n874

BANKING
Batz/Running Press glossary of banking language/78n750
European financial almanac/76n886
Index to bank letters, bulletins, & reviews/ 78n751; 78n752
Rock/Money, banking & macroeconomics/ 79n873
Thorndike/Thorndike ency of banking & financial tables/75n958

BAPTIST CHURCH
Directory of the Amer Baptist Church in the USA/79n1061
Townsend/South Carolina Baptists, 1670-1805/75n431

BARBERINI, MAFFEO
Lavin/Seventeenth cent Barberini documents ... of art/77n866

BARNES, DJUNA
Messerli/Djuna Barnes: bibliog/77n1198

BAROQUE ART
Lavin/Seventeenth cent Barberini documents & inventories of art/77n866

BARTENDERS' MANUALS
Grossman/Grossman's gd to wines, spirits, & beers/75n1673/6th ed./78n1456

BARTH, JOHN
Vine/John Barth: bibliog/78n1131
Weixlmann/John Barth: bibliog/77n1199

BARTHELME, DONALD
Klinkowitz/Donald Barthelme: cklist/78n1132

BASEBALL
Appel/Baseball's best/79n706
Balzer/Official baseball register/79n707
Baseball encyclopedia/75n729; 77n673
Cohen/World series/77n674
Grobani/Guide to baseball lit/76n702
Hollander/Complete hndbk of baseball/79 n708
Neft/Sports ency: baseball/75n733; 78n610
New York Times bk of baseball hist/76n703
Official baseball gd/Sporting News/78n612
Official baseball rules/75n730; 76n704
Official world series records/75n731; 76 n705; 77n675
Reidenbaugh/100 yrs of National League baseball/77n676
Scholl/Running Press glossary of baseball language/78n613
Sporting News official baseball record bk/75 n732; 77n677
Tanner/Official major league baseball playbook/75n734
Turkin/Official ency of baseball/77n678

BASEBALL CARDS
Clark/Complete bk of baseball cards/77n930

BASEBALL PARKS
Shannon/Ballparks/76n706

BASKETBALL
Clark/Illustrated basketball dict for young people/79n709
Hollander/Complete hndbk of pro basketball 1977/77n679
Hollander/Pro basketball ency/78n614

BASKETBALL (cont'd)
National Basketball Assn official gd/Curran/76n707
National Basketball League official gd/Winick/77n680

BATMAN
Fleisher/Encyclopedia of comic bk heroes/77n1167

BATTLESHIPS
See Warships

BAUM, L. FRANK
Hanff/Bibliographia Oziana/77n1187

BEATLES
Castleman/All together now/77n978
Castleman/Beatles again?/79n997

BEAUTY, PERSONAL
Maclay/Total beauty catalog/79n1491
Morini/Encyclopedia of health & beauty/77n1497
Wilkens/Secrets from the super spas/77n1525

BEEBE, WILLIAM
Berra/William Beebe: bibliog/78n1271

BEER
Grossman/Guide to wines, beers, & spirits/78n1456
Jackson/World gd to beer/79n1517
Tudor/Wine, beer & spirits/77n1522
Weiner/Taster's gd to beer/78n1461

BEER CANS
Cady/Beer can collecting/77n929
Martells/Beer can collector's bible/77n936

BEETHOVEN, LUDWIG VAN
Briggs/Collector's Beethoven/79n982
MacArdle/Beethoven abstracts/75n1158

BEETLES
Headstrom/Beetles of America/78n1329

BEHAVIOR, GROUP
Morrison/Collective behavior/77n707

BEHRMAN, SAMUEL NATHANIEL
Klink/Maxwell Anderson & S. N. Behrman/78n925

BEINECKE COLLECTION (Yale)
Beinecke rare bk & manuscript library/76n57

BELGIUM
Belgium's 500 largest companies/76n895

BELLOW, SAUL
Nault/Saul Bellow: bibliog/78n1133
Sokoloff/Saul Bellow/75n1352

BELLOWS, GEORGE
Mason/Lithographs of G. Bellows/79n899

BENNETT, ARNOLD
Miller/Arnold Bennett: bibliog/78n1166

BEOWULF
Tinker/Translations of Beowulf/76n1267

BEREAVEMENT
Bernstein/Books to help children cope with separation & loss/79n744
Fulton/Death, grief & bereavement/78n1425

BERGSON, HENRI
Gunter/Henri Bergson: bibliog/76n1107

BERKELEY, GEORGE
Keynes/Bibliography of G. Berkeley/77n1027

BERNAYS, EDWARD L.
Larson/Public relations/79n804

BERRYMAN, JOHN
Arpin/John Berryman: ref gd/77n1200
Stefanik/John Berryman: bibliog/76n1228

BEST SELLERS
Hackett/80 yrs of best sellers/78n37

BETJEMAN, JOHN
Stapleton/Sir John Betjeman: bibliog/76n1268

BIBLE
Beers/Children's illust'd Bible dict/78n989
Blair/Abingdon Bible hndbk/76n1095
Cambridge hist of the Bible/Ackroyd/76n1097
Catalogue de la bibliotheque de L'Ecole Biblique et archeologique Francaise, Jerusalem/76n19
Eerdmans' family ency of the Bible/Alexander/79n1065
Expositor's Bible commentary, v10/78n992
Heim/Reader's companion to the Bible/76n1101
Hiers/Reader's gd to the Bible/79n1069
Interpreter's dict of the Bible/77n1044
Leon-Dufour/Dictionary of biblical theology/75n1230
May/Oxford Bible atlas/75n1232
Megivern/Bible interpretation/79n1043
Miller/Topical Bible concordance/78n993
Monser/Topical index & digest of the Bible/75n1231
Nelson's compl concordance of the new Amer Bible/Hartdegen/78n994
Nelson's new compact illust'd Bible dict/79n1071
Pfeiffer/Baker's pocket atlas of the Bible/75n1233
Rhymer/Bible in order/77n1047
Soulen/Handbook of biblical criticism/78n997
Staudacher/Lector's gd to biblical pronunciations/76n1102
Unger/Unger's gd to the Bible/76n1103
Wycliffe Bible ency/77n1050
Zondervan pict ency of the Bible/Tenney/76n1104

BIBLE. N.T.
Barclay/New Testament words/75n1228
Brown/New internat'l dict of New Testament theology, vI/77n1043
Bullinger/Critical lexicon & concordance to the English & Greek New Testament/78n990
Hastings/Dictionary of the New Testament/75n1229
Hickie/Greek-English lexicon to the New Testament/79n1068
Kissinger/Sermon on the Mount/77n1045
Kubo/Reader's Greek-English lexicon of the New Testament .../77n1046
New internat'l dict of New Testament theology, v2/78n995
Rienecker/Linguistic key to the Greek New Testament, v1/78n996
Thayer/Greek-English lexicon of the New Testament/78n998
Theological dict of the New Testament, vX/77n1048

BIBLE, O.T.
Botterweck/Theological dict of the Old Testament, v1/76n1096; 79n1064
Childs/Old Testament bks for pastor & teacher/78n991
DeVries/Yesterday, today & tomorrow/76n1098
Einspahr/Index to Brown, Driver & Briggs Hebrew lexicon/77n1042
Hebrew-English lexicon of the Bible/76n1100
Martin/Syntactical & critical concordance to Baruch and Jeremiah/79n1070
Morrish/Concordance of the Septuagint/78n981
Owens/Genesis/79n1072
Vine/Expository dict of words/79n1074
Walton/Chronological charts of the Old Testament/79n1075

BIBLE AS LITERATURE
Warshaw/Bible-related curriculum matls/77n1049

BIBLE CHARACTERS
Barr/Who's who in the Bible/76n1094

BIBLE IN HYMNS
Spencer/Hymn & scripture selection gd/79n1063

BIBLE IN LITERATURE
Chapman/Index of names in *Pearl*, .../79n1251
Looper/Byron & the Bible/79n1234
Shaheen/Biblical refs in Faerie Queene/77n1245

BIBLE LANDS
Avi-Yonah/Encyclopedia of archaeological excavations in the Holy Land, vIII/79n393

BIBLE LANDS (cont'd)
Frank/Hammond's atlas of the Bible lands/79n1066
Grollenberg/Penguin shorter atlas of the Bible/79n1067
Oxford Bible atlas/May/75n1232
Pfeiffer/Baker's pocket atlas of the Bible/75n1233

BIBLE QUOTATIONS
Garvey/Concise treasury of Bible quotations/76n1099

BIBLIOGRAPHERS
Immroth/Ronald Brunlees McKerrow/75n266
Roper/Alfred William Pollard/77n283

BIBLIOGRAPHIC SERVICES
Watson/On-line bibliographic services/79n267

BIBLIOGRAPHY
Afflerbach/Emerging field of sociobibliography/78n214
Anderson/Universal bibliographic control/76n195
Brenni/Essays on bibliog/76n196
Davinson/Bibliographic control/76n197
Dunkin/Bibliography: tiger or fat cat?/76n198
Gore/Bibliography for beginners/75n244
LC/Composite MARC formats/78n216
National & internat'l library planning/Vosper/77n271
Prospects for change in bibliographic control/78n215

BIBLIOGRAPHY
Toomey/World bibliography of bibliographies/78n5
Weeks/Bibliography of 17th cent bibliographies/79n5

BIBLIOGRAPHY, NATIONAL
  AFRICA
African bks in print/76n13
  AUSTRALIA
Australian bks in print/75n6; 79n9
Borchardt/Australian bibliog/77n22
  BRAZIL
Bassches/Bibliography of Brazilian bibliographies/79n1
  CANADA
Canadian bks in print/75n8; 77n23; 77n24; 79n11
Canadiana/79n12
Subject gd to Canadian bks in print 1973/75n9
  CHILE
Williams/Allende yrs: union list of Chilean imprints/78n11

BIBLIOGRAPHY, NATIONAL (cont'd)
FRANCE
L'Edition de langue française catalogue cumulatif 76/78n8
Répertoire des livres de langue française disponibles/77n26
GREAT BRITAIN
Allison/Titles of English (& of foreign bks printed in England), v1, 1475-1640/77n333/v2, 1641-1700/78n9
British bks in print/75n7; 76n15; 79n10
Short-title catalogue of bks, v2, I-Z, 2nd ed/77n27
Small press record of bks/76n11
Whitaker's five-yr cum bk list/75n14
Whitaker's three-yr cum bk list 1973-75/78n10
INDIA
Indian bks in print/75n10; 75n12
Kalia/Bibliography of bibliographies on India/76n5
Kaul/Early writings on India/77n325
Reference catalogue of Indian bks in print/75n11
Supplement to ref catalogue of Indian bks in print in English/76n18
IRELAND
Allison/Titles of English (& of foreign bks printed in England), author's name, pseudonym or initials, v1, 1475-1640/77n333
Short-title catalogue of bks, v2, I-Z, 2nd ed/77n27
ITALY
Catalogo dei libri in commercio/77n25; 78n7
NEW ZEALAND
New Zealand bks in print/76n17
PHILIPPINES
Bernardo/Philippine retrospective natl bibliog 1523-1699/76n14
Tubangui/Catalog of Filipiniana at Valladolid/76n279
SCOTLAND
Allison/Titles of English (& of foreign bks printed in England), v1 1475-1640/77n333
Short-title catalogue of books, v2, I-Z, 2nd ed/77n27
SPAIN AND LATIN AMERICA
Libros en venta/76n16
UNITED STATES
American bk publishing record/75n4
Books in print/76n7; 79n6
Books in series 1966-75/78n1/Suppl/79n2
Bruntjen/Checklist of Amer imprints for 1831/76n8/for 1832/78n6
Children's bks in print/75n196; 76n154
Large type bks in print/77n18
LC/Monographic series/76n12

BIBLIOGRAPHY, NATIONAL (cont'd)
UNITED STATES (cont'd)
Paperbound bks in print/76n9
Publishers' trade list annual/76n10; 79n7
Schreiner-Yantis/Genealogical bks in print/76n421
Small press record of bks/76n11; 79n39
Sources/79n40
Subject gd to bks in print/77n19; 79n8
Subject gd to children's bks in print/75n197; 76n155
Thompson/New Sabin/75n5; 77n20; 77n21

BIBLIOGRAPHY OF LIBRARY ECONOMY
Jordan/Cannons' bibliog . . .: author index/77n167

BIBLIOMETRICS
Donohue/Understanding scientific lit/75n278

BIBLIOTHECA BODMERIANA
Manuscrits et autographes français/75n68
Manuscrits français du Moyen Age/76n59

BIBLIOTHERAPY
Bernstein/Books to help children cope with separation & loss/79n744
Dreyer/Bookfinder/78n1100
Rubin/Bibliotherapy sourcebk/79n307
Rubin/Using bibliotherapy/79n308
Wilkin/Survival themes in fict for children and young people/79n1197
Zaccaria/Bibliotherapy in rehabilitation . . ./79n309

BICULTURAL EDUCATION
Reilly/Selected bibliog of bicultural classroom matls for Mexican Amer studies/79n686
Schon/Bicultural heritage/79n462
Trueba/Bilingual bicultural educ for Spanish speaking/78n548

BICYCLING
Bridge/Freewheeling/75n735
Browder/American biking atlas & touring gd/75n736
DeLong/DeLong's gd to bicycles & bicycling/75n738
New York AYN Council/American youth hostels bike-hike bk/77n681
Schwinn bicycle service manual/75n1754
Sloane/New compl bk of bicycling/75n744

BIG BEND NATIONAL PARK
Schmidly/Mammals of trans-Pecos Texas/78n1333

BILINGUAL EDUCATION
Bibliography of lang arts matls for native North Americans: bilingual/78n587
Cartel anno bibliog of bilingual bicultural matls/78n589

BILINGUAL EDUCATION (cont'd)
Directory of Title VII ESEA bilingual educ programs/78n557
Evaluation instruments for bilingual educ: bibliog/77n575
Teacher training bibliog: matls for bilingual bicultural teacher educ/77n583
Trueba/Bilingual bicultural educ for Spanish speaking in the US: bibliog/78n548

BILLINGS, WILLIAM
Nathan/William Billings/78n909

BIOCHEMISTRY
Annual review of biochemistry/Snell/76 n1339
Kirschenbaum/Atlas of protein spectra in the ultraviolet & visible regions/75 n1451
Stenesh/Dictionary of biochemistry/77n1331

BIOENGINEERING
Annual review of biophysics & bioengineering/Mullins/76n1348
Graf/Reston ency of biomedical engineering terms/78n1395

BIOETHICS/Walters/Biography of bioethics/76n1520; 78n1385; 78n1386

BIOGRAPHICAL FILMS
Emmens/Famous people on film/78n957

BIOGRAPHY
See also under specific topics
Biography (periodical)/79n136
Biography news/75n117
Blue book/76n95
Celebrity register/Blackwell/75n118
DeFord/Who was when?/77n363
Dictionary of biography/Robinson/76n100
Dictionary of internat'l biog/78n112
Hammerton/Concise universal biog/77n121
Hart/100: most influential persons in hist/79 n397
International who's who 1974-75/76n101
International who's who 1975-76/76n102
Kulkin/Her way/77n719
Lewytzkyj/Who's who in the socialist countries/79n143
Men of achievement, 1977/78n113
New York Times biog'l service/79n141
Rosenfelt/Strong women/78n599
Thevet/Les Vrais pourtraits et views des homme illustres/75n120
Thomas/Universal pronouncing dict of biog & mythology/77n1056
Vincent/Dictionary of biog/76n103
Who did what/Howat/75n121
Who was who in America, with world notables, vVI, 1974-76/77n142
Who's who in the world/77n123
Who's who in the world, 4th ed/79n142

BIOGRAPHY (cont'd)
Who's who of Amer women/79n771
World who's who of women/77n124
Slocum/Biographical dictionaries & related works, 2nd suppl/79n134
INDEXES
Author biogs master index/La Beau/79n135
Biographical dictionaries master index/La Beau/76n91; 77n120
Chicorel/Index to biogs/76n93
Contemporary authors cum index/79n139
Falk/Personal name index to NYT index, 1851-1974/77n40
Marquis who's who pubs index to all bks 1974/76n92
Nicholsen/People in bks/78n110
Rothenberg/Index of scientific writings on creativity/76n94
Ruffner/Eponyms dictionaries index/78n111
Silverman/Index to young readers' collective biogs, 2nd ed/76n1200

BIOLOGISTS
American men & women of sci: biology/78 n1212

BIOLOGY
See also Life sciences
Biological & agric'l index/Brooks/76n1370
Biological sciences: dissertations/77n1344
Egan/Topics-aids: biology/79n682
Haensch/Dictionary of biology: English-German-French-Spanish/78n1275
Keleti/Handbook of micromethods for biological sciences/75n1462
Kirk/Library research gd to biology/79 n1335
Thompson/Index to illus of the natural world/78n1277

BIOMEDICINE
Chen/Biomedical, scientific & tech bk reviewing/78n1381
Medi-KWOC index/76n1540

BIOPHYSICS
Annual review of biophysics & bioengineering/Mullins/76n1348

BIRD EGGS AND NESTS
Harrison/Field gd to birds' nests in US/76 n1422
Harrison/Field gd to the nests, eggs, & nestlings of British & European birds/77n1380

BIRD FEEDING
Dennis/Complete gd to bird feeding/76n1417

BIRD WATCHING
Ferguson-Lees/Guide to bird-watching in Europe/77n1376
Kitching/Birdwatcher's gd to wildlife sanctuaries/77n1382
McElroy/Habitat gd to birding/75n1506

BIRD WATCHING (cont'd)
Pettingill/Guide to bird finding East of the Mississippi/78n1320

BIRDS
See also Ornithology; names and types of birds
Ali/Handbook of the birds of India & Pakistan, v10/77n1373
Audubon Soc field gd to North Amer birds: Eastern region/Bull/78n1315
Audubon Soc field gd to North American birds: Western region/Urvardy/78n1323
Birds of western North Amer/Carlson/75n1500
Blake/Manual of neotropical birds, vI/78n1316
Brudenell-Bruce/Birds of the Bahamas/76n1415
Bruun/Dell ency of birds/75n1501
Bruun/Larousse gd to birds of Britain & Europe/79n1369
Bull/Birds of the New York area/77n1373
Campbell/Dictionary of birds in color/76n1416
Clarke/Birds of the West/77n1375
Clements/Birds of the world/75n1502; 79n1370
Cramp/Handbook of the birds of Europe, v1/79n1371
De Schauensee/Guide to the birds of Venezuela/79n1372
Dorst/Life of birds, trans Galbraith/76n1418
ffrench/Guide to the birds of Trinidad & Tobago/75n1504
Fisher/Thorburn's birds/77n1377
Gooders/Great bk of birds/76n1419
Green/Minnesota birds/76n1420
Gruson/Checklist of the world's birds/77n1379
Harris/Field gd to the birds of Galapagos/76n1421
Imhof/Alabama birds/78n1319
King/Field gd to the birds of South-East Asia/76n1423
Leck/Birds of New Jersey/76n1424
Lowery/Louisiana birds/75n1505
Mackenzie/Complete outdoorsman's gd to birds of eastern North Amer/77n1383
Mayr/Birds of the SW Pacific/79n1374
Morcombe/Australian bush birds in colour/76n1426
Oberholser/Bird life of Texas/Kincaid/76n1427
Penny/Birds of Seychelles . . . /76n1428
Peterson/Field gd to Mexican birds/75n1509
Peterson/Field gd to the birds of Britain & Europe/76n1429
Ridgely/Guide to the birds of Panama/77n1385
Rising/Songbirds of eastern & central states/78n1321

BIRDS (cont'd)
Robertson/Birds in New Zealand/76n1430
Rogers/Encyclopedia of cage & aviary birds/77n1386
Scott/World atlas of birds/75n1511
Short/Birds of the world/77n1387
Small/Birds of Calif/75n1510; 76n1432
Stringer/Identification gd to cage & aviary birds/79n710

BIRDS IN ART
Anker/Bird bks & bird art/75n1025
Stanley/Birds of the world on stamps/75n1091

BIRDS OF AMERICA
Fries/Double elephant folio/75n46

BIRMINGHAM, AL
Fussell/Demographic atlas of Birmingham/77n754
Sumrall/Map abstract of trends in calls for police service/79n742

BIRTH CONTROL
See Family planning

BISHOPS
Liederbach/America's 1000 bishops/75n1226

BLACK ACTORS AND ACTRESSES
Mapp/Directory of blacks in performing arts/79n1016

BLACK AUTHORS
Bailey/Broadside authors & artists/75n1334
Fairbanks/Black Amer fict/79n1215
Matthews/Black Amer writers, 1773-1949/76n398
Popkin/Modern black writers/79n1186
Rush/Black Amer writers past & present/76n1226
Shockley/Living black Amer authors/75n1349

BLACK COLLEGES
Beaumont/Handbook for recruiting at trad'l black colleges/75n653
Chambers/Black higher educ in US/79n628

BLACK DRAMATISTS
Arata/Black Amer playwrights/77n986
Hatch/Black playwrights 1823-1977/79n1009

BLACK LIBRARIANS
Handbook of black librarianship/78n142

BLACK LITERATURE
Chapman/Index to black poetry/76n1211
Clark/Black lit resources/77n1188
Fairbanks/Black Amer fict/79n1215
Whitlow/Black Amer lit/75n1336

BLACK NAMES
See African names

BLACK NATIONALISM
Helmreich/Afro-Americans & Africa/78n386

BLACK POETS
Mandelik/Concordance to the poetry of Langston Hughes/76n1240

BLACK SINGERS
Turner/Afro-American singers/79n977

BLACK WOMEN
Williams/American black women in the arts & social sciences/79n454

BLACKS
Abajian/Blacks in selected newspapers and censuses: index/78n385
Afro-American ency/Rywell/76n377
Aptheker/Documentary hist of Negro people in US, 1933-45/75n810
Blockson/Black genealogy/78n397
Clack/Black lit resources/77n1188
Dunn/Black Americans/76n397
Ebony handbook/75n812
Ford/Guide to the black apple/79n600
Hughes/Pictorial hist of black Americans/75n814
MacGregor/Blacks in the US armed forces/79n452
Madubuike/Handbook of African names/78n424
McLaughlin/Black parents' hndbk/77n1495
Negro in Amer hist/75n815
Ploski/Negro almanac/77n433
Smythe/Black Amer ref bk/77n435
  BIBLIOGRAPHY
Abajian/Blacks & their contribution to the American West: union list/76n342
Barry/Marketing & black consumer/77n807
Bibliographic gd to black studies/77n2
Blazek/Black experience/79n448
Davis/Black family in the US/79n449
Davis/Black woman in Amer society/76n396
Dictionary catalog of Negro collection of Fisk Univ library/76n376
Dunmore/Black children & their families/77n715
Glenn/Black rhetoric/77n1122
Mills/Black world in lit for children/76n160; 77n1159
Obudho/Black-white racial attitudes/77n427
Philadelphia. Library/Afro-Americana, 1553-1906/75n816
Rollock/Black experience in children's books/76n163
Smith/Afro-American history/75n360
Szwed/Afro-American folk culture/79n453
Taylor/Blacks in Minnesota/77n437
Whitlow/Black Amer literature/75n1336
Williams/Howard Univ bibliog of African & Afro-Amer religious studies/78n979
  BIOGRAPHY
Brignano/Black Americans in autobiography/75n811

BLACKS (cont'd)
  BIOGRAPHY (cont'd)
Ellison/William Wells Brown & Martin R. Delany/79n450
Greene/Black defenders of America/75n813
Profiles of black mayors in America/Fox/79n542
Richardson/Great black Americans/77n434
Significant Amer blacks/Jacobs/77n127
Spradling/In black & white: Afro-Americans in print/77n436
Who's who among black Americans/Matney/77n438
Who's who of the colored race/Mather/77n439
  PERIODICALS
Analytical gd & indexes:
  Alexander's Magazine/75n29
  Colored American Magazine/75n30
  Voice of the Negro/75n31
Birkos/African & black Amer studies writers gd/77n431
Combined retrospective index set to journals in hist 1838-1974/78n334
Grant/Indexes to *The Competitor*/79n451
Jacobs/Antebellum black newspapers/77n432
Ojo-Ade/Analytic index of *Présence Africaine*/78n276

BLACKS IN FILMS
Powers/Blacks in Amer movies/76n1051
Sampson/Blacks in white & black/78n950

BLATHWAYT ATLAS
Black/Blathwayt atlas, v2/76n367

BLAVATSKY, H. P.
Conger/Combined chronology for use with the Mahatma letters to A. P. Sinnett/75n1235

BLIND
See also Visually handicapped
Bauman/Blindness, visual impairment, deaf-blindness/79n1449
International catalog, aids & appliances for blind & visually impaired persons/Clark/75n1637
International gd to aids & appliances for blind & visually impaired persons/78n1406
Directories of agencies serving the visually handicapped in US/77n1480
For younger readers: braille & talking bks/79n338
Gill/International register of research on blindness & visual impairment/79n1469
Schauder/Libraries for the blind/79n241
Strom/Library services to the blind & physically handicapped/78n237
Talking bk topics/79n339
Talking bks adult/79n340

BLISS BIBLIOGRAPHIC CLASSIFICATION
Bliss bibliographic classification:
  Intro & auxiliary schedules/78n224
  Class J/78n225
  Class P/78n226
  Class Q/78n227

BLOOD
Bessis/Corpuscles/75n1642

BOARD GAMES
Arnold/Illustrated bk of table games/76n741

BOATS
  See also Navigation; Sailing; Seamanship; Yachting
Arighi/Wildwater touring/75n745
BUC book/Used boat directory/76n708
BUC's new boat directory/77n682
Chapman/Piloting, seamanship & small boat handling/76n709
Dempsey/Complete gd to outboard motor service & repair/77n683
Fillingham/Complete bk of canoeing & kayaking/76n710
Getchell/Mariner's catalog/75n748; 76n711
Jenkinson/Wild rivers of North America/75n632
Johnson/Boating facts & feats/77n684
Martenhoff/Powerboat hndbk/76n712
Pilkington/Waterways in Europe/75n625
Putz/Mariner's catalog/76n713

BODLEIAN LIBRARY
Hassall/Treasures from the Bodleian/77n29
Ohlgren/Illuminated manuscripts & bks in the Bodleian library/79n68
Steele/Independent Mexico/75n312

BODY, HUMAN
Encyclopedia of health & the human body/Newman/79n1483
Woman's body/79n1494

BODY LANGUAGE
Bauml/Dictionary of gestures/76n1167

BOEHM, EDWARD
Palley/Porcelain art of Boehm/77n889

BOLOGNA CHILDREN'S BOOK FAIR
Illustrators of children's bks/78n811

BOMBERS
Jones/US bombers/76n1682

BOOK AUCTIONS
Munby/British bk sale catalogues 1676-1800/79n60

BOOK COLLECTING
Arnott/Actors: sales catalogs/76n52
Bookman's price index/78n48
Bradley/Book collector's hndbk of values/77n62

BOOK COLLECTING (cont'd)
Cohen/Official gd to comic bks & big little books/75n66
Feisenberger/Scientists: sales catalogs/76n55
Francis/Whitman at auction/79n1225
Haller/Book collector's fact bk/77n63
Heard/Bookman's gd to Americana/78n49
Iacone/Pleasures of bk collecting/77n64
Jenkins/Works of genius/76n53
Lewis/Book browser's gd/76n54
Magee/Infinite riches/75n67
Overstreet/Comic bk price gd/77n1171
Peters/Book collecting/78n50
Reynolds/Bookhunter's gd to the West, SW/79n56
Schatzki/Children's books/75n1322
7000 old books/78n51
Steele/Independent Mexico/75n312
Szladits/Owen D. Young/75n69
Tannen/How to identify & collect Amer first editions/77n65
Webber/Books about books/75n70; 76n56
Zempel/First edition?/79n57

BOOK DESIGN
Agner/Books of WAD: bks by W. A. Dwiggins/78n52
Brady/Eric Gill/75n71
Gill/Bibliography of Eric Gill/75n72
Hammelmann/Book illustrators in 18th cent England/77n66
Ray/Illustrator & the bk in England from 1790 to 1914/77n67

BOOK JOBBERS
International Publications Service/International publications (catalogs)/75n13
Jobbers directory/78n205
Wertheimer/Books in other languages/78n206

BOOK OF MORMON
Ludlow/Companion to your study/77n1018
Matthews/Who's who/78n987
Topical gd to the scriptures of the Church of LDS/79n1073

BOOK REVIEWS
American bk review/79n1216
B-J paperback bk gd/Blow/77n195
Canadian bk review annual/Tudor/77n196
Children's lit review/77n1150
Gardner/Choice . . . 1964-74/77n198; 79n179
Harper's lost reviews/77n1184
Human (and anti-human) values in children's books/77n1154
Kliatt paperback bk gd/Hiatt/75n199
Kutler/Reviews in Amer hist/76n316
LJ bk review/77n200; 79n182
Magill/Magill's literary annual/79n1185
Perkinson/Review of educ/76n587

BOOK REVIEWS (cont'd)
Reference & subscription books reviews/78n150; 78n151; 79n183
Rowen/Reviews in European hist/76n363
INDEXES
America: hist & life/Boehm/76n329
Book review digest/76n30
Book review digest: index 1905-74/77n37
Book review index/Tarbet:
   1969/76n31
   1970/76n32
   1971/75n32
   1973/75n33
   1974/76n33
   1976/78n21
Bowles/Index to critical film reviews ... reviews of bks abt films/76n1062
Brewster/Index to bk reviews in hist'l periodicals/76n303; 77n368; 79n405
Current bk review citations/77n39
Hart/Multi-media indexes/76n679
Matos/Guide to reviews of bks from & abt Hispanic America/77n341; 77n342
National Library Service cum bk review index 1905-74/77n44
New York Times Book Review index, 1896-1970/75n172
Reference sources/78n26
Rzepecki/Social sci periodicals/79n346
Tarbert/Children's bk review index/76n1196; 77n1147; 79n1196
Van Balen/Geography & earth sciences/79n579; 79n580

BOOK SELECTION
Cabeceiras/Multimedia library/79n244
Carter/Building library collections/75n219
Collection building (periodical)/79n189
Collection developmt policy/79n193
Koops/Developments in collection bldg in univ libraries in Western Europe/79n197
Lunati/Book selection/76n186
Pope/Sex & the undecided librarian/75n269
Slote/Weeding library collections/76n203
Spiller/Book selection/75n220
Urquhart/Regulation & stock control in libraries/78n171
Wertheimer/Books in other languages/78n206

BOOK SELECTION AIDS
See under types of libraries; subjects

BOOK TALKS
Gillespie/More juniorplots/79n228
Spirt/Introducing more bks/79n235

BOOK THEFTS
Bahr/Book theft & library security systems/79n250

BOOKMOBILES
Hu/Benefit-cost analysis of alternative library delivery systems/77n248

BOOKS
Rath/Care & conservation of collections/78n321
Rider/Story of books & libraries/77n282
PRICES
American bk prices current ... index/75n61
American bk prices current/77n68
Bookman's price index/78n48
Bradley/Book collector's hndbk of values/77n62
Francis/Whitman at auction/79n1225
Heard/Bookman's gd to Americana/78n49
Mandeville/Used bk price gd/75n62; 79n58
McGrath/Bookman's price index/79n59
7000 old books/78n51
Standard old bk value gd/79n62

BOOKS (data base)
Settel/Subject descrip of books/79n282

BOOKS AND READING
See also Best sellers; Book selection; Censorship; Children's literature; Reading
Books for you/77n232
Cohan/Readers advisory service/76n134
Downs/Books and history/75n136
Downs/Famous books/76n133
Fadiman/Lifetime reading plan/79n691
Jacques/Leisure reading for adults/78n596
Lyman/Literacy and the nation's libraries/78n144
Lyman/Reading & the adult new reader/78n234
Nominated for survival: classics?/75n173
Parker/College on your own/79n632
Varlejs/Young adult lit in the seventies/79n220
JUVENILE
Adell/Guide to non-sexist children's books/77n1142
Betrand/Books with options/77n1143
Cullinan/Literature and young people/78n1099
Dreyer/Bookfinder/78n1100
Fader/New hooked on books/78n586
Hotchkiss/African-Asian reading gd for children & young adults/77n1152
Jacob/Independent reading grades one thru three/77n652
Jacob/Independent reading grades one thru three/76n158
Johnson/Start early for an early start/77n225
Larrick/Parent's gd to children's reading/77n1157
Owen/Smorgasbord of books/76n161
Polette/E is for everybody/77n1161
Weber/Good reading/79n693
Withrow/Gateways to readable books/77n1166

BOOKS IN SERIES
Baier/Titles in series/75n2
Books in series in the US 1966-75/78n1/ Suppl/79n2
Girls series books/79n1213
LC/Monographic series/76n12
Rosenberg/Young people's lit in series/78 n1122
Van Zant/Selected US gov series/79n126

BOOKSELLING
Anderson/Bookselling in America & the world/76n40
Book trade in Canada/79n48
Bowker annual/79n172
Hackett/80 yrs of best sellers/78n37
Manual on bookselling/75n47
Mumby/Publishing & bookselling/75n48
Parks/John Dunton & the English bk trade/77n55
Taubert/Book trade of the world/77n51
Women's gd to books/75n855
  DIRECTORIES
American bk trade directory/76n47; 79n46
Directory of multiple bookstore owners/75 n53; 76n48
Empresa del libro en America Latina/75n57
Halpern/International classified directory of dealers in sci fiction/76n50
Jobbers directory/78n205
Reynolds/Bookhunter's gd to the West, SW/79n56
Reynolds/Bookhunter's gd to the NE/78n47
Zell/African bk world & press/79n45

BOSTON
Appleton/Boston births, baptisms, marriages, & deaths 1630-99, & births 1700-1800/79n474
Lankevich/Boston/75n507
McGlenen/Boston marriages from 1700-1809/78n406

BOTANY
  See also Plant names; Plants; Flowers, etc.
Atlas of flora of Great Plains/78n1283
Cunningham/Common plants/78n1279
Howes/Dictionary of useful & everyday plants/75n1463
Miller/Root anatomy & morphology/76n1372
Shosteck/Flowers & plants/75n1464
Swift/Botanical classifications/76n1371

BOTANY, MEDICINAL
  See also Herbs
Bianchini/Health plants of the world/79n1351
Keys/Chinese herbs/77n1505
Krochmal/Guide to the medicinal plants of the US/75n1466
Millspaugh/American medicinal plants/76n1377
Moerman/American medical ethnobotany/78 n1280

BOTANY, MEDICINAL
Thomason/Medicines from the earth/79 n1354

BOTSWANA
Stevens/Historical dict of Botswana/76n248

BOTTLES
Baldwin/Collectors gd to patent medicine bottles/75n1078
Kovel/Official bottle price list/75n1083
Munsey/Illustrated gd to collecting bottles/77n921

BOWDOIN COLLEGE MUSEUM OF ART
Norris/Medals & plaquettes/77n914

BOXING
Burrill/Who's who in boxing/75n753
McCallum/Encyclopedia of world boxing champions/77n686

BOYS' CLUBS
Kujoth/Boys' & girls' bk of clubs/76n696

BRADBURY, RAY
Nolan/Ray Bradbury companion/76n1229

BRADFORD, WILLIAM
Gallagher/Early Puritan writers/77n1185

BRAILLE
For younger readers: braille & talking bks/79n338

BRAND NAMES
  See Trade marks

BRASSES
Schiffer/Brass book/79n937

BRAZIL
Bassches/Bibliography of Brazilian bibliographies/79n1
Brazilian-American business review/78n708
Fitzgibbon/Brazil (chronology)/75n340
Lombardi/Brazilian serial docs/75n109
McCarthy/Developing libraries in Brazil/76 n216

BREWERIES
Weiner/Taster's gd to beer/78n1461

BRIDGE (card game)
Frey/Official ency of bridge/78n615
Goren/Goren's bridge complete/75n768

BRISTOL (Great Britain)
Hargreaves-Mawdsley/Bristol & America: first settlers in the colonies/79n485

BRITISH ARTISTS
Rothenstein/Modern English painters/76 n937

BRITISH AUTHORS
Buckley/Victorian poets & prose wroters/78 n1155
Sharp/Dict of English authors/79n1232

BRITISH COLUMBIA
Kosloff/Plants & animals of the Pacific NW/ 77n1346

BRITISH DIARIES
Batts/British MSS of 19th cent/77n405

BRITISH DRAMA
Connoly/English drama/79n1007
English drama to 1660/Penninger/77n988
English drama, 1660-1800/Link/78n926
English drama, 1900-50/Mikhail/78n729
English drama & theatre, 1800-1900/ Connoly/79n1007
Fordyce/Caroline drama/79n1008
Logan/New intellectuals/78n927
Logan/Popular school/76n1032
Reader's adviser, v2/Sypher/78n1090
Wells/English drama/76n1264

BRITISH DRAMATISTS
Tucker/Bibliography of writings by & abt John Ford & Cyril Tourneur/78n932

BRITISH FICTION
Beasley/English fict 1660-1800/79n1227
Evans/Guide to prose fict in the *Tatler* & the *Spectator*/78n1163
Halperin/Plots & characters in the fict of Austen, the Brontës & Eliot/77n1229
Johnson/Plots & characters in the fict of 18th cent English authors/78n1164
Leeming/Who's who in Jane Austen & the the Brontës/75n1377
Rosa/Contemporary fict in America & England/78n1105

BRITISH LITERARY PERIODICALS
Bennett/Victorian periodicals/79n1226
McGuffie/Samuel Johnson in the British press/77n1236

BRITISH LITERARY TOURS
Eagle/Oxford literary gd to the British Isles/ 78n1159
Harting/Literary tour gd to England & Scotland/77n1223

BRITISH LITERATURE
See also names of authors; titles, e.g., Beowulf, etc.; English literature; Commonwealth literature, etc.
Bateson/Guide to English & Amer lit/78n1088
Bond/Eighteenth century/76n1257
Buckley/Victorian poets & prose writers/78 n1155
Doyle/Guide to basic info in Engl lit/77n1220
Fordyce/Caroline drama/79n1008
Friedman/English lit 1660-1800/76n1259
Johnson/Plots & characters in the fict of 18th cent English authors/78n1164; 79n1229
Manual of writings in Middle Engl/77n1224
New Cambridge bibliog of English lit/Watson/76n1260

BRITISH LITERATURE (cont'd)
Patterson/Literary research guide/77n1126
Ruoff/Crowell's hndbk of Elizabethan & Stuart lit/76n1262
Schweik/Reference sources in English & Amer lit/78n1093
Tominaga/Iris Murdoch & Muriel Spark/77 n1221
Tucker/Modern British lit/76n1263
Ward/Literary reviews in British periodicals 1821-26/78n1157
White/English literary journal to 1900/78 n1158
Woolmer/Checklist of the Hogarth Press, 1917-38/77n1222

BRITISH LITERATURE ON RECORDS
Salley/Selected sound recordings of Amer, British, & European lit in English/78 n1091

BRITISH MUSEUM
Collectors & collections/Camber/79n878

BRITISH NOVELS
Abernethy/English novel explication, suppl I/ 77n1227
Bell/English novel 1578-1956/76n1256
Cassis/Twentieth cent English novel/78n1162
Stanton/Bibliography of modern British novelists/79n1230
Watt/British novel/75n1378
Wiley/British novel/75n1379

BRITISH POETRY
Beale/Old & Middle English poetry to 1500/ 77n1219
Cline/Index to criticisms of British & Amer poetry/75n1332
Foxon/English verse, 1701-50/76n1265

BRITISH POETS
Buckley/Victorian poets & prose writers/ 78n1155

BROAD SYSTEM ORDERING
Coates/Broad system of ordering/79n300

BROADCASTING
See Mass media

BROADSIDE PRESS
Bailey/Broadside authors & artists/75n1334

BROADSIDES
Hummel/More Virginia broadsides/76n346

BROADWAY STAGE
Salem/Guide to critical reviews: musical 1909-74/78n940

BROKEN HOMES
Bernstein/Books to help children cope with separation & loss/79n744

BRONTË, ANNE
Halperin/Plots & characters in the fiction of
 .../77n1229

BRONTË, CHARLOTTE
Halperin/Plots & characters in the fiction of
 .../77n1229
Watt/British novel/75n1378

BRONTË, EMILY
Barclay/Emily Brontë criticism/75n1382
Halperin/Plots & characters in the fiction of
 .../77n1229
Leeming/Who's who in Jane Austen & the Brontës/75n1377

BRONTË FAMILY
Pinion/Brontë companion/76n1269

BROOKS, VAN WYCK
Vitelli/Van Wyck Brooks/78n1134

BROWN, WILLIAM WELLS
Ellison/W. W. Brown & M. R. Delany/79n450

BROWNING, ROBERT AND ELIZABETH
East/Browning music/75n1137
Kelley/Brownings' correspondence/79n1233

BRUNET, JACQUES-CHARLES
McKeon/Classification system of Brunet/78n221

BRYANT, WILLIAM CULLEN
Phair/Bibliography of W. C. Bryant & his critics/76n314

BUCKS COUNTY, PA
Davis/Genealogical & personal hist of Bucks County/76n429
Roberts/Early Friends families of upper Bucks/76n439

BUDDHISM
Humphreys/Popular dict of Buddhism/77n1038
Upasak/Dictionary of early Buddhist monastic terms/77n1040
Yoo/Books on Buddhism/77n1036

BUDDHIST ART
Williams/Outlines of Chinese symbolism/78n1018

BUILDING
See also Construction industry; House construction
Brooks/Illustrated encyclopedic dict of bldg & construction terms/77n1577
Harris/Dictionary of architecture & construction/76n938
Love/Construction manual/75n1766
Merritt/Building construction hndbk/76n1620
O'Brien/Construction inspection handbk/76n1621
Putnam/Architectural & bldg trades dict/75n1021

BUILDING (cont'd)
Schwicker/International dict of bldg construction/76n1618
Scott/Dictionary of bldg/75n1760
US Natl Bureau of Stds/Building technology publications/78n1519

BUILDING LAWS
Hopf/Designer's gd to OSHA/76n1605
Jensen/Fire protection for the design profession/77n1578

BULBS (botany)
Vance/Home gardener's gd to bulb flowers/75n1709
Doerflinger/Complete bk of bulb gardening/75n1700

BULGAKOV, MIKHAIL
Proffer/International bibliog of works by & about M. Bulgakov/78n1197

BULGARIAN LITERATURE
Mihailovich/Modern Slavic literatures/... literary criticism, vII, Bulgarian/78n1199

BULLETIN OF BIBLIOGRAPHY
Cumulative index (1897-1975)/78n22

BURROUGHS, EDGAR RICE
Roy/Guide to Barsoom/78n1135

BURROUGHS, WILLIAM S.
Goodman/W. S. Burroughs: bibliog/77n1201

BURUNDI
Weinstein/Historical dict of Burundi/77n312

BUSINESS
See also Corporations; Finance; Management; Secretaries; Small business, etc.
Dow Jones-Irwin business almanac/Levine/78n715
 ATLASES
Business atlas of western Europe/76n838
Business control atlas of the US & Canada/75n899
Cleartype business control atlas of the US & Canada/77n763
Economic atlas of Nebraska/Lawson/78n695
 BIBLIOGRAPHY
Bibliographic gd to business & economics/77n3
Brown/Canadian business & economics/77n765
Business books & serials in print/78n697
Daniells/Business info sources/77n767
Vernon/Use of mgmt & business lit/77n772
Wasserman/Encyclopedia of business info sources/78n705
Wright/Texas sources/78n316
 DICTIONARIES
Ammer/Dictionary of business & economics/78n706

BUSINESS (cont'd)
DICTIONARIES (cont'd)
McCaffrey/Language of business/75n885
Moore/Dictionary of business, finance, & investment/76n830
Tver/Gulf publishing company dict of business & science/75n886
Zahn/Euro dict of economics & business: German-English-French/75n887

DIRECTORIES
Africano/Businessman's gd to the Middle East/79n815
Business & financial planning tables desk bk/77n791
Ewing/Writing for results in business, gov, & the professions/75n889
Guide to natl practices in western Europe/75n890
Try us: natl minority business/76n837
Wasserman/Encyclopedia of geographic info/79n813
Women-owned businesses/77n788

HISTORY
Business hist collection/Dallas Public Library/76n822

PERIODICALS
Business periodicals index/76n839
Media gd intl: Europe/77n784
Media gd intl: Middle East & Africa/77n785

BUSINESS EDUCATION
Barron's... admissions tests for grad study in business/Jaffe/76n597

BUSINESS ENTERPRISES
Directory of state & fed funds for business development/78n710
Hagendorf/Tax gd for buying & selling a business/77n854
Hansen/Guide to buying or selling a business/76n866
Romaine/Guide to Amer trade catalogs, 1744-1900/78n703
Rubel/Guide to selling a business/78n739
Rubel/Guide to venture capital sources/78n753
Smollen/Source gd for borrowing capital/78n754

BUSINESS ETHICS
Jones/Bibliography of business ethics/78n701

BUSINESS LAW
Kintner/Primer on the law of mergers/75n892
Ross/New ency'ic dict of business law—with forms/76n831

BUSINESS LIBRARIES
Campbell/Manual of business library practice/76n166

BUSINESS MATHEMATICS
Skrapek/Mathematical dict for economics & business admin/78n707

BUSINESS NAMES
See also Trade names
Trade names dict/77n787

BUSINESS PEOPLE
Business people in the news, vol L/77n795

BUSINESS RECORDS
Directory of business archives in the US & Canada/77n780
Hoffman/Alphanumeric filing rules for business docs/79n819

BUSINESS SCHOOLS
Miller/Barron's gd to grad business schools/79n659

BUSINESS SERVICES
Business services & info/79n817
Campbell/Business info services/76n852
Grant/Directory of business & financial services/77n800

BUSINESS TRAINING PROGRAMS
Wasserman/Training & developmt organizations directory/79n814

BUSSES
Baldwin/Observer's bk of commercial vehicles/76n1663

BUTTERFLIES
Klots/Field gd to the butterflies of North America/78n1330
Neill/Butterflies afield in the Pacific NW/78n1331
Riley/Field gd to the butterflies of the West Indies/77n1391
Smart/International butterfly bk/76n1441
Watson/Dictionary of butterflies & moths in color/76n1442

BUTTONS
Houart/Buttons/79n936

BRYON, GEORGE GORDON
Looper/Byron & the Bible/79n1234
Santucho/Lord Byron: bibliog, 1807-1974/78n1167

BYZANTINE ART
Allen/Literature on Byzantine art 1892-1967, v2/77n860

BYZANTINE STUDIES
Harvard Univ catalogue... Dumbarton Oaks Research Library/76n294

CABINET OFFICERS
Vice-presidents & cabinet members: biogs/ 76n340

CABINET SYSTEM
See Legislative bodies

CABLE TELEVISION
Rivkin/Cable TV: fed regulations/76n1179

CACTI
Bechtel/Cactus identifier/78n1486
Innes/Complete hndbk of cacti & succulents/ 78n1286
Lamb/Colorful cacti of Amer deserts/76 n1385

CAGE BIRDS
Rogers/Encyclopedia of cage & aviary birds/ 77n1386
Stringer/Identification gd to cage & aviary birds/79n710

CAIN
Gilreath/CAIN online user's gd/77n255

CALCULATING MACHINES
Sipple/Calculator user's gd & dict/77n1582

CALDECOTT AWARD
Newbery & Caldecott medal bks/77n1192

CALIFORNIA
California environmental directory/78n1346
DeWitt/Anti-Filipino movements in Calif: bibliog/77n442
Durrenberger/California: patterns on the land/77n543
Held/Rise of the public library in Calif/75 n186
Henke/California legal research hndbk/76 n516
Hoskin/California experience/79n388
Parker/Personal name index to Orton's "Records of the Calif men in the war of the rebellion 1861-1867"/79n492
Rocq/California local history/77n394
Spinazze/Index to the Argonauts of Calif/ 76n441
Trzyna/California handbook/76n492
Weber/Select bibliog to Calif Catholic lit/76 n1079

FLORA
Abbott/Marine algae of Calif/77n1365
Clarke/Edible & useful plants of Calif/79 n1366
Niehaus/Field gd to Pacific states wildflowers/ 77n1361
Young/Wildflowers of the redwood empire/ 77n1363

GUIDEBOOKS
Dills/Best restaurants of Los Angeles & So. Calif/77n1541
Killeen/Best restaurants of San Francisco & No. Calif/77n1542
Mobil travel gd: Calif & the West/79n602
North/Underwater Calif/77n699
Rapoport/California catalogue/78n529
Sunset travel gd to So Calif/75n617

CALIFORNIA INDIANS
Bean/California Indians/78n676
Heizer/Bibliography of Calif Indians/78 n679
Heizer/California (hndbk of No Amer Indians v8)/79n785
Heizer/California Indian hist/76n804
Heizer/Indians of Calif/77n740
Kroeber/Handbook of the Indians of Calif/ 78n683
Walsh/John Peabody Harrington . . . field- notes/77n734

CALIFORNIA MISSIONS
Camphouse/Guide-book to the missions of Calif/76n545

CALLIGRAPHY
Hyde/Dictionary for calligraphers/78n810; 79n896

CAMBODIAN LANGUAGE
See Khmer language

CAMBRIDGE. UNIVERSITY. LIBRARY
Union catalogue of scientific libraries, Cambridge/76n1313

CAMEROON
DeLancey/Bibliography of Cameroon/76 n249
LeVine/Historical dict of Cameroon/75 n318

CAMPAIGN FUNDS
Dollar politics/75n490
GAO/Alphabetical listing of 1972 presiden- tial campaign receipts/75n498
Sobel/Money & politics/75n496

CAMPBELL COUNTY, VA
Our Quaker friends of ye olden time/77 n454

CAMPGROUNDS
AA gd to camping . . . on the continent/79 n711
Campground guide/76n717
European campgrounds & trailer parks/76 n536
Landi/Bantam great outdoors gd to the US & Canada/79n712
Rand McNally campground & trailer park gd/ 79n714
Steinberg/Camper's favorite campgrounds/75 n598
Trailer Life's RV gd/75n600; 76n723; 77n689

CAMPING
See also Backpacking; Hiking; Outdoor life
AA gd to camping . . . on the continent/79n711
Bearse/Canoe camper's hndbk/76n714
Bergaust/National outdoorsmen's ency/76n715
Bridge/Tourguide to the Rocky Mountain wilderness/76n716
Explorers Ltd. source bk/Perrin/78n616
Kaysing/Robin Hood hndbk/75n756
Knap/Family camping hndbk/77n687
Landi/Bantam great outdoors gd to the US & Canada/79n712
Oberrecht/Great outdoors catalog/78n621
Ormond/Outdoorsman's hndbk/76n719
Power/Camper's hndbk/75n635
Robinson/San Bernardino mtn trails/76n720
Schaffer/Tahoe Sierra/76n721
Stout/Backpacking with small children/76n722
Winnett/Sierra south: California's Sierra/76n725

CANADA
Artibise/Western Canada since 1870/79n375
Canada year bk/78n303
Canadian almanac & directory/78n304
Canadian bk review annual/Tudor/77n196
Canadian bks in print/75n8; 77n23; 77n24; 79n11
Canadian serials directory/78n14
Canadiana/79n12
Colombo's Canadian references/78n305
Corpus almanac of Canada/Fawcett/77n335
Directory of assns in Canada/75n343; 76n65; 79n82
Directory of Canadian museums/79n83
Hamilton/Macmillan bk of Canadian place names/79n625
Harder/Illustrated dict of place names, US & Canada/77n551
Henderson/Guide to basic ref matls for Canadian libraries/79n180
Jarvi/Canadian selection/79n181
National atlas of Canada/76n534
National trade . . . assns of the US & Canada/Colgate/77n87
Rand McNally road atlas/75n636
Ryder/Canadian ref sources/76n6
Subject gd to Canadian bks in print/75n9
Union list of serials indexed by PAIS held by Canadian libraries/78n78
   BIOGRAPHY
Dictionary of Canadian biog/76n109; 78n116
Leonard/Women's who's who of America: US & Canada, 1914-15/77n122
MacMillan/Contemporary Canadian composers/77n971

CANADA (cont'd)
   BIOGRAPHY (cont'd)
Ukrainians in North Amer/Shtohryn/76n107
Who was who among North Amer authors 1921-31/77n1183
   ECONOMIC CONDITIONS
Brown/Canadian business & economics/77n765
Dick/Economic hist of Canada/79n800
Oxford regional economic atlas/77n764
   ENVIRONMENT
Schwartz/Climate advisor/79n1417
Sparrow/Annotated bibliog of Canadian air pollution literature/77n1420
   HISTORY
Directory: hist'l societies/77n386
Morley/Ontario & the Canadian North/79n376
Sloane/Winnipeg/75n393
Thibault/Bibliographia Canadiana/75n394
Toye/Supplement to Oxford companion to Canadian hist & literature/75n1412
Wright/Genealogical reader: NE US & Canada/75n434
   LIBRARIES
Bird/Library telecommunications directory/78n134
Canadian library directory: fed/75n159
Canadian library systems & networks/75n254
Directory of library assns in Canada/78n137
Federal gov libraries in Canada/78n202
Jackson/Century of service/77n157
Parch/Directory of newspaper libraries/77n182
Research collections in Canadian libraries/76n169
   POLITICS
Evans/Women in fed politics/76n482
Saywell/Canadian annual review of politics/75n338; 76n500
   POSTAGE STAMPS
Boggs/Postage stamps & postal hist of Canada/75n1089
Howes/Canadian postage stamps & stationery/75n1090
Walburn/Official catalog of Canadian precancels/78n860
   RELIGION
Piepkorn/Profiles in belief/78n970
Yearbook of Amer & Canadian churches/Jacquet/76n1089
Who was who among North Amer authors/77n1183

CANADIAN CHILDREN'S LITERATURE
See Children's literature

CANADIAN FICTION
Fee/Canadian fiction/77n1255

230–Subjects

CANADIAN INDIANS
Helm/Indians of the subArctic/77n741

CANADIAN LITERATURE
See also French Canadian literature; names of individual authors
Canadian essays & collections index/77n1253
Canadian essay & lit index/77n1135
Gnarowski/Concise bibliog of English-Canadian lit/79n1260
Moyles/English-Canadian lit to 1900/77n1257
Toye/Suppl to Oxford companion to Canadian hist & literature/75n1412

CANADIAN MUSIC
Jarman/Canadian music/77n957

CANADIAN POETRY
League of Canadian Poets: catalogue/77n1254
Stevens/Modern English-Canadian poetry/79n1261

CANOEING
Bearse/Canoe camper's hndbk/76n714
Fillingham/Complete bk of canoeing & kayaking/76n710

CAPE VERDE ISLANDS
McCarthy/Guinea-Bissau & Cape Verde Islands/79n353

CAPITAL
Smollen/Source gd for borrowing capital/78n754

CARD CATALOGS (libraries)
Future of card catalogs/ARL/76n189
Hoffman/What happens in library filing?/77n270

CARD GAMES
Ainslie's complete Hoyle/76n740
Goren/Goren's bridge complete/75n768

CARD TRICKS
Hugard/Encyclopedia of card tricks/76n744

CARDIOLOGY
Gutgesell/Atlas of pediatric echocardiography/79n1446

CAREER EDUCATION
See Vocational education

CAREERS
See Occupations; Vocational guidance

CARGO HANDLING
Jane's freight containers/Finlay/78n1546

CARIBBEAN
Caribbean investment hndbk/Jonnard/75n916
Chang/Annotated bibliog of Caribbean bibliographies in English/77n337
Comitas/Complete Caribbeana 1900-75/79n377

CARIBBEAN (cont'd)
Fielding's gd to the Caribbean/Harman/75n620
Lux/Historical dict of the British Caribbean/76n282
Schwartz/Climate advisor/79n1417

CARNIVAL GLASS
Hand/Collector's ency of carnival glass/79n925
Klamkin/Collector's gd to carnival glass/77n920

CAROLINE DRAMA
Fordyce/Caroline drama/79n1008

CARTOGRAPHY
Bibliographia cartographica/Zogner/78n511
Lock/Geography & cartography: hndbk/77n555

CASTLES
Long/Castle hotels of Europe/79n618

CATALOGING AND CLASSIFICATION
Akers/Simple library cataloging/78n217
Allen/Manual of European languages for librarians/77n189
Daily/Cataloging phonorecordings/76n188
Dowell/Cataloging with copy/77n253
Foster/Managing the catalog dept/77n254
Future of card catalogs/ARL/76n189
Hoffman/Descriptive cataloging in a new light/78n219
Hoffman/Small library cataloging/79n272
Hyman/Analytical access/79n261
INIS: authority list for corporate entries/79n273
INIS: descriptive cataloguing samples/79n274
LC/Composite MARC formats/78n216
Olsen/Index to LC *Cataloging Service Bulletin*/78n223
Piercy/Commonsense cataloging/76n192
Ranganathan/Cataloguing practice/76n193
Sayre/Illustrated gd to ISBD M/77n259
Smith/Practical approach to serials cataloging/79n283
Tillin/Standards for cataloging nonprint materials/77n261
Verona/Corporate headings/77n262
Wynar/Introduction to cataloging & classification/77n264

CATALOGING COPY
Computext book guides:
  Business & economics/76n824
  Conference publications/76n20
  Government publications/76n82
  Law/76n509
  Medicine/76n1515
  Technology/76n1310
Dowell/Cataloging with copy/77n253

Subjects—231

CATHEDRALS
Houghton/Guide to the British cathedrals/ 75n1018

CATHER, WILLA
Lathrop/Willa Cather: checklist/76n1230

CATHOLIC CHURCH
Bangert/Bibliographical essay on Society of Jesus/77n1021
Byers/Readings for town & country church workers: bibliog/76n1072
Catholic almanac/Foy/76n1086
Catholic encyclopedia/77n1037
Liebard/Clergy & laity/79n1040
Liederbach/America's thousand bishops/75n1226
Megivern/Worship & liturgy/79n1044
New Catholic ency: suppl/76n1085
Steel/Sources for Roman Catholic & Jewish genealogy & family history/78n421
Weigle/Penitente bibliog/77n1035

CATHOLIC LITERATURE
Clancy/English Catholic books, 1641-1700/ 75n1216
Weber/Bibliography to Calif Catholic lit, 1856-1974/76n1079

CATHOLIC SCHOOLS
Ganley's Catholic schools in America/75n683; 77n600

CATS
Bloomfield/Concise dict of cats/79n1522
Cat catalog/Fireman/77n1527
Hazen/Dell ency of cats/75n1682
Schneck/Complete home medical gd for cats/77n1531

CATTLE
Müller-Hayes/Bibliography of Criollo cattle of the Americas/79n1524

CATV
Ellmore/Illustrated dict of broadcast-CATV-telecommunications/79n1162
Thomassen/CATV & its implications for libraries/75n242

CB RADIO
King/Underground buying gd for hams, CBers/78n749
Len Buckwalter's CB channel directory/78n1083

CEBUANO LITERATURE
Mojares/Cebuano lit: bibliog/78n1195

CELLO
Cowling/Cello/76n1014
Kenneson/Bibliography of cello ensemble music/76n1016

CELLS
Motta/Microanatomy of cell & tissue surfaces/ 79n1336

CELTIC LITERATURE
Bromwich/Medieval Celtic lit/76n1258

CENSORSHIP
Anderson/Problems in intellectual freedom & censorship/75n229
Busha/Intellectual freedom primer/78n266
Haight/Banned books/79n310
Intellectual freedom manual/75n154
MacCafferty/Right to know/77n1104
McShean/Running a message parlor/79n311
Oboler/Fear of the word/75n238
Pope/Sex & the undecided librarian/75n269
Tucker/Suitable for children?/77n1165

CENSUS
Bentley/Index to 1800 census of Massachusetts/79n478
Bibliography & reel index: microfilm ed of US census 1790-1970/77n755
Demographic yrbk/UN/76n814
Directory of fed stats for local areas/79n788
Lunt/Key to publications of the US census, 1790-1887/78n685
Pocket data bk, USA/78n693
Potter/Index to 1820 North Carolina census/ 79n493
Register/State census of North Carolina 1784-87/79n494
US Library of Congress/General censuses & vital stats in Americas/75n875

CENTRAL AMERICA
Cook/Stratigraphic atlas of North & Central America/78n513
Hardaway/Central Amer by recreation vehicle/76n558

CERAMICS
See also Pottery; Porcelain
Bibliography: clay/75n1039
Campbell/Pottery & ceramics/79n946
Savage/Illustrated dict of ceramics/75n1040

CERVANTES, MIGUEL DE
Torbert/Cervantes' place-names/79n1293

CHAD
Decalo/Historical dict of Chad/78n283

CHAIRS
Darty/Chairs/75n1074
Pollack/Chairs/79n923

CHAMBER MUSIC
Hinson/Piano in chamber ensemble/79n991

CHAMBERS OF COMMERCE
Brazilian-American business review: directory/78n708

CHAPLAINS
US naval chaplains, 1957-70/75n1854

CHARACTERS IN LITERATURE
Berry/Plots & characters in major Russian fiction, v1/78n1196/v2/79n1282
Carrington/Plots & characters in the fict of W. D. Howells/77n1205
Fisher/Who's who in children's books/76n1198
Freeman/Dictionary of fictional characters/75n1326
Gerber/Plots & characters in the fict of T. Dreiser/78n1137
Glasheen/Third census of Finnegans Wake/78n1177
Halperin/Plots & characters in the fiction of J. Austen, Brontës & G. Eliot/77n1129
Hartnoll/Who's who in Shaw/76n1287
Hayashi/John Steinbeck: dict of his fict characters/77n1213
Holderness/Who's who in D. H. Lawrence/77n1237
Irvine/How to pronounce names in Shakespeare/76n1035
Jerrold/Descriptive index to Shakespeare's characters/77n1241
Johnson/Dictionary of famous names in fict, drama, poetry, hist, & art/76n1186
Johnson/Plots & characters in the fict of 18th cent English authors, vI/78n1164/vII/79n1229
Leeming/Who's who in Henry James/77n1207
Leeming/Who's who in Thomas Hardy/76n1275
Levith/What's in Shakespeare's names/79n1252
McCullen/Dictionary of the characters in G. Meredith's fiction/78n1179
Penzler/Detectionary: biog dict . . . detective & mystery fiction/78n1104
Rajec/Study of names in lit/79n1182
Scott/Who's who in Chaucer/76n1270
Swan/Who's who in fiction?/77n1178
West/Index of proper names in French Arthurian prose romances/79n1275

CHARITIES
Directory of agencies/77n711
Guide to global giving/77n712

CHARLEMAGNE
Langston/Pedigrees of . . . Charlemagne's descendants, v2/75n425

CHARLES, PRINCE OF WALES
Paget/Lineage & ancestry of Prince Charles/78n420

CHARLOT, JEAN
Morse/Jean Charlot's prints: catalogue/77n882

CHATTERTON, THOMAS
Warren/Descriptive . . . bibliog of Chatterton/78n1168

CHAUCER, GEOFFREY
Baird/Bibliography of Chaucer/78n1169
Baugh/Chaucer/78n1170
Dillon/Chaucer dict/75n1383
Scott/Who's who in Chaucer/76n1270

CHAVEZ, CESAR
Fodell/Cesar Chavez & United Farm Workers/75n976

CHEESE
Eekhof-Stork/World atlas of cheese/77n1543
Gourmet's dict of cheeses/77n1546
Jones/World of cheese/77n1547
O'Keefe/Cheese buyer's hndbk/79n1532

CHEMICAL EDUCATION
Blaser/College chemistry faculties/78n1252
Frazer/Resource bk on chemical educ in the United Kingdom/77n1312

CHEMICAL ELEMENTS
Encyclopedia of electro-chemistry of the elements/Bard,v1/75n1450/Bard, v3/76n1343/Bard, v11/79n1318/Plambeck, v10/78n1249

CHEMICAL ENGINEERS
Miles/American chemists & chemical engineers/78n1257

CHEMICAL FORMULARIES
Chemical formulary, vXX/Bennett/78n1254

CHEMICAL INDUSTRY
Charnley/European chemical industries/76n896

CHEMICAL KINETICS
US Natl Bureau of Stds/Vibrationally excited hydrogen halides/75n1455
Westly/Chemical kinetics of the gas phase combustion of fuels/78n1241

CHEMICAL LASERS
Gross/Handbook of chemical lasers/78n1255

CHEMICAL PROCESSES
Ash/Formulary of paints & other coatings/79n1320
Considine/Chemical & process technology ency/75n1755
Encyclopedia of chemical processing & design/McKetta/78n1247
Guthrie/Process plant estimating evaluation & control/75n1810

CHEMICAL RESEARCH
Abstracts of papers: Amer Chem Society/76n1338
Americal Chem Soc directory of grad research/78n1251
Davis/Information retrieval in chemistry/75n276

CHEMICAL TECHNOLOGY
Codd/Chemical technology: . . . v VIII/77 n1575

CHEMICALS
Verschueren/Handbook of environmental data on organic chems/79n1322

CHEMISTRY
Annual review of lignin chemistry/Pearl/77 n1334
Annual review of physical chemistry/Eyring/76n1340
BIBLIOGRAPHY
Selected titles in chemistry/79n1317
Woodburn/Using the chem lit/76n1347
DICTIONARIES
Bard/Encyclopedia of electrochemistry of the elements, v1/75n1450
Callaham/Russian-English chemical & polytechnical dict/76n1341
Concise chem & tech dict/Bennett/76n1342
Hampel/Glossary of chem terms/77n1330
Hawley/Condensed chem dict/78n1248
Yamada/Sanyo's tri-lingual glossary of chem terms: English-Japanese-Chinese/78n1250
HANDBOOKS
Chen/New hndbk of chem/77n1332
Handbook of chem & physics/Weast/76 n1344
Kaye/Tables of physical & chem constants . . . /75n1458
Nemeth/Chemical tables/77n1333
Stark/Formula book 2/77n1313
Strauss/Handbook for chem technicians/77 n1335

CHEMISTS
American men & women of sci: chemistry/78n1213
Miles/American chemists & chemical engineers/78n1257

CHESNUTT, CHARLES W.
Ellison/C. W. Chesnutt: ref gd/78n1336

CHESS
Betts/Chess/75n767
Brace/Illustrated dict of chess/79n715
Sunnucks/Encyclopedia of chess/78n622
US Chess Federation/Official rules of chess/76n746

CHICANO LITERATURE
Lomeli/Chicano perspectives in lit/78n1128

CHICAGO
Banes/Sweet home Chicago/75n602
Chicago: chronology/Furer/75n508
Chicago women's directory/76n790
Ligare/Illinois women's directory/79n765

CHICANOS
Cabello-Argandona/Chicana: bibliographic study/77n440
Dunn/Chicanos: study gd/76n400
Heisley/Annotated bibliog of Chicano folklore/78n1013
Mexican-American bibliographies/Cortes/75 n822
Mexican-Americans: bibliog/Univ of Houston Libraries/76n401
Pino/Mexican Americans: bibliog/76n402
Quintana/Current bibliog on Chicanos/76 n403
Reilly/Selected . . . bibliog of bicultural classroom matls for Mexican Amer studies/79n686
Schon/Bicultural heritage/79n462
Talbot/Comprehensive Chicano bibliog/75 n824
Trejo/Bibliografia Chicana/76n404
Woods/Reference matls on Mexican Americans: bibliog/77n441

CHILD ABUSE
Interdisciplinary glossary on child abuse & neglect/79n747
Kalisch/Child abuse & neglect/79n748

CHILD MENTAL HEALTH
Berlin/Bibliography of child psychiatry & child mental health/77n1457
US facilities & programs for children with severe mental illnesses/79n1436

CHILD PSYCHOLOGY
Catalog of J. Piaget archives/76n1492
Pitts/Concept developmt . . . the God concept in the child/79n752

CHILD STUDY
Annotated bibliog for child & family developmt programs/79n743
Harris/Developmental tasks resource gd for elementary school children/77n651
Review of child developmt research/Horowitz/76n1501
Who's who . . . child developmt professionals/77n606
Wilson/Bibliography of child study: 1898-1912/76n1489

CHILDREN
Archuleta/Hyperactive child/75n1645
Broadribb/Modern parents' gd to baby & child care/75n1647
Caplan/Parents' yellow pages/79n745
Child health ency/Feinbloom/76n1543
Cody/Your child's ears, nose & throat/76 n1544

CHILDREN (cont'd)
Family life & child developmt . . . bibliog/
78n655
Garoogian/Child care issues . . ./78n656
Green/Sigh of relief/79n1485
Handbook of pediatrics/Silver/77n1486
Spock/Baby & child care/77n1499
　DISEASES
Common symptom guide/Wasson/77n1484
　MINORITIES
Dunmore/Black children & their families/
77n715
McLaughlin/Black parents' hndbk/77n1495
　SOCIAL CONDITIONS
National children's directory/Bundy/78
n659

CHILDREN'S ENCYCLOPEDIAS
Britannica junior encyclopaedia/78n64
Compton's encyclopedia/75n74
Compton's precyclopedia/75n75
Junior Pears ency/Blishen/79n73
New book of knowledge/77n75
Purnell's first ency in colour/78n66
Rand McNally's children's ency/78n67
World book ency/78n70

CHILDREN'S LIBRARIES
See also School libraries
Baker/School & public library media programs for children & YAs/78n178
Baskin/Special child in the library/77n216
Broderick/Library work with children/78n181
Burke/Children's library service: school or public/75n192
Dyer/Cooperation in library serv to children/
79n208
Fasick/Children using media/79n209
Johnson/Start early for an early start/77n225
Ray/Library serv to children/79n215
Richardson/Children's services of public
libraries/79n216
Wilkinson/Canadian juvenile fict & the library
market/77n1259
　SELECTION AIDS
Buttlar/Building ethnic collections/78n376
Chambers/Hey Miss! You got a book for me?/
79n226
Gillespie/Best bks for children/79n230
Mills/Black world in lit for children/77n1159
Rollock/Black experience in children's bks/76
n163

CHILDREN'S LITERATURE
See also Books and reading; Children's
encyclopedias; Illustrated books; Storytelling; Young adult literature
Bader/American picturebks/78n1119
Blishen/Thorny paradise: writers on writing for
children/77n1145

CHILDREN'S LITERATURE (cont'd)
Carlson/Enrichment ideas/77n642
Children's literary almanac/75n1344
Cullinan/Literature & young people/78n1099
Fisher/Who's who in children's bks/76n1198
Gillespie/More juniorplots/79n228
Huck/Children's lit in the elementary school/
77n1153
James/Children's bks of yesterday/77n1155
Kelley/In pursuit of values/75n1346
Lukens/Critical hndbk of children's lit/77
n1158
MacCann/Cultural conformity in bks for
children/78n1120
Macleod/Children's literature/79n1191
Polette/E is for everybody/77n1161
Rudman/Children's literature/79n1193
Spirt/Introducing more bks/79n235
Sutherland/Children & books/79n218
Tucker/Suitable for children?/77n1165
Waggoner/Hills of faraway/79n1206
Wheelbarger/Children's lit handbk/75n1323
Wilkinson/Canadian juvenile fict & the library
market/77n1259
Yonkers Public Library/Gd to subjects &
concepts in picture bk format/75n1348
　AUTHORS AND ILLUSTRATORS
Hopkins/More bks by more people/75n1345
Illustrators of children's bks/Bologna Ch Bk
Fair/78n811
Jones/Children's authors/77n1125
Kingman/Illustrators of children's bks 1967-
76/79n898
LaBeau/Children's authors & illustrators/
77n1156
Profiles/77n1258
Sarkissian/Children's authors & illustrators:
index/79n1194
Something abt the author, v9/77n1162/
v 10/77n1163
Stewart/Taylors of Ongar: bio-bibliog/76
n1201
Thomson/Kate Greenaway: catalogue/78
n1161
Ward/Illustrators of bks for young people/76
n944
Yesterday's authors of bks for children,
v1/Commire/78n1102
　AWARDS AND PRIZES
Children's bk showcase/CBC/75n1343; 76
n1222
Children's bks: awards & prizes/77n1148;
78n1098
Children's bks of the year/CSA/77n1149
Moss/Children's bks of the yr/77n1126
Newbery & Caldecott medal bks, 1966-75/
77n1192
Notable children's bks 1940-70/78n1121

CHILDREN'S LITERATURE (cont'd)
BIBLIOGRAPHY
Children's bks in print/75n196; 76n154
Children's bks in rare bk div of LC/76n1197
Gottlieb/Early children's bks & their illustration/77n70
Haviland/Children's lit, 2nd suppl/79n233
Leif/Children's lit: bibliog/78n1101
Meacham/Information sources in children's lit/79n234
Monson/Research in children's lit/77n1160
Schatzki/Children's bks/75n1322
Subject gd to children's bks in print/75n197; 76n155

BOOK REVIEWS
Children's lit review/77n1150; 77n1151
Human values in children's bks/77n1154
Tarbert/Children's bk review index/76n1196; 77n1147; 79n1196

PUBLISHING
Boyle/Children's media market place/79n225
Gottlieb/Publishing children's bks in America/79n1214

SELECTION AIDS
Adell/Guide to non-sexist children's bks/77n1142
Baskin/Notes from a different drummer/78n179
Betrand/Books with options: bibliog of non-stereotyping . . . /77n1143
Best of the best/77n1144
Bibliography of bks for children/Baron/79n223
Davis/Liberty Cap: non-sexist matls/79n227
Dreyer/Bookfinder/78n1100
Gillespie/Best bks for children/79n230
Haviland/Children's bks of internat'l interest/79n232
Hotchkiss/African-Asian reading gd/77n1152
Jacob/Independent reading grades 1-3/77n652
Larrick/Parent's gd to children's reading/77n1157
Libros en español/79n1190
Markun/Bibliography: bks for children/75n1347
McDonough/Canadian bks for children/77n1256
McDonough/Canadian bks for young people/79n1192
Mills/Black world in lit for children/76n160; 77n1159
Polette/Celebrating with bks/78n191
Rollock/Black experience in children's bks/76n163
Schmidt/Children's bks on Africa & their authors: bibliog/76n1199
Schon/Books in Spanish for children & YAs/79n1292

CHILDREN'S LITERATURE (cont'd)
SELECTION AIDS (cont'd)
Wilkin/Survival themes in fict for children/79n1197
Wilkinson/Canadian juvenile fiction & the library market/77n1259
Withrow/Gateways to readable bks/77n1166

CHILDREN'S LITERATURE IN SERIES
See Books in series

CHILDREN'S LITERATURE ON FILM
Greene/Multi-media approach to children's lit/79n231

CHILDREN'S LITERATURE ON PHONORECORDS
Greene/Multi-media approach to children's lit/79n231

CHILDREN'S PLAYS
Kreider/Index to children's plays in collections/78n939

CHILDREN'S POETRY
Brewton/Index to poetry for children & YA 1970-75/79n1189
Childhood in poetry, 2nd suppl/77n1146
Smith/Subject index to poetry for children & YA 1957-75/79n1195

CHILDREN'S RIGHTS
See Juvenile rights

CHILDREN'S TELEVISION
Clark/Children's television/79n1177

CHILE
Bibliographical notes for . . . military coup in Chile/76n497
Sobel/Chile & Allende/75n524
Williams/Allende years/78n11

CHINA
Association for Asian Studies/Dictionary of Ming biog, 1368-1644/77n398
Blair/Development in the People's Republic of China/78n296
China: administrative atlas/78n523
China & the US 1964-72/Yim/76n502
China: survey of lit/79n368
Cho/Japanese writings on communist Chinese law/79n564
Chou/Oracle bone collections in the US/78n318
Dean/Science & technology in the developmt of modern China/75n299
Destenay/Nagel's ency-guide: China/75n331
Felber/American's tourist manual for People's Republic of China/77n565
Hsieh/Chinese historiography on revolution of 1911/76n361
Kamachi/Japanese studies of modern China since 1953, suppl vol for 1953-69/77n319

CHINA (cont'd)
Lieberthal/Research gd to central party meetings in China/77n524
MacMurray/Treaties . . . with China, 1894-1919/75n536
Parker/American dissertations on foreign educ, v VI/77n578
Posner/China: resource gd/78n297
Shulman/Doctoral dissertations on China/79n369
Skinner/Modern Chinese society/75n302
Times atlas of China/Geelan/76n535
US Bureau of Economic Analysis/Provinces of People's Republic of China/79n370
Vanderstappen/T. L. Yuan bibliog of Western writings on Chinese art & archaeology/77n865
Wang/Cultural revolution in China/77n320

CHINESE AMERICANS
Tung/Chinese in America/75n825
Young/Chinese in Hawaii/75n826

CHINESE ART
Vanderstappen/T. L. Yuan bibliog of Western writings on Chinese art . . ./77n865
Williams/Outlines of Chinese symbolism & art motives/75n1001; 78n1018

CHINESE AUTHORS
Chu/Twentieth cent Chinese writers/78n1185

CHINESE LANGUAGE
Chi/Chinese-English dict/78n1051
Ching/201 Chinese verbs/79n1130
Dobson/Dictionary of Chinese particles/75n1263
Dunn/Chinese-English & Eng-Chinese dictionaries in LC/79n1131
Karlgren/Analytic dict of Chinese & Sino-Japanese/76n1151
Lin Yutang/Chinese-English dict/75n1264
Norman/Concise Manchu-English lexicon/79n1132
Rose-Innes/Beginners' dict of Chinese-Japanese characters/78n1052

CHINESE LITERATURE
Bailey/Guide to Chinese poetry & drama/75n1413
Chu/Twentieth cent Chinese writers/78n1185
Gibbs/Bibliography of studies & translations of modern Chinese lit, 1918-42/76n1293
Kaufman/Musical refs in Chinese classics/77n948
Paper/Guide to Chinese prose/75n1414

CHINESE PERIODICALS
Bibliography of Chinese newspapers & periodicals in European libraries/77n318
Chinese periodicals in . . . Australian Natl Univ/75n39
Lo/Chinese newspapers published in North America 1854-1975/79n455

CHIPPENDALE STYLE
Hummel/Winterthur gd to American Chippendale furniture/78n853

CHIROPRACTICS
Klein/Chiropractic: bibliog/78n1424

CHOICE
Gardner/Choice: cumulation/77n198; 79n179

CHOLESTEROL
Kraus/Dictionary of sodium, fats, & cholesterol/76n1577

CHORAL MUSIC
May/Avant-garde choral music: bibliog/78n895
Nardone/Choral music in print/75n1132; 77n960

CHRISTIAN ART
Sill/Handbook of symbols in Christian art/76n926

CHRISTIAN NAMES
Weekley/Jack and Jill/76n482
Withycombe/Oxford dict of English Christian names/78n426

CHRISTIANITY
Barker/Who's who in church hist/79n1076
Douglas/New internat'l dict of the Christian Church/79n1056
Eerdman's hndbk to the hist of Christianity/Dowley/78n985
Littel/Macmillan atlas hist of Christianity/77n1020
Livingstone/Concise Oxford dict of the Christian Church/79n1058

CHRISTIANS IN AFRICA
Ofori/Christianity in tropical Africa/78n973

CHROMATOGRAPHY
Denney/Dictionary of chromatography/78n1244
Deyl/Bibliography of liquid column chromatography/78n1239
Macek/Bibliography of paper & thin-layer chromatography/77n1324
Scott/Thin-layer chromatography abstracts/75n1453

CHROMOSOMES
de Grouchy/Clinical atlas of human chromosomes/79n1444

CHRONOLOGY, HISTORICAL
American almanac/Linton/78n348
Bicentennial almanac/Linton/76n331
Clements/Chronology of US/76n333
DeFord/Who was when?/77n363
Freeman-Grenville/Chronology of African hist/75n391
Freeman-Grenville/Chronology of world hist/76n304

CHRONOLOGY, HISTORICAL (cont'd)
Grun/Timetables of history/76n305
Jensen/America in time/78n349
Leonard/Day by day: the '40s/79n403
Millgate/Almanac of dates/78n88
Storey/Chronology of the medieval world/75n353

CHUMASH
Anderson/Bibliography of Chumash & their predecessors/79n773

CHURCH AND STATE
Menendez/Church-state relations: bibliog/77n1028

CHURCH FURNISHINGS
Dirsztay/Church furnishings/79n912

CHURCH HISTORY
Constable/Medieval monasticism: bibliog/77n1025

CHURCH LIBRARIES
Barber/Minister's library/75n1213; 77n235
Corrigan/Periodicals for religious educ centers & parish libraries/77n1026
McMichael/Library & resource center in Christian educ/78n195
Smith/Getting bks off the shelves/77n241

CHURCH MUSIC
Conely/Guide to improvisation: . . . for church organists/76n999
Davidson/Dictionary of Protestant church music/76n995
MusiCatalog/78n902

CHURCH OF ENGLAND
Barber/Index to letters . . . of Frederick Temple/77n1041
Bill/Catalogue of manuscripts in Lambeth Palace Library/77n1023
Keynes/Bibliography of G. Berkeley Bishop of Cloyne/77n1027
Sayers/Calendar of papers of C. T. Longley/77n1033

CHURCH OF JESUS CHRIST OF THE LATTER-DAY SAINTS
See Mormons

CHURCHES
Madden/Religious gd to Europe/76n1071
Weis/Colonial clergy & the colonial churches of New England/78n416

CINEMA
See Film theaters; Films

CIO
Fink/State labor proceedings: bibliog, 1885-1974/78n767
Woodbridge/AFL & CIO pamphlets, 1889-1955/78n774

CIRCUS
Sokan/Bibliographic catalog of the circus/78n930

CITIES AND TOWNS
Comparative atlas of America's great cities/77n728
Hoehn/Union list of Sanborn fire insurance maps (Alabama to Missouri)/78n764

CITIZEN ACTION GROUPS
See also Politics, Practical
Hutcheson/Citizen groups in local politics/77n523
Strauss/How to get things changed/75n515

CITRUS PLANTS
Knorr/Citrus diseases & disorders/76n1401

CIVIL ENGINEERING
Directory of computer software applications/79n1561
Holstrom/Index to pubs of institution of civil engineers/78n1516
Merritt/Standard hndbk for civil engineers/77n1576
Schwicker/International dict of bldg construction/76n1618
TVA/Flood damage prevention/75n1756
US Corps of Engineers/Shore protection manual/75n1816
Zilly/Handbook of environmental civil engineering/76n1619

CIVIL ENGINEERS
Marshall/Biographical dict of railway engineers/79n1585

CIVIL RIGHTS
See also Human rights
Alexander/State-by-state gd to women's legal rights/76n512
Burke/Civil rights/75n796
Eichman/Bibliography of AV matls reflecting a civil liberties theme/78n495
Fisher/Free at last: bibliog of M. L. King, Jr./78n444
Fraenkel/Rights we have/75n481
Gager/Women's rights almanac/75n849
Karis/From protest to challenge: African politics in So Africa 1882-1964/78n471
Law/Rights of the poor/75n559
Levine/Rights of students/75n560
Neuborne/Rights of candidates & voters/77n504
Rosengart/Rights of suspects/75n562
Ross/Rights of women/75n563
Wynne/South African political matls/78n472
von Pfeil/Juvenile rights since 1967/76n510

CIVIL SERVICE
Federal career directory/77n626
Guide to fed career lit/77n596

CIVILIZATION
Bullock/Harper dict of modern thought/78n83
Garber/Concise ency of ancient civilizations/79n404
Kurtz/World gd to antiquities/76n299

CLARKE, JEREMIAH
Taylor/Thematic catalog of the works of J. Clarke/78n910

CLASSICAL LITERATURE
Classical world bibliography of . . .
Greek drama & poetry/79n1262
Philosophy, religion, & rhetoric/79n1080
Vergil/79n1264
Thompson/Bibliography of dissertations in classical studies/78n551

CLASSICISTS
Carrubba/Directory of college & univ classicists in the US & Canada/75n677

CLASSIFICATION OF ARTIFACTS
Chenhall/Nomenclature for museum cataloging/79n269

CLASSIFICATION OF BOOKS
Bliss bibliographic classification:
Intro & auxiliary schedules/78n224
Class J/78n225
Class P/78n226
Class Q/78n227
Bloomberg/Introduction to classification & number bldg in Dewey/77n250
Dewey classification & subj index for cataloging & arranging the bks & pamphlets of a library/78n228
Foskett/Subject approach to info/79n270
General classification systems in a changing world/79n271
Henderson/Major classification systems/78n218
Langridge/Classification & indexing in the humanities/77n256
LC classification schedules: cum of additions & changes/Savage/77n257
Maltby/Classification in the 1970's/78n220
McKeon/Classification system of Jacques-Charles Brunet/78n221
National Library of Medicine classification/79n276
NTIS subj classification/78n1526
Olson/Author-number index to the LC classification schedules/79n277
Olson/Biographical subj index to the LC classification schedules/79n278
Olson/Classified index to persons in the LC classification schedules/79n279
Olson/Geographical name index to the LC classification schedules/79n280
Olson/Subject keyword index to the LC classification schedules/79n281

CLASSIFICATION OF BOOKS (cont'd)
Poole/Documents Office classification/79n123
Vickery/Classification & indexing in science/77n263

CLASSIFICATION OF KNOWLEDGE
See Knowledge, classification of

CLAVICHORD
Boalch/Makers of the harpsichord & clavichord 1440-1840/76n1012

CLAY
Bibliography: clay/75n1039
Chappell/Potter's compl bk of clay & glazes/79n947

CLEMENS, SAMUEL LANGHORNE
See Twain, Mark

CLERGY
Weis/Colonial clergy & the colonial churches of New England/78n416
Weis/Colonial clergy of Virginia, North Carolina & South Carolina/77n479

CLEVELAND, OH
Vexler/Cleveland: chronological hist/78n361
Wynar/Ethnic groups in Ohio: emphasis on Cleveland/76n393

CLEVELAND MUSEUM OF ART
Cleveland Museum of Art/European paintings before 1500/76n917

CLIMATOLOGY
Climates of the states/Natl Oceanic & Atmospheric Admin/76n1477
Grayson/Bibliography of lit on North American climates/76n1478
Hastenrath/Climatic atlas of tropical Atlantic & Eastern Pacific oceans/79n1414
Lawson/Climatic atlas of Nebraska/79n1415
Pollack/Weather/79n1416
Ruffner/Climates of the states/79n1413
Ruffner/Weather almanac/75n1568; 78n1353
Schwartz/Climate advisor/79n1417
Sunrise & sunset tables US/78n1354
Weather atlas of the US/Baldwin/76n1479

CLIMBING
See Mountaineering

CLOCKS AND WATCHES
Bromley/Clockmaker's library/79n934
Cutmore/Watch collector's hndbk/77n898
Distin/American clock: pictorial survey 1723-1900/78n867
Erhardt/Clock/79n935
Nutting/Clock bk: . . . antique clocks/77n901

CLOTHING AND DRESS
Kleeberg/Butterick fabric hndbk/76n875
Linton/Modern textile & apparel dict/75n964

CLOUGH, ARTHUR HUGH
Scott/Early editions of A. H. Clough/78n1171

CLUBS
Circle of Friends/78n79
Kujoth/Boys' & girls' bk of clubs & organizations/76n696

COAL INDUSTRY
Munn/Coal industry in America/79n846

COAL MINING
Tompkins/Strip-mining for coal/75n1815

COBOL
Brophy/COBOL programming/77n288

CODICES
Turner/Typology of the early codex/79n70

COINS
Andrews/Fell's internat'l coin bk/75n1060; 77n902
Angus/Fell's gd to coins & money tokens of the world/75n1061
Brunk/World countermarks on medieval & modern coins/77n905
Catalogue of the world's most popular coins/ Reinfeld/78n844
Coin world almanac/77n907
Craig/Coins of the world 1750-1850/77n908
Domestic & foreign coins manufactured by mints of the US 1793-1976/79n919
Krause/Standard catalog of world coins/75n1068; 76n969
Rosichan/Stamps & coins/75n1052
Yeoman/Current coins of the world/75n1072; 77n916

ANCIENT
Crawford/Roman republican coinage/76n966
Klawans/Reading & dating Roman imperial coins/78n847
Kraay/Archaic & classical Greek coins/77n912

INVESTMENTS
Deutch/High profits without risk/77n910
Sinclair/How the experts buy & sell gold bullion, gold stocks & gold coins/76n862

FOREIGN COUNTRIES
Bressett/Guide bk of English coins, 19th & 20th centuries/77n904
Buttrey/Guide bk of Mexican coins 1822 to date/78n843
Charlton/Standard catalogue of Canadian coins/75n1062
Clark/Token coinage of Guatemala/75n1063
Coole/Ch'i heavy sword coins & pieces of the Chou era/78n845
Guttag/J. Guttag collection of Latin American coins/75n1065
Hazlitt/Coinage of the European continent/ Oikonomides/76n968
Seppa/Coins of Ecuador/75n1070
Stockney/Coins & paper money of Nicaragua/75n1071
Vogt/Std catalogue of Mexican coins/79n920

COINS (cont'd)
UNITED STATES
Attinelli/Bibliography of Amer numismatic auction catalogues, 1828-75/77n903
Walter Breen's ency of US & colonial proof coins/79n918
Brown/Guide to the grading of US coins/76n965
Cline/Standing liberty quarters/77n906
Crosby/Early coins of America/75n1064
Culver/Guidebook of Franklin Mint issues/76n967
Davis/Complete bk of US coin collecting/77n909
Durst/Comprehensive gd to Amer colonial coinage/78n846
Loring/Monographs on varieties of US large cents 1795-1803/77n913
Noe/Silver coinage of Massachusetts/75n1069
Sheldon/Penny whimsy: descriptive classification with tables of rarity & value/77n915
Yeoman/Handbook of US coins/77n917; 78n848; 79n921

COLERIDGE, SAMUEL TAYLOR
Caskey/S. T. Coleridge/79n1235
Haven/S. T. Coleridge: bibliog, v1/77n1230

COLLECTIBLES AS INVESTMENTS
Durst/Collector-investor gdbk & inventory/78n831

COLLECTING
Barber/Ceramic, furniture, & silver collectors' glossary/78n830
Dorn/Insider's gd to antiques, art, & collectibles/75n1050
Durst/Collector-investor gdbk & inventory/78n831
Franklin/Antiques & collectibles/79n913
Hake/Encyclopedia of political buttons/75n1095
Hammond/Pictorial price gd to American antiques . . . /79n914
Hotchkiss/Limited edition collectibles/75n1085
Kovels' collector's gd to limited editions/75n1086
Liu/American sporting collector's hndbk/77n935; 78n832
Lowery/Backyard treasure hunting/75n1051
Miller/Wallace-Homestead flea market price guide/78n833
Patterson/Collector's gd to relics & memorabilia/75n1058

COLLECTION DEVELOPMENT
See Book selection
See also Libraries—acquisitions; Library resources

COLLECTIVE BARGAINING
Abell/Collective bargaining in higher educ/ 78n161
Allen/Collective bargaining in higher educ/ 75n639
Rothman/Bibliography of collective bargaining in hospitals & related facilities/77n840
Schlipf/Collective bargaining in libs/76n184
Weatherford/Collective bargaining & the academic librarian/77n207

COLLECTIVISM
Morrison/Collective behavior: bibliog/77n707

COLLEGE AND SCHOOL JOURNALISM
Directory of the college student press in America/75n1299

COLLEGE AND UNIVERSITY LIBRARIES
Abell/Collective bargaining in higher educ/ 78n161
Books for college libraries/76n141
Branscomb/Teaching with books/75n178
Brevik/Open admissions & the academic library/78n162
Bryan/University libraries in Britain/77n201
Cowley/Libraries in higher educ/77n202
Farber/Academic library: essays/75n180
Fussler/Research libraries & tech/75n181
Gore/Farewell to Alexandria/77n205
Grieder/Acquisitions/79n245
Jefferson/College library/79n196
Johnson/Libraries for teaching, libraries for research/78n261
Josey/New dimensions for academic library service/76n138
McCullough/Approval plans & academic libraries/78n165
McInnis/New perspectives for ref service in academic libraries/79n296
Mitchell/Cost analy of library functions/79n256
Mount/University sci & engineering libraries/ 77n239
Novak/Running out of space—what are the alternatives?/79n258
Oboler/Ideas & the univ library/78n167
Schad/Probs developg academic lib colls/75n212
Smith/Library stats coll & univ/78n170
Steele/Steady-state, zero growth & the academic library/79n200
Thompson/Intro to univ lib admin/75n182
Urquhart/Regulation & stock control in libraries/78n171
ADMINISTRATION
Baumol/Econ of academic libs/75n176
Booz/Organization & staffing of libs Columbia Univ75n177

COLLEGE AND UNIVERSITY LIBRARIES (Cont'd)
ADMINISTRATION (cont'd)
Durey/Staff mgmt univ & coll libs/77n203
Edwards/Role of the beg libr'n in univ libs/ 77n204
Ellsworth/Planning manual academic lib bldgs/75n179
Lee/Emerging trends in lib organ/79n198
Lyle/Administration of the college library/ 76n139
Marchant/Participative mgmt in academic libraries/78n164
Martin/Budgetary control in academic libraries/79n199
Young/Planning, programming, budgeting systems in academic libraries/77n208
INSTRUCTION IN USE
Comprehensive program of user educ for the general libraries, Univ of Texas/78n233
Hardesty/Use of slide-tape presentations in academic libraries/79n195
Kirkendall/Putting library instruction in its place/79n290
Rader/Faculty involvement in library instruction/78n169
Rader/Library instruction in the '70s/78n236
Ward/Southeastern bibliographic instruction directory/79n169

COLLEGE LEARNING RESOURCE CENTERS
See Learning Resource Centers

COLLEGE-LEVEL EXAMINATION PROGRAM
College placement & credit by exam/77n614

COLLEGE STUDENTS
Johnson/Freshman's friend/77n585

COLLEGES AND UNIVERSITIES
See also Community colleges; Higher education; Student aid; Students

Also under subjects Business education; Medical schools
Askew/Small college: hndbk/75n640
Beach/Bibliog gd to Amer coll & univ/76n575
Blackwell/College law digest/75n564
Dressel/Hndbk of academic eval/77n633
Gabriel/Summary bibliog of hist of universities of Great Britain & Ireland/75n645
Guide to prof developmt opportunities for college & univ administrators/Irwin/76 n648
USOE/Facilities inventory/75n719

COLLEGES AND UNIVERSITIES (cont'd)
ADMISSION REQUIREMENTS
Admissions, financial aid & placement . . .
  College Board/77n607
American Schools Assoc/Directory of college
  transfer info/75n672
Barron's hndbk of college transfer info/
  Proia/76n636
Chronicle Guidance Pubs/College counseling
  for transfers & careers/75n655
College admissions data serv hndbk/79n651
College placement & credit by exam/77
  n614; 79n654
Zuker/Peterson's gd to admissions/77n627
FACULTIES
Academic who's who . . . in British Isles/77
  n641
AIBS directory of bioscience depts & faculties US & Canada/77n1293
Guthrie/Graduate programs & faculty in reading/77n618
National faculty directory 1976/77n622
Carrubba/Directory of college & univ
  classicists in US & Canada/75n677
DIRECTORIES—U.S.
Accredited institutions of postsecondary
  educ/76n632
Barron's gd to grad schools: social sci &
  psychology/76n634
Barron's profiles of American colleges . . .
  Descriptions v1/76n638; 79n649
  Midwest/76n639
  Northeast/76n640
  South/76n641
  West/76n642
Basic info abt higher educ institutions in the
  middle states region/75n675
Blaze/Guide to alternative colleges/76n643
Cass/Comparative gd to Amer colleges/77
  n611; 78n567; 79n650
Cass/Counselors' comparative gd to Amer
  colleges/77n612
College charts/76n645
College hndbk/Watts/77n613; 79n652
Colleges classified/76n647
Hawes/New Amer gd to colleges/78n565
Hinckley/Peterson's travel gd to colleges/79
  n658
Lovejoy's college gd/77n621
Peterson's annual guides to undergrad &
  grad study/77n623; 79n663
Peterson's annual guides to grad study/79
  n662
Podolsky/Education directory, colleges &
  universities/79n664
Randax educ gd/77n624
Randax grad school directory/77n625
Songe/American universities & colleges/79
  n640

COLLEGES AND UNIVERSITIES (cont'd)
DIRECTORIES—U.S. (cont'd)
US HEW/Education directory/76n655
Yale Daily News/Insider's gd to colleges/79
  n665
DIRECTORIES—INTERNATIONAL
Directory of No & So American universities/
  Zils/79n667
Garraty/New gd to study abroad/79n641
Handbook on internat'l study for US
  nationals/77n589; 78n574
Higher educ in United Kingdom: hndbk for
  students from overseas/78n575
International gd to the academic market
  place/76n572
Study abroad/76n615
Summer study abroad/Cohen/77n590
US college programs abroad/Cohen/77n591
World gd to universities: pt 1/77n593/pt 2/
  79n668
World list of universities/77n594
World of learning/76n617
MINORITIES AND HANDICAPPED
Chambers/Black higher educ in the US/79
  n628
Feingold/College gd for Jewish youth/79
  n459
Gollay/College gd for students with disabilities/78n564
PROGRAMS AND COURSES
Bayerl/Interdisciplinary studies in the humanities: directory/78n560
Cohen/Summer study abroad/77n590
Cohen/US college sponsored programs
  abroad/77n591
College hndbk index of majors/79n653
College programs for high school students/
  76n646
Directory of US college degrees for part-time
  students/Pitchess/75n676
Gordon/On-campus, off-campus degree programs for part-time students/77n616
Guide to four-yr college majors/76n613
Guide to two-yr college majors/76n649
Innovative grad programs directory/77n619
Lewchuk/National register of internships/75
  n679
Parker/College on your own/79n632
Yellow pages of undergrad innovations/75
  n682

COLLINS, WILKIE
Beetz/Wilkie Collins/79n1236

COLOMBIA
Davis/Historical dict of Colombia/78n306

COLOR IN NATURE
Smithe/Naturalist's color gd/76n1366

COLOR PRINTS
Havlice/World paintings index/78n816
Smith/Index to reproductions of Amer paintings/78n820

COLOR THEORY
Buckley/Color theory/76n914

COLORADO
COIN: indexed cklist to Colorado state pubs/78n95
Denver Public Library/Catalog/76n344
Directory of Colorado manufacturers/77n824
Jones/Colorado grubstake '76/76n347
Kolsar/Bibliography of Colorado State Univ imprints/78n12
Mitterling/Guide to the Edward C. Weatherly papers 1890-1936/76n349
Mitterling/Guide to the Harper M. Orahood papers 1861-1908/76n350
Mitterling/Guide to the Henry M. Teller papers 1862-1908/76n351
Walton/Colorado: practical gd/75n506
Weber/Rocky Mtn flora/77n1359
Wilkins/Colorado railroads/76n1674

COLORADO STATE UNIVERSITY
Kolsar/Bibliography of CSU imprints/78n12

COLORED AMERICAN
Jacobs/Antebellum black newspapers . . . indices, 1827-1841/77n432

COLORED AMERICAN MAGAZINE
Analytical gd & indexes . . . 1900-09/75n30

COLUMBIA PICTURES, INC.
Larkin/Hail, Columbia/76n1048

COLUMBIA UNIVERSITY LIBRARIES
Organization & staffing of the libs of Columbia Univ/75n177

COMBUSTION OF FUELS
Westly/Chemical kinetics of the gas phase combustion of fuels: bibliog/78n1241

COMIC BOOKS
Cohen/Official gd to comic bks . . . /75n66
Crawford/Crawford's ency of comic bks/79n1198
Fleisher/Encyclopedia of comic bk heroes, v1/77n1167/v2/77n1168
Gifford/British comic catalogue/77n1169
Horn/World ency of comics/77n1170
Kempkes/International bibliog of comics lit/75n1312
Overstreet/Comic bk price gd/77n1171

COMMEMORATIVE PLATES
Bradford bk of collector's plates/77n918

COMMERCE
Brazilian-American business review/78n708
Business atlas of western Europe/76n838
Chisholm's hndbk of commercial geog/Blake/76n832
Directory of US importers/79n833
Doing business abroad/77n782
Exporters directory: US buying gd/79n834
FAO trade yrbk/79n835
Foreign trade marketplace/Schultz/78n734
Jonnard/Exporter's financial & marketing hndbk/76n867
Landau/European directory of market research surveys/76n868
MEI marketing economics gd/Hong/76n869

COMMERCIAL CORRESPONDENCE
Brusaw/Business writer's hndbk/79n816
Hill/Hill's manual of social & business forms/77n794

COMMERCIAL LAW
Karr/Condominium buyer's gd/75n948
Rejnis/Everything tenants need to know . . . /75n933

COMMODITY EXCHANGES
Balachandran/Guide to trade & securities statistics/78n727
Gould/Dow Jones-Irwin gd to commodities trading/75n914
Reidy/Guide to world commodity markets/78n728; 79n831
Wasserman/Commodity prices/75n920
Woy/Commodity futures trading/77n806
Wyckoff/International stock & commodity exchange directory/76n863

COMMODITY MARKET
Trade yearbook/78n740

COMMON LAW
Blaustein/Bibliography on the common law in French/75n546

COMMON MARKET
See European Economic Community

COMMONWEALTH LITERATURE
Ferres/Modern commonwealth lit/79n1184
New/Critical writings on Commonwealth lit: bibliog/76n1182

COMMONWEALTH OF NATIONS
Bindoff/Research in progress in English & hist in Britain/77n406
Tett/Professional organizations in the Commonwealth/77n88
Bloomfield/Commonwealth elections/78n476

COMMUNICATION
Aitchison/Unesco thesaurus/79n344
Brightbill/Communications & the US Congress/79n1159

COMMUNICATION (cont'd)
Buteau/Nonprint matls on communication/77n1103
Cassata/Reader in library communication/78n232
Catalog of the communications library, Univ of Illinois/76n1166
Ceynar/Creativity in the communicative arts/76n1161
Communication abstracts/79n1158
Feezel/Selected . . . resources in speech communication: bibliog/77n1121
McGarry/Communication knowl & the librarian/76n117
McGarry/Communication studies/75n156
Key/Nonverbal communication/78n1074
Kuhn/Annotated bibliog of Aspen Institute publications/78n543
Richstad/Mass communication & journalism in the Pacific Islands/79n1160
Root/Communication directory/76n1171
Unger/Literature survey of communication systems/78n1509
Waldhart/Communication research in library & info science/76n127
World communications: 200 country survey/76n1160

COMMUNICATION DISORDERS
Nicolosi/Terminology of communication disorders/79n1175

COMMUNICATIONS INDUSTRY
See Mass media

COMMUNISM
Donovan/Chinese communist matls at the Bureau of Investigation, Taiwan/78n473
Lewytzkyj/Who's who in the socialist countries/79n143
Lieberthal/Research gd to central party . . . meetings in China/77n524
Phan Tien Chau/Vietnamese communism/77n525
Shaffer/Periodicals on socialist countries on Marxism: index of Eng pubs/78n467
South Vietnam . . .
  v3/Millet/75n527
  v4/Millet/75n528
  v5/Sobel/75n529
  v7/Knappman/75n530
Wang/Cultural revolution in China/77n320
Whetten/Current research in comparative communism: bibliog'ic gd/78n468
Yearbook on internat'l communist affairs/75n531

COMMUNITY COLLEGES
Cass/Comparative gd to two yr colleges/78n567
Guide to two-yr college majors/76n649
Schwartz/Community educ bibliog/79n634

COMMUNITY COLLEGES (cont'd)
Thomson/Learning resource centers in community colleges/77n206
Veit/Community college library/76n140
Vocational-tech periodicals for community college libraries/77n210

COMMUNITY EDUCATION
See also Continuing education
Catalog of resource matl on community educ/79n678
Schwartz/Community educ bibliog/79n634
USOE/Catalogue of fed programs related to community educ/78n571

COMMUNITY SERVICES
Watkins/International who's who in community services/75n800

COMPARATIVE EDUCATION
World gd to higher educ/77n592

COMPARATIVE LIBRARIANSHIP
Balnaves/Australian libraries/76n212
Chaplin/Organization of the library profession/75n255
Fjällbrant/User educ in libraries/79n312
Foskett/Reader in comparative librarianship/78n249
Garry/Canadian libraries in their changing environment/79n313
Gidwani/Comparative librarianship: in honor of D. N. Marshall/75n256
Guide for the conversion of school libraries into media centres/79n210
Harvey/Comparative & internat'l library sci/79n314
Huq/Librarianship & Third World/78n251
Ingram/Libraries and the challenge of change/76n213
Jovanovic/Guide to Yugoslav libraries/76n214
Key/Library automation: the Orient & South Pacific/77n289
Koops/Developments in collection bldg in univ libraries in Western Europe/79n197
Kumar/Research libraries in developing countries/75n257
Lewanski/Guide to Polish libraries/76n215
McCarthy/Developing libraries in Brazil/76n216
National & internat'l library planning/77n271
Sable/International studies in librarianship/75n258
Simsova/Handbook of comparative librarianship/76n217
Stevens/Japanese & US research libraries at the turning point/78n250
Welch/Toshokan: libraries in Japanese society/77n272
Wijasuriya/Barefoot librarian: Southeast Asia, ref to Malaysia/76n218

COMPETENCY BASED EDUCATION
Competency based educ sourcebk/78n577
COMPETITOR
Grant/Indexes to *The Competitor*/79n451
COMPOSERS
Anderson/Charles T. Griffes/79n981
Anderson/Contemporary Amer composers: biog dict/77n970
ASCAP symphonic catalog/78n921
Briggs/Collector's Beethoven/79n982
Brown/Carlo D'Ordonez/79n983
Bull/Index to biogs of contemp composers/75n1152
Burke/Collector's Haydn/79n984
Composium directory of new music/78n907
Eagon/Catalog of published concert music by Amer composers/75n1124
Gilder/Dictionary of composers & their music/79n963
Hughes/American composers/75n1117
Jacobi/Contemporary Amer composers/76n1005
Jenkins/Thematic catalogue . . . of G. B. Sammartini/78n908
MacMillan/Contemporary Canadian composers/77n971
Moldon/Bibliography of Russian composers/78n896
Nathan/William Billings/78n909
Parker/Musical biography/76n1006
Significant Amer musicians, composers, & singers/Meltzer/77n135
Stern/Women composers/79n988
Taylor/Thematic catalog of . . . J. Clarke/78n910
Tischler/K. B. Jirak: catalog/76n1011

COMPOST
Campbell/Let it rot!/76n1582

COMPRESSORS
PTFE seals in reciprocating compressors/76n1654

COMPUTER-BASED SERVICES
Divilbiss/Negotiating for computer services/79n301
International directory of computer info system services/75n1775

COMPUTER EDUCATION
Association for Computing Machinery/Graduate assistantship directory/75n673
Spencer/Guide to teaching abt computers in secondary schools/75n716

COMPUTER INDUSTRY
Computer industry review/75n960
Computer review/75n961
Minicomputer review/75n965
Peripherals review/75n966
Worldwide directory of computer companies/75n898

COMPUTER-OUTPUT MICROFILM
Gildenberg/Computer-output-microfilm systems/75n1770
Saffady/Computer-output microfilm/79n333

COMPUTER PROGRAMMING
Brophy/COBOL programming: for librarians/77n288
Brown/FORTRAN to PL/1 dictionary/76n1624
Davis/Illustrative computer programming for libraries/75n275
Directory of computer software applications: civil engineering/79n1561/energy/79n1562
Harrison/Data-structures & programming/75n1771
Ledgard/Programming proverbs for FORTRAN programmers/76n1628
Lee/Computer programs in environmental design/75n1551
Stock/Bibliography of programming languages/75n1777
vanCleemput/Computer aided design of digital systems: bibliog/77n1587

COMPUTER SCIENTISTS
American men & women of science: . . . computer science/78n1216
Who's who in computer educ & research/Hsiao/77n1588

COMPUTERS
Automatic data processing hndbk/Diebold Group/78n713
Burton/Dictionary of microcomputing/78n1521
Carter/Guide to ref sources in the computer sciences/75n273
Chandor/Dictionary of computers/79n1560
Computer security hndbk/75n1768
Encyclopedia of computer sci/Ralston/77n1579
Encyclopedia of computer sci & tech: v1/Belzer/76n1626/v2-v6/78n1523
Helms/Literature in digital signal processing/77n1580
International directory of computer info system services/75n1772
MacCafferty/Computer security/78n1525
Maynard/Dictionary of data processing/77n1581
McCabe/PCC's ref bk of personal & home computing/79n1549
Prenis/Running Press glossary of computer terms/78n1527
Robinson/Documentation stds manual for computer systems/75n1773
Schlossberg/Home computer hndbk/79n1564
Sippl/Computer dict/75n1774
Sippl/Data communications dict/77n1583

COMPUTERS (cont'd)
Sippl/Microcomputer dict & gd/77n1584
Soucek/Microprocessors & microcomputers/77n1585
Spencer/Computer acronym hndbk/75n1775
Spencer/Computer dict/75n1776
Terminals review/75n967
US Dept of Commerce/Annotated bibliog . . . resource sharing computer networks/Woods/77n1586
US Natl Bureau of Stds/Technical gd to computer-communications interface standards/75n1778
vanCleemput/Computer aided design of digital systems: bibliog/77n1587
Way things work bk of the computer/75n1779
Weik/Standard dict of computers & info processing/78n1529

COMPUTERS AND LAW
Duggan/Law & the computer/75n548

COMPUTERS AND MUSIC
Kostka/Bibliography of computer applications in music/75n1129
Ward/Electronic music circuit gdbk/76n1635

CONCRETE CONSTRUCTION
Fintel/Handbook of concrete engineering/75n1759
Waddell/Concrete construction hndbk/75n1761

CONDEMNED BOOKS
Haight/Banned books/79n310

CONDOMINIUMS
Karr/Condominium buyer's gd/75n948

CONFEDERATE STATES OF AMERICA
Crown/Confederate postal hist/77n923
Gibson/J. Davis . . . & treaties with Indian tribes/79n420
Wakelyn/Biographical dict/78n364
Warner/Biographical register/76n341

CONFERENCE PROCEEDINGS
See Congresses and conventions

CONGO
Thompson/Historical dict of Congo/76n250

CONGRESSES AND CONVENTIONS
Bibliographic gd to conf pubs/77n4
Union list of conf proceedings in libraries of the Fed Republic of Germany . . ./79n27

CONJURING
See Magic (conjuring)

CONNECTICUT
Barbour/Families of Hartford/78n396
Cummings/Fairfield county/76n547
Directory of foundations/77n80

CONNECTICUT (cont'd)
Flaste/NY Times gd to children's entertainment/77n559
Gannett/Geographic dict of Connecticut & Rhode Island/79n596
Jacobus/Families of ancient New Haven/75n422
Jacobus/History . . . of families of old Fairfield/77n466
Trumbull/Indian names in Connecticut/75n457
Tyler/Connecticut loyalists/78n415

CONRAD, JOSEPH
Briggum/Concordance to *Almayer's Folly*/79n1237
Parins/Concordance to *Lord Jim*/77n1231

CONSERVATION
See also Environmental sciences
Catalog of the conservation library: Denver Public Library/76n1457
Conservation directory/77n1412
Fahl/North Amer forest . . .hist/78n1483
Harrah/Conservation-ecology: resources/76n1465

CONSERVATISM
Murphy/Directory of conservative . . . serials & freelance markets/79n88
Solara/Key influences in the Amer right/75n482

CONSTELLATIONS
Cleminshaw/Beginner's gd to the skies/79n1314

CONSTITUTIONAL CONVENTIONS
State constitutional conventions . . .
Canning/1959-76/78n457
Yarger/1959-75/77n522

CONSTITUTIONS
Constitutions of countries of world/Blaustein/78n427
Rana/Writings on Indian constitution/75n565
Swindler/Sources . . . of US constitutions/75n566; 79n536

CONSTRUCTION INDUSTRY
See also Building; House construction
Burgess/Construction industry hndbk/75n1757
Cutler/Handbook of housing systems/75n1764
Godel/Sources of construc info/78n1517
Lytle/American metric constr hndbk/77n1567
Ward/Construction info source & ref gd/75n1762

CONSULTANTS
Wasserman/Consultants directory/77n789/New consultants, suppl/77n790

CONSULTANTS (cont'd)
Who's who in consulting/75n902

CONSUMER CREDIT
Miller/Thesaurus of terms in . . . credit/79n872

CONSUMER EDUCATION
Bendick/Catalog of economy & ecology/76n882
Biegel/Best yrs catalogue/79n839
Bruck/Access: for disabled Americans/79n840
Consumers index to product evaluations & info sources/75n943; 77n812
Co-op Hndbk Collective/Food co-op hndbk/76n872
CU/Guide to consumer services: financial, professional/78n747
David/Reference gd for consumers/77n813
Denenberg/Shopper's gdbk to insurance/75n945
Dorfman/Consumer's arsenal/77n814
Fargis/Consumer's hndbk/76n873
Gotsick/Information for everyday survival/77n815
Jurgensen/How to live better on less/76n874
Karnaookh/Shortage survival hndbk/75n947
Karr/Condominium buyer's gd/75n948
Kiernan/Shrinks, etc./75n1591
Kleeberg/Butterick home decorating hndbk/77n941
Krochmal/Making it: do it for less/76n876
Medicine show/75n1649
Rejnis/Everything tenants need to know . . . /75n933
Rosenbloom/Consumer complaint gd/75n934
Rowse/Help/79n107
Sylvia Porter's money bk/76n877
Thomas/Guide to sources/75n935
Thorelli/Consumer info hndbk/75n936
Wasserman/Consumer sourcebk/79n844
White/Angry buyer's complaint directory/75n939
Winter/Consumer's dict of cosmetic ingredients/75n940; 77n818
Yearbook of consumer electronics/Belt/75n1791

CONSUMER PRODUCT SAFETY ACT
ABC's of CPS Act/75n929

CONSUMER PROTECTION
ABC's of the Consumer Product Safety Act/75n929
Capital contacts in consumerism/78n745
Consumer protection directory/Osberg/76n871
Consumer sourcebook/75n931
Directory of consumer protection . . . agencies/Trzyna/75n932
Silva/Justice for Calif consumer/77n816

CONSUMER PROTECTION (cont'd)
US Consumer Affairs Office/State consumer action/75n937
US HEW/Directory: . . . consumer offices/75n938; 77n817

CONSUMERS
Barry/Marketing & black consumer: bibliog/77n807

CONTAINER GARDENING
Yand/Terrace gardener's hndbk/76n1602

CONTAINERIZATION
Jane's freight containers/Finlay/78n1546

CONTESTS
Stuart/Who won what when/79n100

CONTINENTS
Smith/Mesozoic . . . paleocontinental maps/78n1357

CONTINUING EDUCATION
Continuing education: programs/78n568
Wasserman/Training & developmt organizations directory/79n814
Yearbook of . . . continuing educ/76n606; 78n581

CONTROL VALVES
Hutchison/ISA hndbk of control valves/77n1608

CONVENTIONS
Official meeting facilities gd/75n586

CONVERSATION
Veley/Catching up/79n101

CONVICT SHIPS
Coldham/English convicts/78n399

COOKING
Arkin/Kitchen wisdom/78n1467
Axford/English lang cookbks/77n1539
Complete cookery ency/75n1686
Eekhof-Stork/World atlas of cheese/77n1543
Fitzgibbon/Food of the Western world/77n1544
Gourmet's dict of cheeses/77n1546
Handbook of food preparation/Amer Home Economics Assn/76n1571
Hardwick/Fundamentals of quantity food preparation/76n1572
Hering's dict of classical . . . cookery/76n1573
Jones/World of cheese/77n1547
Martin/International dict of food/75n1693
McClane/Encyclopedia of fish cookery/78n1475
New Larousse gastronomique/Montague/78n1476
Patten/Books for cooks: bibliog/77n1549
Recipe index/Forsman/75n1694
Tarr/Up-with-wholesome . . . recipes & household formulas/77n1550

Subjects—247

COOKING (cont'd)
Tudor/Cooking for entertaining/77n1551
Wasserman/Don't ask your waiter/79n1534
Wilson/Complete food catalogue/78n1480
World atlas of food/Hale/75n1695

COOLBRITH, INA
Rodehamel/Ina Coolbrith/75n252

COOLIDGE, ARCHIBALD CARY
Bentinck-Smith/Building a great library/77n276

COOPERATIVE SOCIETIES
Community market/75n942
Food co-op directory/78n711

COPTIC LANGUAGE
Cerny/Coptic etymological dict/78n1053

COPYRIGHT
Complete gd to new copyright law/79n63
Copyright law symposium . . .
   number 21/76n41
   number 22/78n54
   number 23/78n53
Essential elements of copyright clearinghouse/78n55
Heilprin/Copyright & photocopying/79n64
Henry/Copyright info technology public policy, pt I/78n56/Pt 2/78n57
Hurst/Copyright: how to register . . . /78n58
Hurst/Your intro to music-record copyright . . . /78n59
Johnston/Copyright hndbk/79n65
King Research, Inc/Library photocopying in the US/79n318
Library photocopying/79n319
McCormick/Williams & Wilkins case/76n42
Nasri/Crisis in copyright/77n50
White/Copyright dilemma/79n320

CORPORATE ENTRY (cataloging)
Verona/Corporate headings/77n262

CORPORATE INFORMATION POLICY
Automatic data processing hndbk/Diebold Group/78n713

CORPORATE SOCIAL RESPONSIBILITY
Bibliography/Bank of America/78n696
Handbook/Human Resources Network/76n898
Uhr/Social responsibility in marketing/78n744

CORPORATIONS
Angel/Directory of Inter-Corporate ownership/76n893
Arpan/Directory of foreign manufacturers in the US/76n894
Belgium's 500 largest companies/76n895
Corporate profiles/77n798
Directors' . . . ency manual/77n773
Directory of Amer firms operating in foreign countries/77n779

CORPORATIONS (cont'd)
Directory of companies required to file . . . with SEC . . . /79n832
Directory of corporate affiliations/77n781
Europe's 5000 largest companies/76n897
1500 largest companies in Finland/76n892
Hernes/Multinational: gd/78n698
Jane's major companies of Europe/78n758
Kintner/Primer on law of mergers/75n892
1000 largest companies in . . .
   Denmark/76n889
   Norway/76n890
   Sweden/76n891
Standard & Poor's register of corps/79n811
Strharsky/Bibliographical notes for . . . transnational corps & Third World/76n828
Walker's manual of western corps/79n812
Weston/Treasurer's hndbk/78n722

CORPUSCLES
Bessis/Corpuscles/75n1642

CORRECTIONAL INSTITUTIONS
See also Prisons
American Correctional Assn/Directory of juvenile & adult correctional depts . . ./77n709

CORRESPONDENCE SCHOOLS
Continuing educ/78n568
Gordon/on-campus, off-campus degree programs for part-time students/77n616
Guide to independent study through correspondence instruction/76n621
Jones/Correspondence educ'l directory/78n569
Parker/College on your own/79n632

COSMETICS
Ash/Formulary of cosmetic preparations/78n1253
Krochmal/Guide to natural cosmetics/75n1677
Rinzler/Cosmetics/78n1256
Rose/Herbal body book/77n1524
Winter/Consumer's dict of cosmetic ingredients/75n940; 77n818

COSMONAUTS
See Astronauts

COST CONTROL
Higgins/Cost reduction from A-Z/77n774

COSTUME
Cunnington/Costume of household servants . . . Middle Ages to 1900/76n979
Leese/Costume design in movies/78n952

COTES, FRANCIS
Johnson/F. Cotes: compl edition/78n817

COTTON, JOHN
Gallagher/Early Puritan writers/77n1185

COUNCIL ON LIBRARY RESOURCES
20th annual report/78n157

COUNSELING
Hyde/Hotline!/77n105
Zimpfer/Group work in helping professions/77n1444

COUNTRY MUSIC
Artis/Blue grass/76n1022
Illustrated ency/Dellar/78n917
Osborne/55 years of recorded country-western music/77n980
Stambler/Encyclopedia of folk, country, & western music/76n1031

COUNTY GOVERNMENT
County year bk/76n494
Matthews/County info systems directory/78n464

COURTAULD INSTITUTE OF ART, LONDON
Checklist of painters 1200-1976/79n905

COURTS
American bench/Reincke/79n570
Chase/Biographical dict of fed judiciary/77n541
Tompkins/Court organization/75n549
US court directory/79n529

CRABBE, GEORGE
Bareham/Bibliography of G. Crabbe/79n1238

CRAFTS
See also Needlework projects; Weaving; etc.
Andrew/Arco ency of crafts/79n939
Bibliography: enamel/75n1048
Bibliography: glass/75n1049
Bibliography: wood/75n1044
Blandford/Country craft tools/75n1030
Chicorel index to crafts/76n954
Harwell/Crafts for today/75n1035
Index to how to do it info/78n24
Make it yourself/Harding/79n945
Rose/Illustrated ency of crafts/79n940
Schneider/Crafts of the No Amer Indians/75n1037
Scott/Crafts business ency/79n941
Shields/Make it: index to projects/76n956
Turner/Index to handicrafts/76n955
Weingarten/Selling your crafts . . . Los Angeles/75n1038
CATALOGS AND DIRECTORIES
ACC/Directory of courses/75n1029
Art & crafts market/Lapin/78n874
Boyd/Mail-order crafts catalogue/76n948
Brabec/Guide to craft world/76n949
Catalogue of South/Phillips/75n98
Colin/Craft sources/76n950
Contemporary crafts market place/American Crafts Council/76n951

CRAFTS (cont'd)
CATALOGS AND DIRECTORIES (cont'd)
Coyne/By hand: schools/75n1031
Craft shops USA/75n1032
Craft suppliers: fiber/75n1041
Eddy/Alternative shopping/75n1033
Glassman/National gd to craft supplies/76n952
Glassman/NY gd to craft supplies/75n1034
Lapin/Craftworker's market/79n938
Marietta College crafts directory/77n895
Rosenbloom/Craft supplies supermarket/76n953
Rosenbloom/Kits and plans/75n1036
Weills/Goodfellow catalog/78n875

CRANE, STEPHEN
Baron/Concordance to poems of Crane/Katz/76n1231
Crosland/Concordance to complete poetry of Crane/76n1232

CRASH VEHICLES
Vanderveen/Fire & crash vehicles/77n1622

CRC HANDBOOKS
Composite index/79n1304

CREATIVE ABILITY
Arasteh/Creativity in human developmt/78n1361
Rothenberg/Index of scientific writings on creativity/76n94; 77n1296

CREATIVE WRITING
Ireland/Index to inspiration/77n94

CREDIT MANAGEMENT
D&B hndbk of credits/75n956

CREOLE DIALECTS
Bibliography of Pidgin & Creole/77n1060

CRETE
Davaras/Guide to Cretan antiquities/77n349

CRICKET
Golesworthy/Encyclopedia of cricket/76n766

CRIES
Beall/Kaufrufe und strabenhandler/78n806

CRIME AND CRIMINALS
See also Criminal justice; Juvenile delinquency; Law enforcement
Crime & juvenile delinquency/79n574
Davis/Criminological bibliographies/79n575
Hopkins/Organized crime/75n827
Index to abstracts on crime/79n576
Kelly/Jack the Ripper/75n828
Kinton/Criminology, law enforcement/75n829
Franke/America's 50 safest cities/75n833
Parker/Violence in the US/75n834

Subjects—249

CRIME AND CRIMINALS (cont'd)
Radzinowicz/Criminology & the admin of criminal justice: bibliog/78n499
Wright/Use of criminology lit/75n838
NY Radical Feminists/Rape/75n850
Wolfgang/Criminology index/76n780
Wright/Use of criminology lit/75n838

CRIME PREVENTION
Clifford/Security!/75n832

CRIMINAL INVESTIGATION
US Dept of Justice/Science of fingerprints/75n836
US Dept of Justice/Crime scene search/75n835

CRIMINAL JUSTICE
See also Crime and criminals; Law enforcement
Parisi/Sources of ... stats/79n577
O'Brien/Directory of ... info sources/78n506
Radzinowicz/Criminology & admin of criminal justice: bibliog/78n499
Rush/Dictionary of criminal justice/78n502
Search Group, Inc/Dictionary of criminal justice data terminology/78n503
US Natl Criminal Justice Ref Service/Thesaurus/78n504
US Natl Criminal Justice Info & Stats Service/Sourcebk of ... statistics/75n837; 78n491

CRIMINAL LAW
Bond/Plea bargaining/76n514
Bailey/Complete manual of criminal forms/76n513
Rosengart/Rights of suspects/75n562

CRIMINOLOGY
See Crime and criminals

CRIOLLO CATTLE
Müller-Hayes/Bibliography/79n1524

CROATIAN EMIGRE LITERATURE
Prpic/Croation books ... in exile/75n823

CROCHETING
Chicorel index to crafts/76n954
Halevy/Knitting & crocheting pattern index/78n878
Mariano/Encyclopedia of knitting & crochet patterns/78n879

CROSS REFERENCES (cataloging)
Subject cross ref gd/77n260

CROSSWORD PUZZLES
Bailie/British crosswd puzzle dict/79n1122
Pulliam/NY Times crosswd puzzle dict/76n1135
Schwartz/Funk & Wagnalls crosswd puzzle wd finder/75n1265

CROSSWORD PUZZLES (cont'd)
Swanfeldt/Crossword puzzle dict/78n1047
Whitfield/Webster's new world crosswd puzzle dict/78n1049

CROWS
Goodwin/Crows of the world/77n1378

CRYPTOGRAPHY
Shulman/Annotated bibliog/77n1105

CRYSTALS
Pearl/Gems, minerals, crystals, & ores/78n1360

CUBA
Perez/Cuban revolutionary war/77n400

CULTS
Spiritual community gd/Khalsa/79n1087

CUMBERLAND, GEORGE
Bentley/Bibliography of G. Cumberland .../76n1271

CUNNINGHAM, J. V.
Gullans/Bibliography of published works/75n1353

CURIOSITIES
Bongartz/New England records/79n386
Brandon/Weird America/79n1085
Burnam/Dictionary of misinformation/77n89
Cornell/Great internat'l disaster bk/77n98
Felton/Best, worst, & most unusual/77n92
Felton/More best, worst & most unusual/77n93
Kane bk of famous first facts/75n93; 77n95
Macksey/Book of women's achievements/78n671
McWhirter/Guinness bk of phenomenal happenings/77n99
McWhirter/Guinness bk of world records/77n100
McWhirter/Guinness bk of young recordbreakers/77n101
Passel/Best, encore/78n89
Sandow/Durations/79n99
Veley/Catching up/79n101
Wallechinsky/Book of lists/78n94
Worth/Complete super trivia ency/79n104

CURRENT INDEX TO JOURNALS IN EDUCATION
Finding list of journals in CIJE/78n583

CUTTER, CHARLES AMMI
Miksa/C. A. Cutter/78n153

CYTOLOGY
Index of tissue culture/Stahl/78n1423

CZECHOSLOVAK LITERATURE
Mihailovich/Modern Slavic lits/78n1199

CZECHOSLOVAKIA
Hejzlar/Czechoslovakia 1968-69/76n269

DAG HAMMARSKJOLD COLLECTION
Kamenetsky/Guide to . . . collection on developing nations/78n273

DAHOMEY
Decalo/Historical dict of Dahomey/77n313

DAIRY INDUSTRY
Spencer/Economic hist of milk marketing/75n926

DALLAS, TX
Korkmas/Directory of services for young children/75n799
Open Dallas/75n613; 78n81

DANCE
Bibliographic gd to dance/77n5
Clarke/Encyclopedia of dance/79n1019
Dance world/76n1037
Frost/Encyclopedia of physical educ . . . dance/78n607
Jacobson/Dance horizons travel gd/79n615
Kaprelian/Aesthetics for dancers/78n924
McLean/Annotated bibliog of Oceanic music & dance/79n960
Norton/Dance directory/79n1017
Raffe/Dictionary of dance/76n1036

DANCE BANDS
Rust/American dance band discography/76n994

DANCE IN FILMS
Parker/Guide to dance in film/79n1038

DANISH LITERATURE
Henriksen/Karen Blixen-Isak Dinesen/79n1265

DANTE (Alighieri)
Companion to Divine Comedy/Grandgent/76n1296
Locock/Biographical gd to Divina Commedia/76n1297

DARIO, RUBEN
Ellis/Critical approaches to R. Dario/76n1299
Woodbridge/R. Dario: bibliog/76n1303

DARWIN, CHARLES
Carroll/Annotated calendar of letters/77n1345
Freeman/Works of C. Darwin: hndlist/78n1272

DATA BASES
See also Machine-readable bibliographic data
Atherton/Librarians & online services/79n299
Christian/Electronic library/79n261
Directory of data files . . . /Natl Tech Info Service/76n1625; 78n1521
Inventory of . . . services available to US House of Representatives/78n99
Schneider/Survey of commercially available computer-readable biblio'ic data bases/75n283

DATA BASES (cont'd)
Settel/Subject descrip of bks/79n282
Yska/Final report on data bases for environmental info/79n304

DATA PROCESSING
Automatic data processing hndbk/Diebold Group/78n713
Brandon/Data processing mgmt/76n1623
Computer security hndbk/75n1768
Gildersleeve/Organizing & documenting data processing info/78n1524
Hayes/Handbook of data processing for libraries/76n230
Lancaster/Proceedings of 1973 clinic on library applications of data processing/75n282
Maynard/Dictionary of data processing/77n1581
Pratt/Information economics/77n292
Pratt/On-line age: proceedings of EUSIDIC Conf, Oslo/77n293
Schulz/Data systems dict/79n1565
Sippl/Data communications dict/77n1583
Weik/Standard dict of computers/78n1529
Wittman/Dictionary of data processing . . . /79n1566

DAVIS, JEFFERSON
Gibson/J. Davis & . . . treaties with Indian tribes/79n420

DAYS
See also Holidays
Emmens/AV gd to Amer holidays/79n1086
Gregory/Anniversaries & holidays/76n1108

DEAF
See also Hearing disorders
Bauman/Blindness, visual impairment, deaf-blindness/79n1449
Fellendorf/Bibliography on deafness/79n1455

DEATH
See also Bereavement
Fulton/Death, grief & bereavemt/78n1425
Harrah/Funeral service/77n704
Miller/Death: bibliog'l gd/78n1426
Poteet/Death & dying: bibliog/78n1427
Sell/Dying & death: bibliog/78n1428

DEATHS, REGISTERS OF
Birth, marriage, death—on record/78n654

DEBATE
Kruger/Argumentation & debate/76n1177

DECADENCE (literary movement)
Dowling/Aestheticism & decadence/78n1089

DECORATIVE ART
Dirsztay/Church furnishings/79n912
Fleming/Dictionary of decorative arts/78n828
Osborne/Oxford companion to dec arts/76n946

DECORATIVE ART (cont'd)
Stafford/Illustrated dict of ornament/76n924
Studio dict of design/75n1023

DEEDS
Nelson/Patents & deeds of NJ, 1664-1703/77n471

DEGREES, ACADEMIC
Baker/Earned degrees conferred/76n633

DELANY, MARTIN R.
Ellison/W. W. Brown & M. R. Delany/79n450

DELAWARE
Bibliography of Delaware/78n311
Gannett/Gazetteer of MD & DE/77n463
Gehring/Delaware papers, 1664-82/79n484
Olmsted/Index to 1850 census/78n407

DELAWARE BAY
Plunguian/Comprehensive bibliog/75n1525

DELAWARE VALLEY
Cramer/Museum Council . . . gd to museums/77n76

DEMOGRAPHY
Bibliography of land settlemt/79n787
Bilsborrow/Population in planning/78n684
Chang/Taiwan demography/75n871
Demographic yrbk/76n814; 77n760
Desai/Survey of research in demography/77n756
Dobyns/Native Amer hist'l demography/77n736
Fussell/Demographic atlas of Birmingham/77n754
Goode/Population explosion/75n872
International Migration Review cum index/79n794
LC/General censuses in Americas/75n875
McEvedy/Atlas of world pop hist/79n786
Murray/Atlas of Atlanta/75n880
Population & demography: bibliog/78n686
Population activists hndbk/75n514
Population problems in Africa/75n294
Shaw/Migration theory & fact/77n757
Triche/Population explosion/76n813
Trzyna/Population: internat'l directory/77n713
UN/Demographic yrbk/76n814
Zelinsky/Bibliographic gd to population geography/77n758

DENMARK
Denmark: handbk/76n270
1000 largest companies/76n889
Scandinavian political studies/76n501

DENTAL SCHOOLS
Admission requirements/77n1479

DENTISTRY
Wischnitzer/Barron's gd to med, dental, & health sci careers/78n1409
Zebooker/Your teeth, your dentist/75n1651

DENVER PUBLIC LIBRARY
Catalog of conservation library/76n1457

DEPRECIATION
Depreciation gd/76n911

DERMATOLOGY
Weinberg/Color atlas of pediatric dermatology/76n1541

DESERTS
Larson/Sierra Club gd to deserts of SW/78n1270

DESIGN PROTECTION
Kase/Designs/76n1648

DETECTIVE AND MYSTERY STORIES
Barnes/Best detective fiction/76n1202
De Waal/World bibliog of Sherlock Holmes . . . /76n1205
Herman/Corpus delicti of mystery fiction/76n1207
Mundell/Detective short story/75n1327
Penzler/Detectionary/78n1104
Smith/Clock-and-dagger bibliog/77n1174
Steinbrunner/Encyclopedia of mystery & detection/77n1177
Tracy/Encyclopaedia Sherlockiana/78n1172
Young/Georges Simenon: checklist/77n1179

DETECTIVES IN LITERATURE
Penzler/Detectionary: biog dict/78n1104

DETROIT, MI
Vexler/Detroit: chron & doc hist/78n362

DETROIT PUBLIC LIBRARY
Thomson/Kate Greenaway: catalogue/78n1161

DEUTERIUM
Vasaru/Deuterium & heavy water/77n1341

DEWEY, JOHN
Boydston/Checklist of writings about J. Dewey/75n642

DEWEY, MELVIL
Vann/Melvil Dewey/79n188

DEWEY DECIMAL CLASSIFICATION
Dewey/Classification & subj index/78n228
General classification systems/79n271
Henderson/Major classification systems/78n218

DIAGNOSIS (medical)
See also Internal medicine
Common symptom gd/Wasson/77n1484
Encyclopedia of common diseases/77n1472
Galton/Complete bk of symptoms/79n1484

DIAGNOSIS (medical) (cont'd)
Gardner/Good Housekeeping dict of symptoms/77n1493
Hart/French's index of differential diagnosis/75n1630
Horwitz/Index of suspicion in . . . diseases/76n1531
Krupp/Current med diagnosis & treatment/75n1609
Miller/Symptoms: ency/77n1496
Physician's handbook/Krupp/77n1488
Taylor's self-help med gd/78n1418
Vickery/Take care of yrself/78n1432

DIAGNOSTIC TESTS (medical)
French/Guide to diagnostic procedures/76n1529

DIAL
Zingman/Dial: author index/76n1221

DIARIES
Batts/British manuscript diaries of 19th cent/77n405

DIBDIN, THOMAS FROGNALL
Neuburg/T. F. Dibdin/79n187

DICKENS, CHARLES
Churchill/Bibliography of Dickensian criticism/76n1272
Partlow/Dickens studies annual/75n1384

DICTATORS
Egan/Kings, rulers & statesmen/78n332

DICTIONARIES, POLYGLOT
Elsevier's telecommunication dict in six languages/77n1117
Glossary of conf terms/Unesco/76n1138
Suryakanta/Sanskrit-Hindi-Engl dict/77n1098

DIEGUENO INDIANS
Almstedt/Bibliography/75n802

DIET
See also Reducing diets
Ashley/Dictionary of nutrition/77n1469
Casale/Diet food finder/76n1569
Konishi/Exercise equivalents of food/75n1690
Kraus/Basic food . . . calorie counter/75n1691
Kraus/Basic food . . . carbohydrate counter/75n1692

DIET IN DISEASE
Lagua/Nutrition & diet therapy/76n1525

DIGITAL ELECTRONICS
Helms/Literature in digital signal processing/77n1580
van Cleemput/Computer aided design of digital systems/77n1587; 78n1528

DINESEN, ISAK
Henriksen/Karen Blixen-Isak Dinesen/79n1265

DIPTERA
Delfinado/Catalog . . . of Oriental region/78n1328

DIRECT DELIVERY OF BOOKS
Kim/Books by mail/78n143

DIRECTORIES
Greenfield/National directory of addresses/79n86

DISABLED
See Handicapped

DISADVANTAGED CHILDREN
McCormick/Primary educ for disadvantaged: annotated bibliog/77n576

DISARMAMENT
Burns/Arms control/79n550
Dupuy/Documentary hist of arms control/75n1835
Meeker/Proliferation of nuclear weapons/75n1836
Ridgeway/NPT: current issues in nuclear proliferation/79n559
Roswell/Arms control . . . & econ planning/75n1837
SIPRI yrbk, world armaments/76n505

DISASTERS
Annual summary of . . . natural disasters/Unesco/76n1469
Cornell/Great internat'l disaster bk/77n98
Manning/Disaster technology/77n705
Nash/Darkest hours/78n86

DISCARDING OF BOOKS
Slote/Weeding library collections/76n203
Urquhart/Regulation & stock control/78n171

DISCOVERIES (in geography)
Newby/Rand McNally atlas of exploration/76n298

DISEASES
Common symptom gd/Wasson/77n1484
Encyclopedia of common diseases/77n1472
Horwitz/Index of . . . treatable diseases/76n1531
Locke/Virus diseases/79n1490

DISNEY, WALT
Finch/Art of Walt Disney/75n1190
Maltin/Disney films/75n1195
Munsey/Disneyana/75n1098

DISRAELI, BENJAMIN
Stewart/Disraeli's novels/76n1273

DISSENT
Liber/Nonconformity . . . in Ukrainian SSR/79n549

DISSERTATIONS, ACADEMIC
Comprehensive dissertation index/75n688
Reynolds/Guide to theses & dissertations/76n583
Sugden/Graduate thesis/75n696

DISTILLERIES
Barleycorn/Moon-shiners manual/76n1560

DIVINE COMEDY (Dante)
Companion to Divine Comedy/Grandgent/76n1296
Locock/Biographical gd to Divina Commedia/76n1297

DIVING, SUBMARINE
Zanelli/Sub-aqua illust'd dict/78n634

DIVORCE
Birth . . . marriage . . . death-on the record/78n654
Eddy/What you should know about marriage, divorce, . . . in Louisiana/75n556
Israel/Bibliography on divorce/76n782
Mayer/Divorce & annulment/77n716
McKenney/Divorce: bibliog/76n783
Women in transition/76n785

DOCUMENTATION
See Information science

DOCUMENTS LIBRARIES
Harleston/Administration of gov docs collections/75n214
Schorr/Government docs in library lit/78n131

DOGS
Ashworth/Dell ency of dogs/75n1678
Bernstein/Dog digest/77n1526
Chrystie/Pets/75n1679
Complete dog bk/76n1564
Glover/Standard gd to pure-bred dogs/79n1523
McClean gd to kennels/75n1683
Schneck/Complete home med gd/77n1532
Sessions/Dog owner's med manual/77n1533
Sprung/"Popular dogs"/76n1565
Sprung/Dog lovers complete gd/77n1535
Swedrup/Pocket ency of dogs/77n1538
White/Sewell's dog's med dict/78n1466
Woodhouse/Encyclopedia of dogs/79n1526

DOLL HOUSES
O'Brien/Collector's gd to dollhouses/75n1099
Rosner/Inside the world of . . . dollhouses/77n938

DOLLS
DeWein/Collectors ency of Barbie dolls/78n866

DOLPHINS
Coffey/Dolphins, whales & porpoises/78n1332

DOLPHINS (cont'd)
Truitt/Dolphins & porpoises/75n1521

DOLPHY, ERIC
Simosko/Eric Dolphy/75n1164

DOMESDAY BOOK
Darby/Domesday gazetteer/76n368

DOMESTIC ANIMALS
Spaulding/Veterinary gd for animal owners/77n1534
Encyclopedia of animal care/West/78n1462

D'ORDONEZ, CARLO
Brown/Carlo D'Ordonez/79n983

DOSTOEVSKII, FEDOR M.
Berry/Plots & characters in major Russian fict/79n1282

DOVER, NH
Dover Hist'l Soc/Vital records, 1686-1850/79n482

DOYLE, ARTHUR CONAN
Tracy/Encyclopaedia Sherlockiana/78n1172
DeWaal/World bibliog S. Holmes/76n1205

DRACULA FILMS
Glut/Dracula book/76n1046

DRAFT, MILITARY
See Military service

DRAMA
See also American drama; British drama; etc.
Boyer/Texas collection of comedias sueltas/79n1006
Chicorel theater index to plays/78n937
Connor/Ottemiller's index to plays/77n996
NYPL/Catalogue of theatre & drama collections, pt III, non-book/77n989
Salem/Drury's gd to best plays/79n1018
Samples/Drama scholars' index to plays & filmscripts/75n1187
Theatre/drama & speech index/76n1044

DRAMATIC CRITICISM
Eddleman/American drama criticism, suppl II/77n987
Palmer/European drama xriticism/Suppl/75n1324/2nd ed/78n941

DRAMATISTS
Meltzer/Significant Amer authors, poets, & playwrights/77n126
Vinson/Contemporary dramatists/75n1189; 78n946

DRAWINGS
Gibbons/Catalogue of Italian drawings in . . . Princeton Univ/78n808
LC/American Revolution in drawings . . . /77n373

DREAMS
Robinson/Dreamer's dict/75n1583
DREISER, THEODORE
Gerber/Plots & characters in . . . Dreiser/78 n1137
Pizer/Theodore Dreiser: bibliog/76n1233
DROSOPHILA
Herskowitz/Bibliography of genetics/75n1460
DRUG ABUSE
Advena/Drug abuse bibliog/75n1652; 76 n1547
Andrews/Bibliography of drug abuse/78 n1435
Annotated bibliog of papers from Addiction Research Center/79n1496
Bibliography on women/76n788
Bludworth/300 most abused drugs/75n1653
Burkhalter/Nursing care of . . . drug abuser/ 76n1528
Christenson/Women & drug use/76n791
Drug abuse films/75n1654
Iiyama/Drug use among minorities/77n1504
Kline/Psychotropic drugs/75n1656
Patterson/Study gd for emergency med . . . technicians/75n1633
US Natl Inst on Drug Abuse/Primary prevention: gd to lit/78n1446
Wales/Drug abuse law review/75n1658
Winek/Everything . . . abt drug abuse/75n1659
DRUG MANUFACTURERS
Pharmaceutical mfgrs of US/78n1442
DRUGS
AMA drug evaluations/79n1495
American drug index/Billups/78n1434
APha drug names: index/77n1500
Bogomolny/Handbook on 1970 Fed Drug Act/76n1549
Current drug hndbk/Falconer/78n1436
Fate of drugs in the organism/Hirtz/78n1437
Fazey/Aetiology of psychoactive substance use/79n1454
Fisher/Dictionary of drugs/77n1501
Fraunfelder/Drug-induced ocular side effects/ 77n1502
Glasby/Encyclopedia of antibiotics/78n1438
Graedon/People's pharmacy/78n1439
Griffith/Drug info for patients/79n1497
Handbook of non-prescrip drugs/78n1440
Honigfeld/Psychiatric drugs/79n1498
Hopkins/Principal drugs/79n1499
Jones/Good Housekeeping gd to medicines & drugs/79n1488
Kastrup/Facts and comparisons/79n1500
Loebl/Nurse's drug hndbk/79n1501
Long/Essential gd to prescrip drugs/78n1441
Massett/Everyman's gd to drugs/76n1550
Modell/Drugs in current use/76n1551
National drug code directory/79n1505

DRUGS (cont'd)
National formulary/76n1552
Parish/Doctors & patients hndbk/79n1492
Rubinstein/Doctor's gd to nonprescrip drugs/ 79n1503
Safford/Psychedelics ency/78n1445
Sewell/Guide to drug info/78n1443
Shirkey/Pediatric drug hndbk/79n1504
Smith/Medication gd/78n1444
Stern/Prescription drugs . . . side effects/77 n1506
DRYDEN, JOHN
Latt/John Dryden: bibliog/77n1232
Zamonski/Annotated bibliog/76n1274
DuBOIS, W. E. B.
Aptheker/Annotated bibliog/75n356
Partington/W. E. B. DuBois: bibliog/78n387
DUCKS
Merne/Ducks, geese & swans/76n1425
DUMBARTON OAKS
Harvard Univ dict catalogue of Byzantine collection of Dumbarton Oaks Library/ 76n294
DUNBAR, PAUL LAURENCE
Metcalf/P. L. Dunbar: bibliog/76n1234
DUNTON, JOHN
Parks/J. Dunton & Engl bk trade/77n55
DURAND, ASHER
Lawall/A. B. Durand/79n907
DURKHEIMIAN SCHOOL
Nandan/Durkheimian school: bibliog/78n645
DUTCH IN U.S.
Clough/Dutch uncles & New England cousins/ 78n398
New York manuscripts: Dutch/Van Laer/75 n428
DWIGGINS, WILLIAM A.
Agner/Books of WAD: bibliog/78n52
DYES
Axford/Weaving, spinning, & dyeing/76n947
Grae/Nature's colors/75n1042
Krochmal/Complete illust'd bk of dyes/75 n1043

EAKINS, THOMAS
Rosenzweig/T. Eakins collection of Hirshhorn Museum . . . /78n787
EARLY CHILDHOOD EDUCATION
See also Head Start
Harbin/Curriculum matls: bibliog/78n595
Johnson/Start early for an early start/77 n225
Monahan/Free . . . matls for preschool . . . / 78n597

EARTH SCIENCES
Annual review of earth & planetary sciences/ Donath/76n1468
Planet we live on: ency/77n1424
Stiegler/Dictionary of earth sciences/78n1352
Van Balen/Geography & earth sciences pubs/ 79n579; 79n580

EAST AFRICA
Howell/East African community/78n290
Killick/Economics of East Africa/77n770

EAST ASIA
Recommended East Asian core collection/ Scott/76n259
Yang/East Asian resources/79n367
Giles/Glossary of ... Far East/75n317

EASTERN EUROPE
American bibliog of Slavic ... studies/75 n303; 76n271; 76n272; 78n307
Birkos/East European & Soviet economic affairs: bibliog/76n821
Blejwas/East central European studies/75 n335
East central & SE Europe/Horecky/77n192
Horak/Russia, USSR, Eastern Europe/79n378
Kanet/Soviet & East European foreign policy/ 75n534
Lewytzkyj/Who's who in socialist countries/ 79n143
Zalewski/Guide to ref matls: Russia & East Europe/75n310

EATING AND DRINKING IN ART
Pollack/Dining & drinking/79n902

ECHINODERMS
Grzimek's animal life ency, v3/75n1523

ECHOCARDIOGRAPHY
Gutgesell/Atlas of pediatric echocardiography/ 79n1446

ECOLOGY
Annual review of ecology/Johnston/76n1357
Burke/Guide to ecology info/77n1403
Chicorel index to environment/76n1451
Grzimek's ency of ecology/78n1344
Lewis/Ecology field glossary/78n1345
Schultz/Bibliography of quantitative ecology/ 77n1409

ECONOMIC EDUCATION
Dawson/Government & economy/75n710
Hughes/Economic educ/78n699
Leamer/Suggestions for a basic economics library/75n200
Lewis/Educational games ... /75n703
Owen/Guide to grad study in economics ... / 79n661

ECONOMIC GEOGRAPHY
Chisholm's hndbk of commercial geog/ Blake/76n832
Earney/Researchers' gd to iron ore/75n569
Muller/Locational analysis & economic geog/ 79n578

ECONOMIC LIBRARIES
Lackner/Directory of economic libraries in Canada/79n239

ECONOMIC PLANNING
European directory of economic ... planning/ 76n833

ECONOMICS
Ammer/Dictionary of business & economics/ 78n706
Bibliographic gd ... /77n3
Catalogue of ... Dept of Trade & Industry/ 77n766
Cohen/Special bibliog in monetary economics/ 79n871
Computex bk guides: business & economics/ 76n824
Goldsmith'-Kress lib of economic lit, v1/77 n768/v2/76n823/79n801
Hutchinson/History of economic analysis/ 77n769
International bibliog of economics/75n882; 78n700
Mai/Men & ideas in economics/79n876
Moffat/Economics dict/77n776
Palgrave/Dictionary of political economy/77 n778
Palmer/Economic arithmetic ... /79n807
Skrapek/Mathematical dict ... /78n707
Strharsky/Bibliographical notes ... Third World/76n828
Tega/Management & economics journals/ 78n704
Zahn/Euro dict of economics & business: German-Engl-French/75n887
Zaremba/Mathematical economics ... /79 n808
AFRICA
Economic cooperation ... /75n289
Implementation ... of developmt activities/ 75n292
Income ... generation/75n293
EUROPE AND EASTERN EUROPE
Sources of European economic info/76n827; 79n798
Horchler/Hungarian economic reforms/79 n802
Birkos/East European ... economic affairs/ 76n821
Kazmer/Russian economic hist/79n803
O'Relley/Soviet-type economic systems/79 n806

ECONOMICS (cont'd)
  NORTH AMERICA
Brown/Canadian business & economics/77n765
Dick/Economic hist of Canada/79n800
Orsagh/Economic hist of US prior to 1860/76n826
Oxford regional econ atlas: US & Canada/77n764
  THIRD WORLD
Annotated bibliog . . . India/79n797
Chen/Economic conditions . . . Asia/79n799
DEVINDEX Canada/79n822
Latin America: economic hist/79n805

ECONOMICS AND FOREIGN POLICY
Amstutz/Economics & foreign policy/79n796

ECONOMISTS
American men & women of sci: economics/75n900
Mai/Men & ideas in economics/76n840; 79n876

EDITING
NY Times manual of style/Jordan/77n116
Olsen/Preparing the manuscript/77n117

EDUCATIONAL ASSOCIATIONS
Educational media organizations/76n619
Lopez/Directory of educ assns/79n642
Piele/Directory of organizations in educ'l mgmt/78n556

EDUCATION
  See also Alternative education; Art education; Bilingual education; Colleges and universities; Community colleges; Community education; Correspondence schools; Early childhood education; Elementary education; Exceptional children; Folk schools; Gifted students; Higher education; International education; Multicultural education; Outdoor education; Private schools; Progressive education; Schools; Secondary education
Catalog of fed assistance programs/78n554
Chisholm/Education bk list/76n577
Educational media yrbk/76n599; 79n669
Educational programs that work/77n599
Federal funding gd/Marshall/78n558
15th to 18th cent rare bks . . . /78n540
Grant/Digest of educ'l stats/76n600
Hamilton/Directory of educ'l stats/76n579
Handbook on contemp educ/Goodman/77n636
Harman/Politics of educ/76n580
Herbst/History of Amer educ/75n646
McCarthy/International list articles on hist of educ/78n584
National comparison local school costs/76n601

EDUCATION (cont'd)
National school market index/76n602
Ralston/Education: gd/78n546
Review of educ/Perkinson/76n587
Rosentiel/Education & anthropology/79n782
Spear/Urban educ/79n635
Standard educ almanac/Greene/75n658
Stoops/Handbook of educ'l admin/77n639
US Office Educ/Catalog of fed programs. . . community educ/78n371
US Dept HEW/Directory of . . . data tapes/77n597
US Office Educ/Facilities inventory/75n719
Woodbury/Guide to educ'l info/77n584
Zeidner/Private elementary & secondary educ/78n552
  DICTIONARIES
Aitchison/Unesco thesaurus/79n344
Educational technology/78n578
Key words in educ/Collins/76n594
Page/International dict of educ/79n639
Unesco: IBE educ thesaurus/77n587
US Dept HEW/Combined glossary/76n596
  DIRECTORIES
Directory of educ div of HEW/76n618
Directory of European Council of Internat'l Schools/78n573
Educational marketer yellow pages/77n659
Klein/Guide to Amer educ'l directories/76n582
Lewchuk/National register of internships . . . /75n679
Mitchell/Stopout!/79n643
Norback/Educational market place/78n555
Patterson's Amer educ/Elliott/76n663
Porter/Education directory: state . . . officials/79n646
Public educ directory/79n647
National school directory/75n684
Technician educ yrbk/76n605
  FOREIGN STUDY
Garraty/New gd to study abroad/79n641
Higher educ in United Kingdom/78n575
How to live in Britain/78n576
Maher/Schools abroad . . . /76n614
Study abroad: . . . courses/76n615
Summer study abroad/Cohen/77n590
US college sponsored programs abroad/Cohen/77n591
US Dept HEW/American students & teachers abroad/McIntyre/76n616
  MINORITIES
Cordasco/Immigrant children in Amer schools/78n539
Gollnick/Multicultural educ: bibliog/78n541
Multicultural educ/Giese/78n598
  PERIODICALS
Arnold/Education-psychology journals/76n584

EDUCATION (cont'd)
  PERIODICALS (cont'd)
  Camp/Guide to periodicals . . . /76n585
  Education index/Hewitt/76n609
  Finding list of journals indexed in CIJIE/78
    n583
  Hamilton/Education journals: . . . Harvard
    Grad School of Educ/76n586
  Index to Asian educ'l periodicals/76n589
  Krepel/Education . . . serials/78n542
EDUCATION, INTERNATIONAL
  See International education
EDUCATIONAL ACCOUNTABILITY
  Bibliography on accountability/75n641
  Competency based educ sourcebk/78n577
  Dressel/Handbook of academic eval/77n633
  Evaluation studies/77n635
  TenBrink/Evaluation/75n717
EDUCATIONAL EQUALIZATION
  Quay/In pursuit of equality . . . /79n633
  Resources in women's educ'l equality/79n759
  Sourcebook of equal educ'l opportunity/78
    n580
  Yearbook of equal educ'l opportunity/76
    n607
EDUCATIONAL FILMS
  See also specific subjects, e.g., Korea;
    science; etc.
  Educators gd to free films/Horkheimer/76
    n669
  Kislia/Let's see it again/76n680
  Parlato/Superfilms: award-winning educ'l
    films/77n1013
EDUCATIONAL LAW
  Gatti/Encyclopedic dict of school law/76
    n592
EDUCATIONAL RESEARCH
  Berry/Bibliographic gd . . . /76n576
  Comprehensive dissertation index/75n688
  Kirschner/Doctoral research in educ'l media/
    76n581
  Reynolds/Guide to theses & dissertations:
    bibliog/76n583
  US Office Educ/Bibliography of research
    studies/75n650
  Wolcott/Ethnographic approaches to research
    in educ: bibliog/77n747
EDUCATIONAL TECHNOLOGY
  Educational technology: . . . glossary/78n578
  International yearbk/77n637
  Taggart/Guide to sources . . . /76n686
EDUCATIONAL TELEVISION
  Carlson/Educational TV . . . /75n1192
  NAEB public telecommunications directory/
    79n1163

EDUCATIONAL TESTS
  Buros/English tests/76n562
  Buros/Foreign lang tests/76n563
  Buros/Mathematics tests/76n565
  Buros/Reading tests/76n567
  Buros/Social studies tests/76n569
  Buros/Science tests/76n568
  Buros/Vocational tests/76n570
  Encyclopedia of educ'l eval/Anderson/76
    n590
  Reviews of . . . tests in Engl/Grommon/77
    n653
  US Natl Center for Health Stats/Rationale
    . . . of vocabulary test/75n718
EDUCATIONAL TOURS
  Eisenberg/Learning vacations/79n655; 79
    n656
EDUCATORS
  Academic who's who, . . . British Isles/77
    n641
  Boydston/Checklist of writings abt J. Dewey/
    75n642
  Directory of Amer scholars/75n690
  Leaders in educ/75n692
  Ohles/Biographical dict of Amer educators/
    79n695
  Significant Amer historians & educators/
    Mandel/77n131
  Who's who biog school district officials/78
    n602
EGYPT
  University of Michigan/Educ'l media resources
    on Egypt/79n351
EISENHOWER, DWIGHT D.
  Cumulated indexes to public papers/79n416
  Schoenebaum/Political profiles/79n527
ELASTOMERS
  Harper/Handbook of plastics . . . /77n1614
ELDERLY
  Biegel/Best yrs catalogue/79n839
  Norback/Older American's hndbk/79n738
  Sourcebook on aging/79n740
  Tripp/Senior citizens/79n843
ELECTIONEERING
  Kaid/Political campaign communication/75
    n462
  Neuborne/Rights of candidates & voters/77
    n504
ELECTIONS
  America votes 12/Scammon/78n449
  Bain/Convention decisions & voting records/
    75n487
  Bloomfield/Commonwealth elections/78
    n476

ELECTIONS (cont'd)
Congressional Quarterly's gd/76n475/Suppl/ 78n452
Mackie/International almanac of electoral hist/75n473
Senate campaign info/79n528

ELECTORAL BEHAVIOR
Rose/Electoral behavior/75n474
Rouyer/Economic, soc & voting characteristics of Idaho precincts/75n504

ELECTRIC INSULATORS
Grzegorczyk/Handbook of plastics in electronics/75n1784

ELECTRIC POWER
Metz/Information sources in power engineering/77n1400
Smith/Efficient electricity use/77n1600; 79n1389

ELECTRIC POWER PLANTS
Inventory of power plants in the US/79n1408

ELECTRIC TRANSFORMERS
Stigant/J&P transformer bk/75n1790

ELECTRICAL ENGINEERING
Fink/Standard hndbk/79n1546
Index to IEEE pubs/75n1718
Jay/IEEE std dict . . . terms/79n1569
Say/Electrical engineer's ref bk/76n1632
US Natl Bureau of Stds/Index of internat'l stds/75n1719

ELECTRICAL WIRING
Garland/National electrical code/78n1532
Kurtz/Lineman's & cableman's hndbk/77n1594
Summers/NFPA hndbk/76n1634

ELECTRICITY AND MAGNETISM
Gartrell/Electricity . . . & animal magnetism/77n1591
Mottelay/Bibliographical hist . . ./76n1631

ELECTROCARDIOGRAPHY
Lyon/Basic hndbk/78n1413

ELECTROCHEMISTRY
Encyclopedia of electrochemistry of the elements:
  Bard/v1/75n1450
  Bard/v3/76n1343
  Bard/v11/79n1318
  Plambeck/v10/78n1249
Davies/Dictionary/78n1242

ELECTRONIC APPLIANCES
King/Underground buying gd for . . . hobbyists/78n749

ELECTRONIC CALCULATING MACHINES
Feldzamen/Calculator hndbk/75n1769

ELECTRONIC CIRCUITS
Douglas/Sourcebook of organ circuits/77n1590
Furlow/Circuit design/75n1781
Goodman/Indexed gd/75n1782
Guidebook/75n1785
Handbook of components for electronics/Harper/78n1533
Harper/Handbook of thick film hybrid microelectronics/75n1786
Jensen/Handbook of circuit analysis languages & techniques/77n1592
Lenk/Hndbk of designs/77n1595
Motorola/Microprocessor applications manual/77n1598
Sessions/Master hndbk . . . practical electronic circuits/77n1599
Stout/Handbook of operational amplifier circuit design/77n1601
van Cleemput/Computer aided design of digital systems/78n1528
Ward/Electronic music circuit gdbk/76n1635

ELECTRONIC COMPONENTS
Handbook/78n1533

ELECTRONIC DATA PROCESSING
See Data processing

ELECTRONIC INDUSTRY
Telephone directory/77n825
Who's who in electronics/77n832
Yearbook of consumer electronics/Belt/75n1791

ELECTRONIC MEASUREMENTS
Herrick/Oscilloscope handbk/75n1787
Moon/Simplified gd to . . . test procedures/77n1596
Robinson/Handbook of electronic instrumentation/75n1788

ELECTRONIC OFFICE MACHINES
Sippl/Calculator user's gd/77n1582

ELECTRONIC ORGANS
Douglas/Sourcebook of electronic organ circuits/77n1590

ELECTRONIC TECHNICIANS
Carr/C.E.T. license hndbk/77n1589
Kaufman/Handbook/77n1593

ELECTRONICS
Dummer/Electronic inventions/78n1530
Electronics designers' hndbk/Giacoletto/78n1531
Fink/Electronics engineers' hndbk/76n1629
Graf/Electronic databk/76n1630
Graf/Modern dict of electronics/79n1568
Grolle/Electronic technician's hndbk/75n1783
Jay/IEEE std dict/79n1569
Markus/Electronics dict/79n1590
Ludwig/Illus'd hndbk elect tables/78n1534

ELEMENTARY EDUCATION
Elementary . . . free curriculum matls/Suttles/ 76n676
McCormick/Primary educ for disadvantaged/ 77n576
Harris/Developmental tasks resource gd/77n651
Zeidner/Private elementary . . . educ: bibliog/ 78n552

ELIOT, GEORGE
Baker/G. Eliot-G. H. Lewes Library, London/ 78n1160
Fulmer/George Eliot/79n1239
Hartnoll/Who's who in G. Eliot/78n1173

ELLISON, RALPH WALDO
Covo/Blinking eye/75n1354

ELVES
Arrowsmith/Field gd to little people/78 n1008

EMBLEMS
Clapp/Professional ethics & insignia/75n79

EMERGENCY AID
Manning/Disaster technology/77n705

EMERGENCY MEDICAL SERVICES
See First aid; Medical emergencies

EMIGRATION AND IMMIGRATION
Buenker/Immigration & ethnicity/78n375
Coldham/English convicts in colonial Amer/ 78n399
Cordasco/Immigrant children . . ./78n539
Pap/Portuguese in the US/78n391
Shaw/Migration theory & fact/77n757

EMPERORS
Rowland-Entwistle/Famous kings . . ./78 n333

EMPLOYEE TRAINING
International resource directory: . . . training & developmt profession/79n861

EMPLOYEES
Franklin/Human resources developmt/79 n858

EMPLOYEES, PUBLIC
See Public employees

EMPLOYEES' REPRESENTATION
Abell/Collective bargaining in higher educ/ 78n161
Marchant/Participative mgmt in libraries/78 n164

EMPLOYMENT
See also Job vacancies; Occupations; Student employment
Directory of overseas summer jobs/77n835
Employment & earnings/77n836
MacCafferty/Employment relations in UK/77 n837

EMPLOYMENT (cont'd)
Manpower research . . . projects/77n838
Murphy/Where's what: fed investigators/77 n839
Occupational outlook for college grads/78 n771; 79n862
Pogrebin/Getting yours: . . . working woman/ 76n796
Salmon/Job hunter's gd . . . 8 Amer cities/79 n864
Sprague/Finding a job: for middle aged & retired/79n865
Summer employmt directory/77n842; 79 n867
Yeomans/Jobs/78n778

EMPLOYMENT AGENCIES
Directory of exec recruiters/79n856
International directory of exec recruiters/ 76n834; 79n859

ENAMELS
Bibliography: enamel/75n1048

ENCYCLOPEDIAS, GENERAL
Cadillac modern ency/75n73
Collier's ency/79n71
Encyclopaedia Britannica-Yrbk of sci/78 n1220
Encyclopedia Americana/77n72
Encyclopedia internat'l/77n73
Great world ency/77n74
Great Soviet ency/75n76
Horsley/New Hutchinson 20th cent ency/79 n72
Kister/Encyclopedia buying gd/77n71; 79 n74
Merit students ency/Halsey/79n75
New Caxton ency/79n76
New Columbia ency/Harris/76n60
New ency Britannica/75n77; 79n77
New std ency/Downey/76n61
Pears cyclopaedia/76n62; 79n78
Pears' shilling cyclopaedia/79n79
Petite ency Larousse/78n65
Random House ency/78n68
University desk ency/78n69

ENCYCLOPEDIAS, JUVENILE
See Children's encyclopedias

ENDOCRINOLOGY
Year in endocrinology/Ingbar/78n1420

ENERGY
Annual review/77n1415
Bemis/Energy gd/78n1337
Brown/Energy info resources/76n1464
Buyer's gd: energy/75n1546
Crabbe/World energy bk/79n1392
Directory of computer software applications/Grooms/79n1562
Encyclopedia of energy/Lapedes/77n1411
Energy: resources in US/75n1547; 79n1382

ENERGY (cont'd)
Energy atlas: who's who/78n1347
Energy directory/75n1548
Energy: dissertation index/78n1351
Energy fact bk/77n1417
Energy index/75n1557; 79n1383
Energy info abstracts/77n1401
Energy info locator/77n1413
Hsieh/Energy: bibliog/78n1340
Hsieh/Energy ref sources/77n1405
McRae/Energy sourcebk/79n1386
Metz/Information sources in power engineering: gd/77n1400
Morrison/Energy: bibliog/77n1407; 79n1387
US House/Energy facts/75n1544

ENERGY CONSERVATION
Lee/Bibliography of energy conservation in architecture/78n803
Lee/Encyclopedia of energy-efficient bldg design/78n1518
Smith/Efficient electricity use/77n1600; 79n1389
Sobel/Energy crisis/75n1543

ENERGY CONSUMPTION
Energy demand studies/Basile/79n1398
Weiner/Energy prod & consump in paper industry/79n1327

ENERGY POLICY
Energy policy-making/Rycroft/79n1384

ENERGY SOURCES
Clegg/New low-cost sources for the home/76n1458
Foster/Homeowner's gd to solar heating/77n1419
Harrah/Alternate sources of energy/76n1454
Pesko/Solar directory/77n1414
Standard terms of energy economy/79n1390
Synerjy/79n1391
Wade/Homegrown energy/76n1466

ENERGY SPECIALISTS
Energy-related doctoral scientists/79n1385
Powell/Ontario energy catalogue/79n1388

ENERGY TECHNOLOGY
Considine/Energy tech hndbk/78n1349

ENGINEERING
Annual bk of ASTM stds/76n1604
Auger/Engineering eponyms/76n1651
Bolz/Handbooks of tables/75n1713
Directory of engineering educ/77n588
Encyclopedia of how it works/Clarke/78n1501
Eshback/Handbook of engineering/77n1566
Gieck/Engineering formulas/78n1505
Kverneland/World metric stds/79n1547
Kyed/Scient'ic, eng'g & med soc pubs/77n1285
Kyed/Scient'ic, tech & eng'g soc pubs/77n1430

ENGINEERING (cont'd)
Malinowsky/Science & eng'g lit/77n1286
Metz/Information sources in power eng'g/77n1400
Mildren/Use of eng'g literature/77n1568
Mount/Guide to basic info/78n1500
Lodewijk/Way things work/75n1712
Perry/Engineering manual/77n1569
Sneddon/Encyclopaedic dict of mathematics/78n1504
US Natl Park Serv/Historic Amer eng'g/781499

ENGINEERING INSTRUMENTS
See Automatic control

ENGINEERING LIBRARIES
Mount/University sci & eng'g libraries/77n239

ENGINEERS
Bell/Biographical index of British engineers/76n1606
Who's who of British engineers/75n1720

ENGLAND
See Great Britain

ENGLISH AS A FOREIGN LANGUAGE
Bibliography of lang arts matls for native North Americans/78n587
Davis/English lang & orientation programs/78n561
Forinash/Reader developmt bib/78n592
Goldstein/Teaching Engl as 2nd lang/76n678

ENGLISH AUTHORS
See British authors

ENGLISH DRAMA
See American drama; British drama

ENGLISH FICTION
See also American fiction; British fiction
Beasley/English fict 1660-1800/79n1227
Chronological bibliog of Engl lang fict in LC/75n1325
Dyson/English novel/75n1376
Ford/Victorian fiction/79n1229
Messerli/Index to periodical fict in English/78n1103
Reader's advisor, v1: Amer & British fiction/75n1314

ENGLISH LANGUAGE
Allen/Linguistics & Engl linguistics/78n1024
Brasch/Comprehensive annot'd bibliog of Amer black English/75n1245
Frank/Plan for dict of Old Engl/75n1248
Moorman/Editing Middle Engl manuscript/76n1113

ENGLISH LANGUAGE (cont'd)
DICTIONARIES
Barlough/Archaicon/75n1256
Barnhart/World bk dict/77n1075
Bernstein's reverse dict/76n88
Byrne's dict of unusual words/75n1257
Concise heritage dict/78n1034
Funk & Wagnalls . . .
    Comprehensive std internat'l dict/75
      n1251
    Standard college dict/78n1035
    Standard desk dict/78n1036
Hornby/Oxford student's dict/79n1098
Hunsberger/Quintessential dict/79n1125
Illustrated heritage dict/78n1027
Kidney/Nelson's new compact Webster's dict/79n1099
Landau/Doubleday dict/76n1120
Kister/Dictionary buying gd/78n1028
Merriam-Webster dict/77n1077
Merriam-Webster dict for lg print users/78n1037
Oxford advanced learner's dict/75n1260
Oxford illust'd dict/Coulson/76n1117
Pocket dict/79n1103
Random House dict/79n1104
Reid/Writer's cue/75n1261
Scribner-Bantam Engl dict/Williams/78n78
6,000 words: suppl to Webster's 3rd new internat'l dict/77n1068
Webster's new 20th cent dict/79n1096
Webster's new world dictionary:
    College ed/76n1125
    Compact school/79n1105
    Large print ed/79n1106
    Pocket-sized/79n1126
Word book/Ellis/78n1039
Wyld/Universal dict/79n1097
Zettler/-Ologies & -isms/79n1128
DICTIONARIES, JUVENILE
American heritage school dict/79n1107
Bennett/New color-picture dict/79n1108
Grosset starter picture dict/77n1076
HBJ school dict/79n1109
Holmes/Super dict/79n1110
Jenkins/My first picture dict/78n1029
Macmillan dict for children/Halsey/76n1120
Magic world of words/Halsey/79n1111
Ogle/Golden picture dict/78n1030
Scott, Foresman beginning dict/77n1078
Thorndike Barnhart intermediate dict/76n1122
Webster's concise family dict/77n1079
Webster's intermediate dict/79n1112
Webster's new elementary dict/Merriam/76n1123
Webster's new students dict/Merriam/76n1124
Weston/Oxford children's dict/77n1080
Wright/Rainbow dict/79n1113

ENGLISH LANGUAGE (cont'd)
DICTIONARIES, JUVENILE (cont'd)
Xerox intermediate dict/75n1255
ETYMOLOGY
Coleridge/Dictionary of the first words in the Engl lang/77n1072
Morris dict of word . . . origins/78n1032
Shorter Oxford Engl dict on hist'l principles/75n1252
Supplement to Oxford Engl dict/77n1073
Sykes/Concise Oxford dict/77n1074
FOREIGN WORDS AND PHRASES
Mawson/Dictionary of foreign terms/76n1118
Pei/Dictionary of foreign terms/76n1119
GLOSSARIES, VOCABULARIES, ETC.
Dale/Living word vocabulary/77n1066
Thorndike/Teacher's word bk/77n586
GRAMMAR AND USAGE
Bell & Cohn's hndbk of grammar/77n1086
Burns/Annotated bibliog on texts on writing skills/77n1067; 78n588
Crews/Random House hndbk/79n128
Day/Creative writing/79n630
Ehrlich/Concise index to Engl/75n1287
Follett/Modern Amer usage/75n1288
Hudson/Dictionary of diseased Engl/79n1123
Johnson/How to achieve competence in Engl/77n1087
Mager/Encyclopedic dict of Engl usage/75n1289
Morris/Harper dict/76n1130
Nickles/Dictionary of do's & don'ts/75n1290
Shaw/Dictionary of problem words/76n1131
Smith/Dictionary of Engl word-roots/77n1085
Sparkes/Dict of collectivity nouns/76n1136
Stratton/Handbook of English/77n1088
Vizetelly/Desk-bk of errors/76n1132
Witherspoon/Common errors/75n1291
IDIOMS AND COLLOQUIALISMS
Adams/Language of railroader/79n1114
Allen/Linguistic atlas of Midwest/76n1115; 77n1058
Anderson/Book of slang/76n1127
Beck/Rail talk/79n1115
Beeton/Dictionary of Engl usage in Africa/77n1083
Branford/Dictionary of So African Engl/79n1116
Cowie/Oxford dict of idiomatic Engl/77n1069
Flexner/I hear America talking/78n1031
Freeman/Concise dict of Engl idioms/77n1070
Leigh/Glossary of words used in dialect of Cheshire/75n1258

ENGLISH LANGUAGE (cont'd)
  IDIOMS AND COLLOQUIALISMS (cont'd)
Partridge/Dictionary of catch phrases/78n1046
Partridge/Macmillan dict of hist'l slang/76n1128
Pederson/Manual for dialect research/75n1250
Phythian/Concise dict of Engl slang/77n1071
Savaiano/2001 Spanish & Engl idioms/77n1101
Wentworth/Dictionary of Amer slang, suppl/76n1129
Wilkes/Dictionary of Australian colloquailisms/79n1117
  PRONUNCIATION, SYLLABICATION, ETC.
Deighton/Handbook of Amer Engl spelling/79n1124
Kahn/Word bk/76n1133
Lass/Dictionary of pronunciation/77n1084
Norback/Misspeller's dict/75n1259
Sharp/Follett vest-pocket/79n1127
Leslie/20,000 words/78n1048
  RHYME, ETC.
Kloe/Dictionary of onomatopeic sounds/78n1045
Modglin/Rhymer ... for poets/79n1126
Whitfield/Songwriters' rhyming dict/76n1137
  STUDY AND TEACHING
Brownell/Directory of resources for study of Engl in Japan/77n1062
Buros/English tests/76n562
Daniels/International visual dict/75n652
English lang programs in US/75n668
Goldstein/Teaching Engl as a 2nd lang/76n678
NCTE gd to teaching matls/75n704; 76n682
Parnwell/Oxford picture dict: French/79n1101/Spanish/79n1100
  SYNONYMS
Boyer/Nelson's new compact Roget's thesaurus/79n1118
Doubleday Roget's thesaurus/Landau/78n1040
Family word finder/77n1081
Laird/Webster's new world thesaurus/76n1134
Reid/Verb synonyms/75n1253
Right word/79n1119
Roget's internat'l thesaurus/78n1041
Schiller/In other words/79n1120
Schiller/Junior thesaurus/79n1121
Webster's collegiate thesaurus/77n1082
Webster's new dict of synonyms/75n1254

ENGLISH LITERATURE
  See also names of authors; American literature; British literature; Canadian literature; Commonwealth literature, etc.
Altick/Selective bibliog for study of Engl & Amer lit/76n1180
Bindoff/Research in progress in Engl & hist in Britain, Ireland, Canada/77n406
Crane/Engl lit 1660-1800, v2/75n1374
DeLaura/Victorian prose/75n1372
Doyle/Guide to basic info sources/77n1220
Ferres/Modern Commonwealth lit/79n1184
Ford/Pelican gd, v7: Modern Age/75n1373
Friedman/English lit 1660-1800/76n1259
Gerstenberger/4th directory of periodicals/76n1193
Gillie/Longman companion/76n1261
Gunn/Mexico in Amer & Brit letters/75n1311
McNamee/Dissertations in Engl & Amer lit, suppl 2/75n1313
NCTE gd to teaching matls/76n682
New Cambridge bibliog of Engl lit:
  Pickles/v5, index/78n1156
  Watson/v1, 600-1600/75n1375; 76n1260
Patterson/Literary research gd/77n1126
Reader's advisor, v1/75n1314
Schweik/Reference sources in Engl & Amer lit/78n1093
Vitale/Basic tools of research: gd/78n1094
Webster's new world companion to Engl & Amer lit/77n1131
Year's work in Engl studies, v55/Redmond/79n1187

ENGLISH POETRY
Cline/Index to criticisms of British & Amer poetry/75n1332

ENOCH PRATT FREE LIBRARY
Martin/Adults & Pratt Library/75n188

ENTERTAINERS
Significant Amer entertainers/Tegland/77n129

ENTOMOLOGY
Annual review, v20/Smith/76n1409
Leftwich/Dictionary/77n1390

ENVIRONMENTAL EDUCATION
Boesch/Careers in the outdoors/76n598
Harrah/Conservation-ecology: resources/76n1465
Matthews/Resource matls for environmental mgmt & educ/77n1399

ENVIRONMENTAL ENGINEERING
Bond/CRC hndbk of environmental control, v3: water & treatmt/75n1536
Encyclopedia of environmental sci & eng'g/Pfafflin/78n1343

ENVIRONMENTAL ENGINEERING (cont'd)
Environmental engineers' hndbk:
  v2, air pollution/76n1459
  v3, land pollution/76n1460
Harrah/Alternate sources of energy/76n1454
Lee/Bibliography of energy conservation in architecture/78n803
Lee/Encyclopedia of energy-efficient bldg design/78n1518
Liptak/Environmental engineers' hndbk, v1: water/75n1540

ENVIRONMENTAL LAW
Barros/International law of pollution/75n1535
Environmental regulation hndbk/75n1538
Grieves/International law & the environment: bibliog/76n1453
Schwartz/Environmental law: gd/78n1341

ENVIRONMENTAL SCIENCES
See also Conservation; Human ecology; Pollution
Allaby/Dictionary of environment/79n1393
Bennett/Environmental lit/75n1556
Burchell/Environmental impact hndbk/77n1416
Burk/Environmental concerns/78n1338
Buyer's gd to environmental media/75n1545
California environmental directory/78n1346
Catalog of conservation library: Denver PL/76n1457
Chicorel index to environment/76n1451
Collias/Atlas of phy & chem properties of Puget Sound/75n1576
Conservation directory/77n1412
Cross/Handbook on environmental monitoring/75n1537
EIS: key to impact statements/79n1395
Environment abstracts/75n1558; 79n1396
Environment USA/75n1549
Environment index/75n1559; 79n1397
Environmental quality abstracts/77n1402
Glossary of the environment, French & German equivalents/78n1342; 79n1394
Gunn/Bibliography of Naval Arctic Research Lab/75n1524
Holum/Topics in environmental problems/79n1398
International directory of behavior research/Beckman/75n1550
Jones/Index of human ecology/75n1560
Lee/Computer programs/75n1551
McGraw-Hill ency/75n1533
Meshenberg/Environmental planning/77n1406
Minneapolis PL Catalog/Environmental Conservation Library/75n1531
NY Times cum index: environment/79n1399
Owings/Environmental values/77n1408

ENVIRONMENTAL SCIENCES (cont'd)
Plunguian/Bibliography on Delaware Bay/75n1525
Sumek/Environmental mgmt & politics/75n1526
Thomas/Biological indicators of environmental quality/75n1528
US Air Force/Environmental-socioeconomic data sources/Kavaliunas/78n1350
US. Army/Glossary of terms/75n1534
US Environmental Data Serv/Bibliography of urban mod of atmosphere . . ./75n1529
US Environmental Protection Agency/Indexed bibliog of . . . reports/76n1456
US Natl Oceanic & Atmospheric Admin: Bibliography of NY bight/75n1563
Publications/75n1561
Verschueren/Handbook of environmental data on organic chems/79n1322
Wilson/World directory of environmental research centers/75n1552
Wolff/Information sources/75n1553
World directory of organizations/Trzyna/78n1348
World environmental directory/76n1467
Yska/Final report on data bases . . . /79n304
Zilly/Handbook of environmental civil eng'g/76n1619

ENVIRONMENTAL TOXICOLOGY
See Toxicology

EPISCOPAL CHURCH
Benton/Church cyclopaedia/76n1080
Harper/Episcopalian's dict/76n1083

EPONYMS
Auger/Engineering eponyms: . . . in mechanical eng'g/76n1651
Ruffner/Eponyms dictionaries index/78n111

EQUAL OPPORTUNITY IN EDUCATION
See Educational equalization

EQUAL RIGHTS AMENDMENT
ERA: bibliog'ic study/78n496

ERASMUS
Margolin/Neuf années . . . Erasmienne/78n1003

ERIC
Goodman/Thesaurus of ERIC/76n593
Tessier/Feasibility of . . . access to data/79n266

EROTIC LITERATURE
Hoffman/Analytical survey of . . . erotica/75n1321

ESEA TITLE VII
Directory of . . . bilingual educ/78n557

ESKIMO LANGUAGE
Survey of materials/Johnson/78n1026

ESKIMOS
Lass-Woodfin/Books on Amer Indians & Eskimos/79n464

ESPIONAGE
Blackstock/Intelligence, espionage, & covert operations/79n501
DeVore/Spies & all that/79n502

ESQUIRE
Baron/Author index/77n1190

ESTONIA
Parming/Bibliography of Engl sources/75 n305; 76n273

ESTONIAN AMERICANS
Pennar/Estonians in America/76n405

ETCHINGS
Kennedy/Etched work of Whistler/79n897

ETHIOPIA
Brown/Ethiopian perspectives/79n352
Hidaru/Short gd to Ethiopia: bibliog/77n314

ETHNIC PRESS
Directory of ethnic publishers/78n378
Kowalik/Polish press in Amer/79n465
McLaren/Ontario newspapers/75n1300
Weres/Directory of Ukrainian publishing/78n392
Wynar/Encyclopedic directory of newspapers/77n430

ETHNIC STUDIES
See also particular groups, e.g., Asian Americans; Blacks; Chicanos; German Americans; Jews; Ukrainian Americans, etc. Also Minorities
Allsworth/Soviet Asia: bibliogs/77n345
Barton/Brief ethnic bibliog/77n421
Bodnar/Ethnic hist in Pennsylvania/76n386
Buenker/Immigration & ethnicity/78n375
Buttlar/Building ethnic collections/78n376
Cashman/Bibliography of Amer ethnology/77n422
Coe/Folklife & the fed gov/79n1083
Cohen/Multi-ethnic media/76n387
Collnick/Multi-cultural educ/78n541
Cordasco/Immigrant children in Amer schools/78n539
Directory of ... librarians/78n136
Ethnic serials at Univ of Calif libraries/Bullock/78n379
Ethnic studies bibliog/78n377
Ethnic studies resource kit/Haley/77n418
Gagala/Economics of minorities/77n423
International Migration Review cum index/79n794
Johnson/Directory of special programs for minority group members/75n801
Johnson/Ethnic Amer minorities/77n424
Kinton/American ethnic groups/76n390

ETHNIC STUDIES (cont'd)
Kipel/Ethnic directory of NJ/79n445
Lebar/Ethnic groups of SE Asia/76n810
Levitan/Minorities in the US/76n391
Miller/Comprehensive bibliog of Amer minorities/77n425
Miller/Handbook of Amer minorities/77n419
Multicultural educ/Giese/78n598
Nation of nations/77n420
Oaks/Minority studies: bibliog/77n426
Pap/Portuguese in the US/78n391
US Bureau of Labor/Directory of data ... minorities/77n429
Van Why/Adoption bibliog/78n657
Wasserman/Ethnic info sources/77n428
Wynar/Encyclopedic directory of ethnic newspapers in the US/77n430
Wynar/Encyclopedic directory of organizations in the US/76n394
Wynar/Ethnic groups in Ohio/76n393
Wynar/Guide to ethnic museums.../79n446

ETHNOBOTANY
Moerman/American med ethnobotany/78n1280

ETHNOHISTORY
Guide to ethnohistorical sources/Cline/76n889

ETHNOLOGY
Abler/Canadian Indian bibliog/75n863
Anderson/Revised bibliog of Chumash/79n773
Baldwin/Yoruba of SW Nigeria/77n735
Cashman/Bibliography of Amer ethnology/77n422
Ethnographic bibliog of No Amer/77n738
Survey of research in sociology/77n702
Tindale/Aboriginal tribes of Australia/75n870
Troisi/Santals: bibliog/77n746
Weekes/Muslim peoples/79n772
Wolcott/Ethnographic research in educ/77n747

ETHNOMUSICOLOGY
Frisbie/Music & dance research of SW US Indians/78n890

ETHNOPSYCHOLOGY
Favazza/Anthropological ... themes in mental health: bibliog/78n1373

ETHOLOGY
See Animal behavior

ETIQUETTE
Post/New Emily Post's etiquette/76n1109

EUCLID
Thomas-Stanford/Early eds of Euclid's elements/78n63

EUROPE
Bartholomew-Scribner atlas/Browne/75n575
Cook/European political facts/76n460; 79n505
Directory of European assns, pt1/77n77/pt2/76n66
Europa yearbook/76n265
European parliament digest/75n471
Kelly/Bibliography in hist of European women/77n401
Mitchell/European hist'l stats/76n815
Reviews in European hist/Rowen/76n363

ECONOMICS AND INDUSTRY
Business atlas/76n838
Charnley/European chem industries/76n896
European financial almanac/76n886
European offshore oil/77n1418
Europe's 5000 largest companies/76n897
Franko/Petroleum industry/77n1404
Jane's major companies of Europe/Love/78n758
Sources of European economic info/76n827; 79n798

TRAVEL GUIDES
AA gd to camping . . . /Kelly/79n711
European campgrounds/76n536
Fielding's travel gd to Europe/77n567
Fielding's low-cost Europe/75n623
Fielding's selective shopping gd/76n537
Let's go: budget gd/79n617
Madden/Religious gd/76n1071
Pilkington/Waterways in Europe/75n625
Simpson/Country inns/77n568; 79n622
Myra Waldo's travel gd/75n629
Whitman's off season travel gd/77n571

EUROPEAN COMMUNITIES
Duic/Europa admin: directory/78n475
European communities yrbk/79n506
Jeffries/Guide to publications/79n119

EUROPEAN COUNCIL OF INTERNATIONAL SCHOOLS
Directory . . . /76n611

EUROPEAN ECONOMIC COMMUNITY
Duic/Europa admin: directory/78n475
Gurland/Common market: gd for Americans/76n865
Kitter/US and EEC/75n924
Paxton/Dictionary/79n809

EUROPEAN PARLIAMENT
European parliament digest/75n471

EUTHANASIA
Triche/Euthanasia controversy/77n1467

EVANS-PRITCHARD, EDWARD EVANS
Bibliography of writings . . . /76n803

EVERSON, WILLIAM
Bartlett/W. Everson: bibliog/78n1138

EVOLUTION
Grzimek's ency/78n1274

EXCAVATIONS (archaeology)
Avi-Yonah/Encyclopedia of excavations in the Holy Land/77n347
Stillwell/Princeton ency of classical sites/77n350

EXCEPTIONAL CHILDREN
Baskin/Special child in the library/77n216
Directory/79n644
Glassman/Utilizing resources in handicapped services field: directory/75n687
Yearbook of special educ/76n608; 77n640

EXECUTIVES
Bricker's internat'l directory of . . . development programs/76n644; 77n609
Directory of exec recruiters/79n856
International directory of exec recruiters/76n834; 79n859

EXERCISE
Chapman/Physiology of physical stress/76n1514

EXISTENTIALISM
Lapointe/Gabriel Marcel & his critics/78n1001
Lapointe/Maurice Merleau-Ponty & his critics/78n1002

EXOBIOLOGY
See Life on other planets
See also UFOs

EXPLORERS
Newby/Rand McNally atlas of exploration/76n298

EXPORT MARKETING
Doing business abroad: . . gd to Washington/77n782
Exporters Directory/US buying gd/79n834
Foreign trade marketplace/Schultz/78n734
Guide to natl practices in western Europe/75n890
Jonnard/Exporter's financial & marketing hndbk/76n867
Joyner/International businessman's gd to official Washington/75n894

EXPRESSIONISM (art)
Spalek/German expressionism in fine arts: bibliog/78n786

FABLES
Tyler/Concordance to fables of Jean de la Fontaine/75n1418

FACE THE NATION
Face the nation/76n1156-58

FACSIMILE TRANSMISSION
MacCafferty/Fax & teletext/78n238

FACTS ON FILE
Five-yr index/77n500

FAERIE QUEENE
Rose/Spenser's art/76n1290

FAIRIES
Arrowsmith/Field gd to the little people/78n1008
Briggs/Encyclopedia of fairies/78n1009

FALLACIES
Ward/Dictionary of common fallacies/79n102

FAMILY COUNSELORS
Register: Amer Assoc of Marriage & Family Counselors/79n753

FAMILY FARMS
Seymour/Guide to self-sufficiency/78n1447
Vivian/Manual of practical homesteading/76n849

FAMILY LIFE EDUCATION
Annotated bibliog for child & family/79n743
Dunmore/Black children & their families/77n715
Family life & child developmt/78n655
Garoogian/Child care issues for parents & society/78n656
Lopata/Family factbook/79n749
Milden/Family in past time/79n751
Selective gd to matls for mental health & family life educ/77n1442

FAMILY PLANNING
Atkins/AV resources for population educ & family planning/77n714
Directory, family planning service sites/79n1468
Lyle/International family planning progs/79n750

FANTASY
Post/Atlas of fantasy/75n1328
Waggoner/Hills of faraway/79n1206

FARM MANAGEMENT
Christian/Agricultural enterprises/79n1512
Wheeler/Tax desk bk for farming/77n855

FARM PRODUCE
Bibliography of food/79n1511
Production yearbk/FAO/76n846
Trade yearbook/78n740

FARMS
See Family farms; Farm management; Ranches

FASHION
Calasibetta/Fairchild's dict/76n978
Lambert/World of fashion/77n940

FATS IN FOOD
Kraus/Dictionary of sodium, fats, . . . /76n1577

FAULKNER, WILLIAM
Brown/Glossary of Faulkner's South/77n1202
McHaney/W. Faulkner: ref gd/77n1203
Petersen/Each in its ordered place/76n1235

FEATURE FILMS
American Film Inst catalog/77n1006
Limbacher/Feature films on 8mm & 16mm/78n959

FEDERAL AID
A-V connection/78n245
Catalog of fed educ programs/78n554
Catalog of fed youth programs/78n658
Encyclopedia of US gov benefits/79n96
Federal funding gd for . . . educ/Marshall/78n558
US Office Educ/Catalog of fed programs . . . community educ/78n571

FEDERAL DRUG ACT
Bogomolny/Handbook . . . /76n1549

FEDERAL LOAN GUARANTEES
Catalog of programs/79n874

FEE-BASED INFORMATION SERVICES
Proceedings of . . . library services workshop, Syracuse, NY/78n258
Warken/Directory/78n138

FELLINI, FEDERICO
Price/F. Fellini/79n1025

FEMINISM
Forschl/Feminist resources for schools/78n593
Myerson/Margaret Fuller/79n767
SHARE: directory/77n183; 79n167

FENWICK'S COLONY
Shourds/History & genealogy of . . . /77n476

FERNS
Lakela/Ferns of Florida/78n1284
Nakaike/Enumeratio pteridophytarum Japonicarum/76n1379

FERTILITY, HUMAN
Freedman/Sociology of human fertility/76n771

FESTIVALS
Calendar of festivals/78n1019
Wasserman/Festivals sourcebk/78n77

FICTION
Cooper/Cumulative index to MFS/77n1137
Post/Atlas of fantasy/75n1328
Smith/Cumulated fiction index/77n1176
Swan/Who's who in fiction?/77n1178
Tennyson/Index to 19th-cent fict/78n1107

FIELD CROPS
Wellman/Dictionary of tropical Amer crops/78n1453

Subjects—267

FIESTA DINNERWARE
Huxford/Collectors ency/79n949

FIGHTER PLANES
Knaack/Encyclopedia of US Air Force aircraft/79n1593

FILING SYSTEMS
Hoffman/What happens in library filing?/77n270
Hoffman/Alphanumeric filing rules for business/79n819

FILIPINO AMERICANS
Alcantara/Filipinos in Hawaii/78n388
DeWitt/Anti-Filipino movemts in Calif/77n442
Norell/Literature of Filipino-Amer/77n443

FILM ACTORS AND ACTRESSES
See also Actors and actresses
Aros/Actor gd to the talkies/78n953
Parish/Film actors gd: West Europe/78n960
Parish/Hollywood character actors/78n1037
Parish/Hollywood players: the '30s/77n1016/'40s/77n1015
Pitts/Hollywood on record/79n975
Ragan/Who's who in Hollywood 1900-76/78n965
Schuster/Motion picture performers/77n1003
Stewart/Filmarama, v1/76n1070/v2/78n966
Thomson/Biographical dict of film/77n1017
Truitt/Who was who on screen/75n1212; 78n967

FILM ADAPTATIONS
Daisne/Filmographic dict of world lit, suppl/79n1033
Emmens/Short stories on film/79n1034
Enser/Filmed bks & plays/77n1001
Greene/Multi-media approach to children's lit/79n231

FILM AWARDS
Parlato/Superfilms/77n1013
Rickard/Oscar movies from A-Z/79n1030

FILM DIRECTORS AND PRODUCERS
Birkos/Soviet cinema/77n1007
Finch/Art of Walt Disney/75n1190
Hochman/American film directors/75n1210
Niver/D. W. Griffith/75n1197
Parish/Film directors/76n1058
Parish/Film director's gd: West Europe/78n961
Price/Federico Fellini/79n1025
Rosenfeldt/Ken Russell/79n1027
Rosenfeldt/Richard Lester/79n1028
Smith/Women who make movies/76n1069
Thomson/Biographical dictionary of film/77n1017
Truitt/Who was who on screen/75n1212
Tuska/Close up/78n968
Willis/Films of Howard Hawks/76n1060

FILM DISTRIBUTORS
Emmens/Non-theatrical film distributors/76n174
Film-Makers' Cooperative catalogue/76n1056

FILM EDUCATION
American Film Institute gd to college courses/77n1004; 79n1029

FILM INDUSTRY
Costner/Motion pict market place/77n1005
Fitzgerald/Universal Pictures/78n949
Kowalski/Women & film/77n1002
Larkin/Hail, Columbia/76n1048

FILM LIBRARIES
Directory of 16mm film collections/76n206
Rehrauer/Film user's hndbk/76n182
Weber/North Amer film directory/77n186

FILM SCRIPTS
Poteet/Published radio, TV & film scripts/76n1165
Samples/Drama scholars' index to plays & filmscripts/75n1187

FILM THEATERS
Stoddard/Theatre architecture/79n1011

FILMS
See also Feature films; Western films; Educational films; Gangster films
Arijon/Grammar of the film lang/78n947
Ash/Motion pict film editor/75n1207
Batty/Retrospective index to film periodicals/76n1061
Bawden/Oxford companion to film/77n997
Bowles/Index to critical film reviews/76n1062
Callaghan/Van Nostrand Reinhold manual of film-making/75n1203
Cowie/80 yrs of cinema/78n948
Dyment/Literature of the film/77n1000
Film lit index/76n1063; 77n1014
Film Review/Speed/77n998; 79n1039
Film Review digest/Brownstone/76n1064
Gerlach/Critical index/75n1209
Halliwell/Filmgoer's bk of quotes/75n1191
Halliwell/Filmgoer's companion/76n1025; 79n1023
Halliwell's film gd/78n958
Heinzkill/Film criticism: index/76n1065
International film gd/Cowie/76n1047; 77n999
International index to film periodicals/Jones/76n1066
MacCann/New film index/76n1067
Maynard/Classroom cinema/79n685
Mehr/Motion pictures, TV, & radio: ... manuscript collections in US/79n1165
Motion pictures: catalog/78n951
Moulds/International index to film periodicals/75n1211
Pichard/Companion to the movies/75n1199

FILMS (cont'd)
Piper/Personal filmmaking/76n1049
Public library subj headings for 16mm motion pictures/75n227
Ragan/Who's who in Hollywood/78n965
Rehrauer/Cinema booklist, suppl 1/79n1026
Sampson/Blacks in white & black/78n950
Sheahan/Moving pict: bibliog/75n1193
World ency of film/Smith/76n1053
  FILMOGRAPHIES
Adams/Shoot-em-ups/79n1031
American Film Inst catalog: feature films/77n1006
American folklore films/77n1052
Aros/Title gd to talkies/79n954
Cowie/World filmography/79n1032
Daisne/Filmographic dict of world lit, suppl/79n1033
Dawson/Women's films in print/76n1055
Emmens/Short stories on film/79n1034
Enser/Filmed books & plays/77n1001
Film-Makers' Cooperative catalogue/76n1056
Films: catalog for schools, colleges & libraries/77n1008
Films on art/79n1035
Fox/Jewish films in the US/77n1009
Glut/Dracula book/76n1046
Last whole film catalog/77n1010
Lee/Reference gd to fantastic films/75n1194
Limbacher/Feature films on 8mm & 16mm/75n1208; 78n959
Maltin/Disney films/75n1195
Minus/Films: 1000 public domain films/75n1196
Parish/Great spy pictures/75n1198
Parker/Guide to dance in film/79n1038
Rehrauer/Short film/76n1059
World filmography/Cowie/78n964

FILMS FOR CHILDREN
Artel/Positive images/78n955
Gaffney/More films kids like/79n1024
Zornow/Movies for kids/75n1200

FILMSTRIPS
Educators gd to free filmstrips/Horkheimer/76n670; 77n649
Index to 35mm filmstrips/76n695

FILTERS
Hilburn/Manual of filter design/75n1807

FINANCE
Brealey/Bibliography of finance/75n955
Broster/Glossary of appl mgmt & financial stats/76n908
Buckley/Executive's digest of financial research/79n825
Business people in news/77n795
Business & financial tables/77n791
Childs/Encyclopedia of long-term financing & capital mgmt/77n821

FINANCE (cont'd)
Cohen/Special bibliog in monetary economics & finance/79n871
Cost of personal borrowing/77n822
Directors'... ency manual/77n773
Directory of state & fed funds for business developmt/78n710
European financial almanac/76n886
Facts & figures on gov finance/77n823
Grant/Directory of business & financial services/77n800
Levine/Financial analyst's hndbk/76n887
Moffat/Concise bk of business finance/77n775
Moore/Dictionary of business, finance, & investmt/76n830; 77n777
Rubel/Guide to venture capital/75n957; 78n753
Smollen/Source for borrowing capital/78n754
Thorndike ency of banking & financial tables/75n958
Weston/Treasurer's hndbk/78n722
Who's who in finance/75n903

FINANCE, PERSONAL
Guide to consumer services/78n747
Miller/Thesaurus of terms in consumer credit/79n872
Stillman/Guide to personal finance/76n878
Sylvia Porter's money book/76n877

FINE ARTS
  See Arts

FINE ARTS MUSEUM OF SAN FRANCISCO
Bennett/Five centuries of tapestry/78n861

FINGERPRINTS
US Dept of Justice/Science of fingerprints/75n836

FINITE ELEMENT METHOD
Whiteman/Bibliography for finite elements/76n1603; 77n1562

FINLAND
1500 largest companies/76n892
Scandinavian political studies/76n501

FINNEGANS WAKE
Glasheen/Third census/78n1177
Hart/Concordance/76n1276
O Hehir/Classical lexicon/78n1178

FIRE DAMAGES IN LIBRARIES
Morris/Managing the library fire risk/76n118

FIRE EXTINCTION
Kuvshinkoff/Fire sciences dict/78n1503

FIRE FIGHTING VEHICLES
Vanderveen/Fire & crash vehicles/77n1622

FIRE PREVENTION
Fire protection gd on hazardous matls/75
  n1714
Jensen/Fire protection for design profession/
  77n1578

FIRE RESISTANT TEXTILES
Reeves/Handbook/76n1649

FIREARMS
  See also Handguns; Machine guns; Rifles
Archer/Jane's pocket bk of rifles/79n1607
Byron/Firearms price gd/78n849
Chapel/Gun collector's hndbk/78n850
Flayderman/Flayderman's gd to antique
  Amer firearms/78n851
Foss/Infantry weapons/78n1468
Guns & ammo/75n777
Guns illust'd/77n690
Hogg/Encyclopedia of infantry weapons of
  World War II/78n1569
Hogg/Military small arms/78n1558
Jane's infantry weapons/Archer/78n1570
Rice/Outdoor life gun bk/76n758
Rywell/Confederate guns/76n971
Small arms of world/Ezell/79n1608/Smith/
  75n1839
Steinwedel/Gun collector's fact bk/76n972
Wahl/Gun trader's gd/76n759

FIRST AID
  See also Medical emergencies
Arnold/Check list for emergencies/75n1646
Green/Sigh of relief/79n1485

FIRST EDITIONS
First edition?/Zempel/79n57
Tannen/How to identify Amer 1st eds/77n65

FISHERIES
International directory of fish tech institutes/
  78n757
US Natl Marine Fisheries Serv/Fisheries of
  US/75n969; 78n761/Publications/75n970
World list of aquatic sci, suppl 2/79n1529

FISHERY PRODUCTS
US Natl Marine Fisheries Service . . .
  Processors/75n968
  Wholesale dealers/75n928

FISHES
  See also Aquariums; Freshwater fishes;
    Marine fishes; Tropical fishes
Branson/Fishes of Red River, KY/75n1512
Dahlberg/Guide to coastal fishes, GA/76n1434
Eddy/Northern fishes/75n1513
Lindberg/Fishes of the world/75n1514
Simon & Schuster's compl gd . . . aquarium
  fishes/79n704
Somerton/Field gd to fish of Puget Sound/77
  n1388
Wheeler/Fishes of the world/76n1437

FISHING
Alaska fishing gd/75n758; 76n726
Bates/Fishing: ency gd/75n759
Clotfelter/Hunting & fishing/75n721
Dunaway/Modern saltwater fishing/76n728
Gingrich/Fishing in print/75n760
Henkin/Fly tackle/77n692
Henkin/Complete fisherman's catalog/78
  n623
Knap/Where to fish & hunt in North Amer/
  76n729
McClane's new std fishing ency/75n761
Oberrecht/Great outdoors catalog/78n621
Veniard/Fly dressers' gd/75n762
Whole fishing catalog/79n716
Wisner/Complete gd to . . . fishing eqmt/77
  n693

FITZGERALD, F. SCOTT
Bruccoli/Apparatus for . . . Great Gatsby/75
  n1355
Crosland/Concordance to . . . Great Gatsby/
  76n1236
Duggan/Fitzgerald-Hemingway annual/79
  n1212

FLAGS
Campbell/Book of flags/76n449
Davis/Third Reich/76n1676
Schnapper/American symbols/75n444
Smith/Flags through the ages/77n486

FLIGHT TRAINING
Kershner/Flight instructor's manual/76n731
Reithmaier/Instrument pilot's gd/76n733

FLOOD DAMAGE
Flood damage prevention/75n1756

FLOODS
World catalogue of . . . floods/78n1358

FLORENCE
Weaver/Chronology of music in Florentine
  theater 1590-1750/79n995

FLORIDA
Fleming/Wild flowers/78n1290
Marks/Who was who in Florida/75n125
Morris/Florida place names/75n452
Warmke/Caribbean seashells/77n1396
Wood/New Florida atlas/75n583

FLORISTRY
Stevenson/Encyclopedia of floristry/75n927

FLOWER GARDENING
Doerflinger/Complete bk of bulb gardening/
  75n1700
Foster/Organic flower gardening/76n1586
Hay/Color dict of flowers/76n1587
Perry/Gardening in color/77n1559
Pizzetti/Flowers/76n1599
Sperka/Growing wildflowers/75n1708
Vance/Home gardener's gd to bulb flowers/
  75n1709

FLOWERS
Gibbs/Chemotaxonomy of flowering plants/ 75n1476
Hutchinson/Families of flowering plants/75n1477
Huxley/Flowers of Greece/79n1343
Language & sentiment of flowers/75n1244
Patraw/Flowers of SW mesas/79n1345
Perry/Simon & Schuster's compl gd to plants and flowers/77n1559
Reader's Digest ency of garden plants & flowers/78n1494
Shosteck/Flowers & plants/75n1464

FLUID MECHANICS
Annual review of fluid mechanics/Van Dyke/ 77n1602; 77n1603

FLUORESCENCE
Passwater/Guide to fluorescence/76n1352

FLUTE MUSIC
McGowan/Italian baroque sonatas/79n992
Pellerite/Handbook of lit for flute/79n993

FLY TYING
Bay/How to tie freshwater flies/76n727
Veniard/Fly dressers' gd/75n762

FM RADIO STATIONS
Elving/FM atlas & directory/79n1171

FOGARTY, JOHN E.
Healey/John E. Fogarty/75n251

FOLGER SHAKESPEARE LIBRARY
Wright/Of books & men/78n265

FOLK MEDICINE
Bricklin/Practical ency of natural healing/ 78n1433

FOLK SCHOOLS
Paulston/Folk schools in soc change/75n647

FOLKLIFE
Coe/Folklife & fed gov/79n1083
Szwed/Afro-American folk culture/79n453

FOLKLORE
American folklore films/77n1052
Arrowsmith/Field gd to little people/78n1008
Briggs/Encyclopedia of fairies/78n1009
Brunvand/Folklore: research gd/78n1010
Dundes/Folklore theses/78n1011
Flanagan/American folklore: bibliog/78n1012
Heisley/Annotated bibliog of Chicano folklore/78n1013
LC/Folklore from Africa: bibliog/77n1057
Lockwood/Yugoslav folklore/77n1053
Probert/Lost mines of West: bibliog/78n358
Thompson/Folktale/78n1015
Williams/Outlines of Chinese symbolism/78n1018

FOOD
Balfour/Good earth almanac/76n1567
Doyle/Complete food hndbk/78n1469
Feinman/Catalog of food/78n1471
McGraw-Hill ency of food . . . /78n1452
New Larousse gastronomique/Montagne/78n1476
Peterson/Encyclopedia of food sci/79n1533
Robertson/Spices, condiments, . . . other delicacies/76n1578
Tilson/Mail order food gd/78n1478
Wasserman/Don't ask your waiter/79n1534
Wilson/Complete food catalogue/78n1480
Woodward/Food catalog/79n1536
World atlas of food/Hale/75n1695

COMPOSITION AND TABLES
Adams/Encyclopedia of food/79n1529
Deskins/Everyone's gd . . . /76n1570
Food & nutrition/75n1687
Food composition tables: bibliog/78n1472
Fryer/Dictionary of food suppls/77n1545
Handbook of food prep/76n1571
How to buy food for economy/76n883
Konishi/Exercise equivalents of food/75n1690
Kraus/Basic food . . . calorie counter/75n1691; 75n1692
Kraus/Dictionary of protein/76n1576
Kraus/Dictionary of sodium, fats, . . . /76n1577
Nutritive value of Amer foods/Adams/77n1548
Ockerman/Source bk for food scientists/79n1531
Wade/Brand-name hndbk of protein, . . . /78n1479
Watt/Handbook of nutritional content of foods/77n1552

FOOD, WILD
See also Plants, edible
Angier/Field gd to edible wild plants/75n1465
Clarke/Edible & useful plants of Calif/79n1366
Hall/Wild food trailgd/77n1350
Knutsen/Wild plants you can eat/76n1575
Peterson/Field gd to edible wild plants/79n1367
Tomikel/Edible wild plants of PA & NY/75n1470

FOOD ADDITIVES
Winter/Consumer's dict of food additives/79n1535

FOOD COOPERATIVES
Food co-op directory/78n711
Food co-op hndbk/76n872
Vellela/Food co-ops for small groups/76n880

FOOD SERVICE
See also Cooking
Hardwick/Fundamentals of quantity food preparation/76n1572
Hering's dict of classical & modern cookery . . . /Bickel/76n1573
Wilkinson/Complete bk of cooking eqmt/76n1580

FOOD INDUSTRY AND TRADE
Bibliography of food & agri'l marketing/79n1511
FAO/Production yrbk/76n846; 79n1515
Rechcigl/World food problem/76n847
Sobel/World food crisis/76n848
Thomas grocery register/77n830
World food crisis: directory/Trzyna/78n1481

FOOD TECHNOLOGY
Bender/Dictionary of . . . food tech/78n1468
Codd/Chemical technology/77n1575
Elsevier's dict of food sci/Morton/78n1470
Johnson/Encyclopedia . . . /76n1574
Peterson/Encyclopedia of food sci/79n1533

FOOTBALL
CFL 74/Walker/75n764
Football register/Douchant/76n735
Grobani/Guide to football lit/76n736
Lorimer/Football book/79n717
Mendell/Who's who in football/75n765
Nelson/Illustrated football rules/77n694
NFL's official ency'ic hist of prof football/75n766; 78n624
Olgin/Illustrated football dict for young people/77n695
Pro football/76n734
Sporting News' natl football gd/76n737; 78n625
Sports ency: pro football/Neft/76n738
Sullivan/Pro football A to Z/76n739
Treat/Encyclopedia of football/78n626

FORD, GERALD R.
Lankevich/Gerald R. Ford/79n414

FORD, JESSE HILL
White/J. H. Ford: checklist/76n1237

FORD, JOHN
Tucker/Bibliography of writings abt J. Ford & C. Tourneur/78n932

FORD, PAUL LEICESTER
DuBois/P. L. Ford/78n155

FORD MOTOR CO.
Wagner/Ford trucks since 1905/79n1558

FOREIGN TRADE
See Commerce

FORESTRY
Davis/North Amer forest hist/78n1482
Fahl/North Amer forest & conservation hist/78n1483
FAO/Forestry/76n845
FAO/Yearbook of forest products/76n850
Forest serv directory/79n1537
Forest tree seed directory/77n1367
Kinch/Forestry theses/79n1538
Louden/Short rotation trees/78n1484
Sykes/Forest fertilization/77n1321

FORMOSA
Lebar/Ethnic groups of insular SE Asia, v2/76n810

FORMULAS
Dick's ency of practical receipts . . . /76n1638
Stark/Formula book/76n1645; 77n1313
Tarr/Up-with-wholesome, . . . household formulas/77n1550

FORSTER, EDWARD MORGAN
McDowell/E. M. Forster/79n1240

FORTRAN
Brown/FORTRAN to PL/1 dict/76n1624
Ledgard/Programming proverbs/76n1628

FOSSILS
Day/Guide to fossil man . . . /79n784
Hamilton/Larousse gd to . . . fossils/78n1359
Macdonald/Sabre-tooth cats . . . /75n1577
Tidwell/Common fossil plants west North Amer/76n1386

FOUNDATION ENGINEERING
Winterkorn/Foundation eng'g hndbk/76n1622

FOUNDATIONS (philanthropic)
Broce/Directory of OK foundations/75n78
Directory of Fellows/77n78
Directory of foundations in CT/77n80
Directory of foundations in ME/77n81
Directory of foundations in MA/77n79; 79n92
Directory of foundations in NH/77n82
Directory of foundations in RI/77n83
Directory of foundations in VT/77n84
Directory of research grants/78n73
Foundation Center/Foundation grants index/79n85
Foundation Center source bk/Beck/76n571
Foundation directory/76n620; 78n74
International foundation directory/75n82
National directory of art support/78n793
National directory of grants . . . in arts/Millsaps/77n86
Mitchell/Directory of NJ foundations/78n80
Trustee$ of wealth: Taft gd/77n595

272—Subjects

FOUNDING
Foseco foundryman's hndbk/77n1612
FOUR-WHEEL DRIVE VEHICLES
See Trucks
FRANCE
Caswell/Coutumes of France in LC/79n563
Cooke/France, 1789-1962/76n364
Edition de langue francaise catalogue/78n8
Heinz/French 5th Republic/75n519
Ponchie/French periodical index/77n45; 79n25
Répertoire des livres de langue française disponibles/77n26
Scholberg/Bibliographie des francais dan l'Inde/77n399
Thompson/Bibliography of French revolutionary pamphlets/76n365
Tully/France: for women/76n560
Wylie/France: events 1968/75n309
FRANCHISES
Directory of franchising organizations/77n799; 78n709
Franchise annual/79n829
Franchise opportunities hndbk/79n830
US Dept of Commerce/Franchise opportunities hndbk/77n804
US Small Business Admin/Franchise index/75n919
FRANCIS A. COUNTWAY LIBRARY, BOSTON
Chen/Applications of OR models to libraries/77n236
FRANKLIN, BENJAMIN
Barbour/Concordance to . . . Poor Richard/75n1356
FRANKLIN MINT
Culver/Guidebook of issues/76n967
FREDERIC, HAROLD
O'Donnell/Bibliography of writings/76n1239
FREE MATERIAL
Aubrey/Selected free matls for teachers/77n647
DuVall/Free matls & educ/79n681
Educators guide to free . . .
   Audio matls/Berg/78n591
   Films/Horkheimer/76n669
   Filmstrips/Horkheimer/76n670; 77n649
   Guidance matls/Saterstrom/76n671
   Health & PE/Horkheimer/76n672
   Science/Saterstrom/76n673
   Social studies/Suttles/76n674
   Tapes/Wittich/76n675
Elementary teachers gd to free curriculum matls/Suttles/76n676; 79n689
Feinman/Catalog of free things/77n91
Free & inexpensive learning matls/77n650

FREE MATERIAL (cont'd)
Index to free periodicals/77n41
Kislia/Let's see it again/76n680
Monahan/Free . . . matls for preschool/78n597
Shaffer/Career educ pamphlets/77n654
Shaffer/Sources of free teaching matls/77n655
Sources/78n3
FREE THOUGHT
Brown/Freethought in the US/79n1079
FREEDOM OF INFORMATION
Anderson/Privacy & public disclosure/77n531
Michael/Working on the system/75n104
FREEDOM OF THE PRESS
Knappman/Government & the media/75n494
FRENCH AMERICANS
Pula/French in America/76n406
FRENCH AUTHORS
Alden/French XX bibliog/79n1266
Bonnefoy/Dictionnaire de littérature francaise contemporaine/79n1269
FRENCH CANADIAN DIALECT
Clapin/Dictionnaire Canadien-Francais/76n1140
Dionne/Le parler populaire des Canadiens Francais/76n1141
FRENCH CANADIAN LITERATURE
Tougas/Checklist of printed matls/75n1411
FRENCH CANADIANS
Riseborough/Canada & the French/76n504
FRENCH DRAMA
SantaVicca/Four French dramatists/75n1417
FRENCH LANGUAGE
Atkins/Collins-Robert French-Engl dict/79n1134
Bassan/Annotated bibliog of French lang/77n1260
Brueckner's French contextuary/76n1139
Dubois/Modern French-Engl dict/79n1135
Einhorn/Old French/76n1142
Gerber/Dictionary of French idioms/78n1054
Hamlyn French dict/78n1055
Henstock/First French dict/75n1265
Lipton/French bilingual dict/75n1266
Marks/English-French dict of slang/76n1143
Miller/700 French idioms/77n1089
New contemp French-Engl dict/75n1267
Nutting/Cortina-Grosset basic French dict/77n1090
Petit Larousse illustre/78n1056
Putnam's contemp French dict/75n1268

FRENCH LANGUAGE (cont'd)
Switzer/Follett vest-pocket French dict/79n1136
US Dept of State/English-French glossary/78n1057

FRENCH LITERATURE
Alden/French XX bibliog/79n1266
Baker/Introduction to library research in French lit/79n1268
Bassan/Annotated bibliog of French lang & lit/77n1260
Bonnefoy/Dictionnaire de littérature française contemporaine/79n1269
Mahaffey/Concise bibliog/77n1262
Martin/Bibliographie du genre romanesque français 1751-1800/78n1186
Modern French lit/Popkin/78n1187
Reid/Concise Oxford dict/78n1188
Taylor/Littérature occitane du moyen age/79n1274
Tyler/Concordance to fables of Jean de la Fontaine/75n1418
West/Index of proper names in French Arthurian prose romances/79n1275

FRENCH LITERATURE IN TRANSLATION
Bowe/French lit in Amer trans/79n1270

FRESHWATER FISHES
Carlander/Handbook of freshwater fishery biology, centrarchid fishes/78n1325
Favre/Larousse dict of freshwater aquarium/79n700
Hoedeman/Naturalists' gd to fresh-water aquarium fish/75n1668
Identification gd to freshwater tropical aquarium fish/79n702
Matthes/Bibliography of African freshwater fish/75n1515
McClane's field gd to North Amer fishes/79n1376
Paysan/Guide to aquarium fishes/76n1559

FREUD, SIGMUND
Grinstein/S. Freud's writings/78n1363
Rothget/Abstracts of ... psychological works of S. Freud/75n1596

FRICK COLLECTION
Illustrated catalogue, v VIII, enamels .../78n868

FRISBEE
Johnson/Firsbee: practitioner's manual/76n767

FROST, ROBERT
Crane/Robert Frost/75n1357
Lentricchia/R. Frost: bibliog/77n1204
van Egmond/Critical reception of R. Frost/75n1358

FROUDE, JAMES ANTHONY
Goetzman/J. A. Froude/79n432

FRUIT
Gunn/World gd to tropical drift seeds/77n1349
Montgomery/Seeds & fruits .../78n1285
Peterson/How to know wild fruits/75n1467

FRYE, NORTHROP
Denham/Frye/75n1410

FULLER, HENRY BLAKE
Silet/H. B. Fuller & H. Garland/78n1125

FULLER, MARGARET
Myerson/Margaret Fuller/79n757

FUNERAL SERVICE
Harrah/Funeral service: bibliog/77n704

FUNGI
See also Mushrooms
Coker/Gasteromycetes of Eastern US & Canada/76n1396
Wyllie/Mycotoxic fungi .../79n1477

FUR TRADE
White/Fur trade in Minnesota/79n409

FURNITURE
Bishop/How to know Amer antique furniture/75n1073
Darty/Chairs/75n1074
Filbee/Dictionary of country furn/79n922
Gaines/Woman's Day dict of antique furn/75n1075
Grow/Old house catalogue/78n852
Hummel/Winterthur gd to Amer Chippendale furn/78n853
Kirk/Early Amer furn/75n1076
Morningstar/Early Utah furniture/78n854
Myers/Furniture repair & refinish/75n1795
Semple/Introductory gd to Midwest antiques/78n840
Voss/Antique Amer country furn/79n924
Williamsburg collection/75n1077

FUSED SALT SYSTEMS
Plambeck/Encyclopedia of electrochemistry, v X/78n1249

FUTURISM
Andreoli-deVillers/Futurism & the arts/77n861
Future: gd to info sources/79n112
McHale/Futures directory/79n113

G. ROBERT VINCENT VOICE LIBRARY, MICHIGAN
Dictionary catalog/Cluley/76n293

GADGETS
Grossinger/Book of gadgets/75n92

GALAXIES
de Vaucouleurs/2nd ref catalogue of bright galaxies/77n1306
Sandage/Galaxies & the universe/77n1311

GALLUP POLL
Gallup/Gallup poll/79n507

GAMBIA
Gailey/Historical dict/76n251

GAMBLING
Scarne/Scarne's new compl gd/76n745

GAME AND GAME BIRDS
Elman/Hunter's fld gd ... No Amer/75n776
Ovington/Wildlife illust'd/76n1414
Rue/Game birds of No Amer/75n779

GAMES
  See also Mathematical recreations
Anderson/SportSource/77n663
Belch/Contemporary games/75n697
Diagram Group/Way to play/76n742
Frisbee practitioner's manual/Johnson/76n767
Grunfeld/Games of the world/76n743
Lewis/Educational games ... in economics/75n703
Official rules of sports & games/76n700
Official Scrabble players dict/79n727
Rules of the game/75n728
Steven Caney's play bk/76n764
Turner/Index to outdoor sports, games, & activities/79n699

GANDHI, MAHATMA
Satyaprakash/Gandhiana/78n298

GANGSTER FILMS
Parish/Great gangster pictures/77n1011

GARDENING
  See also Container gardening; flower gardening; Greenhouses; Horticulture; House plants; Indoor gardening; Organic gardening; Vegetable gardening
Bailey/Good Housekeeping basic gardening/75n1697
Brimer/Home gardener's gd to trees/77n1553
Campbell/Let it rot!/76n1582
Faust/NY Times bk of gardening/76n1584
Fogg/History of popular garden plants/78n1491
Hay/Practical gardening ency/79n1540
Healey/Gardener's gd to plant names/76n1588
Hersey/Flowering shrubs/75n1702
Hudak/Gardening with perennials/77n1555
Kramer/Free earth gd/75n1704
Leggett/Complete garden/76n1594
Link/Whole seed catalog/77n1557
Marshall Cavendish illust'd ency/79n1541
Perry/Gardening in colour/77n1559

GARDENING (cont'd)
Plants & flowers/75n1705
Powell/Avant gardener/76n1601
Reader's Digest ency of garden plants & flowers/78n1494
Reader's Digest illust'd gd/79n1542
Rice/How to eat better & spend less/75n1706
Riker/Gardener's catalogue/75n1707
Rottenberg/Guide to buying plants/78n1495
Schroeder/Green thumb directory/78n1496
Seymour/Guide to self-sufficiency/78n1447
Stangle/Chilton's ency of gardening/77n1560
Stone Soup/Green world: gd/77n1561
Wallach/Reluctant weekend gardener/75n1710
Wyman/Saturday morning gardener/75n1711
Wyman's gardening ency/78n1498

GARDENS
Guide to public gardens/Garden Club of Amer/78n526
Leblanc/Pelican gd to gardens of Louisiana/75n610
Logan/Traveller's gd to No Amer gardens/75n633

GARFIELD, JAMES A.
LC/Index to ... papers/75n372

GARLAND, HAMLIN
Bryer/H. Garland & the critics/75n1359
Silet/H. B. Fuller & H. Garland/78n1125

GAS CHROMATOGRAPHY
Signeur/Guide to lit, v3/76n1346

GAS INDUSTRY
European offshore oil yrbk/77n1418

GASKELL, ELIZABETH
Selig/E. Gaskell: ref gd/78n1174
Welch/E. Gaskell: bibliog/78n1175

GAY, JOHN
Klein/J. Gay/75n1385

GAY MEN
Katz/Gay Amer hist/78n652

GEESE
Merne/Ducks, geese & swans/76n1425

GENEALOGICAL SOCIETIES
Meyer/Directory of genealogical societies in the USA & Canada/79n471

GENEALOGY
  See also Heraldry; Marriage registers; Registers of births; Ship passenger lists
  Also under names of families; place names
Amer Genealogical Res Inst/How to trace your family tree/76n420
Barrow/Genealogist's gd/79n466

GENEALOGY (cont'd)
Beard/How to find your family roots/79n467
Filby/American & Brit genealogy & heraldry/77n449
Helmbold/Tracing your ancestry/77n450/Logbook/77n451
Kaminkow/Genealogies in the LC: bibliog, suppl/78n394
Langston/Pedigrees of some of emperor Charlemagne's descendants/75n425
McNaughton/Book of kings/76n446
Oregon Hist'l Soc microfilm gd/75n384
NYPL/Dictionary catalog of local hist & genealogy div/75n382
Peskett/Discover your ancestors/79n468
Schreiner-Yantis/Genealogical bks in print/76n421
Skalka/Tracing, charting your family hist/76n422
Sperry/Survey of Amer genealogical periodicals/79n472
Stevenson/Search & research/79n470
Towle/Genealogical periodical annual index/79n473
Wellauer/Guide to foreign genealogical research/77n452
Westin/Finding your roots/78n395
Wright/Genealogical reader: NE US & Canada/75n434
    CANADA
De Ville/Acadian church records/76n430
    GERMANY
Hall/Atlantic bridge to Germany/75n417
Smith/American genealogical resources in German archives/78n412
Smith/Encyclopedia of German-Amer genealogical research/77n478
    GREAT BRITAIN
Burke/Genealogical & heraldic hist of commoners of Grt Britain & Ireland/78n393
Burke/General armory of England, Scotland, Ireland & Wales/77n483
Burke's family index/78n418
Camp/Everyone has roots: Engl genealogy/79n438
Cox/Parish registers of England/75n436
Debrett's peerage/Montague-Smith/78n419
Filby/American & British genealogy & heraldry/77n449
Gibson/Wills & where to find them/75n437
Hamilton-Edwards/In search of British ancestry/75n438
Loyd/Origins of Anglo-Norman families/76n445
Norman people/76n447
Paget/Lineage & ancestry of Prince Charles/78n420
Steel/Sources for Roman Catholic & Jewish genealogy & family hist/78n421

GENEALOGY (cont'd)
    GREAT BRITAIN (cont'd)
Thomson/Catalogue of British family histories/78n422
Turton/Plantagenet ancestry . . . /76n444
    IRELAND
Black/Your Irish ancestors/75n435
Burke/Genealogical & heraldic hist of the commoners of Grt Britain & Ireland/78n393
Burke's Irish family records/78n417
O'Hart/Irish pedigrees/77n481
Rottenberg/Finding our fathers: Jewish genealogy/78n408
    UNITED STATES
American genealogist/77n453
Appleton/Boston births, baptisms, marriages, & deaths 1630-99/79n474
Austin/Genealogical dict of RI/79n475
Barbour/Families of early Hartford, CT/78n396
Barnes/Marriages & deaths Baltimore, 1796-1816/79n477
Barnes/Maryland marriages/76n423; 79n476
Bell/Our Quaker friends . . . /77n454
Blockson/Black genealogy/78n397
Bolin/Ohio Valley hist/77n455
Bolton/Real founders of New England/75n408
Boulton/Founders: . . . before 1701/77n456
Brumbaugh/Maryland records/76n424
Bunker/Long Island genealogies/77n457
Burke's Amer families with British ancestry/76n425
Burke's presidential families of USA/76n426
Chalkley/Chronicles of Scotch-Irish settlemts in Virginia/75n409
Chapman/Annals of Newberry (SC)/75n410
Chapman/Marriages of Isle of Wight County, VA, 1628-1800/77n458
Clift/Kentucky marriages, 1797-1865/75n411
Clough/Dutch uncles & New Engl cousins/78n398
Coldham/English convicts in colonial Amer/75n412; 78n399
Cumrine/Virginia court records in SW Pennsylvania/75n413
Davis/Genealogical & pers hist of Bucks County, PA/76n429
Davis/Genealogical register of Plymouth families/76n428
DeVille/Louisiana recruits 1752-58/75n414
du Bellet/Some prominent VA families/77n459
Egle/Early PA land records/77n460
Esker/Source records from DAR magazine/76n431
Ericson/Nacogdoches-gateway to TX/75n415
Felldin/Index to 1820 census of VA/77n461

GENEALOGY (cont'd)
UNITED STATES (cont'd)
Fernow/Records of New Amsterdam from 1653-74/77n462
Flavell/Ohio area key/78n401
Flavell/Ohio genealogical periodical index/78n400
Francis/Lost links/76n432
Gannett/Gazetteer of Maryland & Delaware/77n463
Green/Historic families of Kentucky/76n433
Greenwood/Researcher's gd to Amer genealogy/75n416
Hamlin/They went thataway/75n418
Hardy/Colonial families of the southern states of America/75n419
Harris/Biographical hist of Lancaster County (PA)/75n420
Harrison/Settlers by Long Grey Trail/76n434
Heavener/German New River settlemt, VA/77n464
Heiss/Encyclopedia of Amer Quaker genealogy, v7, abstracts/78n402
Hill/History of Henry County, VA/77n465
Hills/History of Mayflower planters . . . /76n435
Hotten/Original lists of persons of quality/75n421
Jacobus/Families of ancient New Haven/75n422
Jacobus/History of families of old Fairfield/77n466
Jaussi/Genealogical records of Utah/75n423
Johnston/West Virginians in Amer Revolution/78n403
Jordan/Colonial & revolutionary families of PA/79n488
Judd/Voyages to Hawaii before 1820/75n424
Kaylor/Abstracts of land grant surveys of . . ., VA, 1761-91/77n467
Lackey/Frontier claims in lower South/78n404
Lee/Lee of Virginia, 1642-1892/75n426
Linn/Annals of Buffalo Valley, PA/76n436
Littell/Family records . . . Passaic Valley/77n468
Marine/British invasion of MD/78n405
Maryland rent rolls/77n469
Mayflower families thru 5 generations/77n470
Mullins/Republic of TX: poll lists for 1846/75n427
Nead/Pennsylvania-German in Maryland/76n437
Nelson/Patents . . . NJ, 1664-1703/77n471
NY manuscripts: Dutch/Van Laer/75n428
North Carolina/Muster rolls of War of 1812/77n472

GENEALOGY (cont'd)
UNITED STATES (cont'd)
Parker/Personal name index to Ortons . . . records of Calif in War of Rebellion/79n492
Passano/Index of source records of MD/75n429
Pearson/Genealogies of . . . 1st settlers of . . . Schenectady (NY)/77n473
Pearson/Genealogies of . . . 1st settlers of . . . Albany (NY)/77n474
Portnov/US gd to family records/79n469
Plymouth church records/76n438
Register/Index to the 1830 census of GA/75n430
Roberts/Early Friends families of Bucks, PA/76n439
Robertson/Kansas territorial settlers of 1860/77n475
Rupp/Collection of upwards of 30,000 names/76n440
Scott/Abstracts from the *Pennsylvania Gazette*/78n410
Scott/Buried genealogical data/78n411
Scott/Genealogical data from NY newspapers/78n409
Shourds/History & genealogy of Fenwick's Colony/77n476
Shurtleff/Records of Plymouth Colony/77n477
Spinazze/Index to Argonauts of Calif/76n441
Strassburger/Pennsylvania German pioneers/76n442
Tepper/Emigrants to PA, 1641-1819/78n414
Tepper/Emigrants to PA . . . ship passenger lists/76n443
Tepper/Passengers to America/78n413
Townsend/South Carolina Baptists, 1670-1805/75n431
Tyler/Connecticut loyalists/78n415
US Dept of State/Census of pensioners for revolutionary or military services/75n432
Van Voorhis/Old and new Manogahela/75n433
Weis/Colonial clergy and churches of New England/78n416
Weis/Colonial clergy of VA, NC, SC/77n479
Winborne/Colonial hist of Hartford County, NC/77n480

GENESIS (Bible)
Owens/Genesis/79n1072

GENETICS
Annual review of genetics/77n1342
Herskowitz/Bibliography on genetics of drosophila/75n1460
King/Dictionary of genetics/76n1356

GEOCHEMISTRY
Wolfson geochem atlas of England/Webb/ 79n1419

GEOGRAPHERS
Geographers biobibliog studies . . .
  v1/Freeman/78n536
  v2/Freeman/79n626
Yearbook of Assoc of Pacific Coast Geogs/ 77n556; 79n582

GEOGRAPHY
Chisholm's hndbk of commercial geog/Blake/ 76n832
Lock/Geography & cartography/77n555
Muller/Locational analysis & economic geog . . ., suppl/79n578
Van Balen/Geography pubs/79n579; 79n580
ATLASES
Atlas of Japan/75n573
Atlas of Mississippi/Cross/75n574
Bartholomew-Scribner atlas of Europe/ Browne/75n575
Chi-Bonnardel/Atlas of Africa/75n576
Hammond internat'l world atlas/75n577
Highsmith/Atlas of Pacific NW/75n578
McEvedy/Penguin atlas of ancient hist/77n357
Road atlas of Grt Britain/75n579
Robinson/Atlas of Wisconsin/75n580
US Military Academy, West Point/Atlas of landforms/75n581
Webster's atlas & zip code directory/75n582
Wood/New Florida atlas/75n583
BIBLIOGRAPHY
Aiyepeku/Geographical lit on Nigeria/75n567
Alexander/Guide to atlases suppl/78n510
Ball/Bibliography for geographic educ/77n547
Bederman/Africa: bibliog/75n568
Bibliographia cartographica/Zogner/78n511
Geographers biobibliog'l studies/Freeman/ 78n536
Harris/Bibliography of geog/77n548
Harris/Guide to geograph'l bibliogs in Russian/76n522
Saveland/Inventory of research in geog'ic educ/77n549
Sukhwal/South Asia: bibliog/76n523
Wheeler/Bibliography on geographic thought, philosophy, & methodology/77n550
DICTIONARIES
DeSola/Geographic glossary/76n520
Gannett/Geographic dict of CT & RI/79n596
Gannett/Geographic dict of MD/79n594
Gannett/Geographic dict of NJ/79n595
Gazetteer of Scotland/Munro/75n572
Moore/Dictionary of geog/79n581
von Engeln/Story key to geog'ic names/77n553

GEOLOGY
See also Earth sciences
American Geological Inst/Dictionary of geological terms/77n1425
Andriot/Guide to US gov maps/78n1355
Challinor/Dictionary of geology/76n1471
Cook/Stratigraphic atlas of No & Central America/78n513
Encyclopedia of world geology/77n1426
Harbaugh/Geology gd to Calif/75n1564
International stratigraphic gd/78n1356
Kasbeer/Bibliog of cont'l drift/75n1565
Lapedes/McGraw-Hill ency of geological sciences/79n1418
Smith/Mesozoic & cenozoic paleocontinental maps/78n1357
Titratsoo/Oilfields of the world/75n1566
Whitten/Penguin dict of geology/77n1427
Woolley/Illustrated ency of mineral kingdom/ 79n1423

GEOMETRY
Santalo/Integral geometry . . . /78n1229

GEOPHYSICS
Corliss/Strange phenomena/75n91

GEORGIA
Register/Index to 1830 census/75n430
Simpson/Georgia history: bibliog/77n395
Utley/Placenames of Georgia/76n459

GEOTHERMAL ENERGY
Geothermal world directory/Tratner/79n1403

GERMAN AMERICAN LITERATURE
Tolzmann/German-Amer lit/78n1191

GERMAN AMERICAN NEWSPAPERS
Arndt/German lang press of Americas/77n444

GERMAN AMERICANS
Heavener/German New River settlement, VA/ 77n464
Richards/Pennsylvania-German in Revolutionary War/79n495
Smith/American genealogical resources in German archives/78n412
Smith/Encyclopedia of German-Amer genealogical research/77n478
Tolzmann/German-Americana: bibliog/76n407

GERMAN LANGUAGE
Farrell/Dict of German synonyms/78n1058
Hamlyn German dict/78n1059
Keller/German word family dict/79n1137
Putnam's contemp German dict/75n1269
Oxford-Harrap std German-Engl dict/Jones/ 79n1138
Schöffler/New Schöffler-Weis German & Engl dict/75n1270
Stern/Hndbk of Engl-German idoms/75n1271
Zotter/Cortina-Grosset basic German dict/ 77n1091

GERMAN LANGUAGE SERIALS
Union list of German lang serials in libraries of the Fed Republic of Germany/79n381

GERMAN LITERATURE
See also names of authors
Albrecht/Internationale bibliographie zur geschichte der deutschen literatur . . . /79n1276
Garland/Oxford companion to German lit/77n1263
German lit Widener library shelflist/76n1295
Gillespie/Catalogue of persons in Germanic heroic lit/75n1420
Tolzmann/German-Amer lit/78n1191

GERMAN POETRY
Bartlett/Word index to R. M. Rilke's German lyrical poetry/79n1277

GERMANY
Ambrosi/Where great German wines grow/77n1518
Davies/German army hndbk/75n1848
Davis/Flags . . . Third Reich/76n1676
Deutsches bibliotheksadressbuch/78n135
Fout/German history & civilization/75n395
Gebhardt/Special collections in German libraries/78n194
Hall/Atlantic bridge to Germany, v1/75n417
Lenton/German warships of WWII/77n1650
Merritt/Politics, economics, & society in two Germanies/79n379
Price/Federal Republic of Germany/79n380
Schwerin/Bibliography of German lang legal monograph series/79n567
Smith/American genealogical resources in German archives/78n412
Snyder/Encyclopedia of Third Reich/77n402
Spalek/German expressionism in fine arts: bibliog/78n786
Stachura/Weimar era & Hitler/79n430

GERSHWIN, GEORGE
Schwartz/George Gershwin: bibliog & discog/76n1010

GESTURE
Bauml/Dictionary of gestures/76n1167

GHANA
Afre/Ashanti region of Ghana/76n252

GHOSTS
Coxe/Haunted Britain/75n622
Hallam/Ghosts' who's who/78n1377

GIFT-BOOKS (annuals, etc.)
Kirkham/Indices to Amer literary annuals and gift books/77n1191

GIFTED STUDENTS
Laubenfels/Gifted student/79n631

GILBERT AND SULLIVAN
Moore/Handbook/76n1009

GILL, ERIC
Brady/Eric Gill/75n71
Gill/Bibliography of E. Gill/75n72

GIRLS' CLUBS
Kujoth/Boys' & girls' bk of clubs/76n696

GISSING, GEORGE
Collie/G. Gissing: bibliog/77n1233
George Gissing/75n1386

GLASGOW
Hendry/Social hist of branch library developmt/76n224

GLASS
Ash/Dictionary of British antique glass/77n896
Bibliography: glass/75n1049
Ehrhardt/Cut glass price gd/75n1079
Florence/Collectors ency of depression glass/78n855
Hand/Collector's ency of carnival glass/79n926
Klamkin/Collector's gd to carnival glass/77n920
Klamkin/Depression glass/75n1081
Miller/Wallace-Homestead price gd to antiques & pattern glass/78n838
Newman/Illustrated dict of glass/79n926
Oliver/American antique glass/78n856

GLAZES
Chappell/Potter's compl bk of clay & glazes/79n947

GLIDING
America's soaring bk/76n730
Soaring directory/78n638

GOD
Pitts/Concept developmt & . . . God concept in the child/79n752

GOGOL', NIKOLAI V.
Berry/Plots & characters in major Russian fict, vII/79n1282

GOLD
Persons/Investor's ency of gold, . . ./76n860
Sinclair/How experts buy & sell gold bullion . . . /76n862

GOLDEN COCKEREL PRESS
Bibliography 1921-41/77n52
Chambers/Cook-A-Hoop/77n53

GOLDSMITHS
Grimwade/London goldsmiths 1697-1837/77n899

Subjects—279

GOLDSMITHS' LIBRARY OF ECONOMIC LITERATURE, LONDON
Canney/Catalog, v2/76n823
Microfilm collection, vI/77n768

GOLF
Elliott/Who's who in golf/77n696
Encyclopedia of golf/Steel/76n748
Evans/Encyclopedia of golf/75n769
Simms/World of golf/79n718
Ward-Thomas/World atlas of golf/77n697

GONCHAROV, IVAN A.
Berry/Plots & characters in major Russian fiction/79n1282

GORDON, CAROLINE
Golden/F. O'Connor & C. Gordon/78n1123

GORGAS, AMELIA GAYLE
Johnston/A. G. Gorgas/79n186

GOSPEL MUSIC
See also Hymns; Sacred songs
Gordon/New gospel treasure select-a-song/77n955

GOVERNMENT AID
Catalog of fed domestic assistance/77n109

GOVERNMENT DOCUMENTS LIBRARIES
See Documents libraries

GOVERNMENT LENDING
Directory of state & fed funds for business developmt/78n710

GOVERNMENT PUBLICATIONS
See also International agencies; United Nations; countries, by name
ALA/Directory of gov doc collections/75n157
Bibliographic gd to gov pubs foreign/77n7
Harleston/Administration of gov docs collections/75n214
Inventory of . . . services available to US House of Representatives/78n99
Schorr/Government docs in library lit/78n131
Sources/78n3
    FEDERAL
Bibliographic gd to gov pubs/77n6
Buchanan/Cumulative subj index to Monthly Catalog/75n102
Catalog of fed domestic assistance/77n109
Computex bk gds: gov pubs/76n82
Consolidated . . . Monthly Catalog/78n96
Cumulative subj gd to US gov bibliogs/Kanely/77n112
Declassified Docs Quarterly catalog/77n113
Declassified docs retrospective collection/78n97
Downey/US fed official pubs/79n115
Federal program evaluations/79n116
Field/Bibliography . . . Cong prints 1911-69/79n117

GOVERNMENT PUBLICATIONS (cont'd)
    FEDERAL (cont'd)
Giefer/Water pubs of state agencies, suppl/77n1428
Government ref bks/Schorr/77n106; 79n125
Index to Civil Serv Comm info/77n114
Index to US gov periodicals/75n103; 76n37
LC/Popular names of US gov reports/77n115
Leidy/Popular gd to gov pubs/77n107
Morehead/Intro to US public docs/76n83; 79n120
National union catalog of US gov pubs/75n105
Newsome/New gd to popular gov pubs/79n121
Norback/Everything you can get from the gov for free/76n84
Palic/Government pubs: bibliog'ic tools/77n108
Poole/Documents office classification/79n123
Poole/1909 cklist . . . /75n107
Reference list of AV matls produced by US gov/79n124
Government ref bks/Schorr/79n125; 77n106/Wynkoop/75n108
US General Accounting Office/Federal info sources/77n110
US government manual/76n86
US Supt of Docs/GPO sales pubs ref file/78n100
Van Zant/Selected US gov series/79n126
Yannarella/US gov scientific & tech periodicals/77n1295
    STATE
Check-list of VA state pubs/79n114
COIN: cklt to CO state pubs/78n95
Parish/State gov ref pubs/75n106

GOVERNMENT PURCHASING
Businessman's gd to dealing with fed gov/75n888
Government prod prime contractors directory/77n826
Ruder/Businessman's gd to Washington/76n836
US gov purchasing & sales directory/79n821

GOVERNMENTAL LIBRARIES
Federal gov libraries in Canada/78n202
World directory of admin libraries/77n187

GOVERNORS
Gateley/Register of governors of USA/76n339
Kallenbach/American state governors/78n458
Phillips/Governors of Tennessee/79n534
Sobel/Biographical directory of governors of the US/79n543
Solomon/Governors of states/75n505

280–Subjects

GRADUATE SCHOOLS
   See also specific fields, e.g., Business schools; Medical schools, etc.
Peterson's annual gds to grad study/79n662
Tomlinson/Guide to grad studies in Great Britain/76n665

GRAFFITI
Reisner/Encyclopedia of graffiti/76n63

GRAINS
Karel/Dried grasses, grains, gourds, pods & cones/76n1590
Rachie/Millets & minor cereals/75n1696

GRAMOPHONE CO., GERMANY
Bennett/Catalogue of vocal recordings from 1898-1925 Gramophone Co/79n969

GRAND TETON NATIONAL PARK
Shaw/Field gd to vascular plants/77n1356

GRANTS-IN-AID
Annual register of grant support/75n667; 79n80
Directory of research grants/76n610; 78n73
Encyclopedia of US gov benefits/76n829
Foundation Center/Grants index/79n85
Foundation Center source bk: v1, documentation/Beck/76n571
Foundation directory/78n74
Grant Info System/Faculty alert bulletin/75n669
Grants register/Turner/76n612
Human Resources Network/How to get money for...
   Arts & humanities, drug abuse, health/Nowlan/76n623
   Conservation & community developmt/Nowlan/76n624
   Education fellowships/Nowlan/76n625
   Youth, elderly, handicapped/Nowlan/76n626
Human Resources Network/User's gd to funding resources/Nowlan/76n627
National directory of grants in arts/Millsaps/77n86
National Endowmt for Arts/gd to programs/76n628
NSF factbook/76n603
Scurlock/Government contracts & grants for research/76n653
Trustee$ of wealth/Brodsky/77n595
US Natl Park Serv/Historic preservation grants-in-aid catalog/77n877
White/Grants: how to find out/78n78

GRAPHIC ARTS
   See also Calligraphy; Etchings; Illustrators; Prints
Beall/Kaufrufe und strabenhandler/78n806
Graphic artists guild, directory/78n809
Muehsam/Guide to basic info sources in visual arts/79n888

GRAPHIC ARTS (cont'd)
Penrose graphic arts internat'l/76n943
Pollack/Animal kingdom/79n901/Dining & drinking/79n902

GRAPHIC SYMBOLS
Modley/Handbook of pictorial symbols/78n812

GRAPHOLOGY
Landrum/Who's who in graphology.../78n1378

GRASS, GUNTER
Everett/Select bibliog/75n1419; 76n1294
O'Neill/G. Grass: bibliog/77n1264

GRASSES
Beard/Turfgrass bibliog 1672 to 1972/79n1347
Clifford/Identifying grasses/79n1348
Gould/Grasses of Texas/77n1364
Karel/Dried grasses, grains, gourds, pods & cones/76n1590
Knobel/Field gd to grasses, sedges, & rushes/79n1349
Meyer/Ornamental grasses/76n1597
Pohl/How to know the grasses/76n1350

GRAVES, ROBERT
Presley/R. Graves manuscripts at So Illinois Univ/77n1234

GREAT BRITAIN
Abse/Art galleries of Brit & Ireland/77n868
Barefoot/Community (health) services/79n1458
Black/Blathwayt atlas, v2: commentary/76n367
Directory of Brit assns & assns in Ireland/75n80; 78n72
Hogg/Museums of England/75n81
Lock/General sources of stats/77n751
McClure/British place-names in their hist'l setting/75n451
Reaney/Dictionary of British surnames/77n489; 79n500
Road atlas of Grt Brit/75n579
Vexler/England (chronology)/75n336
Wolfson geochem atlas of England/Webb/79n1419
   ARMED FORCES
Bruce/Annotated bibliog of Brit army 1660-1914/77n1641
May/Badges & insignia of Brit armed services/76n1678
   BIBLIOGRAPHY
Allison/Titles in English/77n333; 78n9
British bks in print/75n7; 76n15; 79n10
Short-title catalogue of bks printed in England, v2/Pollard/77n27
Small press record of bks/76n11
Whitaker's five-yr cum bk list/75n14
Whitaker's three-yr cum bk list/78n10

Subjects—281

GREAT BRITAIN (cont'd)
   BIOGRAPHY
Compact ed of dict of natl biog/77n147
Lives of Stuart Age/Urdang Assoc/77n412
Lives of Tudor Age/Hoffman/78n369
Reel/Index to biogs of Englishmen 1000-1485 in dissertations/76n370
Who's who/75n132; 79n145
   ECONOMIC CONDITIONS
Aslib Transport & Planning Group/New directions in transport sources of info/77n1617
Chaloner/British economic & soc hist: bibliog/77n407
Harrison/Warwick gd to Brit labour periodicals/78n768
Hepple/Bibliography of lit on Brit & Irish labour law/76n904
MacCafferty/Inflation in UK/78n702
Palmer/Economic arithmetic, stat sources, 1700-1850/79n807
   EDUCATION
Academic who's who/77n641
Frazer/Resource bk on chem educ in UK/77n1312
Gabriel/Summary bibliog of hist of univ of Grt Britain & Ireland to 1800/75n645
Priestley/British qualifications/76n664
Tomlinson/Guide to grad studies in Grt Britain/76n665
   FLORA AND FAUNA
Fisher/Thorburn's birds/77n1377
Harrison/Field gd to nests, eggs, nestlings of British & European birds/77n1380
Phillips/Wild flowers of Britain/79n1346
   GENEALOGY AND HERALDRY
See Genealogy; Heraldry

   GOVERNMENT PUBLICATIONS
Cumulative index to HMSO pubs/77n111
Index to correspondence of Foreign Off/79n557; 79n558
List of Admiralty records, v7/78n479
Public Record Office . . .
   v1, Africa/78n480
   v3, America/78n481
Pemberton/British official pubs/75n110
   HISTORY
Annual bibliog of Brit & Irish hist/77n404
Anglo-Saxon England/Clemoes/77n403
Batts/British manuscript diaries of 19th cent/77n405
Bell/Dissertations on Brit hist/76n366
Brown/Bibliography of Brit hist 1789-1851/78n368
Chaloner/British economic & soc hist/77n407
Coldham/English convicts in colonial Amer, v2/78n399
Darby/Domesday gazetteer/76n368
Elton/Annual bibliog of Brit & Irish hist/79n431

GREAT BRITAIN (cont'd)
   HISTORY (cont'd)
Gross/Bibliography of Engl hist to 1485/77n408
Guth/Late-Medieval England/77n409
Hanham/Bibliography of Brit hist 1851-1914/77n410
Harvard Univ Library/British hist/76n369
Havighurst/Modern Engl/77n411
Nicholls/19th cent Britain 1815-1914/79n433
Pargellis/Bibliography of Brit hist: 1714-89/78n370
Powell/English hist'l facts 1485-1603/79n434
Simpson/Manuscript catalogue of Library of Royal Commonwealth Society/77n413
Who's who in hist, Engl 1789-1837/Treasure/76n371
Wiener/Great Britain: hist of domestic policy 1689-1973/76n372
Wilkinson/High Middle Ages in Engl/79n435
   POLITICS AND GOVERNMENT
Bellamy/Dictionary of labour biog/79n547
Bidwell/Bidwell's gd to gov ministers, 1900-72/75n517
Blackstone/Social policy & admin in Britain/78n703
Cook/Sources in Brit pol hist, 1900-51/78n477
General index to reports from committees of House of Commons, 1715-1801/75n476
Guardian directory of pressure groups/78n478
Hellicar/Prime Ministers of Britain/79n548
Sainty/Home Office officials, 1782-1870/76n499
Stenton/Who's who of Brit members of Parliament, 1832-1885/78n482
Year bk of social policy in Britain/75n337
   PUBLISHING
Bibliography of Golden Cockerel Press/77n52
Chambers/Cook-A-Hoop/77n53
Gifford/British comic catalogue, 1847-1974/77n1169
Hammelmann/Book illustrators in 18th cent England/77n66
Parks/John Dunton & Engl bk trade/77n55
Ray/Illustrator & bk 1790-1914/77n67
Tomkinson/Select bibliog of modern presses in Grt Brit & Ireland/77n56

GREAT GATSBY
Crosland/Concordance/76n1236

GREAT LAKES
Mobil travel gd/79n603

GREAT PLAINS
Atlas of flora/78n1283
Mobil travel gd: NW & Grt Plains/79n606

GREECE
Classical world bibliog of Greek & Roman hist/79n402
Coulson/Annotated bibliog of Greek & Roman art, . . . /77n862
Huxley/Flowers of Greece & Aegean/79n1343
Melas/Greek experience/75n1020
Michaelides/Music of ancient Greece/79n965

GREEK DRAMA
Classical world bibliog of Greek drama & poetry/79n1262

GREEK LANGUAGE
Gall/Layman's Engl-Greek concordance/76n1144
Wharton/Etymological lexicon of classical Greek/76n1145

GREEK LITERATURE
Willcock/Companion to Iliad/77n1265

GREEK POETRY
Classical world bibliog of Greek drama & poetry/79n1265

GREEN, BEN K.
Wilson/Ben K. Green: bibliog/78n1139

GREENAWAY, KATE
Thomson/Kate Greenaway: catalogue/78n1161

GREENE, CHARLES
Makinson/Guide to work of Greene & Greene/76n939

GREENE, HENRY
Makinson/Guide to work of Greene & Greene/76n939

GREENHOUSES
Abraham/Organic gardening under glass/76n1581

GRIEF
See Bereavement

GRIFFES, CHARLES T.
Anderson/C. T. Griffes/79n781

GRIFFIN, D. W.
Niver/D. W. Griffin/75n1197

GROCERY TRADE
Thomas grocery register/77n830

GROUNDS MAINTENANCE
Conover/Grounds maintenance hndbk/78n1490

GROUP PSYCHOTHERAPY
Zimpfer/Group work in the helping professions: bibliog/77n1444

GROUP RELATIONS TRAINING
Pfeiffer/Reference gd to hndbks & annuals/78n1372

GUADALUPE MOUNTAINS NATIONAL PARK
Schmidly/Mammals of trans-Pecos Texas/78n1333

GUIANA MAROONS
Price/Guiana Maroons: bibliog/78n677

GUIDED MISSILES
Gatland/Missiles & rockets/77n1647
Knaack/Encyclopedia of USAF aircraft & missile systems/79n1593
Taylor/Missiles of the world/78n1571

GUINEA (Republic)
O'Toole/Historical dict/79n354

GUINEA-BISSAU
McCarthy/Guinea-Bissau & Cape Verde Islands/79n353

GUITAR
Purcell/Classic guitar, lute, & vihuela discog/78n905

GUNS
See Firearms

GUYANA
McDowell/Bibliography of lit from Guyana/76n1302

GYNECOLOGY
Benson/Handbook of obstetrics & gynecology/75n1626
Obstetrics & gynecology annual/Wynn/77n1487

HAGUE PEACE CONFERENCE
Proceedings . . . of 1899 & 1907, index/Scott/78n437

HAITI
Bissainthe/Dictionnaire de bibliog haitienne, suppl/75n295
Perusse/Historical dict/78n308

HALL-MARKS
Grimwade/London goldsmiths 1697-1837/77n899

HALLS OF FAME
Appel/Baseball's best/79n706
Big bk of halls of fame in US & Canada: sports/Soderberg/78n603

HALLUCINOGENIC DRUGS
Safford/Psychedelics ency/78n1445

HALLUCINOGENIC PLANTS
Menser/Hallucinogenic & poisonous mushroom fld gd/78n1301
Schultes/Hallucinogenic plants/78n1281

HANDGUNS
Millard/Handbook on identification of revolvers & pistols/76n756
Nonte/Pistol & revolver gd/76n757

HANDICAPPED
Appleby/Training progs & placemt services/79n852
Baskin/Notes from a different drummer/78n179
Bruck/Access: gd for disabled Americans/79n840
Choosing & using phonograph records for physical educ/79n679
Eckstein/Handicapped funding directory/79n1507
Gollay/College gd for students with disabilities/78n564
Materials on creative arts . . . for persons with handicapping conditions/79n684
Sex & the handicapped: bibliog/78n1391
Weiss/Access to the world/79n623

HANDICAPPED CHILDREN
Directory of AV training matls/75n699
Glassman/Utilizing resources in handicapped services: directory/75n687
Instructional matls for handicapped/Thorum/77n644

HANDICRAFTS
See Crafts

HANOVER COUNTY, VA
Bell/Our Quaker friends/77n454

HARDY, THOMAS
Leeming/Who's who in Hardy/76n1275
Purdy/Thomas Hardy/79n1241

HARKNESS COLLECTION
LC/Harkness Collection in LC/75n313

HARMONY
Schillinger/Encyclopedia of rhythms/78n900

HARPER'S MAGAZINE
Harper's lost reviews: notes by L. Hutton, J. K. Bangs . . . /77n1184

HARPSICHORD
Bedford/20th cent harpsichord music/75n1120
Boalch/Makers of harpsichord & clavichord/76n1012

HARRINGTON, JOHN PEABODY
Walsh/J. P. Harrington: Indian fieldnotes/77n734

HARRIS, ROY
Strassburg/Roy Harris/75n1159

HARSUSI LANGUAGE
Johnstone/Harsusi lexicon/79n1139

HARTFORD COUNTY, NC
Winborne/Colonial & state hist/77n480

HARVARD UNIVERSITY
Elliot/Descriptive gd to archives/77n634
Shipton/Sibley's Harvard grads, 1768-1771/76n667

HARVARD UNIVERSITY LIBRARY
Catalogue of bks & manuscripts, pt2, Italian, 16th cent bks/76n58
Bentinck-Smith/Building a great library/77n276
German lit Widener library shelflist/76n1295
Russian revolutionary lit collection: microfilm/77n416

HAWAII
Alcantara/Filipinos in Hawaii/78n388
Clay/Hawai'i garden tropical exotics/78n1488/Tropical shrubs/78n1489
Day/Books about Hawaii/78n313
Judd/Voyages to Hawaii before 1860/75n424
Matsuda/Japanese in Hawaii/77n445
Pukui/Place names in Hawaii/75n453

HAWAIIAN LANGUAGE
Andres/Dictionary/75n1280
Pukui/Pocket Hawaiian dict/76n1153

HAWAIIAN LITERATURE
Judd/Hawaiian lang imprints, 1822-99/79n389

HAWKES, JOHN
Hryciw/J. Hawkes: bibliog/78n1140
Scotto/Three contemp novelists: J. Hawkes, J. Heller, T. Pynchon/78n1124

HAWKS, HOWARD
Willis/Films of H. Hawks/76n1060

HAWTHORNE, NATHANIEL
Clark/Nathaniel Hawthorne/78n1141; 79n1220

HAYDN, FRANZ JOSEPH
Burke/Collector's Haydn/79n984

HAYNE, PAUL HAMILTON
De Bellis/S. Lanier, H. Timrod, & P. H. Hayne/79n1210

HAZARDOUS SUBSTANCES
Fire protection gd/75n1714
Fritsch/Household pollutants gd/79n1400
Saz/Dangerous properties of industrial matls/76n1650

HEAD
Lore/Atlas of head & neck surgery/75n1644

HEAD START
Directory of AV training matls/75n699
Directory of instruc'l matls/VanEtten/75n700
Glassman/Utilizing resources in handicapped services field/75n687

HEADS OF STATE
See also Dictators; Emperors; Kings and rulers; Presidents
Countries of world & leaders/76n461; 78n433
Egan/Kings, rulers, statesmen/78n332
Rulers & govs of the world, 1492-1929/ Spuler/78n434

HEALTH CARE
See Medical care

HEALTH CARE ORGANIZATIONS
See Medical care organizations

HEALTH CARE PERSONNEL
See Medical personnel

HEALTH CARE TRAINING
See Medical schools

HEALTH EDUCATION
See also Medicine, popular
Ardis/AV source directory/79n1467
Ash/Health: multimedia gd/77n1454
Brantz/Health sci AV resource list/79n1451
Completed research in health, PE, & recreation, v18/Thomas/78n606
Educators gd to free health, PE, & recreation matls/Horkheimer/76n672
Shugar/Educator's internat'l gd to free health AV teaching aids/79n687

HEALTH FACILITIES
Directory of adult day care centers/79n1506
Directory of architects for health facilities/ 78n791
US medical directory/Alperin/79n1471
US Natl Center for Health Stats/Health resource stats: manpower & facilities/78 n1419

HEALTH RESORTS
Wilkens/Secrets from super spas/77n1525

HEALTH SCIENCES
See Medical sciences

HEALTH SERVICES
See Medical care

HEALTH SERVICES ADMINISTRATION
Catalog of library of Amer Hospital Assn/ 77n1460

HEARING
Brown/Dictionary of speech & hearing, anatomy & physiology/76n1523; 77 n1470

HEARING DISORDERS
See also Deaf
Information Center for Hearing, Speech, etc/ Hearing, speech, & commication disorders: citations/75n1518
Nicolosi/Terminology of comm disorders/79 n1175

HEATING
Zurick/Air conditioning, heating & refrig dict/79n1549

HEAVY WATER
Vasaru/Deuterium & heavy water: bibliog/ 77n1341

HEBRAICA
Brisman/History & gd to Judaic bibliog/79 n458

HEBREW LANGUAGE
Ben Abba/Signet Hebrew-Engl dict/79n1140
Sivan/New Bantam-Megiddo Hebrew & Engl dict/78n1060

HEBREW LITERATURE
Hebrew printing & bibliog/78n38

HEBREW SCRIPTURES
Einspahr/Index to Brown, Driver & Briggs Hebrew lexicon/77n1042
Hebrew-Engl lexicon of the Bible/76n1100

HELICOPTERS
Brown/Helicopter directory/77n1619
Taylor/Helicopters of the world/78n1508

HELLER, JOSEPH
Scotto/Three contemp novelists: J. Hawkes, J. Heller, T. Pynchon/78n1124

HEMATOLOGY
Block/Text-atlas of hematology/77n1455

HEMINGWAY, ERNEST
Duggan/Fitzgerald-Hemingway annual/79 n1212
Hanneman/Suppl to E. Hemingway: bibliog/ 76n1239
Harmon/Understanding E. Hemingway: gd/ 78n1142
Wagner/E. Hemingway: ref gd/78n1143

HENRY COUNTY, VA
Hill/History/77n465

HERALDRY
Anson/Mottoes & badges of families, regiments, schools, societies, etc. British & foreign/77n482
Briggs/National heraldry of world/76n448
Burke/Genealogical & heraldic hist of commoners of Grt Brit & Ireland/78n393
Burke/General armory of Engl, Scotland, Ireland, & Wales/77n483
Child/Heraldic design/77n484
Clark/Introduction to heraldry/75n440
Dirsztay/Church furnishings/79n912
Filby/American & Brit genealogy & heraldry/ 77n449
Grant/Manual of heraldry/77n485
Johnson/Handbook of Amer coats of arms/ 75n441
Kelly/Irish family names, ... crests & mottoes/ 77n487

HERALDRY (cont'd)
Morant/General armory two/75n442
Pinches/Royal heraldry of Engl/75n443
Schnapper/American symbols/75n444
Smith/Flags through the ages & across the world/77n486
Von Volborth/Heraldry of the world/75n445
Wagner/Historic heraldry of Britain/76n450

HERBERT, GEORGE
Di Cesare/Concordance to writings of Herbert/78n1176

HERBS
Dugdale/Modern Amer herbal/79n1351
Gabriel/Herb identifier & hndbk/77n1348
Hylton/Rodale herb bk/75n1481
Keys/Chinese herbs/77n1505
Law/Concise herbal ency/75n1482
Loewenfeld/Complete bk of herbs & spices/75n1484
Miller/Shaker herbs/78n1298
Morton/Herbs & spices/78n1299
Muenscher/Garden spice & wild pot-herbs/79n1353
Rose/Herbal body bk/77n1524
Sanecki/Complete bk of herbs/75n1485
Sybil Leek's bk of herbs/75n1483

HEREDITY
Rosenfield/New environment-heredity controversy/75n793

HESSE, HERMANN
Mileck/H. Hesse: biog & bibliog/78n1190

HIEROGLYPHICS
Budge/Egyptian hieroglyphic dict/79n1133

HIGH FIDELITY
Records in review, annual/78n906

HIGHER EDUCATION
   See also Colleges and universities; Correspondence schools; Graduate schools; Grants-in-aid; Student aid; Students
Allen/Collective bargaining/75n639
Altbach/Comparative higher educ abroad: bibliog/77n573
Altbach/Higher educ in developing nations/76n573
Askew/Small college: hndbk/75n640
Chambers/Black higher educ in US/79n628
Directory of research grants/78n73
International ency of higher educ/79n638
Keeslar/Financial aids for higher educ/78n563
Quay/Research in higher educ: bibliog/78n545
World gd to higher educ/77n592; 79n668
Yearbook of higher educ/Greene/75n661

HIGHWAYS
Baker/Hndbk of highway eng'g/76n1662

HIGHWAYS (cont'd)
US Fed Highway Admin/Highway stats/78n1552

HIKING
   See also Backpacking
Amer Youth Hostels bike-hike bk/77n681
Bridge/America's backpacking bd/75n754
Hart/Walking softly in the wilderness/78n617
Reifsnyder/Foot-loose in the Swiss Alps/75n626
Rudner/Huts & hikes in Dolomites/75n628

HILLINGDON PROJECT
Totterdell/Effective library: report on Hillingdon Project on public lib effectiveness/77n215

HIMALAYA
Ohashi/Flora of eastern Himalaya/77n1355

HINDI LANGUAGE
Aggarwal/Bibliography of studies/79n1141
Platts/Dictionary of Urdū, classical Hindī, & English/78n1071

HINDUISM
Stutley/Harper's dict of Hinduism/78n983

HIRSHHORN MUSEUM
Rosenzweig/Thomas Eakins collection/78n787

HISPANIC LITERATURE
   See Latin American literature

HISTOLOGY
Di Fiore/New atlas of histology/79n1445
Motta/Microanatomy of cell & tissue surfaces/79n1336

HISTORIANS
Significant Amer historians & educators/Mandel/77n131

HISTORIC AMERICAN BUILDINGS SURVEY
Historic bldgs of Massachusetts/77n874

HISTORIC PRESERVATION
   See also Restoration of buildings
Kettler/Historic preservation law: bibliog/77n536
National Trust for Historic Preservation/Guide to historic preservation programs/78n353
   Supplement/78n352
   Historic preservation plans/78n344
Nylander/Fabrics for historic bldgs/78n862
Rath/Historic preservation: bibliog/77n381
Smith/Critical bibliog of bldg conservation/79n892
Tubesing/Architectural preservation in US/79n894
US Natl Park Service/Historic preservation grants-in-aid catalog/77n877

HISTORIC SITES
Laws/Guide to Natl Trust in Devon & Cornwall/79n616
Lord/American travelers' treasury/78n527
Swetnam/Guidebook to historic western PA/78n360
US Natl Park Service/
  Here was the revolution/Unrau/78n336
  Historic Amer eng'g record catalog/78n1499
  National register of historic places/77n387
  Presidents from Washington to Ford/78n337
  Signers of the Constitution/78n338

HISTORICAL MUSEUMS
Rath/Interpretation/79n400

HISTORICAL RESEARCH
Barzun/Modern researcher/78n322
Bindoff/Research in progress in Engl & hist in Brit, Ireland, Canada, etc/77n406
Doctoral dissertations in hist/77n360
McCoy/Researching & writing in hist/75n347
Moss/Oral hist prog manual/75n348
Sanderlin/Writing the hist paper/76n286
Thoyts/How to decipher & study old docs/76n287
Wilson/Research gd in hist/75n349

HISTORICAL SOCIETIES
McDonald/Directory of hist'l societies in the US & Canada/77n386; 79n413

HISTORIOGRAPHY
Birkos/Historiography, method, hist teaching: bibliog/76n284
Stephens/Historiography: bibliog/76n292

HISTORY
  See also individual countries; Chronology, historical; Local history; Military history; Oral history
Annual register/75n84
Brewster/Index to bk reviews in hist'l periodicals/76n303; 77n368; 79n405
CBS news almanac/Westerman/77n97
Facts on File five-yr index/77n500
Facts on File yrbk/78n84
Reader's Digest almanac/78n91
Statesman's yr-bk/75n87
Trotsky/News dict/77n498
What they said in . . . /77n96
World factbook/75n89
Year bk of world affairs/75n90
  ANCIENT
Avi-Yonah/Illustrated ency of classical world/77n364
Cambridge ancient hist:
  plates to vI & vII/79n396
  v2, pt2, Middle East & Aegean/Edwards/76n357

HISTORY (cont'd)
  ANCIENT (cont'd)
Classical world bibliog of Greek & Roman hist/79n402
Garber/Concise ency of ancient civilizations/79n404
Harvard Univ Library/Ancient hist/76n295
Hawkes/Atlas of early man/78n327
Kurtz/World gd to antiquities/76n299
McEvedy/Penguin atlas of ancient hist/77n357
  MEDIEVAL
Ferguson/Bibliography of Engl translations from medieval sources/75n350
Powell/Medieval studies/78n325
Storey/Chronology of medieval world/75n353
Wilkinson/High Middle Ages in Engl/79n435
  MODERN
Bayliss/Bibliographic gd to two world wars/78n329
Bloomberg/WWII: bibliog/76n289
Cronon/Second WW & atomic age/76n290
Enser/Subject bibliog of WWII/78n330
Mayer/Two world wars: MSS collections in UK/78n326
New Cambridge modern hist, v1: Renaissance/76n288
Palmer/Dictionary of mod hist/77n365
  WORLD
Atlas of discovery/Roberts/75n351
Barraclough/Times atlas of world hist/79n583
Day/History: hndbk/78n324
DeFord/Who was when?/77n363
Freeman-Grenville/Chronology of world hist/76n304
Grun/Timetables of hist/76n305
Kinder/Anchor atlas of world hist/76n297; 79n401
Langer/New illust'd ency of world hist/76n300
My first world hist atlas/77n358
Sanderson/Sea battles/76n301
Shepherd's hist'l atlas/75n352
Uden/Longman illust'd companion to world hist/77n356
Unstead's dict of history/77n367

HITLER, ADOLPH
Stachura/Weimar era & Hitler 1918-33/79n430

HOBBIES
  See specific hobbies: Collecting; Crafts, etc.

HOCKEY
Complete hndbk of pro hockey/Hollander/77n698
Fischlers' hockey ency/76n749

Subjects—287

HOCKEY (cont'd)
Gitler/Ice hockey A to Z/79n719
Hockey register/Spink/78n627
Hollander/Complete ency of hockey/76n750
Pro & amateur hockey gd/75n770
Ronberg/Hockey ency/75n771
Styer/Encyclopedia of hockey/75n772
Walker/Illustrated hockey dict for young people/78n628

HOFMANNSTHAL, HUGO VON
Sondrup/Konkordanz zu den Gedichten . . . / 79n1278

HOGARTH PRESS
Woolmer/Checklist 1917-38/77n1222

HOLIDAYS
Cordello/Celebrations/78n1020
Emmens/AV gd to Amer holidays/79n1086
Gregory/Anniversaries & holidays/76n1108
Hopkins/Do you know what day tomorrow is?/77n643
Oxbridge omnibus of holiday observances around the world/78n1021
Polette/Celebrating with bks/78n191

HOLLYWOOD
Ragan/Who's who in Hollywood 1900-76/78n965

HOLMES, SHERLOCK
See Sherlock Holmes

HOLOCAUST
Cargas/Holocaust/79n436
Roskies/Teaching holocaust to children/76n685
Szajkowski/Illustrated sourcebk on holocaust/79n438

HOME DECORATION
See Interior decoration

HOME HEALTH AGENCIES
Council of Home Health Agencies/Directory of . . . medicare providers/76n1534; 78n1404

HOME REPAIRS
See House maintenance

HOMER, WINSLOW
Davis/W. Homer: bibliog/77n863

HOMONYMS
Newhouse/Encyclopedia of homonyms/78n1033

HOMOSEXUALITY
See also Gay men; Lesbians
Bullough/Bibliog of homosexuality/78n650
Directory of homosexual organizations & pubs/76n1507; 78n651
Katz/Gay Amer hist/78n652
Parker/Homosexuality bibliog/78n653

HOMOSEXUALITY (cont'd)
Sanders/Gay source/79n741
Young/Male homosexual in lit: bibliog/77n1128

HONDURAS
Meyer/Historical dict/77n344

HONG KONG
Parker/American dissertations on foreign educ, vVI, China, Hong Kong, Far East/77n578

HOOKER, THOMAS
Gallagher/Early Puritan writers/77n1185

HOOVER, HERBERT
Tracey/H. Hoover, bibliog/78n448

HOPI INDIANS
Laird/Hopi bibliog/79n777

HOPKINS, GERALD MANLEY
Dunne/G. M. Hopkins: bibliog/77n1235

HORSE RACING
Ainslie's ency of thoroughbred handicapping/79n720
Drager/Most glorious crown/76n751

HORSEMANSHIP
Illustrated glossary of horse eqmt/77n1529
Johnson/International riding/75n773
Summerhays' ency for horsemen/77n1537

HORSES
Davidson/Horseman's veterinary advisor/75n1661
Edwards/Complete bk of horse/75n1680
Ensminger/Complete ency of horses/78n1463
Goodall/Horses of the world/75n1681
Green/Color of horses/76n725
McKibbin/Horse owner's hndbk/78n1464
Pady/Horses & horsemanship/75n1684
Price/Whole horse catalog/79n1525
Roberts/Horse world catalog/78n1465
Rossdale/Horse's health from A to Z/75n1663
Stratton/International horseman's dict/76n1566
Summerhays' ency for horsemen/Walker/77n1537

HORTICULTURE
See also Gardening
Bailey/Hortus third/78n1485

HOSPITAL LIBRARIES
Catalog of lib of Amer Hospital Assn/77n1460
Phinney/Librarian and patient/78n196

HOSPITAL LITERATURE
Dunlap/Hospital lit subj headings/78n229

HOSPITALS
See also Health facilities
American Hospital Assn gd to health care fld/78n1402
Cumulative index of hospital lit/Dunlap/78n1422
Directory of high-energy radiotherapy centres/78n1403
Selected bibliog for ambulatory health care computer applications/76n1519
Rothman/Bibliography of collective bargaining in hospitals/77n840

HOTELS
Hotel & travel index/75n584
Long/Castle hotels of Europe/79n618
Neuer/Inn book/75n612
Official hotel & resort gd/Rubin/75n588
Simpson/Country inns: European ed/77n568; 79n622
Who's who among innkeepers/75n901
World travel directory/Korsant/75n591

HOTTEN LIST
Hotten/Original lists of persons of quality/75n421

HOURS OF LABOR
Baum/Practical gd to flexible working hours/75n981

HOUSE CONSTRUCTION
Browne/Housebuilding bk/75n1763
Kern/Owner-built home/76n1640
Krieger/Homeowner's ency of house construction/79n1571
Schuler/Encyclopedia of home bldg & decoration/76n1642

HOUSE FURNISHINGS
Faulkner/Los Angeles home furnishing, decorating & accessory buying gd/75n1102
Grow/Old house catalogue/78n852
Hoffman/Fairchild's dict of home furnishings/75n1105
Kleeberg/Butterick fabric hndbk/76n875
Nylander/Fabrics for historic bldgs/78n862
Schuler/Homeowner's directory/79n1573

HOUSE MAGAZINES
Gebbie house magazine directory/76n24

HOUSE MAINTENANCE
Consumer Guide/Whole house catalog/78n1537
Fahy/Home remedies/76n1639
Liles/Good Housekeeping gd to fixing things/75n1794
NY Times gd to home repairs without a man/Gladstone/75n1793
Scharff/Complete bk of home remoding/76n1641
Schipf/Home repair & improvemt/75n1796
Schuler/5,000 ques answered abt maintaining, repairing your home/78n1535

HOUSE MAINTENANCE (cont'd)
Schuler/Homeowner's directory/79n1573
Schuler/Home renovation/75n1797
Singer/Dictionary of household hints/75n1798
Slater/Things your mother never taught you/75n1799
Tarr/Up-with-wholesome . . . household formulas/77n1550
Treves/Homeowner's compl gd/75n1800
Ubell/Recipes for home repair/75n1801
Waugh/Handyman's ency/78n1536
Zarchy/Modern woman's fix it yrself hndbk/75n1802

HOUSE PAINTING
Banov/Book of successful painting/76n1636
Wheeler/Interior painting, wallpapering, paneling/75n1106

HOUSE PLANTS
Baines/ABC of indoor plants/75n1698
Beckett/Illustrated ency of indoor plants/78n1487
Fitch/Complete bk of houseplants under lights/76n1585
Hay/Dictionary of house plants/75n1701
Herwig/Treasury of houseplants/77n1554
Kramer/How to identify & care for houseplants/76n1591
Kramer/Indoor trees/76n1592
Kramer/Pit n' pot grower's bk/76n1593
Kramer/Seasonal gd to indoor gardening/77n1556
McDonald/Color hndbk of house plants/77n1558
McDonald/World bk of house plants/76n1595
Menage/Growing exotic plants indoors/76n1596
Mott/Total bk of house plants/76n1598
Nicholls/Plant buyer's hndbk/78n1493
Poincelot/Gardening indoors with house plants/76n1600
Sunset Books/How to grow house plants/75n1703
Wickham/Indoor garden/78n1497

HOUSEHOLD APPLIANCES
Squeglia/All abt repairing major household appliances/76n1644

HOUSING
Cutler/Handbook of housing systems/75n1764
Harrison/Houses/75n1765
Paulus/Housing/75n1767
Statistical yrbk of HUD/77n829

HOVERCRAFT
Jane's surface skimmers/McLeavy/78n1547

HOWARD, ROBERT ERVIN
Lord/Last Celt/79n1218

Subjects—289

HOWELLS, WILLIAM DEAN
Carrington/Plots & characters in fiction of W. D. Howells/77n1205
Eichelberger/Published comment on Howells through 1920/77n1206

HUDSON, W. H.
Payne/W. H. Hudson: bibliog/78n1273

HUGHES, LANGSTON
Mandelik/Concordance to poetry/76n1240

HUMAN BIOLOGY
Rand McNally atlas of body & mind/77n1456

HUMAN BODY
See Body, human

HUMAN CHROMOSOMES
See Chromosomes

HUMAN ECOLOGY
Jones/Index of human ecology/75n1560
Zilly/Handbook of environmental civil eng'g/76n1619

HUMAN RIGHTS
Christiano/Human rights organizations/76n470
Ginger/Human rights organizations & periodicals/75n475; 78n431
Liber/Nonconformity & dissent in Ukrainian SSR/79n549

HUMAN SERVICES
Queens College/College progs for paraprofessionals/76n652

HUMANITARIANS
Significant Amer social reformers/Miekina/77n138

HUMANITIES
Allsworth/Soviet Asia/77n345
American humanities index/78n20
Bayerl/Interdisciplinary studies in the humanities/78n560
Bolte/Libraries & arts & humanities/79n146
Chicorel index to abstracting services: humanities & soc sciences/76n34
Hazfeld/Periodical indexes in soc sci & humanities/79n345
Guide to Indian periodical lit, v6, soc sci & humanities/76n35
Humanities: bibliog of dissertations accepted by Indian universities/77n323
Humanities index/76n36
Raben/Computer-assisted res in humanities/78n76
Rogers/Humanities/75n174
Stevens/Reference bks in soc sci & humanities/78n4

HUNGARIAN AMERICANS
Szeplaki/Hungarians in America/76n408

HUNGARY
Bakó/Guide to Hungarian studies/75n304
Horchler/Hungarian economic reforms/79n802
Hungarian hist & lit: classification schedule/76n274

HUNGER
Rechcigl/World food problem/76n847
Sobel/World food crisis/76n848
World food crisis: directory/Trzyna/78n1481

HUNTING
Alaska hunting gd/75n774; 76n753
Bauer/Hunting with camera/75n775
Carmichel/Modern rifle/76n755
Clotfelter/Hunting & fishing/75n721
Elman/Hunter's fld gd to game birds & animals of No Amer/75n776
Guns & ammo/75n777
Oberrecht/Great outdoors catalog/78n621
Peterson's hunting annual/75n778
Rice/Outdoor life gun data bk/76n758
Rue/Game birds of No Amer/75n779
Strung/Complete hunter's catalog/79n721

HUNTINGTON LIBRARY
Wright/Of books and men/78n265

HUTTON, LAURENCE
Harper's lost reviews/77n1184

HYDRAULICS
Brater/Handbook of hydraulics/77n1604
Schwicker/International dict of bldg construction/76n1618

HYDROFOILS
Jane's surface skimmers/McLeavy/78n1547

HYDROLOGY
Andriot/Guide to US gov maps: geologic & hydrologic/78n1355
Geraghty/Water atlas of US/75n1567
Giefer/Sources of info in water resources/77n1429
Giefer/Water pubs of state agencies, suppl/77n1428
Summers/Isotopes of water: bibliog/77n1430
US Environmental Data Serv/Bibliog of the urban mod of atmosphere & hydrologic environment/75n1529
WMO/International glossary of hydrology/76n1472
World catalogue of large floods/78n1358

HYMNS
See also Gospel music; Sacred songs
Spencer/Hymn & scripture selection gd/79n1063
Gordon/New gospel treasure select-a-song/77n955
Mason/Hymn-tunes of Lowell Mason/77n959

HYPERACTIVE CHILDREN
Archuleta/Hyperactive child/75n1645
Winchell/Hyperkinetic child/76n1490

ICELANDIC LITERATURE
Mitchell/Bibliography of Icelandic lit in translation/77n1266

IDAHO
Nelson/Idaho local hist/78n357
Rouyer/Economic, soc & voting characteristics/75n504

ILIAD
Willcock/Companion to Iliad/77n1265

ILLINOIS
Burks/Mayflies or Ephemeroptera/76n1439
Chronology & doc hndbk/79n423
Descriptive inventory of archives/79n406
Downs/Guide to IL lib resources/75n18
Frison/Stoneflies of IL/76n1440
Mohlenbrock/Guide to vascular flora/77n1354

ILLITERACY
Lyman/Literacy & nation's libraries/78n144

ILLUSTRATED BOOKS
Edison/Thoreau MacDonald: design & illustration/75n991
Gottlieb/Early children's bks & their illustration/77n70
Pollard/Fine books/75n65
Ray/Illustrator & bk in Engl 1790 to 1914/77n67

ILLUSTRATORS
Dykes/50 grt western illustrators: checklist/76n940
Hammelmann/Book illustrators in 18th cent England/77n66
Illustrators of children's bks/78n811
Kingman/Illustrators of children's bks/79n898

IMAGE INTERPRETERS
US Naval Air Systems Command/Image interpretation eqpmt catalog/75n971

IMPEACHMENTS
Grayson/Impeachmt congress/75n491
Impeachment & US Congress/75n492
US House Com on Judiciary/Impeachment, selected matls on procedure/75n499

IMPERIAL COLLEGE OF TROPICAL AGRICULTURE, TRINIDAD
Catalogue of Univ of West Indies/76n1555

IMPORTING
Directory of US importers/79n833

INCOME TAX
Clergy's fed income tax gd/75n982
Holzman/Take it off!/75n983

INCOME TAX (cont'd)
Kess/Practical gd to indiv income tax/75n985
Kess/Practical gd to tax planning/75n984
Sommerfeld/Dow Jones-Irwin gd to tax planning/75n986

INCUNABULA
Goff/Incunabula in Amer libraries/75n64
Pollard/Fine books/75n65

INDENTURED SERVANTS
Hargreaves-Mawdsley/Bristol & Amer: first settlers in colonies of No Amer/79n485

INDEPENDENT SCHOOLS
See Private schools

INDEXING
Borko/Indexing concepts & methods/79n330
Brown/Introduction to subj indexing . . .
 v1, Subject analysis/77n251
 v2, UDC & Chain/77n252
Buchanan/Glossary of indexing terms/77n170
Chicorel index to abstracting & indexing services/76n34
Davis/Information retrieval in chemistry/75n276
Gilbert/Picture indexing for local hist/75n224
Harrod/Indexers on indexing/79n331
Hoyle/Indexing terms for physical educ/79n674
Langridge/Classification & indexing in humanities/77n256
Marshall/On equal terms: thesaurus for non-sexist indexing/79n275
Perica/Newspaper indexing/76n191
Physics & astronomy classification/79n1334
PRECIS index system/78n222
Ramsden/Introduction to index lang construction/75n228
Soergel/Indexing langs & thesauri/76n194
Vickery/Classification & indexing in science/77n263

INDIA
Ali/Handbook of the birds of India & Pakistan, v10/77n1373
Gazetteer of India/76n261
Gidwani/Guide to ref matls on India/77n322
Guide to Indian periodical lit, v6/76n35
Indian books/75n12
Indian bks in print/75n10
Indian periodicals in print/75n40
Minister of Info/India: ref annual/76n262; 77n324
Kalia/Bibliography of bibliogs on India/76n5
Kaul/Early writings on India/77n325
Reference catalogue of Indian bks in print/75n11
Sharma/India & Indians/75n301

INDIA (cont'd)
ECONOMIC AND SOCIAL
CONDITIONS
Annotated bibliog on econ hist/79n797
Bose/Bibliography on urbanization/78n641
Chekki/Social system of modern India/76 n260
Dasgupta/Women on Indian scene/77n321
Desai/Survey of res in demography/77n756
Troisi/Santals: bibliog/77n746
HISTORY
Abidi/50 yrs of Indian hist'l writings/76 n359
Gustafson/Sources on Punjab hist/76n360
Kurian/Historical & cultural dict/77n326
Satyaprakash/Gandhiana/78n298
Satyaprakash/Karnataka/79n371
Scholberg/Bibliography of French in India/ 77n399
Sources for hist of British India in 17th cent/ Khan/76n362
POLITICS AND GOVERNMENT
Chandidas/India votes/75n518
Documents on India's foreign policy/76 n503
Fazal-e-Rab/J. P. movement & emergence of Janata Party/79n545
Ghosh/Indian political movemt 1919-71: bibliog/78n483
Kumar/Committees & commissions in India/ 78n484; 79n546
Rana/Writings on Indian constitution/75 n565

INDIAN LITERATURE
Karkala/Bibliography of Indo-Engl lit, 1800- 1966/77n1267
Lal/Annotated Mahabharata bibliog/75n1421
Naqvi/Indian response to lit in Engl/75n1422
Narang/Kalidas bibliog/77n1268

INDIAN OCEAN
US CIA/Indian Ocean atlas/78n519

INDIANA
Baker/Indiana place names/76n453
Bolin/Ohio Valley hist: bibliog/77n455
McPherson/Wild food plants/78n1312
Thompson/Indiana authors & their bks 1917- 66/76n354

INDIANS OF MIDDLE AMERICA
Breedlove/Guide to holdings of Stanford Univ/75n864
Handbook of Middle Amer Indians/77n749
McGlynn/Middle Amer anthropology/77n733

INDIANS OF NORTH AMERICA
See also Native Americans; California Indians; Plains Indians; languages, e.g., Menomi'ni, Salish; tribes, e.g., Apache, Diegueno, Hopi, Navaho, Ojibwa
Abler/Canadian Indian bibliog/75n863

INDIANS OF NORTH AMERICA (cont'd)
American Indian: bibliog/75n803
Encyclopedia of Indians/75n866
Ethnographic bibliog of No Amer/77n738
Helm/Indians of SubArctic: bibliog/77n741
North Amer Indians: diss index/78n383
Oppelt/SW pottery: bibliog/78n680
Ray/Indians of ME & Atlantic provinces: bibliog/78n681
Schneider/Crafts of No Amer Indians/75 n1037
Smith/Indians of US & Canada: bibliog/76 n414
Wolf/Indians of No & So Amer: bibliog/78 n682

INDIANS OF SOUTH AMERICA
Price/Guiana Maroons/78n677
Wolf/Indians of No & So Amer: bibliog/78 n682

INDIC LITERATURE
Banerji/Companion to middle Indo-Aryan lit/78n1192

INDIVIDUAL PSYCHOLOGY
Mosak/Bibliography for Adlerian psychology/ 76n1488

INDIVIDUALIZED INSTRUCTION
Wehmeyer/School librarian as educator/77 n229

INDO-ARYAN LITERATURE
Banerji/Companion to middle Indo-Aryan lit/78n1192

INDONESIA
Dalton/Indonesia handbk/79n372
Ricklefs/Indonesian manuscripts in Great Britain/79n69
Tairas/Indonesia: bibliog/77n327

INDONESIAN LANGUAGE
Echols/English-Indonesian dict/76n1150

INDOOR GARDENING
Herwig/Treasury of house-plants/77n1554
Kramer/Pit n' pot grower's bk/76n1593
Kramer/Seasonal gd to indoor gardening/77 n1556
McDonald/Color hndbk of house plants/77 n1558
Wickham/Indoor garden/78n1497

INDUSTRIAL CHEMISTRY
Reigel/Handbook of industrial chem/75n1452

INDUSTRIAL ENGINEERING
Becker/Plant mgr's hndbk/75n1805
Guthrie/Process plant estimating eval & control/75n1810
Juran/Quality control hndbk/75n1811
Kovalenko/English-Russian reliability & quality-control dict/78n1502

INDUSTRIAL ENGINEERING (cont'd)
Lewis/Facilities & plant eng'g hndbk/75n1812
Moffat/Plant engineer's hndbk of formulas, charts & tables/75n1813

INDUSTRIAL MICROBIOLOGY
Progress in industrial microbiology/Hockenhull/76n1365

INDUSTRIAL NOISE
Faulkner/Handbook of industrial noise control/77n1606

INDUSTRIAL POLLUTION
Sax/Industrial pollution/76n1463

INDUSTRIAL PROPERTY
Kase/Designs: gd to design protection/76n1648
Warden/Annual of industrial property law/76n519

INDUSTRIAL RELATIONS
Morris/Bibliography of industrial relations in railroad industry/76n905

INDUSTRIAL RESEARCH LABORATORIES
Industrial research laboratories/76n1323; 78n1218

INDUSTRIAL SAFETY
Fire protection gd on hazardous matls/75n1714
Industrial safety hndbk/Handley/78n1538
Saz/Dangerous properties of industrial matls/76n1650

INDUSTRIAL SOCIOLOGY
Dubin/Handbook of work, organization & society/77n792

INDUSTRIAL TOURS
US Travel Serv/USA plant visits/78n762

INDUSTRY AND MANUFACTURING
Arpan/Directory of foreign mfgrs in US/76n894
Belgium's 500 largest companies/76n895
Business people in the news/77n795
Catalogue of translator's lib of dept of trade & industry, vI, authors/77n766
Directory of CO mfgrs/77n824
Directory of TX mfgrs/78n755
Europe's 5000 largest companies/76n897
1500 largest companies in Finland/76n892
Government prod prime contractors directory/77n826
Harris Michigan mfgrs industrial directory/77n827
Heasley/Production fig bk for US cars/78n756
Holtje/National directory of mfgrs' reps/79n845
Marketing economics key plants/77n783

INDUSTRY AND MANUFACTURING (cont'd)
National referral serv for industry/76n899
Ohio mfgrs industrial directory/78n759
1000 largest companies in Denmark/76n889
1000 largest companies in Norway/76n890
1000 largest companies in Sweden/76n891
US foamed plastics markets & directory/78n760
US industrial outlook/79n848
US Travel Serv/USA plant visits/78n762
Who's who in finance & industry/75n903

INDUSTRY TRAINING PROGRAMS
Wasserman/Training & developmt organizations directory/79n814

INFANT DEATH
Archuleta/Sudden Infant Death Syndrome: bibliog/76n1512

INFANTRY WEAPONS
Foss/Infantry weapons of world/78n1568
Hogg/Encyclopedia of infantry weapons of WWII/78n1569
Jane's infantry weapons/Archer/78n1570

INFLATION
Sobel/Inflation & Nixon admin/75n495; 76n820
MacCafferty/Inflation in UK/78n702

INFORMATION CENTERS
Bundy/Alternatives to trad lib services/79n286
Turick/Community info serv in libraries/79n292

INFORMATION INDUSTRY ASSOCIATION
Information sources: directory/78n45

INFORMATION NETWORKS
Brown/Nonprint media info networking/78n247
Hall/On-line info retrieval/78n242
MacCafferty/User educ/78n235
Pratt/On-line age/77n293
US Dept of Commerce/Annotated bibliog on resource sharing computer networks/Woods/77n1586

INFORMATION RESOURCE MANAGER
Automatic data processing hndbk/Diebold Group/78n713

INFORMATION SCIENCE
See also Library science
Adams/Information for sci & tech/75n134
Advances in info systems sci/Tou/78n1520
Anderson/Universal bibliographic control/76n195
Annual review of info sci & tech/78n141; 79n171
Arnold/Management of info dept/79n249

Subjects—293

INFORMATION SCIENCE (cont'd)
Auger/Use of reports lit/76n1306
Basova/Publications on theoretical foundations of info sci/76n229
British sci'fic documentation services/78n1217
Clason/Elsevier's dict of lib sci/79n158
Coates/Broad System of Ordering/79n300
Continuing educ opportunities for lib, info, & media personnel/77n273
Davinson/Bibliographic control/76n197
Debons/Information science/75n277
Directory of continuing educ opportunities/78n256
Donohue/Understanding sci'fic lit/75n278
Encyclopedia of lib & info sci/76n129; 78n133; 79n159
EURIM II: European conf on application of res/78n267
FID publications: bibliog/77n166
Garfield/Essays of an info scientist/79n302
Hammer/Information age/77n155
Hershfield/Effecting change in lib educ/75n264
Index to users studies/76n124
Information mgmt in the '80s/79n303
Journal of Documentation index, v1-30/78n158
Kilgour/Library & info cumindex/78n147
Klempner/AV matls in support of info sci curricula/79n305
Kochen/Integrative mechanisms in lit growth/76n114
Kruzas/Encyclopedia of info systems & services/75n165
Kunz/Methods of analysis & evaluation of info needs/79n263
Lanzing/Library, documentation & archives serials/77n36
Library literature/78n148
LIST/Wasserman/76n125
MacCafferty/Library-info sci/78n129
MacCafferty/Annotated bibliog of automation in libraries & info sci/77n168
Montgomery/Document retrieval systems/76n234
Pratt/On-line age/77n293
Raffin/Marketing of info services/79n154
Rayward/Universe of information/77n258
Reynolds/Reader in lib & info services/76n235
Salton/Dynamic info & lib processing/77n295
Schultz/Thesaurus of info sci terminology/79n161
Sherrod/Information systems & networks/76n235
Slater/Assessing the need for short courses in lib-info work/78n353
Tou/Information systems, COINS IV/76n237
van Rijsbergen/Information retrieval/77n296

INFORMATION SCIENCE (cont'd)
Waldhart/Communication research in lib & info sci/76n127
Walker/Natural lang in info sci/79n337
Watson/On-line bibliog'ic services/79n267
Weiss/Many faces of info sci/79n157
Wersig/Terminology of documentation/77n172
Williams/Simulation activities in lib, communication & info sci/78n128
Wolfe/Economics of tech info systems/75n881

INFORMATION SCIENCE AS A PROFESSION
Minor/Alternative careers in info-lib services/79n324
Raffin/Information worker/78n127
Sullivan/Opportunities in lib & info sci/78n259

INFORMATION SCIENCE ASSOCIATIONS
Fang/International gd to lib, archival, & info sci associations/77n176

INFORMATION SERVICES
Arnold/Management of the info dept/79n249
Bidmead/Use of computers in libraries & info centres/77n287
Childers/Information-poor in Amer/76n199
Directory of libraries providing computer-based info serv in NY/79n163
Ein/Whole Washington hndbk/76n881
Harvey/Specialised info centres/77n237
Kochen/Information for the community/77n267
Kruzas/Encyclopedia of info systems & services/79n166
Martin/Library serv to disadvantaged/76n201
Proceedings of the info broker-free lance librarian: workshop/78n258
Raffin/Marketing of info services/79n154
Sohmer/Call for action: NY/76n884
Warken/Directory of fee-based info services/78n138

INFORMATION STORAGE AND RETRIEVAL SYSTEMS
See also Data bases; Library automation
ASIS/Proceedings: innovative developmts in info systems/75n272
Atherton/Librarians & online serv/79n299
Bidmead/Use of computers in libraries & info centres/77n287
Brophy/COBOL programming/77n288
Carter/Guide to ref sources in computer sciences/75n273
Davis/Illustrative computer programming for libraries/75n275
Davis/Information retrieval in chem/75n276

INFORMATION STORAGE AND
RETRIEVAL SYSTEMS (cont'd)
Directory of computerized data files/Natl
 Tech Info Serv/76n1625
Divilbliss/Economics of lib automation/78
 n241
Donohue/Understanding sci'fic lit/75n278
Gildenberg/Computer-output-microfilm
 systems/75n1770
Gilreath/CAIN online user's gd/77n255
Hall/On-line info retrieval/78n242
International directory of computer info
 system serv/75n1772
Kochen/Principles of info retrieval/75n279
Lancaster/Information retrieval on-line/75
 n280
Lancaster/Use of computers in lit searching/
 77n290
MacCafferty/User educ/78n235
Meadow/Analysis of info systems/75n281
Metcalf/Information retrieval, 1876-1976/77
 n291
Pratt/Information economics/77n292
Pratt/On-line age/77n293
Proceedings of clinic on lib applications of
 data processing/Lancaster/75n282
Salton/Dynamic info & library processing/
 77n295
Schneider/Survey of . . . computer-readable
 bibliog'ic data bases/75n283
Thesaurus of agric'l terms/77n1517
UNESCO: IBE educ thesaurus/77n587
US Dept HEW/Directory of fed agency educ
 data tapes/77n597
US Natl Aeronautics & Space Admin/NASA
 thesaurus/77n1563
van Rijsbergen/Information retrieval/77
 n296
Williams/Computer-readable bibliog'ic data
 bases/78n243

INFRARED SPECTROMETRY
Dolphin/Tabulation of infrared spectral data/
 79n1321

INIS
 See International Nuclear Information
 System

INLAND NAVIGATION
US Coast Guard/Light lists/78n1551

INSCRIPTIONS
Oikonomides/Abbreviations in Greek inscrip-
 tions/76n285

INSECTS
Bland/How to know the insects/79n1379
Chinery/Field gd to insects of Britain & No
 Europe/75n1516
Delfinado/Catalog of diptera of Oriental
 region . . . /78n1328

INSECTS (cont'd)
Dickens/World of moths/75n1517
Grzimek's animal life ency, v2/76n1404
Johnson/Insects that feed on trees & shrubs/
 77n1389
Tweedie/Atlas of insects/75n1518

INSIGNIA, MILITARY
Britton/US military shoulder patches/77
 n1629
May/Badges & insignia of British armed
 services/76n1678
Rosignoli/Army badges & insignia of WWII,
 book 1/77n1644/Book 2/77n1645

INSTITUTE FOR SEX RESEARCH,
INDIANA UNIVERSITY
Catalog of social & behavioral sci section/76
 n1493

INSTRUCTIONAL MATERIALS CENTERS
 See also School libraries; Learning
 resource centers
Blazek/Influencing students toward media
 center use/77n217
Chibnall/Organisation of media/77n152
College learning resources progs/78n163
Hug/Instructional design & media program/
 77n224
Merrill/Criteria for planning the college &
 univ learning resources center/78n166
Thomson/Learning resource centers in com-
 munity colleges/77n206

INSTRUCTIONAL MEDIA
Aubrey/Selected free matls for classroom
 teachers/77n647
AV market place/78n553
Blake/Great perpetual learning machine/77
 n648
Buteau/Nonprint matls on communication/
 77n1103
Carlson/Enrichment ideas/77n642
Catalog of US gov produced AV matls/76
 n668
Directory of AV training matls/75n699
Directory of selected instructional matls/
 VanEtten/75n700
Dunbar/Curriculum matls exhibited at
 ASCD annual conf/78n590
Dwyer/Guide for improving visualized instruc-
 tion/75n711
Educational marketer yellow pages/77n659
Educational media organizations directory/
 76n619
Educational media yrbk/Brown/75n656;
 76n599; 79n669
Educators gd to free tapes, scripts & tran-
 scriptions/Wittich/76n675
El-Hi textbooks in print/75n701; 76n677
Elementary teachers gd to free curriculum
 matls/Suttles/76n676

INSTRUCTIONAL MEDIA (cont'd)
Free & inexpensive learning matls/77n650
Guide to educ'l & learning aids/Meyer/78n594
Harris/Developmental tasks resource gd for elementary school children/77n651
Hart/Multi-media indexes, . . . /76n679
Hendershot/Programmed learning . . . bibliog/75n702
Index to instruc'l media catalogs/75n689
Media & young adult/78n190
Media review digest/Wall/78n585
National school market index/76n602
Norback/Educational market place/78n555
Ohliger/Media & adult learning: bibliog/77n577
Rufsvold/Guides to educ'l media/78n600
Selecting educ'l eqmt & matls/Deans/77n645
Schrank/Seed catalog/75n706
Shaffer/Sources of free teaching matls/77n655
Sive/Selecting instruc'l media/79n688
Spache/Good reading for poor readers/75n707
Superka/Values educ sourcebk/77n646
Suttles/Elementary teachers gd to free curriculum matls/79n689
Tom Swift & his electric Engl teacher/75n708
US Dept HEW/Aids to media selection/77n657
Walker/Teaching media skills/78n188

INSTRUCTIONAL TECHNOLOGY
Burlingame/Library & media/79n251
Cantwell/Instructional tech/75n698
Dodge/AV resources for teaching instruc'l tech/79n680

INSTRUMENTAL MUSIC
Carnovale/20th cent music for trumpet & orchestra: bibliog/76n1013
Goodman/Instrumental music gd/78n891
Selfridge-Field/Venetian instrumental music from Gabrieli to Vivaldi/76n984

INSTRUMENTATION (engineering)
See Automatic control

INSURANCE
Casey/Life insur desk bk/76n901
Cockerell/British insur business/79n849
Davids/Dictionary of insur/79n850
Denenberg/Shopper's gdbk to life insur, health insur/75n945
Fordney/Insurance hndbk for medical office/78n1410
Gregg/Life & health insur hndbk/75n972
Hoehn/Union list of Sanborn fire insur maps (Alabama to Missouri)/78n764
Lloyd's calendar/76n902

INSURANCE (cont'd)
Nelli/Bibliography of insur hist/79n851
List of worthwhile life & health insur bks/77n833
Singer/Medical risks/78n1416

INTEGRATED CIRCUITS
See Electronic circuits

INTELLIGENCE SERVICE
See also Espionage; Spies
Blackstock/Intelligence, espionage, . . . & covert operations/79n501
DeVore/Spies & all that/79n502
National basic intelligence factbk/79n508

INTELLIGENCE TESTS
Buros/Intelligence tests/76n564

INTERIOR DECORATION
See also House furnishings
Banov/Book of successful painting/76n1636
Carleton Varney decorates from A to Z/79n942
Faulkner/Los Angeles home furnishings, decorating & accessory buying gd/75n1102
Grow/Old house catalogue/78n852
Hatje/1601 decorating ideas for modern living/75n1104
Hoffman/Fairchild's dict of home furnishings/75n1105
Kleeberg/Butterick home decorating hndbk/77n941
Schuler/Homeowner's directory/79n1573
Schuler/Encyclopedia of home bldg & decoration/76n1642
Studio dict of design & decoration/75n1023
Wheeler/Interior painting, wallpapering, & paneling/75n1106
Wilson/First compl home decorating catalogue/77n942

INTERLIBRARY LOANS
ARL/Access to periodical resources/75n230
ARL/Methods of financing interlib loan services/75n231
ARL/System for interlib communications/75n232
Thomson/Interlibrary loan policies/76n202

INTERNAL MEDICINE
Annual review of medicine/Creger/76n1527
Hart/French's index of differential diagnosis/75n1630
Krupp/Current medical diagnosis & treatmt/75n1609

INTERNATIONAL AGENCIES
See also individual names of agencies, e.g., European Communities; Hague Peace Conference; League of Nations; United Nations

INTERNATIONAL AGENCIES (cont'd)
Atherton/International organizations/78n428
Documents of internat'l organizations/78n98
Human rights organizations & periodicals/78n431
IFLA/Sources, organization of internat'l documentation: UN & intergovernmental organizations/75n259
International bibliog, info, documentation/79n118
Science & gov report internat'l almanac/Greenberg/78n435

INTERNATIONAL AGREEMENTS
Vambery/Cumulative list of treaties & internat'l agreements, UN, v2/79n560

INTERNATIONAL CONFERENCES
Glossary of conf terms: Engl., Fr, Arabic/Unesco/76n1138

INTERNATIONAL EDUCATION
Altbach/Comparative higher educ abroad: bibliog/77n573
Directory of European Council on Internat'l schools/76n611
Handbook on internat'l study/77n589; 78n574
Parker/American dissertations on foreign education . . .
  v6/77n578
  v7/77n579
  v9/78n544
Tysse/International educ: Amer experience/75n649; 78n549
von Klemperer/International educ/75n666

INTERNATIONAL FEDERATION FOR DOCUMENTATION
FID publications: 80 yr bibliog/77n166
FID yearbk/76n73

INTERNATIONAL FEDERATION OF LIBRARY ASSOCIATIONS
IFLA annual/79n315
Koops/IFLA's first fifty yrs/79n316

INTERNATIONAL LABOUR OFFICE
Pease/Consolidated index to ILO legislative series/78n772
Thesaurus of descriptors used for info processing in ILO library/77n171

INTERNATIONAL LAW
Delupis/Bibliography of internat'l law/77n535
Gamboa/Dictionary of internat'l law & diplomacy/75n554
International law of pollution/Barros/75n1535

INTERNATIONAL LIBRARY CONFERENCE, KINGSTON, JAMAICA
Ingram/Libraries & challenge of change/76n213

INTERNATIONAL MIGRATION REVIEW
Cumulative index/79n794

INTERNATIONAL NUCLEAR INFORMATION SYSTEM
INIS: authority list for corp entries/79n273
INIS: descriptive cataloguing samples/79n274

INTERNATIONAL ORGANIZATIONS
See International agencies

INTERNATIONAL READING ASSOCIATION
IRA directory/75n670

INTERNATIONAL RELATIONS
Amstutz/Economics & foreign policy/79n796
Cortada/Bibliographic gd to Spanish diplomatic hist 1460-1977/79n551
Donovan/US & Soviet policy in Middle East/75n532
Gordon/Atlantic alliance/79n552
Groom/International relations theory/79n553
Index to correspondence of (British) Foreign Office/79n557; 79n558
Kanet/Soviet & East European foreign policy/75n534
Kreslins/Foreign affairs bibliog/77n528
LaBarr/Study of internat'l politics/77n529
McLane/Soviet-Asian relations/75n537
McLane/Soviet Middle-East relations/75n538
Middle East: US policy, Israel, oil & Arabs/75n539
Morley/Japan's foreign policy, 1868-1941/75n540
Parker/SALT II/75n541
Pfaltzgraff/Study of internat'l relations/78n487
Schulz/International & regional politics in Middle East & No Africa/78n488
US CIA/National basic intelligence factbk/78n274
Wright/Essay collections in internat'l relations/78n490
Yearbook of UN/79n514
Year bk of world affairs/Keeton/76n507; 79n513

INTERNATIONAL STANDARD BIBLIOGRAPHIC DESCRIPTION
Sayre/Illustrated gd to ISBD M/77n259

INTERNATIONAL STANDARD BOOK NUMBER
International ISBN publishers' index/79n54

INTERNATIONAL TRADE
Directory of US importers/79n833
Exporters directory-US buying gd/79n834
FAO trade yrbk/79n835

Subjects—297

INTERNATIONAL TRADE (cont'd)
Haiek/Mideast business gd/79n818

INTERNATIONAL WOMEN'S YEAR
World conf documents index/78n672

INTERNS (public service)
Directory of public serv internships/78n562
Mitchell/Stopout! Working ways to learn/79n643

INTERORGANIZATIONAL STUDIES
Bell/Annotated bibliog/78n640

INTERPERSONAL RELATIONS
Pfeiffer/Reference gd to handbks & annuals/78n1372

INVENTIONS
Carter/Dictionary of inventions & discoveries/77n1288
De Bono/Eureka! Hist of inventions/76n1307
Dummer/Electronic inventions 1745-1976/78n1530
Encyclopedia of how it works/Clarke/78n1501
How it works/78n1208

INVENTORS
Significant Amer inventors/Quinn/77n133

INVERTEBRATES
Grzimek's animal life ency, v1/76n1403
Kozloff/Keys to marine invertebrates of Puget Sound/76n1412

INVESTMENTS
Balachandran/Guide to trade & securities statistics/78n727
Brealey/Bibliography of finance & investmt/75n955
Childs/Encyclopedia of long-term financing & capital mgmt/77n821
Corporate profiles/77n798
Directory of companies required to file . . . with SEC/79n832
Durst/Collector-investor gdbk & inventory/78n831
Franchise annual/79n829
Franchise opportunities hndbk/79n830
Gould/Dow Jones-Irwin gd to commodities trading/75n914
Handbook of wealth mgmt/Barnes/78n729
Hansen/Guide to buying or selling a business/76n866
Hardy/Dun & Bradstreet's gd to your investments/75n915; 76n855
Investment companies/76n857
Jonnard/Caribbean investmt hndbk/75n916
Levine/Financial analyst's hndbk/76n887
Moore/Dictionary of business, finance, & investment/76n830; 77n777
Mutual funds almanac/78n730
Noddings/Dow Jones-Irwin gd to convertible securities/75n917

INVESTMENTS (cont'd)
Persons/Investor's ency of gold, silver & precious metals/76n860
Reidy/Guide to world commodity markets/79n831
Roalman/Investor relations hndbk/75n918
Rubel/Guide to venture capital sources/78n753
Rubel/Guide to venture capital sources/75n957
Wiesenberger/Investment companies/77n805
William Rickenbacker's savings & investmt guide/77n803

IONS
Anderson/Bibliography & index experimental range & stopping power data, v2/79n1329

IOWA
Harris/Guide to manuscripts/75n380

IRAN
Allsworth/Soviet Asia: bibliog/77n345
Behn/Kurds in Iran/78n284

IRELAND
Abse/Art galleries of Brit & Ireland/77n868
Allison/Titles of Engl (& of foreign bks printed in England): . . . author's name, pseudonym or initials, v1, 1475-1640/77n333
Black/Your Irish ancestors/75n435
Burke/Burke's Irish family records/78n417
Burke/General armory of Engl, Scotland, Ireland & Wales/77n483
Edwards/Atlas of Irish hist/75n396
Egon Ronay's Lucas gd/79n613
Elton/Annual bibliog of Brit & Irish hist/77n404; 79n431
Hajducki/Railway atlas of Ireland/76n1672
Hepple/Bibliography of lit on Brit & Irish labour law/76n904
Kelly/Irish family names/77n487
Short-title catalogue of bks printed in Engl, Scotland, & Ireland & Engl bks printed abroad 1475-1640, v2/77n27
Tomkinson/Select bibliog of principal modern presses . . . in Grt Brit & Ireland/77n56
Treasures of Brit & Ireland/78n534
Who's who, what's what & where in Ireland/75n133

IRISH LITERATURE
Finneran/Anglo-Irish lit/78n1193
Harmon/Select bibliog study of Anglo-Irish lit/79n1280
Kersnowski/Bibliography of modern Irish & Anglo-Irish lit/77n1269
McKenna/Irish lit, 1800-1975/79n1281

IRON ORE
Earney/Researchers' gd/75n569

IRREGULAR SERIALS AND ANNUALS
Bowker serials bibliog suppl/77n33

IRVING, WASHINGTON
Myers/Worlds of W. Irving, 1783-1859/76n1241
Springer/W. Irving: ref gd/77n1208

ISIS
ISIS cum bibliog/77n1283

ISLAM
Abdulrazak/Arabic hist'l writing/78n366
al-Qazzaz/Women in Middle East & No Africa/78n279
Arab islamic bibliog/Grimwood-Jones/78n278
Geddes/Analytical gd to bibliographies on Arabian Peninsula/75n291
Geddes/Analytical gd to bibliographies on Islam, Muhammad, & the Qur'an/75n290
Littlefield/Islamic Near East & No Africa/78n281
Martin/No Amer collections of Islamic manuscripts/79n382
Ofori/Islam in Africa south of Sahara/79n1051
Pearson/Index Islamicus/75n345; 77n303; 79n383
Poonawala/Biobibliog of Isma'ili lit/79n1052
Wismer/Islamic Jesus: bibliog/78n980
Zoghby/Islam in Sub-Saharan Africa/79n1055

ISMA'ILI LITERATURE
Poonawala/Biobibliography/79n1052

ISRAEL
DeVore/Arab-Israeli conflict: bibliog/77n417
Litvinoff/Israel, 2500 BC-1972/75n328
Sobel/Israel & Arabs/75n525

ISRAELI-ARAB CONFLICT
See Arab-Israeli conflict

ITALIAN AMERICANS
Cordasco/Italian Americans/79n456
Cordasco/Italian-American experience/76n409
Cordasco/Italian community & its language in US/76n410
Diodati/Writings on Italian-Americans/76n411

ITALIAN ART
Venturi/Storia dell'arte italiana: index/77n871

ITALIAN LANGUAGE
Berberi/Cortina-Grosset basic Italian dict/77n1092
Bocchetta/Follett vest-pocket Italian dict/79n1142
Hamlyn Italian dict/78n1061

ITALIAN LANGUAGE (cont'd)
Ragazzini/English-Italian, Ital-Engl dict/75n1272
Reynolds/Concise Cambridge Italian dict/76n1154

ITALIAN LITERATURE
Alfonsi/Annotated bibliog of Moravia criticism/77n1270
Italian hist & lit/76n275
Catalog of Petrarch Collection in Cornell Univ Library/76n1298
Rotunda/Motif-index of Italian novella in prose/75n1423

ITALY
Brody/Music gd to Italy/79n956
Catalogo dei libri in commercio/77n25; 78n7
Dogo/Treasures of Italy/78n531
Italian hist & literature/76n275
Kane/Italy A to Z/78n532
Rudner/Huts & hikes in Dolomites/75n628

JACK THE RIPPER
Kelly/Jack the Ripper/75n828

JAMAICA
Sangster/Jamaica/75n621

JAMES, HENRY
Leeming/Who's who in H. James/77n1207
Ricks/H. James: bibliog of secondary works/76n1242
Stafford/Name, title & place index to writings of H. James/76n1243

JAMES, WILLIAM
Skrupskelis/W. James: ref gd/78n1004

JAPAN
Atlas of Japan/75n573
Introductory bibliog for Japanese studies/76n263
Jentschura/Warships of Imperial Japanese navy, 1869-1945/79n1602
Lu/Sources of Japanese hist/75n392
Morley/Japan's foreign policy, 1868-1941/75n540
Nippon:charted survey of Japan/77n328
Shulman/Doctoral dissertations on Japan & Korea/77n329
Stevens/Japanese & US research libraries at the turning point/78n250
Ward/Allied occupation of Japan/75n544
Welch/Toshokan: libraries in Japanese society/77n272

JAPANESE AMERICANS
Herman/Japanese in America/75n818
Ichioka/Buried past: bibliog/75n819
Matsuda/Japanese in Hawaii: bibliog/77n445

JAPANESE ART
Roberts/Dictionary of Japanese artists/78 n825
Ysuda/Handbook of Japanese art/78n797

JAPANESE DRAMA
Pronko/Guide to Japanese drama/75n1178

JAPANESE LANGUAGE
All-romanized Engl-Japanese dict/75n1273
Rose-Innes/Beginners' dict of Chinese-Japanese characters/78n1052

JAPANESE LITERATURE
Hisamatsu/Biographical dict of Japanese lit/77n1271

JAPANESE POETRY
Rimer/Guide to Japanese poetry/77n1272

JAVANESE LANGUAGE
Horne/Javanese-Engl dict/75n1283

JAYAPRAKASH NARAYAN MOVEMENT
Fazal-e-Rab/J. P. movement & emergence of Janata Party/79n545

JAZZ MUSIC
Case/Illustrated ency of jazz/79n996
Feather/Encyclopedia of jazz in '70s/78n915
Gitler/Jazz masters of '40s/75n1162
Gold/Jazz talk/76n1025
Hadlock/Jazz masters of '20s/75n1163
Kinkle/Complete ency of popular music & jazz 1900-50/75n1171
Meeker/Jazz in movies: musicians 1917-77/78n919
Rust/Jazz records 1897-1942/79n1000
Simosko/Eric Dolphy/75n1164

JEFFERSON, THOMAS
Index to Jefferson papers/78n441

JERUSALEM
Bahat/Historical atlas of Jerusalem/76n356
Gilbert/Jerusalem hist atlas/79n440

JESUITS
Bangert/Bibliographical essay on hist of . . . /77n1021

JESUS CHRIST
Watlington/Christ our Lord/79n1045

JEWETT, CHARLES COFFIN
Harris/Age of Jewett/76n209

JEWISH LITERATURE
See Hebraica; Judaica

JEWS
American Jewish yr bk/75n321; 76n378
Atid bibliog/79n457
Bibliographical essays in medieval Jewish studies/77n1022
Brickman/Jewish community in Amer/78 n389

JEWS (cont'd)
Cohen/Jewish organizations: worldwide/76 n379
Comay/Who's who in Jewish hist after the Old Testament/75n397
Epper/International bibliog of Jewish affairs/77n297
Feingold/College gd for Jewish youth/79 n459
Fox/Jewish films in US/77n1009
Gilbert/Jewish hist atlas/78n371
Goodman/Aspects of Jewish life/76n381
Gross/1001 ques & answers abt Judaism/79n1062
Jewish bk annual/76n382
Kaganoff/Dictionary of Jewish names/78n423
Marcus/Index to pict collection of Amer Jewish Archives/79n460
Mason/Directory of Jewish archival institutions/76n383
New std Jewish ency/Wigoder/78n285
Postal/American Jewish landmarks/78n528; 79n609
Robinson/Guide to Jewish hist under Nazi impact/75n398
Rockland/Jewish yellow pages/77n820
Roskies/Teaching holocaust to children/76 n685
Rottenberg/Finding our fathers: genealogy/78n408
Sable/Latin Amer Jewry/79n461
Singerman/Jewish & Hebrew onomastics/78 n425
Singerman/Jews in Spain & Portugal/76n384
Steel/Sources for Roman Catholic & Jewish genealogy/78n421
Strassfeld/Second Jewish catalog/78n390
Wigoder/Encyclopedic dict of Judaica/75 n320

JIRAK, KAREL BOLESLAV
Tischler/K. B. Jirák: catalog of his works/76n1011

JOB TRAINING
See Occupational training

JOB VACANCIES
Salmon/Job hunter's gd/79n864
Sprague/Finding a job: for the middle-aged & retired/79n865
Summer employment directory of US/O'Brien/79n867
Yeomans/Jobs/78n778

JOBS
See Occupations

JOHN SIMON GUGGENHEIM MEMORIAL FOUNDATION
Directory of fellows/77n78

JOHNSON, EDWARD
Gallagher/Early Puritan writers/77n1185

JOHNSON, LYNDON B.
Cumulated indexes to public papers of L. B. Johnson/78n418

JOHNSON, SAMUEL
McGuffie/S. Johnson in Brit press, 1749-84/77n1236

JONES, DAVID
Rees/David Jones/79n1242

JONES, JAMES
Hopkins/J. Jones: checklist/76n1244

JONSON, BEN
Bates/Concordance to poems of B. Jonson/79n1243
Brock/Ben Jonson/75n1387
Chalfant/Ben Jonson's London/79n1244
Di Cesare/Concordance to poems of Ben Jonson/79n1245

JOURNAL OF DOCUMENTATION
Index to vols 1-30/78n158

JOURNAL OF INDIAN HISTORY
Abidi/Fifty yrs of Indian hist'l writings: index/76n359

JOURNAL OF LIBRARY HISTORY
Davis/Index ... 1966-76/79n190

JOURNAL OF THE AMERICAN STATISTICAL ASSOCIATION
Index to vols 61-72, 1966-77/78n694

JOURNALISM
Abbreviations in African press/75n1297
Alternatives: gd to newspapers/Akeroyd/77n104
Anderson/Research gd in journalism/75n1292
Angione/Associated Press stylebk & libel manual/79n127
Brigham/History & bibliog of Amer newspapers, 1690-1820/77n1110
Conlin/American radical press, 1880-1960/75n1293
Directory of college student press in Amer/75n1299
Gardner/Press of Latin Amer/75n1294
Gibbney/Labor in print: gd to the ... labor press in Australia/76n903
Kato/Japanese research on mass communication/75n1295
McLaren/Ontario ethno-cultural newspapers, 1835-1972/75n1300
Meyer/Guide to Long Island news media/75n1301
Nordland/Names & numbers: journalist's gd/79n1164
Richstad/Mass communication & journalism in Pacific Islands/79n1160
Richstad/Pacific Islands press/75n1303
Webb/Washington Post deskbk on style/79n133

JOURNALISM (cont'd)
Weiner/News bureaus in US/75n1304
White/Editing by design/75n1298
Wynar/Encyclopedic directory of ethnic newspapers & periodicals in US/77n430

JOURNALISTS
Kermani/John Ashbery: bibliog/77n864
McCoy/Theodore Schroeder/75n1296
Professional directory of writers/75n1302
Who was who in journalism/79n1170
Working press of nation/75n1305

JOYCE, JAMES
Gifford/Notes for Joyce/75n1388
Glasheen/Third census of Finnegans Wake/78n1177
Hart/Concordance to Finnegans Wake/76n1276
O Hehir/Classical lexicon for Finnegans Wake/78n1178

JUDAICA
See also Hebraica; Jews; Judaism
American Jewish yrbk/75n321; 76n378
Bibliographical essays in medieval Jewish studies/77n1022
Brisman/History & gd to Judaic bibliog/79n458
Epper/International bibliog of Jewish affairs/77n297
Goodman/Aspects of Jewish life/76n381
Grossfeld/Bibliography of Targum lit/79n1049
Jewish book annual/76n382; 75n323
Wigoder/Ency dict of Judaica/75n320

JUDAISM
Gross/1001 ques & answers abt Judaism/79n1062

JUDGES
See also Courts
Chase/Biographical dict of fed judiciary/77n541
Reincke/American bench/79n570
US court directory/79n529

JUGS
Paton/Jugs/78n872

JULIUS CAESAR (play)
Velz/Tragedy of Julius Caesar/79n1253

JUNG, CARL GUSTAV
Rothgeb/Abstracts of collected works/79n1431
Vincie/C. G. Jung & analytical psychology/78n1365

JUNIOR COLLEGES
See Community colleges

JUSTICE, ADMINISTRATION OF
See Law enforcement
See also Courts; Crime and criminals; Criminal justice

JUVENILE DELINQUENCY
Crime & juvenile delinquency/79n574
Index to abstracts on crime & juvenile delinquency/79n576
National directory of runaway programs/78n660

JUVENILE RIGHTS
von Pfeil/Juvenile rights since 1967/76n510

KAFKA, FRANZ
Flores/Kafka bibliog/78n1189

KALAMAZOO COUNTY, MI
Chapman/Directory of community resources/75n512/Suppl/75n513

KALIDAS
Narang/Kalidas bibliog/77n1268

KANSAS
Robertson/Kansas territorial settlers of 1860 . . . /77n475

KASHMIR
Gazetteer of Kashmir & Ladak/75n332

KENNEDY, JOHN F.
Cumulated indexes to papers of . . . : J. F. Kennedy/79n417
Newcomb/J. F. Kennedy: bibliog/78n446

KENNELS
McClean/McClean gd to kennels/75n1683

KENTUCKY
Barbour/Mammals of KY/75n1519
Bolin/Ohio Valley hist: bibliog/77n455
Chronology & documentary hndbk/79n424
Clift/Kentucky marriages, 1797-1865/75n411
Green/Historic families/76n433
Karan/Atlas/78n520

KENYA
Barlow/English-Kikuyu dict/77n1093
Howell/East African community/78n290
Killick/Economics of East Africa/77n770

KHMER LANGUAGE
Headley/Cambodian-Engl dict/79n1129
Huffman/English-Khmer dict/79n1143
Jacob/Concise Cambodian-Engl dict/75n1284

KIKUYU LANGUAGE
Barlow/English-Kikuyu dict/77n1093

KING, CHARLES BIRD
Cosentino/Paintings of C. B. King (1785-1862)/78n815

KING, MARTIN LUTHER, JR.
Fisher/Free at last: bibliog/78n444

KINGS AND RULERS
See also Dictators; Emperors; Heads of state
Egan/Kings, rulers & statesmen/78n332
McNaughton/Book of kings/76n446
Rowland-Entwistle/Famous kings & emperors/78n333
Spuler/Rulers & gov of world, v2/78n434/v3/79n512

KIPLING, RUDYARD
Knowles/Kipling primer/75n1389

KITCHEN EQUIPMENT
Arkin/Kitchen wisdom/78n1467
Beard/Cooks' catalogue/76n1568
Knees/Butterick kitchen eqpmt hndbk/78n1474
Wilkinson/Complete bk of cooking eqpmt/76n1580
Wilson/Complete food catalogue/78n1480

KITCHEN REMODELING
How to remodel your kitchen/76n1637

KNITTING
Halevy/Knitting & crocheting pattern index/78n878
Mariano/Encyclopedia of knitting & crochet stitch patterns/78n879

KNIVES
Ehrhardt/Encyclopedia of old pocket knives/75n1092
Latham/Knives & knifemakers/75n1093
Strung/Encyclopedia of knives/77n894

KNOWLEDGE, CLASSIFICATION OF
Batty/Knowledge & its organization/77n150
Kemp/Nature of knowledge/77n159

KORAN
Penrice/Dictionary & glossary/78n982

KOREA
Butler/Films for Korean studies/79n373
Shulman/Doctoral dissertations on Japan & Korea/77n329

KOREAN AMERICANS
Kim/Koreans in America/75n821

KOSSUTH, LOUIS
Szeplaki/L. Kossuth "The Nation's Guest": bibliog/77n382

KRESS LIBRARY OF BUSINESS AND ECONOMICS, HARVARD UNIVERSITY
Goldsmiths'-Kress Library of Econ Lit/77n768

KURDISTAN
Behn/Kurds in Iran/78n284

KUSAIEAN LANGUAGE
Lee/Kusaiean-English dict/77n1094

LA FONTAINE, JEAN DE
Tyler/Concordance to fables & tales/75n1418

LABOR
Baum/Practical gd to flexible working hrs/75n981
Baer/Labor arbitration gd/75n973
Bergman/Handbook of manpower stats for So Dakota/75n974
Bibliography on . . . humanisation of work/79n854
Biographical dict of Amer labor leaders/Fink/75n975
Business people in the news: industry, finance, & labor/77n795
Dwyer/Labor educ in US: bibliog/78n765
Fodell/Cesar Chavez & UFW/75n976
Harrison/Warwick gd to Brit labour periodicals 1790-1970/78n768
Hepple/Bibliography of lit on Brit & Irish labour law/76n904
Pease/Consolidated index to ILO legislative series (1919-70)/78n772
Pflug/Guide to archives of labor hist/75n979
Register of labor organizations/79n863
US Bureau of Labor Statistics
    Handbook of methods for surveys/78n691
    Handbook of labor stats/77n843
    Monthly Labor Review: index/78n776
    Productivity: bibliog/78n777
US Dept of Labor/Library catalog/76n907
Year bk of labour stats/77n848

LABOR ECONOMICS
Azevedo/Labor economics/79n853

LABOR UNIONS
    See Trade unions

LABORATORY ANIMALS
Andrla/Abstracts of alternatives to lab animals/76n1369

LABORATORY TESTS
French/Guide to diagnostic procedures/76n1529

LABOUR PARTY
Bellamy/Dictionary of labour biog/79n547

LADAK
Gazetteer of Kashmir & Ladak/75n332

LAFAYETTE, MARQUIS DE
Gottschalk/Lafayette: gd to letters, . . . /76n317

LAGOONS
Middlebrooks/Lagoon info source bk/79n1580

LAMBETH PALACE LIBRARY (GREAT BRITAIN)
Barber/Index to papers of Frederick Temple/77n1041
Bill/Catalogue of manuscripts/77n1023
Sayers/Calendar of papers of Charles Thomas Longley/77n1033

LANCASTER COUNTY, PA
Harris/Biographical hist/75n420

LAND GRANTS
Kaylor/Abstracts of land grant surveys of . . . Virginia, 1761-91/77n467
Nugent/Cavaliers & pioneers/79n491

LAND POLLUTION
Environmental engineers' hndbk, v3/76n1460

LAND REFORM
Land Tenure Center/Land tenure & agrarian reform in Africa & Near East/77n1514

LAND SETTLEMENT
Bibliography of land settlement/79n787
International Inst for Environment & Development/Human settlements: bibliog/77n730/Reports/77n731
Yalan/Design of agricultural settlements/77n732

LAND TENURE
Land Tenure Center/Land tenure & agrarian reform in Africa & Near East/77n1514
Sutton/Indian land tenure/76n806

LAND USE
Land use planning abstracts/76n1462; 79n1404
Paylore/Arid lands research institutions/79n1405

LANDLORD AND TENANT
Maryland rent rolls: Baltimore/77n469
Rejnis/Everything tenants need to know . . . /75n933

LANGUAGE ARTS
Bibliography of lang arts matls for native No Americans/78n587
Burns/Annotated bibliog on texts on writing skills/77n1067; 78n588
Day/Creative writing in classroom/79n630
Far West Lab/Reading & lang arts/79n683
Reviews of selected pub'd texts in Engl/Grommon/77n653

LANGUAGE DISABILITIES
Nicolosi/Terminology of communication disorders/79n1175

LANGUAGES
Allen/Manual of European langs for librarians/77n189
Brewer/Dictionaries, encys/76n1114

LANGUAGES (cont'd)
Buros/Foreign lang tests/76n563
Catalogue of translator's lib of dept of trade/77n766
Survey of matls for study of uncommonly taught langs/Johnson/78n1026
Walford/Guide to foreign lang courses & dictionaries/79n1092
Wilson/Public Affairs Info Serv/Foreign lang indexes/75n477
World's langs catalog/79n1093

LANIER, SIDNEY
De Bellis/S. Lanier, H. Timrod, & P. H. Hayne/79n1210

LARDNER, RING W.
Bruccoli/Ring W. Lardner: bibliog/77n1209

LARVAE
Smith/Guide to marine coastal plankton .../79n1381

LATERAL THINKING
De Bono/Wordpower: dict/78n1043

LATIN AMERICA
Brownrigg/Colonial Latin American manuscripts .../79n443
Clouston/CILA: acq of Latin Amer lib matls/75n210
Coelho/Holdings of Stanford Univ libs on Latin Amer languages/75n1247
Delpar/Encyclopedia of Latin Amer/75n316
Directory of eng'g educ institutions: Africa, Asia, Latin America/77n588
Dorn/Latin America, Spain, & Portugal: paperback bks/77n305
Gardner/Press of Latin Amer/75n1294
Gropp/Bibliography of Latin Amer bibliog/77n339
Handbook of Latin Amer studies/Stewart/75n296
Hanson/Dissertations on Iberian & Latin Amer history/77n361
Harding/Latin Amer review of bks/76n280
Hawkins/Teacher's resource hndbk/77n340
Latin America: econ hist/79n805
Libros en venta/76n16
Lyday/Bibliography of Latin Amer theater/79n1010
Matos/Guide to reviews of bks from & abt Hispanic America/77n341; 77n342
Poston/Nonformal educ in Latin America: bibliog/77n580
Saulniers/Women in . . . Africa & Latin Amer/79n261
Sobel/Latin America/75n342
UN/Latin Amer initialisms . . . /75n344
Wilgus/Historiography of Latin Amer/76n373

LATIN AMERICA (cont'd)
Wilgus/Latin Amer, Spain & Portugal/79n384
Wilgus/Latin Amer bks/75n297

LATIN AMERICAN LITERATURE
Amago/Centeno collection/79n1285
Bleznick/Sourcebk for Hispanic lit & lang/75n1426
Coll/Indice informativo de la novela hispanoamericana/79n1287
Foster/Modern Latin Amer lit/76n1301
Foster/20th cent Spanish-Amer novel/76n1300
Freudenthal/Index to anthologies of Latin Amer lit in English translation/78n1194
LC/Archive of Hispanic lit on tape/75n1429
Shaw/Latin Amer lit in English trans/77n1273

LATIN LANGUAGE
Dictionary of medieval Latin . . . /Latham/76n1149
Glare/Oxford Latin dict/77n1095; 79n1144

LATIN STUDIES
McGuire/Introduction to medieval Latin studies/79n1091

LATVIAN AMERICANS
Karklis/Latvians in America/75n820

LAW
See also Common law; Courts; Criminal law; International law; Maritime law
Anderson/Privacy & public disclosures . . . /77n531
Anderson/Anglo-Scandinavian law dict . . . professional & commercial practice/78n500
Backe/Concise Swedish-Engl glossary of legal terms/75n552
Bibliographic gd to law/77n8
Blackwell/College law digest/75n564
Boner/Reference gd to Texas law/77n532
Casey/Lawyer's desk bk/76n515
Computex bk guides: law/76n509
Cunningham/Para-legal & lawyer's library/75n555
Davison/Bibliography of law-related curriculum matls/78n494
Davison/Media: law-related AV matls/77n534
Dorman/Running Press dict of law/77n538
Duggan/Law & computer/75n548
Eddy/What you should know abt marriage, divorce, . . . in Louisiana/75n556
Egbert/Multilingual law dict/79n568
Family legal advisor/75n557
Gifis/Law dictionary/76n511
Gordon/Legal word bk/79n569
Hanna/Complete layman's gd/75n558

LAW (cont'd)
Hein's legal periodical check list/79n565
Henke/California legal research hndbk/76n516
Index to legal periodicals/Sahanek/78n508
Kelly/Directory of law-related educ projects/79n571
Kettler/Historic preservation law/77n536
Klein/Admin of justice in courts/77n537
Laska/Tennessee legal res hndbk/79n573
Law/Rights of the poor/75n559
Legal secretary's ency'id dict/Prentice Hall/78n501
Levine/Rights of students/75n560
Pederson/Checklist of Amer Bar Assn matls . . . /78n498
Philo/Lawyers desk ref: . . . for personal injury action/76n517
Reilly/Legal secretary's word finder/75n561
Ross/Rights of women/75n563
Shain/Legal first aid/76n508
Sletwold/Sletwold's manual of documents for legal secretary/77n533
  FOREIGN COUNTRIES
Blaustein/Bibliography on common law in French/75n546
Caswell/Coutumes of France in LC/79n563
Cho/Japanese writings on communist Chinese law/79n564
Encyclopedia of Soviet law/Feldbrugge/75n553
Nguyễn/Vietnamese legal matls/79n566
Schwerin/Bibliography of German lang legal monograph series/79n567
Valderrama/Law & legal lit of Peru/78n493
Walsh/Martial law in Philippines/75n551

LAW ENFORCEMENT
  See also Criminal justice
Felkenes/Law enforcement: bibliog/78n497
Franke/America's 50 safest cities/75n833
Gunn/Glossary handbk for law enforcement educ/75n831
Kinton/Criminology, law enforcemt & offender treatment/75n829
Klein/Administration of justice in courts/77n537
Kobetz/Law enforcemt & criminal justice educ directory/76n779
Prostano/Law enforcement/75n830
Sumrall/Map abstract of trends in calls for police serv: Birmingham, AL/79n742

LAW LIBRARIES
Cunningham/Para-legal & lawyer's library/75n555
Werner/Manual for prison law libraries/77n242

LAW SCHOOLS
Epstein/Barron's gd to law schools/79n657
Pre-law hndbk: ABA-approved law schools/78n507
Tseng/Law schools of world/79n572

LAWRENCE, D. H.
Holderness/Who's who in Lawrence/77n1237

LAWRENCE, T. E.
Meyers/T. E. Lawrence: bibliog/76n1277

LAWYERS
Parker directory of attorneys/77n539
Who's who in Amer law/Marquis/78n509

LEADERSHIP
Stogdill/Handbook of leadership/75n797

LEAGUE OF CANADIAN POETS
Catalogue of members/77n1254

LEAGUE OF NATIONS
Birchfield/Consolidated catalog of pubs/78n429
Reno/League of Nations documents/75n112; 77n501

LEARNED SOCIETIES
World gd to scien'ic assns & learned societies/75n1436; 79n89

LEARNING DISABILITIES
Bush/Dictionary of reading & learning disabilities/75n651
Chicorel abstracts to reading & learning disabilities/78n582; 79n690
Lee/Learning disabilities . . . /79n692
Mann/Handbook in diagnostic teaching/76n690
Mauser/Assessing learning disabled/79n672

LEARNING RESOURCE CENTERS
Bennie/Learning centers/79n206
Burlingame/College learning resource center/79n192
Burlingame/Library and media/79n251
College learning resources programs/78n163
Merrill/Criteria for planning the college & univ learning resources center/78n166
Schuster/Library-centered approach to learning/79n325

LEE, RICHARD
Lee/Lee of Virginia, 1642-1892/75n426

LEFTIST PERIODICALS
Landwehr/Student's gd to leftist periodicals/76n25

LEGAL SECRETARIES
Legal secretary's ency'ic dict/Prentice Hall/78n501
Reilly/Legal secretary's word finder & desk bk/75n561
Sletwold/Manual of docs & forms/77n533

LEGENDS
Robinson/Myths & legends of all nations/77 n1055

LEGISLATIVE BODIES
European parliament digest/75n471
Herman/Parliaments of the world/77n495
Paxton/World legislatures/76n465

LESBIANS
Damon/Lesbian in lit: bibliog/76n1506
Grier/Lesbiana/78n674
Katz/Gay Amer hist/78n652
Women loving women: bibliog/77n1127

LESOTHO
Haliburton/Historical dict/78n286

LESTER, RICHARD
Rosenfeldt/Richard Lester/79n1028

LEVI-STRAUSS, CLAUDE
Lapointe/C. Levi-Strauss & critics/79n779

LEWES, GEORGE HENRY
Baker/G. Eliot–G. H. Lewes Library: catalogue, London/78n1160

LEWIS, C. S.
Christopher/C. S. Lewis/75n1390

LEWIS, WYNDHAM
Morrow/Bibliography of writings of W. Lewis/79n1246
Pound/W. Lewis/79n1247

LEYH, GEORG
Dosa/Libraries in political scene/75n250

LIBERALISM
Murphy/Directory of conservative & libertarian serials/79n88

LIBERTARIAN MOVEMENT
Murphy/Directory of conservative & libertarian serials/79n88

LIBERTY
Eichman/Selective bibliog of AV matls reflecting a civil liberties theme/78n495

"LIBRARIAN"
Pearson/"Librarian": selections from column of that name/77n281

LIBRARIANS
Armour/Happy bookers/77n149
Certification model for prof school media personnel/AASL/77n218
Dosa/Libraries in political scene/75n250
Edwards/Role of beginning librarian in univ libraries/77n204
Faculty status for academic librarians/76 n136
Professional & non-professional duties in libraries/76n181
Ricking/Personnel utilization in libraries/76 n183

LIBRARIANS (cont'd)
Warken/Directory of fee-based info services/ 78n138
  BIOGRAPHY
Charles A. Cutter/78n153
Cole/Ainsworth R. Spofford/76n208
Cummings/Bio-bibliographical directory of women librarians/78n154
DuBois/Paul L. Ford/78n155
Dictionary of Amer library biog/79n185
Directory of ethnic studies librarians/78 n136
Harris/Age of Jewett/76n209
Healey/John E. Fogarty/75n251
Johnston/Amelia G. Gorgas/79n186
Neuburg/Thomas F. Dibdin/79n187
Rodehamel/Ina Coolbrith/75n252
SHARE: feminist library workers/77n183; 79n167
Shores/Quiet world: L. Shores/76n210
Trejo/Who's who of Spanish heritage librarians in US/77n185
Vann/Melvil Dewey/79n188
Who's who in librarianship & info sci/Landau/ 75n253

LIBRARIANS' UNIONS
Guyton/Unionization/76n177
Schlipf/Collective bargaining in libraries/76 n184
Weatherford/Collective bargaining & academic librarian/77n207

LIBRARIANSHIP
  See Library science

LIBRARIES
  See also specific types, e.g., Children's; Church; College and university; Governmental; Medical; Newspaper; Private; Public; School; Seamen's; Special, etc.
Dosa/Libraries in political scene/75n250
Estabrook/Libraries in post-industrial society/ 78n119
Libraries & life of mind in Amer/78n122
Mathews/Libraries for today & tomorrow/77 n162
Penland/Library as a learning serv center/79 n153
Thomassen/CATV & its implications for libraries/75n242
  ACQUISITIONS
Cabeceiras/Multimedia library/79n244
Clarke/Acquisitions from the Third World/ 76n173
Clouston/CILA: ... acq of Latin American library matls/75n210
Collection mgmt/78n156
Fothergill/Non-book matls in libraries/79 n148
Fry/Publishers & libraries/78n35

LIBRARIES (cont'd)
  ACQUISITIONS (cont'd)
Futas/Library acq policies & procedures/78 n204
Gore/Farewell to Alexandria/77n205
Grieder/Acquisitions/79n245
Jobbers directory/78n205
Katz/Guide to magazine & serial agents/77 n199
Kent/Resource sharing in libraries/75n211
Kim/Policies of publishers/77n177; 79n247
Low/Acquisition of maps published by US gov/77n245
Library acquisitions: practice & theory/78 n159
McCullough/Approval plans & academic libraries/79n165
METRO CAP catalog/78n149
Schad/Problems in developing academic library collections/75n212
  CIRCULATION
Kim/Books by mail/78n143
Hu/Benefit-cost analy of alternative library delivery systems/77n248
  COST ANALYSIS
Mitchell/Cost analy of library functions/79n256
  CULTURAL PROGRAMS
Bolte/Libraries & arts & humanities/79n146
Robotham/Library programs/77n163
  DIRECTORIES
American library directory/75n158; 77n174; 79n165
Bird/Library telecommunications directory Canada & US/78n134
Directory of libraries providing computer-based info services in NY metro area/79 n163
METRO directory of members/77n179
Warken/Directory of fee-based info services/78n138
  EQUIPMENT AND SUPPLIES
Library Technology Reports/Sourcebk of library technology/77n193
  EVALUATION
Altman/Data gathering... for performance measures in public libraries/78n172
Lancaster/Measurement & eval of library services/78n121
National inventory of lib needs/78n124
Wools/Evaluation techniques for school library-media programs/79n221
  FOREIGN COUNTRIES
Balnaves/Australian libraries/76n212
Bettelheim/Worldwide directory of fed libraries/75n169
Bryan/University libraries in Brit/77n201
Canadian library directory: fed gov/75n159
Canadian library systems & networks/75n254
Cowley/Libraries in higher educ/77n202
Deutsches bibliotheksadressbuch/78n135

LIBRARIES (cont'd)
  FOREIGN COUNTRIES (cont'd)
Directory of med libraries in British Isles/78 n198
Downs/British lib resources/75n148
Federal gov libraries in Canada/78n202
Garry/Canadian libraries in their changing encironment/79n313
Jackson/Century of service: US & Canada/ 77n157
Key/Library automation, the Orient & So Pacific/77n289
Lewanski/Guide to Polish libraries & archives/76n215
Morris/Parliament & public libraries/78n175
Steele/Major libraries of world/77n184
Welch/Toshokan: libraries in Japanese society/ 77n272
World directory of admin libraries/77n187
World gd to libraries/75n168
  HANDBOOKS AND YEARBOOKS
Ladenson/American library laws, 2nd suppl/ 79n174
Meyers/Insurance manual for libraries/78 n145
Morris/Managing the library fire risk/76 n118
Murphy/Handbook of lib regs/78n146
Withers/Standards for lib serv: internat'l survey/76n123
  PUBLIC RELATIONS
Baeckler/PR for pennies/79n284
Hannaford/Promotion planning/76n200
Kies/Problems in lib public relations/75 n235
  SPECIAL COLLECTIONS
Kemp/Manuscript solicitation for libraries/ 79n246

LIBRARIES AND HANDICAPPED
Strom/Library services to blind & physically handicapped/78n237

LIBRARIES AND MINORITIES
Josey/Opportunities for minorities in librarianship/78n257

LIBRARIES AND READERS
Lyman/Literacy & nation's libraries/78n144
Lyman/Reading & adult new reader/78n234

LIBRARIES AND SCHOOLS
Wehmeyer/School librarian as educator/77 n229

LIBRARY ADMINISTRATION
Baumol/Economics of academic libraries/ 75n176
Brown/Joetta community lib/76n146
Emery/Staff communication in libraries/76 n176
Evans/Management techniques for librarians/ 77n246

LIBRARY ADMINISTRATION (cont'd)
Goldberg/Systems approach to lib program developmt/78n207
Goodell/Libraries & work sampling/76n112
Hamburg/Library planning & decision-making systems/75n213
Harleston/Administration of gov docs collections/75n214
Harvey/Specialised info centres/77n237
Hicks/Managing multimedia libraries/78n208
Holroyd/Studies in library mgmt . . .
    v2/76n178
    v3/77n247
    v4/78n209
Hu/Benefit-cost analy of alternative library delivery systems/77n248
Kemper/Directorship by objectives/78n210
Lancaster/Measurement & eval of lib services/78n121
Lee/Emerging trends in lib organization/79n198
Lee/Library budgeting/78n211
Lowell/Library mgmt cases/76n179
Lubans/Reader in lib systems analysis/76n180
Lyle/Administration of college lib/76n139
Management educ/75n215
Martin/Budgetary control in academic libs/79n199
Pearson/Learning resource centers/75n216
Perkins/Branch library serv/79n259
Shimmon/Reader in library mgmt/77n249
Shonyo/Library mgmt/78n313
Spyers-Duran/Management probs in serials work/75n217
Stueart/Library mgmt/78n212
Thompson/Introduction to univ library admin/75n182
Tsuneishi/Issues in library admin/75n218
Zachert/Simulation teaching of lib admin/76n185

LIBRARY AND SOCIETY
Schuman/Social responsibilities & libraries/77n164

LIBRARY ARCHITECTURE
Ellsworth/Planning manual for academic lib bldgs/75n179
Hannigan/Media center facilities design/79n211
Holt/Architectural strategy for change/77n214
Ward/New library bldgs/76n204
Novak/Running out of space—what are the alternatives?/79n258
Schell/Reader on the library bldg/76n205
Thompson/Planning & design of lib bldgs/77n145; 79n260

LIBRARY ASSISTANTS
See Library technicians

LIBRARY ASSOCIATIONS
Directory of lib assns in Canada/75n160; 78n137
Fang/International gd to library, archival, & info sci assns/77n176

LIBRARY AUTOMATION
See also Data bases; Information storage and retrieval systems
Atherton/Librarians and online servs/79n299
Bidmead/Use of computers in libraries: proceedings of conf by Aslib/77n287
Brophy/COBOL programming: for librarians/77n288
Christian/Electronic library/79n261
Davis/Illustrative computer programming for libraries/75n275
Divilbliss/Economics of library automation/78n241
Divilbliss/Negotiating for computer services/79n301
Dranov/Automated library circulation systems/79n288
Gough/Systems analysis in libraries/79n254
Hayes/Handbook of data processing for libraries/76n230
Key/Library automation: Orient & South Pacific/77n289
Kimber/Automation in libraries/76n231
Lancaster/Applications of minicomputers to library problems/76n232
Lancaster/Use of computers in lit searching/77n290
MacCafferty/Annotated bibliog of automation in libraries & info sci/77n168
Martin/Library automation/76n233
Pitkin/Serials automation in US: bibliog/77n169
Proceedings of 1973 clinic on lib applications of data processing/Lancaster/75n282
Salmon/Library automation systems/77n294
Watson/On-line bibliog'ic services/79n267

LIBRARY CATALOGS
Collison/Published library catalogues/75n17
Keller/Union catalogs & lists/75n249

LIBRARY-COLLEGE
Branscomb/Teaching with bks/75n178
Schuster/Library-centered approach to learning/79n325
Shores/Generic bk/79n155

LIBRARY COMMISSIONS
National Com on Libraries & Info Sci/Annual report/79n151

LIBRARY CONFERENCES
Bonn/Changing times: changing libraries/79n147
Josey/Information society/79n149

308—Subjects

LIBRARY COOPERATION
Anders/Libraries & lib services in SE/77n148
ASLA report on interlibrary cooperation/ 77n173; 79n162
Dyer/Cooperation in lib serv to children/79n208
Black/Directory of academic lib consortia/ 77n209
Information thru cooperative action: services in metro Washington/77n156
MacCafferty/Fax & teletext/78n238

LIBRARY EDUCATION
Adamovich/Reader in lib technology/76n175
Bramley/World trends in lib educ/76n219
Cassata/Administrative aspects of educ for librarianship/76n220
Conroy/Library staff developmt & continuing educ/79n322
Directory of continuing educ opportunities for library-info-media personnel/77n273; 78n256
Directory of institutions offering progs for library tech assistants/77n175
Edwards/In-service training in Brit libraries/ 79n254
Evaluation of alternative curricula: school library media educ/76n221
Hershfield/Effecting change in lib educ/75n264
Houser/Search for a scientific profession/79n323
Klempner/AV matls in support of info sci curricula/79n305
Michael/Continuing professional educ in librarianship: bibliog/76n222
Sage/Continuing library educ/78n252
Slater/Assessing need for short courses in library-info work/78n253
Stone/Continuing educ resource bk/78n254
Virgo/Continuing library educ/78n255
Warncke/Planning library workshops & institutes/77n274
White/Historical intro to lib educ/77n275

LIBRARY FINANCE
Frase/Library funding & public support/75n137
Improving state aid to pub libraries/78n173
Lee/Library budgeting/78n211
Martin/Budgetary control in academic libraries/79n199
Prentice/Public library finance/78n176

LIBRARY HISTORY
Basler/Muse & the librarian/75n260
Bentinck-Smith/Building a great library: Harvard/77n276
Brewster/American overseas lib tech assistance/77n277
Carroll/Library at Mt Vernon/79n326

LIBRARY HISTORY (cont'd)
Dale/Carl H. Milam & UN Library/77n278
Davis/*Journal of Library Hist* index 1966-76/79n190
Ellsworth/Landmarks of lib lit, 1876-1976/ 77n279
Goldstein/Milestones to the present/79n327
Harris/American lib hist/79n328
Harris/Guide to research in Amer lib hist/ 76n223
Hendry/Social hist of branch library developmt, ref to Glasgow/76n224
Jackson/Century of service: US & Canada/ 77n157
Jackson/Libraries & librarianship in the West/ 75n267
Johnson/History of libraries in western world/77n280
Johnson/Libraries for teaching, libraries for research/78n261
Keeling/British library hist: bibliog/76n225
Laugher/Thomas Bray's grand design/75n268
Pearson/Librarian: selections from the column of that name/77n281
Rider/Story of bks & libraries/77n282
Rogers/Story of a small town library/75n270
Roper/Alfred William Pollard/77n283
Skallerup/Books afloat & ashore/75n271
Smith/Oak from an acorn/78n262
Stone/American lib developmt 1600-1899/ 78n263
Sullivan/Carl H. Milam & ALA/77n284
Thomison/History of ALA/79n329
Wright/Oral antecedents of Greek librarianship/78n264
Wright/Of books and men/78n265

LIBRARY HUMOR
Armour/Happy bookers/77n149

LIBRARY INFORMATION NETWORKS
Canadian lib systems & networks/75n254
Goldstein/Library networks/75n139
Hamilton/Multitype lib cooperation/78n120
Kruzas/Encyclopedia of info systems & services/79n166
Martin/Library networks/77n161; 79n150
New governance structure for OCLC/Arthur D. Little, Inc./79n257
Sherrod/Information systems & networks/ 76n235
Stevens/Japanese & US research libraries at the turning point/78n250

LIBRARY INSTRUCTION
Beeler/Evaluating library use instruction/77n265
Carey/Library guiding/75n233
Cleary/Discovering bks & libraries/78n182

Subjects—309

LIBRARY INSTRUCTION (cont'd)
Comprehensive prog of user educ ... Univ of Texas at Austin/78n233
Cook/New library key/76n110
Downs/How to do library research/76n111
Fjällbrant/User educ in libraries/79n312
Gates/Guide to use of bks & libraries/75n138
Gibson/Finding info in library/77n223
Hardesty/Use of slide-tape presentations in academic libraries/79n195
Hart/Instruction in school media center use/79n212
Kirkendall/Putting library instruction in its place/79n290
Knight/1-2-3 gd to libraries/77n160
Library instruction progs, Wisconsin directory/76n132
Lolley/Your library/75n143
Lubans/Educating the library user/75n237
Lubans/Progress in educating library user/79n291
Morse/Concise gd to lib research/76n119
Neal/NY library instruction progs/77n180
Paradis/Research hndbk/75n695
Peterson/Library instruction gd/75n239
Rader/Faculty involvemt in lib instruction/78n169
Rader/Library instruction in the '70s/78n236
Shapiro/Teaching yrself in libraries/79n217
Walker/Teaching media skills/78n188
Ward/Southeastern bibliog'ic instruction directory/79n169

LIBRARY JOURNAL
Library Journal bk review/77n200; 79n182

LIBRARY OF CONGRESS
Basler/Muse & the librarian/75n260
Cole/LC in perspective/79n237
Goodrum/Library of Congress/75n204
Library of Congress as the national bibliog'ic center/77n238

LIBRARY OF CONGRESS CATALOGING SERVICE BULLETIN
Olsen/Index to LC Cataloging Serv Bulletin: nos. 1-120/78n223

LIBRARY OF CONGRESS CLASSIFICATION
Elrod/Index to LC classification/76n190
Olson/Author-number index to LC schedules/79n277
Olson/Biographical subj index to LC schedules/79n278
Olson/Classified index to persons in LC schedules/79n279
Olson/Geographical name index to LC schedules/79n280
Olson/Subject keywrd index to LC schedules/79n281

LIBRARY OF CONGRESS SUBJECT HEADINGS
Chan/LC subj headings/79n268

LIBRARY PERSONNEL
Conroy/Library staff developmt & continuing educ/79n322
Durey/Staff mgmt in univ & college libraries/77n203
Edwards/Role of beginning librarian in univ libraries/77n204
Ricking/Personnel utilization in libraries/76n183

LIBRARY PUBLICATIONS
Wasserman/Library bibliogs & indexes/76n128

LIBRARY REPORTS
Gore/To know a library/79n194

LIBRARY REPROGRAPHIC SERVICES
Directory of lib reprographic services/75n161
LaHood/Reprographic services in libraries/77n286
MacCafferty/Fax & teletext/78n238
New/Reprography for librarians/76n228
Nitecki/Directory of lib reprographic services/77n181
Whitestone/Photocopying in libraries/79n293

LIBRARY RESOURCES
Ash/Subject collections/76n131
Association for Asian Studies/South Asian library resources in No Amer: conf papers/77n244/Survey/77n243
Directory of PA library resources/75n162
Directory of ref & research lib resources systems in NY state/75n163
Downs/Guide to IL library resources/75n18
Downs/British library resources/75n148
Gebhardt/Special collections in German libraries/78n194
Guide to local hist'l matls in south central NY state/77n392
Horecky/East central & SE Europe: library & archival resources in No Amer/77n192
Howell/Special collections in libraries of the SE/79n164
Josey/Handbook of black librarianship/78n142
Kent/Resource sharing in libraries/75n211
Smith/Library resources in Scotland/75n166
Suffolk parochial libraries: catalogue/79n77
Wagle/Guide to res collections in microform in Univ of Toronto library/76n143
Williams/Guide to res collections of NYPL/77n194

LIBRARY RULES AND REGULATIONS
Murphy/Handbook of library regulations/78n146

LIBRARY SCHOOLS
Davis/Association of Amer Library Schools, 1915-68/75n262
Davis/Comparative hist'l analy of three assns of professional schools/75n263

LIBRARY SCIENCE
See also Comparative librarianship; Information science; Libraries
Advances in librarianship, v7/78n140
Atkinson/Librarianship: intro/75n135
Gates/Introduction to librarianship/77n154
Hammer/Information age/77n155
Hug/Strategies for change in info programs/ 75n140
Jackson/Century of service/77n157
Jeffreys/Art of the librarian/75n141
Katz/Library Lit ...
 -4/75n142
 -5/76n113
 -6/77n158
 -8/79n173
Lyman/Literacy & nation's libraries/78n144
Maidment/Librarianship/76n115
Marshall/Of, by & for librarians/75n144
McCrimmon/American library philosophy/76n116
McGarry/Communication knowl & librarian/ 76n117
Myers/Women in librarianship/76n120
National inventory of lib needs/78n124
National library & info services/78n125
Orr/Libraries as communication systems/78n126
Plotnik/Library life-Amer style/76n121
Schuman/Social responsibilities & libraries/ 77n164
Shera/Introduction to lib sci/77n165
Thompson/History of principles of librarianship/79n156
Thompson/Library power/75n146
Williams/Simulation activities in lib, communication & info sci/78n128
 BIBLIOGRAPHY
FID publications, 1895-1975/77n166
International bibliog of bk trade & librarianship/77n54
Lanzing/Library, doc & archives serials/77n36
MacCafferty/Library-information sci/78n129
Magnotti/Master's theses in lib sci 1960-69/ 76n126/1970-74/78n130
Schlachter/Library sci dissertations, 1925-72/ 75n150
Taylor/Library & info studies in UK & Ireland, 1950-74/78n132

LIBRARY SCIENCE (cont'd)
 DICTIONARIES AND ENCYCLOPEDIAS
Clason/Elsevier's dict of lib sci, info & documentation in six langs/79n158
Encyclopedia of lib & info science ...
 v9/75n152
 v11/76n129
 v14-22/78n133
 v23-25/79n159
Harrod/Librarians' glossary of terms/79n160
 HANDBOOKS
Cave/Rare bk librarianship/77n191
Handbook of black librarianship/78n142
Kent/Reading the Russian lang/75n155
Lock/Manual of lib economy/78n123
McGarry/Communication studies/75n156
Taylor/Librarian's hndbk/79n175
 INDEXES
Jordan/Cannons' bibliog of lib economy, author index/77n167
Journal of Documentation index to v1-30/ 78n158
Kilgour/Library & info cumindex/78n147
Library lit/78n148
 RESEARCH
Carpenter/Statistical methods for librarians/ 79n336
Chen/Applications of operations research models to libraries/77n236
Daiute/Library operations research/75n261
EURIM II: European conf/78n267
Freeman/Index to research in school librarianship 1960-74/78n184
Kunz/Methods of analysis & eval of info needs/79n263
Wasserman/LIST, v4/75n149/v5/76n125
Simpson/Basic statistics for librarians/76n122
Srikantaiah/Introduction to quantitative research methods for librarians/78n268
Waldhart/Communication research in library & info sci/76n127
 YEARBOOKS
ALA yearbook/77n188; 78n139; 79n170
Annual review of info sci & tech/78n141
Bowker annual of library & bk trade info/77n190; 79n172
Council on Library Resources/annual report/ 78n157
Voight/Advances in librarianship/75n153

LIBRARY SCIENCE AS A PROFESSION
Chaplin/Organization of lib profession/75n255
Josey/Opportunities for minorities in librarianship/78n257
Minor/Alternative careers in info-library serv/ 79n324

Subjects—311

LIBRARY SCIENCE AS A PROFESSION (cont'd)
Proceedings of info broker-free lance librarian-new careers-new lib services workshop, Syracuse, NY/78n258
Raffin/Information worker/78n127
Sullivan/Opportunities in lib & info sci/78n259

LIBRARY SECURITY SYSTEMS
Bahr/Book theft & lib security systems/79n250

LIBRARY SERVICE TO BLIND
Schauder/Libraries for the blind/79n241
Strom/Library serv to blind & physically handicapped/78n237

LIBRARY SERVICE TO CHILDREN
Dyer/Cooperation in lib serv to children/79n208
Gillespie/More juniorplots/79n228
Ray/Library serv to children/79n215
Richardson/Children's services of public libraries/79n216
Spirt/Introducing more bks/79n235

LIBRARY SERVICE TO DISADVANTAGED
Martin/Library serv to disadvantaged/76n201

LIBRARY SERVICE TO MINORITIES
Buttlar/Building ethnic collections/78n376
Chambers/Hey miss! you got a bk for me?/79n226
Correy/Library community services/79n287
Hanna/People make it happen/79n289
Library & info services for special groups/75n236
Peterson/Library serv to Spanish speaking/79n202

LIBRARY SERVICE TO PHYSICALLY HANDICAPPED
Bramley/Outreach/79n285
Correy/Library community serv/79n287
Prentiss/Improving lib serv to blind, & physically handicapped in NY state/75n240

LIBRARY STATISTICS
National inventory of lib needs/78n124
Smith/Library stats of colleges & universities/78n170
Wisconsin Dept of Public Instruction/Public, academic & special lib service record/75n167

LIBRARY TECHNICIANS
Adamovich/Reader in lib technology/76n175
Bloomberg/Introduction to public services/78n231
Bloomberg/Introduction to tech services/75n247; 77n269
Borkowski/Library tech assistant's hndbk/77n151

LIBRARY TECHNICIANS (cont'd)
Chirgwin/Library assistant's manual/79n321
Christianson/Paraprofessional . . . staff in special libraries/75n203
Directory of institutions offering programs . . . / 77n175
Wisdom/Introduction to lib services/75n147

LIBRARY TECHNOLOGY
Library Technology Reports/Sourcebk of lib technology/77n193

LIBRARY USE STUDIES
Wilson/Community elite & public lib/78n177

LIFE ON OTHER PLANETS
Sable/Exobiology/79n1337

LIFE SCIENCES
See also Agriculture; Biology; Medicine
AIBS directory of biosci depts . . . in US & Canada/77n1293
Martin/Dictionary of life sci/78n1276
McGraw-Hill dict of life sci/77n1347
Retrospective index to theses of Grt Britain & Ireland 1716-1950, v3 life sci/79n1306
Smit/History of life sci: bibliog/76n1354

LINGUISTIC GEOGRAPHY
Allen/Linguistic atlas of upper midwest/76n1115; 77n1058
Mather/Linguistic atlas of Scotland/76n1116

LINGUISTICS
Allen/Linguistics & Engl linguistics/78n1024
Brasch/Comprehensive bibliog of Amer black English/75n1245
Coelho/Holdings of Stanford Univ on Latin Amer languages . . . /75n1247
Gazdar/Bibliography of contemp linguistic research/79n1089
Guide to programs in linguistics/77n1063
Katzner/Languages of the world/76n1110
Kloss/Linguistic comp of nations of the world: central & western So Asia/76n1112
MacCafferty/Thesauri & thesauri construction/79n1090
Pei/Dictionary of linguistics/77n1061
Voegelin/Classification and index of world's languages/78n1022
Walker/Natural language in info sci/79n337

LINGUISTS
Bronstein/Biographical dict of phonetic sciences/79n1157
Cirtautas/Nicholas Poppe/79n1088

LIONEL TRAINS
Greenberg/Greenberg's price gd to Lionel trains:
 O & 0-27 trains, 1945-77/78n870
 O & 0-27 trains, 1915-42; std gauge trains, 1906-40/78n869
McComas/Collectors gd & hist to Lionel trains/77n943

LIQUOR
Alexis Lichine's new ency of wines & spirits/ 76n1562
Barleycorn/Moon-shiners manual/76n1560
Tudor/Wine, beer and spirits/77n1522

LITERACY PROGRAMS
Right to read & nation's libraries/75n241
Smith/Getting people to read/75n715

LITERARY CHARACTERS
See Characters in literature

LITERARY CRITICS
Borklund/Contemporary literary critics/79 n1207

LITERARY MAGAZINES
See also Little magazines
Bennett/Victorian periodicals/79n1226
Chielens/Literary journal in Amer 1900-50/ 78n1109
Ward/Literary reviews in British periodicals 1821-26/78n1157
White/English literary journal to 1900/78 n1158

LITERARY PRIZES
Children's bks: awards & prizes/77n1148; 78n1098
Literary & library prizes/77n178
Moss/Children's bks of yr/77n1126
Newbery & Caldecott medal bks, 1966-75/ 77n1192

LITERARY RESEARCH
Harmon/Scholar's market/76n1194
Kehler/Problems in literary research: gd to ref works/76n1181
Patterson/Literary research gd: bibliog of ref bks & periodicals . . . /77n1126
Vitale/Basic tools of research: gd for students of English/78n1094

LITERATURE
See also American literature; British literature; Children's literature; English literature; French literature, etc.; names of authors
Heiney/Essentials of contemp lit of the Western world/75n1309
  ATLASES
Post/Atlas of fantasy/75n1328
  BIBLIOGRAPHY
Coleman/Epic & romance criticism/75n1310
Dowling/Aestheticism & decadence/78n1089
Mundell/Detective short story/75n1327
Negley/Utopian lit/79n1181
Reader's adviser, v2, 12th ed/Sypher/78n1090
Sween/Bibliography of sci fict/75n1329
Tuck/Encyclopedia of sci fict & fantasy thru 1968/75n1330
Young/Male homosexual in lit/77n1128

LITERATURE (cont'd)
  BIBLIOGRAPHY (cont'd)
Women loving women/77n1127
  DICTIONARIES AND
  ENCYCLOPEDIAS
Beckson/Literary terms/76n1184
Cassell's ency of world lit/75n1315
Cuddon/Dictionary of literary terms/78n1097
de Vries/Dictionary of symbols & imagery/ 77n1129
Encyclopedia of world lit in 20th cent, v4/ Ungar/76n1185
Freeman/Dictionary of fictional characters/ 75n1326
Fuchs/Classics illust'd dict/75n1317
Peer/Terms of literary study/75n1318
Timperley/Encyclopaedia of literary & typographical anecdote/78n42
  HANDBOOKS AND YEARBOOKS
Borklund/Contemporary literary critics/79 n1207
Brown/Reader's companion to world lit/75 n1307
Bryfonski/20th cent literary criticism, v1/79 n1183
Contemporary literary criticism . . .
  v2/75n1319
  v3/76n1188
  v4/76n1189
  v5/77n1130
Handy/20th cent criticism/75n1320
Hoffman/Analytical survey of Anglo-Amer traditional erotica/75n1321
Ward/Longman companion to 20th cent lit/ 76n1190
Walker/20th-cent short story explication, suppl 2 to 2nd ed/75n1331

LITERATURE IN TRANSLATION
Bowe/French lit in early Amer translation/ 79n1270
Freudenthal/Index to anthologies of Latin Amer lit in Engl translation/78n1184
Reader's adviser, v2, 12th ed/Sypher/78n1090
Salley/Selected sound recordings of Amer, Brit, & European lit in Engl/78n1091

LITHOGRAPHS
Mason/Lithographs of George Bellows/79 n899

LITTLE MAGAZINES
Access index to little magazines/Burke/78n19
Bloomfield/Author index to selected Brit "little magazines" 1930-39/77n1133
Chielens/Literary journal in Amer 1900-50/ 78n1109
Comprehensive index to Engl-lang little magazines 1890-1970/77n1136
Directory of small magazines-press editors & publishers/79n52

LITTLE MAGAZINES (cont'd)
England/British directory of little magazines & small presses/75n24
Goode/Index to Commonwealth little magazines 1970-73/77n1139/1974-75/77n1138
Goode/Indexes to Amer little magazines 1900-19/76n1191
Higgins/Whole COSMEP catalog/75n25
International directory of little magazines & small presses/75n26; 78n46
New periodicals index/78n25
Small press record of bks in print/79n39

LIVINGSTONE, DAVID
Casada/Dr. David Livingstone & Sir Henry Morton Stanley: bibliog/77n309

LOANS
Catalog of fed loan guarantee programs/79n874
Cost of personal borrowing in US/77n822

LOBBYISTS
Directory of regist'd lobbyists & lobbyist legislation/76n477
Guardian directory of pressure grps/78n478
Washington lobby/75n500
Washington lobbyist-lawyers directory/79n531

LOCAL GOVERNMENT
See also Municipal government
Andriot/Township atlases of US/78n462
Hutcheson/Citizen groups in local politics/77n523

LOCAL HISTORY
Crouch/Directory of state & local hist periodicals/78n351
Flavell/Ohio area key/78n401
Gilbert/Picture indexing for local hist/75n224
Hobbs/Local hist & library/75n265
Lackey/Frontier claims in lower South/78n404
NYPL/Dictionary catalog of local hist & genealogy div/75n382
NYPL/US local hist catalog/75n383
Rath/Interpretation/79n400
Thompson/Local hist collections/79n176
Weinstein/Collection, use & care of hist'l photographs/78n888

LOCATIONAL ANALYSIS
Muller/Locational analy & economic geog, suppl 1971-77/79n578

LOCKS AND LOCKSMITHING
Roper/Complete hndbk of locks & locksmithing/77n1570

LOCOMOTIVE BUILDERS
Marshall/Biographical dict of railway engineers/79n1585

LOCOMOTIVES
Casserley/Observer's bk of Brit steam locomotives/76n1669
Long/Catalogue of steam locomotive types/75n1833

LOGIC (symbolic)
Greenstein/Dictionary of logical terms & symbols/79n1563

LONDON, JACK
Sherman/Jack London: ref gd/78n1144
Woodbridge/Jack London/75n1360

LONDON
Banks/Penguin gd to London/79n611
Chalfant/Ben Jonson's London/79n1244
Collins' illust'd atlas of London/76n533
Kadish/London on $500 a day/76n559
Lucie-Smith/First London catalogue/75n949

LONDON STAGE
Busby/British music hall: illust'd who's who/78n942
Highfill/Biographical dict of actors, . . . & other stage personnel in London 1660-1880/76n1045
Wearing/London stage 1890-99/77n990

LONGLEY, CHARLES THOMAS
Sayers/Calendar of papers of C. T. Longley, Archbishop of Canterbury/77n1033

LORCA, FEDERICO GARCÍA
Laurenti/Federico García Lorca y su mundo/75n1427
Pollin/Concordance to plays & poems of F. G. Lorca/76n1305

LORD JIM
Parins/Concordance to Conrad's Lord Jim/77n1231

LOS ANGELES
Dills/Best restaurants of Los Angeles & So Calif/77n1541
Goldman/Nothing new: gd to 2nd hnd shopping/75n946
Hugo/Guide to art resources in LA/78n792
Los Angeles & its environs in 20th cent/75n381
Mayer/Los Angeles: 1542-1976/79n427
Partridge/Bargain hunting in LA/75n953

LOUGHLIN POTTERY COMPANY, OH
Huxford/Collectors ency of Fiesta with Harlequin & Riviera/79n949

LOUISIANA
De Ville/Louisiana recruits 1752-58/75n414

LOUISIANA (cont'd)
Eddy/What you should know abt marriage, divorce, . . . in Louisiana/75n556
Leblanc/Pelican gd to gardens of Louisiana/75n610
Louisiana almanac/Calhoun/76n490
Remy/Louisiana sports ency/78n609

LOVE
Liebard/Love & sexuality/79n1041

LOVECRAFT, H. P.
Shreffler/H. P. Lovecraft companion/78n1145

LOWENS, IRVING
Lowens/Music in Amer & Amer music/79n987

LUMMIS, CHARLES F.
Sarber/Charles F. Lummis/79n1221

LUNENBERG COUNTY, VA
Bell/Cumberland parish: Lunenberg Co., VA 1746-1816/75n406
Bell/Sunlight on the southside: lists of tithes, Lunenberg Co., VA, 1748-83/75n407

LUTE
Purcell/Classic guitar, lute & vihuela discog/78n905

LUTHERAN CHURCH
Yearbook of Amer Lutheran Church/Mickelson/76n1090
Lutheran cyclopedia/77n1039

LYLE, GUY R.
Farber/Academic library: essays in honor of G. R. Lyle/75n180

MacDONALD, THOREAU
Edison/Thoreau MacDonald: catalog of design/75n991

MACHEN, ARTHUR
Goldstone/Bibliography of A. Machen/75n1391

MACHINE GUNS
Archer/Jane's pocket bk of rifles & light machine guns/79n1607
Small arms of the world/Ezell/79n1608; Smith/75n1839

MACHINE-READABLE BIBLIOGRAPHIC DATA
Hyman/Analytical access/79n261
MacCafferty/User educ/78n235
Settel/Subject descrip of bks/79n282
Tessier/Feasibility of maintaining . . . access to data archives thru ERIC/79n266
Williams/Computer-readable bibliog'ic data bases/78n243

MACHINE-SHOP PRACTICE
Oberg/Machinery's hndbk/76n1653
Weingartner/Machinists' ready ref/75n1808; 79n1575

MACHINE-TOOLS
Tool & mfg'g engineers hndbk/77n1611

MACHINERY
Encyclopedia of how it works/Clarke/78n1501

MACROECONOMICS
Rock/Money, banking & macroeconomics/79n873

MAGIC
Doerflinger/Magic catalogue/79n722
Gill/Magic as a performing art: bibliog/78n637
Kaye/Catalog of magic/79n723

MAGNETISM
Gartrell/Electricity, magnetism, & animal magnetism: checklist, 1600-1850/77n1591
Mottelay/Bibliographical hist of electricity & magnetism/76n1631

MAGNETS
Moskowitz/Permanent magnet design & application hndbk/77n1597

MAHABHARATA
Lal/Annotated Mahabharata bibliog/75n1421

MAIL ORDER CATALOGS
Boyd/Mail-order crafts catalogue/76n948
De La Iglesia/Catalogue of Amer catalogues/75n944
De La Iglesia/New catalogue of catalogues/77n819; 78n746
Feinman/Catalog of food/78n1471
Hart/Catalog of unusual/75n100
Hodupp/Shopper's gd to museum stores/79n842
Lyons/Whole world catalog/75n950
Moller/Original world-wide mail order shoppers' gd/75n952
Robertson/Spices, condiments, delicacies/76n1578
Rockland/Jewish yellow pages/77n820
Romaine/Guide to Amer trade catalogs, 1744-1900/78n703
Strassfeld/Second Jewish catalog/78n390
Tilson/Mail order food gd/78n1478
Weills/Goodfellow catalog of wonderful things: crafts/78n875
Wilson/Complete food catalogue/78n1480
Wilson/First compl home decorating catalogue/77n942
Woodward/Food catalog/79n1536

MAILER, NORMAN
Adams/Norman Mailer: bibliog/76n1245
Sokoloff/Bibliography of N. Mailer/75n1361

MAINE
Baker/Maine shipbuilding/75n376
Banks/Maine during the Federal & Jeffersonian period: bibliog/76n343
Clark/Maine during colonial period/75n378
Directory of foundations/77n81
Dow/Maine postal hist & postmarks/77n924
Jordan/Maine in Civil War: bibliog'l gd/77n393
Ring/Maine bibliographies/75n386
Ray/Indians of Maine & Atlantic provinces: bibliog'l gd/78n681

MALAYSIA
Wijasuriya/Barefoot librarian: SE Asia/76n218

MALI
Imperato/Historical dict of Mali/78n287

MALLARME, STEPHANE
Morris/Stephane Mallarmé/79n1272

MALORY, THOMAS
Dillon/Malory handbk/79n1248
Kato/Concordance to works of Sir T. Malory/75n1392

MAMMALS
See also Marine mammals
Banfield/Mammals of Canada/76n1443
Barbour/Mammals of Kentucky/75n1519
Burt/Field gd to mammals: No Amer species/77n1392
DeBlase/Manual of mammology/75n1520
Findley/Mammals of New Mexico/77n1393
Grzimek's animal life ency:
  v11, mammals II/76n1406
  v12, mammals III/76n1407
Hanzak/Encyclopedia of animals/76n1408
Morcombe/Australian marsupials & other native mammals/76n1445
Schmidly/Mammals of trans-Pecos Texas/78n1333
Truitt/Dolphins & porpoises/75n1521
Walker/Mammals of the world/76n1446

MAN, PREHISTORIC
Day/Guide to fossil man/79n784
Hawkes/Atlas of early man/78n327

MANAGEMENT
Bakewell/Management principles & practices/79n869
Baum/Practical gd to flexible working hrs/75n981
Broster/Glossary of applied mgmt & financial statistics/76n908
Coveney/Glossary of German & Engl mgmt terms/78n779

MANAGEMENT (cont'd)
Dyer/Project mgmt: bibliog/78n780
Finch/Concise ency of mgmt techniques/78n781
Franklin/Human resources developmt in the organization/79n858
French/Dictionary of mgmt/76n909
Hanson/Executive & mgmt developmt for business & gov/77n849
Herbert/Management educ & developmt/79n870
Lindemann/Encyclopaedic dict of mgmt & mfg'g terms/75n884
Murrell/Bibliography of sources & applications/76n910
Rogalin/Women's gd to mgmt/77n850
Sandeau/Selective mgmt bibliog/77n851
Tega/Management & economics journals/78n704
Vernon/Use of mgmt & business lit/77n772

MANAGEMENT TRAINING PROGRAMS
Wasserman/Training & developmt organizations directory/79n814

MANCHU LANGUAGE
Norman/Concise Manchu-Engl lexicon/79n1132

MANDELSTAM, OSIP
Koubourlis/Concordance to poems of O. Mandelstam/75n1425

MANILA
Merrill/Flora of Manila/77n1353

MANNERS AND CUSTOMS (LCSH 8)
See Popular customs

MANNHEIM, KARL
Remmling/Sociology of Karl Mannheim: bibliog/76n773

MANUFACTURERS REPRESENTATIVES
Holtje/National directory of mfgrs' reps/79n845

MANUFACTURING
Lindemann/Encyclopaedic dict of mgmt & mfg'g terms/75n884

MANUFACTURING PROCESSES
Dick's ency of practical receipts & processes .../76n1638
Tool & mfg'g engineers hndbk/77n1611

MANUSCRIPTS
Batts/British manuscript diaries of 19th cent/77n405
Bill/Catalogue of manuscripts in Lambeth Palace Library/77n1023
Brichford/Manuscripts gd to collections at Univ of IL at Urbana-Champaign/77n28
Brownrigg/Colonial Latin Amer manuscripts in Obadiah Rich collection/79n443

MANUSCRIPTS (cont'd)
Catalogue of Arabic manuscripts in Princeton Univ Library/78n60
Corbett/Catalogue of medieval & Renaissance manuscripts of Univ of Notre Dame/79n66
Cripe/American manuscripts 1763-1815: index/78n61
Kuckett/Modern manuscripts: manual/77n352
Hassall/Treasures from Bodleian Library/77n29
Kemp/Manuscript solicitation for libraries, special collections, . . . /79n246
Knight/Guide to manuscripts in Natl Maritime Museum/79n408
Manuscripts collections of MN Hist'l Society/78n339
Manuscrits et autographes francais/75n68
Manuscrits francais du moyen age/76n59
Martin/North Amer collections of Islamic manuscripts/79n382
Marx/Bibliographical studies & notes on rare bks & manuscripts in Jewish Theological Seminary of Amer/79n67
Ohlgren/Illuminated manuscripts & bks in Bodleian Library/79n68
Plante/Monastic manuscript microfilm project/75n15
Rath/Care & conservation of collections: bibliog/78n321
Revell/15th cent Engl prayers: list of manuscripts/77n1030
Ricklefs/Indonesian manuscripts in Great Britain/79n69
Sanjian/Catalogue of medieval Armenian manuscripts in US/78n62
Simpson/Manuscript catalogue of Royal Commonwealth Society/77n413
Sinclair/Prières en ancien français/79n1273
Sizer/Guide to selected manuscript collections in Univ of Arkansas lib/77n355
Swigger/Guide to resources for study of recent hist of US . . . libs of the Univ of Iowa . . . /78n354
Turner/Typology of early codex/79n70

MAO TSE-TUNG
Starr/Post-liberation works of Mao Zedong: bibliog & index/78n474

MAORI LANGUAGE
Reed/Concise Maori dict/77n1096

MAP LIBRARIES
Carrington/Map collections in US & Canada/79n236
Drazniowsky/Map librarianship: readings/76n167
Larsgaard/Map librarianship/79n240

MAP LIBRARIES (cont'd)
Low/Acquisition of maps & charts published by US gov/77n245
Nichols/Map librarianship/77n240
World directory of map collections/77n554
Madden/Wonderful world of maps/79n588

MARC
US Library of Congress/Composite MARC formats/78n216

MARCEL, GABRIEL
Lapointe/G. Marcel & critics: bibliog/78n1001

MARIHUANA
Waller/Marihuana: bibliog/77n1507

MARINE ALGAE
Abbott/Marine algae of California/77n1365
Hillson/Seaweeds: illust'd gd/78n1303
Lee/Seaweed hndbk/79n1357
Waaland/Common seaweeds of Pacific Coast/78n1304

MARINE ANIMALS
Halstead/Poisonous & venomous marine animals of world/79n1380

MARINE AQUARIUMS
Cox/Tropical marine aquaria/75n1666
Hargreaves/Tropical marine aquarium/79n701
Stevenson/Complete bk of saltwater aquariums/75n1667

MARINE ENGINEERING
Marine environmental eng'g hndbk/Cross/76n1668

MARINE FISHES
Gordon/Guide bk to marine fishes of Rhode Island/76n1435
Hoese/Fishes of Gulf of Mexico/78n1326
Identification gd to marine tropical aquarium fish/79n703
McClane's fld gd to saltwater fishes of No Amer/79n1377
Muus/Collins gd to sea fishes of Britain/76n1436
Stevenson/Complete bk of saltwater aquariums/75n1667
Ursin/Guide to fishes of temperate Atlantic Coast/79n1378

MARINE INVERTEBRATES
Smith/Guide to marine coastal plankton & marine invertebrate larvae/79n1381
Voss/Seashore life of Florida & the Caribbean/78n1335

MARINE LIFE
Burton/Living sea: illust'd ency/77n1371

MARINE MAMMALS
Coffey/Dolphins, whales & porpoises: ency/78n1332

MARINE POLLUTION CONTROL
Marine environmental eng'g hndbk/Cross/ 76n1668

MARITIME HISTORY
Knight/Guide to manuscripts in Natl Maritime Museum/79n408
Lloyd/Atlas of maritime hist/76n1688; 78n328

MARITIME LAW
US Natl Oceanic & Atmospheric Admin/ Oceans of the world/75n550

MARKETING
Barry/Marketing & black consumer: bibliog/ 77n807
Dillon/Handbook of internat'l marketing/77n808
European retail trades/77n809
Ferber/Basic bibliog on marketing research/ 76n864
Handbook of marketing research/Ferber/ 75n923
Jackson/Marketing profitability analysis/79n836
Landau/European directory of market research surveys/76n868
Marketing doctoral dissertation abstracts/ Shawver/78n736
Marketing economics gd/Hong/76n869; 79n837
Marketing economics key plants/77n783
Michman/Marketing channel strategy: bibliog/ 77n810
Michman/Market segmentation/79n838
Pingry/Industrial marketing: bibliog/78n737
Research & developmt directory/76n835
Rothberg/New product planning mgmt of marketing R&D interface/78n738
Shapiro/Marketing terms/75n925
South Amer markets review/77n811
Spencer/Economic hist of milk marketing & pricing/75n926
Twedt/Personality research in marketing: bibliog/78n743
Uhr/Social responsibility in marketing: bibliog/78n744

MARRIAGE
Eddy/What you should know abt marriage, divorce, . . . in Louisiana/75n556
Mayer/Divorce & annulment in 50 states/77n716

MARRIAGE AND THE FAMILY
See also Family life education
Aldous/International bibliog of research in marriage & family, 1965-72/76n781
Olson/Inventory of marriage & family lit 1973-74/76n784

MARRIAGE COUNSELORS
Register: Amer Assn of Marriage & Family Counselors/79n753

MARRIAGE REGISTERS
Acklen/Tennessee records/75n405
Appleton/Boston births, marriages, & deaths 1630-99, & births 1700-1800/79n474
Barnes/Marriages & deaths from Baltimore newspapers 1796-1816/79n477
Barnes/Maryland marriages, 1634-1777/76n423
Barnes/Maryland marriages 1778-1800/79n476
Bell/Cumberland Parish: Lunenberg Co, VA 1746-1816/75n406
Birth . . . marriage . . . death—on the record: directory of 288 primary sources in 50 states & overseas/78n654
Chapman/Marriages of Isle of Wight Co, VA, 1628-1800/77n458
Clift/Kentucky marriages, 1797-1865/75n411
Hollowak/Index to marriages & deaths in (Baltimore) Sun . . .
1837-50/79n486
1851-60/79n487
McGlenen/Boston marriages from 1700-1809/ 78n406
Steel/Sources for Roman Catholic & Jewish genealogy/78n421

MARSH ECOLOGY
Ursin/Life in & arnd freshwater wetlands/76n1367

MARSHALLESE LANGUAGE
Abo/Marshallese-Engl dict/78n1062

MARSUPIALS
Michael Morcombe's Australian marsupials & other native mammals/76n1445

MARTIAL ARTS
Logan/Handbook of martial arts & self-defense/76n768
Winderbaum/Martial arts ency/78n639

MARVELL, ANDREW
Guffey/Concordance to Engl poems of A. Marvell/75n1393

MARXISM
Lapointe/Maurice Merleau-Ponty & his critics: bibliog/78n1002
Shaffer/Periodicals on socialist countries & on Marxism: index/78n467

MARYLAND
Barnes/Maryland marriages, 1634-1777/76n423/1778-1800/79n476
Brumbaugh/Maryland records: colonial, revolutionary, . . . /76n424

MARYLAND (cont'd)
Bundy/Prison group directory, MD-DC/76 n777
Chronology & doc handbk of state of Maryland/79n425
Gannett/Gazetteer of MD & DE/77n463
Gannett/Geographic dict of MD/79n594
Marine/British invasion of MD/78n405
Passano/Index of source records/75n429
Thompson/Atlas of MD/79n593
Thompson/Economic & social atlas of MD/76n491

MASON, LOWELL
Mason/Hymn-tunes of L. Mason: bibliog/77n959

MASS MEDIA
Authors in the news/77n1108
Brightbill/Communications & US Congress/79n1159
Diamant/Broadcast communications dict/75n1201; 79n1161
Ellmore/Illustrated dict of broadcast-CATV-telecommunications/79n1162
Field/Professional broadcast writer's hndbk/75n1204
Friedman/Sex role stereotyping in mass media: bibliog/78n1075
Head/Bibliography of African broadcasting/76n1164
Kato/Japanese research on mass communication/75n1295
Media report to women: index-directory/77n1107
Mehr/Motion pictures, TV, & radio: union catalogue of manuscript collections in the US/79n1165
Richstad/Mass communication & journalism in Pacific Islands/79n1160
Rivers/Aspen hndbk on media/77n1102
Sterling/Mass media: Aspen Inst gd/79n1166
World communications: 200-country survey/76n1160
Writings of Marshall McLuhan/77n1106

MASSACHUSETTS
Bentley/Index to 1800 census/79n478
Committee for New England Bibliog/Massachusetts: bibliog of hist/77n391
Directory of foundations in Massachusetts/Fubini/79n92
Directory of foundations in Commonwealth of Massachusetts/77n79
Historic bldgs/77n874
Shurtleff/Records of Plymouth Colony/77n477

MASTERS, EDGAR LEE
Flanagan/Edgar L. Masters: Spoon River poet & his critics/76n1246

MATERIALS
Annual review of matls sci/Huggins/v5/77n1564/v6/77n1565
Brady/Materials hndbk/78n1539
Clauser/Encyclopedia-hndbk of matls, parts & finishes/78n1540

MATERIALS HANDLING
Davis/Information sources in transportation, matl mgmt, & physical distribution: bibliog/78n1545

MATHEMATICAL ASSN OF AMERICA
Combined membership list of AMS, MAS, SIAM/79n1308

MATHEMATICAL ORGANIZATIONS
Mathematical sciences administrative directory/79n1309

MATHEMATICAL RECREATIONS
Schaaf/Bibliography of recreational math/79n1310

MATHEMATICAL REVIEWS
Author index 1965-72/76n1331
Index of math papers, reviews for 1973/76n1332

MATHEMATICIANS
American men & women of sci: physics, astronomy, math, . . . /78n1216
Combined membership list of AMS, MAS, & SIAM/79n1308

MATHEMATICS
  BIBLIOGRAPHY
Dorling/Use of math'l lit/78n1223
Schaaf/High school math library/77n1305
Wheeler/Mathematics library/79n1311
Whiteman/Bibliography for finite elements/76n1603; 77n1562
  DICTIONARIES
Encyclopedic dict of math/Mathematical Society of Japan/78n1227
James/Mathematics dict/77n1302
Lapedes/McGraw-Hill dict of physics & math/79n1332
Lohwater/Russian-Engl dict of math'l sci/76n1333
  ENCYCLOPEDIAS
Andrews/Theory of partitions/78n1224
Gellert/VNR concise ency of math/78n1228
McEliece/Theory of info & coding/78n1225
Miller/Symmetry & separation of variables/78n1226
Santalo/Integral geometry & geometric probability/78n1229
Shapiro/Mathematics ency/78n1230
  HANDBOOKS
Assaf/Handbook of math'l calculations for sci students & researchers/75n1440
Lerro/Basic mathematics/77n1303

MATHEMATICS (cont'd)
  HANDBOOKS (cont'd)
Penguin bk of tables/75n1441
Tuma/Technology math hndbk/76n1334
  INDEXES
Author index of Mathematical Reviews 1965-72/76n1331
Index of math'l papers: Mathematical Reviews for 1973/76n1332
Mathematics Teacher cum index, 1966-75/78n1233

MATHEMATICS TEACHER
Mathematics Teacher cum index, 1966-75/78n1233

MATHEMATICS TESTS
Buros/Mathematics tests & reviews/76n565

MATHER, RICHARD
Gallagher/Early Puritan writers: ref gd/77n1185

MAUGHAM, WILLIAM SOMERSET
Bason/Bibliography of writings of W. S. Maugham/75n1394

MAYFLIES
Burks/Mayflies or Ephemeroptera of Illinois/76n1439

MAYORS
Profiles of black mayors in Amer/Fox/79n542

McCULLERS, CARSON
Kiernan/K. A. Porter & C. McCullers: ref gd/77n1211

McKERROW, RONALD BRUNLEES
Immroth/R. B. McKerrow/75n266

McLUHAN, MARSHALL
Writings of M. McLuhan/77n1106

MEAD, MARGARET
Gordon/Margaret Mead: bibliog/78n678

MEASURING INSTRUMENTS
Clason/Elsevier's dict of measuremt & control in six languages/79n1544

MECHANICAL ENGINEERING
Auger/Engineering eponyms/76n1651
Baumeister/Marks' std hndbk for mechanical engineers/79n1577

MEDALS
Culver/Guidebook of Franklin Mint issues/76n967
Dusterberg/Official inaugural medals of Presidents of the US/77n911
Norris/Medals & plaquettes from Molinari collection at Bowdoin College/77n914
Vogt/Standard catalog of Mexican coins, paper money & medals/79n920

MEDICAL CARE
Aday/Development of indices of access to medical care/77n1453
Barefoot/Community services/79n1458
Hendin/World almanac whole health gd/79n1487
Linde/Whole health catalog/79n1489
Litman/Sociology of medicine & health care: bibliog/78n1388
Medicine show/75n1649
NIH factbk/77n1481
Popenoe/Wellness/79n1493
Profiles of financial assistance programs/79n1509
Selected bibliog & abstracts for ambulatory health care computer applications/76n1519
US Congress/Discursive dict of health care/77n1477
Williamson/Improving med practice & health care/79n1457

MEDICAL CARE ORGANIZATIONS
American Hospital Assn gd to health care field/78n1402
Ash/Health: multimedia gd/77n1454
Directory of adult day care centers/79n1506
Directory of home health agencies certified as medicare providers/78n1404
Directory of soc & health agencies of NY city/75n798; 79n1508
Kruzas/Medical & health info directory/78n1407
National health directory/78n1408
Organizing for health care/75n1631
Wasserman/Health organizations of US, Canada, internationally/76n1539; 79n1472

MEDICAL ECONOMICS
Ackroyd/Health & med economics/79n795
Andrews/Bibliography of socioeconomic aspects of medicine/76n1511
Medical socioeconomic research sources/75n1616

MEDICAL EDUCATION
Eidelberg/Health sciences video directory/78n1405
Hospital-health care training media profiles/76n1532
National medical AV center catalog: AV for health scientist/78n1390
Williamson/Improving med practice & health care/79n1457
Wischnitzer/Barron's gd to med, dental, & allied health sci careers/75n1635; 78n1409
Zubkoff/Bibliography of audiotapes & tape-slide progs applicable to undergrad med educ/75n1621

MEDICAL EMERGENCIES
See also First aid
Green/Sigh of relief/79n1485
Henderson/Emergency med gd/79n1486
Noble/Emergency med services/75n1617
Pascoe/Quick ref to pediatric emergencies/
 75n1632
Patterson/Study gd for emergency med &
 drug abuse technicians/75n1633
Travelers' gd to US-certified doctors abroad/
 77n1482

MEDICAL ETHICS
Walters/Bibliography of bioethics/v2/78
 n1385; v3/78n1386
Duncan/Dictionary of med ethics/79n1461
Triche/Euthanasia controversy, 1812-1974:
 bibliog/77n1467

MEDICAL JURISPRUDENCE
Lane/Doctor's lawyer: legal hndbk/76n1533
Mersky/Manual on med lit for law librarians/
 75n1610
Wecht/Legal medicine annual/78n1412

MEDICAL LIBRARIES
Basler/Health sciences librarianship/78n197
Chen/Sourcebk on health sci librarianship/
 78n193
Cheshier/Principles of med librarianship/77
 n1483
Directory of health sci libraries in US/76
 n1535
Directory of med libraries in Brit Isles/78
 n198
Login new title abstracts/75n1615
Magyary-Kossa/Medical librarian?/75n207
Morton/Use of med literature/75n1611
Phinney/Librarian & patient/78n196

MEDICAL LITERATURE
See also Medicine–bibliography
Chen/Biomedical, sci'if & tech bk reviewing/
 78n1381
Dunlap/Hospital lit subj headings/78n229
Morton/Use of med lit/79n1441
National Library of Medicine classification/
 79n276

MEDICAL MICROBIOLOGY
Jawetz/Review of med microbiology/79n1475
Zinsser microbiology/Joklik/77n1491

MEDICAL OFFICE MANAGEMENT
Fordney/Insurance hndbk for med office/78
 n1410

MEDICAL PERSONNEL
American Hospital Assn/Health manpower:
 bibliog/75n1613
Health manpower: bibliog/77n1463
US med directory/Alperin/79n1471
Who's who in health care/79n1473

MEDICAL SCHOOLS
Barron's how to prepare for MCAT med college admission test/Seibel/77n608
Brown/Getting into med school/75n1636;
 77n610
Nelson/Medical school admission/75n1639
Zubkoff/Bibliography of audiotapes & tape-
 slide progs applicable to undergrad med
 education/75n1621

MEDICAL SCIENCE
See Medicine

MEDICAL STATISTICS
Singer/Medical risks/78n1416
US Natl Center for Health Stats/Health
 resources stats/78n1419
Health technology: issues/78n1411

MEDICAL WRITING
Lane/Writer's gd to med journals/76n1537
Stylebook-editorial manual/AMA/78n1382

MEDICARE PROVIDERS
Directory of home health agencies certified
 as medicare providers/76n1534; 78n1404

MEDICINE
 ABBREVIATIONS
Garb/Abbreviations & acronyms in med &
 nursing/77n1475
Hughes/Dictionary of abbreviations in med &
 health sciences/78n1396
Roody/Medical abbreviations & acronyms/78
 n1415
Schertel/Abbreviations in medicine/79n1466
 BIBLIOGRAPHY
Bibliography of the hist of med/79n1450
Bowker's med bks in print/75n1612; 76
 n1513; 77n1458
Catalogue of Tavistock Joint Library/76n1521
Computex bk guides: medicine/76n1515
Login new title abstracts/75n1615
Kyed/Scientific, eng'g & med societies pubs
 in print/77n1285
Medical socioeconomic research sources/75
 n1616
Morton/Use of med lit/75n1611
Shilling/Underwater med & related sci/75
 n1618
 DICTIONARIES AND
 ENCYCLOPEDIAS
Black's med dict/Thomson/76n1522
Brace/Nelson's new compact med dict/79
 n1459
Critchley/Butterworths med dict/79n1460
Curtis/Medical talk for beginners/77n1471
Dorland's pocket med dict/78n1394
Faber med dict/Wakeley/76n1524
Fishbein/Modern home dict of med words/
 77n1473
Kay/Southwestern med dict: Spanish-Engl/
 78n1397

MEDICINE (cont'd)
    DICTIONARIES AND
    ENCYCLOPEDIAS (cont'd)
Livingston's pocket med dict/75n1623
Martin/Concise dict of medicine/76n1526
Medical & health sci word bk/78n1398
Miller/Encyclopedia & dict of med, nursing, & allied health/79n1463
Patterson/Medical terminology from Greek & Latin/79n1464
Rigal/Inverted med dict/78n1399
Roper/New Amer pocket med dict/79n1465
Schmidt/Index of paramedical vocabulary/75n1624
Stedman's med dict/77n1476
Taber's cyclopedic med dict/Thomas/78n1400
Thomson/Thomson's concise med dict/75n1625
US Congress/Discursive dict of health care/77n1477
Willeford/Medical word finder/78n1401
Wingate/Penguin med ency/77n1478
    DIRECTORIES
American men & women of sci: medical & health sciences/76n1542; 78n1215
Directory of med specialists/75n1638
Travelers' gd to US-certified doctors abroad/77n1485
Wechsler/Handbook of med specialties/77n1490
    HANDBOOKS AND YEARBOOKS
Arano/Medieval health hndbk/77n69
Chatton/Handbook of med treatment/75n1627
Franklin/Guide to med math/75n1629
Hart/French's index of differential diagnosis/75n1630
Krupp/Current med diagnosis & treatment/75n1609
Medical & health annual/78n1414
Physician's handbk/Krupp/77n1488
Standard med almanac/78n1417
    INDEXES
Cumulative index to nursing & allied health lit/79n1479

MEDICINE, MILITARY
Brown/Neuropsychiatry & war/77n1459

MEDICINE, POPULAR
Arnold/Check list for emergencies/75n1646
Bricklin/Practical ency of natural healing/78n1433
Broadribb/Modern parents' gd to baby & child care/75n1647
Child health ency/Feinbloom/76n1543
Cody/Your child's ears, nose & throat/76n1544
Curtis/Medical talk for beginners/77n1471
Encyclopedia of common diseases/Prevention Magazine/77n1472
Encyclopedia of health & human body/Newman/79n1483

MEDICINE, POPULAR (cont'd)
Fishbein/Handy home med adviser & concise med ency/75n1648
Fishbein/Modern home dict of med words, with descrip . . . of commonly used tests/77n1473
Galton/Complete bk of symptoms & what they can mean/79n1484
Gardner/Good Housekeeping dict of symptoms/77n1493
Griffith/Drug info for patients/79n1497
Harrison/Traditional medicine/77n1462
Illustrated family med ency/Combs/78n1429
Jones/Good Housekeeping gd to medicines & drugs/79n1488
Linde/Whole health catalog/79n1489
Locke/Virus diseases/79n1490
Medicine show/75n1649
Miller/Symptoms: compl home med ency/77n1496
Morini/Simona Morini's ency of health & beauty/77n1497
New illust'd med ency for home use/Rothenberg/76n1545
Nourse/Ladies' Home Journal family med gd/75n1650
Parish/Doctors & patients hndbk of medicines & drugs/79n1492
Philbrook/Medical bks for the layperson: bibliog/77n1466
Pomeranz/Mothers' & fathers' med ency/78n1430
Popenoe/Wellness/79n1493
Rothenberg/New Amer med dict & health manual/76n1546
Taylor/Dr. Taylor's self-help med gd/78n1418
Vickery/Take care of yourself/78n1432
Wingate/Penguin med ency/77n1478
Woman's body/79n1494
Zebooker/Your teeth, your dentist & your health/75n1651

MEDICINE, PREVENTIVE
Linde/Whole health catalog/79n1489
Popenoe/Wellness/79n1493

MEDICINE, PSYCHOSOMATIC
Dunbar/Emotions & bodily changes: survey of lit/77n1461

MEDIEVAL HISTORY
    See History
    See also Middle Ages

MEDITATION
Alibrandi/Meditation hndbk/77n1446
Spiritual community gd/Khalsa/79n1085
Revell/15th cent Engl prayers & meditations: descrip list/77n1030

MELVILLE, HERMAN
Tanselle/Checklist of editions of Moby-Dick 1851-1976/78n1146

MENOMINI LANGUAGE
Bloomfield/Menomini lexicon/76n1148

MENOTTI, GIAN CARLO
Grieb/Operas of G. C. Menotti: bibliog/76 n1008

MENTAL DEFICIENCY
Grossman/Manual on terminology & classification in mental retardation/75n1590
Tymchuk/Mental retardation dict/75n1585

MENTAL HEALTH
Allen/Mental health almanac/79n1435
Ann Landers ency/79n1427
Favazza/Anthropological & cross-cultural themes in mental health: bibliog/78 n1373
Kiernan/Shrinks/75n1591
Selective gd to matls for mental health & family life educ/Mental Health Matls Center/77n1442
US Natl Inst of Mental Health/Mental health directory/78n1374
Wiener/Consumer's gd to psychotherapy/76 n1502
Williams/Environmental pollution & mental health/75n1530

MENTAL HEALTH FACILITIES
US facilities & programs for children with severe mental illnesses/79n1436

MENTAL HYGIENE
See Mental health

MENTAL ILLNESS
Milt/Basic hndbk on mental illness/75n1594

MENTAL TESTS
Buros/Tests in print II/75n1601
Goldman/Directory of unpublished experimental mental measures/75n1600; 79 n1430
Mauser/Assessing the learning disabled/79 n672

MENTALLY HANDICAPPED
Mauser/Assessing the learning disabled/79 n672

MERCHANDISING
Auerbach gd to retail point-of-sale systems/ 75n921

MERCHANT SHIPS
Talbot-Booth's merchant ships/79n1588

MERCURY (planet)
Cross/Atlas of Mercury/78n1235

MEREDITH, GEORGE
Collie/George Meredith: bibliog/75n1395
McCullen/Dictionary of characters in G. Meredith's fiction/78n1179
Olmsted/George Meredith: bibliog/79n1249

MERGERS
Kintner/Primer on law of mergers/75n892

MERLEAU-PONTY, MARUICE
Lapointe/M. Merleau-Ponty & his critics: bibliog/78n1002

MERTON, THOMAS
Breit/T. Merton: bibliog/75n1215
Dell'Isola/T. Merton: bibliog/76n1073

METABOLISM
Year in metabolism/Freinkel/78n1421

METAL CASTINGS
Foseco foundryman's hndbk/Foundry Services Ltd/77n1612

METAL WORK
Oxford Univ/Catalogue of Anglo-Saxon ornamental metalwork, 700-1100/75n994
Morgenstern/Metalcrafting ency/77n892

METAL WORKING MACHINERY
Daniels/Press brake & shear hndbk/76n1652

METALLURGY
Metals ref bk/Smithells/77n1613
SAE & ASTM/Unified numbering system for metals & alloys/76n1612
Tyrkiel/Dictionary of physical metallurgy/ 79n1578

METALS
Metals ref bk/Smithells/77n1613
Non-ferrous metal data/76n900
Staudhammer/Atlas of binary alloys/75n1454
SAE & ASTM/Unified numbering system for metals & alloys/76n1612

METEORITES
Buchwald/Handbook of iron meteorites/77 n1432

METEOROLOGY
Ruffner/Weather almanac/75n1568
US Naval Weather Serv Command/Worldwide marine weather broadcasts/75n1569
Villeneuve/Glossaire de meteorologie et de climatologie/75n1570

METEOROLOGICAL INSTRUMENTS
World Meteorological Organization/Annotated bibliog on precipitation msmt instruments/ 75n1571

METHODIST CHURCH
Rowe/Methodist union catalog: pre-1976 imprints/76n1078; 77n1032; 79n1054

METRIC SYSTEM
Chisholm/Units of weight & measure/76 n1315
Feirer/SI metric hndbk/78n1231
Hartsuch/Think metric now!/75n1715
Higgins/Metric hndbk for teachers/75n712
Johnstone/For good measure/76n1316

METRIC SYSTEM (cont'd)
Kverneland/World metric stds for eng'g/79n1547
Lewis/Metric & other conversion tables/75n1716
Lytle/American metric construction hndbk/77n1567
Metric manual/76n1318
Metric system gd/76n1319
Metric system gd bulletins/76n1320
Metric yearbk/78n1232
Metrication hndbk/77n1304
Semioli/Conversion tables for SI metrication/75n1717

METRO CAP
METRO CAP catalog: coop acq program/78n149

METROPOLITAN AREAS
Comparative atlas of America's great cities/77n728

METROPOLITAN GOVERNMENT
Murphy/Urban politics/79n539
White/Reforming metro gov: bibliog/76n496

METROPOLITAN OPERA
Peltz/Metropolitan Opera annals/79n994

MEXICAN AMERICANS
See Chicanos

MEXICANS
Schon/Bicultural heritage/79n462

MEXICO
Camp/Mexican political biogs 1935-75/78n485
Hofstadter/Mexico 1946-73/75n341
Illustrated Mexico vacation gd/McCready/75n630
Kendall/Art of Pre-Columbian Mexico/75n988
Millon/Urbanization at Teotihuacan/75n404
Rand McNally road atlas/75n636
Schwartz/Climate advisor/79n1417
Steele/Independent Mexico/75n312
Tully/Mexico: for women/77n569
US LC/Harkness collection in LC/75n313
Wilhelm/Guide to all Mexico/75n631
Wilhelms' gd to all Mexico/79n624

MEXICO IN LITERATURE
Gunn/American & British writers in Mexico/75n1308
Gunn/Mexico in American & British letters/75n1311

MIAMI
Buchanan/Miami: chron doc hist/79n421
Steiman/Guide to restaurants/78n530

MICHIGAN
Beer/Michigan legal lit/75n545

MICHIGAN (cont'd)
Gibson/Artists of early Michigan/76n935
Harris Michigan mfgrs industrial directory/77n827
Michigan stat'l abstract/78n688
Romig/Michigan place-names/75n454
Sommers/Atlas of Michigan/78n522

MICROANALYSIS
Keleti/Handbook of micromethods for biological sciences/75n1462
McCrone/Particle atlas/75n1433

MICROBIOLOGY
Annual review/Starr/76n1358
Hahn/Guide to lit for industrial microbiologist/75n1459
Jawetz/Review of medical microbiology/79n1475
Lennette/Manual of clinical microbiology/76n1362
Zinsser microbiology/Joklik/77n1491

MICROCOMPUTERS
Burton/Dictionary of microcomputing/78n1521
Sippl/Microcomputer dict & gd/77n1584
Soucek/Microprocessors & microcomputers/77n1585

MICROFORM SERVICES
Microfilm source bk/75n58
Veaner/Microform market place/75n60

MICROFORMS
See also Reprints (publications)
American Assn of Community & Junior Colleges/Microform hndbk/Gaddy/76n226
Bahr/Microforms: librarians' view/79n332
Diaz/Microforms in libraries: reader/76n227
Dranov/Microfilm: librarians' view/77n285
Gildenberg/Computer-output-microfilm systems/75n1770
Guide to microforms in print/79n36
International microfilm source bk/77n61
Plante/Monastic manuscript microfilm project/75n15
Russian revolutionary lit collection Houghton Library, Harvard Univ/77n416
Saffady/Computer-output microfilm/79n333
Saffady/Micrographics/79n334
Subject gd to microforms in print/79n42
Teague/Microform librarianship/79n335
Union list of selected microforms in libraries in NY metro area/77n31
Veaner/International microforms in print/75n16

MICRONESIA
Marshall/Micronesia, 1944-74: bibliog of anthropological matls/77n744

MICRONESIAN LANGUAGES
Lee/Kusaiean-Engl dict/77n1094

MICROORGANISMS
Weiner/Microorganism control/78n1263

MICROPROCESSORS
Motorola/Microprocessor applications manual/77n1598
Soucek/Microprocessors & microcomputers/77n1585

MICROWAVES
Bibliography of microwave optical tech/Harvey/78n1266

MIDDLE AGE
Sprague/Finding a job: resource for middle-aged & retired/79n865

MIDDLE AGES
Hughes/Medieval music/76n988
Powell/Medieval studies/75n325

MIDDLE ATLANTIC STATES
Mobil travel gd/79n604

MIDDLE EAST
Africano/Businessman's gd to Mid East/79n815
al-Qazzaz/Women in Mid East & No Africa/78n279
Arab Islamic bibliog/Grimwood-Jones/78n278
Atiyeh/Contemporary Mid East, 1948-73/77n308
Avi-Yonah/Encyclopedia of archaeological excavations in Holy Land/77n347
Cambridge ancient hist, 3rd, v2, Mid East & Aegean/Edwards/76n357
Catalogue of Arabic manuscripts, Princeton Univ Library/78n60
DeVore/Arab-Israeli conflict: bibliog/77n417
Donovan/US & Soviet policy in Mid East, 1957-66/75n532
Drabek/Politics of African & Mid Eastern states: bibliog/78n470
Geddes/Analytical gd to bibliogs on Arab fertile crescent/76n253
Haiek/Mideast business gd/79n818
Legum/Middle East contemp survey/79n355
Littlefield/Islamic Near East & North Africa/78n281
McLane/Soviet Mid East relations/75n538
Middle East & No Africa 1975-76/76n266
Middle East & No Africa 1976-77/77n311
Middle East yrbk/79n356
Middle East: US policy, Israel, oil & Arabs/75n539
Rubner/Middle East conflict from 1973-76/79n358
Schulz/International & regional politics in Mid East & No Africa/78n488

MIDDLE EAST (cont'd)
Shimoni/Political dict of Mid East/75n523
Simon/Modern Mid East/79n359
Union catalogue of Arabic serials & newspapers in Brit libraries/78n29
US CIA/Atlas of issues in Mid East/75n330

MIDDLE ENGLISH LITERATURE
Chapman/Index of names in Pearl, Purity, Patience, & Gawain/79n1251

MIDDLE STATES ASSOC. OF COLLEGES AND SECONDARY SCHOOLS
Crawford/Guide to middle states school in . . .
  Delaware, DC, MD, etc/76n656
  New Jersey/76n657
  New York/76n658
  Pennsylvania/76n659

MIGRATION
International Migration Review cum index/79n794

MIGUÉIS, JOSÉ CLAUDINO RODRIGUES
Kerr/Miguéis—to the 7th decade/79n1289

MILAM, CARL H.
Dale/C. H. Milam & UN Library/77n278
Sullivan/C. H. Milam & ALA/77n284

MILITARY BIOGRAPHY
Martell/World military leaders/75n1844
Significant Amer military leaders/Miekina/77n134
Webster's Amer military biogs/79n1592
Who was who in Amer hist/military/77n1636

MILITARY HISTORY
Banks/World atlas of military hist, v1 to 1500/75n1842
Bruce/Annotated bibliog of Brit army 1660-1914/77n1641
Cavalry Journal/Armor cum indexes 1888-1968/75n1841
Dupuy/Encyclopedia of military hist/78n331
Eakin/Colonial Amer & War for Independence/78n343
Keegan/Who's who in military hist/77n1635
Parkinson/Ency of modern war/78n1559
Pericoli/1815: armies at Waterloo/75n1850
US Dept of Army/Guide to US Army museums & historic sites/77n1646
Young/Atlas of second World War/Natkiel/75n1843

MILITARY INDUSTRIAL COMPLEX
Meeker/Military-industrial complex/75n464

MILITARY PARAPHERNALIA
Johnson/Collector's gd to militaria/78n871

MILITARY SCIENCE
Garber/Modern military dict/77n1627
Lowe/Dictionary of military terms: Chinese-English/79n1595

MILITARY SCIENCE (cont'd)
Quick/Dictionary of weapons & military terms/75n1838
US Dept of Air Force/Dictionary of basic military terms: Soviet view/77n1628
US Immigration Serv/Foreign versions of Engl names & titles/75n250

MILITARY SERVICE
Anderson/Conscription: bibliog/77n1625

MILITARY SERVICE ETIQUETTE
Swartz/Service etiquette/78n1563

MILLER, ARTHUR
Hayashi/Index to A. Miller criticism/77n1210

MILTON, JOHN
Boswell/Milton's library/76n1278
Hunter/Milton ency/79n1250

MILWAUKEE, WI
Lankevich/Milwaukee: chron hist/78n355

MIME
See Pantomime

MIND AND BODY
Rand McNally atlas of body & mind/77n1456

MINERALOGY
See also Crystals; Ores; Precious stones; Rocks
Brown/Illustrated gd to common rocks & their minerals/77n1431
Court/Minerals: nature's fabulous jewels/76n1480
Desautels/Rocks & minerals/75n1572
Firsoff/Rockhound's hndbk/76n1481
Hamilton/Larousse gd to minerals, rocks & fossils/78n1359
Klaits/When you find a rock/77n1434
Kohland/Guide to mineral identification/79n1421
MacFall/Minerals & gems/77n1435
Mason/World of rocks & minerals/77n1436
O'Donoghue/Encyclopedia of minerals & gemstones/77n1437
Pearl/Gems, minerals, crystals, & ores/78n1360
Pough/Field gd to rocks & minerals/77n1438
Ridge/Annotated bibliogs of mineral deposits in Africa, Asia, & Australasia/77n1439
Roberts/Encyclopedia of minerals/75n1573
Shaub/Treasures from the earth/76n1482
Sorrell/Minerals of world/75n1574
Tindall/Collector's gd to rocks & minerals/77n1440
Villard/Gemstones & minerals/75n1101
Woolley/Illustrated ency of mineral kingdom/79n1423

MINERALS IN THE BODY
Fryer/Dictionary of food supplements/77n1545

MINES AND MINERAL RESOURCES
Probert/Lost mines & buried treasures of the West: bibliog/78n358
Ridge/Annotated bibliogs of mineral deposits in Africa, Asia, & Australasia/77n1439

MINIATURE OBJECTS
Rosner/Inside the world of miniatures & dollhouses/77n938

MINICOMPUTERS
Lancaster/Applications of minicomputers to library & related problems/76n232

MINISTERS' LIBRARIES
Barber/Minister's library/79n1047

MINNESOTA
Brook/Reference gd to Minnesota hist/75n377
Gebhard/Guide to architecture/79n890
Taylor/Blacks in Minnesota/77n437
White/Fur trade in Minnesota/79n409

MINNESOTA HISTORICAL SOCIETY
Manuscripts collections, guide no 3/78n339

MINNESOTA MULTIPHASIC PERSONALITY INVENTORY
Butcher/Handbook of cross-natl MMPI research/77n1447
Dahlstrom/MMPI hndbk/76n1498; 76n1499
Taulbee/MMPI inventory: bibliog/78n1364

MINORITIES
See also Ethnic studies
Cole/Minority organizations/79n444
Gagala/Economics of minorities/77n423
Gollnick/Multi-cultural educ & ethnic studies in US/78n541
Iiyama/Drug use & abuse among US minorities: bibliog/77n1504
Johnson/Ethnic Amer minorities: media & materials/77n424
Johnson/Directory of special programs for minority group members/75n801
Johnson/Directory of special programs . . . career info, financial aid, etc/76n389
Katz/Handbook of major Soviet nationalities/76n385
Miller/Handbook of Amer minorities/77n419
Miller/Comprehensive bibliog for study of Amer minorities/77n425
Minority group media gd/78n1076
Multicultural educ, bibliog for teachers/Giese/78n589
Oaks/Minority studies: bibliog/77n426
Riseborough/Canada & French/76n504
Schlachter/Minorities & women/79n762

MINORITIES (cont'd)
Sourcebk of equal educ'l opportunity/78n580
Trueba/Bilingual bicultural educ for Spanish speaking in US: bibliog/78n548
Try us: natl minority business directory/76n837
US Bureau of Labor Stats/Directory of data sources on racial & ethnic minorities/77n429

MINORITIES IN LITERATURE
Inglehart/Image of pluralism in Amer lit: bibliog/76n388

MISSILES
See Guided missiles

MISSIONS
Encyclopedia of missions/Dwight/76n1081
Mission hndbk: No Amer Protestant ministries overseas/75n1221; 78n986

MISSISSIPPI
Atlas of Mississippi/Cross/75n574

MISSISSIPPI VALLEY HISTORICAL REVIEW
Fifty-yr index, 1914-64/75n371

MOBY DICK
Tanselle/Checklist of eds of Moby-Dick 1851-1976/78n1146

MODEL TRAINS
Greenberg's price gd to Lionel trains/78n869; 78n870

MODELS AND MODELMAKING
Cardwell/Index of model periodicals/78n876

MODERN ART
Charmet/Concise ency of modern art/75n997
Sandberg/Annual of new art & artists/75n1006

MODERN DANCE
McDonagh/Complete gd to modern dance/77n995

MODERN FICTION STUDIES
Cooper/Cumulative index 1955-75/77n1137

MODERN HISTORY
See History

MOKILESE LANGUAGE
Harrison/Mokilese-Engl dict/78n1063

MOLECULAR BIOLOGY
Evans/Glossary of molecular biol/76n1355

MOLLUSKS
See also Shells
Grzimek's animal life ency: mollusks & echinoderms/75n1523

MONASTERIES
Madden/Religious gd to Europe/76n1071

MONASTICISM AND RELIGIOUS ORDERS
Constable/Medieval monasticism: bibliog/77n1025

MONETARY ECONOMICS
Cohen/Special bibliog in monetary economics & finance/79n871

MONEY
Rock/Money, banking & macroeconomics/79n873

MONG NJUA LANGUAGE
Lyman/Dictionary of Mong Njua/76n1152

MONGOLIA
Allsworth/Soviet Asia: bibliog/77n345

MONMOUTH COUNTY, NJ
Van Benthuysen/Monmouth Co: bibliog, 1676-1973/76n355

MONONGAHELA TERRITORY
Van Voorhis/Old & new Monongahela/75n432

MONROE COUNTY, NY
Malo/Landmarks of Rochester & Monroe/75n1019

MONTANA
Miller/Ghost towns of Montana/76n552

MONTGOMERY COUNTY SCHOOL DISTRICT, MD
Gillespie/Model school dist media program/78n185

MONTHLY CATALOG OF U.S. GOVERNMENT PUBLICATIONS
Consolidated clothbnd ed of Monthly Catalog: Jan '75-Sept '75/78n96

MONTHLY LABOR REVIEW
US Bureau of Labor Stats/Monthly Labor Review: index, 1971-75/78n776

MOONSHINE
Barleycorn/Moon-shiners manual/76n1560

MOORE, MARIANNE
Abbott/Marianne Moore: bibliog/78n1147

MORAVIA, ALBERTO
Alfonsi/Annotated bibliog of Moravia criticism in Italy . . . /77n1270

MORMONS
See also Book of Mormon
Bitton/Guide to Mormon diaries & autobibliogs/78n971
Flake/Mormon bibliog 1830-1930/79n1048

MORTGAGES
Miller/Thesaurus of terms in mortgage & consumer credit/79n872

MOSSES
Flowers/Mosses: Utah & West/75n1487

MOTHERS
Mothers of achievemt in Amer hist 1776-1976/77n396

MOTHS
Watson/Dictionary of butterflies & moths in color/76n1442

MOTION PICTURES
See Films

MOTORCYCLE RACING
Carrick/Encyclopaedia of motor-cycle sport/78n635
Rivola/Racing motorcycles/79n1557

MOTORCYCLES
Alth/All about motorcycles/76n1617
Bishop/Sachs engine service/75n1740
Chilton's compl gd to motorcycles & motorcycling/75n737
Chilton's motorcycle labor gd/75n1741
Chilton's motorcycle repair manual/75n1742
Chilton's new repair & tune-up guide:
　Hodaka/75n1743
　Kawasaki/75n1744
　Suzuki/75n1745
Ducati serv-repair hndbk/75n1746
Engle/Complete motorcycle bk/75n739
Griffin/Motorcycles/75n740
Lockwood/Motorcycle repair ency/75n1747
Lovin/Complete motorcycle nomad/75n741
Perry/Road rider/75n742
Radlauer/Motorcyclopedia/75n743
Tragatsch/Complete illust'd ency of world's motorcycles/78n1515
Vanderveen/Motorcycles to 1945/77n1623

MOUNT McKINLEY
Washburn/Tourist gd to Mt McKinley/75n618

MOUNT VERNON
Carroll/Library at Mt Vernon/79n326

MOUNTAINEERING
Bunting/Climbing/75n755
Krawczyk/Mountaineering: bibliog/78n618
Lyman/Field bk of mountaineering & rock climbing/76n718
Petzoldt/Wilderness hndbk/75n757
Schneider/Climber's sourcebk/77n688
Unsworth/Encyclopaedia of mountaineering/76n724

MOVEMENT EDUCATION
Pizzitello/Annotated bibliog on movement educ/78n547

MOVIE STARS
See Film actors and actresses

MOVING-PICTURES
See Films

MUGS AND TANKARDS
Stratton/Mugs & tankards/78n873

MULTICULTURAL EDUCATION
Gollnick/Multi-cultural educ & ethnic studies in US/78n541
Multicultural educ, bibliog for teachers/Giese/78n598
Van Why/Adoption bibliog & multi-ethnic sourcebk/78n657

MUNICIPAL GOVERNMENT
Kraemer/Municipal info systems directory/78n463
Municipal gov ref sources/79n537
Municipal year bk/76n495; 79n538

MURDOCH, IRIS
Tominaga/I. Murdoch & M. Spark: bibliog/77n1221

MURRY, JOHN MIDDLETON
Lilley/Bibliog of J. M. Murry/76n1279

MUSEUM LIBRARIES
Collins/Libraries for small museums/79n238

MUSEUM OF MODERN ART
Barr/Painting & sculpture in the Museum 1929-67/79n877

MUSEUM STORES
Hodupp/Shopper's gd to museum stores/79n842

MUSEUMS
American Assn of Museums/Statistical survey of museums in US & Canada/78n71
Chenhall/Nomenclature for museum cataloging/79n269
Cramer/Museum Council of Philadelphia gd to museums in Delaware Valley/77n76
Directory of Canadian museums & related institutions/79n83
Hogg/Museums of England/75n81
Hudson/Directory of world museums/76n67
Jones/Halls of fame/78n75
Liebe/Indexes to NY State Museum Bulletins, 1888-1973/76n930
McDarrah/Museums in NY/79n93
Museums of the world/76n68
National Endowment for the Arts/Museums USA/76n69
Wasserman/Museum media/75n83

MUSHROOMS
Bigelow/Mushroom pocket fld gd/75n1486
Guild/Alaskan mushroom hunter's gd/78n1300
Major/Collecting & studying mushrooms/76n1397

MUSHROOMS (cont'd)
Menser/Hallucinogenic & poisonous mushroom fld guide/78n1301
Miller/Mushrooms of No Amer/78n1302
Rinaldi/Complete bk of mushrooms/75n1489
Smith/Field gd to western mushrooms/76n1398
Stamets/Psilocybe mushrooms/79n1355
Thiers/California mushrooms/76n1399
Tribe/Mushrooms in the wild/79n1356

MUSIC
AMERICAN
American music before 1865 in print & on records: discog/77n964
Dichter/Handbook of early Amer sheet music 1768-1889/79n1001
Eagon/Catalog of published concert music by Amer composers/75n1124
Frisbie/Music & dance research of SW US Indians/78n890
Horn/Literature of Amer music in bks & folk music collections: bibliog/78n893
Jackson/US music/75n1128
Lowens/Music in America/79n987
Mead/Doctoral dissertations in Amer music/76n990
Pavlakis/American music hndbk/75n1150
Rowell/American organ music on records/77n966
Showalter/Music bks of Ruebush & Kieffer, 1866-1942/76n992
BIBLIOGRAPHY
Bibliographic gd to music/77n9
Board of Music Trade of USA/Complete catalogue of sheet music & musical works/75n1121
Chicorel bibliog to bks on music & musicians/76n985
Duckles/Music ref & research matls/75n1123
East/Browning music/75n1137
Fenlon/Catalogue of printed music & music manuscripts before 1801/77n953
Hodgson/Music titles in translation/77n956
Kostka/Bibliography of computer applications in music/75n1129
Krummel/Guide for dating early published music/75n1118
Marco/Information on music:
   v1, basic & universal sources/76n989
   v2, Americas/78n894
Mathieson/Bibliography of sources for study of ancient Greek music/75n1131
Meggett/Music periodical lit/79n961
Mixter/General bibliog for music research/76n991
Olmsted/MLA catalog of cards for printed music 1953-72/75n1138
Pollin/Music for Shelley's poetry/75n1133
Selective music lists: vocal solos, vocal ensembles/77n961

MUSIC (cont'd)
DICTIONARIES AND ENCYCLOPEDIAS
Busby/Musical manual or tech directory/78n898
Eisler/World chronology of music hist/75n1139
Fink/Languages of 20th cent music/76n996
Hopkins/Downbeat music gd/79n957
Jacobs/New dict of music/75n1140
Karp/Dictionary of music/75n1141
Leuchtmann/Dictionary of terms in music/79n964
Moore/Complete ency of music/75n1142
Picerno/Dictionary of musical terms/78n899
Randel/Harvard concise dict of music/79n966
Schillinger/Encyclopedia of rhythms/78n900
Shapiro/Encyclopedia of quotations abt music/79n967
Vinton/Dictionary of contemp music/75n1143
Westrup/New college ency of music/77n969; 79n968
DISCOGRAPHY
Cooper/International bibliog of discographies: classical music & jazz & blues/76n986
Foreman/Systematic discog/75n1135
Gray/Bibliography of discographies, v1/79n970
Greenfield/Penguin stereo record gd/79n971
Halsey/Classical music recordings for home & library/77n965
Records in review/Carter/76n1000
Stahl/Selected discog of solo song/77n967
White House record library/75n1136
FOREIGN COUNTRIES
Jarman/Canadian music: cklt 1950-73/77n957
Kaufman/Musical refs in Chinese classics/77n948
Mathieson/Bibliography of sources for study of ancient Greek music/75n1131
McLean/Annotated bibliog of Oceanic music & dance/79n960
Michaelides/Music of ancient Greece/79n965
Nulman/Concise ency of Jewish music/76n997
Selfridge-Field/Venetian instrumental music from Gabrieli to Vivaldi/76n984
Stone/African music & oral data/77n962
HANDBOOKS AND YEARBOOKS
Adelmann/Musical Europe/75n1144
British music yrbk/76n998
Brody/Music gd to . . .
   Austria & Germany/77n945
   Belgium, Luxembourg, Holland & Switzerland/78n889
Limbacher/Film music/75n1147

MUSIC (cont'd)
    HANDBOOKS AND YEARBOOKS (cont'd)
Donington/Interpretation of early music/75n1145
Donington/Performer's gd to baroque music/75n1146
International music gd/77n946
Handbuch der musikalischen literatur: reprint of 1817 ed & 10 suppls/Whistling/76n987
    HISTORY
Eisler/World chronology of music hist/75n1139
Hughes/Medieval music/76n988
New Oxford hist of music . . .
    v7/75n1148
    v10/75n1149
Sternfeld/Music in modern age/75n1151
Weaver/Chronology of music in Florentine theater 1590-1750/79n995
    INDEXES
Berkowitz/Popular titles & subtitles of musical compositions/76n983
Edson/Organ preludes/75n1153
Maleady/Record & tape reviews index/75n1154

MUSIC, POPULAR (songs, etc.)
    See also names of performers; American songs; Country music; Dance bands; Jazz music; Rock music; Songs; Soul music

    Also Sheet music
Armitage/Annual index to pop music record reviews/75n1169; 77n976; 77n977
Brohaugh/Songwriter's market/79n978
Craig/Sweet & lowdown/79n985
Denisoff/Songs of protest, war & peace/75n1122
Edwards/Top 10's & trivia of rock & roll & rhythm & blues 1950-73/76n1023/Suppl 1974/76n1024
80 yrs of Amer song hits/75n1170
Goldstein/Oldies but goodies: rock 'n' roll yrs/78n916
Havlice/Popular song index/76n1026/Suppl/79n980
Kinkle/Complete ency of pop music & jazz 1900-50/75n1171
Limbacher/Song list/75n1130
Nite/Rock on/79n998
Osborne/Popular & rock records 1948-78/79n999
Popular music periodicals index/75n1172
Propes/Golden oldies/75n1173
Rolling Stone record review/75n1174
Rust/American dance band discog 1917-42/76n994
Shapiro/Popular music/75n1175

MUSIC, POPULAR (songs, etc.) (cont'd)
Shestack/Country music ency/75n1176
Stambler/Encyclopedia of folk, country, & western music/76n1031
Stambler/Encyclopedia of pop, rock, & soul/76n1030; 78n920
Tudor/Popular music periodicals index/75n1172; 77n983

MUSIC AND LITERATURE
East/Browning music/75n1137
Gooch/Musical settings of late Victorian & modern British lit/77n954
Kaufman/Musical refs in Chinese classics/77n948
Pollin/Music for Shelley's poetry/75n1133
Shapiro/Encyclopedia of quotations abt music/79n967

MUSIC EDUCATION
Harris/Music educ/79n959
School music program/75n1119

MUSIC HALLS
Brody/Music gd to Italy/79n956

MUSIC IN FILMS
Limbacher/Film music/75n1147

MUSIC LIBRARIES
Bradley/Reader in music librarianship/75n201
Phillips/Selected bibliog of music librarianship/76n170

MUSIC PUBLISHING
Brohaugh/Songwriter's market/79n979
Dichter/Handbook of early Amer sheet music 1768-1889/79n1001
Hurst/Your intro to music-record copyright, contracts . . . /78n59
Nardone/Organ music in print/76n1018
Showalter/Music bks of Ruebush & Kieffer, 1866-1942/76n992

MUSIC SYNTHESIZERS
Ward/Electronic music circuit gdbk/76n1635

MUSICAL INSTRUMENTS
Diagram Group/Musical instruments of world: ency/77n968
Marcuse/Survey of musical instruments/76n1017
Martin/Complete musician/77n949

MUSICAL NOTATION
Risatti/New music vocabulary/76n1001

MUSICAL REVUES, COMEDIES, ETC.
Busby/British music hall: Illust'd who's who/78n942
Drone/Index to opera & musical comedy synopses . . . /79n979
Green/Encyclopedia of musical theatre/77n992

MUSICAL REVUES, COMEDIES, ETC. (cont'd)
Laufe/Broadway's greatest musicals/79n1004
Salem/Guide to critical reviews: the musical 1909-74/78n940
Woll/Songs from Hollywood musical comedies: dict/77n984

MUSICIANS
Chicorel bibliog to bks on music & musicians/76n985
Claghorn/Biographical dict of Amer music/75n1155
Fisher/Heroes of music/75n1156
Hixon/Women in music: bibliog/76n1002
International who's who in music & musicians' directory/76n1004; 79n1002
Parker/Musical biog/76n1006
Significant Amer musicians, composers, & singers/Meltzer/77n135
Skowronski/Women in Amer music/79n962
York/Who's who in rock music/79n1003

MUSLIMS
Weekes/Muslim peoples/79n772

MUTUAL FUNDS
Investment companies 1975/76n857
Mutual funds almanac/78n730
Weisenberger Investment Co serv investment companies: annual compendium .../77n805

MYCOLOGY
Mycological Society of Amer/Mycological gdbk/75n1488

MYCOTOXICOLOGY
Wyllie/Mycotoxic fungi, mycotoxins, mycotoxicoses/79n1477

MYSTICISM
Ferguson/Illustrated ency of mysticism & the mystery religions/79n1057

MYTHOLOGY
Gupta/From Diatyas to Devatas in Hindu mythology/75n1239
Harnsberger/Gods and heroes: Greek & Roman/78n1016
Kravitz/Who's who in Greek & Roman mythology/78n1017
Lal/Annotated Mahabharata bibliog/75n1421
Palmer/Dictionary of mythical places/77n1054
Peradotto/Classical mythology/75n1240
Robinson/Myths & legends of all nations/77n1055
Thomas/Universal pronouncing dict of biog & mythology/77n1056
Tripp/Meridian hndbk of classical mythology/75n1242

NACOGDOCHES, TX
Ericson/Nacogdoches-Gateway to Texas/75n415

NAMES, GEOGRAPHICAL
Palmer/Dictionary of mythical places/77n1054
Room/Place-names of world/75n455
von Engeln/Story key to geographic names/77n553

STATES AND COUNTRIES
Baker/Indiana place names/76n453
Carlson/Nevada place names/76n454
Gannett/Gazetteer of Maryland & Delaware/77n463
Gannett/Gazetteer of Virginia & W Virginia/76n455
Gordon/Gazetteer of the state of PA/76n456
Hamilton/Macmillan bk of Canadian place names/79n625
Harder/Illustrated dict of place names, US & Canada/77n551
Johnston's gazetteer of Scotland/76n457
McArthur/Oregon geographic names/76n458
McClure/British place-names in their hist'l setting/75n451
Morris/Florida place names/75n452
Phillips/Washington state place names/77n552
Probert/Lost mines & buried treasurs of the West: bibliog & place names/78n358
Pukui/Place names in Hawaii/75n453
Romig/Michigan place-names/75n454
Shirk/Oklahoma place names/75n456
Swift/Vermont place-names/78n535
Trumbull/Indian names in CT/75n457
Utley/Placenames of GA/76n459

NAMES, PERSONAL
Browder/New age baby name bk/75n446
Chuks-orji/Names from Africa/75n447
Irvine/How to pronounce names in Shakespeare/76n1035
Kaganoff/Dictionary of Jewish names/78n423
Kelly/Irish family names .../77n487
Lederman/Russian-Engl dict of suppositional names/76n1147
Levith/What's in Shakespeare's names/79n1252
Maduluike/Handbook of African names/78n424
Puckett/Black names in America/77n488
Rajec/Study of names in lit/79n1182
Reaney/Dictionary of British surnames/77n489; 79n500
Rule/What's in a name?/75n449
Sanyika/Know & claim your African name/77n490

NAMES, PERSONAL (cont'd)
Sharp/Handbook of pseudonyms & personal nicknames/76n451
Singerman/Jewish & Hebrew onomastics: bibliog/78n425
US Immigration Serv/Foreign versions . . . of Engl names & titles/75n250
Weekley/Jack & Jill: Christian names/76n452
West/Index of proper names in French Arthurian prose romances/79n1275
Withycombe/Oxford dict of Engl Christian names/78n426

NANTUCKET ISLAND
Burroughs/Nantuckett: gd with tours/75n603

NASA
NASA factbk/76n1608

NATHAN BURKAN MEMORIAL COMPETITION
Copyright law symposium/78n53; 78n54

NATIONAL AGRICULTURAL LIBRARY
Thesaurus of agric'l terms . . . /77n1517

NATIONAL ASSOCIATION OF EDUCATIONAL BROADCASTERS
NAEB public telecommunications directory/79n1163

NATIONAL COMMISSION ON LIBRARIES AND INFORMATION SCIENCE
Annual report 1975-76/79n151

NATIONAL ENDOWMENT FOR ARTS
National Endowment for Arts/Gd to programs 1975-76/76n628

NATIONAL GALLERY, LONDON
Potterton/National Gallery, London/79n880

NATIONAL GEOGRAPHIC
Underhill/Handy key to your "Natl Geographics"/78n1278

NATIONAL INSTITUTES OF HEALTH
NIH factbook/77n1481

NATIONAL LEAGUE OF PROFESSIONAL BASEBALL CLUBS
Reidenbaugh/100 years of NL baseball/77n676

NATIONAL LENDING LIBRARY FOR SCIENCE AND TECHNOLOGY
Barr/Essays on info & libraries/76n207

NATIONAL LIBRARY OF MEDICINE
NLM classification/79n276

NATIONAL MARITIME MUSEUM
Knight/Guide to manuscripts/79n408

NATIONAL SCIENCE FOUNDATION
NSF factbook/76n603

NATIONAL SECURITY
Murphy/Where's what: info for fed investigators/77n839

NATIONAL SONGS
Shaw/National anthems of world/77n950

NATIONAL TRANSPORTATION SAFETY BOARD
Federal aviation regs for pilots/79n1584

NATIONAL UNIVERSITY EXTENSION ASSOCIATION
Guide to independent study thru correspondence instruction/76n621

NATIONALISM
Katz/Handbook of major Soviet nationalities/76n385

NATIVE AMERICAN LITERATURE
Jacobson/Contemporary Native Amer lit/78n1127

NATIVE AMERICANS
See also Indians of North America

Also names of tribes
American Indian ref bk/78n380
Bibliography of lang arts matls for native No Americans/78n587
Dobyns/Native Amer hist'l demography/77n736
Dockstader/Great No Amer Indians/78n381
Dunn/American Indians: study gd/76n412
Frisbie/Music & dance research of SW US Indians/78n890
Gibson/Jefferson Davis & Confederacy & treaties concluded by Conf States with Indian tribes/79n420
Hill/Office of Indian Affairs, 1824-80/75n804
Hirschfelder/American Indian & Eskimo authors/75n805
Hodge/Bibliography of contemp No Amer Indians/77n742
Johnson/Guide to Amer Indian docs in Congressional Series Set: 1817-99/78n382
Klein/Reference ency of the Amer Indian/75n808; 79n463
Lass-Woodfin/Books on Amer Indians & Eskimos/79n464
Mandel/Significant Amer Indians/77n132
Marquis/Guide to America's Indians, ceremonies, reservations & museums/75n806
Monthan/Art & Indian individualists/76n936
Narratives of captivity among Indians of No America/75n807
Perkins/Native Amer of No America: bibliog/76n805
Prucha/US Indian policy/79n526
Smith/Indians of US & Canada: bibliog/76n414

NATIVE AMERICANS (cont'd)
Sutton/Indian land tenure: bibliog/76n806
Terrell/American Indian almanac/76n811
US Economic Developmt Admin/Federal & state Indian reservations & trust areas/75n809
Washburn/American Indian & US/75n369

NATO
US Dept of Defense/Nuclear weapons & NATO/77n1626

NATURAL HISTORY
Jorgensen/Sierra Club naturalist's gd to southern New England/79n1338
Lewis/Ecology fld glossary/78n1345
Nature-sci annual/76n1321
Palmer/Fieldbook of natural hist/76n1364
Thompson/Index to illustrations of natural world/78n1277

NATURALISTS
Baetzenr/Naturalists' directory internat'l/76n1368

NAVAHO INDIANS
Iverson/Navajos: bibliog/77n743
Kari/Navajo reading bibliog/76n413

NAVAL AVIATION
Swanborough/US Navy aircraft since 1911/78n1577

NAVAL BATTLES
Pemsel/History of war at sea/79n1604
Rohwer/Chronology of war at sea 1939-45/75n542
Sanderson/Sea battles/76n301

NAVAL HISTORY
Pemsel/History of war at sea/79n1604
Rohwer/Chronology of war at sea, 1939-45/75n542
Smith/World War II at sea: bibliog/77n1652

NAVAL OFFICERS
Register of commissioned & warrant officers of US Navy/79n1606

NAVAL SCIENCE
Noel/Naval terms dict/79n1603
Wedertz/Dictionary of naval abbreviations/78n1572

NAVIES
Breyer/Guide to Soviet navy/79n1599
Couhat/Combat fleets of world/77n1648; 79n1600
Dulin/Battleships/77n1649
Ireland/Warships of the world/78n1574
Jane's fighting ships/Moore/78n1575
Jentschura/Warships of Japanese navy, 1869-1945/79n1602
Kemp/Oxford companion to ships and the sea/78n1549

NAVIES (cont'd)
Leather/World warships in review 1860-1906/78n1576
Polmar/Ships & aircraft of US fleet/79n1605

NAVIGATION
Farwell's rules of nautical road/Bassett/78n1573
Reed's nautical almanac & tide tables/79n726
Townsend/Amateur navigator's hndbk/75n752
US Coast Guard/Light lists/78n1551

NEAR EAST
Bacharach/Near East studies hndbk/78n280
Land tenure & agrarian reform in Africa & the Near East: bibliog/77n1514
Littlefield/Islamic Near East & No Africa/78n281

NEBRASKA
Lawson/Agricultural atlas/78n1448
Lawson/Climatic atlas/79n1415
Lawson/Economic atlas/78n695

NECK
Lore/Atlas of head & neck surgery/75n1644

NEEDLEWORK PROJECTS
Chicorel index to crafts: needlework, crocheting & tie-dyeing/76n954
Clabburn/Needleworker's dict/77n890
Dillmont/Complete ency of needlework/79n944
Harding/Make it yourself/79n945
Swan/Wintherthur gd to Amer needlework/78n880

NEGROES
See Blacks

NEPAL
Ali/Handbook of birds of India & Pakistan, ... Nepal/77n1373

NETHERLANDS
Agricultural sci in Netherlands/76n1556
Stichting Drukwerk in de Marge/Bibliografie (small presses)/79n41

NETWORK ANALYSIS
US Dept Commerce/Annotated bibliog of lit on resource sharing/Woods/77n1586

NEUROANATOMY
Lockard/Desk ref for neuroanatomy/79n1462
Miller/Atlas of central nervous system in man/79n1448

NEUROLOGY
Centennial vol of Amer Neurological Assn/Denny-Brown/76n1510
International ency of psychiatry, psychology, psychoanalysis & neurology/Wolman/78n1367

NEUROPSYCHIATRY
Brown/Neuropsychiatry & war/77n1459

NEUROSCIENCE
Annual review/79n1474

NEVADA
Carlson/Nevada place names/76n454

NEW AMSTERDAM
Fernow/Records of New Amsterdam from 1653-74/77n462
Scott/Register of S. Lachaire, notary public, 1661-62/79n496

NEW ENGLAND
Bolton/Real founders of New England/75n408
Bongartz/New England records/79n386
Bryfonski/New England beach bk/76n544
Chapin/Guide to recommended country inns of New England/75n604/New rev gd/76n546
Clough/Dutch uncles & New Engl cousins/78n398
Goodrich/Enjoying summer theatres of New England/75n1184
Guide to newspaper indexes in New Engl/79n22
Index to New Engl periodicals/79n23
Hechtlinger/Pelican gd to historic homes ... revolutionary Amer: New England/77n561
Jorgensen/Sierra Club naturalist's gd to So New England/79n1338
Miser/Factory store gd to all New England/75n951
Scott/Genealogical data from colonial NY newspapers/78n409
Weis/Colonial clergy & colonial churches of New England/78n416

NEW GUINEA
Hays/Anthropology in New Guinea highlands: bibliog/77n739

NEW HAMPSHIRE
Directory of foundations/77n82
New Hampshire's role in Amer Revolution 1763-89: bibliog/76n352

NEW HAVEN, CT
Jacobus/Families of ancient New Haven/75n422

NEW JERSEY
Crawford/Guide to middle states schools/76n657
Flaste/NY Times gd to children's entertainment: NY, NJ, CT/77n559
Gannett/Geographic dict/79n595
Kipel/Ethnic directory of NJ/79n445
Littell/Family records of first settlers of Passaic Valley/77n469
Mitchell/Directory of NJ foundations/78n80

NEW JERSEY (cont'd)
Nelson/Patents & deeds ... 1664-1703/77n471
Newberry/New Jersey/78n315
Shourds/History & genealogy of Fenwick's Colony/77n476
Wright/Directory of NJ newspapers, 1765-1970/79n21

NEW MEXICO
Findley/Mammals of NM/77n1393
Grove/New Mexico newspapers/76n22
Wolf/Bibliography of NM state politics/76n493

NEW ORLEANS, LA
Griffin/Pelican gd to New Orleans/75n608

NEW THOUGHT (religion)
Beebe/Who's who in new thought/79n1077

NEW YORK, NY
Alpern/Pratt gd to planning & renewal for New Yorkers/75n857
Ballard/Directory of Manhattan office bldgs/79n889
Britchky/Restaurants of NY/75n1685; 79n599
Bull/Birds of NY area/77n1374
Boston Women's Collective/NY women's yellow pages/79n767
Directory of soc & health agencies/75n798; 76n774
1866 gd to NY city/76n541
Ford/Guide to black apple/79n600
Goldstone/History preserved: gd to landmarks & hist'ic districts/75n607
Hughes/New York theatre annual/79n1020
Locus: directory of galleries & art sources/77n869
McDade/Directory of soc & health agencies of NY city/79n1508
McDarrah/Museums in NY/79n93
New York art yrbk/78n796
Postal/Jewish landmarks/79n609
Shaw/New York for children/75n614
Shepard/Going out in NY/75n615
Sohmer/Call for action: survival kit for New Yorkers/76n884
Union list of selected microforms in libraries in NY metro area/77n31
Wolfe/New York: gd to ... architecture & history/77n563
Womanpower Project/NY women's directory/75n854
Yeadon/New York bk of bars, pubs & taverns/77n1523

NEW YORK (state)
Bunker/Long Island genealogies/77n457
Cary/NYCLU gd to women's rights/79n763
Clough/Dutch uncles & New Engl cousins/78n398

NEW YORK (state) (cont'd)
Crawford/Guide to middle states schools/76n658
Flaste/NY Times gd to children's entertainment/77n559
Guide to local hist'l matls in libraries of NY state/77n392
New York: chronology/Furer/75n709
Neal/NY library instruction programs: directory/77n180
New York manuscripts: Dutch/Van Laer/75n428
Rifkind/Mansions, mills, & main streets/76n554
Tomikel/Edible wildplants of PA & NY/75n1470

NEW YORK ACADEMY OF DESIGN
Naylor/Exhibition record: 1861-1900/75n993

NEW YORK BIGHT
US Natl Oceanic & Atmospheric Admin/Bibliography/75n1563

NEW YORK FREEDOM'S JOURNAL
Jacobs/Antebellum black newspapers: indices/77n432

NEW YORK HISTORICAL SOCIETY
Catalogue of Amer portraits/76n918

NEW YORK PUBLIC LIBRARY
Beyond the lions: gd to NYPL/75n189
Catalog of theatre & drama collections/77n989
Dictionary catalog of art & architecture division/76n919
Dictionary catalog of prints division/76n920
Williams/Guide to research collections/77n194

NEW YORK STATE MUSEUM
Liebe/Indexes to Museum Bulletins, 1888-1973/76n930

NEW YORK TIMES
New York Times cum subj & personal name index: environment/79n1399/Women/79n769
Falk/Personal name index, 1851-1974/77n40

NEW YORKER
Johnson/Index to lit, v46-50/77n42

NEW ZEALAND
Anderson/New Zealand in maps/79n597
Key/Library automation: Orient & South Pacific/77n289
New Zealand bks in print/76n17
Taubert/Book trade of world: Americas, Australia, New Zealand/77n51

NEW ZEALAND (cont'd)
Wards/New Zealand atlas/78n524
Who's who/Traue/79n144

NEWARK, NJ
Rice/Newark: chron & doc hist/78n359

NEWBERY AWARD
Newbery & Caldecott medal bks/77n1192

NEWMAN, ROBERT LOFTIN
US Smithsonian Institution/R. L. Newman/75n995

NEWS AGENCIES
Weiner/News bureaus in US/78n1077

NEWS CORRESPONDENTS
Hudson's Washington news media contact directory/Hudson/76n1169

NEWS MEDIA AND GOVERNMENT
Knappman/Government & media in conflict/75n494

NEWSLETTERS
See also Periodicals and serials
National directory of newsletters/79n18
Newsletter yrbk-directory/Hudson/78n16

NEWSPAPER LIBRARIES
Whatmore/Modern news library/79n243
Parch/Directory of newspaper libraries in US & Canada/77n182

NEWSPAPERS
Alternatives: gd to newspapers/Akeroyd/77n104
Arndt/German lang press of Americas: hist & bibliog/77n444
Brigham/History & bibliog of Amer newspapers, 1690-1820/77n1110
Directory of college student press in Amer/78n15
Editor & publisher internat'l yr bk/78n44
Feuereisen/Presse in Afrika/75n912
Grove/New Mexico newspapers/76n22
Guide to newspaper indexes in New Engl/79n22
Jacobs/Antebellum black newspapers: indices/77n432
Kowalik/Polish press in America/79n465
Media gd internat'l: newspapers/77n786
Meyer/Guide to Long Island news media/75n1301
Milner/Newspaper indexes: gd/78n1079
Perica/Newspaper indexing for hist'l societies . . ./76n191
Richstad/Pacific Island press/75n1303
Webber/World list of natl newspapers/78n1080
Wright/Directory of NJ newspapers, 1765-1970/79n21
Wynar/Encyclopedic directory of ethnic newspapers/77n430

NEWSPRINT
Pollock/Newsprint/78n1260

NICARAGUAN LITERATURE
Ellis/Critical approaches to Ruben Dario/ 76n1299
Woodbridge/Ruben Dario: bibliog/76n1303

NICKNAMES
See Pseudonyms

NIGERIA
Aguolu/Nigeria: bibliog, 1901-71/75n285
Aguolu/Nigerian civil war/75n390
Aiyepeku/Geographical lit on Nigeria, 1901-70/75n567
Baldwin/Yoruba of SW Nigeria/77n735
Orimoloye/Biographia Nigeriana/78n117

NIN, ANAÏS
Franklin/Anaïs Nin/75n1416

NINETEENTH-CENTURY FICTION
Tennyson/Index to . . . v1-30/78n1107

NIXON, RICHARD M.
Bremer/Richard M. Nixon: chronology/76n332
Presidency 1974/76n487
Sobel/Inflation & the Nixon admin/75n495

NOBEL PRIZE
Opfell/Lady laureates/79n770

NOISE
Floyd/Bibliography of noise/76n1452
Faulkner/Handbook of industrial noise control/77n1606

NONBOOK MATERIALS
See Audiovisual media

NON-FERROUS METALS
Non-ferrous metal data/76n900

NORRIS, FRANK
Crisler/Frank Norris: ref gd/76n1247

NORTH AFRICA
al-Qazzaz/Women in Mid East & No Africa/78n279
Littlefield/Islamic Near East & No Africa/78n281
Middle East & No Africa/76n266
Schulz/International politics in Mid East & No Africa: gd to info sources/78n488

NORTH AMERICA
Burt/Field gd to mammals/77n1392
Cook/Stratigraphic atlas of No & Central America/78n513
Emerson/American Museum of Natl Hist gd to shells/77n1394
Jarrett/Stamps of Brit No Amer/76n975
Jenkinson/Wild rivers of No Amer/75n632
Johnsgard/Waterfowl of No Amer/77n1381
Logan/Traveller's gd to No Amer gardens/75n633

NORTH AMERICA (cont'd)
Mackenzie/Complete outdoorsman's gd to birds/77n1383
Palmer/Handbook of No Amer birds: waterfowl/77n1384
Prenton/No American trees: hndbk/77n1370
Sutton/Wilderness areas of No Amer/75n637
Weber/No Amer film & video directory/77n186

NORTH CAROLINA
Clay/North Carolina atlas/76n531
Muster rolls of soldiers of War of 1812/77n472
Potter/Index to 1820 NC census/79n493
Register/State census of NC 1784-87/79n494
Robertson/Kansas territorial settlers of 1860 . . . born in TN, VA, NC, SC/77n475
Weis/Colonial clergy of VA, NC, SC/77n479

NORTHEASTERN STATES
Mobil travel gd: NE states/79n605
Wright/Genealogical reader: NE US & Canada/75n434

NORTHERN IRELAND
Deutsch/Northern Ireland 1921-74/76n276
Fedden/National Trust gd to Engl, Wales & No Ireland/76n556
Maltby/Government of No Ireland 1822-1972/75n521

NORTHWESTERN STATES
Mobil travel gd: NW and Great Plains states/79n606

NORWAY
1000 largest companies/76n890
Scandinavian political studies: yrbk/76n501

NORWEGIAN AMERICANS
Andersen/Norwegian-Americans/76n415

NOTARIES
Rothman/Notary public practices & glossary/79n562
Scott/Register of S. Lachaire, notary public of New Amsterdam/79n496

NOVELISTS
Stanton/Bibliography of modern Brit novelists/79n1230
Vinson/Contemporary novelists/77n1182

NOVELS
Bell/English novel 1578-1956: chklst of 20th cent criticism/76n1256
Bradley/Index to Waverley novels/76n1283
Cassis/20th cent Engl novel: bibliog/78n1162
Childers/Tales from Spanish picaresque novels/79n1286
Foster/20th cent Spanish-Amer novel: bibliog'ic gd/76n1300
McNutt/18th cent gothic novel: bibliog/76n1209

NOVELS (cont'd)
Stewart/Disraeli's novels reviewed/76n1273

NUCLEAR ENERGY
Hagan/Bibliography on atomic energy levels & spectra/78n1267
Slattery/Index of US nuclear stds/79n1406

NUCLEAR POWER PLANTS
Klema/Public reg of site selection/79n1409

NUCLEAR PROLIFERATION TREATY
Meeker/Proliferation of nuclear weapons & nonproliferation treaty/75n1836
Ridgeway/NPT: current issues/79n559

NUCLEAR SCIENCE
Annual review of nuclear sci/Segre/76n1349
INIS: Atomindex: internat'l abstracting service/77n1339
INIS: authority list for corp entries/79n273
INIS: descrip cataloguing samples/79n274
INIS: thesaurus/79n1298
International directory of certified radioactive matls/77n1340
Vasaru/Deuterium & heavy water: bibliog/77n1341

NUCLEAR WEAPONS
Meeker/Proliferation of nuclear weapons & nonproliferation treaty/75n1836
Nuclear proliferation factbk/79n1407
Ridgeway/NPT: current issues/79n559
US Dept of Defense/Nuclear weapons & NATO: survey of lit/77n1626

NUMISMATICS
See Coins

NURSING
Burkhalter/Nursing care of alcoholic & drug abuser/76n1528
Cumulative index to nursing & allied health lit/79n1479
Cumulative index to nursing lit/75n1640; 77n1492
French/Guide to diagnostic procedures/76n1529
Garb/Abbreviations & acronyms in medicine & nursing/77n1475
Hospital-health care training media profiles/76n1532
Livingstone's dict for nurses/Roper/75n1622
Miller/Encyclopedia & dict of med, nursing & allied health/79n1463
Thompson/Bibliography of nursing lit, 1961-70/75n1619

NURSING HOMES
Council of Home Health Agencies/Directory of home health agencies certified as medicare providers/76n1534; 78n1404

NURSING SCHOOLS
State-approved schools of nursing:
RN/76n1538
LPN-LVN/77n631

NUTRITION
Adams/Encyclopedia of food & nutrition/79n1529
Ashley/Dictionary of nutrition/77n1469
Bender/Dictionary of nutrition & food tech/78n1468
Casale/Diet food finder/76n1569
Deskins/Everyone's gd to better food & nutrition/76n1570
Doyle/Complete food hndbk/78n1469
Food & nutrition/75n1687
Fryer/Dictionary of food supplements/77n1545
Goldbeck/Dieter's companion/77n1494
Kaplan/Selected bibliog of nutrition matls/75n1689
Lagua/Nutrition & diet therapy ref dict/76n1525
McGraw-Hill ency of food, agri, & nutrition/78n1452
Nutrition Search, Inc/Nutrition almanac/77n1498
Nutritive value of Amer foods/Adams/77n1548
Ockerman/Source bk for food scientists/79n1531
Watt/Handbook of nutritional content of foods/77n1552

OBADIAH RICH COLLECTION
Brownrigg/Colonial Latin Amer manuscripts .../79n443

OBSTETRICS
Benson/Handbook of obstetrics & gynecology/75n1626
Obstetrics & gyn annual/Wynn/77n1487

O'CASEY, SEAN
Ayling/Sean O'Casey/79n1279

OCCULT
See also Astrology; Dreams; Ghosts; Magic; Parapsychology; Psychic experiences; Superstitions; Zodiac
Biteaux/New consciousness/76n1508
Brandon/Weird America/79n1084
Cavendish/Encyclopedia of unexplained/75n1604
Chaplin/Dictionary of occult & paranormal/78n1375
Coxe/Haunted Britain/75n622
Day/Occult illust'd dict/77n1451
Shepard/Occultism update/79n1439

OCCULT (cont'd)
Shepard/Encyclopedia of occultism & parapsychology/79n1440
Walker/Man & beasts within: ency/78n1379

OCCUPATIONAL DISEASES
International directory of occupational safety & health services/79n860

OCCUPATIONAL SAFETY
Comprehensive bibliog on pregnancy & work/79n1452
International directory of occupational safety & health services/79n860
Miller/Occupational safety, health & fire index/78n770
Peck/Occupational safety & health/75n978

OCCUPATIONAL TRAINING
See also Business training programs; Employee training; Industry training programs; Management training programs
International resource directory: worldwide gd . . . to training & development profession/79n861
Training film profiles/76n687

OCCUPATIONS
See also Vocational guidance
Career gd to prof assns/77n834
Dictionary of occupational titles/79n855
Joseph/Complete out-of-doors job, business, & professional gd/75n977
Lederer/Guide to career educ/77n629
Lingfelter/Vocations in fict: bibliog/76n1208
Lovejoy/Lovejoy's career & vocational school guide/79n666
Nicholsen/People in books/78n110
Occupational outlook for college grads/78n771; 79n862
Phelps/New career options for women: bibliog/78n773
Shaffer/Career educ pamphlets/77n654
Standard occupational classification manual/79n868/Index/79n866
US Bureau of Labor Stats/Occupational outlook hndbk/77n844
US Civil Serv Commission/Federal career directory/77n626
US Civil Serv Commission/Guide to fed career lit/77n596
US Dept of Labor/Guide to local occupational info/77n845

OCEAN ENGINEERING
Index of SNAME publications/76n1655
Trillo/Jane's ocean technology/79n1545
US Corps of Engineers/Shore protection manual/75n1816
US Natl Oceanic & Atmospheric Admin/Ocean eng'g & oceanography tech lit collection/75n1817

OCEAN LINERS
Emmons/Atlantic liners/75n1828
Emmons/Pacific liners, 1927-72/75n1829
Miller/Guide to No Amer passenger ships/79n1586
Morris/American sailing coasters of No Atlantic/75n1830

OCEANIA
McLean/Annotated bibliog of Oceanic music & dance/79n960

OCEANOGRAPHY
Barton/Atlas of sea/75n1575
Collias/Atlas of physical & chem properties of Puget Sound/75n1576
Unesco/Equalant I & Equalant II: oceanographic atlas/76n1484
Estok/Union list of oceanographic expeditions/77n1441
Smith/Handbook of marine sci/76n1470
US Natl Oceanic & Atmospheric Admin/Ocean eng'g & oceanography tech lit collection/75n1817

OCEANS
Hastenrath/Climatic atlas of tropical Atlantic & Pacific Oceans/79n1414
Rand McNally atlas of oceans/78n517

OCLC
Arthur D. Little, Inc./New governance structure for OCLC/79n257

O'CONNOR, FLANNERY
Golden/F. O'Connor & C. Gordon: ref gd/78n1123

OFFICE BUILDINGS
Ballard/Directory of Manhattan office bldgs/79n889

OFFICE PRACTICE
Hill/Hill's manual of soc & business forms/77n794
Nanassy/Reference manual for office workers/78n717
Sabin/Gregg ref manual/78n718
Simpson/Tested secretarial techniques . . . /75n893

OFFSHORE DRILLING
European offshore oil & gas yrbk/77n1418

OHIO
Alt/Encyclopedia of Ohio assns/79n90
Clark/Ohio art & artists/77n857
Flavell/Ohio area key/78n401
Flavell/Ohio genealogical gd/79n483
Flavell/Ohio genealogical periodical index/78n400
Ohio mfgrs industrial directory/78n759
Wynar/Ethnic groups in Ohio: bibliog'ical gd/76n393

OHIO VALLEY
Bolin/Ohio Valley hist: bibliog/77n455

OJIBWA INDIANS
Tanner/Ojibwas: bibliog/77n745

OKINAWA
Walker/Flora of Okinawa . . . /77n1358

OKLAHOMA
Boce/Directory of Oklahoma foundations/75n78
Morris/Historical atlas of Oklahoma/78n356
Shirk/Oklahoma place names/75n456
Statistical abstract of Oklahoma/79n790

OLD AGE ASSISTANCE
Norback/Older American's hndbk/79n738
Sourcebook on aging/79n740

OLD PROVENCAL LITERATURE
Taylor/Littérature occitane du moyen age/79n1274

OLYMPIC GAMES
de Groote/Olympic sports official album/77n664
McWhirter/Guinness bk of Olympic records/76n697

OMAN
Anthony/Historical & cultural dict of Oman & emirates of eastern Arabia/77n315

O'NEILL, EUGENE
Atkinson/E. O'Neill/75n1362

ONOMATOPOEIA
Kloe/Dictionary of onomatopeic sounds, . . . in Engl & Spanish/78n1045

ONTARIO (province)
Morley/Ontario & Canadian North/79n376
Powell/Ontario energy catalogue/79n1388

OPERA
Alexander/Operanatomy/76n1021
Barlow/Dictionary of opera & song themes/78n911
Chusid/Catalog of Verdi's operas/75n1165
de Schauensee/Collector's Verdi & Puccini/79n986
Drone/Index to opera, operetta & musical comedy synopses . . . /79n979
Eaton/Opera production II/75n1166
England/Favorite operas by German & Russian composers/75n1167
England/Favorite operas by Italian & French composers/75n1168
Forbes/Opera from A to Z/78n912
Grieb/Operas of G. C. Menotti: bibliog/76n1008
May/Companion to opera/78n913
New Kobbe's compl opera bk/77n972
Northouse/20th cent opera in Engl & the US/77n973

OPERA (cont'd)
Orrey/Encyclopedia of opera/77n974
Peltz/Metropolitan Opera annals/79n994
Teasdale/Handbook of 20th cent opera/78n914
Weaver/Chronology of music in Florentine theater 1590-1750/79n995
Who's who in opera/77n975

OPERATIONAL AMPLIFIERS
Stout/Handbook of operational amplifier circuit design/77n1601

OPERATIONS RESEARCH
Chen/Applications of operations research models to libraries/77n236
Moder/Handbook of operations research/79n820
Zaremba/Mathematical economics & operations research/79n808

OPERETTA
Moore/Handbook of Gilbert & Sullivan/76n1009

OPTICAL TECHNOLOGY
Bibliography of microwave optical tech/Harvey/78n1266

OPTICS
Driscoll/Handbook of optics/79n1333
Harburn/Atlas of optical transforms/77n1338
Levi/Handbook of tables for applied optics/76n1351

ORACLE BONES
Chou/Oracle bone collections in US/78n318

ORAHOOD, HARPER M.
Mitterling/Guide to H. M. Orahood papers 1861-1908/76n350

ORAL COMMUNICATION
Feezel/Selected print & nonprint resources in speech communication: bibliog/77n1121
Kirshenblatt-Gimblett/Speech play: resources for studying linguistic creativity/77n1123

ORAL HISTORY
Davis/Oral hist: from tape to type/78n323
Dictionary catalog of G. R. Vincent Voice Library at Michigan State Univ/Cluley/76n293
Meckler/Oral hist collections/76n302
Moss/Oral hist program manual/75n348
Waserman/Bibliography on oral hist/77n383

ORAL TRADITION
Stone/African music & oral data/77n962

ORANGE COUNTY, NY
Gocek/Orange Co., NY/75n379

ORCHESTRAL MUSIC
ASCAP symphonic catalog/78n921

ORCHESTRAL MUSIC (cont'd)
Downes/New York Philharmonic gd to the symphony/78n922
Farish/Orchestral music in print/79n990
Hopkins/Downbeat music gd/79n957

OREGON
Brandt/Oregon biog index/77n390
Loy/Atlas of Oregon/78n521
Kosloff/Plants & animals of Pacific NW/77n1346
McArthur/Oregon geographic names/76n458
Niehaus/Field gd to Pacific states wildflowers/77n1361
Oregon Hist'l Society microfilm gd/75n384
Young/Wildflowers of redwood empire/77n1363

ORES
Pearl/Gems, minerals, crystals, & ores: ency/78n1360

ORGAN MUSIC
Conely/Guide to improvisation: . . . for church organists/76n999
Edson/Organ preludes: suppl/75n1153
Nardone/Organ music in print/76n1018
Rowell/American organ music on records/77n966

ORGANIC COMPOUNDS
Dictionary of organic compounds/78n1246/Suppl/78n1245

ORGANIC FOOD
Stoner/Organic directory/76n885

ORGANIC GARDENING
Abraham/Organic gardening under glass/76n1581
Encyclopedia of organic gardening/79n1539

ORGANIZED CRIME
Hopkins/Organized crime/75n827

ORIENTAL LITERATURE
De Bary/Guide to Oriental classics/76n1187
Prusek/Dictionary of Oriental lit/75n1316; 77n1274

ORNAMENT AND DECORATING
See Decorative art

ORNE, JERROLD
Poole/Academic libraries by yr 2000/78n168

ORNITHOLOGY
See also Birds
Coues/American ornithological bibliog/75n1503
Rowley/Bird life/76n1431
Studer's popular ornithology/78n1322
Van Tyne/Fundamentals of ornithology/78n1324

ORWELL, GEORGE
Meyers/George Orwell: bibliog/78n1180

OSBORNE, JOHN
Northouse/John Osborne: ref gd/76n1280

OSCAR AWARDS
Pickard/Oscar movies from A-Z/79n1030

OSCILLOSCOPES
Herrick/Oscilloscope hndbk/75n1787

OSHA
Hopf/Designer's gd to OSHA/76n1605
Miller/Occupational safety, health & fire index/78n770
Petersen/OSHA compliance manual/76n906

OSLER, WILLIAM
Nation/Annotated checklist of Osleriana/78n1389

OSTEOPATHS
Directory of osteopathic specialists/76n1536

OTLET, PAUL
Rayward/Universe of info: work of P. Otlet/77n258

OUT-OF-PRINT BOOKS
Best buys in print/79n32
Books on demand author gd/79n33
Books on demand subj gd/79n34
Books on demand title gd/79n35
Robinson/Buy bks where—sell bks where/79n61

OUTBOARD MOTORS
Dempsey/Complete gd to outboard motor serv & repair/77n683

OUTDOOR EDUCATION
Swan/Research in outdoor educ/79n636

OUTDOOR LIFE
Bergaust/National outdoorsmen's ency/76n715
Perrin/Explorers Ltd source bk/78n616
Hart/Walking softly in wilderness/78n617
Joseph/Complete out-of-doors job, business, & prof gd/75n977
Kaysing/Robin Hood hndbk/75n756
Knap/Complete outdoorsman's hndbk/75n724
Knap/Family camping hndbk/77n687
Landi/Bantam great outdoors gd to US & Canada/79n712
Oberrecht/Great outdoors catalog/78n621
Ormond/Outdoorsman's hndbk/76n719
Petzoldt/Wilderness hndbk/75n757
Schipf/Outdoor recreation/77n669
Turner/Index to outdoor sports, games, & activities/79n699

340–Subjects

OWLS
Burton/Owls of the world/75n1507
Walker/Book of owls/75n1508

OXFORD, ENGLAND
Woolley/Clarendon gd to Oxford/76n561

OXFORD ENGLISH DICTIONARY
Supplement to Oxford Engl dict/77n1073

OZ BOOKS
Hanff/Bibliographia Oziana/77n1187

PACIFIC HISTORICAL REVIEW
Hager/Cumulative index to v I-XLIII, 1932-74/77n388

PACIFIC ISLANDS
Richstad/Mass communication & journalism in Pacific Islands/79n1160
Richstad/Pacific Islands press/75n1303

PACIFIC NORTHWEST
Highsmith/Atlas of Pacific NW/75n578
Hines/Index of archived resources for a folk-life & cultural hist . . . /78n1014
Somerton/Field gd to fish of Puget Sound/77n1388
Hastenrath/Climatic atlas of tropical Atlantic & Eastern Pacific Oceans/79n1414

PADDLE TENNIS
Squires/Complete bk of platform tennis/75n783

PAINE, THOMAS
Stephans/Paine collection of . . . American Philosophical Society/78n443

PAINT
Ash/Formulary of paints & other coatings/79n1320

PAINTERS
See also names of painters
Beazley/Attic black-figure vase-painters/79n903
Checklist of painters 1200-1976/Courtauld Inst of Art/79n905
Lucas/Bibliography of water colour painting & painters/78n819
Norman/19th cent painters & painting/79n908
Rothenstein/Modern Engl painters: Wood to Hockney/76n937
Rosenzweig/Thomas Eakins collection of Hirshhorn Museum/78n787
Sparrow/Women painters of world/77n859
Waterhouse/Roman baroque painting: list of painters . . . /77n886
Wehlte/Materials & techniques of painting/77n887

PAINTINGS
Barr/Painting & sculpture in Museum of Modern Art/79n877
Cleveland Museum of Art/European paintings before 1500/76n917
Deusch/German painting of 16th cent/75n1027
European paintings in collection of Worcester Art Museum/75n992
Havlice/World paintings index/78n816
Keaveney/American painting/75n1028
Lloyd/Catalogue of earlier Italian paintings in Ashmolean Museum/78n818
Lovell/Annotated bibliog of Chinese painting catalogues . . . /75n989
Naylor/National Academy of Design exhibition record: 1861-1900/75n993
Norman/19th cent painters & painting/79n908
Smith/Index to reproductions of Amer paintings . . . /78n820
Unesco/Illustrated inventory of famous dismembered works of art . . . /76n945
Waterhouse/Roman baroque painting: list of principal painters . . . /77n886
Zeri/Italian paintings in Walters Art Gallery/77n888

PAKISTAN
Abernethy/Pakistan: bibliog/76n264
Ali/Handbook of birds of India & Pakistan, . . . /77n1373
Gustafson/Pakistan & Bangladesh: bibliog/77n330
Siddigi/Press directory of Pakistan/76n1172

PALAUAN LANGUAGE
McManus/Palauan-English dict/78n1064

PALEOGRAPHY
Oikonomides/Abbreviations in Greek inscriptions/76n285

PALEONTOLOGY
Day/Guide to fossil man/79n784
Levi-Setti/Trilobites: photographic atlas/76n1363
Macdonald/Sabre-tooth cats . . . /75n1577

PALESTINE QUESTION
Khaliki/Palestine & Arab-Israeli conflict/75n535
Palestine question/79n503

PALI LITERATURE
Banerji/Companion to middle Indo-Aryan lit/78n1192

PALLAVICINO, BENEDETTO
Flanders/Thematic index to works/76n1007

PAMPHLETS
Catalogue of Tract collection of St. David's Univ College, Lampeter/77n369

Subjects—341

PAN-AFRICANISM
Skurnik/Sub-Saharan Africa/78n292

PANAMA
Ridgely/Guide to birds/77n1385

PANAMA CANAL TREATY
Bray/Controversy over a new canal treaty: bibliog/78n486

PANERO, LEOPOLDO
Ruiz-Fornells/Concordance to poetry/79n1291

PANTOMIME
International mimes & pantomimists directory/75n1177

PAPER
Leif/International sourcebk of paper hist/79n38

PAPER CHEMISTRY
Ewing/Care & maintenance of paper machine clothing/78n1258
Louden/Foam & foam control/79n1324
Louden/Mathematical modeling/79n1326
Louden/Odors & odor control/77n1315
Louden/Paper mill sludge . . . /77n1316
Louden/Permanence/79n1325
Louden/Pulping of bagasse . . . /77n1314
Louden/Wet pressing/77n1317
Macek/Bibliography of paper & thin-layer chromatography/77n1324
Pollock/Analytical methods: cooking liquors/77n1325
Pollock/Corrosion of pulp & paper mill eqmt/77n1326
Pollock/Newsprint/78n1260
Pollock/Pitch/77n1327
Pollock/Retention of fillers . . . /77n1318
Pollock/Runnability of printing papers/77n1319
Pollock/Tall oil/78n1259
Pollock/Wood waste/77n1320
Sykes/Forest fertilization/77n1321
Sykes/White water-saveall s/77n1322
Weiner/Coating eqmt & processes/77n1323
Weiner/Dry strength of paper/78n1261
Weiner/Drying of paper & board/78n1262
Weiner/Microorganism control/78n1263
Weiner/Microscopy of pulp & paper/77n1328
Weiner/Nonsulfur pulping/78n1265
Weiner/Process control, instrumentation/79n1328
Weiner/Protective & decorative coatings for paper/77n1329
Weiner/Wet strength of paper/78n1264
Weiner/Energy production & consumption/79n1327

PAPER MONEY
Beresiner/Collector's guide/78n933

PAPER MONEY (cont'd)
Hessler/Comprehensive catalog of US paper money/75n1066
Pick/Standard catalog of world paper money/76n970
Stockney/Coins & paper money of Nicaragua/75n1071
Vogt/Standard catalog of Mexican coins, paper money & medals/79n920

PAPERBACK BOOKS
Blow/B-J paperback bk gd/77n195
Dorn/Latin America, Spain, & Portugal: bibliog of paperbk bks/77n305
Gillespie/Paperback bks for young people/79n229
Hiatt/Kliatt paperback bk gd/75n199
Wynar/Reference bks in paperback/77n17

PAPERWEIGHTS
Selman/Paperweights for collectors/77n922

PARACHUTING
Horan/Index to parachuting 1900-75/79n724

PARAPSYCHOLOGY
See also Occult; Psychic experiences
Biteaux/New consciousness/76n1508
Cavendish/Encyclopedia of unexplained/75n1604
King/Psychic & religious phenomena limited/79n1438
Regush/PSI: other world catalogue/76n1509
Rolls/Research in parapsychology/75n1606
Shepard/Encyclopedia of occultism & parapsychology/79n1440
Walker/Man & beasts within: ency/78n1379
White/Surveys in parapsychology/77n1452

PARENTING
See Children
See also Family life education

PARISH REGISTERS
Steel/Sources for Roman Catholic & Jewish genealogy & family hist/78n421

PARLIAMENTARY GOVERNMENT
See Legislative bodies

PARLIAMENTARY PRACTICE
Deschler's rules of order/77n494
Dod's parliamentary companion/75n469
Keesey/Modern parliamentary procedure/75n472
Place/Parliamentary procedures simplified/77n497
Unesco/Glossary of conf terms: Engl, French, Arabic/76n1138
US House/Impeachment selected matls on procedure/75n499

PARTICIPATORY MANAGEMENT
Marchant/Participative mgmt in academic libraries/78n164

342—Subjects

PARTICLES
McCrone/Particle atlas/75n1433
PASCAL, BLAISE
Davidson/Concordance to Pascal's Pensees/77n1261
PASSAIC VALLEY
Littell/Family records . . . of 1st settlers/77n468
PASSENGER LISTS
See Ship passenger lists
PATENT LAWS
Kase/Designs: lit on design protection/76n1648
PATER, WALTER H.
Wright/Bibliography of writings/76n1281
"PEARL POET"
Chapman/Index of names in Pearl, Purity, Patience, & Gawain/79n1251
PEDDLERS
Beall/Kaufrufe: cries & itinerant trades/78n806
PEDIATRIC PHARMACOLOGY
Shirkey/Pediatric drug hndbk/79n1504
PEDIATRICS
Pascoe/Quick ref to pediatric emergencies/75n1632
Silver/Handbook of pediatrics/77n1486
PENITENTES
Weigle/Penitente bibliog/77n1035
PENNSYLVANIA
Bodnar/Ethnic hist in PA: bibliog/76n386
Crawford/Guide to mid states schools in PA/76n659
Documentary hist of . . . constitution/77n371
Egle/Early PA land records/77n460
Gordon/Gazetteer of PA/76n456
Jordan/Colonial & revolutionary families of PA/79n488
Linn/Annals of Buffalo Valley, 1755-1855/76n436
Rupp/Collection of 30,000 names/76n440
Scott/Abstracts from Pennsylvania Gazette, 1748-55/78n410
Scott/Buried genealogical data/78n411
Swetnam/Guidebook to historic western PA/78n360
Tepper/Emigrants to PA 1641-1819/76n443; 78n414
Tomikel/Edible wild plants of PA/75n1470
PENNSYLVANIA GAZETTE
Scott/Abstracts . . . 1748-55/78n410
PENNSYLVANIA GERMANS
Nead/Pennsylvania-German in settlement of Maryland/76n437

PENNSYLVANIA GERMANS (cont'd)
Richards/Pennsylvania-German in Revolutionary War/79n495
Strassburger/Pennsylvania-German pioneers/76n442
PENSIONS
CCH/Guidebook to pension planning/78n748
US Dept of State/Census of pensioners for revolutionary or military services (1840)/75n432
PENTAGON PAPERS
Knappman/Government & media in conflict/75n494
PEOPLE'S REPUBLIC OF BENIN
Decalo/Historical dict of Dahomey/77n313
PEOPLE'S REPUBLIC OF CHINA
See China
PERCEPTION
Carterette/Biology of perceptual systems/75n1588
Emmett/Perception: bibliog/78n1362
PERCUSSION MUSIC
Weerts/Original manuscript music for wind & percussion instruments/75n1134
PERENNIALS
Hebb/Low maintenance perennials/76n1589
Hudak/Gardening with perennials/77n1555
PÉREZ GALDÓS, BENITO
Woodbridge/B. P. Galdós: bibliog/77n1277
PERFORMING ARTS
Celebrity Services/Contact bk/76n1041
Handel/National directory for performing arts & civic centers/76n1043; 79n1014
Handel/National directory for performing arts-educational/79n1015
Highfill/Biographical dict of actors . . . in London 1660-1880/76n1045
Mapp/Directory of blacks in performing arts/79n1016
Perry/Performing arts resources/76n1039; 78n936; 79n1005
Whalon/Performing arts research/77n991
PERIODICALS AND SERIALS
See also Newsletters; Newspapers
Alkire/Periodical title abbrevs/78n13
ARL/Access to periodical resources/75n230
Fry/Publishers & libraries/78n35
Macmillan/Serials in transition/79n19
Mayes/Periodicals admin in libraries/79n265
National periodicals center/79n152
Pitkin/Serials automation in US/77n169
Serials Librarian/78n160
Serials updating serv annual/79n191
Smith/Practical approach to serials cataloging/79n283

PERIODICALS AND SERIALS (cont'd)
Spyers-Duran/Management problems in serials work/75n217
Woodward/Factors affecting renewal of subscriptions/79n248
BIBLIOGRAPHY
Akeroyd/Alternatives: gd to newspapers, magazines, etc./77n104
Arndt/German lang press of Americas: 1732-1968/77n444
Carnahan/Guide to alternative periodicals/79n111
Edgar/History & bibliog of Amer magazines 1810-20/76n1162
Madden/19th cent periodical press in Britain: 1901-71/78n1078
Spahn/From radical left to extreme right/77n506
Tronik/Israeli periodicals & serials in Engl & other Western languages/75n20
DIRECTORIES
Black/Advertiser's gd to scholarly periodicals/79n16
Ayer directory of pubs/75n21
Bowker serials bibliog suppl/75n22; 77n33
Buckeye/International subscrip agents/79n49
Business media guide international:
　Africa/75n905
　Asia/75n906
　Europe/75n907; 75n908
　Latin America/75n909
　North America/75n911
　Newspaper & newsmagazines/75n910
Canadian serials directory/78n14
Devers/Guide to special issues & indexes of periodicals/77n34
Directory of small magazine-press editors & publishers/75n23
Directory of college student press in Amer/78n15
England/British directory of little magazines & small presses/75n24
Gebbie House magazine directory/76n24
Higgins/Whole COSMEP catalog/75n25
International directory of little magazines & small presses/75n26; 78n46
International subscrip agents/75n56
Irregular serials & annuals/77n35
Katz/Guide to magazine & serial agents/77n199
Landwehr/Student's gd to leftist periodicals/76n25
Media guide international. Edition: business/professional publications . . .
　Asia/78n724
　Europe/77n784
　Latin America/78n725
　Middle East/77n785
　Newspapers & news magazines/77n786

PERIODICALS AND SERIALS (cont'd)
DIRECTORIES (cont'd)
Murphy/Directory of conservative & libertarian serials/79n88
National directory of newsletters & reporting services/79n18
New serial titles 1950-70/76n26
Serials updating serv annual/Forman/76n23
Sources of serials/78n17
Standard periodical directory/78n18
Ulrich's internat'l periodicals directory/75n27; 76n27; 79n20
Woodworth/Guide to current British journals/75n28
Wynar/Encyclopedic directory of ethnic newspapers & periodicals in US/77n430
INDEXES
Access index to little magazines/76n28; 77n19
Bibliographic index/76n29
Bloomfield/Author index to selected British "little magazines" 1930-39/77n1133
Chicorel index to abstracting & indexing services/76n34
Cumulative index to periodical lit/77n38
Devers/Guide to special issues & indexes of periodicals/77n34
Guide to Indian periodical lit/76n35
Hazfeld/Periodical indexes in soc sci & humanities/79n345
Index to free periodicals/77n41
Index to New Engl periodicals/79n23
Index to US gov periodicals/75n103; 76n37
Kujoth/Subject gd to humor: . . . from 365 periodicals/77n1141
Marconi/Indexed periodicals/77n43
Monthly periodical index/79n24
National Library Serv cum bk review index/1905-74/77n44
New periodicals index/78n25
Ponchie/French periodical index/77n45; 79n25
SELECTION AIDS
Katz/Magazines for libraries/75n171; 79n17
Richardson/Periodicals for school media programs/79n184
Vocational-tech periodicals for community college libraries/77n210
UNION LISTS
Bullock/Ethnic serials at selected Univ of Calif libraries/78n379
Campo/Maine union list of serials/78n27
Danky/Undergrounds: union list of alternative periodicals/75n99
Metropolitan area gd to serials: Washington, DC/78n28
Quintero-Mesa/Latin Amer serial documents: v12, Venezuela/79n26
Regan/Serials: . . . in libraries in NY area/76n38

PERIODICALS AND SERIALS (cont'd)
UNION LISTS (cont'd)
Shelton/South Dakota union list of serials/ 75n43
Union catalogue of Arabic serials in British libraries/78n29
Union list of conf proceedings in libraries of Germany/79n27
Union list of German lang serials in libraries of Germany/79n381
Union list of serials holdings: USC Library/ 76n39
Union list of serials in libraries of Germany/ 78n30
Union list of serials indexed by PAIS held by Canadian libraries/78n31
Wajid/Periodicals in humanities: union catalogue ... in Delhi libraries/75n44

PERSIAN GULF
Gulf handbook/79n614
Nyrop/Area hndbk for Persian Gulf states/ 79n357

PERSIAN LANGUAGE
Steingass/Comprehensive Persian-Engl dict/ 79n1145
Wollaston/English-Persian dict/79n1146

PERSONAL DEVELOPMENT
Ann Landers ency/79n1427
Gotsick/Information for everyday survival/ 77n815
Matson/Psychology Today omnibk of personal developmt/79n1428

PERSONALITY TESTS
Buros/Personality tests & reviews/76n566
Butcher/Handbook of cross-natl MMPI research/77n1447
Dahlstrom/MMPI hndbk/76n1498
Good/Practical gd to MMPI/76n1499

PERSONNEL MANAGEMENT
Murphy/Where's what: info for fed investigators/77n839

PESTS
Cornwell/Pest control in bldgs/75n1532

PETRARCH
Petrarch: catalog cf ... Cornell Univ Library/ 76n1298

PETROLEUM INDUSTRY
Crook/Oil terms/77n1410
European offshore oil & gas yrbk/77n1418
Franko/Petroleum industry in western Europe/77n1404
Titratsoo/Oilfields of world/75n1566
Whole oil world oil directory/78n763

PETS
Dolensek/Practical gd to impractical pets/ 77n1528

PETS (cont'd)
Pommery/What to do till the vet comes/77 n1530
Stein/Great pets!/77n1536

PEWTER
Kerfoot/American pewter/77n900

PHARMACOLOGY
See also Drugs
AMA drug evaluations/79n1495
Annual review of pharmacology/Elliott/76 n1548
Banes/Chemist's gd to drug analysis/75n1449
Fraunfelder/Drug-induced ocular side effects & drug interactions/77n1502
Garb/Undesirable drug interactions/75n1655
Hirtz/Fate of drugs in the organism: bibliog/ 78n1437
Keys/Chinese herbs/77n1505
Kline/Psychotropic drugs/75n1656
Meyers/Review of med pharmacology/75 n1657; 79n1502
Parish/Doctors & patients hndbk of medicines & drugs/79n1492
Smith/Handbook of ocular pharmacology/ 76n1554

PHENOMENOLOGY
Brandon/Weird America/79n1084
Corliss/Strange phenomena/75n91
Cornell/It happened last year!/75n85
Stewart/Exploring phenomenology/75n1238

PHILADELPHIA
Gales/Bicentennial Philadelphia/75n606
Marion/Bicentennial city: walking tours/75 n611

PHILIPPINE LITERATURE
Mojares/Cebuano literature: bio-bibliog/78 n1195

PHILIPPINES
Bernardo/Philippine retrospective natl bibliog 1523-1699/76n14
Lebar/Ethnic groups of insular SE Asia/76 n810
Netzorg/Philippines in WWII/78n299
Saito/Philippine research matls/75n311
Tubangui/Catalog of Filipiniana at Valladolid/ 76n279
Vreeland/Area hndbk for Philippines/78n300
Walsh/Martial law/75n551

PHILOSOPHERS
Erickson/Aristotle's rhetoric/76n1106
Gunter/Henri Bergson: bibliog/76n1107
Lapointe/G. Marcel & his critics: bibliog/78 n1001
Lapointe/M. Merleau-Ponty & his critics: bibliog/78n1002
Lapointe/J.-P. Sartre & his critics: bibliog/77 n1051

PHILOSOPHERS (cont'd)
Margolin/Neuf années de bibliographie Erasmienne/78n1003
Skrupskelis/William James: ref gd/78n1004
Woodbridge/Alfred N. Whitehead: bibliog/78n1005

PHILOSOPHY
American Philosophical Soc yrbk/76n1105
Bechtle/Dissertations in philosophy . . . 1861-1975/79n1078
Blavatsky/Theosophical glossary/75n1234
Brown/Freethought in US/79n1079
Classical world bibliog of philosophy/79n1080
Conger/Combined chronology for use with Mahatma letters to A. P. Sinnett . . . /75n1235
Dictionary of hist of ideas: index/75n1236
Encyclopedia of philosophy/Edwards/75n1237
Guerry/Bibliography of philosophical bibliogs/78n1000
Jack/New age dict/78n1007
Lacey/Dictionary of philosophy/78n1006
McKirahan/Plato & Socrates/79n1081
Nauman/Dictionary of Asian philosophies/79n1082
Stewart/Exploring phenomenology/75n1238

PHOENIX, AZ
Buchanan/Phoenix: chron hist/79n422

PHONETICS
Bronstein/Biographical dict of phonetic sci/79n1157

PHONORECORD INDUSTRY
Kastlemusick directory for collectors of recordings/79n972

PHONORECORD PERFORMERS
See Recording artists

PHONORECORDS
See also Phonotapes; Recording artists
Anderson/Charles T. Griffes/79n981
Armitage/Annual index to pop music record reviews/75n1169; 77n976; 77n977
Bennett/Catalogue of vocal recordings from 1898-1925 German catalogues of Gramaphone Co/79n969
Briggs/Collector's Beethoven/79n982
Burke/Collector's Haydn/79n984
Castleman/Beatles again?/79n997
Daily/Cataloging phonorecordings/76n188
de Schauensee/Collector's Verdi & Puccini/79n986
Dictionary catalog of G. R. Vincent Voice Library . . . /Cluley/76n293
Educators gd to free audio & video matls/Berg/78n591
Gray/Bibliography of discogs/79n970

PHONORECORDS (cont'd)
Greenfield/Penguin stereo record gd/79n971
High Fidelity/Records in review/78n906
Index to educ'l records/76n693
Maleady/Record & tape reviews index/75n1154; 76n1003; 79n973
Moses/Collectors' gd to Amer recordings 1895-1925/78n901
MusiCatalog/78n902
Osborne/Popular & rock records/79n999
Osborne/Record album price gd/78n903
Osborne/Record albums 1948-78/79n974
Osborne/Record collector's price gd/78n904
Popular music periodicals index/75n1172
Propes/Golden oldies/75n1173
Rolling Stone record review/75n1174
Rust/Jazz records 1897-1942/79n1000
Salley/Selected sound recordings of Amer, Brit, & European lit in Engl/78n1091
Soderbergh/78 RPM records & prices/79n976
Tudor/Popular music periodicals index/75n1172; 77n983
Turner/Afro-American singers/79n977

PHONOTAPES
Maleady/Index to record & tape reviews/79n973
Maleady/Record & tape reviews index/75n1154; 76n1003
McKee/Directory of spoken-voice audio-cassettes/76n681; 77n660

PHOTOCOPYING
See also Library reprographic services; Reprographic services (library)
Heilprin/Copyright & photocopying/79n64
King Research, Inc./Library photocopying in US/79n318
Library photocopying & US copyright law of 1976/79n319
Whitestone/Photocopying in libraries/79n293

PHOTOGRAPHERS
Mathews/Early photographs & early photographers/75n1111
Gilbert/Collecting photographica/77n932
Leekley/Moments: Pulitzer Prize photographs/79n953
McDarrah/Stock photo & assignment source bk/78n884
Novotny/Picture sources 3/76n942
Photographs: Sheldon Memorial Art Gallery, Univ of Nebraska/78n886
Wall/Directory of British photographic collections/79n955
Weinstein/Collection, use, & care of hist'l photographs/78n888
Welling/Collector's gd to 19th cent photographs/77n939

PHOTOGRAPHY
Artist's & photographer's market/77n856
Bauer/Hunting with a camera/75n775
Consumer Guide/Complete buying gd to photographic eqmt/75n1107
Encyclopedia of practical photography/79n951
Fossett/Screen printing photographic techniques/75n1108
Gassan/Handbook for contemp photography/75n1109
Gilbert/Collecting photographica/77n932
Hedgecoe/Photographer's hndbk/79n952
Hosking/Wildlife photography/75n1110
Mathews/Early photographs & early photographers/75n1111
Milar/Photographer's market/79n954
Photographic Magazine eqmt buyer's gd/75n1112
Photography market place/76n980
Pittaro/Compact photo lab index/78n883
Pittaro/Photo lab index, lifetime edition/76n982
Sanders/Photography yr bk/75n1113
Shull/Hole thing/75n1114
Snyder/Photography catalog/78n887
Stroebel/Dictionary of contemp photography/75n1115
Sturge/Neblette's hndbk of photography & reprography/78n885
Swedlund/Photography/75n1116
Time-Life/Photography year/76n981

PHYSICAL DISTRIBUTION OF GOODS
Davis/Information sources in transportation, matl mgmt, & physical distribution/78n1545

PHYSICAL EDUCATION
Choosing & using phonograph records for physical educ, recreation . . . /79n679
Educators gd to free health, phy educ & recreation matls/Horkheimer/76n672
Frost/Encyclopedia of phys educ, . . . /78n607
Hoyle/Indexing terms for phys educ/79n674
Hoyle/Physical educ-sports index/79n676
Kirby/Physical educ index/79n675
Pizzitello/Annotated bibliog on movement educ/78n547
Thomas/Completed research in health, phys educ, & recreation/78n606

PHYSICAL FITNESS
Frost/Encyclopedia of phys educ, fitness, & sports/78n607

PHYSICAL SCIENCES
Daintith/Dictionary of phys sciences/78n1207
Retrospective index to theses of Gt Brit & Ireland 1716-1950: phys sci/78n1222

PHYSICALLY HANDICAPPED
See also Blind; Deaf; Handicapped; Visually handicapped
Bramley/Outreach/79n285
Strom/Library services to blind & physically handicapped/78n237

PHYSICIANS
See Medicine

PHYSICISTS
American men & women of sci: physics . . . /78n1216
Besancon/Encyclopedia of physics/75n1456
Coblans/Use of physics lit/77n1336
Denney/Dictionary of spectroscopy/75n1457
Dictionary of physics/79n1331
Encyclopaedic dict of physics/77n1337
Gray/New dict of physics/76n1350
Handbook of chemistry & physics/76n1344
Harburn/Atlas of optical transforms/77n1338
INIS Atomindex/77n1339
Kaye/Tables of phys'l & chem constants/75n1458
Lapedes/McGraw-Hill dict of physics & math/79n1332
Physics & astronomy classification scheme/79n1334
Pitt/Penguin dict of physics/78n1269

PHYSIOLOGY
Comroe/Annual review/76n1359

PIAGET, JEAN
Catalog of Jean Piaget archives, Univ of Geneva/76n1492

PIANO
Hinson/Piano teacher's source bk/76n1015

PIANO MUSIC
Chang/Team piano repertoire/77n952
Faurot/Concert piano repertoire/75n1126
Friskin/Music for piano/75n1127
Hinson/Piano in chamber ensemble/79n991
Rezits/Pianist's resource gd; piano music in print/76n1019

PIANOS
Schmeckel/Piano owner's gd/75n1161

PICASSO
Kibbey/Picasso/79n906

PICTURE BOOKS FOR CHILDREN
Bader/American picturebks/78n1119
Polette/E is for everybody: manual/77n1161

PICTURE DICTIONARIES
Grosset starter pict dict/77n1076
Parnwell/Oxford pict dict of Amer English:
  English-Spanish/79n1100
  French/79n1101
  Monolingual/79n1102

PICTURES
See also Color prints; Photographs; Prints
Evans/Picture researcher's hndbk/76n928
Gilbert/Picture indexing for local hist/75n224
Hart/Picture reference file . . .
   vI, compendium/77n883
   vII, humor/78n813
Index to art reproductions in bks/75n1010
Marcus/Index to picture collection of American Jewish Archives/79n460
McDarrah/Stock photo & assignmt source bk/78n884
Novotny/Picture Sources 3: collections of prints & photos/76n942
Pollack/Animal kingdom/79n901
Thompson/Index to illustns of natural world/78n1277
Underhill/Handy key to your "National Geographics"/78n1278

PIDGIN ENGLISH
Bibliography Pidgin & Creole langs/77n1060

PIERPONT MORGAN LIBRARY
Pierpont Morgan Library/Major acquisitions, 1924-74/75n19

PILGRIM COMPANY OF LEYDEN
Dexter/England & Holland of Pilgrims/79n481

PILOTS (aeronautics)
See Air pilots

PITTSBURGH, PA
Vexler/Pittsburgh: chron hist/78n363

PLACE NAMES
See Names, geographical

PLAINS INDIANS
Hoebel/Plains Indians/79n775

PLANCK, MAX
Max Planck: bibliog/78n1268

PLANETARY SCIENCES
Annual review of earth & planetary sciences/Donath/76n1468

PLANETS
Cross/Atlas of Mercury/78n1235
de Callatay/Atlas of planets/76n1336

PLANKTON
Smith/Guide to marine coastal plankton/79n1381

PLANNING
See also Regional planning
Bibliography of land settlement/79n787
Bilsborrow/Population in developmt planning/78n684
Dumouchel/Dictionary of developmt terminology/76n799

PLANNING (cont'd)
European directory of economic & corp planning/76n833
Management & control of growth/Scott/76n801

PLANT DISEASES
Annual review of phytopathology/Baker/76n1375
Beale/Bibliography of plant viruses/77n1513

PLANT ENGINEERING
Elonka/Standard operators' manual/76n1646

PLANT MAINTENANCE
Maintenance eng'g hndbk/Higgins/78n1542

PLANT NAMES
Cunningham/Common plants: . . . nomenclature/78n1279
Durant/Who named the daisy?/78n1289
Healey/Gardener's gd to plant names/76n1588
Howes/Dictionary of useful & everyday plants/75n1463
Shosteck/Flowers & plants/75n1464
Terrell/Checklist of names of 3000 vascular plants of economic importance/79n1340

PLANT PHYSIOLOGY
Annual review of plant physiology/Briggs/76n1376

PLANT VIRUSES
Beale/Bibliog of plant viruses/77n1513

PLANTAGENETS
Turton/Plantagenet ancestry . . . /76n444

PLANTS
Thompson/Index to illus of natural world/78n1277
   BUYING GUIDES
Riker/Gardener's catalogue/75n1707
Rottenberg/Guide to buying plants/78n1495
Schroeder/Green thumb directory/78n1496
   DICTIONARIES AND ENCYCLOPEDIAS
Bailey/Hortus third/78n1485
Coon/Dictionary of useful plants/76n1373
Fogg/History of pop garden plants from A-Z/78n1491
Kramer/Picture ency of small plants/79n1339
Moerman/American med ethnobotany/78n1280
Reader's Digest ency of garden plants & flowers/78n1494
Usher/Dictionary of plants used by man/76n1374
   HANDBOOKS AND FIELDGUIDES
Atlas of flora of Grt Plains/78n1283
Batson/Guide to genera of native ferns & seed plants of Eastern No Amer/79n1341

PLANTS (cont'd)
    HANDBOOKS AND FIELDGUIDES (cont'd)
Fassett/Spring flora of WI/77n1352
Huxley/Flowers of Greece & Aegean/79n1343
Kosloff/Plants & animals of Pacific NW/77n1346
Merrill/Flora of Manila/77n1353
Mohlenbrock/Guide to vascular flora of Illinois/77n1354
Ohashi/Flora of eastern Himalaya . . . /77n1355
Perry/Simon & Schuster's compl gd to plants & flowers/77n1351
Shaw/Field gd to vascular plants of Grand Teton Natl Park/77n1356
Van Bruggen/Vascular plants of SD/77n1357
Walker/Flora of Okinawa & So Ryukyu Is/77n1358
Weber/Rocky Mtn flora/77n1359
Welsh/Utah plants/75n1471
Willis/Handbook to plants in Victoria, Australia/75n1472

PLANTS, EDIBLE
    See also Food, wild
Angier/Color fld gd to common wild edibles/78n1311
Benoliel/NW foraging/76n1381
Clarke/Edible & useful plants of CA/79n1366
Freitus/160 edible plants/76n1384
Hall/Wild food trailgd/77n1350
Knutsen/Wild plants you can eat/76n1575
McPherson/Wild food plants of IN/78n1312
Peterson/Field gd to edible wild plants/79n1367
Tomikel/Edible wild plants of PA & NY/75n1470

PLANTS, MEDICINAL
    See Botany, medical

PLANTS, ORNAMENTAL
Healey/Gardener's gd to plant names/76n1588
Hebb/Low maintenance perennials/76n1589

PLANTS IN THE CITY
Page/Wild plants in city/76n1380

PLAQUES AND PLAQUETTES
Norris/Medals & plaquettes . . . at Bowdoin College/77n914

PLASTIC SURGERY
Honolulu index of plastic surgery/79n1480
Leuz index of plastic surgery/79n1481
Zeis index & hist of plastic surgery/79n1482

PLASTICS
Harper/Handbook of plastics & elastomers/77n1614
Hilado/Flammability hndbk for plastics/76n1656

PLASTICS (cont'd)
International patents digest of foamed plastics/76n1657
Patterson/Plastics bk list/77n1615

PLASTICS INDUSTRY
US foamed plastics markets & directory/76n1658; 78n760

PLATES (tableware)
Bradford bk of collector's plates/77n918

PLATH, SYLVIA
Lane/Sylvia Plath/79n1222

PLATO
McKirahan/Plato & Socrates/79n1081

PLAY
Steven Caney's play bk/76n764

PLAYWRIGHTS
    See Dramatists

PLEA BARGAINING
Bond/Plea bargaining/76n514

PLOTS (drama, novels, etc.)
Berry/Plots & characters in major Russian fiction/78n1196; 79n1282
Halperin/Plots & characters in fict of J. Austen, Brontës & G. Eliot/77n1129
Johnson/Plots & characters in the fict of 18th cent Engl authors/78n1164; 79n1229
Magill's literary annual/79n1185

PLUMBING
Jacobson/Plumbing dict/77n1616

PLYMOUTH, MA
Davis/Genealogical register of Plymouth families/76n428
Mayflower families thru five generations/77n470
Plymouth church records 1620-1859/76n438
Shurtleff/Records of Plymouth Colony, 1633-89/77n477

POE, EDGAR ALLAN
Hyneman/Edgar A. Poe/75n1364
Pollin/Poe, creator of words/75n1365

POETRY
    See also American poetry; English poetry, etc.
Chapman/Index to black poetry/76n1211
Chicorel index to poetry in anthologies & collections/76n1212
Deutsch/Poetry handbk/75n1333
Marcan/Poetry themes/79n1200
Preminger/Princeton ency of poetry & poetics/76n1213
Smith/Granger's index to poetry/79n1201

POETS
Chapman/Index of names in Pearl, Purity, Patience, & Gawain/79n1251
Kay/International who's who in poetry/79n1199
Vinson/Contemporary poets/76n1214

POISONING
See also Toxicology
Gosselin/Clinical toxicology of commercial products: acute poisoning/77n1485
US Food & Drug Admin/Handbk of common poisonings in children/78n1431

POISONOUS ANIMALS
Biery/Venomous arthropod hndbk/78n1327
Caras/Venomous animals of world/76n1411
Halstead/Poisonous & venomous marine animals of world/79n1380

POISONOUS PLANTS
Menser/Hallucinogenic & poisonous mushrm field gd/78n1301
Muenscher/Poisonous plants of US/76n1378
Tampion/Dangerous plants/78n1282

POLAND
Davies/Poland: past & present/78n372
Lewanski/Guide to Polish libraries/76n215

POLICE
See Law enforcement

POLISH AMERICANS
Zurawski/Polish Amer hist & culture: bibliog/76n416

POLISH LITERATURE
Mihailovich/Modern Slavic literatures: Polish/78n1199

POLISH NEWSPAPERS
Kowalik/Polish press in Amer/79n465

POLITICAL ACTION GROUPS
See also Citizen action groups; Lobbyists
Guardian directory of pressure grps/78n478

POLITICAL PARTIES
Bain/Convention decisions & voting records/75n487
Chester/Guide to political platforms/79n519
Foner/Democratic republican societies, 1790-1800/78n439
Johnson/National party platforms/75n493; 79n520
National party conventions, 1831-1972/77n515

POLITICAL PRISONERS
Liber/Nonconformity & dissent in Ukrainian SSR/79n549

POLITICAL SCIENCE
See also under countries, e.g., US—politics and government
BIBLIOGRAPHY
Blackey/Modern revolutions & revolutionists: bibliog/77n359
Blaustein/Independence docs of the world/79n518
Harmon/Political sci bibliogs/75n460; 77n492
Harmon/Developing the lib collection in political sci/77n491
Holler/Information sources of political sci/76n463
International bibliog of political sci/75n461
Kaid/Political campaign communication/75n462
Murphy/Urban politics/79n539
Stephans/Thomas Paine collection in the Library of Amer Philosophical Soc/78n443
Universal reference system/75n465
DICTIONARIES AND ENCYCLOPEDIAS
Beck/Political sci thesaurus/76n464
Hyams/Dictionary of modern revolution/75n466
Laqueur/Dictionary of politics/75n467
Paxton/World legislatures/76n465
Plano/Political sci dict/75n468
Raymond/Dictionary of politics/79n504
Worldmark ency of the nations/77n306
HANDBOOKS AND YEARBOOKS
Cook/European political facts 1848-1918/79n505
Countries of world & leaders/76n461; 78n433
Engle/National govs around world/75n470
European parliament digest/75n471
Greenstein/Handbook of political sci/76n466
Herman/Parliaments of world/77n495
News dictionary/76n467; 77n498
Political events annual/79n509
Political hndbk of world/76n468; 79n510
US CIA/National basic intelligence factbk/78n274
Wates/Visual approach to Brit & Amer gov/75n458
Williams/Modules in security studies/75n459
Year bk of world affairs/76n507; 79n513
INDEXES
ABC Pol Sci/Garrison/78n436
Facts on File index 1971-75/77n500

POLITICIANS
See also Governors; Mayors; etc.
Atwood/Who's who in Alaskan politics/79n540

POLITICIANS (cont'd)
Bellamy/Dictionary of labour biog/79n547
Camp/Mexican political biogs 1935-75/78n485
Cook/Sources in Brit political hist 1900-51/78n477
CQ/Members of Congress since 1789/78n454
Edgar/Biographical directory of SC House of Reps 1692-1973/75n484
Evans/Women in fed politics/76n482
Karis/From protest to challenge: doc hist of African politics in So Africa 1882-1964/78n471
Lichtenstein/Political profiles: Kennedy yrs/78n440
Morris/Who was who in Amer politics/75n486
Schoenebaum/Political profiles: Eisenhower yrs/79n527
Who's who in Amer politics/76n480; 78n465
Who's who in government/78n466
Women in public office/77n508; 79n544

POLITICS
See Political science

POLLARD, ALFRED WILLIAM
Roper/Alfred W. Pollard: his essays/77n283

POLLUTION
See also Air pollution; Land pollution; Noise; Water pollution
Barros/International law of pollution/75n1535
Fritsch/Household pollutants gd/79n1400
Rudd/Environmental toxicology/79n1401
Sittig/Pollutant removal hndbk/75n1542
Williams/Environmental pollution & mental health/75n1530

POLYGLOT GLOSSARIES
Allen/Manual of European langs for librarians/77n189
Wersig/Terminology of documentation: in English, French, German, Russian, & Spanish/77n172

POLYNESIAN LANGUAGES
Carroll/Nukuoro lexicon/75n1282
Reed/Concise Maori dict/77n1096

POLYVINYL CHLORIDE
Nass/Encyclopedia of PVC/79n1574

POOLE, HENRY W.
Steele/Independent Mexico/75n312

POOR
Childers/Information-poor in America/76n199
Law/Rights of the poor/75n559
Martin/Library serv to disadvantaged/76n201

POOR RICHARD'S ALMANAC
Barbour/Concordance/75n1356

POPE, ALEXANDER
Bedford/Concordance to poems/76n1282

POPPE, NICHOLAS
Cirtautas/Nicholas Poppe/79n1088

POPULAR CULTURE
Abstracts of pop culture/79n1084
Coe/Folklife & fed gov/79n1083

POPULAR CUSTOMS
Language & sentiment of flowers/75n1244

POPULAR MUSIC (songs, etc.)
See Music, popular (songs, etc.)

POPULATION
See Demography

PORCELAIN
Palley/Porcelain art of Edward Boehm/77n889

PORPOISES
Coffey/Dolphins, whales & porpoises/78n1332
Truitt/Dolphins & porpoises/75n1521

PORTER, KATHERINE ANNE
Kiernan/Katherine A. Porter & Carson McCullers: ref gd/77n1211

PORTRAITS
Catalogue of Amer portraits/76n918
Hummel/Portraits & statuary of Virginians .../79n879
NY Historical Society/Catalogue of Amer portraits/76n918

PORTUGAL
Dorn/Latin Amer, Spain, & Portugal: bibliog/77n305
Hanson/Dissertations on Iberian & Latin Amer history/77n361
Wilgus/Latin America, Spain & Portugal/79n384

PORTUGUESE AMERICANS
Pap/Portuguese in US/78n391

PORTUGUESE LITERATURE
Kerr/Miguéis—to 7th decade/79n1289

POST OFFICES
Directory of post offices/79n84

POSTAGE STAMPS
Allen/Stamp collector's gd to Europe/75n1087
Blake/Boston postmarks to 1890/75n1088
Boggs/Postage stamps & postal hist of Canada/75n1089
Brazer/Essays for US adhesive postage stamps/78n859
Crown/Confederate postal hist/77n923
Dow/Maine postal hist & postmarks/77n924
Felix/Identify your stamps/79n930

Subjects—351

POSTAGE STAMPS (con['d])
Howes/Canadian postage stamps & stationery/75n1090
Ilma/Funk & Wagnalls gd to world of stamp collecting/79n931
Jarrett/Stamps of Brit No Amer/76n975
Linn's world stamp almanac/79n932
Rosichan/Stamps & coins/75n1052
Stanley/Birds of world on stamps/75n1091
Walburn/Official catalog of Canada precancels/78n860

POSTAL SERVICE
Boggs/Postage stamps & postal hist of Canada/75n1089
Crown/Confederate postal hist/77n923
Dow/Maine postal hist & postmarks/77n924
Wiltsee/Pioneer miner & the pack mule express/77n925

POSTMARKS
See Postage stamps

POTTERY
See also Ceramics; Porcelain
Campbell/Pottery & ceramics/79n946
Chappell/Potter's compl bk of clay & glazes/79n947
Evans/Art pottery of US/75n1080
Fournier/Illustrated dict of practical pottery/78n881
Godden/British pottery: illust'd gd/77n919
Hamer/Potter's dict of matls & techniques/77n891
Harbin/Blue & white stoneware, pottery & crockery/79n948
Huxford/Collectors ency of fiesta . . . /79n949
Kovel's collectors' gd to Amer art pottery/75n1082
Oppelt/Southwestern pottery: bibliog/78n680
Ray/Collectible ceramics/75n1084

POWER PLANTS
See Electric power plants

POWER TOOLS
Drake/Everyone's bk of hand & small power tools/75n1792

PRAKIT LITERATURE
Banerji/Companion to mid Indo-Aryan lit/78n1192

PRAVDA
Index to Pravda/76n498; 79n515

PRAYERS
Revell/15th cent Engl prayers . . . list of manuscripts in British library/77n1030

PRECANCELS
Noble official catalog of bureau precancels/76n976

PRECANCELS (cont'd)
Walburn/Official catalog of Canada precancels/76n977; 78n860

PRECIOUS METALS
Persons/Investor's ency of gold, silver, precious metals/76n860
Sinclair/How experts buy & sell gold bullion, gold stocks, coins/76n862

PRECIOUS STONES
Arem/Color ency of gemstones/79n1420
Gubelin/Color treasury of gemstones/77n1433
O'Donoghue/Ency of minerals & gemstones/77n1437
Pearl/Gems, minerals, etc: ency/78n1360
Schumann/Gemstones of world/79n1421
Villard/Gemstones & minerals/75n1101
Webster/Gems/76n1483

PRECIPITATION (meteorology)
World Meteorological Organization/Annotated bibliog on precipitation measurement instruments/75n1571

PRECIS
PRECIS index system/78n222

PRECISION ENGINEERING
Davidson/Handbook of precision eng'g: forming processes/75n1804/Production eng'g/75n1805

PRE-COLUMBIAN ART
Kendall/Art of Pre-Columbian Mexico/75n988

PREGNANCY
Comprehensive bibliog on pregnancy & work/79n1452
McLaughlin/Black parents' hndbk/77n1495

PREJUDICES
Obudho/Black-white racial attitudes: bibliog/77n427

PRESCHOOL EDUCATION
See Early childhood education

PRÉSENCE AFRICAINE
Ojo-Ade/Analytic index/78n276

PRESERVATION OF PLANT MATERIALS
Karel/Dried grasses, grains, gourds/76n1590

PRESIDENTIAL ELECTIONS
Bain/Convention decisions & voting records/75n487
Presidential elections since 1789/77n516

PRESIDENTS
Egan/Kings, rulers & statesmen/78n332
 UNITED STATES
Bassett/Profiles & portraits of Amer presidents/77n1509

PRESIDENTS (cont'd)
UNITED STATES (cont'd)
Biographical directory of US executive branch 1774-1977/78n451; 79n541
Bremer/Richard M. Nixon: chron/76n332
Burke's presidential families of USA/76n426
Cumulated indexes to public papers of the presidents of the US:
D. D. Eisenhower/79n416
J. F. Kennedy/79n417
L. B. Johnson/79n418
Dusterberg/Official inaugural medals of the presidents of US/77n911
Gibson/Name & subj index to presidential chronology series: Washington to Ford/79n419
Index to T. Jefferson papers/78n441
Kane/Facts abt the presidents/77n514
Lankevich/Gerald R. Ford/79n414
Newcomb/John F. Kennedy: bibliog/78n446
Papers of Woodrow Wilson/78n442
Presidential vetoes 1789-1976/79n525
Presidency 1964/76n487
Significant Amer presidents/Buske/77n136
Sobel/Presidential succession/76n488
Tracey/Herbert Hoover–bibliog/78n448
US Natl Park Serv/Presidents from the inauguration of Washington to Ford: historic places/78n337

PRESS
See also Journalists; News correspondents
Hudson's Washington news media contact directory/76n1169
Siddigi/Press directory of Pakistan/76n1172
Weiner/Syndicated columnists/76n1173

PRESS BRAKES
Daniels/Press brake & shear hndbk/76n1652

PRESSURE GROUPS
See Citizen action groups

PREVENTIVE MEDICINE
See Medicine, preventive

PRIMARY EDUCATION
See Elementary education
See also Early childhood education

PRIME MINISTERS
Hellicar/Prime ministers of Britain/79n548

PRINCETON UNIVERSITY
Catalogue of Arabic manuscripts in the Garrett Collection/78n60
Gibbons/Catalogue of Italian drawings in art museum/78n808
Leitch/Princeton companion/79n671
McLachlan/Princetonians 1748-68/78n601

PRINTERS
Hudak/Early Amer women printers & publishers 1639-1820/79n30

PRINTERS (cont'd)
Timperley/Encyclopaedia of literary & typographical anecdotes/78n42

PRINTING
Anderson/Private press work/79n28
Biegeleisen/Art directors workbk of type faces/77n880
Blumenthal/Art of printed bk 1455-1955/75n63
Blumenthal/Printed bk in Amer/78n32
Clair/History of European printing/78n33
Collins/Authors & printers dict/75n51
Cotton/Typographical gazetteer/77n881
Febvre/Coming of the book/78n34
Gerulaitis/Printing & publishing in 15th cent Venice/78n36
Hebrew printing & bibliog/78n38
Pollard/Fine books/75n65
Reilly/Dictionary of colonial Amer printer's ornaments & illustns/77n884
Skillin/Words into type/75n113
Steinberg/500 yrs of printing/75n49
Type for books/77n885
Van Nostrand Reinhold/Type specimen bk/76n44

PRINTS
See also Color prints; Lithographs
American printmakers/75n1024
Blakemore/Who's who in modern Japanese prints/76n931
Donson/Prints & print market: hndbk/78n807
Ebert/Old Amer prints for collectors/75n1026
Mason/Lithographs of George Bellows/79n899
Mason/Print ref sources: bibliog/76n941
Morse/Jean Charlot's prints: catalogue/77n882
New York Public Library/Dict catalog of prints div/76n920
Novotny/Picture Sources 3/76n942
Shapiro/Fine prints: collecting, etc./78n814
Unesco/Catalogue of reproductions of paintings 1860-1973/76n916
US Library of Congress/American Revolution in drawings & prints: checklist 1765-90/77n373

PRINTS AS AN INVESTMENT
Donson/Prints & the print market: hndbk/78n807
Shapiro/Fine prints: collecting/78n814

PRISON LIBRARIES
Rubin/US prison library services/75n208
Werner/Manual for prison law libraries/77n242

PRISON REFORM
Bundy/National prison directory: profiles of prison reform groups/76n778; 77n710; 78n505
Bundy/Prison group directory: Maryland-Washington metro area/75n839; 76n777

PRISONS
See also Correctional institutions
Tompkins/Furlough from prison/75n840

PRIVACY
Anderson/Privacy & public disclosure under Freedom of Info Act/77n531
Latin/Privacy/78n271
US Office of Fed Register/Protecting your right to privacy/78n492

PRIVACY ACT OF 1974
US Office of Fed Register/Protecting your right to privacy/78n492

PRIVATE PRESSES
See also Small presses
Anderson/Private press work/79n28
Bibliog of Golden Cockerel Press 1921-41/77n52
Chambers/Cook-A-Hoop: sequel to Chanticleer, . . . /77n53
Directory of private presses & letterpress printers & publishers/79n51

PRIVATE SCHOOLS
Bunting & Lyon's gd to private schools/77n598
Directory of European Council of Intern'l schools/78n573
Ganley's Catholic schools/75n683; 77n600
Handbook of private schools/77n601
Herbert/Getting skilled: gd to private trade & tech schools/77n628
Maher/Schools abroad/76n614
NATTS directory of accredited private trade & tech schools/77n630
Private independent schools/75n685
Private schools illust'd/77n603
Zeidner/Private elementary & secondary educ: bibliog/78n552

PROBABILITIES
Ross/Index to statistics & probability/75n877; 75n878; 76n819

PROCEEDINGS OF CONFERENCES
See Congresses and conventions

PROCEEDINGS OF SCIENTIFIC CONFERENCES
See Scientific conferences

PROCESS CONTROL
Weiner/Process control: instrumentation/79n1328

PROCESSING (libraries)
Kaiser/Handling special matls in libraries/75n248
Magrill/Library tech services/78n244
Bloomberg/Introduction to tech services for library technicians/75n247; 77n269

PRODUCTION ENGINEERING
Considine/Process instruments & controls hndbk/75n1803
Davidson/Handbook of precision eng'g: production eng'g/75n1805

PROFESSIONAL ETHICS
Clapp/Professional ethics & insignia/75n79

PROFESSIONAL SERVICES
CU/Guide to consumer services: financial & professional services/78n747
Hendin/World almanac whole health gd/79n1487

PROGRAMMED INSTRUCTION
Hendershot/Programmed learning bibliog/75n702

PROGRESSIVE EDUCATION
Winick/Progressive educ movement/79n637

PROJECT MANAGEMENT
Dyer/Project mgmt: bibliog/78n780

PROSTAGLANDIN
Sparks/Prostaglandin abstracts/75n1641

PROSTITUTION
Bullough/Bibliog of prostitution/78n643

PROTEINS
Barbara Kraus dict of protein/76n1576
Kirschenbaum/Atlas of protein spectra . . . /75n1451

PROTESTANT CHURCHES
Read/Brazil 1980/75n1224
Mission hndbk/75n1221; 78n986
Mead/Handbk of denominations in US/76n1087

PROVERBS
Whiting/Early Amer proverbs/79n103

PSEUDONYMS
Atkinson/Dictionary of pseudonyms & pen-names: writers in Engl/76n1183; 78n1096
Chu/20th cent Chinese writers & pen names/78n1185
Dawson/Nicknames & pseudonyms . . . of persons in hist, lit/75n448
Sharp/Handbook of pseudonyms & personal nicknames: suppl/76n451

PSYCHIATRISTS
Biographical directory of . . . Amer Psychiatric Assn/75n1603; 78n1368

PSYCHIATRY
American Psychiatric Assn/Psychiatric glossary/76n1494
Arieti/American hndbk of psychiatry/76n1497
Biographical directory of Amer Psychiatric Assn/75n1603
Brown/Neuropsychiatry & war/77n1459
Eysenck/Handbook of abnormal psychology/75n1589
Group for Advancemt of Psychiatry/Index of publications/75n1602
Klein/Reference ency of Amer psychology & psychiatry/76n1500
Krauss/Encyclopaedic hndbk of medical psychology/78n1370
Markle/Author's gd to journals in psychology, psychiatry/78n1369
Masserman/Handbook of psychiatric therapies/75n1593
Novello/Practical hndbk of psychiatry/75n1595
Rothget/Abstracts of . . . compl psychological works of Freud/75n1596
Small/Concise ency of psychology & psychiatry/79n1429
Solomon/Handbook of psychiatry/75n1597
Wing/Measurement & classification of psychiatric symptoms/75n1599
Wolman/International ency of psychiatry, psychology, . . . /78n1367

PSYCHIC EXPERIENCES
King/Psychic & religious phenomena/79n1438

PSYCHICAL RESEARCH
See Parapsychology

PSYCHOANALYSIS
Annual of psychoanalysis/75n1587
Grinstein/Index of psychoanalytic writings/76n1503
Langs/Technique of psychoanalytic psychotherapy/75n1592
Laplanche/Language of psychoanalysis/75n1581
Rycroft/Critical dict of psychoanalysis/75n1584
Vincie/C. G. Jung & analytical psychology: bibliog/78n1365
Wolman/International ency of psychiatry, . . . psychoanalysis & neurology/78n1367

PSYCHOHISTORY
deMause/Bibliog of psychohistory/76n1487

PSYCHOLOGICAL TESTS
Buros/Intelligence tests/76n564
Buros/Personality tests/76n566
Buros/Tests in print/75n1601
Chun/Measures for psychological assessmt/76n1486

PSYCHOLOGICAL TESTS (cont'd)
Goldman/Directory of unpub experimental mental measures/75n1600

PSYCHOLOGISTS
Catalog of J. Piaget archives, Univ of Geneva/76n1492
Nordby/Guide to psychologists & concepts/76n1504
Zusne/Names in hist of psychology/76n1505

PSYCHOLOGY
Barron's gd to grad schools: soc sci & psychology/76n634
Watson/History of psychology & behavioral sciences/79n1426
BIBLIOGRAPHY
Bibliographic gd to psychology/77n10
Crabtree/Bibliography of aggressive behavior/79n1424
Selective gd to matls for mental health & family life educ/77n1442
Watson/Eminent contributors to psychology: bibliog/75n1579; 77n1443
DICTIONARIES AND ENCYCLOPEDIAS
Berger/Dictionary of psychology: Engl-German/78n1366
International ency of psychiatry, psychology, . . . /Wolman/78n1367
Kinkade/Thesaurus of psychological index terms/76n1495
Klein/Reference ency of Amer psychology & psychiatry/76n1500
Psychology ency/75n1582
Robinson/Dreamer's dict/75n1583
Small/Concise ency of psychology & psychiatry/79n1429
HANDBOOKS AND YEARBOOKS
Annual review of psychology/Rosenzweig/76n1496
Carterette/Biology of perceptual systems/75n1588
Encyclopaedic hndbk of medical psychology/Krauss/78n1370
Eysenck/Handbook of abnormal psychology/75n1589
Grossman/Manual on terminology & classification in mental retardation/75n1590
Kiernan/Shrinks, etc./75n1591
Milt/Basic handbk on mental illness/75n1594
Psychological abstracts info services: manual/78n1371
Wilkening/Psychology almanac/75n1598
PERIODICALS AND SERIALS
Arnold/Education-psychology journals: scholar's gd/76n584
Markle/Author's gd to journals in psychology/78n1369

PSYCHOLOGY (cont'd)
PERIODICALS AND SERIALS (cont'd)
Tompkins/Serials in psychology & allied fields/77n1445
INDUSTRIAL
Dunnette/Handbook of industrial & organizational psychology/77n1448

PSYCHOLOGY, POPULAR
See also Mental health; Personal development; Self-culture
Ann Landers ency/79n1427
Matson/Psychology Today omnibook of personal development/79n1428

PSYCHOLOGY, RELIGIOUS
Capps/Psychology of religion: gd/77n1024

PSYCHOPHARMACOLOGY
Fazey/Aetiology of psychoactive substance use/79n1454
Honigfeld/Psychiatric drugs/79n1498

PSYCHOTHERAPY
Chessick/Technique & practice of intensive psychotherapy/75n1578
Kiernan/Shrinks, etc./75n1591
Masserman/Handbook of psychiatric therapies/75n1593
Wiener/Consumer's gd to psychotherapy/76n1502
Zimpfer/Group work in helping professions/77n1444

PUBLIC ADMINISTRATION
Asiedu/Public admin in Engl-speaking West Africa: bibliog/78n469
Mosher/Basic docs of Amer public admin 1776-1950/78n438
Duic/Europa admin: directory of admin/78n475
Simpson/Guide to library research/77n852

PUBLIC AFFAIRS INFORMATION SERVICE BULLETINS
Cumulative subject index 1915-74/78n23

PUBLIC DISCLOSURE
See Freedom of information

PUBLIC EMPLOYEES
Dwoskin/Rights of public employee/79n252
Tice/Employee relations bibliog/79n857

PUBLIC HEALTH
Barefoot/Community services (Grt Brit)/79n1458
Cornwell/Pest control in bldgs/75n1532
Deblock/Elsevier's dict of public health: in six languages/78n1393
Hospital-health care training media profiles/76n1532
McDade/Directory of soc & health agencies of NYC/79n1508

PUBLIC HEALTH (cont'd)
Profiles of financial assistance programs/79n1509

PUBLIC LANDS
US Bureau of Land Mgmt/Public land stats/78n692

PUBLIC LIBRARIES
Brooks/Public lib in non-trad education/75n183
Du Mont/Reform & reaction/79n201
Held/Rise of public library in Calif/75n186
Howard/Local power & community library/79n255
Library connection: essays/78n174
Morris/Parliament & public libraries/78n175
Shera/Foundations of public library/75n190
Standards for public libraries/79n203
Wellisch/Public library & fed policy/75n191
Wilson/Community elite & public library/78n177
ADMINISTRATION
Altman/Data gathering . . . for performance measures in public libraries/78n172
Brown/Joetta community library: admin/76n146
Dwoskin/Rights of public employee/79n252
Perkins/Branch library serv/79n259
ARCHITECTURE
Holt/Architectural strategy for change: remodeling/77n214
COMMUNITY SERVICES
Baeckler/GO, PEP, and POP!: 250 ideas for lively libraries/77n211
Correy/Library community services/79n287
Davies/Public libraries as culture & soc centers/75n184
Hanna/People make it happen/79n289
Martin/Adults & Pratt Library/75n188
Turick/Community info serv in libraries/79n292
FINANCE
Improving state aid to public libraries/78n173
Prentice/Public library finance/78n176
GUIDES
NYPL/Beyond the lions: gd/75n189
REPORTS AND INQUIRIES
Berelson/Library's public: report of public library inquiry/77n213
Totterdell/Effective library: report of Hillingdon Project/77n215
SELECTION AIDS
Books for public libraries/76n147
Jarvi/Canadian selection/79n181
Science & tech: purchasing gd/76n148
YOUTH SERVICES
Barnes/Youth library work/77n212
Edwards/Fair garden & swarm of beasts/75n185

PUBLIC LIBRARY TRUSTEES
Young/Library trustee/79n204

PUBLIC OPINION POLLS
Gallup/Gallup poll 1972-77/79n507

PUBLIC RELATIONS
Barbour/Who's who in public relations/77n1109
Larson/Public relations, E. L. Bernayses/79n804
Weiner/Professional's gd to public relations services/76n1159

PUBLIC SCHOOLS
See also Education
Maeroff/NY Times gd to suburban public schools/77n602
US HEW/Education directory: public school systems/77n605

PUBLIC SERVICES (libraries)
Bloomberg/Introduction to public services for library technicians/78n231
Cassata/Reader in library communication/78n232
Childers/Information-poor in Amer/76n199
Lyman/Reading & adult new reader/78n234
Martin/Library services to disadvantaged/76n201
Robotham/Library programs/77n163
Strom/Library services to blind & physically handicapped/78n237

PUBLIC SPEAKING
Humes/Speaker's treasury of anecdotes abt the famous/79n1174
Ireland/Index to inspiration/77n94

PUBLIC WELFARE
Patti/Management practice in social welfare: bibliog/77n708

PUBLISHERS AND PUBLISHING
See also Microforms; Private presses; Small presses
Benjamin/Candid critique of bk publishing/79n29
Business of publishing: PW anthology/77n47
Dessauer/Book publishing: what it is, what it does/75n45
Eastman/Education for publishing: directory of courses/77n48
Fries/Double elephant folio: Audubon's birds/75n46
Fry/Publishers & libraries: scholarly & research journals/78n35
Greenfeld/Books: from writer to reader/77n49
Hill/Into print: gd to writing/78n39
Mumby/Publishing & bookselling/75n48
Nasri/Crisis in copyright/77n50
Taubert/Book trade of world/77n51

PUBLISHERS AND PUBLISHING (cont'd)
Vanier/Market structure & business of bk publishing/75n50
  BIBLIOGRAPHIES
Alternative press index/76n78
International bibliog of bk trade & librarianship/77n54
Bibliog of Golden Cockerel Press 1921-41/77n52
Chambers/Cock-A-Hoop: sequel to Chanticleer, Pertelote, . . . /77n53
Hebrew printing & bibliog/78n38
Madden/19th cent periodical press in Britain: bibliog/78n1078
Parks/John Dunton & Engl bk trade/77n55
Small press record of bks in print/79n39
Sources: gd to print & nonprint matls/78n3; 79n40
Stichting Drukwerk in de Marge/Bibliografie/79n41
Tomkinson/Select bibliog of principal mod presses public & private Grt Brit & Ireland/77n56
Woolmer/Checklist of Hogarth Press, 1917-38/77n1222
  DICTIONARIES AND ENCYCLOPEDIAS
Ceux Qui Font L'Édition: Dictionnaire biographique de l'édition et des arts graphiques/79n50
Móra/Wörterbuch des verlagswesens in 20 sprachen/75n52
Orne/Language of foreign bk trade/77n57
Peters/Bookman's glossary/76n46
Stiehl/Dictionary of bk publishing/79n44
  DIRECTORIES
American bk trade directory/76n47; 79n46
American publisher's directory/79n47
Book publishers directory/78n43
Clarke/International academic & specialist publishers directory/77n58
Directory of ethnic publishers/78n378
Directory of private presses & letterpress printers/79n51
Directory of publishing opportunities/75n54; 76n49
Directory of Western bk publishing . . . /75n55; 77n59
Editor & publisher internat'l yr bk/78n44
Empresa del libro en America Latina/75n57
Information sources: directory of Information Industry Assn/78n45
International directory of little magazines & small presses/75n26; 78n46
International directory of scholarly publishers/79n53
International literary marketplace/77n60
International microfilm source bk/77n61
Joan/Guide to women's publishing/79n764
Literary market place/76n51

PUBLISHERS AND PUBLISHING (cont'd)
   DICTIONARIES AND
   ENCYCLOPEDIAS (cont'd)
Microfilm source bk/75n58
Publishers' internat'l directory/75n59; 79n55
Sources of serials: publisher & corp author directory/78n17
Veaner/Microform market place/75n60
Zell/African bk world & press–directory/79n45
   HANDBOOKS AND YEARBOOKS
Association of Amer Publishers/Industry statistics/77n46
Book trade in Canada/79n48
Bowker annual of library & bk trade info/77n190
International ISBN publishers' index/79n54
Kim/Policies of publishers/77n177; 79n247
Timperley/Encyclopaedia of literary & typographical anecdote/78n42
Writer's market/77n1132; 79n1168
   HISTORY
Blumenthal/Printed bk in Amer/78n32
Clair/History of European printing/78n33
Febvre/Coming of the book/78n34
Gerulaitis/Printing & publishing in 15th cent Venice/78n36
Hudak/Early Amer women printers & publishers/79n30
Stowell/Early Amer almanacs/78n40
Tebbel/History of bk publishing in US/76n43; 79n31
Winterich/Early Amer bks & printing/76n45
   JUVENILE
Boyle/Children's media market place/79n225
Gillespie/Paperback bks for young people/79n229
Gottlieb/Publishing children's bks in Amer 1919-76/79n1214

PUBLISHING EDUCATION
Eastman/Education for publishing: . . . directory of courses/77n48

PUCCINI, GIACOMO
de Schauensee/Collector's Verdi & Puccini/79n986

PUERTO RICAN LITERATURE
Hill/Puerto Rican authors/75n1424

PUERTO RICO
Brown/Puerto Rico: checklist matls Univ of CT Library/77n336

PUERTO RICANS
Puerto Ricans: bibliog/76n417
Tuck/Heroes de Puerto Rico/75n374

PUGET SOUND
Collias/Atlas of phys & chem properites/75n1576
Somerton/Field gd to fish/77n1388

PULITZER PRIZE
Leekley/Moments: Pulitzer Prize photographs/79n953

PUMPING MACHINERY
Karassik/Pump handbk/77n1610

PUNJAB
Gustafson/Sources on Punjab hist/76n360

PUNS
Crosbie/Crosbie's dict of puns/78n1042

PURCHASING
Basil/Purchasing info sources/78n732

PURITANS
Gallagher/Early Puritan writers: ref gd/77n1185

PVC
   See Polyvinyl chloride

PYNCHON, THOMAS
Scotto/Three contemp novelists/78n1124

QUAKERS
Bell/Our Quaker friends . . . Cedar Creek Meeting, Virginia/77n454
Heiss/Encyclopedia of Amer Quaker genealogy/78n402
Roberts/Early Friends families of Upper Bucks, PA/76n439

QUALITY CONTROL
Juran/Quality control hndbk/75n1811
Kovalenko/English-Russian reliability & quality-control dict/78n1502

QUOTATIONS
Battista/Quotoons/79n94
Burke/Dictionary of contemp quotations/77n90
Cory/Quote unquote/79n95
Garvey/Concise treasury of Bible quotations/76n1099
Great treasury of Western thought/78n85
Halliwell/Filmgoer's bk of quotes/75n1191
Humes/Speaker's treasury of anecdotes abt the famous/79n1174
Kenin/Dictionary of biog'l quotation/79n97
Mackay/Scientific quotations/79n1302
Murphy/Crown treasury of relevant quotations/79n98
Neil/Concise dict of religious quotations/75n1219
Partnow/Quotable woman 1800-1975/79n768
Peter/Peter's quotations/78n87
Reader's Digest treasury of modern quotations/76n75
Shapiro/Encyclopedia of quotations abt music/79n967
Spiegelman/Whole grains/75n95

QUOTATIONS (cont'd)
What they said in 1975/77n96

QUR'AN
Geddes/Analytical gd to bibliogs on Islam, Muhammad, & the Qur'an/75n290

RACE AWARENESS
Obudho/Black-white racial attitudes: bibliog/77n427

RACISM IN CHILDREN'S BOOKS
MacCann/Cultural conformity in bks for children/78n1120

RADIATION STERILIZATION
International Atomic Energy Agency/Manual on radiation sterilization of . . . matls/75n1461

RADIO
Amos/Radio, TV & audio tech ref bk/79n1567
Broadcast antenna systems hndbk/75n1780
Collins/Radio amateur's hndbk/75n1206; 77n1113; 78n1084
Dunning/Tune in yesterday: ency of old-time radio/78n1081
King/Underground buying gd for hams, CBers, . . . /78n749
McCavitt/Radio & TV/79n1173
Mehr/Motion pictures, TV, & radio: catalogue of MSS collections in US/79n1165
Specialized communications techniques for radio amateur/76n1633

RADIO, SHORT WAVE
Bennett/Complete short wave listener's hndbk/75n1202

RADIO AND MUSIC
Jacobs/Musica: 1st gd to classical music on Amer radio stations/77n947

RADIO BROADCASTING
Dictionary of radio & TV terms: Engl-German/77n1111
Filsinger/National radio publicity directory/76n1176
World radio & TV hndbk/77n1112

RADIO IN PUBLICITY
Radio contacts/77n1115

RADIO INDUSTRY
Ellmore/Illust'd dict of broadcast-CATV-telecommunications/79n1162

RADIO PROGRAMS
Pitts/Radio soundtracks: ref gd/77n1114
Radio contacts/77n1115

RADIO SCRIPTS
Educators gd to free tapes, scripts & transcriptions/76n675
Poteet/Published radio, TV, & film scripts: bibliog/76n1165

RADIO STATIONS
Elving/FM atlas & station directory/79n1171
Jones/North Amer radio-TV station gd/76n1170
Krompotich/Traveling FM radio gd/78n1082
Lay/Interstate gd to good listening/79n1172

RADIOACTIVE SUBSTANCES
International directory of certified radioactive matls/77n1341

RADIOLOGY
Bureau of Radiological Health publications index/79n1478
Johnson/Atlas of gallium-67 scintigraphy/75n1643

RADIOTHERAPY
Directory of high-energy radiotherapy centres/78n1403

RAILROAD CARS
Forney/Railroad car builder's pictorial dict/76n1671

RAILROAD ENGINEERS
Marshall/Biographical dict of railway engineers/79n1585

RAILROADS
Adams/Language of railroader/79n1114
Baker/Collector's bk of railroadiana/77n928
Beck/Rail talk/79n1115
Cors/Railroads/76n1670
Dubin/More classic trains/75n1832
Hajducki/Railway atlas of Ireland/76n1672
Jane's world railways/Goldsack/78n1548
Klamkin/Railroadiana: gd/77n934
Marshall/Rail facts & feats/75n1834
McComas/Collector's gd & hist to Lionel trains/77n943
Morris/Bibliog of industrial relations in railroad industry/76n905
Nock/Railways in transition from steam 1940-65/76n1673
Schleicher/Model railroading hndbk/77n944
Wilkins/Colorado railroads: chron developmt/76n1674

RAILROAD TRAVEL
Wojtas/Rand McNally gd to travel by train/75n590

RALLIDAE (birds)
Ripley/Rails of the world/79n1375

RANCHES
See also Family farms; Farm management
Farm, ranch & countryside gd/75n594
Wheeler/Tax desk bk for farming & ranching/77n855

RAND SCHOOL
Guide to MSS collection of Tamiment Library/79n517

RANGE MANAGEMENT
Vallentine/US-Canadian range mgmt/79n1527

RAPE
Barnes/Rape: bibliog/78n673
Kemmer/Rape & rape-related issues: bibliog/78n675
New York Radical Feminists/Rape/75n850

RARE BOOK LIBRARIES
Cave/Rare bk librarianship/77n191

RARE BOOKS
See also Incunabula
Beinecke rare bk & manuscript library: gd/76n57
Bookman's price index/78n48
Gottlieb/Early children's bks & their illustration/77n70
Harvard College Library/Catalogue of bks & manuscripts; Italian 16th cent/76n58
Heard/Bookman's gd to Americana/78n49
Magee/Infinite riches/75n67
Marx/Bibliographical studies & notes on rare bks in Jewish Theological Seminary of Amer/79n67
Shaaber/16th cent imprints in libraries of Univ of PA/77n30
Thomas-Stanford/Early editions of Euclid's Elements/78n63

READER'S GUIDE TO PERIODICAL LITERATURE
Cumulative index 1959-70/77n38

READING
Berger/Rates of comprehension: bibliog/77n574
Curry/Searching professional lit in reading/76n689
Far West Lab/Reading & lang arts: products from NIE/79n683
Searls/How to use WISC scores in reading diagnosis/76n691
Sheridan/Sex differences & reading: bibliog/77n581
Spache/Good reading for poor readers/75n707
Thorndike/Teacher's word bk of 20,000 words found most frequently ... children and young people/77n586
Withrow/Gateways to readable bks: graded list of bks for adolescents/77n1166

READING (adult education)
Fadiman/Lifetime reading plan/79n691
Forinash/Reader developmt bibliog/78n592
Jacques/Leisure reading for adults/78n596
Reader developmt bibliog/76n683; 76n684

READING DISABILITY
Bush/Dictionary of reading & learning disabilities/75n651
Chicorel abstracts to reading & learning disabilities/78n582; 79n690
Chicorel index to reading disabilities/76n692
Lee/Learning disabilities with emphasis on reading/79n692

READING EDUCATION
Guthrie/Graduate programs in reading/77n618

READING TESTS
Buros/Reading tests/76n567

REAL ESTATE
Boyce/Real estate appraisal terminology/76n851
Casey/Real estate investmt tables/76n853
Gross/Concise desk gd to real estate practice/77n801

REAL PROPERTY
Gushee/Financial capitalization rate tables ... for real estate appraisal/76n854
Harrison/Houses/75n1765
Johnsich/Modern real estate dict/77n802
Real estate investments & how to make them/76n861
Volpe/Running Press glossary of real estate language/78n782

RECLAMATION OF DISTURBED LANDS
Czapowskyj/Annotated bibliog on ecology & reclamation of disturbed areas/78n1339

RECORDER MUSIC
McGowan/Italian baroque solo sonatas .../79n992

RECORDING ARTISTS
Castleman/All together now/77n978
Castleman/Beatles again?/79n997
Pitts/Hollywood on record/79n975
York/Who's who in rock music/79n1003

RECREATION
Anderson/SportSource/77n663
Choosing & using phonograph records for phys educ, recreation, ... /79n679
Educators gd to free health, phys educ & recreation matls/76n672
Great escape/75n722
Nueckel/Selected gd to sports & recreation bks/75n726
Swan/Research in outdoor educ/79n636

RECREATION (cont'd)
Thomas/Completed research in health, phys educ, & recreation . . . /78n606
Turner/Index to outdoor sports, games, & activities/79n699
US HEW/Handbk for recreation/77n667
Schipf/Outdoor recreation/77n669

RECREATIONAL VEHICLES
Leavy/Recreational vehicles: gd/78n619
Nulsen/More miles, less gas/76n770
Trailer Life's RV campground & services directory/77n689

RECRUITING OF EMPLOYEES
See also Employment agencies
Beaumont/Handbook for recruiting at trad'l black colleges/75n653
Directory of exec recruiters/79n856
International directory of exec recruiters/76n834; 79n859

REDFORD, ROBERT
Spada/Films of R. Redford/78n963

REDUCING DIETS
Goldbeck/Dieter's companion/77n1494
Goldberg's diet catalog/78n1473
Smith/Dieter's checklist/76n1579

REFERENCE BOOKS
Bell/Reference bks/79n178
Chandler/How to find out/75n3
Cottam/Writer's research hndbk/78n102
Doyle/Reference resources: systematic approach/77n266
Gibson/Finding info in library/77n223
Henderson/Guide to basic ref matls for Canadian libraries/79n180
Hillard/Where to find more/78n239
Katz/Introduction to ref work/75n245; 79n294
Library of Congress main reading rm ref collection subj catalog/77n32
Nordling/Dear faculty: gdbk to high-school library/77n227
O'Brien/Basic gd to research sources/77n13
Palic/Government pubs: bibliog'ic tools/77n108
Paradis/Research hndbk/75n695
Peterson/Reference bks for elementary & jr high school libraries/76n162
Reader's advisor/78n2
Reference & subscrip bks reviews/76n135; 78n150; 79n183
Reference sources/78n26
Ryder/Canadian ref sources/76n6
Schorr/Government ref bks/77n106; 79n125
Sheehy/Guide to ref bks/77n14
Stevens/Reference bks in soc sci & humanities/78n4
Taylor/Basic ref sources/75n246

REFERENCE BOOKS (cont'd)
Texas Lib Assn/TX ref sources/77n521
Walford/Guide to ref matl/77n15; 79n4
Wynar/American Ref Bks Annual/75n1; 76n1
Wynar/Best ref books/77n16
Wynar/Reference bks in paperbk/77n17
Wynar/Guide to ref bks for school media centers, Suppl/77n234
Ziskind/Reference readiness/78n152

REFERENCE SERVICES (libraries)
See also Information services
Atherton/Librarians & online services/79n299
Bundy/Investigative methods for info specialists/75n243
Cohan/Readers advisory serv: booklists/76n134
Doyle/Reference resources: systematic approach/77n266
Hillard/Where to find more/78n239
Hillard/Where to find what/76n130
Katz/Introduction to ref work/75n245; 79n294
Kochen/Information for the community/77n267
Lancaster/Use of computers in lit searching/77n290
McInnis/New perspectives for ref serv in academic libraries/79n296
Murfin/Reference service/78n240
Shores/Reference as the promotion of free inquiry/77n268

REFRIGERATION
Zurick/Air conditioning, heating, & refrig dict/79n1549

REGIONAL PLANNING
Land use planning abstracts/76n1462; 79n1404

REGISTERS OF BIRTHS
Appleton/Boston births, marriages, . . . 1630-99, 1700-1800/79n474
Birth . . . marriage . . . death—on the record: 50 states and overseas/78n654
Steel/Sources for Roman Catholic & Jewish genealogy/78n421

RELIABILITY (engineering)
Kovalenko/English-Russian reliability & quality-control dict/78n1502

RELIGION
ATLASES
al Faruqi/Historical atlas of religions of world/76n1091
Gaustad/Historical atlas of religion in Amer/77n1019
BIBLIOGRAPHY
Adams/Reader's gd to grt religions/78n969

RELIGION (cont'd)
BIBLIOGRAPHY (cont'd)
Barber/Minister's library/75n1213
Breit/Thomas Merton/75n1215
Capps/Psychology of religion/77n1024
Clancy/English Catholic bks, 1641-1700/ 75n1216
Classical world bibliog of philosophy, religion . . . /79n1080
O'Brien/Bibliography of festschriften in religion . . . /76n1074
Ofori/Black African trad'l religions & philosophy: bibliog'ic survey/77n1029
Regazzi/Guide to indexed periodicals in religion/76n1075
Religious bks & serials in print/79n1053
Religious reading/76n1076; 78n974; 78n975
Sayre/Index of festschriften in religion/75 n1217
Thompson/Studies of Chinese religion/77 n1034
Turner/Bibliography of new religious movemts in primal societies, black Africa/78n977
Williams/Howard Univ bibliog of African . . . religious studies/78n979
BIOGRAPHY
Barker/Who's who in church hist/79n1076
Beebe/Who's who in new thought/79n1077
Bowden/Dictionary of Amer religious biog/ 78n999
Liederbach/America's thousand bishops/75 n1226
Who's who in religion/76n1093
DICTIONARIES AND ENCYCLOPEDIAS
Douglass/New internat'l dict of Christian Church/75n1218
Ferguson/Illustrated ency of mysticism & mystery religions/79n1057
Kauffman/Baker's pocket dict of religious terms/76n1084
Neil/Concise dict of religious quotations/75 n1219
Oxford dict of the Christian Church/75 n1220
Rice/Eastern definitions: ency of religions of Orient/79n1059
DIRECTORIES
Deemer/Ecumenical directory of retreat & conf centers/75n1225
Directory of religious organizations in USA/ 79n1060
Khalsa/Spiritual community gd/79n1085
Madden/Religious gd to Europe/76n1071
Melton/Directory of religious bodies in US/ 78n984
HANDBOOKS AND YEARBOOKS
Karpinski/Religious life of man/79n1050
Mead/Handbook of denominations in US/76 n1087

RELIGION (cont'd)
HANDBOOKS AND YEARBOOKS (cont'd)
Mission handbk/75n1221
New spiritual community gd for No America/ 75n1222
Piepkorn/Profiles in belief: religious bodies of US & Canada/78n970
Pilgrim's gd to planet earth/75n1223
Read/Brazil 1980/75n1224
Rosten/Religions of America/76n1088
Yearbook of Amer & Canadian churches/76 n1089

RELIGIOUS EDUCATION
Newland/Resource gd for adult religious educ/ 75n1214
Pitts/Concept developmt & God concept in the child/79n752
Thomson/Resource gd for adult religious educ/76n1077
Weld/World directory of theological educ by extension/75n1227

REMBRANDT (HARMENSZOON VAN RIJN)
Broos/Index to formal sources of Rembrandt's art/79n904

REMOTE CONTROLLED AIRCRAFT
See ROBOT AIRCRAFT

RENAISSANCE
New Cambridge modern hist, 1493-1520/ 76n288

REPAIRING
Schuler/How to fix almost everything/76 n1643

REPORT WRITING
Brusaw/Business writer's hndbk/79n816
Cordasco/Research & report writing/75n693
Cottam/Writer's research hndbk/78n102
Ewing/Writing for results in business, gov, & professions/75n889
Fleischer/Bibliographic citations for nonprint matls/76n87
MLA handbook/79n131
Morse/Complete gd to organizing & documenting research papers/75n694
Nordling/Dear faculty: . . . gdbk to highschool library/77n227
O'Brien/Basic gd to research sources/77n13
Paradis/Research hndbk/75n695
Turabian/Student's gd for writing research papers/78n105
van Leuen/Handbook for scholars/79n132

REPRINTS (publications)
See also Microforms
Books on demand author gd/79n33
Books on demand subj gd/79n34
Books on demand title gd/79n35

REPRINTS (publications) (cont'd)
Davis/Guide to reprints/79n37
International bibliog of reprints/78n41

REPROGRAPHIC SERVICES (library)
King Research/Library photocopying in US/79n318
LaHood/Reprographic services in libraries/77n286
Library photocopying & US copyright law of 1976/79n319
New/Reprography for librarians/76n228
Nitecki/Directory of lib reprographic services/77n181
Whitestone/Photocopying in libraries/79n293

REPROGRAPHY
Neblette's hndbk of photography & reprography/78n885

REPTILES
Brown/Reptiles & amphibians of West/76n1447
Cogger/Reptiles & amphibians of Australia/78n1336
Conant/Field gd to reptiles & amphibians of North America/76n1448
Czajka/State laws regulating collection of reptiles & amphibians in US/76n1449
Grzimek's animal life ency: reptiles/76n1405
Henderson/Checklist to amphibians & reptiles of Belize, Central America/77n1397

REPUBLIC OF CHINA
See Taiwan

RESCUE VEHICLES
Vanderveen/Fire & crash vehicles/77n1622

RESEARCH
Researchers gd to Washington/78n82
Scurlock/Government contracts & grants for research/76n653
Sugden/Graduate thesis/75n696
van Leuen/Handbook for scholars/79n132

RESEARCH AND DEVELOPMENT
Greenberg/Science & gov report interna'l almanac/78n435

RESEARCH CENTERS
Inventory of info resources & services available to US House of Reps/78n99
Inventory of major research facilities in European community/79n87
Palmer/Research centers directory/76n629

RESEARCH LIBRARIES
See also College and university libraries
Fussler/Research libraries & tech/75n181
Goodrum/Library of Congress/75n204
Inventory of info resources & services available to US House of Reps/78n99

RESEARCH LIBRARIES (cont'd)
Johnson/Libraries for teaching, libraries for research/78n261
Kumar/Research libraries in developing countries/75n257
Research collections in Canadian libraries/76n169
Stevens/Japanese & US research libraries at the turning point/78n250
Wagle/Guide to research collections in microform in Univ of Toronto Library/76n143
Williams/Guide to research collections of NYPL/77n194
Wright/Of books and men/78n265

RESTAURANTS
Britchky/Restaurants of New York/75n1685; 77n1540; 79n599
Dills/Best restaurants of Los Angeles & So Calif/77n1541
Foster/New York Times correspondents' choice: restaurants around the world/75n1688
Killeen/Best restaurants of San Francisco & No Calif/77n1542
Rice/Where to eat in America/78n1477
Steiman/Guide to restaurants of greater Miami/78n530

RESTORATION OF BUILDINGS
Grow/Old house catalogue: products, services, & suppliers for restoring, decorating, etc./78n852
Nylander/Fabrics for historic bldgs/78n862
Smith/Critical bibliog of bldg conservation/79n892
Tubesing/Architectural preservation in US/79n894

RETAIL TRADE
Auerbach gd to retail point-of-sale systems/75n921
European retail trades/77n809

RETIREMENT
Buckley/Retirement hndbk/75n930; 79n841
Sprague/Finding a job: middle-aged & retired/79n865

RETIREMENT INCOME
CCH/Guidebook to pension planning/78n748

REVOLUTIONS
Blackey/Modern revolutions & revolutionists: bibliog/77n359
Hyams/Dictionary of modern revolution/75n466

RHETORIC
Classical world bibliog of philosophy, religion, & rhetoric/79n1080

RHODE ISLAND
Austin/Genealogical dict/79n475
Directory of foundations/77n83

RHODE ISLAND (cont'd)
Gannett/Geographic dict of CT & RI/79n596
Gordon/Guide bk to marine fishes of RI/76n1435

RHODESIA
Pollak/Rhodesia-Zimbabwe/78n291

RHYTHM
Winick/Rhythm: bibliog/76n993

RIFLES
See also Firearms
Archer/Jane's pocket bk of rifles & light machine guns/79n1607
Carmichel/Modern rifle/76n755

RIGHT AND LEFT (political science)
Kehde/American left, 1955-70: union catalog of pamphlets/77n505
Spahn/From radical left to extreme right: bibliog of periodicals/77n506

RIGHTS OF ALL
Jacobs/Antebellum black newspapers: indices/77n432

RIIS, JACOB A.
Fried/Jacob A. Riis: ref gd/78n644

RILKE, RAINER MARIE
Bartlett/Word index to Rainer M. Rilke's German lyrical poetry/79n1277

RIMBAUD, ARTHUR
Carter/Concordance to oeuvres complètes of Arthur Rimbaud/79n1271

RIVER RUNNING
Arighi/Wildwater touring/75n745
Jenkinson/Wild rivers of No Amer/75n632

RIVERS
Hogan/Rivers of the West/76n521

ROBBE-GRILLET, ALAIN
Fraizer/Alain Robbe-Grillet/75n1415

ROBINSON, EDWIN ARLINGTON
Lippincott/Bibliography of writings & criticisms of Edwin A. Robinson/75n1366

ROBOT AIRCRAFT
Taylor/Jane's pocket bk of remotely piloted vehicles/79n1594

ROCHESTER COUNTY, NY
Malo/Landmarks of Rochester & Monroe County/75n1019

ROCK MUSIC
Castleman/All together now: Beatles discog/77n978
Castleman/Beatles again?/79n997
Edwards/Top 10's & trivia of rock & roll . . . /76n1023; 76n1024
Gillet/Rock almanac/77n979
Goldstein/Oldies but goodies: rock 'n' roll yrs/78n916

ROCK MUSIC (cont'd)
Logan/Illustrated ency of rock/78n918
Nite/Rock on: illust'd ency of rock 'n roll/76n1029; 79n998
Osborne/Popular & rock records 1948-78/79n999
Propes/Golden goodies: gd to 50's & 60's rock & roll record collecting/77n981
Stambler/Encyclopedia of pop, rock, & soul/76n1030; 78n920
York/Who's who in rock music/79n1003

ROCKETS
Gatland/Missiles & rockets/77n1647

ROCKINGHAM COUNTY, VA
Kaylor/Abstracts of land grant surveys, 1761-91/77n467

ROCKS
See also Mineralogy
Brown/Illustrated gd to common rocks & minerals/77n1431
Deeson/Collectors ency of rocks & minerals/75n1094
Desautels/Rocks & minerals/75n1572
Hamilton/Larousse gd to minerals, rocks & fossils/78n1359
Klaits/When you find a rock/77n1434
Mason/World of rocks & minerals/77n1436
Pearl/Gems, minerals, crystals, & ores: ency/78n1360
Pough/Field gd to rocks & minerals/77n1438
Shaub/Treasures from the earth/76n1482
Tindall/Collector's gd to rocks & minerals/77n1440

ROCKY MOUNTAINS
Bridge/Tourguide to Rocky Mtn wilderness/76n716

RODENTS
Hanney/Rodents: lives & habits/76n1444

ROETHKE, THEODORE
Moul/T. Roethke's career: bibliog/78n1148

ROLLING STONE
Rolling Stone record review/75n1174

ROMAN ART
Coulson/Annotated bibliog of Greek & Roman art, architecture, & archaeology/77n862

ROMAN CATHOLICS
See Catholic Church

ROMANIAN AMERICANS
Wertsman/Romanians in Amer: chron/76n418

ROMANIAN LANGUAGE
Vorvoreanu/Romanian phrase bk/75n1286

ROME (ancient)
Classical world bibliog of Greek & Roman history/79n402
Coulson/Annotated bibliog of Greek & Roman art, architecture, & archaeology/77n862

ROOTS (botany)
Miller/Root anatomy & morphology: gd to lit/76n1372

ROSES
Browne/Rose-lover's gd/75n1699

ROSSETTI, CHRISTINA
Crump/Christina Rossetti: ref gd/77n1238

ROTH, PHILIP
Rodgers/Philip Roth/75n1367

ROYAL COMMONWEALTH SOCIETY
Simpson/Manuscript catalogue of the Library/77n413

ROYAL FAMILIES
McNaughton/Book of kings: genealogy/76n446

RUBBER
Heinisch/Dictionary of rubber/76n1647

RUBENS, PETER PAUL
Illustrated catalogue raisonne of work of Peter P. Rubens/75n990

RUGS, ORIENTAL
Fokker/Oriental carpets for today/75n1103

RUIZ, JUAN
Mignani/Concordance to J. Ruiz/79n1290

RUNAWAY CHILDREN
National directory of runaway programs/78n660

RURAL CHURCHES
Byers/Readings for town & country church workers: bibliog/76n1072

RURAL CONDITIONS
Yalan/Design of agric'l settlements/77n732

RURAL DEVELOPMENT
US Dept of Agri/Rural developmt lit: bibliog/77n1515

RUSKIN, JOHN
Beetz/John Ruskin: bibliog/77n1239

RUSSELL, KEN
Rosenfeldt/Ken Russell/79n1027

RUSSIA
Boisture/Sources of support for research on Russia & the USSR/76n277
Horak/Russia, USSR, & Eastern Europe/79n378
McCauley/Russian revolution & Soviet state 1917-21: documents/76n374

RUSSIA (cont'd)
Wieczynski/Modern ency of Russian & Soviet history/79n442

RUSSIAN AMERICANS
Wertsman/Russians in America, 1727-1975: chronology/77n446

RUSSIAN LANGUAGE
Eimermacher/Subject bibliog of Soviet semiotics/78n1025
Coulson/Pocket Oxford Russian-Engl dict/76n1146
Daum/Dictionary of Russian verbs/78n1065
Kent/Reading Russian lang/75n155
Lederman/Russian-Engl dict of suppositional names/76n1147
Muller/English-Russian dict/75n1274
Smirnitsky/Russian-English dict/75n1275

RUSSIAN LITERATURE
See Soviet literatures for literatures of the USSR

Also under national literatures, e.g., Ukrainian literature
Berry/Plots & characters in major Russian fiction/78n1196; 79n1282
Koubourlis/Concordance to poems of Osip Mandelstam/75n1425
Moody/10 bibliogs of 20th cent Russian lit/79n1284
Weber/Modern ency of Russian & Soviet lit/79n1283

RUSSIAN REPUBLIC
See Russia

RUSSIAN STUDIES
See Soviet studies

RYUKYU ISLANDS
Walker/Flora of Okinawa & So Ryukyu Islands/77n1358

SACRAMENTUM MUNDI
Radner/Encyclopedia of theology: sacramentum mundi/76n1082

SACRED SONGS
See also Gospel music; Hymns
Gordon/New gospel treasure select-a-song/77n955
Mason/Hymn-tunes of Lowell Mason: bibliog/77n959

SAILING
See also Boats; Yachting
Budd/Sailing boats of the world/75n746
Encyclopedia of sailing/79n725
McDermott/Sailboat racing rules/75n749
Rousmaniere/Glossary of modern sailing terms/77n685
Shuwall/Running Press glossary of sailing language/78n633

SAILING (cont'd)
Somerville/Sailing/75n751

SAINT DAVID'S UNIVERSITY COLLEGE, LAMPETER
Catalogue of Tract collection/77n369

ST. LOUIS, MO
Vexler/St. Louis/75n510

ST. PAUL, MN
Empson/Street where you live: street names of St. Paul/76n548

SAINTS
Habig/Saints of the Americas/76n1092

SAINTS IN ART
Bles/How to distinguish saints in art . . . /76n925

SALISH LANGUAGE
Hess/Dictionary of Puget-Salish/77n1097

SALT II
Parker/SALT II/75n541

SAMMARTINI, GIOVANNI BATTISTA
Jenkins/Thematic catalogue of works/78n908

SAN BERNARDINO MOUNTAINS
Robinson/San Bernardino Mtn trails/76n720

SAN DIEGO, CA
Mayer/San Diego: chron hist/79n428

SAN FRANCISCO
Killeen/Best restaurants of San Francisco & No Calif/77n1542
Mayer/San Francisco/75n511
Socolich/Bargain hunting in SF/75n954

SANBORN FIRE INSURANCE MAPS
Hoehn/Union list of Sanborn fire insur maps/78n764

SANITARY ENGINEERING
Meinck/Dictionary of water & sewage eng'g/79n1579
Middlebrooks/Lagoon info source bk/79n1580

SANSKRIT LANGUAGE
Apte/Student's Engl-Sanskrit dict/75n1281
Suryakanta/Sanskrit-Hindi-Engl dict/77n1098
Narang/Kalidas bibliog/77n1268

SANTA CLARA COUNTY, CA
Fox/Santa Clara county bk/75n605

SANTALS
Troisi/Santals: bibliog/77n746

SARTON, MAY
Blouin/May Sarton/79n1223

SARTRE, JEAN-PAUL
Lapointe/Jean-Paul Sartre & critics: bibliog/77n1051

SATELLITES (artificial)
See Artificial satellites

SATIRE
Kujoth/Subject gd to humor: from 365 periodicals, 1968-74/77n1141

SAUDI ARABIA
Who's who in Saudi Arabia/78n118

SAVING AND INVESTMENT
Rickenbacker/William Rickenbacker's savings & investment gd/77n803

SAYERS, DOROTHY L.
Harmon/Annotated gd to works/78n1181

SCANDINAVIA
Fraser/Scandinavian education/75n644
Scandinavian political studies/76n501; 79n511

SCHENECTADY, NY
Pearson/Genealogies of . . . 1st settlers of Schenectady 1662-1800/77n473

SCHISTOSOMIASIS
Schistosomiasis: abstracts/78n1392; 79n1442

SCHOLARLY PUBLISHERS
See University presses

SCHOLARS
Directory of Amer scholars/75n690; 79n694
Montgomery/International scholars directory/76n666

SCHOLARSHIPS AND FELLOWSHIPS
Feingold/Scholarships, fellowships & loans/78n566
Directory of public service internships/78n562
Schlachter/Directory of financial aids for women/79n766
Study abroad: internat'l scholarships/76n615

SCHOOL ADMINISTRATORS
Requirements for certification/77n638; 78n579
Who's who biog'l record-school district officials/78n602

SCHOOL LIBRARIES
See also Children's libraries; Instructional materials centers; Learning resource centers
Baker/School & public lib media programs for children & YAs/78n178
Bennie/Learning centers/79n206
Burke/Children's lib serv: school or public/75n192
Davies/School lib media center/75n194
Delaney/Media programs in elementary & middle schools/77n220

SCHOOL LIBRARIES (cont'd)
Evaluating media programs/78n183
Freeman/Pathfinder: gd for school librarian/77n221
Gillespie/Creating a school media program/75n195
Gillespie/Model school district media program/78n185
Guide for conversion of school libraries into media centres/79n210
Hannigan/Media center facilities design/79n211
Hug/Instructional design & media program/77n224
Jones/Survey of school media stds/79n670
Liesener/Systematic process for planning media programs/78n186
Loertscher/Budgeting for school media centers: bibliog/77n226
Marshall/Managing modern school library/77n222
Martin/Principal's hndbk on school lib media center/79n213
Media programs: district & school/76n149
Nickel/Steps to service/76n150
Pearson/Learning resource centers/75n216
Planning & operating media centers: readings/77n228
Prostano/School library media center/78n187
Saunders/Modern school library/76n151
Shapiro/Serving youth/76n152
Wehmeyer/School librarian as educator/77n229
Wehmeyer/School library volunteer/76n153
Woolls/Evaluation techniques for school library: media programs/79n221
  INSTRUCTION IN USE
Blazek/Influencing students toward media center use/77n217
Cleary/Discovering bks & libraries/78n182
Gibson/Finding info in library: Rochelle High School/77n223
Hart/Instruction in school media center use/79n212
Nordling/Dear faculty: gdbk to high-school library/77n227
Peterson/Library instruction gd/75n239
Shapiro/Teaching yrself in libraries/79n217
Walker/Teaching media skills/78n188
  MEDIA EDUCATION
AASL/Certification model for prof school media personnel/77n218
Case/Curriculum alternatives: experiments in school lib media educ/75n193
Chisholm/Media personnel in educ/77n219
Daniel/Process for developing a competency based educ'l program for media professionals/79n207

SCHOOL LIBRARIES (cont'd)
  MEDIA EDUCATION (cont'd)
Evaluation of alternative curricula: school lib media educ/76n221
Freeman/Index to research in school librarianship/78n184
Requirements for certification for elementary schools, secondary schools, junior colleges/77n638; 78n579
  SELECTION AIDS
Adventuring with books/78n189
AUP/University press bks for secondary school libraries/76n164
BAMEG reviews/79n222
Baskin/Notes from different drummer/78n179
Bestern der besten—best of the best/77n1144
Baron/Bibliog of bks for children/79n223
Books for secondary school libraries/77n231
Books for you/77n232
Brown/Core media collection for secondary schools/76n156
Buttlar/Building ethnic collections/78n376
Children's bks in print/75n196; 75n197
Children's bks of the year/77n1149
Elementary school lib collection/76n157; 77n233
Fader/New hooked on books/78n586
Jacob/Independent reading grades 1-3/76n158
Junior high school lib catalog/76n159
Leamer/Suggestions for a basic economics library/75n200
Kliatt paperbk bk gd/Hiatt/75n199
McDonough/Canadian bks for young people/79n1192
Owen/Smorgasbord of bks/76n161
Peterson/Reference bks for elementary & jr high school libraries/76n162
Polette/Celebrating with books/78n191
Richardson/Periodicals for school media programs/79n184
Schaaf/High school math library/77n1305
Schon/Books in Spanish for children & YAs/79n1292
US Dept HEW/Aids to media selection for students & teachers/77n657
Wilgus/Latin America books/75n297
Withrow/Gateways to readable bks: graded list/77n1166
Wynar/Guide to ref bks for school media centers, suppl/77n234

SCHOOL PLAYS
Mersand/Guide to play selection/76n1034

SCHOOLS
 See also Elementary education; Private schools; Secondary schools
Curriculum Info Center/School universe data bk/76n660; 77n604
Hoffman/Guide to fed funds for elementary & secondary educ/76n662

SCHOOLS (cont'd)
Patterson's Amer educ/76n663
Summary of school stats by county/75n686

SCHROEDER, THEODORE
McCoy/T. Schroeder, cold enthusiast/75n1296

SCIENCE
  ABBREVIATIONS
Ocran's acronyms . . . in scientific & tech writing/79n1300
Wennrich/Anglo-Amer & German abbreviations in sci & tech/78n1202; 79n1301
  BIBLIOGRAPHY
Bibliographic gd to technology/77n11
Catalogue of hist of sci collections of Univ of Oklahoma/77n1281
Dasbach/Science for society/78n1204
Grogan/Science & technology/77n1282
ISIS cum bibliog: hist of sci 1913-65/77n1283
Kyed/Scientific, eng'g & med societies publications in print/77n1285
Kyed/Scientific, tech, & eng'g societies publications in print/75n1430
Knight/Sources for hist of sci, 1660-1914/76n1309
Malinowsky/Science & eng'g lit/77n1286
Parker/Information sources in sci & tech/77n1287
Physical sciences: doctoral dissertations by Indian universities 1857-1970/76n1312
Scientific & tech bks & serials in print/78n1205
Wolff/AAAS sci bk list suppl/79n1294
  DICTIONARIES AND ENCYCLOPEDIAS
Carter/Dictionary of inventions & discoveries/77n1288
Chambers/Dictionary of sci & tech/77n1289
Chernukhin/English-Russian polytechnical dict/78n1206
Daintith/Dictionary of phys sciences/78n1207
De Vries/French-Engl sci & tech dict/77n1290
De Vries/German-Engl sci dict/79n1295
Dorian/Dictionary of sci & tech: Engl-German/79n1296
Duncan/Encyclopedia of ignorance/79n1297
Kerrod/Concise color ency of sci/76n1314
Lapedes/McGraw-Hill dict of scientific & tech terms/75n1434; 79n1299
Lapedes/McGraw-Hill ency of sci & tech/78n1210
Lucas/First sci dict/78n1209
Mackay/Scientific quotations/79n1302
SPINES thesaurus: vocabulary . . . for policymaking/78n1211
Tver/Gulf Publishing Co dict of business & science/75n886
US Congress/Science policy: working glossary/77n1291
Van Nostrand's scientific ency/77n1292

SCIENCE (cont'd)
  DIRECTORIES
British scientific documentation services/78n1217
Inventory of major research facilities in European community/79n87
Klein/Guide to Amer scientific & tech directories/77n1284
  HANDBOOKS AND YEARBOOKS
Britannica/Yearbk of sci & future/78n1220
Chen/Biomedical, scientific & tech bk reviewing/78n1381
La Follette/Citizen & sci almanac & bibliog/78n1201
McGraw-Hill yrbk of sci & tech/76n1317
Moses/Practicing scientist's hndbk/79n1303
Nature-science annual/76n1321
  PERIODICALS AND INDEXES
Aitchison/Unesco thesaurus/79n344
Applied sci & tech index/76n1325
Composite index for CRC hndbks/79n1304
Houghton/Scientific periodicals/76n1308
Index to all bks on physical sciences in English 1967-74/75n1438
Kronick/History of scientific & tech periodicals/77n1278
NTIS subj classification/78n1526
Owen/Abstracts & indexes in sci & tech/75n1432
Rothberg/Index of scientific writings on creativity/77n1296
Satyaprakash/Indian sci index/78n1221
Science citation index/76n1326; 76n1327
Yannarella/US gov scientific & tech periodicals/77n1295

SCIENCE AND STATE
Greenberg/Science & gov report internat'l almanac/78n435
Provisional world list of periodicals dealing with sci & tech policies/76n1324

SCIENCE AND TECHNOLOGY
Dean/Science & tech in developmt of modern China/75n299
Sci & tech: purchasing gd for public libraries/76n148
Stonehouse/Science & tech/75n175
US Natl Aeronautics & Space Admin/NASA thesaurus/77n1563

SCIENCE EDUCATION
AAAS sci film catalog/77n1280
Educator's gd to free sci matls/76n673
New Unesco source bk for sci teaching/75n714
Nova/Science adventures on TV/75n1431; 76n1311
NSF factbook/76n603

SCIENCE FAIRS
Stoffer/Science fair projects index/76n1328

368–Subjects

SCIENCE FICTION
Ash/Visual ency of sci fict/79n1202
Ash/Who's who in sci fict/77n1172
Barron/Anatomy of wonder/77n1173
Cole/Checklist of sci fict anthologies/76n1204
Contento/Index to sci fict anthologies/79n1203
Hall/Science fict bk review index/76n1206; 78n1106
Halpern/International classified directory of dealers in sci fict & fantasy bks/76n50
Lord/Last Celt . . . Robert E. Howard/79n1218
Nolan/Ray Bradbury companion/76n1229
Roy/Guide to Barsoom/78n1135
Sween/Bibliography of sci fict/75n1329
Trimble/Star Trek concordance/78n1087
Tuck/Encyclopedia of sci fict & fantasy/75n1330; 79n1204
Tymm/Research gd to sci fict studies/79n1205

SCIENCE FICTION FILMS
Lee/Reference gd to fantastic films/75n1194
Parish/Great sci fict pictures/78n962

SCIENTIFIC APPARATUS
Wynter/Scientific instruments/77n1279

SCIENTIFIC CONFERENCES
Index to scientific & tech proceedings/79n1305
InterDok directory of published proceedings/75n1435
Union catalogue of . . . Cambridge: scientific conf proceedings, 1644-1972/76n1313

SCIENTIFIC LIBRARIES
Mount/University sci & eng'g libraries/77n239
Science & tech: purchasing gd/76n148

SCIENCE TESTS
Buros/Science tests & reviews/76n568

SCIENTIFIC SOCIETIES
Kyed/Scientific, tech & eng'g societies publications in print/75n1430
World gd to scientific assns/75n1436; 79n89

SCIENTISTS
American men & women of sci/75n346; 77n1297; 78n1214; 79n347
Asimov's biog'l ency of sci & tech/77n1298
Barr/Index to biog'l fragments in scientific journals/75n1437
Dictionary of scientific biog/75n1439; 76n1329; 77n1299; 77n1300
ISI's who is publishing in science/77n1294
Quinn/Significant Amer scientists/77n137
Who was who in Amer hist, science & tech/77n1301
Williams/Biographical dict of scientists/76n1330

SCORING (sports)
Richards/Complete hndbk of sports scoring/75n727

SCOTCH HIGHLANDERS
MacLean/Historical account of settlements of Scotch Highlanders prior to the Peace of 1783/79n489

SCOTCH-IRISH
Chalkley/Chronicles of Scotch-Irish settlement in Virginia/75n409

SCOTLAND
Allison/Titles of Engl bks & foreign bks printed in England, 1475-1640/77n333
Burke/General armory of England, Scotland, Ireland & Wales/77n483
Donaldson/Who's who in Scottish hist/75n399
Harting/Literary tour gd to England & Scotland/77n1223
Johnston's gazetteer of Scotland/76n457
Mather/Linguistic atlas of Scotland/76n1116
Munro/Gazetteer of Scotland/75n572
Pollard/Short-title catalogue of bks printed in England, Scotland, & Ireland . . . , 1475-1640/77n27
Smith/Library resources in Scotland/75n166
Stuart/Scottish family hist/79n499
Watt/Biographical dict of Scottish grads to AD 1410/79n441

SCOTT, WALTER
Bradley/Index to Waverley novels/76n1283

SCOTTISH LANGUAGE
Mather/Linguistic atlas of Scotland/78n1023

SCRABBLE (game)
Official Scrabble players dict/79n727

SCULPTURE
Barr/Painting & sculpture in Museum of Modern Art/79n877
Ekdahl/American sculpture: gd to info sources/78n821

SCULPTORS
Krauss/Sculpture of David Smith: catalogue/78n822

SEA
Kemp/Oxford companion to ships & the sea/78n1549

SEA MAMMALS
See Marine mammals

SEA STORIES
Smith/Sea fiction gd/77n1175

SEAMANSHIP
Chapman/Piloting, seamanship & small boat handling/76n709

SEAMEN
Kemp/Oxford companion to ships & the sea/
  78n1549
SEAMEN'S LIBRARIES
Skallerup/Books afloat & ashore/75n271
SEASHELL COLLECTING
  See Shells
SEASHORE BIOLOGY
Voss/Seashore life of Florida & Caribbean/
  78n1335
SEAWEEDS
  See Marine algae
SECONDARY EDUCATION
Bibliography on accountability/75n641
SECONDARY SCHOOLS
Crawford/Guide to mid states schools in
  DE, DC, MD, Puerto Rico, etc/76n656
Crawford/Guide to mid states schools in NJ/
  76n657
Crawford/Guide to mid states schools in NY/
  76n658
Crawford/Guide to mid states schools in PA/
  76n659
National school directory/75n684
Student activities in secondary schools/75
  n648
SECRETARIES
Doris/Complete secretary's hndbk/78n714
Eckersley-Johnson/Webster's secretarial
  hndbk/78n716
Hill/Hill's manual of soc & business forms/77
  n794
Nanassy/Reference manual for office workers/
  78n717
Sabin/Gregg ref manual/78n718
Simpson/Tested secretarial techniques for
  getting things done/75n893
Sletwold/Sletwold's manual of docs & forms
  for legal secretary/77n533
SECURITIES
Balachandran/Guide to trade & securities
  stats/78n727
Noddings/Dow Jones-Irwin gd to convertible
  securities/75n917
SECURITIES AND EXCHANGE
  COMMISSION
Directory of companies required to file annual
  reports with SEC/79n832
Skousen/Introduction to SEC/78n731
SECURITIES EXCHANGE ACT
Securities Reform Act of 1975/76n888
SECURITIES LAW
Folk/Securities law review/76n518

SEEDS
Forest tree seed directory/77n1367
Gunn/World gd to tropical drift seeds &
  fruits/77n1349
Karel/Dried grasses, grains, etc/76n1590
Link/Whole seed catalog/77n1557
Montgomery/Seeds & fruits of plants of
  Canada & NE US/78n1285
Schroeder/Green thumb directory/78n1496
Green world: gd & catalog/77n1561
SELF-CULTURE
  See also Personal development; Psychology, popular
Ann Landers ency/79n1427
SELF DEFENSE
Logan/Handbook of martial arts & self-
  defense/76n768
Winderbaum/Martial arts ency/78n639
SELF-DETERMINATION, NATIONAL
Blaustein/Independence docs of world/79
  n518
SELF-DISCLOSURE
Moss/Bibliographical gd to self-disclosure
  literature/79n1425
SENDER, RAMON J.
King/Ramon J. Sender: bibliog/77n1275
SENIOR CITIZENS
  See Elderly
  See also Aging; Retirement
SEPARATION AND LOSS
  See Bereavement; Broken homes
SEPTUAGINT
Morrish/Concordance of . . . /78n981
SERBOCROATIAN LANGUAGE
Dictionary: Engl-Serbocroation, . . . /78n1067
SERIES, MONOGRAPHIC
  See Books in series
SERMON ON THE MOUNT
Kissinger/Sermon on the Mount: hist &
  bibliog/77n1045
SERMONS
Spencer/Hymn & scripture selection gd/79
  n1063
SERVICE INDUSTRIES
CU/Guide to consumer services: financial &
  professional/78n747
SEWAGE
Meinck/Dictionary of water & sewage eng'g/
  79n1579
SEWING
Carbone/Dictionary of sewing terminology/
  79n943

SEWING MACHINES
Courtney/Butterick sewing machine hndbk/78n877
Jewell/Veteran sewing machines: collector's gd/77n933

SEX
Bustanoby/Dictionary of sexology/75n1580
Catalog of . . . library of Inst for Sex Research, Indiana Univ/76n1493
Sheridan/Sex differences & reading: bibliog/77n581
Sex & handicapped: bibliog/78n1391
Pope/Sex & undecided librarian/75n269

SEX DISCRIMINATION
Forschl/Feminist resources for schools & colleges/78n593
Hughes/Sexual barrier/79n756
Myers/Women in librarianship/76n120

SEX ROLES
Adell/Guide to non-sexist children's bks/77n1142
Bertrand/Bks with options: bibliog of non-stereotyping bks for children/77n1143
Davis/Liberty cap: catalogue of non-sexist matls for children/79n227
Friedman/Sex role stereotyping in mass media: bibliog/78n1075

SHAKERS
Miller/Shaker herbs/78n1298
Richmond/Shaker lit: bibliog/77n1030; 78n976

SHAKESPEARE, WILLIAM
Bergeron/Shakespeare: res gd/76n1284
Berman/Reader's gd to Shakespeare's plays/75n1396
Clark/New century Shakespeare hndbk/75n1398
Dent/World of Shakespeare/75n1397
Irvine/How to pronounce names in Shakespeare/76n1035
Jacobs/Annotated bibliog of Shakespearean burlesques, . . . /77n1240
Jerrold/Descriptive index to Shakespeare's characters/77n1241
Levith/What's in Shakespeare's names/79n1252
McManaway/Selective bibliog of Shakespeare editions, . . . /76n1285
Muir/Shakespeare survey: annual survey/75n1399; 76n1286; 77n1242
Spevack/Harvard concordance to Shakespeare/75n1400
Velz/Tragedy of Julius Caesar/79n1253
Wells/Shakespeare: dict/79n1254

SHAKESPEARE FESTIVALS
Loney/Shakespeare complex; gd to summer festivals in No Amer/76n1042

SHAW, BERNARD
Hardwick/Bernard Shaw companion/75n1401
Hartnoll/Who's who in Shaw/76n1287

SHAW, RALPH
Stevens/Essays for Ralph Shaw/76n211

SHAW CHILDHOOD IN POETRY COLLECTION
Childhood in poetry: catalogue, Florida State Univ/77n1146

SHEET MUSIC
Klamkin/Old sheet music—pic hist/76n1027

SHELLEY, MARY
Lyles/Mary Shelley: bibliog/77n1243

SHELLEY, PERCY BYSSHE
Dunbar/Bibliography of Shelley studies/77n1244
Pollin/Music for Shelley's poetry/75n1133

SHELLS
Abbott/American malacologists/75n1498
Abbott/American seashells/75n1522
Andrews/Shells & shores of TX/78n1334
Angeletti/Seas & their shells/79n927
Dance/Collector's ency of shells/78n857
Emerson/American Museum of Natl Hist gd to shells/77n1394
Fair/Shell collector's gd/77n931
Grzimek's animal life ency: mollusks & echinoderms/75n1523
Humfrey/Sea shells of West Indes/76n973
Kirtisinghe/Sea shells of Sri Lanka/79n928
Lindner/Field gd to seashells of world/79n929
Major/Collecting world sea shells/75n1097
Oliver/Guide to shells/76n974
Radwin/Murex shells of world: illust'd gd/77n1395
Warmke/Caribbean seashells: gd/77n1396

SHEPARD, THOMAS
Gallagher/Early Puritan writers: ref gd/77n1185

SHERLOCK HOLMES
De Waal/World bibliog of Sherlock Holmes & Dr. Watson: list/76n1205
Tracy/Encyclopaedia Sherlockiana/78n1172

SHIP PASSENGER LISTS
Boyer/Ship passenger lists, NY & NJ, 1600-1825/79n480
Hargreaves-Mawdsley/Bristol & America: 1st settlers in No Amer 1654-85/79n485
Hotten/Original lists of persons of quality/75n421
Tepper/Emigrants to PA, 1641-1819/76n443; 78n414
Tepper/Immigrants to mid colonies/79n497
Tepper/Passengers to America/78n413

SHIPBUILDING
Baker/Maine shipbldg/75n376

SHIPPING
Lloyd's calendar/76n902

SHIPS
Blackburn/Illustrated ency of ships, etc/79n1582
Emmons/Atlantic liners/75n1828
Emmons/Pacific liners/75n1829
Kemp/Oxford companion to ships & the sea/78n1549
Miller/Guide to No Amer passenger ships/79n1586
Morris/American sailing coasters of No Atlantic/75n1830
Taggart/Motorboat, yacht or canoe/75n1831

SHKLOVSKY, VIKTOR
Sheldon/Viktor Shklovsky: bibliog/78n1198

SHOCK (mechanics)
Harris/Shock & vibration hndbk/77n1607

SHOOTING
Amber/Handloader's digest/76n754

SHOPPING
See also Consumer education; Mail order catalogs

Camblos/Shopping round mtns/75n941
Community market co-op catalog/75n942
Eddy/Alternative shopping/75n1033
Ein/Whole Washington hndbk/76n881
Fielding's selective shopping gd to Europe/76n537
Goldman/Nothing new: gd to second-hand shopping in Los Angeles/75n946
Hodupp/Shopper's gd to museum stores/79n842
Karnaookh/Shortage survival hndbk/75n947
Lucie-Smith/First London catalogue/75n949
Miser/Factory store gd to New England/75n951
Partridge/Bargain hunting in LA/75n953
Socolich/Bargain hunting in San Francisco/75n954
USDA/How to buy food for economy & quality/76n883

SHOPPING CENTERS
Directory of shopping centers in US & Canada/75n922

SHORES, LOUIS
Shores/Quiet world/76n210

SHORT-LIVED PHENOMENA
See Phenomenology

SHORT STORIES
Bogart/Short story index/76n1210; 77n1134
Chicorel index to short stories/76n1203; 79n1188

SHORT STORIES (cont'd)
Emmens/Short stories on film/79n1034
Walker/20th cent short story explication/75n1331; 78n1108

SHOW BUSINESS
Celebrity Service/Contact bk/76n1041

SICILY
Guido/Sicily: archaeological gd/78n320

SICKLE CELL ANEMIA
Davis/Sickle cell anemia/79n1453
Triche/Sickle cell hemoglobinopathies/75n1620
Triche/Sickle cell hemoglobinopathies: comp bibliog/77n1468

SIDNEY, PHILIP
Donow/Concordance to poems/76n1288

SIERRA LEONE
Foray/Historical dict/78n288

SIERRA NEVADA
Schaffer/Tahoe Sierra: gd to 100 hikes/76n721
Winnett/Sierra south: 100 back-country trips/76n725

SIGNS AND SYMBOLS
Modley/Handbook of pict'l symbols/78n812

SIKKIM
Ali/Handbook of birds of India & Pakistan/77n1373
Gazetteer of Sikhim/75n333

SILVER
Persons/Investor's ency of gold, silver, etc/76n860

SIMENON, GEORGES
Young/G. Simenon: cklist of "Maigret"/77n1179

SIMMS, WILLIAM GILMORE
Kibler/Pseudonymous pubs of W. G. Simms/77n1212

SINGAPORE
Key/Library automation: Orient & South Pacific/77n289

SINGERS
Meltzer/Significant Amer musicians, composers, & singers/77n135
Turner/Afro-American singers/79n977

SINNETT, A. P.
Conger/Combined chron for use with Mahatma letters/75n1235

SKATEBOARDING
Cassorla/Skateboarder's bible/78n636

SKIING
Avis gd to skiing in Europe/76n760
Fehr/Skiing USA/79n728

SKIING (cont'd)
Goeldner/Bibliography of skiing studies/78n629
Liebers/Complete bk of cross-country ski touring/75n784
Mokres/Ski America cheap/75n785

SKIN DIVING
North/Underwater California/77n699
Titcombe/Handbook for professional divers/75n787

SLAVERY
Am I not a man & a brother: antislavery crusade of revolutionary Amer 1688-1788/78n335

SLAVIC LANGUAGES
Herman/Dictionary of Slavic word families/76n1111

SLAVIC LITERATURE
Mihailovich/Modern Slavic lit/78n1199

SLAVIC STUDIES
See also Soviet studies
American bibliog of Slavic & East European studies/75n303; 76n271; 76n272; 78n307
Scholars' gd to Washington, DC for Russian-Soviet studies/78n309
Skoric/Russian ref aids in Univ of Toronto Library/75n306
Zalewski/Guide to selected ref matls: Russia & East Europe/75n310

SLIDES
DeLaurier/Slide buyers gd/75n1003
Irvine/Slide libraries/75n205

SMALL ARMS
See Firearms
See also types of arms: Handguns; Machine guns; Rifles

SMALL BUSINESS
Directory of state & fed funds for business development/78n710
How to run a small business/75n891
Kryszak/Small business index/79n823

SMALL PRESSES
See also Alternative culture; Little magazines; Microforms; Private presses; Publishers and publishing
American bk review/79n1216
Directory of small magazines-press editors & publishers/79n52
International directory of little magazines & small presses/78n46
Small press record of bks in print/79n39
Stichting Drukwerk in de Marge/Bibliografie/79n41

SMITH, DAVID
Krauss/Sculpture of David Smith: catalogue/78n822

SMITHSONIAN INSTITUTION
Nation of nations: people who came to Amer as seen through objects & docs/77n420

SNAKES
Stidworthy/Snakes of world/76n1450

SNOWMOBILES
Dempsey/Complete snowmobile repair hndbook/75n1753

SOARING
See Gliding
America's soaring bk/76n730
Soaring directory/78n638

SOBRIQUETS
See Pseudonyms

SOCCER
Gardner/Illustrated soccer dict for young people/78n630
Hollander/Complete hndbk of soccer/79n729

SOCIAL ACTION
Bank of Amer/Bibliog of corporate social responsibility/78n696
Bibliography: corp responsibility for social problems/75n790
Human Resources Network/Handbk of corp soc responsibility/76n898
Uhr/Social responsibility in marketing: bibliog/78n744

SOCIAL AGENCIES
Directory of soc & health agencies of NY city/76n774; 75n798
Watkins/International who's who in community services/75n800

SOCIAL CHANGE
See also Alternative culture
Alternatives in print/76n79
Bundy/Guide to lit of soc change/78n646

SOCIAL JUSTICE
Mainelli/Social justice/79n1042

SOCIAL MEDICINE
Andrews/Bibliog of socioeconomic aspects of medicine/76n1511
Litman/Sociology of med & health care: bibliog/78n1388

SOCIAL PROBLEMS IN LITERATURE
Brunton/Index to contemp scene/76n21

SOCIAL POLICY
Blackstone/Social policy & admin in Britain: bibliog/77n703

SOCIAL PSYCHOLOGY
Armer/African soc psychology: bibliog/76 n1485

SOCIAL REFORMERS
Fried/Jacob A. Riis: ref gd/78n644
Miekina/Significant Amer soc reformers & humanitarians/77n138

SOCIAL RESPONSIBILITY
See Corporate social responsibility; Social action

SOCIAL SCIENCES
BIBLIOGRAPHY
Afflerbach/Emerging field of sociobibliography/78n214
Allsworth/Soviet Asia: bibliogs/77n345
Almasy/Comparative survey analys/78n270
Burrington/How to find out abt soc sciences/76n238
Freides/Literature & bibliog of soc sciences/75n170
Guide to Indian periodical lit: soc sci & humanities/76n35
Gustafson/Pakistan & Bangladesh: bibliog'ic essays in soc science/77n330
Hazfeld/Periodical indexes in soc sci & humanities/79n345
Heiliger/Bibliog of Soviet soc sci/79n385
Hundsdorfer/Bibliographie zur sozialwissenschaftlichen erforschung Tanzanias/76n256
Latin/Privacy/78n271
London bibliog of soc sci/77n298; 78n272; 79n341
Lu/US gov pubs, soc sci/76n240
Marien/Societal directions & alternatives: critical gd to lit/77n299
McInnis/Social sci research hndbk/76n239
Morrison/Energy: bibliog of soc sci lit/77n1407
Roberts/Use of soc sci lit/78n269
Simon/Modern Mid East: gd soc sci/79n359
Stevens/Reference bks in soc sci & humanities/78n4
White/Sources of info in soc sci/75n284
World list of soc sci periodicals/77n302

BIOGRAPHY
American men & women of sci: soc & behavioral sciences/75n346; 79n347

DICTIONARIES
Aitchison/Unesco thesaurus/79n344
Reading/Dictionary of soc sci/79n342

DIRECTORIES
Barron's gd to grad schools: soc sci & psychology/76n634
Haley/Directory of soc studies-soc sci service organizations/77n300
Levine/American gd to British soc sci resources/77n301

SOCIAL SCIENCES (cont'd)
DIRECTORIES (cont'd)
Sessions/Directory of data bases in soc & behavioral sciences/76n241
World directory of soc sci institutions/79n343

INDEXES
Bloomfield/Social sciences index/77n304
Chicorel index to abstracting & indexing services/76n34
Rzepecki/Book review index to soc sci periodicals/79n346
Social sciences citation index/76n242

SOCIAL SECURITY
Social security programs thruout world/79n875

SOCIAL SERVICE
Directory of agencies: US voluntary, international voluntary, inter-gov/77n711
Guide to global giving/77n712
McDade/Directory of soc & health agencies of NY city/79n1508

SOCIAL STUDIES
Educators gd to free soc studies matls/76n674
Haley/Directory of soc studies-soc sci service organizations/77n300
Social studies curriculum matls data bk/77n656

SOCIAL STUDIES TESTS
Buros/Social studies tests/76n569

SOCIAL WORK
Directory of soc & health agencies of NY city/75n798
Haimes/Helping others/75n841
Markle/Author's gd to journals in . . . social work/78n1369
Patti/Management practice in soc welfare: bibliog/77n708
Romanofsky/Social serv organizations/79n733
Sheppard/Social wrk ref aids in Univ of Toronto libraries/75n842
Turner/Ency of soc work/78n647

SOCIAL WORK EDUCATION
Atkins/AV resources for population educ & family planning/77n714
Li/Social work educ/79n731
Stickney/World gd to soc wk educ/75n665

SOCIAL WORK WITH YOUTH
Bundy/Natl children's directory/78n659
Catalog of fed youth programs/78n658
Korkmas/Directory of serv for young children/75n799

SOCIAL WORKERS
NASW register of clinical soc workers/79n735; 79n736

SOCIALISM
Shaffer/Periodicals on socialist countries & Marxism: index/78n467

SOCIALIST PARTY
Guide to MSS collection of Tamiment library/79n517

SOCIETY FOR INDUSTRIAL AND APPLIED MATHEMATICS
Combined membership list AMS, MAA, & SIAM/79n1308

SOCIETY OF AUTOMOTIVE ENGINEERS
SAE/Cumulative index: SAE papers, 1965-73/76n1609
SAE transactions & lit/76n1611

SOCIOLINGUISTICS
Kirshenblatt-Gimblett/Speech play/77n1123
Williams/Keywords/77n1065
Survey of research in sociology & soc anthropology/77n701

SOCIOLOGY
Bell/Annotated bibliog of interorganizational studies/78n640
Bundy/Guide to lit of soc change/78n646
Contemporary sociology: journal of reviews/76n776
Encyclopedia of sociology/75n794
Inkeles/Annual review/76n775
International bibliog/75n791
Leif/Community power & decision-making/75n792
Mark/Sociology of America: gd/77n706
Matthews/Soviet sociology/79n732
Nandan/Durkheimian school: bibliog/78n645
Remmling/Sociology of Karl Mannheim: bibliographical gd/76n773
Rosenberg/Urban info thesaurus/79n734
Rosenfield/New environment-heredity controversy/75n793
Sanders/Sociologist as detective/75n789
Sussman/Author's gd to journals in sociology/79n737
Van de Merwe/Thesaurus of sociological research terminology/75n795

SOCRATES
McKirahan/Plato & Socrates/79n1081

SODIUM IN FOOD
Kraus/Dict of sodium, fats, & cholesterol/76n1577

SOILS
Greenwood/KWIC index to Commonwealth Bureau of Soils/75n1665

SOLAR ENERGY
Foster/Homeowner's gd to solar heating & cooling/77n1419
Hickok/Handbook of solar & wind energy/76n1461
Martz/Solar energy source bk/79n1410
Pesko/Solar directory/77n1414
Solar age catalog/79n1411
Solar energy & res directory/79n1412

SOMALIA
Castagno/Historical dict of Somalia/76n254
Salad/Somalia/78n289

SONG WRITERS, POPULAR
See Music, popular (songs, etc.)

SONGBIRDS
See Birds

SONGS
See also American songs; Music, popular (songs, etc.)
Barlow/Dictionary of opera & song themes/78n911
Denisoff/Songs of protest, war & peace/75n1122
Espina/Repertoire for solo voice: 13th cent to present/78n892
Nardone/Classical vocal music in print/78n897
Selective music lists: vocal solos, vocal ensembles/77n961
Stahl/Selected discog of solo song/77n967

SOUL MUSIC
Stambler/Ency of pop, rock, & soul/76n1030; 78n920

SOUND
Stephens/International dict of sci & tech: sound/76n1353

SOUND RECORDINGS
See Phonorecords

SOUND RECORDINGS FOR VISUALLY HANDICAPPED
See Blind; Talking books; Visually handicapped

SOUTH, THE
Lackey/Frontier claims in lower South/78n404
Mobil travel gd: SW & S-central area/79n608

SOUTH AFRICA
Karis/From protest to challenge, hist of ... politics in So Africa, 1882-1964/75n520; 78n471
Rosenthal/Ency of So Africa/75n319
Wynne/South African political matls: catalogue/78n472

SOUTH AMERICA
Isenberg/South America: probs & prospects/76n281
Knaster/Women in Spanish Amer: bibliog/78n373
Lombardi/Venezuelan hist: bibliog/78n374
Myra Waldo's travel gd/77n570
Parker/American dissertations on foreign educ, So Amer/78n544

SOUTH ARABIAN LANGUAGES
Johnstone/Harsūsi lexicon & Engl-Harsūsi word-list/79n1139

SOUTH ASIA
Sukhwal/South Asia: geog'ic bibliog/76n523
Wagle/Reference aids to So Asia/79n366

SOUTH CAROLINA
Chapman/Annals of Newberry/75n410
Edgar/Biographical directory of SC House of Reps: 1692-1973/75n484
Robertson/Kansas territorial settlers of 1860 born in TN, VA, NC & SC/77n475
Townsend/South Carolina Baptists, 1670-1805/75n431
Weis/Colonial clergy of VA, NC & SC/77n479

SOUTH DAKOTA
Bergman/Handbook of manpower stats for SD/75n974
Shelton/South Dakota union list of serials/75n43
Van Bruggen/Vascular plants of SD/77n1357

SOUTHEAST
Mobil travel gd: Southeastern states/79n607

SOUTHEAST ASIA
Johnson/Index to SE Asian journals/78n295
Nunn/Southeast Asian periodicals/79n365
Wijasuriya/Barefoot librarian/76n218

SOUTHEAST ASIAN LANGUAGES
Echols/English-Indonesian dict/76n1150
Lyman/Dictionary of Mong Njua/76n1152

SOUTHERN AFRICA
El-Khawas/American-So African relations: bibliog'ic essays/77n526

SOUTHERN ILLINOIS UNIVERSITY
Presley/Robert Graves MSS & letters at SIU/77n1234

SOUTHERN STATES
Hardy/Colonial families of southern states of America/75n419
Knight/Biographical dict of southern authors/79n1219
Stevens/Southern almanac/79n391

SOUTHWEST
Larson/Sierra Club naturalist's gd to deserts of SW/78n1270
Monthan/Art & Indian individualists: southwestern artists/76n936
Oppelt/Southwestern pottery: bibliog/78n680
Patraw/Flowers of SW mesas/79n1345

SOVIET LITERATURES
See also Russian literature; Ukrainian literature
Weber/Modern ency of Russian & Soviet lit/79n1283

SOVIET STUDIES
See also Slavic studies
Matthews/Soviet sociology/79n732
O'Relley/Soviet-type economic systems/79n806
Whetten/Current research in comparative communism: bibliog'ic gd to Soviet system/78n468

SOVIET UNION
See Union of Soviet Socialist Republics

SPACE CRAFT
Wilding-White/Jane's pocket bk of space exploration/78n1510

SPACE FLIGHT
See Astronautics

SPACE MUSEUMS
See Aeronautical and space museums

SPAIN
Cortada/Bibliographic gd to Spanish diplomatic hist 1460-1977/79n551
Dorn/Latin America, Spain, & Portugal: bibliog paperbk bks/77n305
Hanson/Dissertations on Iberian & Latin American hist/77n361
Libros en venta/76n16
Wilgus/Latin America, Spain & Portugal/79n384

SPANISH AMERICA
Knaster/Women in Spanish America: bibliog/78n373

SPANISH AMERICAN DIALECT
Galván/El diccionario del español chicano/79n1150
Vasquez/Regional dict of Chicano slang/76n1155

SPANISH AMERICANS
Natella/Spanish in Amer: chronology/76n419
Trejo/Who's who of Spanish heritage librarians in US/77n185
Who's who among Latin Americans in Washington/77n343

SPANISH LANGUAGE
Arora/Proverbial comparisons . . . in Spanish/ 79n1147
Bleznick/Sourcebk for Hispanic lit & lang/75 n1426
Castillo/University of Chicago Spanish dict/ 78n1070
de Nebrija/Vocabulario de romance en Latin/ 75n1276
Diccionario escolar Larousse/79n1148
Diccionario práctico Larousse/79n1149
Gross/Diccionario moderno Espanol-Ingles/ 78n1068
Gross/Pequeño Larousse ilustrado/79n1151
Hamlyn Spanish dict/78n1069
Kloe/Dictionary of onomatopeic sounds, . . . in Engl & Spanish/78n1045
Laita/Cortina-Grosset basic Spanish dict/77 n1099
Lipton/Spanish bilingual dict/77n1100
New pronouncing dict of Spanish & English languages/75n1277
Putnam's contemp Spanish dict/75n1278
Renty/El Mundo de los negocios/79n1152
Savaiano/2001 Spanish & Engl idioms/77n1101
Simon & Schuster's internat'l dict/75n1279

SPANISH LITERATURE
Amago/Centeno collection/79n1285
Bleznick/Sourcebk for Hispanic lit & lang/75 n1426
Boyer/Texas collection of comedias sueltas/ 79n1006
Childers/Tales from Spanish picaresque novels/ 79n1286
Foster/Manual of Hispanic bibliog/78n1200
González Ollé/Manual bibliográfico de estudios españoles/79n1288
King/Ramon J. Sender: bibliog/77n1275
Laurenti/Federico García Lorca y su mundo/ 75n1427
Manual de bibliografia de la literatura española/75n1428
Mignani/Concordance to Juan Ruiz, libro de buen amor/79n1290
Pollin/Concordance to plays & poems of Federico García Lorca/76n1305
Rudder/Literature of Spain in Engl translation: bibliog/77n1276
US Library of Congress/Archive of Hispanic lit on tape/75n1429
Woodbridge/Benito Pérez Galdós: bibliog/77 n1277

SPANISH POETRY
Ruiz-Fornells/Concordance to poetry of Leopoldo Panero/79n1291

SPANISH SPEAKING AMERICANS
Burma/Spanish-speaking groups in US/75 n817

SPANISH SPEAKING AMERICANS (cont'd)
Peterson/Library serv to Spanish speaking/ 79n202
Spanish speaking in US: gd/76n392
Trueba/Bilingual bicultural educ for Spanish speaking in US: bibliog/78n548

SPANISH STUDIES
González Ollé/Manual bibliográfico de estudios españoles/79n1288

SPARK, MURIEL
Tominaga/Iris Murdoch & Muriel Spark: bibliog/77n1221

SPAS
See Health facilities

SPECIAL EDUCATION
See Exceptional children

SPECIAL INTEREST GROUPS
See Citizen action groups; Political action groups
See also Trade and professional associations

SPECIAL LIBRARIES
See also Types of libraries, e.g., Economic libraries; Map libraries; Museum libraries; Newspaper libraries; Transportation libraries
Arnold/Management of info dept/79n249
Aufdenkamp/Special libraries: gd for mgmt/ 76n165
Bailey/Special librarian as a supervisor/78 n192
Christianson/Paraprofessional & nonprofessional staff in special libraries/75n203
Directory of special libraries & info centers/ 75n164; 78n199
Kaiser/Handling special matls in libraries/75 n248
Ladendorf/Changing role of special librarian in industry, business & gov/75n206
New special libraries/78n200
Rees/Contemporary probs in tech library & info center mgmt/76n168
Schorr/Directory of special libraries in Alaska/ 76n171
Special libraries directory/78n203
Subject directory of special libraries & info centers/76n172; 78n201
Sussman/US Info Serv libraries/75n209

SPECTATOR
Evans/Guide to prose fict in Tatler & Spectator/78n1163

SPECTRUM ANALYSIS
Denney/Dict of spectroscopy/75n1457
Greenwood/Index of vibrational spectra of inorganic . . . compounds/79n1323
Hawkins/Auger electron spectroscopy/79n1316
Yamashita/Atlas of rep stellar spectra/79n1315

SPEECH
Brown/Dictionary of speech & hearing anatomy . . . /76n1523; 77n1470
Tandberg/Research gd in speech/76n1178
Theatre, drama & speech index/76n1044

SPEECH DISORDERS
Information Center for Hearing, Speech, & Disorders of Human Communication/ Hearing, speech, & comm disorders: citations/76n1518
Nicolosi/Terminology of comm disorders/79n1175

SPEECHES, ADDRESSES, ETC.
See also Public speaking
Glenn/Black rhetoric: gd/77n1122
Mitchell/Speech index: collections of world famous orations . . . /78n1085

SPEED READING
Berger/Rates of comprehension: bibliog/77n574

SPELLING
Flesch/Look it up: deskbk of Amer spelling/78n103

SPENDER, STEPHEN
Kulkarni/S. Spender, works & crit/78n1182

SPENSER, EDMUND
Frushell/Contemporary thought on Edmund Spenser: bibliog/76n1289
Heffner/Spenser allusions in 16th & 17th centuries/75n1402
Rose/Spenser's art: companion to . . . Faerie Queene/76n1290
Shaheen/Biblical refs in Faerie Queene/77n1245

SPICES
Loewenfeld/Complete bk of herbs & spices/75n1484
Morton/Herbs & spices/78n1299
Muenscher/Garden spice & wild pot-herbs/79n1353

SPIES
DeVore/Spies & all that/79n502

SPINNING
Axford/Weaving, spinning, & dyeing/76n947

SPIRITUAL LIFE
Dell'Isola/Thomas Merton: bibliog/76n1073
Singh Khalsa/Spiritual community gd/79n1087

SPOFFORD, AINSWORTH RAND
Cole/A. R. Spofford/76n208

SPORTING EQUIPMENT AND MEMORABILIA
Liu/American sporting collector's hndbk/77n935; 78n832
Sugar/Sports collectors bible/79n696

SPORTS
ABCs wide world of sports ency/75n720
Anderson/SportSource/77n663
Arlott/Oxford companion to world sports & games/76n701
Charles/Encyclopedia of sport/77n670
Consumer Guide/Thrill sports catalog/78n605
de Groote/Olympic sports official album/77n664
Frost/Encyclopedia of phys educ, fitness, & sports/78n607
Grosset & Dunlap's all-sports world record book/77n665
Hickok/New ency of sports/78n608
Hollander/Encyclopedia of sports talk/77n671
Hoyle/Physical educ-sports index/79n676
Kirby/Physical educ index/79n675
Mandel/Significant American sport champions/77n139
McWhirter/Guiness sports record bk/77n666
Menke/Encyclopedia of sports/76n698; 79n697; 79n698
Nueckel/Selected gd to sports & recreation books/75n726
Nunn/Sports/77n668
Official AP sports almanac/76n699
Official rules of sports & games/76n700; 78n604
Perrin/Explorers Ltd source bk/78n616
Remy/Louisiana sports ency/78n609
Richards/Complete hndbk of sports scoring & record keeping/75n727
Rules of the game/75n728
Turner/Index to outdoor sports, games, & activities/79n699
Webster's sports dict/77n672

SPORTS CARS
Filby/Specialist sports cars/76n765

SPORTS MUSEUMS
Lewis/Sporting heritage/75n725
Soderberg/Big bk of halls of fame in US & Canada: sports/78n603

SRI LANKA
Ali/Handbk of birds of India & Pakistan, . . . & Sri Lanka/77n1373
Kirtisinghe/Sea shells of Sri Lanka/79n928

STAGE LIGHTING
Stoddard/Stage scenery, machinery, & lighting: gd to info sources/78n931

STAGE SCENERY
Stoddard/Stage scenery, machinery, & lighting: gd to info sources/78n931

STAIN REMOVAL
Moore/How to clean everything/79n1572

STAINLESS STEEL
Peckner/Handbook of stainless steels/78n1544

STANLEY, SIR HENRY MORTON
Casada/Dr. D. Livingstone & Sir H. M. Stanley: bibliog/77n309

STAR TREK
Trimble/Star Trek concordance/78n1087

STARS
Burnham's celestial hndbk/79n1312
Cleminshaw/Beginner's gd to skies/79n1314
Howard/Telescope hndbk & star atlas/76n1337
Moore/Color star atlas/75n1448
Yamashita/Atlas of rep stellar spectra/79n1315

STATE GOVERNMENT PUBLICATIONS
See Government publications

STATE GOVERNMENT
See also names of individual states
Council of State Govs/Book of states/77n519; 79n532
Canning/State constitutional conventions, . . . : bibliog/78n457
Lukowski/State info book/78n461
Principal legislative staff offices/79n535
Solomon/Governors of the states/75n505
State admin officials/78n459
State elective officials & legislatures/78n460
Swindler/Sources & docs of US constitutions/79n536
Vellucci/National directory of state agencies/76n70
Yarger/State constitutional conventions: bibliog/77n522

STATE LIBRARIES
Simpson/State library agencies/79n168

STATION WAGONS
Narus/Great Amer woodies & wagons/79n1555

STATISTICIANS
American men & women of sci: physics, astronomy, math, stats, & computer sci/78n1216

STATISTICS
Carpenter/Statistical methods for librarians/79n336
Simpson/Basic stats for librarians/76n122
US Bureau of Labor Stats/BLS hndbk of methods for surveys & studies/78n691
  BIBLIOGRAPHY
Inter-American Statistical Inst/Bibliog of stat'l sources of Amer nations/75n873
Sources of European economic info/76n827
Subrahamaniam/Multivariate analysis/75n874

STATISTICS (cont'd)
  BIBLIOGRAPHY (cont'd)
US Library of Congress/General censuses & vital stats in the Americas/75n875
Wasserman/Statistics sources/75n879; 78n687
  DICTIONARIES AND ENCYCLOPEDIAS
Webb/New dict of stats/75n876
Broster/Glossary of applied mgmt & finan'l statistics/76n908
  HANDBOOKS, TABLES, AND YEARBOOKS
Directory of fed stats for local areas/79n788
Harvey/Statistics Africa/79n789
Lunt/Key to pubs of US census, 1790-1887/78n685
Michigan stat'l abstract/78n688
Mitchell/European hist'l stats 1750-1970/76n815
Odeh/Pocket bk of stat'l tables/78n689
Statistical abstract of OK/79n790
Showers/World in figures/75n86
Statistical hist of US: from colonial times to the present/78n690
Statistical yearbk/77n761
Unesco stat'l yearbk/76n816
US Bureau of Census/Pocket data bk, USA/78n693
US Bureau of Land Mgmt/Public land stats/78n692
World stats in brief/79n791
Yearbook of natl accounts stats/77n762
  INDEXES
JASA: Journal of Amer Stat'l Assn. index to 1966-77/78n694
Joiner/Current index to stats/79n792; 79n793
Ross/Index to stats & probability, locations & authors/75n877; 75n878; 76n819

STATUES
Hummel/Portraits & statuary of Virginians . . ./79n879

STEAM ENGINES
Norbeck/Ency of Amer steam traction engines/78n1550

STEIN, GERTRUDE
Wilson/G. Stein: bibliog/76n1248

STEINBECK, JOHN
Goldstone/J. Steinbeck: bibliog'l catalogue of A. H. Goldstone Collection/76n1249
Hayashi/J. Steinbeck: dict of his fict'l characters/77n1213
Hayashi/Study gd to Steinbeck/75n1368

STEREOCHEMISTRY
Klyne/Atlas/76n1345

STEVENS, WALLACE
Edelstein/W. Stevens/75n1369

STEVENSON, ROBERT LOUIS
Slater/Robert Louis Stevenson/75n1403

STOCK MARKET
Skousen/Introduction to SEC/78n731
Wyckoff/International stock & commodity exchange directory/76n863

STOCKS
Hirsch/Stock trader's almanac/76n856
Moody's hndbk of common stocks/McDonald/76n859
Mutual funds almanac/78n730
Sinclair/How experts buy & sell gold bullion, gold stocks, etc./76n862

STONEFLIES
Frison/Stoneflies . . . of IL/76n1440

STONEWARE
See Pottery

STOPPING POWER (nuclear physics)
Andersen/Bibliog & index of experimental range & stopping power data/79n1329

STORYTELLING
Baker/Storytelling/79n205
Bauer/Handbook for storytellers/78n180
Cathon/Stories to tell to children/75n198
Pellowski/World of storytelling/79n214
Ziskind/Telling stories to children/77n230

STOWE, HARRIET BEECHER
Ashton/Harriet Beecher Stowe: gd/78n1149
Hildreth/H. B. Stowe: bibliog/77n1214

STRATIGRAPHY
International stratigraphic gd/78n1356

STRAVINSKY, IGOR FEDOROVITCH
de Lerma/I. F. Stravinsky/75n1157

STRESS (physiology)
Chapman/Physiology of phys stress: bibliog/76n1514

STRING MUSIC
Farish/String music in print/75n1125

STRINGED INSTRUMENTS
Purcell/Classic guitar, lute & vihuela discog/78n905

STRIPMINING
Czapowskyj/Annotated bibliog on ecology & reclamation of disturbed areas/78n1339
Munn/Strip mining/75n1814
Tompkins/Strip mining for coal/75n1815

STRUCTURAL ENGINEERING
Directory of computer software applications: civil & structural eng'g/79n1561

STUDENT ACTIVITIES
Student activities in secondary schools/75n648

STUDENT AID
Admissions, financial aid & placemt procedures . . . /77n607
Barron's hndbk of Amer college financial aid/Proia/76n635
Barron's hndbk of junior & community college financial aid/Proia/76n637
Davis/Guide to lit of student financial aid/79n629
Keeslar/Financial aids for higher educ/75n678; 78n563
Lever/How to obtain money for college: gd to sources of financial aid/77n620
Schlachter/Directory of financial aids for women/79n766
Scholarships, fellowships & loans/Feingold/78n566
Student aid-annual/76n654

STUDENT EMPLOYMENT
Directory of overseas summer jobs/77n835
Mitchell/Stopout! Working ways to learn/79n643
Rowland/Student adventure travel & study/77n562
Summer employmt directory of US/77n842

STUDENT LOAN FUNDS
Scholarships, fellowships & loans/Feingold/78n566

STUDENT TEACHING
Tittle/Student teaching/75n659

STUDENT TRAVEL
Eisenberg/Learning vacations/79n656
Eisenberg/Learning vacations: educ'l tours/79n655
Rowland/Student adventure travel & study, USA/77n562

STUDENTS
Gollay/College gd for students with disabilities/78n564
Levine/Rights of students/75n560
    FOREIGN AND EXCHANGE
Davis/English lang & orientation programs in US/78n561
Handbook on internat'l study for US nationals/78n574
Higher educ in UK: hndbk for students from overseas/78n575
How to live in Britain: hndbk for students from overseas/78n576
Spaulding/World's students in US: review of research/77n582

STUDENTS FOR A DEMOCRATIC SOCIETY
Heath/Vandals in bomb factory: hist & lit of SDS/77n503

STYLE MANUALS
Angione/Associated Press stylebk & libel manual/79n127
Burkett/Writing in subj-matter fields/78n101
Crews/Random House hndbk/79n128
Fleischer/Bibliographic citations for nonprint materials/76n87
Fleischer/Style manual for citing microform & nonprint media/79n129
Flesch/Look it up: deskbk of Amer spelling & style/78n103
Hoffman/Bibliog without footnotes/78n104
Leggett/Prentice-Hall hndbk for writers/79n130
MLA handbook/79n131
New York Times manual of style & usage/Jordan/77n116
Polking/Beginning writer's answer bk/79n1169
Quick ref encyclopedia/78n90
Turabian/Student's gd for writing research papers/78n105
van Leuen/Handbook for scholars/79n132
Webb/Washington Post deskbk on style/79n133
Writer's manual/78n106
Zondervan manual of style/78n107

STYRON, WILLIAM
Leon/William Styron/79n1224
West/William Styron: bibliog/78n1150

SUBJECT HEADINGS
Atkins/Cross-ref index/75n222
Brown/Introduction to subj indexing: programmed text/77n251; 77n252
Chan/LC subj headings/79n268
Dunlap/Hospital lit subj headings/78n229
Foskett/Subject approach to info/79n270
Marshall/On equal terms: thesaurus for nonsexist indexing/79n275
Metcalf/Information retrieval, British & Amer 1876-1976/77n291
PRECIS index system/78n222
Public library subj headings for 16mm motion pictures/75n227
Sears list of subj headings/78n230
Settel/Subject descrip of bks/79n282
Subject cross ref gd/77n260
Thesaurus of descriptors used for info processing in ILO library/77n171

SUBMARINES
Anderson/Submarines, diving, & underwater world: bibliog/76n1687
Bagnasco/Submarines of WW II/79n1598

SUB-SAHARAN AFRICA
See Africa, Sub-Saharan

SUBSCRIPTION AGENTS
International subscrip agents/75n56; 79n49
Katz/Guide to magazine & serial agents/77n199

SUCCULENT PLANTS
See also Cacti
Bechtel/Cactus identifier, including succulent plants/78n1486
Innes/Complete hndbk of cacti & succulents/78n1286

SUDAN
Voll/Historical dict of Sudan/79n360

SUDDEN INFANT DEATH SYNDROME
Archuleta/Sudden infant death syndrome: bibliog/76n1512

SUFFOLK, GREAT BRITAIN
Suffolk parochial libraries: catalogue/79n77

SUICIDE
Prentice/Suicide: bibliog/76n772

SUMMER CAMPS
Guide to summer camps & summer schools/76n661
College programs for high school students/76n646
Eisenberg/Learning vacations/79n656
Guide to summer camps & schools/76n661
Rowland/Student adventure travel & study/77n562

SUN–RISING AND SETTING
Sunrise & sunset tables for key cities/78n1354

SUPERINTENDENT OF DOCUMENTS CLASSIFICATION
Poole/Documents Office classification/79n123

SUPERSTITION
Briggs/Ency of fairies/78n1009

SURFING
Filosa/Surfer's almanac: internat'l/78n632

SURGERY
Lore/Atlas of head & neck surgery/75n1644
Surgery annual/Nynus/77n1489

SURINAM
Price/Guiana Maroons: bibliog'l intro/78n677

SURVIVAL TECHNIQUES
Gregory/Good earth almanac survival bk/75n723
Knap/Complete outdoorsman's hndbk/75n724
Petzoldt/Wilderness hndbk/75n757

SWANS
Merne/Ducks, geese & swans/76n1425
Wilmore/Swans of world/76n1433

SWAZILAND
Grotpeter/Historical dict/76n255
SWEDEN
Backe/Concise Swedish-Engl glossary of legal terms/75n552
1000 largest companies/76n891
Scandinavian political studies/76n501
SWIMMING
Besford/Encyclopaedia of swimming/78n631
National lifeguard manual/Cornforth/75n786
SWIMMING POOLS
Cross/Handbook of swimming pool construction, maintenance & sanitation/75n1758
SWITCHING LANGUAGES
Coates/BSO, Broad System of Ordering/79n300
SWITZERLAND
Reifsnyder/Foot-loose in Swiss Alps/75n626
SYMBOLISM
Anderson/Symbolism: bibliog/77n1124
SYMBOLISM IN ART
Bles/How to distinguish saints in art/76n925
Hall/Dictionary of subjects & symbols in art/76n922
Sill/Handbook of symbols in Christian art/76n926
Williams/Outlines of Chinese symbolism/75n1001; 78n1018
SYMBOLISM IN LITERATURE
de Vries/Dictionary of symbols & imagery/77n1129
SYMBOLISM OF FLOWERS
Language & sentiment of flowers/75n1244
SYMPHONIES
Downes/New York Philharmonic gd to symphony/78n922
SYMPTOMS
See Diagnosis (medical)
SYNDICATED COLUMNISTS
Weiner/Syndicated columnists/76n1173
SYNGE, J. M.
Levitt/J. M. Synge/75n1404
Mikhail/J. M. Synge: bibliog/76n1291

TAIWAN
Chang/Taiwan demography/75n871
Parker/American dissertations on foreign educ: bibliog/77n578
TALES
Tyler/Concordance to fables & tales of Jean de la Fontaine/75n1418

TALKING BOOKS
For younger readers: braille & talking bks/79n338
Talking Books adult/79n340
Talking bk topics/79n339
TALL OIL
Pollock/Tall oil/78n1259
TANGANYIKA AFRICAN NATIONAL UNION
Howell/Tanganyika African Natl Union/78n293
TANKS
See also Armored vehicles, military
Chamberlain/British & Amer tanks of WW II/76n1684
TANZANIA
Howell/East African community/78n290
Howell/Tanganyika African Natl Union/78n293
Hundsdorfer/Bibliographie zue sozialwissenschaftlichen erforschung Tanzanias/76n256
Killick/Economics of East Africa/77n770
Kurtz/Historical dict/79n361
TAPESTRY
Bennett/Five centuries of tapestry/78n861
TARGUM LITERATURE
Grossfeld/Bibliog of Targum lit/79n1049
TAROT
Butler/Dictionary of tarot/77n1450
Kaplan/Encyclopedia of tarot/79n1437
TATLER
Evans/Guide to prose fict in *Tatler* . . . /78n1163
TAUBER, MAURICE FALCOLM
Szigethy/M. F. Tauber: bibliog/75n151
TAVERNS
Yeadon/New York bk of bars, pubs . . . /77n1523
Thompson/Saloon: gd to America's great bars, . . . /77n1521
TAVISTOCK INSTITUTE OF HUMAN RELATIONS
Catalogue of Library, London/76n1521
TAXATION
CCH/Federal tax return manual/76n912
Depreciation gd/76n911
Federal tax desk bk/77n853
Hagendorf/Tax gd for buying & selling a business/77n854
Owens/Bibliography on taxation of foreign operations/78n783
Shepards fed tax locator/76n913
Sommerfeld/Dow Jones-Irwin gd to tax planning/75n986

382—Subjects

TAXATION (cont'd)
Wheeler/Tax desk bk for farming & ranching/77n855

TAYLOR FAMILY (authors)
Stewart/Taylors of Ongar . . . bio-bibliog/76n1201

TAZEWELL COUNTY, VA
Schreiner-Yantis/Archives of pioneers of Tazewell Co/75n362

TEACHERS
Cohen/Teaching abroad/78n572
Lance/Teachers' centers exchange directory/78n559
Teacher training bibliog: for bilingual bicultural educ/77n583
Tittle/Student teaching/75n659
Woellner/Requirements for certification/75n660; 76n631; 77n638; 78n579

TEACHING
Meyer/Guide to educ'l & learning aids/78n594
Hoover/Professional teacher's hndbk/75n713

TEACHING WITH FILMS
Maynard/Classroom cinema/79n685

TECHNICAL ASSISTANCE
Brewster/American overseas library tech assistance/77n277

TECHNICAL EDUCATION
See Vocational education

TECHNICAL INFORMATION SERVICES
National referral services for industry: directory/76n899

TECHNICAL LIBRARIES
Campbell/Small tech libraries/75n202
Rees/Contemporary probs in tech library . . . mgmt/76n168
Wolfe/Economics of tech info systems/75n881

TECHNICAL REPORTS
Auger/Use of reports lit/76n1306

TECHNICAL SERVICES (libraries)
See Processing

TECHNICAL WRITING
Brusaw/Business writer's hndbk/79n816
Burns/Annotated bibliog of texts on writing skills/77n1067; 78n588

TECHNOLOGY
Chen/Biomedical, scient'ic & tech bk reviewing/78n1381
Dummer/Electronic inventions 1745-1976/78n1530
Inventory of research facilities in European community/79n87

TECHNOLOGY (cont'd)
BIBLIOGRAPHY
Bibliographic gd/77n11
Computext bk guides: technology/76n1310
Grogan/Science & tech: intro to lit/77n1282
Klein/Guide to Amer scient'ic & tech directories/77n1284
Malinowsky/Science & eng'g lit/77n1286
Parker/Information sources in sci & tech/77n1287
Scientific & tech bks & serials in print/78n1205
BIOGRAPHY
Asimov/Asimov's biog'l ency of sci & tech/77n1298
Who was who in Amer hist—sci & tech/77n1301
DICTIONARIES AND ENCYCLOPEDIAS
Chambers dict of sci & tech/77n1289
de Vries/French-Engl sci & tech dict/77n1290
Dorian/Dictionary of sci & tech: English-German/79n1296
How it works: ency of sci & tech/78n1208
Lapedes/McGraw-Hill dict of scient'ic & tech terms/75n1434; 79n1299
McGraw-Hill ency of sci & tech/Lapedes/78n1210
McGraw-Hill yrbk of sci & tech/76n1317
Ocran's acronyms used in scient'ic & tech writing/79n1300
Shernukhin/English-Russian polytechnical dict/78n1206
SPINES thesaurus/78n1211
Wennrich/Anglo-Amer & German abbreviations in sci & tech/79n1301
PERIODICALS AND INDEXES
Applied sci & tech index/Toom/76n1325
InterDok directory of published proceedings/75n1435
Kronick/History of scient'ic & tech periodicals/77n1278
Owen/Abstracts & indexes in sci & tech/75n1432
Yannarella/US gov scient'ic & tech periodicals/77n1295

TECHNOLOGY AND STATE
Science & gov report internat'l almanac/Greenberg/78n435

TECHNOLOGY TRANSFER
Federal Council for Sci & Tech/Federal tech transfer directory of programs/76n1322
US Natl Sci Foundation/Directory of federal technology/78n1219

TELECOMMUNICATIONS
Ellmore/Illustrated dict of broadcast-CATV-telecommunications/79n1162
Elsevier's telecomm dict in six langs/77n1117

TELECOMMUNICATIONS (cont'd)
NAEB public telecomm directory/79n1163

TELEPHONE DIRECTORIES
Greenfield/National directory of addresses & telephone numbers/79n86

TELESCOPES
Howard/Telescope hndbk . . . /76n1337

TELETYPE IN LIBRARIES
MacCafferty/Fax & teletext/78n238

TELEVISION
See also Cable television; Children's television; Educational television
American Film Inst gd to college courses in film & TV/77n1004; 79n1029
Brown/New York Times ency of TV/79n1176
Dictionary of radio & TV terms: English-German/77n1111
Ellmore/Illustrated dict of broadcast-CATV-telecommunications/79n1162
Hurrell/Van Nostrand Reinhold manual of TV graphics/75n1205
International film gd/Cowie/76n1047; 77 n999
Jones/North Amer radio-TV station gd/76 n1170
McCavitt/Radio & TV/79n1173
Parish/Actors' TV credits/79n1179
Television factbook/78n1086
World radio & TV hndbk/77n1112

TELEVISION ENGINEERING
Amos/Radio, TV & audio tech ref bk/79n1567
Broadcast antenna systems hndbk/75n1780
Shane/All-in-one TV alignmt hndbk/75n1789

TELEVISION PROGRAMS
David/TV season/77n1116
Gianakos/TV drama series programming/79 n1178
Lackmann/TV soap opera almanac/77n1118
Teachers' guides to TV/79n1180
Television contacts/77n1119
Terrace/Complete ency of TV programs/77 n1120
Trimble/Star Trek concordance/78n1087

TELEVISION SCRIPTS
Face the nation: collected transcripts/CBS News/76n1156; 76n1157; 76n1158
Mehr/Motion pics, TV, & radio: union catalogue/79n1165
Poteet/Published radio, TV, & film scripts: bibliog/76n1165

TELLER, HENRY MOORE
Mitterling/Guide to H. M. Teller papers/76 n351

TEMPLE, FREDERICK
Barber/Index to papers of Temple, Archbishop of Canterbury . . . /77n1041

TENNESSEE
Acklen/Tennessee records/75n405
Laska/Tennessee legal research hndbk/79n573
Phillips/Governors of Tennessee/79n534
Robertson/Kansas territorial settlers of 1860 born in TN, VA, NC, & SC/77n475
Smith/Tennessee hist: bibliog/76n353

TENNIS
See also Paddle tennis
Casewit/America's tennis bk/76n761
Duggan/Tennis catalog/79n730
Klein/Tennis player's vacation gd/75n585
Robertson/Encyclopedia of tennis/76n762

TEOTIHUACAN, MEXICO
Millon/Urbanization at Teotihuacan/75n404

TERMINOLOGY ORGANIZATIONS
Krommer-Benz/World gd to terminological activities/79n1095

TERRORISM
Boston/Terrorism: bibliog/78n642
Sobel/Political terrorism/76n462

TESTS, EDUCATIONAL
See Mental tests
See also Intelligence tests; Psychological tests

TEXAS
Andrews/Shells & shores of TX/78n1334
Boner/Reference gd to TX law/77n532
Carrington/Women in early TX/76n337
Directory of TX mfgrs/78n755
Gould/Grasses of TX/77n1364
Mullins/Republic of TX: poll lists for 1846/ 75n427
Texas ref sources/Texas Library Assn/77n521
Wright/Texas sources/78n316
Wright/Texas trade & prof assns/78n712

TEXTBOOKS
El-hi textbks in print/75n701; 76n677
NCTE gd to teaching matls for Engl, grades 7-12/75n704; 76n682
Reinhart/Vocational-tech'l learning matls/75 n705

TEXTILES
Axford/Weaving, spinning, & dyeing/76n947
Kleeberg/Butterick fabric hndbk/76n875
Linton/Modern textile & apparel dict/75n964
Lubell/France: illust'd gd to textile collections in museums/79n950
Nylander/Fabrics for historic bldgs/78n862
Reeves/Fire resistant textiles hndbk/76n1649
Textile hndbk/Amer Home Economics Assn/ 76n879
United Kingdom–Ireland: gd to textile collections/Lubell/78n863
United States & Canada: gd to textile collections/Lubell/78n864

THACKERAY, WILLIAM
Olmsted/Thackeray & 20th-cent critics: bibliog/78n1183

THAILAND
Chety/Research on Thailand in Philippines/79n374
Duncan/Thailand: gd/77n564
Hart/Thailand/78n301
Smith/Historical & cult'l dict/77n331

THEATRE
  BIBLIOGRAPHY
Bibliographic gd to theatre arts/77n12
Guide to play selection: bibliog of modern plays/NCTE-Mersand/76n1034
International mimes & pantomimists directory/75n1177
Kaminsky/Nonprofit repertory theatre in No Amer: bibliog to playbill collection/78n923
Research collections in Canadian libraries/75n1179
Research Libraries of NYPL/Catalog of theatre & drama non-bk collection/77n989
Stoddard/Stage scenery, machinery, & lighting: gd to info sources/78n931
Wearing/London stage 1890-99: calendar of plays/77n990
Wilmeth/American stage to WW I/79n1012
  BIOGRAPHY
Herbert/Who's who in theatre: contemp stage/78n943
Highfill/Biographical dict of actors ... & stage personnel in London, 1660-1800/75n1188; 76n1045; 79n1022
Notable names in Amer theatre/78n945
Young/Famous actors & actresses on Amer stage/76n1033
  CRITICS AND CRITICISM
Comtois/Contemporary Amer theater critics/79n1013
Eddleman/American drama criticism/77n987
Lyday/Bibliography of Latin Amer theater criticism/79n1010
Stanley/Broadway in West End (Grt Brit)/79n1021
  DICTIONARIES AND ENCYCLOPEDIAS
Encyclopedia of world theater/78n933
Green/Encyclopedia of musical theatre/77n992
Sergel/Language of show biz/75n1180
Wehlburg/Theatre lighting: glossary/77n993
  DIRECTORIES
Celebrity Services/Contact bk/76n1041
Goodrich/Enjoying summer theatres of New England/75n1184
Handel/Natl directory of performing arts & civic centers/75n1185

THEATRE (cont'd)
  DIRECTORIES (cont'd)
Loney/Shakespeare complex: gd to summer festivals ... No Amer/76n1042
NY Times directory of theatre/75n1186
  HANDBOOKS AND YEARBOOKS
Hughes/NY theatre annual/79n1020
May/Companion to theatre: Anglo-Amer stage from 1920/76n1038
Roberts/Theatre in Britain/75n1183
Stern/Stagemanagement/75n1182
Stevenson/Tony Award: listing & hist/77n985
Stoddard/Theatre & cinema architecture/79n1011
  INDEXES
Chicorel/Chicorel theater index to plays in anthologies & collections/78n937
Samples/Drama scholars' index to plays & filmscripts/75n1187
Theatre/drama & speech index/76n1044
  THEMATIC INDEXES
Brown/Carlo D'Ordonez/79n983
Flanders/Thematic index to works of B. Pallavicino/76n1007

THEOLOGY
Botterweck/Theological dict of Old Testament/76n1096; 79n1064
Brown/New internat'l dict of New Testamt theology/77n1043; 78n995
Encyclopedia of theology/Radner/76n1082
Leon-Dufour/Dict of biblical theology/75n1230
Theological dict of New Testament/77n1048
  CATHOLIC
Liebard/Clergy & laity/79n1040
Liebard/Love & sexuality/79n1041
Mainelli/Social justice/79n1042
Megivern/Bible interpretation/79n1043
Megivern/Worship & liturgy/79n1044
Watlington/Christ our Lord/79n1045

THEOSOPHY
Blavatsky/Theosophical glossary/75n1234
Conger/Combined chronology for use with Mahatma letters to A. P. Sinnett ... /75n1235

THERMODYNAMICS
James/Dict of thermodynamics/78n1243

THESAURUS CONSTRUCTION
MacCafferty/Thesauri & ... constr/79n1090

THIRD WORLD
Cyr/Filmog of Third World: list/78n956
DEVINDEX Canada/79n822
Drabek/Politics of African & Mid Eastern states: bibliog/78n470
Harrison/Traditional medicine/77n1462
Huq/Librarianship & Third World/78n251

THIRD WORLD (cont'd)
Kamenetsky/Guide to Hammarskjold collection on developing nations/78n273
Landsat index atlas of developing countries/World Bank/78n515
Rihani/Developmt as if women mattered/79n760
Stockholm Internat'l Peace Research Inst/Arms trade with Third World/76n870
Strharsky/Bibliographical notes for . . . transnational corps & Third World/76n828

THOMAS, DYLAN
Lane/Concordance to poems/77n1246

THOMSON, JAMES
Campbell/J. Thomson: bibliog/77n1247

THORBURN, ARCHIBALD
Fisher/Thorburn's birds/77n1377

TIDES
Reed's nautical almanac & tide tables/79n726

TIE-DYEING PROJECTS
Chicorel index to crafts: needlework, crocheting and tie-dyeing/76n954

TIME
Sandow/Durations/79n99
DeVries/Yesterday, today & tomorrow: time & hist in Old Testamt/76n1098
Zelkind/Time research/76n1491

TIMROD, HENRY
De Bellis/S. Lanier, H. Timrod, & P. H. Hayne/79n1210

TISSUE CULTURE
Index of tissue culture/Stahl/78n1423

TITLES OF HONOR
US Immigration Serv/Foreign versions of Engl names & titles/75n250

TITLES OF MUSICAL COMPOSITIONS
Berkowitz/Popular titles & subtitles of musical compositions/76n983

TABACCO
Andrews/Bibliography of drug abuse, alcohol & tobacco/78n1435
Cheek/List of theses . . . on tobacco/75n959
Fazey/Aetiology of psychoactive substance use/79n1454
Gold/Comprehensive bibliog of lit on tobacco/77n1503

TOGO
Decalo/Historical dict of Togo/77n316

TOKENS
Hoch/Canadian tokens & medals/75n1067

TOLKIEN, J. R. R.
Tyler/Tolkien companion/77n1248

TOM SAWYER
Haviland/S. L. Clemens: centennial bibliog/78n1151

TONY AWARD
Stevenson/Tony Award: listing/77n985

TOOLS
Blandford/Country craft tools/75n1030
Drake/Everyone's bk of hand & small power tools/75n1792
Salaman/Dict of tools used in woodworking 1700-1970/77n893

TORONTO, UNIVERSITY LIBRARY
Wagle/Guide to res collections in microform/76n143

TORRES STRAIT ISLANDERS
Coppell/World catalogue of theses . . . abt Aborigines & Torres Strait Islanders/79n774

TOURIST CAMPS, HOSTELS, ETC.
See Campgrounds; Youth hostels

TOURIST TRADE
Goeldner/Travel res bibliog/78n742
Hudman/Analysis & atlas of travel in US/78n735
Lundberg/Tourist business/77n828
Travel market yrbk/77n831

TOURNEUR, CYRIL
Tucker/Bibliog of writings by & abt J. Ford & Cyril Tourneur/78n932

TOWNSHIPS
Andriot/Township atlases of US/78n462

TOXICOLOGY
Driesbach/Handbk of poisoning/75n1628
Fritsch/Household pollutants gd/79n1400
Gosselin/Clinical toxicology of commercial products/77n1485
Rudd/Environmental toxicology/79n1401
Toxic substances sourcebk/79n1402
US Food & Drug Admin/Handbk of common poisonings in children/78n1431
Venomous arthropod hndbk/Biery/78n1327
Wyllie/Mycotoxic fungi . . . /79n1477

TRACK AND FIELD
Nelson/Little red bk: metric conversion for track fan . . . /76n769
Potts/Association of track & field statisticians annual/77n700

TRACTION ENGINES
Norbeck/Ency of Amer steam traction engines/78n1550

TRADE
See Commerce

TRADE AND PROFESSIONAL ASSOCIATIONS
See also Associations
Career gd to prof assns: directory/77n834
Colgate/Directory of Washington reps of Amer assns & industry/79n91
Davis/Comparative hist'l analysis of three assns of prof schools/75n263
Directory of assns in Canada/75n343
Directory of British assns & assns in Ireland/75n80; 78n72
Directory of European assns/76n66; 77n77
Encyclopedia of assns/77n85
Fang/International gd to library, archival, & info sci assns/77n176
FID yearbook/76n73
Kyed/Scientific, tech & eng'g societies publications in print/75n1430
National trade & prof assns of US & Canada & labor unions/Colgate/77n87
Piele/Directory of organizations & personnel in educ'l mgmt/78n556
Sources: gd to print & nonprint matls available from organizations, etc./78n3
Tett/Professional organizations in the Commonwealth/77n88
Texas trade & prof assns & . . . selected organizations/Wright/78n712
World gd to trade assns/75n897

TRADE MARKS
See also Brand names
Book of Amer trade marks/Carter/78n733
Cooper/World of logotypes/77n118
Crowley/New trade names/79n810
Haslam/Marks & monograms of modern movement 1875-1930: gd to artists, designers, etc./78n829
Kase/Trademarks/75n962
Kuwayama/Trademarks & symbols/75n963
Trade names dict/77n787
Trademarks & brand mgmt: annotations/Hill/78n741

TRADE SCHOOLS
See also Vocational education
Herbert/Getting skilled: gd to trade & tech schools/77n628
NATTS directory of accredited trade & tech schools/77n630
US Dept of HEW/Directory of postsecondary schools with occupational programs/77n632

TRADE UNIONS
Abell/Collective bargaining in higher educ: implications for librarians/78n161
Dwyer/Labor educ in US: bibliog/78n765
Fink/Labor unions/78n766
Fink/State labor proceedings: bibliog of AFL, CIO, & AFL-CIO, 1885-1974/78n767

TRADE UNIONS (cont'd)
Gibbney/Labor in print: press in Australia/76n903
Harrison/Warwick gd to British labour periodicals 1790-1970/78n768
Martens/African trade unionism: bibliog/78n769
National trade & prof assns of US & Canada & labor unions/Colgate/77n87
Register of reporting labor organizations/79n863
Rothman/Bibliog of collective bargaining in hospitals . . . /77n840
Soltow/American women & labor movemt, 1825-1974: bibliog/77n841
US Bureau of Labor Stats/Directory of national unions & employee assns/78n775
Who's who in labor/77n847
Woodbridge/AFL & CIO pamphlets, 1889-1955/78n774

TRAFFIC ENGINEERING
Baerwald/Transportation & traffic eng'g hndbk/77n1618

TRAILER PARKS
Rand McNally campground & trailer park gd/79n714

TRAINING PROGRAMS
See Business training programs; Continuing education; Employee training; Industry training programs; Management training programs; Occupational training

TRANSFORMATIONAL GRAMMAR
Ambrose-Grillet/Glossary of . . . /79n1094

TRANSLATING AND INTERPRETING
Fuller/Handbook for translators/75n1249
Van Hoof/International bibliog of translation/75n1246

TRANSLATION SERVICE OF THE BRITISH DEPT OF TRADE AND INDUSTRY
Catalogue of translator's library of . . . : dict, gloss, ency, bks abt lang, etc/77n766

TRANSLATIONS
Index translationum 26/79n3

TRANSLATIONS OF LITERATURE
See Literature in English translation; other literatures, e.g., French literature in translation

TRANSLATORS
Translator referral directory/77n1064

TRANSPORTATION
Cumulative index: SAE papers/SAE/76n1609
Davis/Information sources/78n1545
Ocran/Transportation costs & costing, 1917-73: bibliog/76n825

TRANSPORTATION (cont'd)
Oram/Transportation system mgmt: bibliog of tech reports/77n1620
Rakowski/Transportation economics: gd/77n771
Rand McNally ency of transportation/77n1621

TRANSPORTATION LIBRARIES
Special Libraries Assn/Transportation libraries in US & Canada/79n242

TRAVEL AGENTS
World travel directory/Korsant/75n591

TRAVEL GUIDES
Baedeker's hndbks for travellers: bibliog of Engl editions/76n539
Heise/Travel gdbks in review/79n598
Hotel & travel index/75n584
Jacobson/Dance horizons travel gd to world's dance capitals/79n615
Klein/Tennis player's vacation gd/75n585
Meyer/World traveler's almanac/76n538
Nueckel/Selected gd to travel bks/75n587
Official hotel & resort gd/Rubin/75n588
Official meeting facilities gd/75n586
Pan Am's world gd/75n589; 79n620
Rand McNally traveler's almanac/79n621
Roth/Allergy in the world/79n1476
Suit your spirit: gdbks in review/76n540
Travelers' gd to US-certified doctors abroad/77n1482
Weiss/Access to the world: handicapped/79n623
World travel directory/Korsant/75n591
  AFRICA AND MIDDLE EAST
Boone/West African travels/75n638
(Persian) Gulf handbk/79n614
  ASIA AND AUSTRALIA
Davis/On-your-own gd to Asia/79n612
Lynch/All-Asia gd/79n619
White/Australia/75n619
  EUROPE AND USSR
AA gd to camping & caravanning/Kelly/79n711
Allen/Stamp collectors gd to Europe/75n1087
Brody/Music gd to Italy/79n956
Dogo/Treasures of Italy/78n531
Fielding's low-cost Europe/Fielding/75n623
Let's go: budget gd Europe/79n617
Long/Castle hotels of Europe/79n618
Kane/Italy A to Z/78n532
Louis/Complete gd to Soviet Union/78n533
Pilkington/Waterways in Europe/75n625
Reifsnyder/Foot-loose in Swiss Alps/75n626
Rudner/Huts & hikes in Dolomites/75n628
Simpson/Country inns & back roads/79n622
Tully/France: especially for women/76n560
Waldo/Myra Waldo's travel & motoring gd to Europe/75n629

TRAVEL GUIDES (cont'd)
  EUROPE AND USSR (cont'd)
Whitman's off season travel gd/77n571
  GREAT BRITAIN
Banks/Penguin gd to London/79n611
Coxe/Haunted Britain/75n622
Eagle/Oxford literary gd to Brit Isles/78n1159
Egon Ronay's Britain/75n627; 79n613
Egon Ronay's Lucas gd/79n613
Fedden/National Trust gd to England, Wales & No Ireland/76n556
Harting/Literary tour gd to England & Scotland/77n1223
How to live in Britain: for students from overseas/78n576
Laws/Guide to National Trust in Devon & Cornwall/79n616
Murray/Kings & queens of England/75n624
Simpson/Country inns/79n622
Treasures of Britain & ireland/78n534
Woolley/Clarendon gd to Oxford/76n561
  NORTH AMERICA
Illustrated Mexico vacation gd/McCready/75n630
Jenkinson/Wild rivers of No Amer/75n632
Landi/Bantam great outdoors gd to US & Canada/79n712
Logan/Traveller's gd to No Amer gardens/75n633
Milepost: all-the-North travel gd/75n634
Power/Camper's hndbk/75n635
Rand McNally road atlas/75n636
Sutton/Wilderness areas of No Amer/75n637
Wilhelm/Gd to all Mexico/75n631; 79n624
Wojtas/Rand McNally gd to travel by train/75n590
  SOUTH AMERICA
Fielding's gd to Caribbean plus Bahamas/Harman/75n620
Hardaway/Central America by RV/76n558
Sangster/Jamaica/75n621
  UNITED STATES
Adventure trip gd/75n592
AYH hostel gd & hndbk/76n542; 77n557
Banes/Sweet home Chicago/75n602
Book of the road/76n543
Bryfonski/New Engl beach bk/76n544
Burroughs/Nantucket: gd with tours/75n603
Businessman's entertainment gd/75n593
Chapin/Guide to country inns of New Engl/75n604; 76n546
Farm, ranch & countryside gd/75n594
Ford/Gd to the black apple/79n600
Fox/Santa Clara county bk/75n605
Gales/Bicentennial Philadelphia/75n606
Garden Club of Amer/Gd to public gardens/78n526
Goldstone/History preserved: NY city landmarks & historic districts/75n607

TRAVEL GUIDES (cont'd)
UNITED STATES (cont'd)
Gomer's gd from Atlantic to the Mississippi/77n560
Gomer's gds from Mississippi to Pacific/78n525
Griffin/Pelican gd to New Orleans/75n608
Harting/Literary tour gd in US: NE/79n601
Hechtlinger/Pelican gd to revolutionary Amer: New England/77n561
Hinckley/Peterson's travel gd to colleges/79n658
Illustrated gd to treasures of Amer/75n595
Keown/Lovers' gd to Amer/75n596
Kirk/Washington state natl parks, historic sites, etc/75n609
Leblanc/Pelican gd to gardens of Louisiana/75n610
Lord/American travelers' treasury: gd to nation's heirlooms/78n527
Marion/Bicentennial city: historic Philadelphia/75n611
Metropolitan NY AYH Council/American youth hostels bike-hike bk/77n681
Miser/Factory store gd to all New Engl/75n951
Mobil city vacation & business gd/76n553
Mobil travel guide:
    California & West/79n602
    Great Lakes area/79n603
    Middle Atlantic states/79n604
    Northeastern states/79n605
    Northwest & Great Plains states/79n606
    Southeastern states/79n607
    Southwest & South Central area/79n608
Neuer/Inn bk/75n612
Postal/American Jewish landmarks/78n528
Postal/Jewish landmarks of NY/79n609
Rand McNally auto road atlas/75n597
Rand McNally campground & trailer park gd/79n714
Rapoport/California catalogue: living, working, & traveling . . . /78n529
Rice/Where to eat in America: 30 most-traveled Amer cities/78n1477
Rowland/Student adventure travel & study/77n562
Shaw/NY for children/75n614
Shepard/Going out in NY/75n615
Shosteck/Weekender's gd Washington-Baltimore area/75n616
Simons' list bk: (sights to see in US)/79n610
Steinberg/Camper's favorite campgrounds/75n598
Stember/Bicentennial gd to Amer revolution/75n599
Sunset travel gd to So Calif/75n617
Thompson/Saloon: gd to America's great bars, etc./77n1521

TRAVEL GUIDES (cont'd)
UNITED STATES (cont'd)
Trailer Life's recreational vehicle campgrnd & services gd/75n600
US Natl Park Serv/Gd to historic places of American Revolution/75n601
US Natl Park Serv/Here was the Revolution: historic sites/78n336
US Natl Park Serv/Signers of the Constitution: historic places/78n338
Washburn/Tourist gd to Mt. McKinley/75n618

TRAVEL INDUSTRY
Noe/Travel marketing/79n847

TREASURE HUNTING
Perrin/Explorers Ltd. gd to lost treasure in US & Canada/79n399
Probert/Lost mines & buried treasures of West: bibliog & place names/78n358
Underbrink/Treasure trove: bibliog of . . . gold, lost mines, buried treasure/76n957

TREATIES
Grenville/Major internat'l treaties 1914-73/75n533
MacMurray/Treaties & agreements concerning China, 1894-1919/75n536
Rohn/World treaty index/76n506
Treaties & alliances of world/75n543
US Dept of State/Treaties in force/78n489
Vambery/Cumulative list of treaties & agreements . . . recorded with UN/79n560

TREES AND SHRUBS
Arno/Northwest trees/79n1358
Barber/Trees around us/76n1400
Bean/Trees & shrubs hardy in Brit Isles/75n1490
Brimer/Home gardener's gd to trees & shrubs/77n1553
Clay/Hawai'i garden tropical shrubs/78n1489
Crittenden/Trees of the West/79n1359
Davis/Guide to Alabama trees/77n1366
Forest tree seed directory/77n1367
Gault/Color dict of shrubs/77n1368
Gorer/Trees & shrubs: gd/78n1492
Hersey/Flowering shrubs & small trees/75n1702
Johnson/International bk of trees/75n1491
Kramer/Indoor trees/76n1592
Leathart/Trees of the world/79n1360
Little/Atlas of US trees: hardwoods/78n1305
Louden/Short rotation trees/78n1484
Marx/Leaf prints of Amer trees & shrubs/75n1493
Mitchell/Field gd to trees of Brit & No Europe/75n1492
Mulligan/Woody plants in Univ of Washington Arboretum/79n1361
Newcomb/Newcomb's wildflower gd: wildflowers, flowering shrubs, etc/78n1296

TREES AND SHRUBS (cont'd)
Ornamental conifers/77n1369
Palmer/Western treebook/79n1362
Peterson/Native trees of Sierra Nevada/76n1402
Phillips/Trees of No Amer & Europe/79n1363
Polunin/Trees & bushes of Europe/78n1307
Preston/North Amer trees: hndbk for field use/77n1370
Rehder/Bibliog of cultivated trees & shrubs/79n1364
Rock/Indigenous trees of Hawaiian Islands/75n1494
Simon & Schuster's gd to trees/79n1365
Stephens/Woody plants of No Central plains/75n1469
Vines/Trees of East Texas/78n1308

TRILOBITES
Levi-Setti/Trilobites: photographic atlas/76n1363

TRIVIA
See Curiosities

TROLLOPE, ANTHONY
Hardwick/Gd to A. Trollope/75n1405
Olmsted/Reputation of Trollope/79n1255

TROPICAL CROPS
Catalogue of Imperial College of Tropical Agri, Univ of West Indies/76n1555
Wellman/Dict of tropical Amer crops & their diseases/78n1453

TROPICAL DISEASES
Schistosomiasis: compl lit/78n1392; 79n1442

TROPICAL FISHES
Cox/Tropical marine aquaria/75n1666
Halstead/Tropical fish: maintaining an aquarium/76n1558
Hargreaves/Tropical marine aquarium/79n701
Identification gd to freshwater tropical aquarium fish/79n702
Identification gd to marine tropical aquarium fish/79n703
Julian/Dell ency of tropical fish/75n1669
Zeiller/Tropical marine fishes: Florida & Bahama Islands/76n1438

TROPICAL PLANTS
Clay/Hawai'i garden tropical exotics/78n1488
Clay/Hawai'i garden tropical shrubs/78n1489
Gunn/World gd to tropical drift seeds and fruits/77n1349

TROPICS
Hastenrath/Climatic atlas of tropical Atlantic & eastern Pacific Oceans/79n1414

TRUCKS
Baldwin/Observer's bk of commercial vehicles/76n1663
Chilton's repair & tune-up guide:
    Dodge-Plymouth vans/75n1748
    International Scout/75n1750
    Jeep Wagoneer, Commando & Cherokee/75n1749
Chilton's truck repair manual/75n1751
Hull/Pickup camper manual/75n1752
International catalogue of commercial vehicles/76n1665
Vanderveen/American trucks of early '30s/76n1667
Wagner/Ford trucks since 1905/79n1558

TRUMPET WITH ORCHESTRA
Carnovale/20th cent music for trumpet & orchestra: bibliog/76n1013

TURF MANAGEMENT
Beard/Turfgrass bibliog 1672-1972/79n1347

TURKEY
Allsworth/Soviet Asia: bibliogs of soc sci & humanities on Iranian, Mongolian, & Turkic nationalities/77n345
LC/Ataturk & Turkey/75n526

TURKISH LANGUAGE
Iz/Oxford Engl-Turkish dict/79n1153
Selim/Turkish phrase bk/75n1285

TWAIN, MARK
Gale/Plots & characters in works/75n1370
Haviland/S. L. Clemens: centennial for *Tom Sawyer*, bibliog/78n1151

TYPESETTING
Shapiro/Ency of contemp typesetting/79n43

TYPOGRAPHY
Blumenthal/Art of printed bk 1455-1955/75n63

UFOs
Sable/Exobiology/79n1337

UGANDA
Gray/Uganda: subj gd to official pubs/79n362
Howell/East African community/78n290
Killick/Economics of East Africa/77n770

UKRAINE
Liber/Nonconformity & dissent in Ukrainian SSR, 1955-75/79n549
Pidhainy/Ukrainian Republic in great East-European revolution: bibliog/76n375
Weres/Ukraine, bibliog/75n308

UKRAINIAN AMERICANS
Shtohryn/Ukrainians in No Amer: biog directory/76n107

UKRAINIAN AMERICANS (cont'd)
Wertsman/Ukrainians in Amer: chronology/77n447

UKRAINIAN EMIGRE PRESS
Fedynskyj/Bibliographical index of Ukrainian press outside Ukraine/76n1163
Weres/Directory of Ukrainian publishing houses, periodicals, bkstores, libraries, etc of Ukrainica in Diaspora/78n392

UKRAINIAN LITERATURE
Mihailovich/Modern Slavic lits: criticism: Bulgarian, Czech, Polish, Ukrainian, & Yugoslav/78n1199

UNESCO
Bibliog of pubs issued by Unesco, 1946-71/75n111
Records of General Conf, 1974/79n516

UNIFORMS, MILITARY
See also Insignia, military
Carman/Dictionary of military uniforms/78n1556
Military uniforms in Amer, 1796-1851/78n1553
Mollo/Army uniforms of WW II/75n1849
Mollo/Naval, marine & air force uniforms of WW II/77n1631
Mollo/Uniforms of Amer Revolution/76n1679
Windrow/Military dress of No Amer 1665-1970/75n1840

UNION OF SOVIET SOCIALIST REPUBLICS
Bezer/Russian & Soviet studies/75n334
Boisture/Sources of support for research on Russia & USSR/76n277
Dossick/Doctoral research on Russia & Soviet Union, 1960-75/77n346
Grant/Scholar's gd to Washington, DC for Russian-Soviet studies/78n309
Great Soviet ency/75n76
Horak/Russia, USSR, & Eastern Europe/79n378
Index to Pravda/76n498; 79n515
Jones/Books in Engl on Soviet Union, 1917-73/76n278
Lewytzkyj/Who's who in socialist countries/79n143
Skoric/Russian ref aids in Univ of Toronto Library/75n305
US Dept of Army/USSR: survey of lit/78n310
Zalewski/Guide to selected ref matls: Russia & East Europe/75n310
 ARCHITECTURE
Senkevitch/Soviet architecture, 1917-62/75n1022

UNION OF SOVIET SOCIALIST REPUBLICS (cont'd)
 ARMED FORCES
Breyer/Guide to Soviet navy/79n1599
Green/Observer's Soviet aircraft directory/77n1638
US Dept of Air Force/Dict of basic military terms: Soviet view/77n1628
 ECONOMIC CONDITIONS
Birkos/East European & Soviet economic affairs: bibliog 1965-73/76n821
Kazmer/Russian economic hist/79n803
O'Relley/Soviet-type economic systems/79n806
USSR agriculture atlas/77n1511
 FOREIGN RELATIONS
Donovan/US & Soviet policy in Middle East/75n532
Hunter/Soviet-Yugoslav relations, 1948-72: bibliog/77n527
Kanet/Soviet & East European foreign policy/75n534
McLane/Soviet-Asian relations/75n537; 75n538
McLane/Soviet-Middle East relations/75n538
 GEOGRAPHY AND TRAVEL
Felber/American's tourist manual for USSR/76n557; 77n566
Harris/Guide to geograph'l bibliog & ref wks on Soviet Union/76n522
Louis/Complete gd to Soviet Union/78n533
 HISTORY AND GOVERNMENT
Katz/Handbook of major Soviet nationalities/76n385
McCauley/Russian revolution & Soviet state 1917-21: documents/76n374
Mathews/Soviet government/75n522
Mazour/Modern Russian historiography/77n414
Russian revolutionary lit collection, Harvard Univ: descrip gd to microfilm/77n416
Wieczynski/Modern ency of Russian & Soviet history/77n415; 79n442
 SOCIAL SCIENCES
Allsworth/Soviet Asia: bibliog of soc sci & humanities on Iranian, Mongolian, & Turkic nationalities/77n345
Apanasewicz/Education in USSR: bibliog of Engl-language matls/76n573
Feldbrugge/Encyclopedia of Soviet law/75n553
Heiliger/Bibliog of Soviet soc sci/79n385
Matthews/Soviet sociology/79n732

UNIONIZATION OF PROFESSIONALS
See Collective bargaining

Subjects—391

UNITED ARAB EMIRATES
Anthony/Historical dict of Oman & eastern Arabia/77n315

UNITED FARM WORKERS
Fodell/Cesar Chavez & UFW/75n976

UNITED NATIONS
Annual review of UN affairs/Vambery/78 n432
Chamberlin/Chronology & fact bk of UN/77 n493
Hajnal/Guide to UN organization, documentation, & publishing . . . /79n554
Hufner/UN system—internat'l bibliog/78 n430; 79n555; 79n556
IFLA/Sources, organization, utilization of internat'l documentation: UN & other intergov organizations/75n259
Records of Gen Conf, Paris, 1974: index/79 n516
UN documents index/76n85
Who's who in UN & related agencies/Hawkin/ 76n471
Worldmark ency of nations/77n306
Yearbook of UN/76n469; 77n499; 79n514

UNITED NATIONS LIBRARY
Dale/Carl H. Milam & UN Library/77n278

UNITED STATES
See also particular states and regions, e.g., California; the South

Also under specific subjects, e.g., Genealogy; Minorities; Publishing; Religion; etc.
American stats index: gd to statis'l pubs of US gov/76n818
Bibliography & reel index: gd to US decennial census pubs 1790-1970/77n755
Directory of fed stats for local areas/79n788
Dodd/Historical stats of US, 1790-1970: Midwest/77n750
Encyclopedia of US gov benefits/76n829
Kane bk of famous 1st facts & records in US/77n95
US Bureau of Census/Gd to recurrent & special gov stats/77n752
US Bureau of Census/Historical stats of US: colonial times to 1970/77n753
US fact bk: Amer almanac/76n817
US Office of Mgmt & Budget/Federal statis'l directory/77n759
    ARMED FORCES
Higham/Guide to sources of US military hist/ 76n1675
Greene/Black defenders of America/75n813
MacGregor/Blacks in US armed forces/79n452
Uniformed services almanac/Sharff/77n1632
Uniformed services almanac: reserve forces edition/Sharff/77n1634

UNITED STATES (cont'd)
    ARMED FORCES (cont'd)
Webster's Amer military biogs/79n1592
    BIBLIOGRAPHY AND IMPRINTS
American bk publishing record/75n4
Books in print: authors, titles/76n7; 79n6
Books in series in US/78n1; 79n2
Bruntjen/Checklist of Amer imprints for 1831/76n8
Bruntjen/Checklist of Amer imprints for 1832/78n6
Children's bks in print/75n196; 76n154
Cripe/American MSS 1763-1815: index to . . . auction records & catalogues/78n61
Heard/Bookman's gd to Americana/78n49
Large type bks in print/77n18
LC/Monographic series/76n12
LC/Guide to study of USA, suppl 1956-65/ 77n338
Paperbound bks in print/76n9
Publishers' trade list annual/76n10; 79n7
Schreiner-Yantis/Genealogical bks in print/ 76n421
Small press record of bks/76n11; 79n39
Sources/79n40
Subject gd to bks in print/77n19; 79n8
Subject gd to children's bks in print/75 n197; 76n155
Thompson/New Sabin/75n5; 77n20; 77n21
    BIOGRAPHY
American biogic'l notes/75n122
Biographical cyclopaedia of Amer women/ Cameron/76n104
Boulton/Founders: portraits of persons who came to the colonies . . . before 1701/77 n456
Concise dict of Amer biog/78n114
Dickstader/Great No Amer Indians/78n381
Dictionary of Amer biog/Drake/75n123; 76 n105
Dictionary of Amer biog, suppl/76n106; 78n115
Garraty/Ency of Amer biog/75n124
Leonard/Women's who's who of America/77 n122
McLachlan/Princetonians 1748-1768/78n601
Mothers of achievement in Amer hist, 1776-1976/77n396
Prenton/American biogs/75n373
Shipton/Sibley's Harvard grads, 1768-71/76 n667
Significant Amer blacks/Jacobs/77n127
Significant Amer Indians/Mandel/77n132
Significant Amer women/Meltzer/77n140
Significant Americans/77n141
Ukrainians in No Amer/Shtohryn/76n107
Van Doren/Webster's Amer biogs/75n127
Wakelyn/Biographical dict of Confederacy/ 78n364

UNITED STATES (cont'd)
  BIOGRAPHY (cont'd)
Who was who in Amer hist: arts & letters/77n143
Who was who in Amer hist: sci & tech/77n1301
Who's who among black Americans 1975-76/77n438
Who's who in America/77n144
Who was who in America, with world notables/77n142
Who's who in the East/75n128
Who's who in the Midwest/77n145
Who's who in the South/75n129
Who's who in the South & SW/77n146
Who's who in the West/75n130
Who's who of Amer women/79n771
Who's who of the colored race/Mather/77n439
Willard/American women/75n853
  ECONOMIC CONDITIONS
Orsagh/Economic hist of US prior to 1860: bibliog/76n826
Oxford regional economic atlas: US & Canada/77n764
Schapsmeier/Ency of Amer agri'l hist/77n1516
Sobel/Inflation & Nixon admin/76n820
US Dept Agri/Fact bk of US agri/77n1510
  FOREIGN RELATIONS
Bray/Controversy over a new Canal treaty between US & Panama: bibliog/78n486
China & US 1964-72/Yim/76n502
Donovan/US & Soviet policy in Mid East/75n532
El-Khawas/American-Southern African relations: bibliog/77n526
Fowler/American diplomatic hist since 1890/76n311
Hill/Office of Indian Affairs, 1824-80/75n804
Johnson/Guide to Amer Indian docs in Congressional Series Set/78n382
Middle East: US policy/75n539
Prucha/US Indian policy/79n526
Public Records Office/List of Colonial Office records, v3, America to 1946/78n481
US Dept of State/Treaties in force/78n489
  GENEALOGY
    See Genealogy
  GEOGRAPHY
    See also Travel guides; US Bicentennial
Climates of the states in 2 vols: US/Natl Oceanic & Atmospheric Admin/76n1477
Climates of the states/Ruffner/79n1413
Fullard/Nelson Philip American compact atlas/79n592
Grayson/Bibliog of lit on No Amer climates/76n1478
Hammond bicentennial road atlas/76n549

UNITED STATES (cont'd)
  GEOGRAPHY (cont'd)
Harder/Illustrated dict of place names/77n551
Photo-atlas of US/76n531
Rand McNally auto road atlas of US/75n597
Rand McNally road atlas: US, Canada, Mexico/75n636
Schwartz/Climate advisor/79n1417
Szeplaki/Louis Kossuth "The Nation's Guest": bibliog/77n382
  GOVERNMENT PUBLICATIONS
    See Government Publications
  HISTORIC SITES
Boatner/Landmarks of Amer Revoln/76n326
Hechtlinger/Pelican gd to historic homes & sites of revolutionary Amer/77n561
Lord/American travelers' treasury: gd to nation's heirlooms/78n527
Official gd to historic places/76n327
US Natl Park Serv/Guide to historic places of Amer Revolution/75n601
US Natl Park Serv/Here was the Revolution: historic sites/78n336
US Natl Park Serv/Signers of the Constitution: historic places/78n338
  HISTORY
MacLean/Historical account of settlements of Scotch Highlanders prior to 1783/79n489
Marine/British invasion of Maryland 1812-15/78n405
North Carolina/Muster rolls of soldiers of War of 1812/77n472
Richards/Pennsylvania-German in Revolutionary War/79n495
Sanchez-Saavedra/Gd to Virginia military organizations in Amer Revolution/79n1596
Tyler/Connecticut loyalists/78n415
US Dept State/Census of pensioners for revolutionary or military services (1840)/75n432
    ALMANACS AND HANDBOOKS
Clements/Chronology of US/76n333
Coakley/War of Amer Revolution/76n334
Dupuy/Outline hist of Amer Revolution/76n306
Jensen/America in time: hist yr by yr/78n349
Linton/American almanac/78n348
Linton/Bicentennial almanac/76n331
Schemmer/Almanac of liberty: chron of Amer military anniversaries/76n336
War of the Amer Revolution/US Dept of Defense/77n374
    ATLASES
Atlas of Amer Revolution/Nebenzahl/75n364
Cappon/Atlas of early Amer hist: 1760-90/77n375
Carrington/Battle maps of Amer Revolution/76n321

Subjects—393

UNITED STATES (cont'd)
    HISTORY (cont'd)
        ATLASES (cont'd)
History atlas of our country/77n376
Jackson/Atlas of Amer hist/79n410
Marshall/Campaigns of Amer Revolution: MSS maps/77n377
        BIBLIOGRAPHY
Abajian/Blacks & their contribution to Amer West: union list/76n342
Cassara/History of USA: gd/78n341
De Santis/Gilded age 1877-96/75n357
Dougherty/Writings on Amer hist/76n309; 78n342
Eakin/Colonial Amer & War for Independence/78n343
Ferguson/Confederation, constitution, & early natl period/76n310
Filler/Progressivism & muckraking/77n378
Gottschalk/Lafayette: gd to letters, docs, MSS in US/76n317
Harvard gd to Amer history/75n355
Jordan/Maine in the Civil War/77n393
Koenig/European MSS sources of Amer Revolution/76n319
LC/American Revolution in drawings & prints/77n373
Manuscript sources in LC on Amer Revolution/76n320
Matthews/American diaries in MSS, 1580-1954/75n361
Nebenzahl/Bibliog of printed battle plans of Amer Revolution/76n313
New Hampshire's role in Amer Revolution/76n352
Okinshevich/US hist & historiography in postwar Soviet writings/77n380
Shy/American Revolution/75n359
Smith/Afro-American hist/75n360
Smith/Era of Amer Revolution/76n315
Swigger/Guide to resources for study of US in libraries of Univ of Iowa/78n354
Waserman/Bibliog on oral hist/77n383
Women in US hist/78n347
        BIOGRAPHY
Evans/Weathering the storm: women of Amer Revolution/76n338
Johnston/West Virginians in Amer Revolution/78n403
Notable names in Amer hist/75n126
Significant Amer colonial leaders/Buske/77n128
US Natl Park Serv/Signers of Declaration/75n375
White/Fighters for independence/79n411
Who was who during Amer Revolution/78n365
Who was who in Amer hist: military/77n1636

UNITED STATES (cont'd)
    HISTORY (cont'd)
        DICTIONARIES AND ENCYCLOPEDIAS
American Indian & the US/Washburn/75n369
Boatner/Ency of Amer Revolution/75n365
Dictionary of Amer hist/77n384
Dupuy/People & events of Amer Revolution/75n368
Encyclopedia of Amer hist/Kohlmetz/75n366
Family ency of Amer hist/76n322
Hurwitz/Encyclopedic dict of Amer hist/75n367
Lossing/Harper's ency of US hist, 458 AD to 1915/76n323
Martin/Dictionary of Amer hist/79n412
Morris/Encyclopedia of Amer hist/77n385
Record of America: ref hist/McCarthy/76n324
Sharp/Footnotes to Amer hist/78n346
Watts/Dict of Old West 1850-1900/78n350
        INDEXES
America: hist & life, article abstracts & citations/Boehm/76n328
America: hist & life, 5-yr index/79n415
America: hist & life, index to bk reviews/Boehm/76n329
Clark/Index to maps of Amer Revolution in bks & periodicals/75n370
Combined retrospective index set to journals in hist 1838-1974, US: black hist-elections/78n334
Fifty-yr index: Mississippi Valley Hist'l Review 1914-64/75n371
Hager/Pacific Hist'l Review: cum index . . . 1932-74/77n388
Ireland/Index to Amer: life & customs-18th century/77n389
Parker/Personal name index to Orton's "Records of Calif men in war of rebellion 1861-67"/79n492
Reviews in Amer hist/Kutler/76n316
        LOCAL HISTORY
Crouch/Directory of state & local hist periodicals/78n351
Kaminkow/US local histories in LC: bibliog/76n348
NYPL/Dictionary catalog of local hist & genealogy division/75n382
NYPL/US local history catalog/75n383
Oregon Hist'l Society microfilm gd/75n384
        SOURCES
Am I not a man & a brother: antislavery crusade of revolutionary Amer 1688-1788/78n335
Aptheker/Documentary hist of Negro people in US, 1933-45/75n810

UNITED STATES (cont'd)
    HISTORY (cont'd)
        SOURCES (cont'd)
Commager/Documents of Amer hist/75n354
Guide des sources de l'histoire des états-unis dans les archives françaises/78n367
Historic documents of 1974/76n486
Hughes/Pictorial hist of black Americans/75n814
Lesser/Sinews of independence: strength reports of Continental Army/77n372
Negro in Amer history/75n815
Peckham/Toll of independence: American Revolution/76n335
US Natl Archives/Written word endures: milestone docs of Amer hist/78n340
    NATIONAL SECURITY
Buncher/CIA & security debate/77n510
Burt/Congressional hearings on Amer defense policy/75n489
Meeker/Military-industrial complex/75n464
Parker/SALT II/75n541
Williams/Modules in security studies/75n459
    POLITICS AND GOVERNMENT
        BIBLIOGRAPHY
Johnson/American political sci research gd/79n521
Thompkins/Selection of vice president/75n497
US House/Impeachment, selected matls on procedure/75n499
US Natl Archives/Gd to natl archives of US/75n363
        BIOGRAPHY
Barzman/Madmen & geniuses: VPs of US/75n788
Bassett/Profiles & portraits of Amer presidents/77n509
Biographical directory of US executive branch 1774-1977/78n451; 79n541
Burke's presidential families of USA/76n426
Evans/Women in fed politics/76n482
Kane/Facts abt presidents/77n514
Schoenebaum/Political profiles: Eisenhower years/79n527
Significant Amer gov leaders/Miekina/77n130
Significant Amer presidents of US/Buske/77n136
Vice-presidents & cabinet members/76n340
Who was who in Amer politics/Morris/75n486
Who's who in Amer politics/76n480; 78n465
Who's who in government/78n466
Women in public office/77n508; 79n544
        DICTIONARIES AND ENCYCLOPEDIAS
American gov ency/75n479
Encyclopedia of gov'mental advisory organizations/75n481

UNITED STATES (cont'd)
    POLITICS AND GOVERNMENT (cont'd)
        DICTIONARIES AND ENCYCLOPEDIAS (cont'd)
Plano/American political dict/77n507
        DIRECTORIES
LC/Directory of info resources in US fed gov/75n483
Ruder/Businessman's gd to Washington/76n836
Solara/Key influences in Amer right/75n482
Washington info directory/76n479
        HANDBOOKS AND YEARBOOKS
Bain/Convention decisions & voting records/75n487
Barone/Almanac of Amer politics/75n480; 76n474
Chester/Guide to political platforms/79n519
Congress & the nation/79n523
Dollar politics/75n490
Drossman/Watergate & White House/75n501
Fraenkel/Rights we have/75n481
Impeachment & US Congress/75n492
Kane/Facts abt presidents/77n388; 77n514
Knappman/Government & media in conflict/75n494
Presidential vetoes 1789-1976/79n525
Sobel/Inflation & Nixon admin/75n495
Sobel/Money & politics/75n496
Washington lobby/75n500
US Gen Accounting Office/Alpha listing of 1972 presidential campaign receipts/75n498
US gov manual/76n86; 79n530
Watergate: chron of crisis/75n502
        INDEXES
LC/Index to Garfield papers/75n372
US political sci documents/79n522
        SOURCES
Basic documents of Amer public admin 1776-1950/Mosher/78n438
Democratic republican societies, 1790-1800: sourcebk of constitutions, declarations/Foner/78n439
Ewing/Documentary source bk in Amer gov & politics/76n476
Johnson/National party platforms, 1840-1972/75n493; 79n520
US House/Inaugural addresses of Presidents of US to Nixon/75n389
US political sci documents/78n450
    PUBLISHING
AAP/Industry stats/77n46
American book trade directory/76n47; 79n46
American publishers directory/79n47
Blumenthal/Printed bk in Amer/78n32

UNITED STATES (cont'd)
PUBLISHING (cont'd)
Brigham/History & bibliog of Amer newspapers, 1690-1820/77n1110
Hudak/Early Amer women printers & publishers/79n30
Literary market place/76n51
Stowell/Early Amer almanacs/78n40
RELIGION AND SOCIAL CONDITIONS
Gaustad/Historical atlas of religion in Amer/77n1019
Lerner/Bibliography in hist of American women/77n720
Mark/Sociology of America/77n706
Mead/Handbook of denominations in US/76n1087
Piepkorn/Profiles in belief: religious bodies in US & Canada/78n970
Rosten/Religions of America/76n1088
Yearbook of Amer & Canadian churches/76n1089
TRAVEL GUIDES
See Travel guides
ARMY
Index of administrative pubs/79n1595
Lesser/Sinews of independence: reports of Continental Army/77n372
Marshall/Campaigns of Amer Revolution: atlas of MSS maps/77n377
US Dept of Army/Gd to US Army museums & historic sites/Cary/77n1646

UNITED STATES BICENTENNIAL
America's birthday/75n1243
Gaylord/SIRS Bicentennial special program pkg for Amer Issues Forum/Goldstein/76n325
Gales/Bicentennial Philadelphia/75n606
Lawlor/Bicentennial book/76n551
Marion/Bicentennial city: walking tours of historic Philadelphia/75n611
Media for Bicentennial/77n379
Stember/Bicentennial gd to Amer Revolution/75n599
US Natl Park Serv/Gd to historic places of Amer Revolution/75n601

UNITED STATES CENTRAL INTELLIGENCE AGENCY
Buncher/CIA & security debate/77n510

UNITED STATES CIVIL SERVICE COMMISSION
Index to Civil Serv Com info/77n114

UNITED STATES CONGRESS
CIS/Annual: abstracts of congres'l pubs & legislative histories/77n511
Congress & the nation/79n523

UNITED STATES CONGRESS (cont'd)
Congressional roll call: chron & analysis of votes in House & Senate/76n483; 77n513
CQ/Guide to Congress/77n512
CQ/Members of Congress since 1789/78n454
DePauw/Documentary hist of first fed Congress 1789-91/78n453
Engelbarts/Women in US Congress, 1917-72/75n485
Field/Bibliog & indexes of US Congres'l Committee prints, 1911-1969 . . . /79n117
Grayson/Impeachment Congress/75n491
Schlesinger/Congress investigates: documented hist 1792-1974/76n307
US Congress/Official congres'l directory/76n486; 77n517; 79n122
US Gen Accounting Office/Recurring reports to Congress: directory/77n518

UNITED STATES CONSTITUTION
Documentary hist of ratification of Constitution/77n370; 77n371
Equal Rights Amendment: bibliog'ic study/78n496
Mason/American constitutional developmt/78n445
Millett/Selected bibliog of Amer constitutional history/76n312
Sobel/Presidential succession: Ford, Rockefeller & 25th amendment/76n488
Swindler/Sources & docs of US Constitutions/75n566
US Natl Park Serv/Signers of Constitution: historic places/78n338

UNITED STATES COURTS
See Courts

UNITED STATES DEPARTMENT OF HEALTH, EDUCATION AND WELFARE
Directory of Educ Div/76n618

UNITED STATES DEPARTMENT OF HOUSING AND URBAN DEVELOPMENT
Statistical yrbk/77n829

UNITED STATES DEPARTMENT OF LABOR
US Dept Labor library catalog/76n907

UNITED STATES DEPARTMENT OF THE AIR FORCE
US DAF/US Air Force history/75n1847

UNITED STATES DEPARTMENT OF THE NAVY
Dictionary of naval abbreviations/Wedertz/78n1572
Dulin/Battleships: WW II/77n1649
Polmar/Ships & aircraft of US fleet/77n1651; 79n1605

UNITED STATES DEPARTMENT OF THE NAVY (cont'd)
Register of commissioned & warrant officers of US Navy/79n1606
Smith/American Navy, 1789-1860/75n1851
Smith/American Navy, 1865-1918/75n1852
Smith/American Navy, 1918-41/75n1853
Swanborough/US Navy aircraft since 1911/78n1577
US Dept Navy/Dict Amer naval fighting ships/77n1653
US Dept Navy/US naval chaplains, 1957-70/75n1854

UNITED STATES ENVIRONMENTAL PROTECTION AGENCY
US EPA/Indexed bibliog of research & development reports/76n1456

UNITED STATES LIBRARY OF CONGRESS
See Library of Congress

UNITED STATES MARINE CORPS
US Marine Corps/Marines in Vietnam, 1954-73/75n1855

UNITED STATES NATIONAL AGRICULTURAL LIBRARY
Gilreath/CAIN online user's gd/77n255

UNITED STATES NATIONAL AUDIOVISUAL CENTER
US NAVC/Directory of US gov AV personnel/76n630

UNITED STATES NATIONAL GUARD
Uniformed services almanac: Natl Grd ed/Sharff/77n1633

UNITED STATES NATIONAL MARINE FISHERIES SERVICE
US NMFS/Publications & services/75n970

UNITED STATES OFFICE OF MANPOWER RESEARCH & DEVELOPMENT
Manpower research & developmt projects/77n838

UNITED STATES SENATE
Douth/Leaders in profile: US Senate, 1975 edition/76n484
Senate campaign information/79n528
US Congress/US Senate: hist'l bibliog/78n455

UNITED STATES SUPREME COURT
Anderman/US Supreme Court decisions: index/77n540

UNIVERSAL DECIMAL CLASSIFICATION
Brown/Introduction to subj indexing, v2, UDC/77n252
Computers & UDC/Rigby/76n187

UNIVERSAL DECIMAL CLASSIFICATION (cont'd)
General class systems in changing world/79n271

UNIVERSAL PICTURES
Fitzgerald/Universal Pictures: hist & filmog/78n949

UNIVERSITY OF ARKANSAS LIBRARY
Sizer/Gd to selected MSS collections/77n355

UNIVERSITY OF BIRMINGHAM, MUSIC LIBRARY
Fenlon/Catalogue of printed music & music MSS before 1801 . . . Barber Inst of Fine Arts/77n953

UNIVERSITY OF CALIFORNIA AT LOS ANGELES LIBRARY
McGlynn/Middle Amer anthropology: gd to UCLA collections/77n733

UNIVERSITY OF CONNECTICUT LIBRARY
Brown/Puerto Rico: cklist/77n336

UNIVERSITY OF NEBRASKA AT LINCOLN
Photographs: Sheldon Memorial Art Gallery collections/78n886

UNIVERSITY OF OXFORD
Emden/Biographical register of Univ of Oxford AD 1501-40/75n691

UNIVERSITY OF TEXAS AT AUSTIN
Comprehensive program of user educ for the general libraries/78n233

UNIVERSITY OF TORONTO
Univ of Toronto doctoral theses 1968-75: bibliog/78n550

UNIVERSITY OF WASHINGTON ARBORETUM
Mulligan/Woody plants in Univ Arboretum/79n1361

UNIVERSITY PRESSES
American bk review/79n1216
International directory of scholarly publishers/79n53

UPDIKE, JOHN
Olivas/Annotated bibliog of Updike criticism/76n1250
Sokoloff/John Updike/75n1371

UPPER VOLTA
McFarland/Historical dictionary/79n363

URBAN EDUCATION
Spear/Urban education/79n635

URBAN TRANSPORTATION
Baerwald/Transportation & traffic eng'g hndbk/77n1618

URBAN TRANSPORTATION (cont'd)
Aslib & Library Assn/New directions in transport sources of info: proceedings/77n1617

URBANIZATION
Bibliography of land settlement/79n787
Bose/Bibliography on urbanization in India/78n641
International Inst for Environmt & Development/Human settlements: bibliog/77n730; 77n731

URBANOLOGY
Alpern/Pratt gd to planning & renewal for New Yorkers/75n857
American men & women of sci: urban community sciences/75n858
Antinoro-Polizzi/Ghetto & suburbia/75n859
Bryfogle/City in print: bibliog/77n726; 77n727
Comparative atlas of America's great cities/77n728
Crawford/Handbook of zoning & land use ordinances—with forms/75n860
Dumouchel/Dictionary of developmt terminology/76n799
Hoover/Cities/77n729
Murphy/Urban politics/79n539
Rosenberg/Urban info thesaurus/79n734
Ross/Urban affairs bibliog/76n802
Scott/Management & control of growth/76n801
Urban affairs abstracts/75n861
Whittick/Encyclopedia of urban planning/75n862

URDU LANGUAGE
Platts/Dictionary of Urdu, classical Hindi, & English/78n1071

URQUHART, DONALD
Barr/Essays on info & libraries/76n207

URUGUAY
Willis/Historical dictionary/76n283

USIA
Sussman/US Info Service libraries/75n209

USSR
See Union of Soviet Socialist Republics

UTAH
Jaussi/Genealogical records of Utah/75n423

UTOPIAS
Negley/Utopian literature/79n1181

VALUES EDUCATION
Human (& anti-human) values in children's bks/77n1154
Superka/Values educ sourcebk: bibliog/77n646

VALVES
Hutchison/ISA hndbk of control valves/77n1608
Lyons' ency of valves/77n1609

VARIATIONS (vocal)
Selective music lists: vocal solos, vocal ensembles/77n961

VEGETABLE GARDENING
Faust/NY Times bk of vegetable gardening/76n1583

VEHICLES
Baldwin/Observer's bk of commercial vehicles/76n1663
International catalogue of commercial vehicles/76n1665
Foss/Military vehicles of world/77n1643
Vanderveen/Fire & crash vehicles from 1950/77n1622
Vanderveen/Observer's army vehicles directory to 1940/76n1681
Vanderveen/Tanks & transport vehicles: WW II/76n1686

VENEREAL DISEASES
Goode/Venereal disease bibliog/75n1614; 76n1517

VENEZUELA
De Schauensee/Guide to birds/79n1372
Lombardi/Venezuelan history: bibliog/78n374
Quintero-Mesa/Latin American serial docs: Venezuela/79n26

VENICE
Gerulaitis/Printing & publishing in 15th cent Venice/78n36
Selfridge-Field/Venetian instrumental music from Gabrieli to Vivaldi/76n984

VENOMOUS ANIMALS
See Poisonous animals

VENTURE CAPITAL
Rubel/Guide to venture capital sources/75n957; 78n753
Smollen/Source gd for borrowing capital/78n754

VERDI, GIUSEPPE
Chusid/Catalog of Verdi's operas/75n1165
de Schauensee/Collector's Verdi & Puccini/79n986

VERGIL
Classical world bibliog of Vergil/79n1264
Warwick/Vergil concordance/76n1304

VERMONT
Directory of foundations/77n84
Swift/Vermont place-names/78n535

VETERINARIANS
American men & women of sci: agriculture, animal & vet sciences/75n1660

VETERINARY DRUGS
Rossoff/Handbook of vet drugs/76n1553

VETERINARY MEDICINE
Davidson/Horseman's vet advisor/75n1661
Hurov/Handbook of vet surgical instruments & glossary of terms/79n1543
Merck vet manual/75n1662
Pommery/What to do till the vet comes/77n1530
Rossdale/Horse's health from A to Z/75n1663
Schneck/Complete home med gd for cats/77n1531
Schneck/Complete home med gd for dogs/77n1532
Sessions/Dog owner's med manual/77n1533
Spaulding/Veterinary gd for animal owners/77n1534
West/Encyclopedia of animal care/78n1462

VETOES
Presidential vetoes 1789-1976/79n525

VIBRATION
Harris/Shock & vibration hndbk/77n1607

VICE-PRESIDENTS (United States)
Barzman/Madmen & geniuses/75n488
Tompkins/Selection of the VP/75n497
Vice-presidents & cabinet members: biogs/76n340

VIDEOTAPES
Educators gd to free audio & video matls/Berg/78n591
Goldstein/Video in libraries/78n248

VIETNAM
Cotter/Vietnam/78n302
Nguyen Phuong-Khan/Vietnamese legal matls/79n566
Phan Tien Chau/Vietnamese communism: bibliog/77n525
Whitfield/Historical & cultural dict/77n332

VIETNAMESE WAR
Heath/Mutiny does not happen lightly: lit of Amer resistance to Vietnam war/77n502
Leitenberg/Vietnam conflict/75n463
South Vietnam: US-communist confrontation in SE Asia/75n527;75n528;75n529;75n530
US Marine Corps/Marines in Vietnam/75n1855

VIHUELA
Purcell/Classic guitar, lute & vihuela discog/78n905

VILLAGE STUDIES
Lambert/Village studies/79n778

VINES
Duncan/Woody vines of SE US/76n1383
Newcomb's wildflower gd/78n1296

VINEYARDS
Ambrosi/Where the great German wines grow: gd/77n1518
Fowler/German wine atlas & vineyard register/78n1455

VIOLA
Barrett/Viola/79n989

VIOLENCE IN POLITICS
Manheim/Political violence in US, 1875-1974: bibliog/76n472

VIOLETS
Klaber/Violets of US/78n1292

VIOLIN MUSIC
Creighton/Discopaedia of violin, 1889-1971/75n1160

VIRGINIA
Almanac of VA politics/78n456
Chalkley/Chronicles of Scotch-Irish settlement in VA/75n409
Check-list of VA state pubs/79n114
Cumrine/Virginia court records in SW PA/75n413
duBellet/Some prominent VA families/77n459
Felldin/Index to 1820 census of VA/77n461
Gannett/Gazetteer of VA & West VA/76n455
Hamlin/They went thataway/75n418
Harrison/Settlers by the Long Grey Trail/76n434
Heavener/German New River settlmt/77n464
Hummel/More Virginia broadsides before 1877/76n346
Hummel/Portraits & statuary of Virginians . . ./79n879
Lee/Lee of Virginia, 1642-1892/75n426
Leonard/General Assembly of VA 1619-1978/79n533
Meade/Old churches, ministers & families of VA/79n490
Nugent/Cavaliers & pioneers: abstracts of VA land patents/79n491
Robertson/Kansas territorial settlers of 1860 who were born in TN, VA, NC & SC/77n475
Sanchez-Saavedra/Guide to VA military organizations in Amer Revolution/79n1596
Weis/Colonial clergy of VA/77n479

VIROLOGY/Fraenkel-Conrat/Comprehensive virology, catalogue of viruses/76n1361

VIRUS DISEASES
Locke/Virus diseases/79n1490

VISUAL INSTRUCTION
Dwyer/Guide for improving visualized instruction/75n711

VISUALLY HANDICAPPED
See also Blind

Bauman/Blindness, visual impairment, deaf-blindness/79n1449

Directories of agencies serving the visually handicapped in US/77n1480

For younger readers: braille & talking bks/79n338

Gill/International register of research on blindness & visual impairment/79n1469

International catalog, aids & appliances for blind & visually impaired persons/Clark/75n1637

International gd to aids & appliances for blind & visually impaired persons/78n1406

McGarry/Federal assistance for programs serving visually handicapped/79n1470

Strom/Library services to blind & physically handicapped/78n237

Talking bk topics/79n339

Talking bks adult/79n340

VITAL STATISTICS
Birth . . . marriage . . . death—on the record: directory of . . . records in 50 states & overseas/78n654

Dover Historical Soc/Vital records of Dover, NH 1686-1850/79n482

Meade/Old churches, ministers & families of VA/79n490

Shurtleff/Records of Plymouth Colony, 1633-89/77n477

VITAMINS
Fryer/Dictionary of food supplements: gd for buying vitamins, minerals, etc/77n1545

VOCABULARY
Dale/Living word vocabulary: inventory/77n1066

VOCABULARY TESTS
US Natl Center for Health Stats/Rationale development . . . of basic word vocabulary test/75n718

VOCAL MUSIC
Bennett/Catalogue of vocal recordings from 1898-1925 . . . Gramaphone Co/79n969

Espina/Repertoire for solo voice: gd to works . . . 13th cent to present/78n892

Nardone/Classical vocal music in print/78n897

Selective music lists: vocal solos, vocal ensembles/77n961

VOCATIONAL EDUCATION
See also Occupational training; Trade schools

Appleby/Training programs & placemt services: severely handicapped/79n852

Cass/Comparative gd to two-yr colleges & career programs/78n567

Continuing educ: gd to career developmt programs/78n568

Cordasco/Bibliog of vocational educ/78n538

Guide to two-yr college majors & careers/76n649

Herbert/Getting skilled: gd to trade & tech schools/77n628

Jones/Correspondence educ'l directory/78n569

Lovejoy's career & vocational school gd/79n666

Miller/Guide to eval of educ'l experiences in armed services/76n650

NATTS directory of accredited trade & tech schools/77n630

Queens College, NY/College programs for paraprofessionals: in the human services/76n652

Reinhart/Vocational-technical learning matls/75n705

Shaffer/Career educ pamphlets/77n654

Technician educ yrbk/76n605

US Bureau Labor Stats/Occupational outlook hndbk/77n844

US Dept HEW/Directory postsecondary schools with occupational programs/77n632

US Dept Labor/Guide to local occupational information/77n845

Yearbook of adult & continuing educ/78n581

VOCATIONAL GUIDANCE
See also Occupations

Boesch/Careers in the outdoors/76n598

Chronicle Guidance Pubs/College counseling for transfers & careers/75n655

Educators gd to free guidance matls/76n671

Encyclopedia of careers & vocational guidance/76n590

Hecht/Alternatives to college/76n622

Hopke/Children's dict of occupations/75n709

Johnson/Directory of special programs for minority group members/75n801

Lederer/Guide to career educ/75n657; 77n629

Mitchell/I can be anything: careers & colleges for young women/76n651; 79n660

National Assn of Housing & Redevelopmt Officials/Urban careers gd/75n680

Phelps/New career options for women: bibliog/78n773

VOCATIONAL GUIDANCE (cont'd)
Tiedeman/Key resources in career educ: annotated gd/78n570

VOCATIONAL TESTS
Buros/Vocational tests/76n570

VOICE OF THE NEGRO
Analytical gd & indexes to *Voice of the Negro* 1904-07/75n31

VOLTA REVIEW
Fellendorf/Bibliography on deafness/79n1455

VONNEGUT, KURT
Pieratt/Kurt Vonnegut: bibliog/76n1251

VOTERS
See also Elections
Neuborne/Rights of candidates & voters: ACLU gd/77n504

WAGES
Employment & earnings, states & area/77n836
US Soc Security Admin/Earnings distributions in US/77n846

WALES
Burke/General armory of England, Scotland, Ireland & Wales/77n483
Fedden/National Trust gd to England, Wales & No Ireland/76n556
Wolfson geochemical atlas of England & Wales/Webb/79n1419

WALPOLE, HORACE W.
Hazen/Bibliography of Walpole/75n1406
Lewis/Guide to life of Walpole/75n1407

WALTERS ART GALLERY, BALTIMORE
Zeri/Italian paintings in Walters Art Gallery/77n888

WAR
Parkinson/Encyclopedia of modern war/78n1559
Williams/Atlas of weapons & war/78n1554

WARSHIPS
Couhat/Combat fleets of world/77n1648; 79n1600
Dulin/Battleships: US in WW II/77n1649
Elliott/Allied escort ships of WW II/79n1601
Ireland/Warships of world/78n1574
Jane's fighting ships/Moore/78n1575
Jentschura/Warships of Imperial Japanese navy, 1869-1945/79n1602
Leather/World warships in review 1860-1906/78n1576
Lenton/German warships of 2nd WW/77n1650
Ships & aircraft of US fleet/77n1651; 79n1605

WARSHIPS (cont'd)
US Dept Navy/Dictionary of Amer naval fighting ships/77n1653

WASHINGTON, GEORGE
Carroll/Library at Mt Vernon/79n326

WASHINGTON, DC
Babb/Washington Post gd to Washington/77n558
Bundy/Prison group directory/76n777
Circle of friends/78n79
Colgate/Directory of Washington reps of Amer assns & industry/79n91
Ein/Whole Washington hndbk/76n881
Fisher/Materials for study of Washington: bibliog/76n800
Grayson/Washington IV: directory/76n478
Information thru cooperative action: library services/77n156
McMahan/Washington, DC artists born before 1900/78n824
Researchers gd to Washington/Washington Researchers/78n82
Ruder/Businessman's gd to Washington/76n836
Scholar's gd to Washington, DC for Russian-Soviet studies/78n309
Shosteck/Weekender's gd/75n616

WASHINGTON (state)
Kirk/Washington state natl parks, historic sites, etc/75n609
Kosloff/Plants & animals of Pacific NW: illust'd gd/77n1346
Niehaus/Field gd to Pacific states wildflowers/77n1361
Phillips/Washington state place names/77n552
Washington educ directory/75n671

WASHINGTON PRESS CORPS
Hudson's Washington news media contacts directory/76n1169

WASTEWATER MANAGEMENT
Azad/Industrial wastewater mgmt hndbk/77n1605
Meinck/Dictionary of water & sewage eng'g/79n1579
Middlebrooks/Lagoon info source bk/79n1580
Tchobanoglous/Wastewater mgmt: gd to info sources/77n1421

WATER
Bond/CRC hndbk of environmental control: water supply & treatmt/75n1536
FAO/Water for agriculture/75n1664
Gehm/Handbook of water resources & pollution control/77n1422
Geraghty/Water atlas of US/75n1567
Hawkins/Physical & chem properties of water: bibliog/78n1240

WATER (cont'd)
Meinck/Dictionary of water & sewage eng'g/ 79n1579
Meta Systems/Systems analysis in water resources planning/76n1473
Ralston/Water resources: bibliog/76n1474
Summers/Isotopes of water: bibliog/77n1430
van der Leeden/Ground water: bibliog/76n1475

WATER BIRDS
Baird/Water birds of No Amer/75n1499
Cogswell/Water birds of Calif/78n1317
Johnsgard/Ducks, geese & swans of world/ 79n1373
Johnsgard/Waterfowl of No Amer/77n1381
Merne/Ducks, geese & swans/76n1425
Palmer/Handbook of No Amer birds: waterfowl/77n1384

WATER-COLORS
Lucas/Bibliography of water colour painting & painters/78n819

WATER POLLUTION
Algae abstracts/75n1555
Gehm/Handbook of water resources & pollution control/77n1422
Liptak/Environmental engineers' hndbk: water pollution/75n1540
Louden/Paper mill sludge characteristics, .../77n1316
Summers/Ground water pollution/75n1527
Todd/Polluted groundwater: review of lit/ 77n1423
Unger/Bibliography of water pollution control benefits & costs/76n1455
US Environmental Data Serv/Bibliog of urban modification of hydrologic environment/75n1529
US EPA/Indexed bibliog of res & developmt reports/76n1456
Water quality abstracts/75n1562

WATERGATE
Knappman/Government & media in conflict/ 75n494
Rosenberg/Watergate: bibliog/76n473
Watergate & White House/Drossman/75n501
Watergate: chronology of crisis/75n502; 76n489

WATERLOO, BATTLE OF
Pericoli/1815: armies at Waterloo/75n1850

WAVERLEY NOVELS
Bradley/Index to Waverley novels/76n1283

WEAPON SYSTEMS
Knaack/Ency of US Air Force aircraft & missile systems/79n1593
Pretty/Jane's weapon systems/79n1609

WEAPONS
See Arms and armor; Arms trade; Disarmament; Nuclear weapons; SALT II; Weapon systems

WEATHER
See Climatology

WEATHER SERVICE
US Naval Weather Serv Command/Worldwide marine weather broadcasts/75n1569

WEATHERLY, EDWARD CHRISTOPHER
Mitterling/Guide to E. C. Weatherly papers/ 76n349

WEAVING
Axford/Weaving, spinning, & dyeing/76n947
Craft suppliers: fiber/75n1041
Zielinski/Ency of hand-weaving/78n882

WEEDING (libraries)
See Discarding of books

WEEDS
Brown/Weeds in winter/78n1309
Crockett/Wildly successful plants: hndbk of No Amer weeds/78n1310

WEEKLY ADVOCATE, THE
Jacobs/Antebellum black newspapers: indices to ... The Weekly Advocate (1837) and others/77n432

WEIGHT LOSS
See Reducing diets

WEIGHTS AND MEASURES
See also Metric system; Measuring instruments
Chisholm/Units of weight & measure/76n1315
Johnstone/For good measure: compendium of internat'l weights & measures/76n1316

WEIMAR REPUBLIC
Stachura/Weimar era & Hitler/79n430

WELLS, HERBERT GEORGE
Hammond/H. G. Wells/79n1256

WELTY, EUDORA
Thompson/E. Welty: ref gd/77n1215

WEST, NATHANAEL
Vannatta/N. West: bibliog/77n1216
White/N. West: comp bibliog/76n1252

WEST, THE
Abajian/Blacks & their contribution to Amer West: bibliog & union list/76n342
Clarke/Birds of the West/77n1375
Denver Public Library.Western Hist Dept/ Catalog/76n344
Lamar/Reader's ency of Amer West/78n314
Mobil travel gd: CA & the West/79n602

402–Subjects

WEST, THE (cont'd)
Probert/Lost mines & buried treasures of the West: bibliog & place names/78n358
Society of Amer Travel Writers/Exploring the unspoiled West/76n555
Watts/Dictionary of Old West 1850-1900/78n350

WEST AFRICA
Asiedu/Public admin in English-speaking West Africa: bibliog/78n469
Boone/West African travels/75n638

WEST IN ART
Dykes/Fifty great western illustrators: bibliographic checklist/76n940

WEST INDIES
Humfrey/Sea shells of West Indies/76n973
Riley/Field gd to butterflies of West Indies/77n1391
Warmke/Caribbean seashells/77n1396

WEST VIRGINIA
Gannett/Gazetteer of VA & West VA/76n455
Johnston/West Virginians in Amer Revolution/78n403

WESTERN FILMS
Adams/Shoot-em-ups/79n1031
Eyles/Western/76n1068
Nachbar/Western films: bibliog/76n1050
Parish/Great western pics/77n1012

WESTERN MUSIC
   See Country music

WHALES
Coffey/Dolphins, whales & porpoises: ency/78n1332

WHISTLER, JAMES M.
Kennedy/Etched work/79n897

WHITE, PATRICK
Lawson/P. White/75n1409

WHITEHEAD, ALFRED NORTH
Woodbridge/A. N. Whitehead: bibliog/78n1005

WHITMAN, WALT
Allen/New Walt Whitman hndbk/77n1217
Francis/Whitman at auction 1899-1972/79n1225

WHITTIER, JOHN GREENLEAF
von Frank/Whittier: bibliog/77n1218

WIDOWS
Strugnell/Adjustment to widowhood . . . /75n852

WIESEL, ELIE
Abramowitz/E. Wiesel: bibliog/76n1253

WIFE BEATING
Howard/Wife beating/79n746

WIGHT COUNTY, VA
Chapman/Marriages of Isle of Wight Co, 1628-1800/77n458

WILD FLOWERS
Alaska-Yukon wild flowers gd/75n1473
Blackall/How to know western Australian wildflowers/76n1387
Chickering/Flowers of Guatemala/75n1474
Clark/Wild flowers of Pacific NW/78n1287
Crittenden/Wildflowers of East/78n1288
Dean/Wildflowers of AL . . . /75n1475
Duncan/Wildflowers of SE US/76n1388
Durant/Who named the daisy: dict of No Amer wildflowers/78n1289
Dwelley/Summer & fall wildflowers of New England/79n1342
Fitter/Wild flowers of Britain & No Europe/76n1389
Fleming/Wild flowers of FL/78n1290
Haskin/Wild flowers of Pacific Coast/78n1291
Herdey/Woman's Day bk of wildflowers/77n1360
Klimas/Wildflowers of CT/76n1390
Klimas/Wildflowers of eastern Amer/75n1478
Klimas/Wild flowers of MA/76n1394
Klimas/Wild flowers of New Hampshire & Vermont/76n1391
Klimas/Wild flowers of New Jersey/76n1392
Klimas/Wild flowers of New York/76n1393
Klimas/Wild flowers of Pennsylvania/76n1395
Linn/Eastern No America's wildflowers/79n1344
Mackenzie/Wild flowers of Midwest/78n1293
Mackenzie/Wild flowers of North country/75n1480
Mackenzie/Wild flowers of South/78n1294
Moyle/Northland wild flowers: gd for MN/78n1295
Newcomb's wildflower gd/78n1296
Niehaus/Field gd to Pacific states wildflowers/77n1361
Orr/Wildflowers of western Amer/75n1479
Phillips/Wild flowers of Britain/79n1346
Rickett/Complete index for wild flowers of US/77n1362
Roberts/Born in the spring/78n1297
Sperka/Growing wildflowers/75n1708
Young/Wildflowers of redwood empire/77n1363

WILD FOOD PLANTS
   See Food, wild; Plants, edible

WILDERNESS AREAS
Sutton/Wilderness areas of No Amer/75
n637

WILDLIFE REFUGES
Kitching/Birdwatcher's gd to wildlife
sanctuaries/77n1382

WILLIAMS, CHARLES W. S.
Glenn/Charles W. S. Williams: cklist/77n1249

WILLIAMS, ROGER
Coyle/Roger Williams: ref gd/78n972

WILLIAMS AND WILKINS CASE
McCormick/Williams & Wilkins case/76
n42

WILLIAMSBURG, VA
Williamsburg collection of antique furnishings/75n1077

WILLS
Gibson/Wills and where to find them/75n437

WILSON, WOODROW
Papers of W. Wilson/78n442

WIND ENERGY
Hickok/Handbook of solar & wind energy/
76n1461

WIND INSTRUMENT—MUSIC
Weerts/Original MSS music for wind & percussion instruments/75n1134

WINDOW GARDENING
See Indoor gardening

WINE AND WINE MAKING
Alexis Bespaloff's gd to inexpensive wines/
77n1519
Alexis Lichine's new ency of wines & spirits/
76n1562
Ambrosi/Where the great German wines
grow/77n1518
Born/Concise atlas of wine/75n1670
Churchill/World of wines/75n1671
Donner/Pennypincher's wine gd/75n1672
Dubuigne/Larousse dict of wines of world/
78n1454
Fadiman/Wine buyers gd/79n1516
Fowler/German wine atlas & vineyard register/
78n1455
Frank Schoonmaker's ency of wine/75n1676;
76n1563; 79n1521
Grossman's gd to wines, spirits, & beers/75
n1673; 78n1456
Hugh Johnson's pocket ency of wine/79n1518
Johnson/Wine/76n1561
Kaufman/Whole-world wine catalog/79n1519
Lee/Inexpensive wine/75n1674
Meinhard/International Wine & Food Society's
gd to wines of Germany/78n1457
Melville/Gd to Calif wines/77n1520
Misch/Quick gd to wines of the Americas/78
n1458

WINE AND WINE MAKING (cont'd)
Nelson/Poor person's gd to great cheap
wines/79n1520
New Larousse gastronomique: ency of food,
wine & cookery/Montague/78n1476
Quimme/Signet bk of Amer wine/78n1459
Read/Wines of Spain & Portugal/75n1675
Tudor/Wine, beer and spirits/77n1522
Wasserman/Wines of Italy/78n1460

WINNERS OF CONTESTS, AWARDS,
ETC.
Stuart/Who won what when/79n100

WINNIPEG, MANITOBA
Sloane/Winnipeg/75n393

WISCONSIN
Fassett/Spring flora of Wisconsin/77n1352
Robinson/Atlas of Wisconsin/75n580

WIT AND HUMOR
Fechtner/Encyclopedia of ad-libs, crazy
jokes, etc./78n1044
Kujoth/Subject gd to humor: anecdotes,
. . . from 365 periodicals, 1968-74/77
n1141
Picture ref file: humor, wit, & fantasy/Hart/
78n813
Prochnow/Dict of wit, wisdom, & humor/76
n74

WITCHCRAFT
Witchcraft: collection in Cornell Univ/Crowe/
78n1380

WOLEAIAN LANGUAGE
Sohn/Woleaian-Engl dict/78n1072

WOLFE, THOMAS
Phillipson/Thomas Wolfe: ref gd/78n1153
Reeves/Thomas Wolfe: critical reception/76
n1254

WOLLSTONECRAFT, MARY
Todd/Mary Wollstonecraft: bibliog/77n1250

WOMEN
Partnow/Quotable woman 1800-1975/79
n768
    BIBLIOGRAPHY
Bibliog of women's periodicals/75n844
Catalogs of Sophia Smith Collection, Smith
College/76n789
Davis/Bibliography on women/75n846
Friedman/Women's work & women's studies/
77n717
Goodwater/Women in antiquity/76n792
Kelly/Bibliography in hist of European
women/77n401
King/Women's studies sourcebk/77n718
Krichmar/Women's studies: gd to pubs &
services, library Univ Calif at Santa
Barbara/76n142
Lerner/Bibliog in hist of Amer women/77n720

WOMEN (cont'd)
    BIBLIOGRAPHY (cont'd)
    Lynn/Research gd in women's studies/76
        n795
    Oakes/Guide to soc sci resources in women's
        studies/79n758
    Rosenfelt/Strong women: bibliog of lit for
        high school/78n599
    Schlachter/Minorities & women/79n762
    Stanwick/Political participation of women in
        US/78n447
    Wheeler/Womanhood media suppl/76n798
    Williams/American black women in arts &
        soc sciences/79n454
    Women in US history/78n347
    Women's gd to books/75n855; 77n725
    Woodsworth/Women: gd to sources Univ
        of Toronto libraries/75n856
    BIOGRAPHY
    Berkowitz/Who's who & where in women's
        studies/76n787
    Cameron/Biographical cyclopaedia of Amer
        women/76n104
    Carrington/Women in early Texas/76n337
    Collins/Women artists in America II/76n932
    Evans/Weathering the storm: women of Amer
        Revolution/76n338
    Howes/American women: biogic'l dict of
        notable women/75n849
    Kulkin/Her way: biogs of women for young
        people/77n719
    Leonard/Women's who's who of Amer, 1914-
        15/77n122
    Mothers of achievement in Amer hist, 1776-
        1976/77n396
    Myerson/Margaret Fuller/79n757
    Opfell/Lady laureates: women who won the
        Nobel Prize/79n770
    Significant Amer women/Meltzer/77n140
    Who's who of Amer women/79n771
    Willard/American women/75n853
    World who's who of women/77n124
    DICTIONARIES AND
        ENCYCLOPEDIAS
    Encyclopedia of women: chron/78n668
    Astin/Women: bibliog on their educ &
        careers/75n843; 76n786
    Froschl/Feminist resources for schools &
        colleges: gd/78n593
    Mitchell/I can be anything: careers & colleges
        for young women/76n651; 79n660
    Resources in women's educ'l equality/79
        n759
    Schlachter/Directory of financial aids for
        women/79n766
    EMPLOYMENT
    Bickner/Women at work/75n845
    Foxley/Locating, recruiting & employing
        women/77n793
    Loring/New life options: working woman's
        resource bk/77n721

WOMEN (cont'd)
    EMPLOYMENT (cont'd)
    Phelps/New career options for women: bibliog/
        78n773
    Pogrebin/Getting yours: make the system
        work for working woman/76n796
    HANDBOOKS AND YEARBOOKS
    Alexander/State-by-state gd to women's legal
        rights/76n512
    Boulding/Handbook of intenat'l data on
        women/78n669
    Cary/NYCLU gd to women's rights in NY
        state/79n763
    Gager/Women's rights almanac/75n848
    Good Housekeeping woman's almanac/
        McDowell/78n670
    Macksey/Book of women's achievements/77
        n722; 78n671
    Paulsen/Women's almanac/77n723
    Ross/Rights of women/75n563
    Sherr/American women's gazetteer/77n724
    Tully/France: especially for women/76
        n560
    Woman's body/79n1494
    Women in transition: feminists hndbk on
        separation & divorce/76n785
    INDEXES
    AAUP/Journal index 1882-1975/79n673
    International Women's Yr World Conf docs
        index/78n672
    NY Times cum subj & personal name index:
        women 1965-75/79n769
    SOCIAL CONDITIONS
    Bibliography on women & drug related
        issues/76n788
    Buvinic/Women & world developmt: bibliog/
        78n662
    Christenson/Women & drug use: bibliog/76
        n791
    Davis/Black woman in Amer society: bibliog/
        76n396
    Een/Women & society—citations 3601 to
        6000/79n755
    Jacobs/Women in perspective: gd for cross-
        cultural studies/76n794
    Knaster/Women in Spanish Amer: bibliog
        from pre-Conquest to contemp times/78
        n373
    Rosenberg/Women & society: review of lit
        with bibliog/76n797
    Status of women: bibliog/78n666
WOMEN ARTISTS
    Collins/Women artists in Amer/75n1011; 76
        n932
    Female artists past & present/76n933; 76n934
    Sparrow/Women painters of world/77n859
WOMEN AUTHORS
    Backsheider/Annotated bibliog of 20th cent
        studies of women & lit, 1660-1800/78
        n1154

WOMEN AUTHORS (cont'd)
Schwartz/Articles on women writers: bibliog/78n1092
White/American women writers/79n1211
Women & lit: bibliog/78n1095

WOMEN EXECUTIVES
Rogalin/Women's gd to mgmt/77n850
US Bureau of Census/Women-owned businesses/77n788

WOMEN FILM DIRECTORS
Dawson/Women's films in print: . . . films by women/76n1055
Smith/Women who make movies/76n1069

WOMEN IN DEVELOPING COUNTRIES
al-Qazzaz/Women in Mid East & No Africa/78n279
Dasgupta/Women on Indian scene: bibliog/77n321
Rihani/Development as if women mattered/79n760
Saulniers/Women in development process . . . sub-Saharan Africa & Latin Amer/79n761

WOMEN IN LITERATURE
Backsheider/Annotated bibliog of 20th cent critical studies of women & lit, 1660-1800/78n1154
Myers/Women in lit: criticism of '70s/77n1125
Palmegiano/Women & British periodicals 1832-67: bibliog/78n665
Women loving women: bibliog/77n1127

WOMEN IN MASS MEDIA
Media report to women: what women are doing & thinking abt communication media: index-directory/77n1107

WOMEN IN THE FILM INDUSTRY
Kowalski/Women & film: bibliog/77n1002

WOMEN IN TRADE-UNIONS
Soltow/American women & labor movemt 1825-1974: bibliog/77n841

WOMEN LIBRARIANS
Cummings/Biographical-bibliogic'l directory/78n154
Myers/Women in librarianship/76n120
SHARE, directory of feminist library workers/77n183; 79n167

WOMEN MUSICIANS
Hixon/Women in music: bibliog/76n1002
Skowronski/Women in Amer music/79n962
Stern/Women composers/79n988

WOMEN PHYSICIANS
Chaff/Women in medicine: bibliog/78n1387

WOMEN POLITICIANS
Evans/Women in fed politics: bio-bibliog/76n482

WOMEN POLITICIANS (cont'd)
Stanwick/Political participation of women in US/78n447
Women in public office: biogic'l directory/77n508; 79n544

WOMEN PRINTERS
Hudak/Early Amer women printers & publishers 1639-1820/79n30

WOMEN'S ATHLETIC PROGRAMS
Assoc for Intercollegiate Athletics for Women/AIAW directory/79n648

WOMEN'S FILMS
Artel/Positive images: gd to non-sexist films for young people/78n955
Betancourt/Women in focus/76n1054
Dawson/Women's films in print: gd to films by women/76n1055

WOMEN'S MOVEMENT
DeNoyelles/Women in Calif: gd to organizations & resources/78n667
Harrison/Women's movemt media: gd/76n793
Krichmar/Women's movemt in '70s: bibliog/78n663

WOMEN'S ORGANIZATIONS
Boston Women's Collective/NY women's yellow pages/79n767
Chicago women's directory/76n790
DeNoyelles/Women in Calif: gd to organizations & resources/78n667
Edry/Women's yellow pages/75n847
Ligare/Illinois women's directory/79n765
Womanpower Project/NY woman's directory/75n854

WOMEN'S PRESSES
Joan/Guide to women's publishing/79n764

WONDER WOMAN
Fleisher/Encyclopedia of comic bk heroes, Wonder Woman/77n1168

WOOD
Bibliography: wood/75n1044
Encyclopedia of wood/79n1576

WOODSTOCK, NY
Rogers/Story of a small town library/75n270

WOODWIND MUSIC
Voxman/Woodwind solo & study matl gd/77n963

WOODWORK
Bibliography: wood/75n1044
Blackburn/Illustrated ency of woodworking handtools, etc./75n1045
Hickin/Wood preservation/75n1046
Maguire/Complete bk of woodworking & cabinetmaking/75n1047

WOODWORK (cont'd)
Salaman/Dictionary of tools used in woodworking, 1700-1970/77n893

WOODY PLANTS
Mulligan/Woody plants in Univ of Washington Arboretum/79n1361

WOOLF, LEONARD
Woolmer/Checklist of Hogarth Press, 1917-38/77n1222

WOOLF, VIRGINIA
Majumdar/Virginia Woolf: bibliog of criticism/78n1184
Woolmer/Checklist of Hogarth Press, 1917-38/77n1222

WORCESTER ART MUSEUM, MA
European paintings in collection/75n992

WORDSWORTH, WILLIAM
Bauer/William Wordsworth/79n1257
Stam/Wordsworthian criticism/75n1408

WORK
Bibliography on major aspects of humanisation of work . . . /79n854
Dubin/Handbook of work, organization & society/77n792

WORK SAMPLING
Goodell/Libraries & work sampling/76n112

WORLD HISTORY
See History—world

WORLD POLITICS
Political events annual/79n509
Political handbk of world/79n510
Schulz/International politics in Mid East & No Africa: gd/78n488
Year bk of world affairs/Keeton/79n513

WORLD SERIES (baseball)
Cohen/World series/77n674
Official world series records, 1903-76/77n675

WORLD WAR I
Banks/Military atlas of 1st world war/76n296
Bayliss/Bibliographic gd to two world wars/78n329
Brown/Neuropsychiatry & the war/77n1459
Mayer/Two world wars: gd to MSS collections in UK/78n326
Smith/World war I in air: bibliog & chron/78n1566

WORLD WAR II
Bagnasco/Submarines/79n1598
Bayliss/Bibliographic gd to the two world wars/78n329
Bloomberg/World War II: bibliog/76n289
Cronon/Second world war & atomic age, 1940-73/76n290
Dulin/Battleships/77n1649

WORLD WAR II (cont'd)
Elliott/Allies escort ships of WW II/79n1601
Enser/Subject bibliog of 2nd WW/78n330
Hogg/Ency of infantry weapons/78n1569
Lenton/German warships/77n1650
Liddell Hart/WW II: illust'd hist/79n398
Mayer/Two world wars: gd to MSS collections in UK/78n326
Mollo/Army uniforms/75n1849
Mollo/Naval, marine & air force uniforms/77n1631
Netzorg/Philippines in WW II & to independence/78n299
O'Neill/WW II: documents/77n362
Rand McNally ency/Keegan/78n1560
Rohwer/Chronology of war at sea/75n542
Rosignoli/Army badges & insignia/77n1644; 77n1645
Smith/WW II at sea: bibliog in Engl/77n1652
Weal/Combat aircraft/78n1567
Young/Atlas of WW II/Natkiel/75n1843

WORSHIP PROGRAMS
Spencer/Hymn & scripture selection gd/79n1063

WRESTLING
Clayton/Handbook of wrestling terms & holds/75n788

WRIGHT, FRANK LLOYD
Storrer/Architecture of F. L. Wright/79n893

WRIGHT, LOUIS B.
Wright/Of books and men/78n265

WYOMING
Shaw/Field gd to vascular plants of Grand Teton Natl Park/77n1356

YACHTING
Bavier/New yacht racing rules/75n750
Johnson/Yachting world hndbks/75n747

YAPESE LANGUAGE
Jensen/Yapese-Engl dict/78n1073
Jensen/Yapese ref grammar/79n1154

YEATS, WILLIAM BUTLER
Jochum/W. B. Yeats/79n1258
Malins/Preface to Yeats/76n1292

YIDDISH LANGUAGE
Rosenbaum/Yiddish word bk for English-speaking people/79n1155
Weinreich/Modern Engl-Yiddish dict/79n1156

YORUBAS
Baldwin/Yoruba of SW Nigeria: bibliog/77n735

YOUNG, OWEN D.
Szladits/Owen D. Young/75n69

YOUNG ADULT LIBRARIANSHIP
Barnes/Youth library work/77n212
Edwards/Fair garden & swarm of beasts/75n185
Media & young adult/78n190
Books for the teen/79n224
Fader/New hooked on books/78n586

YOUNG ADULT LITERATURE
Kliatt paperbk bk gd/75n199
Owen/Smorgasbord of bks/76n161
Son of young adult reviewers/77n1164
Varlejs/Young adult lit in the '70s/79n220

YOUTH
Webster/18: teenage catalog/78n661

YOUTH HOSTELS
AYH hostel gd & hndbk/76n542; 77n557
Metropolitan NY AYH Council/American youth hostels bike-hike bk/77n681

YOUTH PROGRAMS
Bundy/National children's directory/78n659
Catalog of fed youth programs/78n658
National directory of runaway programs/78n660

YUGOSLAV AMERICANS
Eterovich/Guide & bibliog to research on Yugoslavs in US & Canada/77n448

YUGOSLAV LITERATURE
Mihailovich/Modern Slavic lits: Bulgarian, Czech, Yugoslav, etc/78n1199

YUGOSLAVIA
Horton/Yugoslavia/79n392
Hunter/Soviet-Yugoslav relations, 1948-72/77n527
Jovanovic/Guide to Yugoslav libraries & archives/76n214
LC/Yugoslavia/75n307
Lockwood/Yugoslav folklore/77n1053

ZEN BUDDHISM
Vessie/Zen Buddhism: bibliog/78n978

ZIMBABWE
Pollak/Rhodesia-Zimbabwe/78n291

ZIP CODE
Webster's atlas & zip code directory/75n582

ZODIAC
Sun/Asian animal zodiac/75n1607

ZONING
Crawford/Handbook of zoning & land use ordinances—with forms/75n860

ZOOLOGY
Fogden/Animals & their colors/75n1495
Leftwich/Dictionary of zoology/75n1497
Wood/Introduction to lit of vertebrate zoology/75n1496

Ref.
Z
1035.1
A55
Index
1975-79

AUG 22 1979